ECONOMETRIC MODELS AND
ECONOMIC FORECASTS

ECONOMETRIC MODELS AND ECONOMIC FORECASTS

Second Edition

Robert S. Pindyck

Massachusetts Institute of Technology

Daniel L. Rubinfeld

University of Michigan

McGraw-Hill Book Company

New York   St. Louis   San Francisco   Auckland   Bogotá   Hamburg
Johannesburg   London   Madrid   Mexico   Montreal   New Delhi
Panama   Paris   São Paulo   Singapore   Sydney   Tokyo   Toronto

This book was set in Times Roman by Science Typographers, Inc. The editors were Bonnie E. Lieberman and M. Susan Norton; the production supervisor was John Mancia. New drawings were done by ECL Art Associates, Inc. The cover was designed by Infield, D'Astolfo Associates.
R. R. Donnelley & Sons Company was printer and binder.

ECONOMETRIC MODELS AND ECONOMIC FORECASTS

890 DODO 898765

Library of Congress Cataloging in Publication Data

Pindyck, Robert S
    Econometric models and economic forecasts.

    Includes indexes.
      1.   Economic forecasting—Mathematical models.
2. Econometrics. I. Rubinfeld, Daniel L., joint
author. II. Title.
HB3730.P54   1981   338.5'44   80-14427
ISBN 0-07-050096-7

to our wives,
Nurit and Gail

סוקדש לנשות'נו –
נור'ת וג''ל

CONTENTS

Preface   xi
Introduction   xiii

Part 1   Single-Equation Regression Models

1   Introduction to the Regression Model   3

1.1   Curve Fitting   3
1.2   Derivation of Least Squares   8
      Appendix 1.1   The Use of Summation Operators   13
      Appendix 1.2   Derivation of Least-Squares Parameter Estimates   16

2   Elementary Statistics: A Review   19

2.1   Random Variables   19
2.2   Estimation   24
2.3   Desirable Properties of Estimators   27
2.4   Probability Distributions   31
2.5   Hypothesis Testing and Confidence Intervals   36
      Appendix 2.1   The Properties of the Expectations Operator   40

3   The Two-Variable Regression Model   46

3.1   The Model   46
3.2   Best Linear Unbiased Estimation   51
3.3   Hypothesis Testing and Confidence Intervals   55
3.4   Analysis of Variance and Correlation   61
      Appendix 3.1   Variance of the Least-Squares Slope Estimator   68
      Appendix 3.2   Maximum-Likelihood Estimation   69
      Appendix 3.3   Some Properties Relating to the Least-Squares
                      Residuals   71

4 The Multiple Regression Model 75

4.1	The Model	75
4.2	Regression Interpretation and Statistics	77
4.3	F Tests, R^2, and Corrected R^2	78
4.4	Multicollinearity	87
4.5	Beta Coefficients and Elasticities	90
4.6	Partial Correlation and Stepwise Regression	91
	Appendix 4.1 Least-Squares Parameter Estimation	96
	Appendix 4.2 Partial Regression Coefficients	97
	Appendix 4.3 The Multiple Regression Model in Matrix Form	99

5 Using the Multiple Regression Model 107

5.1	The General Linear Model	107
5.2	Use of Dummy Variables	111
5.3	The use of t Tests and F Tests for Hypotheses Involving More than One Parameter	116
5.4	Piecewise Linear Regression	126
5.5	Specification Error	128
5.6	The Multiple Regression Model with Stochastic Explanatory Variables	134
	Appendix 5.1 Tests Involving Dummy Variable Coefficients	135

6 Serial Correlation and Heteroscedasticity 139

6.1	Heteroscedasticity	140
6.2	Serial Correlation	152
	Appendix 6.1 Generalized Least-Squares Estimation	164

7 Instrumental Variables and Two-Stage Least Squares 174

7.1	Correlation between an Independent Variable and the Error Term	175
7.2	Errors in Variables	176
7.3	Introduction to Simultaneous Equation Models	180
7.4	Consistent Parameter Estimation	184
7.5	The Identification Problem	186
7.6	Two-Stage Least Squares	191
7.7	Serial Correlation in the Presence of Lagged Dependent Variables	193
	Appendix 7.1 Instrumental-Variables Estimation in Matrix Form	199

8 Forecasting with a Single-Equation Regression Model 203

8.1	Unconditional Forecasting	206
8.2	Forecasting with Serially Correlated Errors	215
8.3	Conditional Forecasting	221
	Appendix 8.1 Forecasting with the Multivariate Regression Model	224

9 Single-Equation Estimation: Advanced Topics 230

9.1	Distributed Lags	231
9.2	Missing Observations	245
9.3	Pooling of Cross-Section and Time-Series Data	252

9.4	Nonlinear Estimation	261
	Appendix 9.1 *Estimating Confidence Intervals for Long-Run*	
	Elasticities	269

10 **Models of Qualitative Choice** **273**

10.1	Binary-Choice Models	274
10.2	Multiple-Choice Models	301
	Appendix 10.1 *Maximum-Likelihood Estimation of the Logit*	
	and Probit Models	310

Part 2 Multi-Equation Simulation Models

11 **Simultaneous-Equation Estimation** **319**

11.1	Types of Equation Systems	320
11.2	The Identification Problem	324
11.3	Single-Equation Estimation	328
11.4	Estimation of Equation Systems	331
11.5	Comparison of Alternative Estimators	338
	Appendix 11. *The Identification Problem in Matrix Form*	339
	Appendix 11.2 *Two-Stage Least Squares in Matrix Form*	344
	Appendix 11.3 *Zellner Estimation in Matrix Form*	347
	Appendix 11.4 *Maximum-Likelihood Estimation of Equation*	
	Systems	349

12 **Introduction to Simulation Models** **354**

12.1	The Simulation Process	356
12.2	Evaluating Simulation Models	360
12.3	A Simulation Example	367
12.4	Model Estimation	374
12.5	Other Kinds of Multi-Equation Simulation Models	378

13 **Dynamic Behavior of Simulation Models** **382**

13.1	Model Behavior: Stability and Oscillations	383
13.2	Model Behavior: Multipliers and Dynamic Response	391
13.3	Tuning and Adjusting Simulation Models	401
13.4	Stochastic Simulation	405

14 **Examples of Simulation Models** **414**

14.1	A Small Macroeconometric Model	415
14.2	An Industry-Wide Econometric Model	440
14.3	Simulation Models for Corporate Financial Planning	447
	Appendix 14.1 *Estimation Method and Data Series for*	
	the Macroeconometric Model	456

Part 3 Time-Series Models

15 **Smoothing and Extrapolation of Time Series** **473**

15.1	Simple Extrapolation Models	473
15.2	Smoothing and Seasonal Adjustment	484

16 Properties of Stochastic Time Series — 493

16.1 Introduction to Stochastic Time-Series Models — 494
16.2 Stationary and Nonstationary Time Series — 497
  Appendix 16.1 The Autocorrelation Function for a Stationary Process — 511

17 Linear Time-Series Models — 514

17.1 Moving Average Models — 515
17.2 Autoregressive Models — 519
17.3 Mixed Autoregressive–Moving Average Models — 526
17.4 Homogeneous Nonstationary Processes: ARIMA Models — 529
17.5 Specification of ARIMA Models — 531
  Appendix 17.1 Stationarity, Invertibility, and Homogeneity — 535

18 Estimation of Time-Series Models — 539

18.1 The Estimation Procedure — 541
18.2 Diagnostic Checking — 548
  Appendix 18.1 Initialization of the Time Series — 552

19 Forecasting with Time-Series Models — 555

19.1 Minimum Mean Square Error Forecast — 556
19.2 Computing a Forecast — 557
19.3 The Forecast Error — 558
19.4 Forecast Confidence Intervals — 559
19.5 Properties of ARIMA Forecasts — 561
19.6 Two Examples — 568

20 Applications of Time-Series Models — 574

20.1 Review of the Modeling Process — 575
20.2 Models of Economic Variables: Inventory Investment — 577
20.3 Forecasting Seasonal Telephone Data — 589
20.4 Combining Regression Analysis with a Time-Series Model: Transfer Function Models — 593
20.5 A Combined Regression–Time-Series Model to Forecast Interest Rates — 595
20.6 A Combined Regression–Time-Series Model to Forecast Short-Term Savings Deposit Flows — 601

Statistical Tables — 606
Solutions to Selected Problems — 612
Indexes — 621
  Subject Index
  Name Index

PREFACE

Comments and suggestions from a large number of users of the first edition have led us to make a number of substantive changes as well as smaller revisions in this second edition. We have incorporated several changes which we feel have pedagogical value, as well as a number of new topics which currently are receiving relatively wide attention. Nonetheless, the book has the same general outline as the first edition.

In terms of content, Part One includes two new chapters. Chapter 2 contains an expanded and more carefully developed review of important statistical concepts, while Chapter 5 contains a number of topics relating to the multiple regression model that were not treated in detail in the first edition. These include the use of t tests, F tests, and dummy variables. In general, we have tried to make the first five chapters more accessible to those with a weak mathematical background by including more algebraic derivations in footnotes, appendixes, and exercises. Also, Chapter 10 now contains a much more extensive discussion of the estimation of models with qualitative dependent variables.

Part Two of the book is unchanged in overall structure, but it does contain a newly estimated and improved macroeconomic model as well as an expansion of the material on corporate planning models (in Chapter 14). Finally, Part Three has been expanded to include an additional chapter in which simple non-stochastic forecasting models are covered. Topics covered in that chapter include techniques for the smoothing and extrapolation of time series, as well as seasonal adjustment methods.

Just as important as these substantive changes is the fact that many examples have been reworked, and the data for a number of them have been included either in the text or in our instructor's manual. The manual also contains answers to all the rather extensive end-of-chapter questions. All the empirical questions relate to data sets given in the text and the manual so that instructors can make direct use of the assignments in their classes.

In preparing the second edition, we have benefited substantially from the comments and criticisms of our colleagues and our students, as well as suggestions given to us from a wide variety of individuals. We should thank Stephen Dietrich and Annette Hall, who helped plan and edit the first edition. Without their extremely valuable support, we would not have had the courage to tackle a second one. Likewise, Bonnie Lieberman and Susan Norton have been of great assistance with the second edition. We can't possibly thank everyone who provided assistance with this revision, but we will give special thanks to Joseph Langsam, who played a crucial role in the development of the instructor's manual; John Neese, who helped develop the new version of the macroeconometric model; and William Keech, David Kendrick, Ed Kuh, Deborah Swift, Carl Van Duyne, and a number of anonymous reviewers who provided numerous helpful comments and suggestions. Also, we would like to mention some of the people who have found minor errors or argued persuasively for one or more changes in the text. They include H. Akhavipour, Peter An, John G. Bell, Abdul Rauf Butt, George Downs, Alan Fox, Jeffrey Frankel, Rob Gerin, Sue Goldstone, Shuh-Tzy Hsu, Mark Kamlet, Robert Kleinbaum, Jan Kmenta, Nancy E. Meiners, Jonathan Shane, Chandler Stolp, Donald Wise, and Kenneth White. Finally, our thanks to Karen Shamban and Judith Jackson for their patience and diligence in typing the final manuscript of this new edition.

Robert S. Pindyck
Daniel L. Rubinfeld

INTRODUCTION

This book is an introduction to the science and art of building and using models. The science of model building consists of a set of tools, most of them quantitative, which are used to construct and then test mathematical representations of portions of the real world. The development and use of these tools are subsumed under the subject heading of econometrics. Econometrics is a well-defined field and therefore relatively easy to describe. The science of model building is a primary concern of this book. The art of model building is, unfortunately, much harder to describe in words, since it consists mostly of intuitive judgments that occur during the modeling process. Unfortunately, since there are no clear-cut rules for making these model-building judgments, the art of model building is more difficult to master. Nonetheless, one of the purposes of this book is to convey the nature of that art to the reader to the extent possible. This will be done in part by examples and by discussions of technique but also by encouraging readers to do what is ultimately necessary to master the art, namely, to build models of their own.

The book focuses upon models of processes that occur in business, economics, and the social sciences in general. These might include models of aggregate economic activity; the sales of an individual firm, or a political process (e.g., estimating the number of votes that a particular candidate can be expected to receive in an election). Discussions of the purposes of building these models are directed toward forecasting and policy analysis, but the reader should bear in mind the general nature of the content.

As one might expect, there are many types of models that can and often have been used for policy analysis and forecasting. This book does not attempt to cover the entire spectrum of model types and modeling methodologies; instead, it concentrates on models that can be expressed in equation form, relating variables quantitatively. Data are then used to estimate the parameters of the equation or equations, and theoretical relationships are tested statistically.

This still leaves a rather wide range of models from which to choose. On one end of this range, one might determine the effect of alternative monetary policies on the behavior of the United States economy by constructing a large, multi-equation econometric model of the economy and then simulating it using different monetary policies. The resulting model would be rather complicated and would presume to explain a complex structure in the real world. On the other end of the range, one might wish to forecast the sales volume of a firm and, believing that those sales follow a strong cyclical pattern, use a time-series model to extrapolate the past behavior of sales.

It is this range of models that is the subject matter of this book. The objective of this book is to give the reader some understanding of the science and art of determining what type of model to build, building the model which is most appropriate, testing the model statistically, and then finally applying the model to practical problems in forecasting and analysis.

1 WHY MODELS?

Many of us often either use or produce forecasts of one sort or another. Few of us recognize, however, that some kind of logical structure, or model, is implicit in every forecast or analysis of a social or a physical system. Consider, for example, a stockbroker who tells you that the Dow Jones Industrial Average will rise next year. The stockbroker might have made this forecast because the Dow Jones average has been rising during the past few years and the broker feels that whatever it was that made it rise in the past will continue to make it rise in the future. On the other hand, the feeling that the Dow Jones Industrial Average will rise next year may result from a belief that this variable is linked to a set of economic and political variables through a complex set of relationships. The broker might believe, for example, that the Dow Jones average is related in a certain way to the gross national product and to interest rates, so that given certain other beliefs about the most probable future behavior of these latter variables, a rise in the Dow Jones average would appear likely.

If we have to find a word to describe the method by which our stockbroker made this forecast, we would probably say that it was intuitive, although the chain of reasoning differed substantially in the two cases cited above. The stockbroker certainly would not say that the forecast was made by building a model of the Dow Jones average; indeed, no equations were written down, nor was any computer used. Nonetheless, in each case, some *implicit* form of model building was involved. A stockbroker who based the optimistic forecast for the Dow Jones average on past increases has in effect constructed a *time-series model* which extrapolates past trends into the future. If, instead, the forecast was based on a knowledge of economics, a model would still be implicitly involved; it would be composed of the relationships that were loosely conceived in the stockbroker's mind as a result of past experience.

Thus, even the intuitive forecaster constructs some type of model even without being aware of doing so. Of course, it is reasonable to ask why one might want to work with an *explicit* model to produce forecasts. Would it be worth the trouble, for example, for our stockbroker to read this book in order to construct an explicit model, estimate it on the computer, and test it statistically? Our response is that there are several advantages to working with models explicitly. Model building forces the individual to think clearly about, and account for, all the important interrelationships involved in a problem. The reliance on intuition can be dangerous at times because of the possibility that important relationships will be ignored or improperly used. In addition, it is important that individual relationships be tested or validated in some way or another. Unfortunately, this is not usually done when intuitive forecasts are made. In the process of building a model, however, a person must test or validate not only the model as a whole but also the individual relationships that make up the model.

When making a forecast, it is also important to provide a statistical measure of confidence to the user of the forecast, i.e., some measure of how accurate one might expect the forecast to be. The use of purely intuitive methods usually precludes any quantitative measure of confidence in the resulting forecast. The statistical analysis of the individual relationships that make up a model, and of the model as a whole, makes it possible to attach a measure of confidence to the model's forecasts.

Once a model has been constructed and fitted to data, a sensitivity analysis can be used to study many of its properties. In particular, the effects of small changes in individual variables in the model can be evaluated. For example, in the case of a model that describes and predicts interest rates, one could measure the effect on a particular interest rate of a change in the rate of inflation. This type of quantitative sensitivity study, which is important both in understanding and in using the model, can be made only if the model is an explicit one.

2 TYPES OF MODELS

In this book we examine three general classes of models that can be constructed for purposes of forecasting or policy analysis. Each involves a different degree of model complexity and structural explanation, and each presumes a different level of comprehension about the real world processes one is trying to model.

Time-series models In this class of models we presume to know nothing about the real world causal relationships that affect the variable we are trying to forecast. Instead we examine the past behavior of a time series in order to infer something about its future behavior. The time-series method used to produce a forecast might involve the use of a simple deterministic model such as a linear extrapolation or the use of a complex stochastic model for adaptive forecasting.

One example of the use of time-series analysis would be the simple extrapolation of a past trend in predicting population growth. Another example would be the development of a complex linear stochastic model for passenger loads on an airline. Models such as this have been developed and used to forecast the demand for airline capacity, seasonal telephone demand, the movement of short-term interest rates, as well as other economic variables. Time-series models are particularly useful when little is known about the underlying process that one is trying to forecast. The limited structure in time-series models makes them most reliable only in the short run, but they are nonetheless rather useful.

Single-equation regression models In this class of models the variable under study is explained by a single function (linear or nonlinear) of explanatory variables. The equation will often be time-dependent (i.e., the time index will appear explicitly in the model), so that one can predict the response over time of the variable under study to changes in one or more of the explanatory variables.

An example of a single-equation regression model might be an equation that relates a particular interest rate, such as the 3-month Treasury bill rate, to a set of explanatory variables such as the money supply, the rate of inflation, and the rate of change in the gross national product. Regression models are often used to forecast not only the movement in short- and long-term interest rates but also many other economic and business variables.

Multi-equation simulation models In this class of models the variable to be studied may be a function of several explanatory variables, which now are related to each other as well as to the variable under study through a set of equations. The construction of a simulation model begins with the specification of a set of individual relationships, each of which is fitted to available data. Simulation is the process of solving these equations simultaneously over some range in time.

An example of a multi-equation simulation model would be a complete model of the United States textile industry that contains equations explaining variables such as textile demand, textile production output, employment of production workers in the textile industry, investment in the industry, and textile prices. These variables would be related to each other and to other variables (such as total national income, the Consumer Price Index, interest rates, etc.), through a set of linear or nonlinear equations. Given assumptions about the future behavior of national income, interest rates, etc., one could simulate this model into the future and obtain a forecast for each of the model's variables. A model such as this can be used to analyze the impact on the industry of changes in external economic variables.

Multi-equation simulation models presume to explain a great deal about the structure of the actual process being studied. Not only are individual relationships specified, but the model accounts for the interaction of all these interrelationships at the same time. Thus, a five-equation simulation model actually contains more information than the sum of five individual regression equations.

The model not only explains the five individual relationships but also describes the dynamic structure implied by the simultaneous operation of these relationships.

The choice of the type of model to develop is a difficult one, involving trade-offs between time, energy, costs, and desired forecast precision. The construction of a multi-equation simulation model might require large expenditures of time and money, not only in terms of actual work but also in terms of computer time. The gains that result from this effort might include the better understanding of the relationships and structure involved as well as the ability to make a better forecast. However, in some cases these gains may be small enough so to be outweighed by the heavy costs involved. Because the multi-equation model necessitates a good deal of knowledge about the process being studied, the construction of such models may be extremely difficult.

The decision to build a time-series model usually occurs when little or nothing is known about the determinants of the variable being studied, when a large number of data points are available (thus making some kind of inference feasible), and when the model is to be used largely for short-term forecasting. Given some information about the processes involved, however, it may not be obvious whether a time-series model or a single-equation regression model is preferable as a means of forecasting. It may be reasonable for a forecaster to construct both types of models and compare their relative performances.

In the course of this book, we plan not only to describe how each type of model is constructed and used, but also to give some insight into the relative costs and benefits involved. Unfortunately, this can be a rather hard problem, as the choice of model type is often not clear. In any case, it seems natural to include a discussion of all three types of models (single-equation regression, multi-equation simulation, and time series) in the confines of a single book.

3 WHAT THE BOOK CONTAINS

The book is divided into three parts, each concentrating on a different class of models. The most fundamental class of models, discussed in the first part of the book, is the single-equation regression model. The econometric methods developed and used to construct single-equation regression models will, with modification, find application in the construction of multi-equation simulation models as well as time-series models. Thus, Part One of this book presents an introduction to the development and estimation of single-equation econometric models.

Chapters 1 and 2 begin with an introduction to the basic concepts of regression analysis, and a review of elementary statistics. The regression model then is developed in detail, beginning with a two-variable model in Chapter 3 and proceeding to the multiple regression model in Chapters 4 and 5. These chapters also develop statistical tests and procedures that can be used to evaluate the properties of a regression model.

The estimation techniques used in simple regression analysis require that certain assumptions be made about both the data and the model. At times, these assumptions break down. Chapters 6 and 7 begin a discussion of what can be done in some of these cases. Chapter 6 deals with heteroscedasticity and serial correlation and includes statistical tests for these problems as well as estimation methods that correct for them. Chapter 7 deals with the problem of correlation between explanatory variables and the implicit error term in the regression model. It concentrates on the development of the instrumental variable and two-stage least-squares estimation techniques.

Chapter 8 discusses the use of a single-equation regression model for forecasting purposes. The chapter discusses not only the methods by which a forecast is produced, but also measures that describe the reliability of a forecast, such as confidence intervals and the error of forecast.

The last two chapters of Part One of the book consider extensions of the regression model. These chapters are somewhat more advanced in nature, and could be skipped by the beginning student. Chapter 9 deals with the problems of missing observations, the estimation of nonlinear models, distributed lag models, and models which pool cross-section and time-series data. Chapter 10 deals with models in which the variable to be explained is qualitative in nature. These include linear probability models, probit models, and logit models.

The foundation of econometrics of Part One is essential for the development of multi-equation simulation models in Part Two of the book. Part Two begins with a chapter on estimation techniques particular to simultaneous equation models. This includes problems of model identification, as well as techniques such as three-stage least squares. Chapters 12 and 13 discuss the methodology of constructing and using multi-equation simulation models. Chapter 12 is an introduction to simulation models, and includes a discussion of the simulation process, methods of evaluating simulation models, alternative methods of estimating simulation models, and general approaches to model construction. Chapter 13 is more technical in nature and discusses methods of analyzing the dynamic behavior of simulation models, including questions of model stability, dynamic multipliers, and methods of tuning and adjusting simulation models. Chapter 13 concludes with a discussion of sensitivity analysis and stochastic simulation.

Part Two closes with a chapter that presents three detailed examples of the construction and use of simulation models. In the first example, a small but complete model of the United States economy is constructed and used for simple policy analysis. The second example develops an industry market model and shows how it can be used to forecast production and prices. The last example shows how simulation techniques can be useful for financial planning in a corporation.

Instructors interested in using some of the econometric models described in Part Two should know about MODSIM, a computer program for simulating macroeconometric models, written by Carl Van Duyne of Williams College and distributed by CONDUIT at the University of Iowa. The program was designed for use in undergraduate and graduate economics courses, and it can perform all the computations normally employed to simulate and systematically evaluate econometric models, including dynamic and static simulation, ex ante forecasting, and the calculation of dynamic multipliers and summary measures of prediction error. The program contains three models of the United States economy: the small macroeconometric model, described in Chapter 14; the complete April 1979 version of the St. Louis model, parts of which are analyzed in Chapter 13; and the simple four-equation macro model in Chapter 12, reestimated using recently revised data. The complete MODSIM package, which includes a magnetic tape of the computer program, User's Manuals, and an Instructor's Guide, is available from CONDUIT, P.O. Box 388, Iowa City, Iowa 52244.

Part Three of this book is devoted to time-series models, which can be viewed as a special class of single-equation regression models. Thus, the econometric tools developed in Part One of the book will find extensive application in Part Three. Part Three begins with Chapters 15 and 16, which discuss basic smoothing and extrapolation techniques, and which introduce the basic properties of random time series, as well as the notion of a time-series model. Chapter 16 also discusses the properties of stationary and nonstationary time series, and the calculation and use of the autocorrelation function.

Chapters 17, 18, and 19 develop the methods by which time-series models are specified, estimated, and used for forecasting. Chapter 17 covers linear time-series models in detail, including moving average models, autoregressive models, mixed models, and finally models of nonstationary time series. Chapter 18 develops regression methods that can be used to estimate a time-series model, as well as methods of diagnostic checking that can be used to ascertain how well the estimated model "fits" the data. Chapter 19 deals with the computation of the minimum mean-square-error forecast, forecast error, and forecast confidence intervals.

The last chapter of Part Three is devoted entirely to examples of the construction and use of time-series models. After we review the modeling process, we construct models of several economic variables and use them to produce short-term forecasts. Finally we demonstrate through examples how models can be constructed that combine time-series with regression analysis.

4 USE OF MATHEMATICAL TOOLS

This book is written on a rather elementary level, and can be understood with only a limited knowledge of calculus and no knowledge of matrix algebra. Mathematical derivations and proofs are generally reserved for appendixes or suppressed entirely. In Part One of the book, the development of the regression model in matrix form is included in the appendixes. Thus most if not all of the book should be accessible to advanced undergraduate students as well as graduate students.

It is desirable that the reader of this book have some background in statistics. Although Chapter 2 contains a brief review of probability and statistics, the student with *no* background in statistics may find parts of the book somewhat difficult. Typically, this book would be used in an applied econometrics or business-forecasting course which a student would take after completing an introductory course in statistics.

5 ALTERNATIVE USES OF THE BOOK

The book is intended to have a wide spectrum of uses. Curriculum uses include an undergraduate or introductory graduate course in econometrics and an undergraduate or graduate course in business forecasting. In addition, this book can be of considerable value as a reference book for people doing statistical analyses of economic and business data or as a text or reference book for the social scientist or business analyst interested in the application of dynamic simulation models to forecasting or policy analysis.

Coverage in an introductory econometrics or business forecasting course must, of course, depend to some extent on the background of the student and the goals of the instructor. Emphasis on the use of econometric techniques for purposes of forecasting with econometric models would provide for one focus, but several alternatives are available. We list several alternative uses of the book below, but stress that the great variety of the material leaves a good deal of discretion to the instructor planning a course outline.

1. Undergraduate Econometrics (one semester)
   a. *Standard*
      Part One: Chapters 1 to 7; portions of Chapters 8 to 10 optional
   b. *Simulation emphasis*
      Part One: Chapters 1 to 8
      Part Two: Chapters 12 to 14
      Both courses would omit all matrix appendixes.
2. First-year graduate econometrics
   a. *One semester*
      Part One: Chapters 1 to 8; Chapters 9 and 10 optional
      Part Two: Chapters 11 to 14
      Portions of the above and the appendixes may be optional.
   b. *Two semesters*
      Part One: Chapters 1 to 10
      Part Two: Chapters 11 to 14
      Part Three: Chapters 15 to 17; portions of Chapters 18 to 20 optional
      Emphasis on either simulation and/or time-series analysis would depend upon the interest of the instructor.

3. Business forecasting (graduate or advanced undergraduate)
   a. *One semester*
      Part One: Chapter 8 plus review of Chapters 1 to 7
      Part Two: Chapters 12 to 14
      Part Three: Chapters 15 to 20 (selected portions)
   b. *Two semesters*
      Part One: Chapters 1 to 8
      Part Two: Chapters 11 to 14
      Part Three: Chapters 15 to 20
4. Quantitative methods for policy analysis
   a. *Undergraduate, one semester*
      Part One: Chapters 1 to 8
      Part Two: Chapters 12 to 14
   b. *Graduate, one semester*
      Part One: Chapters 1 to 8
      Part Two: Chapters 11 to 14
   c. *Graduate, two semesters*
      Part One: Chapters 1 to 8; Chapters 9 and 10 optional
      Part Two: Chapters 11 to 14
      Part Three: Chapters 15 to 20

The book could also be used for courses in quantitative social science modeling (as taught in departments of sociology or political science). Such a course using this book as a text would probably cover most of Parts One and Two.

6 WHAT DISTINGUISHES THIS BOOK FROM OTHERS?

This book attempts to explain the development and use of quantitative models from a broad perspective. Most textbooks on econometrics develop the single-equation regression model as a self-contained and isolated entity. The reader of such a book often infers that statistical regression models are somehow distinct and independent from other aspects of modeling, such as the analysis of a model's dynamic structure or the use of time-series analysis to forecast one or more exogenous variables in the model. This is certainly not the case, as any practitioner of the art knows. In developing a multi-equation simulation model, for example, one must be knowledgeable not only about regression methods but also about how a model's dynamic behavior results from the interaction of its individual equations.

This book develops the techniques and methods for the construction of all three types of models. Thus, the reader becomes aware of the use of single-equation econometrics as a modeling form in itself, as a tool that can be used in the development of multi-equation simulation models, and as a statistical basis for the development of stochastic time-series models for forecasting. The reader also becomes aware that there is more than one type of model and (we hope) gains an understanding of what models are preferable for a particular purpose.

We believe that this wide breadth of coverage is desirable. The simulation and time-series techniques that make up Parts Two and Three of this book are usually presented only at an advanced level. We feel that a strength of this book is that the coverage is broad and includes these advanced techniques but is presented on a level that can be understood and appreciated by the beginning student.

ONE

SINGLE-EQUATION
REGRESSION MODELS

Part One of this book is concerned with the theory and application of econometrics. The different types of models that lend themselves to econometric analysis will be described as we develop materials in the text. We begin our discussion with single-equation regression models, simple in form but quite powerful in terms of the variety of possible business and economic applications. In these models, one variable under study is assumed to be a linear function of several explanatory variables. Single-equation models are important, not only because they can be useful for testing hypotheses and forecasting but also because they form the groundwork for the analysis of simultaneous-equation models and time-series models. Because most of the econometric techniques discussed in Part One of the book are of use in the remaining parts, we have chosen to develop these methods extensively in a manner which is accessible to all students.

The first eight chapters develop the central framework of single-equation econometrics. In Chapter 1, elementary curve-fitting concepts and the notion of least squares are developed. Chapter 2 contains an extensive review of the basic statistical ideas necessary for the analysis that follows. The two-variable model is then used in Chapter 3 as a means of focusing on the statistical properties which might be desired for regression parameter estimates. Emphasis in the chapter is placed on the notion of hypothesis testing and the problem of measuring goodness of fit of a regression line. Chapter 4 extends the regression model to the multiple-variable case. The presence of more than one explanatory variable in the regression model leads to additional econometric problems relating to the interaction of these variables. These problems include the interpretation of regression coefficients and multicollinearity. Some additional regression statistics which help with the interaction problem are also discussed. Chapter 5 extends the discussion of the multiple regression model in a number of directions. Topics considered include the use of different functional forms, dummy variables, t and F tests, and specification error.

The estimation techniques used in the first part of the book depend crucially upon several assumptions relating to the form of the data and to the specification of the model itself. Chapters 6 and 7 deal with several of these assumptions. In Chapter 6 we focus on the possible existence of heteroscedasticity and serial correlation, describing tests for their existence as well as corrections when they are present. In Chapter 7 we concern ourselves with the difficulties which arise when one or more of the explanatory variables is correlated with the error term in the regression model. To correct for this difficulty, we introduce the methods of instrumental variables and two-stage least-squares estimation. Because the problems in this chapter are likely to arise when the model being studied is truly simultaneous in nature, Chapter 7 serves as an important introduction to the material in Part Two of the book (Chapter 11, especially).

Chapter 8 deals with the problem of forecasting within the context of a single-equation model. The means of obtaining a forecast and some measure of the reliability of that forecast are discussed in the case when the explanatory variables are known as well as unknown and in the case when the errors of the regression model are serially correlated. The material in Chapter 8 lays the groundwork for the more advanced analysis of forecasting in Parts Two and Three.

The final two chapters of Part One contain materials of a more advanced nature than the first eight chapters. Chapters 9 and 10 both deal with extensions of the regression model which can be quite important in applied econometric work but which can be skipped by the reader wishing to focus on Parts Two and Three of the book. Chapter 9 contains brief discussions of four econometric issues—distributed lags, missing observations, pooling of cross-section and time-series data, and nonlinear estimation. Any of the four chapter sections can be read independently of the others. Finally, Chapter 10 deals with the estimation of models in which the variable to be studied is qualitative rather than quantitative. The chapter emphasizes how the linear probability, probit, and logit models can be used to study problems involving binary as well as multiple choices. Chapter 10 is self-contained and can be read independently from Chapter 9.

INTRODUCTION TO THE REGRESSION MODEL

In this chapter we begin our discussion of econometrics by concentrating on the development of the two-variable linear regression model. In the first section the notion of curve fitting is discussed with reference to an example based on student grade-point averages. The least-squares criterion for curve fitting is presented and compared with several alternative curve-fitting schemes. In the second section, a detailed derivation of the least-squares estimation procedure is included. The chapter concludes with three elementary applications of the least-squares regression technique.

1.1 CURVE FITTING

Data resulting from the measurement of variables may come from any number of sources and in a variety of forms. Data which describe the movement of a variable over time are called *time-series* data, and may be daily, weekly, monthly, quarterly, or annual. Data which describe the activities of individual persons, firms, or other units at a given point in time are called *cross-section* data. A marketing study dealing with family expenditures at a given time is likely to utilize cross-section data. Cross-section data might also be used to examine a group of business accounting statements for the purpose of estimating patterns of behavior among individual firms in an industry.

Let us assume that we are interested in the relationship between two variables X and Y. In order to describe this relationship statistically, we need a set of observations for each variable and a hypothesis setting forth the explicit mathematical form of the relationship between X and Y. The set of observations is called a *sample*.† We shall be primarily concerned with the case in which the relationship between X and Y is linear, i.e., the relationship between X and Y can best be described by a straight line. Given the assumption of linearity, our objective is to specify a rule by which the "best" straight line fitting X and Y is to be determined.

As an example, assume that we wish to test the hypothesis that the grade-point average of a student can be predicted or explained to a large extent by the income of the parents of that student. Eight sample points were obtained (hypothetically) and are described in Table 1.1 and plotted as a scatter diagram in Fig. 1.1. Many straight lines can be chosen to fit the plotted points. One could connect the points from the lowest X value to the highest X value (line l_1), or one could draw a line by eye which appears to fit the full scatter of points (line l_2). A better rule might be to choose a line so that the sum of the distances (positive and negative) from the points on the graph to the line, measured vertically, is zero. (These distances, known as *deviations*, are shown in Fig. 1.2.) This criterion would assure that deviations that are equal in magnitude and equal in sign are given equal importance. Unfortunately, however, this proce-dure has the undesirable property that deviations which are equal in size but opposite in sign cancel out. As a result one could find a line (or more than one, for that matter) which had associated with it a zero sum of deviations but actually fit the data quite poorly. We could improve on this method if we were to minimize the absolute value of the deviations of the fitted line from the sample points. Implicit in such a procedure is the judgment that the importance of the deviation is proportional to its magnitude. This would provide us with a reasonable measure of how well the data points fit the line, since positive and negative deviations could not cancel out. While the minimization of the sum of absolute deviations is appealing, it does suffer from several disadvantages. First, the procedure is computationally quite difficult to utilize. Second, it is reason-able that large deviations should be treated with relatively greater attention than small deviations. For example, a prediction involving a 2-unit error would probably be considered worse than a prediction involving two errors of 1 unit each.

A procedure does exist which is computationally feasible and which pe-nalizes large errors relatively more than small errors. This procedure is the method of *least squares*. The least-squares criterion is as follows: *The "line of best fit" is said to be that which minimizes the sum of the squared deviations of the points of the graph from the points of the straight line* (with distances measured vertically). We will see in the next chapter that least squares is also convenient in that it permits statistical testing, but at this point we are concerned solely with describing the procedure itself.‡

---

† The sample data are observations which have been chosen from an underlying *population* which represents the true relationship under study.

‡ Least squares (unlike least absolute deviations) has the property of allowing one to obtain estimates of regression parameters which are best linear unbiased and (under some conditions) maximum likelihood. For details, see Chapter 3.

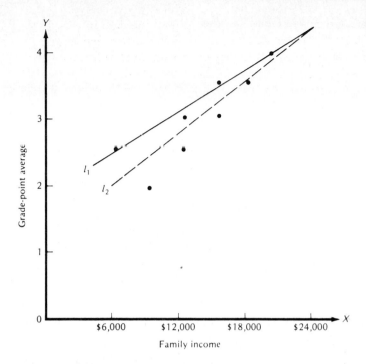

Figure 1.1 Scatter diagram.

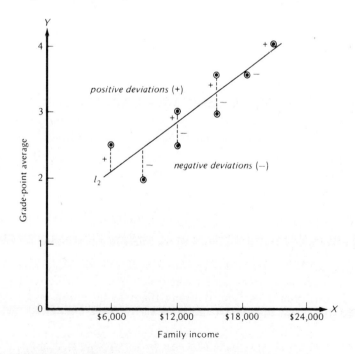

Figure 1.2 Deviations.

Table 1.1 Grade-point average and family income

Y (grade-point average)	X (income of parents in $1,000)
4.0	21.0
3.0	15.0
3.5	15.0
2.0	9.0
3.0	12.0
3.5	18.0
2.5	6.0
2.5	12.0

We will rely heavily on the least-squares estimation procedure in this book, but it is important to realize that other estimation techniques are feasible and occasionally desirable. In part the use of these alternative techniques has been brought about by the relatively recent improvement in computational techniques and efficiency. To digress briefly, we can see how least squares relates to some of these alternative techniques by looking at Fig. 1.3a and b. Figure 1.3a graphs the deviation of a data point from the straight line on the horizontal axis and the "loss" associated with that deviation on the vertical axis. In the case of least squares, we are trying to minimize the sum of squared deviations, so that the loss associated with each individual deviation is that deviation squared. In the case of least-absolute-value estimation, the loss is the absolute value of the deviation. The *loss functions* associated with both least squares and least absolute values are symmetric with respect to the sign of the deviation, but the least-squares loss function penalizes large deviations more than the least-absolute-value loss function does.

One problem that can arise when one is using a least-squares procedure occurs when there is one (or more) large deviation. Assume, for example, that a reporting error was made with respect to the grade-point average of the first student, with a grade of 1.0 being reported rather than the correct figure of 4.0. If line l_2 in Fig. 1.1 were considered as a possible least-squares line, the deviation associated with the first data point would be very large and the deviation squared even larger. The result is that the best-fitting least-squares line will change substantially, with the slope getting flatter since the line must now fit a new set of points. What has happened is that the large penalty associated with least squares has forced the estimation procedure to put great emphasis on the relationship between the straight line and the first data point. The net result is that the slope (and intercept) of the least-squares line is very sensitive to errors of measurement or more generally to data points which lie far from the straight line. We often call such data points *outliers*, defining them to be points more than some arbitrary distance from the regression line.† Of course, outliers may

† We will be able to define outliers more explicitly when we consider the statistical properties of estimators in Chapter 3.

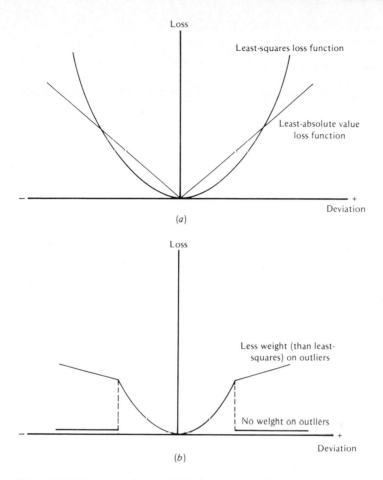

Figure 1.3 (*a*) Loss functions and (*b*) alternative loss functions.

not be the result of measurement error; they may in fact represent important pieces of information about the complexity of the relationship between several variables. Thus, one should never throw out the data point which happens to represent an outlier without further analysis. Indeed, a careful examination of outliers may help us to find mistakes, in which case a correction can be made. But the more general problem is that outliers are likely to suggest that the least-squares line is very sensitive to a small number of data points. This can be seen directly by working out Exercise 1.7, in which the incorrect data point replaces the correct one.

What can be done about the sensitivity of least squares to outliers? The most direct solution is to recalculate the least-squares line when the outlier has been removed. By reporting both the original and the new least-squares slopes and intercepts, we can give a reader a good feeling for the sensitivity of our results to the presence of outliers.† Because the decision about what makes an outlier is an arbitrary one, a better, although more complex, procedure would place a relatively low weight on large deviations. Two examples of such procedures are given in Fig. 1.3*b*, showing loss functions which are less sensitive than least squares to outliers. Since calculations involved with such techniques are more complex and their statistical properties more involved, the matter is not pursued further in this text.‡

1.2 DERIVATION OF LEAST SQUARES

The purpose of constructing statistical relationships is usually to predict or explain the effects on one variable resulting from changes in one or more predictor or explanatory variables. For the scatter of points in Fig. 1.1 we can write the linear equation $Y = a + bX$, where Y, the left-hand variable, is called the *dependent variable* and X, the right-hand variable, is called the *independent variable*. Because we are trying to explain or predict movements in Y, it is natural to choose as our objective the minimization of the vertical sum of the squared deviations from the fitted line.§

In order to obtain the formula for calculating values of a and b using the method of least squares we must use some basic mathematical tools. For those uncertain about the properties of *summation operators*, we suggest a brief review of Appendix 1.1, and for those unsure about the use of partial derivatives in the calculus, we stress that it is not important that one follow all the details of the derivation which follows.

---

† There are problems here, however. For example, it is possible that the newly calculated regression line will have one or more outliers associated with it.

‡ One reason for the complexity of the estimation is that deviations are defined relative to a given straight line. If we were to start with the least-squares line, for example, we would determine which data points should receive less weight after calculating the deviations. The new set of weights would allow us to calculate a new straight line, a new set of deviations, and a new set of weights. The result is that this technique, often called *robust estimation*, involves many iterations rather than a straightforward calculation as in least squares.

§ In general, our decision to write an equation in the form $Y = a + bX$ rather than the reverse form $X = A + BY$ implies that an implicit judgment has been made that movements in the variable Y are "caused" by movements in the variable X and not vice versa. Chapter 7 and Part Two of the book tell us what to do when the causal direction is not so clear. In the grade-point average example, we have assumed implicitly that grade-point average is determined by family income. If we revised our view of causality to one which states that family income is determined by grade-point average, then we would write the equation $X = A + BY$ and our curve-fitting criterion would be adjusted accordingly. Of course, minimizations of the sum of squared vertical and horizontal deviations are not the only least-squares procedures possible. One could minimize the sum of squared deviations measured along any line connecting sample points to the regression line. (An occasional choice is the perpendicular distance.) However, such procedures are more difficult computationally and statistically than the ordinary (vertical-distance) least-squares procedure and will not be pursued further.

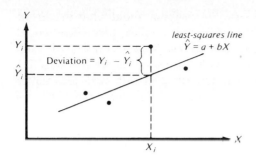

Figure 1.4 Fitted values.

The least-squares criterion (using vertical measurements) can be restated formally as follows:

$$\text{Minimize} \sum_{i=1}^{N} (Y_i - \hat{Y}_i)^2 \tag{1.1}$$

where $\hat{Y}_i = a + bX_i$ represents the equation for a straight line with intercept a and slope b. In this notation Y_i is the actual value of Y for observation i and corresponds to the value of X for that observation, while N is the number of observations. $\hat{Y}_i$, called the *fitted* or *predicted value* of Y_i, is the value of Y on the straight line which is associated with observation X_i. This can be clearly seen in Fig. 1.4, where the deviation is calculated by subtracting the fitted value of Y_i from the actual value. Thus, for each observation on X, there is a corresponding deviation of the fitted from actual value of Y. The sum of squares of these deviations is what we wish to minimize; it will allow us (in Chapter 3) to calculate a measure of how well the straight line fits the data. Finally, the values of a and b are not known and must be estimated from the data to satisfy the least-squares criterion.

The problem is to choose (simultaneously) values for a and b which minimize the expression in Eq. (1.1). This can be done using elementary calculus or algebra. To keep our discussion direct and to the point, we have put all the details of the calculus derivation in Appendix 1.2.† In any case, our analysis tells us that the least-squares solution for the slope and intercept are:

$$b = \frac{N\Sigma X_i Y_i - \Sigma X_i \Sigma Y_i}{N\Sigma X_i^2 - (\Sigma X_i)^2} \tag{1.2}$$

$$a = \frac{\Sigma Y_i}{N} - b\frac{\Sigma X_i}{N} = \bar{Y} - b\bar{X} \tag{1.3}$$

where $\bar{Y}$ and $\bar{X}$ are the sample means of Y and X, respectively.‡

---

† We encourage the reader to follow the derivation to become more familiar with our notation and our use of summation operators.

‡ The *sample mean* and related notions of probability and statistics are reviewed in Chapter 2.

Now consider how the formulas in Eqs. (1.2) and (1.3) simplify in the special case when X and Y both have sample means of 0. First, rewriting (1.3), we notice that

$$a = \overline{Y} - b\overline{X} = 0 \tag{1.4}$$

Thus, when the sample means of X and Y are 0, the intercept of the fitted regression line will be 0. To obtain the corresponding slope estimate in this special case, we divide both the numerator and denominator of Eq. (1.2) by N^2:

$$b = \frac{\Sigma X_i Y_i / N - (\Sigma X_i / N)(\Sigma Y_i / N)}{\Sigma X_i^2 / N - (\Sigma X_i / N)^2}$$

Substituting $\overline{X}$ and $\overline{Y}$ gives

$$b = \frac{\Sigma X_i Y_i / N - \overline{X}\,\overline{Y}}{\Sigma X_i^2 / N - \overline{X}^2}$$

But, $\overline{X} = \overline{Y} = 0$ by definition. Therefore,

$$b = \frac{\Sigma X_i Y_i / N}{\Sigma X_i^2 / N} = \frac{\Sigma X_i Y_i}{\Sigma X_i^2} \tag{1.5}$$

The fact that Eq. (1.5) is less complicated than Eq. (1.2) suggests that it will simplify matters and increase our understanding if we write the least-squares estimates in terms of variables which are expressed as deviations from their respective sample means, whether those means are zero or not.† To do so, we transform the data to deviations form by expressing each observation on X and Y in terms of deviations from their respective means.‡

$$x_i = X_i - \overline{X} \qquad y_i = Y_i - \overline{Y}$$

With this definition, the least-squares slope estimate can be obtained (in the general case) directly from Eq (1.5), since variables x and y have zero mean.

Therefore, we conclude that the least-squares slope estimate is

$$b = \frac{\Sigma x_i y_i}{\Sigma x_i^2} \tag{1.6}$$

The transformation of variables into deviations form is depicted graphically in Fig. 1.5. In Fig. 1.5a the regression line is graphed using the original

---

† The representation of the data in deviations form is done primarily for expositional purposes. Many of the derivations which appear in ensuing chapters will be greatly simplified if deviations data are used. This choice of representation involves no loss of generality.

‡ In Part One we shall always use small letters to refer to variables measured as deviations about their means.

$$\frac{\Sigma x_i}{N} = \frac{\Sigma (X_i - \overline{X})}{N} = \frac{\Sigma X_i}{N} - \overline{X} = \overline{X} - \overline{X} = 0$$

The identical proof holds for the mean of y.

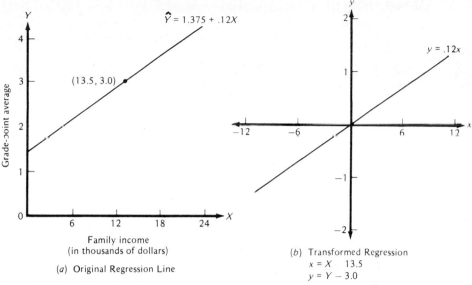

Figure 1.5 Use of deviations form.

observations, while the deviations form is used in Fig. 1.5b. Notice first that the estimated slopes of both regression lines are identical. This is obvious from Eq. (1.6), since only variables in deviations form enter the calculation. However, the intercept of the regression line in Fig. 1.5b is identically equal to 0. This follows from Eq. (1.4) and the fact that $\overline{X}$ and $\overline{Y}$ are equal to 0 by construction. Thus, if we choose to work with data in deviations form, we transform the origin of the regression line but do not alter the slope. Finally, notice that the line in Fig. 1.5b passes through the origin. This is equivalent to the fact that the line in Fig. 1.5a passes through the points of means $(\overline{X}, \overline{Y})$. The proof of this result is left as an exercise for the reader.

Example 1.1   Grade-point average In the grade-point-average example described in the text, the least-squares procedure allows us to obtain an intercept of 1.375 and a slope of .12, yielding the line $\hat{Y} = 1.375 + .12X$.†
The details of the calculations appear in Table 1.2. (The reader should check Fig. 1.1 to see that the resulting equation is quite similar to line l_2, which was determined by careful guesswork.) For any given family income X the regression line allows us to estimate or predict a value for the grade-point average Y. For example, a family income of $12,000 would lead to a predicted grade-point average of $\hat{Y} = 1.375 + .12(12) = 2.815$. While the predicted grade-point average will not necessarily give an accurate guess every time, it will provide a good approximation. For example, we might notice that the two students in the original sample (see Table 1.1) with

---

† Throughout Part I we place a "hat" above the dependent variable to denote the fitted value. We will relax this rule in Parts II and III to simplify the presentation.

Table 1.2 Grade-point average example (calculations)

$\bar{X} = 13.5$ $\bar{Y} = 3.0$

(1) $x_i = X_i - \bar{X}$	(2) $y_i = Y_i - \bar{Y}$	(3) $x_i y_i$	(4) x_i^2
7.5	1.0	7.5	56.25
1.5	.0	.0	2.25
1.5	.5	.75	2.25
−4.5	−1.0	4.5	20.25
−1.5	.0	.0	2.25
4.5	.5	2.25	20.25
−7.5	−.5	3.75	56.25
−1.5	−.5	.75	2.25
$\sum x_i = 0$	$\sum y_i = 0$	$\sum x_i y_i = 19.50$	$\sum x_i^2 = 162.00$

$$b = \frac{\sum x_i y_i}{\sum x_i^2} = .120 \qquad a = \bar{Y} - b\bar{X} = 1.375 \qquad \hat{Y} = 1.375 + .12X$$

parents having incomes of $12,000 had grade-point averages of 3.0 and 2.5. The predicted grade-point average happens to lie between the two actual data points.

The slope in the estimated equation tells us that a $1,000 change in family income will lead to an expected change of .12 in grade-point average. The positive value for the slope is consistent with the hypothesis that students with relatively high grade-point averages come from families with relatively high incomes. The intercept of 1.375 tells us that if family income were projected at $0, the best prediction for grade-point average would be 1.375. Since none of the families in our sample had an income near zero, we do not place much confidence in this result.

We shall examine the two-variable linear regression model in much greater detail in Chapter 3, but it will be instructive at this point to make a final comment about the least-squares procedure. In the model $Y = a + bX$, the slope b is an estimate of dY/dX, the ratio of a change in Y to a change in X. This allows us to interpret the regression slope quite naturally. The interpretation of the intercept, on the other hand, depends on whether sufficient observations near $X = 0$ are available to yield statistically meaningful results. If so, we can interpret the intercept as an estimate of Y when $X = 0$. However, if sufficient observations are not available, the intercept is simply the height of the least-squares line.

Example 1.2 Clothing expenditure† Suppose that we wish to study the relationship between expenditures on clothing and total expenditure on consumption goods. More specifically, we wish to see to what extent

---

† E. Malinvaud, *Statistical Methods of Econometrics* (Paris: North Holland, 1966), pp. 3–7.

movements on clothing expenditures can be predicted by movements in overall consumption expenditures. A study of this kind was constructed in France in 1951. Cross-section data were obtained for 112 households of minor officials living in provincial towns. The two variables measured were clothing expenditure Y and total consumption expenditure X. A decision was made to fit the line $Y = a + bX$, since it was believed that individuals choose their clothing expenditures as a direct function of their total chosen outlays. The estimated equation was

$$\hat{Y} = -1.78 + 1.20X$$

On the basis of the positive sign of the slope coefficient, we can conclude that the data are consistent with the hypothesis of a direct relationship between clothing expenditures and total expenditures.

Example 1.3 Stock prices of public utility companies As part of a larger corporate finance study, it is hypothesized that the price-earnings ratios for public utilities are influenced by their debt-equity ratios. This is reasonable, since one would expect a higher debt-equity ratio to lead to a more variable earning pattern for a company and that this added risk would lead to a lower stock price and thus a lower price-earnings ratio. The model can be expressed formally as

$$Y = a + bX$$

where Y is the price-earnings ratio of the company and
X is its debt-equity ratio.

We expect the coefficient b to have a negative value, but have no *a priori* expectation regarding the value of the intercept. Observations were obtained for variables Y and X for a cross section of public utilities (at a fixed point in time). The linear regression result is

$$\hat{Y} = 10.2 - 4.07X$$

The coefficient of -4.07 appears to confirm the stated hypothesis. However, in order to know how confident we are about the hypothesis in more detail we need to use some of the statistical tests discussed in the next chapter.

APPENDIX 1.1 THE USE OF SUMMATION OPERATORS

Because many elementary propositions in econometrics involve the use of sums of numbers, it will be prove useful to review (or perhaps become acquainted with) summation signs. Throughout the book the capital Greek letter sigma, Σ, represents the summation of the values of each of the observations for a variable. For example, let X represent the variable "family income." Then, using subscript notation,

$$X_1, X_2, \ldots, X_N$$

represents the values taken by each of the N observations of family income. Then total family income $(X_1 + X_2 + \cdots + X_N)$ can be represented as

$$\sum_{i=1}^{N} X_i = X_1 + X_2 + \cdots + X_N \tag{A1.1}$$

The following summation operator rules are useful.

Rule 1 The summation of a constant k times a variable is equal to the constant times the summation of that variable.

$$\sum_{i=1}^{N} kX_i = k \sum_{i=1}^{N} X_i \tag{A1.2}$$

Rule 2 The summation of the sum of observations on two variables is equal to the sum of their summations.

$$\sum_{i=1}^{N} (X_i + Y_i) = \sum_{i=1}^{N} X_i + \sum_{i=1}^{N} Y_i \tag{A1.3}$$

Rule 3 The summation of a constant over N observations equals the product of the constant and N.

$$\sum_{i=1}^{N} k = kN \tag{A1.4}$$

Using the first three rules, we can obtain some useful results concerning means, variances, and covariances of random variables. Since these concepts are discussed more completely in Chapter 2, we will restrict ourselves here to a discussion of algebraic (rather than statistical) properties. First, we define the mean or average of N observations on variable X to be

$$\overline{X} = \frac{1}{N} \sum_{i=1}^{N} X_i \tag{A1.5}$$

Using this definition, we can prove Rule 4.

Rule 4 The summation of the deviations of observations on X about its mean is zero.

$$\sum_{i=1}^{N} \left(X_i - \overline{X} \right) = 0 \tag{A1.6}$$

(See the second footnote on page 10 for proof.) In the text we will have frequent opportunity to use notation in which observations are measured as deviations about their means. To simplify, we use lowercase letters to represent deviations form, that is, $x_i = X_i - \overline{X}$, in which case Rule 4 becomes

$$\sum_{i=1}^{N} x_i = 0 \tag{A1.7}$$

Now we define the sample variance of X to be

$$\text{Var}(X) = \frac{1}{N} \sum_{i=1}^{N} (X_i - \bar{X})^2 \qquad (A1.8)$$

and the sample covariance of X and Y to be

$$\text{Cov}(X, Y) = \frac{1}{N} \sum_{i=1}^{N} (X_i - \bar{X})(Y_i - \bar{Y}) \qquad (A1.9)$$

Using these definitions and our earlier results, we can prove the last two summation rules.

Rule 5 The covariance between X and Y is equal to the mean of the sum of the products of observations on X and Y minus the product of their means

$$\frac{1}{N} \sum_{i=1}^{N} (X_i - \bar{X})(Y_i - \bar{Y}) = \frac{1}{N} \sum_{i=1}^{N} X_i Y_i - \overline{XY} \qquad (A1.10)$$

PROOF The proof is somewhat tedious but quite straightforward.

$$\frac{1}{N} \sum_{i=1}^{N} (X_i - \bar{X})(Y_i - \bar{Y}) = \frac{1}{N} \sum_{i=1}^{N} X_i Y_i - \frac{1}{N} \sum_{i=1}^{N} \bar{X} Y_i$$
$$- \frac{1}{N} \sum_{i=1}^{N} X_i \bar{Y} + \frac{1}{N} \sum_{i=1}^{N} \overline{XY}$$

and using Rule 1, we get

$$\text{Cov}(X, Y) = \frac{1}{N} \sum_{i=1}^{N} X_i Y_i - \frac{1}{N} \bar{X} \sum_{i=1}^{N} Y_i - \frac{1}{N} \bar{Y} \sum_{i=1}^{N} X_i + \frac{1}{N} \sum_{i=1}^{N} \overline{XY}$$

Now, recalling the definition of the mean of X and the mean of Y, we have

$$\text{Cov}(X, Y) = \frac{1}{N} \sum_{i=1}^{N} X_i Y_i - \overline{XY} - \overline{YX} + \frac{1}{N} \sum_{i=1}^{N} \overline{XY}$$

$$= \frac{1}{N} \sum_{i=1}^{N} X_i Y_i - 2\overline{XY} + \overline{XY} \qquad \text{since } \sum_{i=1}^{N} = N\overline{XY} \text{ by Rule 1}$$

$$= \frac{1}{N} \sum_{i=1}^{N} X_i Y_i - \overline{XY}$$

Rule 6 follows easily from Rule 5 since it applies to the case in which X and X again are the two variables.

Rule 6 The variance of X is equal to the mean of the summation of the squares of observations on X minus its mean squared.

$$\frac{1}{N} \sum_{i=1}^{N} (X_i - \bar{X})^2 = \frac{1}{N} \sum_{i=1}^{N} X_i^2 - \bar{X}^2 \qquad (A1.11)$$

Note, incidently, that when X and Y happen to have zero means (as when they are measured as deviations about their means), the definitions of covariance and variance (we have omitted the range of the index here) become

$$\text{Cov}(x, y) = \frac{1}{N} \sum x_i y_i \quad \text{and} \quad \text{Var}(x) = \frac{1}{N} \sum x_i^2$$

In Appendix 2.1 we use summations which apply to two random variables, called *double summations*. Specifically, let N values for each outcome on X_{ij} be a random variable which takes on N values for each outcome on i and j. There will, of course, be N^2 total outcomes. Now we define the double summation of these N^2 outcomes as

$$\sum_{i=1}^{N} \sum_{j=1}^{N} X_{ij} = \sum_{i=1}^{N} (X_{i1} + X_{i2} + \cdots + X_{iN})$$

$$= (X_{11} + X_{12} + \cdots + X_{1N}) + (X_{21} + X_{22} + \cdots + X_{2N})$$

$$+ \cdots + (X_{N1} + X_{N2} + \cdots + X_{NN})$$

The following two double-summation rules will be useful.

Rule 7

$$\sum_{i=1}^{N} \sum_{j=1}^{N} X_i Y_j = \left(\sum_{i=1}^{N} X_i \right) \left(\sum_{j=1}^{N} Y_j \right) \tag{A1.12}$$

Note that the double summation in Rule 7 is very different from the single summation $\sum_{i=1}^{N} X_i Y_i$, which contains N (rather than N^2) terms.

Rule 8

$$\sum_{i=1}^{N} \sum_{j=1}^{N} (X_{ij} + Y_{ij}) = \sum_{i=1}^{N} \sum_{j=1}^{N} X_{ij} + \sum_{i=1}^{N} \sum_{j=1}^{N} Y_{ij} \tag{A1.13}$$

APPENDIX 1.2 DERIVATION OF LEAST-SQUARES PARAMETER ESTIMATES

As stated in the text, our goal is to maximize $\sum (Y_i - \hat{Y}_i)^2$, where $\hat{Y}_i = a + bX_i$ is the fitted value of Y corresponding to a particular observation X_i.

We minimize the expression by taking the partial derivatives with respect to a and to b, setting each equal to 0, and solving the resulting pair of simultaneous equations†

$$\frac{\partial}{\partial a} \sum (Y_i - a - bX_i)^2 = -2\sum (Y_i - a - bX_i) \tag{A1.14}$$

$$\frac{\partial}{\partial b} \sum (Y_i - a - bX_i)^2 = -2\sum X_i (Y_i - a - bX_i) \tag{A1.15}$$

---

† An index does not appear in the summation signs, but the index is assumed to range over all observations $1, 2, \ldots, N$.

Equating these derivatives to zero and dividing by -2, we get

$$\Sigma(Y_i - a - bX_i) = 0 \tag{A1.16}$$

$$\Sigma X_i(Y_i - a - bX_i) = 0 \tag{A1.17}$$

Finally by rewriting Eqs. (A1.16) and (A1.17) we obtain the pair of simultaneous equations (known as the *normal equations*)

$$\Sigma Y_i = aN + b\Sigma X_i \tag{A1.18}$$

$$\Sigma X_i Y_i = a\Sigma X_i + b\Sigma X_i^2 \tag{A1.19}$$

(Recall that N is the number of observations.) Now we may solve for a and b simultaneously by multiplying (A1.18) by ΣX_i and (A1.19) by N:

$$\Sigma X_i \Sigma Y_i = aN\Sigma X_i + b(\Sigma X_i)^2 \tag{A1.20}$$

$$N\Sigma X_i Y_i = aN\Sigma X_i + bN\Sigma X_i^2 \tag{A1.21}$$

Subtracting (A1.20) from (A1.21), we get

$$N\Sigma X_i Y_i - \Sigma X_i \Sigma Y_i = b\left[N\Sigma X_i^2 - (\Sigma X_i)^2\right] \tag{A1.22}$$

from which it follows that

$$b = \frac{N\Sigma X_i Y_i - \Sigma X_i \Sigma Y_i}{N\Sigma X_i^2 - (\Sigma X_i)^2} \tag{A1.23}$$

Given b, we may calculate a from Eq. (A1.18):

$$a = \frac{\Sigma Y_i}{N} - b\frac{\Sigma X_i}{N} \tag{A1.24}$$

EXERCISES

1.1 Assume that you are in charge of the central monetary authority in a mythical country. You are given the following historical data on the quantity of money and national income (both in millions of dollars):

Year	Quantity of money	National income	Year	Quantity of money	National income
1973	2.0	5.0	1978	4.0	7.7
1974	2.5	5.5	1979	4.2	8.4
1975	3.2	6.0	1980	4.6	9.0
1976	3.6	7.0	1981	4.8	9.7
1977	3.3	7.2	1982	5.0	10.0

(a) Plot these points on a scatter diagram. Then estimate the regression of national income Y on the quantity of money X and plot the line on the scatter diagram.

(b) How do you interpret the intercept and slope of the regression line?

(c) If you had sole control over the money supply and wished to achieve a level of national income of 12.0 in 1983, at what level would you set the money supply? Explain.

1.2 Calculate the regression of income on grade-point average in the example described in the chapter, and compare it with the regression of grade-point average on income. Why are the two results different?

1.3 (*a*) Assume that least-squares estimates are obtained for the relationship $Y = a + bX$. After the work is completed, it is decided to multiply the units of the X variable by a factor of 10. What will happen to the resulting least-squares slope and intercept?

(*b*) Generalize the result of part (*a*) by evaluating the effects on the regression of changing the units of X and Y in the following manner:

$$Y^* = c_1 + c_2 Y \qquad X^* = d_1 + d_2 X$$

What can you conclude?

1.4 What happens to the least-squares intercept and slope estimate when all observations on the independent variable are identical? Can you explain intuitively why this occurs?

1.5 Prove that the estimated regression line passes through the point of means $(\overline{X}, \overline{Y})$. *Hint:* Show that $\overline{X}$ and $\overline{Y}$ satisfy the equation $Y = a + bX$, where a and b are defined in Eqs. (1.2) and (1.3).

1.6 How would you interpret the -1.78 value of the intercept in the regression equation of Example 1.2? Explain why the value of the intercept is not likely to be of much practical interest.

1.7 To test for sensitivity of least-squares estimates of intercept and slope to the presence of outliers, perform the following calculations:

1. Reestimate the slope and intercept in Example 1.1 under the assumption that the first observation was (21.0, 1.0) rather than (21.0, 4.0).
2. Reestimate the slope and intercept dropping the first observation from the sample.

(*a*) Describe how the slope and intercept estimates in 1 and 2 compare with those given in the example. A graph of both straight lines would be helpful. Why are least-squares estimates so sensitive to individual data points?

(*b*) Having graphed the least-squares line in case 1, would you conclude that the first data point is an outlier? Discuss.

ELEMENTARY STATISTICS: A REVIEW

The study of econometrics, even in its most applied form, requires a good understanding of the basic concepts of statistics. We assume that most readers have previously studied statistics but realize that some of that knowledge may need updating. Before continuing our study of econometrics with an analysis of the two-variable regression model, we have therefore chosen to review those statistical ideas which will be used at various stages in the text. To help the reader focus attention on important ideas rather than details, we have included the most complicated derivations in Appendix 2.1.

2.1 RANDOM VARIABLES

A *random variable* is a variable that takes on alternative values according to chance. More specifically, a random variable has the property that it assumes different values, each with a probability less than or equal to 1. We can also describe a random variable by examining the process which generates its values. This process, called a *probability distribution*, lists all possible outcomes and the probability that each will occur. We might define a random variable as a function that assigns to each outcome of an experiment a real number. For example, assume that we assign a value of 1 to a coin toss of heads and a value of 0 to a toss of tails (if we use a fair coin the probability of heads will be $\frac{1}{2}$). In this case, we can interpret the value of the coin toss as a random variable; the process generating the random variable is the *binomial probability distribution*.

It is useful to distinguish between discrete and continuous random variables. A *continuous random variable* may take on any value on the real number line,

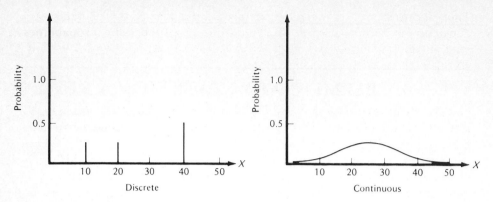

Figure 2.1 Probability functions.

while a *discrete random variable* may take on only a specific number of real values. Figure 2.1 illustrates a discrete and a continuous probability function.

2.1.1 Expected Values

Probability distributions are often described in terms of their means and variances, which, in turn, are defined in terms of the *expectations operator E*. Since we will make use primarily of discrete random variables, let us assume that $X_1, X_2, \ldots, X_N$ represent the N possible outcomes associated with the random variable X. Then the *mean*, or *expected value*, of X is simply a weighted average of the possible outcomes, where the probabilities of the outcomes serve as the appropriate weights. Specifically, the mean of X, denoted μ_X, is defined by

$$\mu_X = E(X) = p_1 X_1 + p_2 X_2 + \cdots + p_N X_N = \sum_{i=1}^{N} p_i X_i \qquad (2.1)$$

where p_i is the probability that X_i occurs, that is, $X = X_i$; $\Sigma p_i = 1$; and $E(\ )$ is the expectations operator.

The mean or expected value should be distinguished from the *sample mean*, which tells us the average of the outcomes obtained in a sample in which a number of observations are chosen (usually at random) from the underlying probability distribution. We denote the sample mean of a set of outcomes on X by $\bar{X}$.

The *variance* of a random variable provides a measure of the spread, or dispersion, around the mean. It is denoted σ_X^2 and (in the discrete case) is defined as

$$\text{Var}(X) = \sigma_X^2 = \sum_{i=1}^{N} p_i [X_i - E(X)]^2 \qquad (2.2)$$

Thus, the variance is a weighted average of the squares of the deviations of outcomes on X from its expected value, with the corresponding probabilities of each outcome occurring serving as weights. The variance in Eq. (2.2) is in itself an expectation, since

$$\sigma_X^2 = E[X - E(X)]^2 \tag{2.3}$$

The (positive) square root of the variance is called the *standard deviation*. As a result, both the variance and the standard deviation of a random variable are nonnegative.

There are a number of properties of the expectations operator which we will find useful in the text, especially when discussing means and variances of random variables. We will not interrupt the central discussion here to prove the results, but we encourage the reader to examine carefully the details described in Appendix 2.1. Three of the major results concerning the expectations operator are as follows:

Result 1

$$E(aX + b) = aE(X) + b$$

where X is a random variable and a and b are constants.

Result 2

$$E[(aX)^2] = a^2 E(X^2)$$

Result 3

$$\text{Var}(aX + b) = a^2 \text{Var}(X)$$

2.1.2 Joint Distributions of Random Variables

To this point we have considered only distributions of a single random variable X. However, it is useful to study briefly joint distributions of X and a second random variable Y. In the discrete case, joint distributions are described by a list of probabilities of occurrence of all possible outcomes on both X and Y. For example, if Y is a random variable which takes on the value 1 if the head of a household has a college education and 0 if not while X is the family income variable described earlier, then the *joint* distribution of X and Y might be:

Outcome	Probability	Outcome	Probability
$X = \$5,000, Y = 1$	0	$X = \$10,000, Y = 0$	$\frac{1}{8}$
$X = \$5,000, Y = 0$	$\frac{1}{4}$	$X = \$15,000, Y = 1$	$\frac{1}{3}$
$X = \$10,000, Y = 1$	$\frac{1}{8}$	$X = \$15,000, Y = 0$	$\frac{1}{6}$

Note that all probabilities are nonnegative and sum to 1.

Just as in the case of a single random variable, the expectations operator is useful for describing the important characteristics of joint distributions. We define the *covariance* of X and Y as the expectation of the product of X and Y when both are measured as deviations about their means;

$$\text{Cov}\,(X, Y) = E\big[(X - E(X))(Y - E(Y))\big] \qquad (2.4)$$

$$= p_{ij} \sum_{i=1}^{N} \sum_{j=1}^{N} [X_i - E(X)][Y_i - E(Y)] \qquad (2.5)$$

where p_{ij} represents the joint probability of X and Y occurring.

The covariance is a measure of the linear association between X and Y. If both variables are always above and below their means at the same time, the covariance will be positive. If X is above its mean when Y is below its mean and vice versa, the covariance will be negative, as in Fig. 2.2. The value of the covariance depends upon the units in which X and Y are measured. As a result we will have frequent occasions on which to use the *correlation coefficient*

$$\rho(X, Y) = \frac{\text{Cov}\,(X, Y)}{\sigma_X \sigma_Y} \qquad (2.6)$$

where σ_X and σ_Y represent the standard deviation of X and Y, respectively.

Unlike covariance, the correlation coefficient is a measure of the association which has been normalized and is *scale-free*. It can be shown that the correlation coefficient will always lie between -1 and $+1$. A positive correlation indicates that the variables move in the same direction, while a negative correlation implies that they move in opposite directions. On the other hand, any two variables which are statistically independent will always have a correlation coefficient of 0.

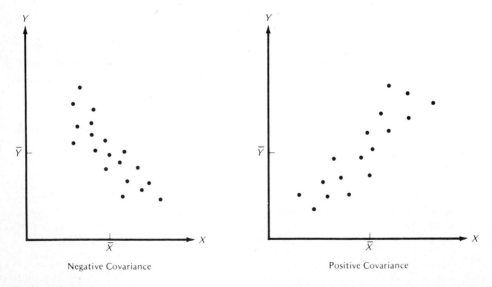

Negative Covariance   Positive Covariance

Figure 2.2 Covariance.

Once again, there are several properties of the expectations operator which are useful when dealing with joint probability distributions. They are stated here and proved in Appendix 2.1.

Result 4 If X and Y are random variables,

$$E(X + Y) = E(X) + E(Y)$$

Result 5

$$\text{Var}(X + Y) = \text{Var}(X) + \text{Var}(Y) + 2\,\text{Cov}(X, Y)$$

2.1.3 Independence and Correlation

In certain special cases the joint probability distribution of X and Y may have the property that the probability of an outcome associated with Y will be unrelated to the outcome associated with X, and vice versa. In this case we say that X and Y are *independent* random variables. As an example, consider the tossing of a fair coin, i.e., a coin for which the probability of heads and the probability of tails are both $\frac{1}{2}$. Assume that the first five tosses are all heads. The probability of tails occurring on the sixth toss will be $\frac{1}{2}$, and this is independent of the previous tosses.

When two variables are independent, calculations involving the expectations operator become simplified. The result is summed up by the two final properties of the expectations operator, proved in Appendix 2.1.

Result 6 If X and Y are independent,

$$E(XY) = E(X)E(Y)$$

Result 7 If X and Y are independent,

$$\text{Cov}(X, Y) = 0$$

Result 7 states that if two random variables are independent, the covariance between them is 0. This makes intuitive sense because independence of X and Y means that there is no relation between the occurrence of outcomes of one variable and outcomes of the other variable. If there is no relationship, we would expect deviations in X about its mean to be unrelated to deviations in Y. Because the correlation between X and Y is also zero when the covariance is zero, we often say that independent variables are uncorrelated.

It is important to realize however, that the result does not hold in the opposite direction. Two variables may be uncorrelated, i.e., have zero covariance, and yet there may be a dependence between the variables. The key here is the fact that covariance and correlation measure *linear* dependence; the variables may be related nonlinearly and yet have a zero covariance.

As an example, assume that X and Y follow the probability distribution

X	-2	-1	0	1	2
Y	4	1	0	1	4

All observations are assumed to occur with equal probability ($\frac{1}{5}$). In this case $E(X) = 0$, $E(Y) = 2$, and

$$\text{Cov}\,(X, Y) = \sum_{i=1}^{5} X_i(Y_i - 2) = 0$$

However, the random variables are certainly not independent. In fact all five joint outcomes listed satisfy the relationship $Y = X^2$, so that there is an exact nonlinear relationship between X and Y.

2.2 ESTIMATION

2.2.1 Estimators of Mean, Variance, and Covariance

Means, variances, and covariances can be measured with certainty only if we know all there is to know about all possible outcomes. Unfortunately, this is an extremely unlikely possibility in applied econometrics. As a result, when we undertake a particular study, we obtain a sample of the relevant information needed. As in our earlier discussion, we will assume that our sample consists of N observations on one or more random variables. Since we cannot know the true mean and variance of a random variable or the true covariance between two random variables, we must use the sample information to obtain the best possible estimates.

Of course our problem is more general than finding estimates for a given sample. Instead we wish to determine a rule which will give a sample estimate for each and every possible sample. To distinguish the single estimate from the more general rule, we call the latter an *estimator*. It is common for students to confuse "estimates" and "estimators," but this confusion can be eliminated if we remind ourselves that estimators are functions or rules while estimates are numbers.

What is entailed in finding the best estimator for any given sample is a somewhat complex issue, discussed in greater detail in Section 2.3. For the moment, let us assume that a minimal requirement for an estimator is that the estimator of a parameter (like the mean or variation) yield estimates closely approximating that parameter. More specifically, we would like the estimator to be *unbiased* in the sense that the *expected value* of the estimator is equal to the parameter itself. As an example, reconsider the sample mean of a random variable X with mean μ_X. The estimator $\overline{X}$ is defined by

$$\overline{X} = \frac{1}{N} \sum_{i=1}^{N} X_i \tag{2.7}$$

To check whether $\overline{X}$ is unbiased, we need to evaluate $E(\overline{X})$ to see whether

$$E(\overline{X}) = \mu_X;$$

$$E(\overline{X}) = E\left(\frac{1}{N} \sum_{i=1}^{N} X_i\right) = \frac{1}{N} E\left(\sum_{i=1}^{N} X_i\right) = \frac{1}{N} \sum_{i=1}^{N} E(X_i)$$

$$= \frac{1}{N} \sum_{i=1}^{N} \mu_X = \frac{1}{N} N\mu_X = \mu_X$$

Now consider how we obtain an unbiased estimator of the variance of a random variable. A reasonable choice for such an estimator is

$$\frac{1}{N} \sum_{i=1}^{N} \left(X_i - \overline{X}\right)^2 \tag{2.8}$$

The problem is that this estimator is biased. As we show in Appendix 2.1, Result 9 (which follows directly from Result 8, shown only in Appendix 2.1), an unbiased estimator of the variance of a random variable (with unknown mean) is given by

$$\frac{1}{N-1} \sum_{i=1}^{N} \left(X_i - \overline{X}\right)^2 \tag{2.9}$$

Why do we divide by $N - 1$ (rather than N) to get an unbiased estimate of the sample variance? The exact answer is given in the proof of the result given in Appendix 2.1, but an intuitive answer can be based on the concept of *degrees of freedom*. Our sample is known to contain N data points. However, in computing the sample variance a necessary first step was the computation of the sample mean. Computing the sample mean places one constraint upon the N data points, the constraint that the N observations sum to N times the computed mean $\overline{X}$. This leaves $N - 1$ unconstrained observations with which to estimate the sample variance given the mean. We will frequently return to the concept of degrees of freedom, and in each case the number of observations minus the number of constraints placed on the data will be the number we are after.

Finally, let us consider how we might obtain an unbiased estimator of the covariance between two random variables. Since the covariance is defined as

$$\text{Cov}\,(X, Y) = E[(X - E(X))(Y - E(Y))]$$

a natural way to estimate the covariance would be to measure the average of the product of the deviations of X and Y about their means, i.e.,

$$\frac{1}{N} \sum_{i=1}^{N} \left(X_i - \overline{X}\right)\left(Y_i - \overline{Y}\right)$$

However, just as in the previous case, this estimator will be biased. To obtain an unbiased estimator we must divide the previous summation by the number of degrees of freedom. In calculating the sum of the product of the deviations in X and Y, there are N observations on the joint outcomes of X and Y, and thus N independent pieces of information. However, *one* piece of information is used to calculate the means of X and Y, the constraint being that the sum of all N observations equals N times the means of X and Y, respectively. As a result there are $N - 1$ degrees of freedom, and the unbiased estimator is

$$\widehat{\text{Cov}}\,(X,\,Y) = \frac{1}{N-1} \sum_{i=1}^{N} (X_i - \bar{X})(Y_i - \bar{Y}) \qquad (2.10)$$

The sample covariance is distinguished from the true covariance by placing a hat ($\wedge$) above the Cov. This is a convention that we will follow frequently in the text.

Finally, we can define the *sample* correlation coefficient between two variables to correspond to the population coefficient defined earlier. The sample correlation coefficient is defined as

$$r_{XY} = \frac{\displaystyle\sum_{i=1}^{N} (X_i - \bar{X})(Y_i - \bar{Y})}{\sqrt{\displaystyle\sum_{i=1}^{N} (X_i - \bar{X})^2 \sum_{i=1}^{N} (Y_i - \bar{Y})^2}} \qquad (2.11)$$

r_{XY} is, of course, a random variable, since its value varies from sample to sample. To distinguish r_{XY} from other more complex measures of correlation we will occasionally call it the *simple correlation* between X and Y. Like its population counterpart, r_{XY} ranges from -1 to $+1$ in value, so that its square lies between 0 and 1. We might note that the simple correlation relates directly to the sample covariance between X and Y as follows:

$$r_{XY} = \frac{\widehat{\text{Cov}}\,(X,\,Y)}{\sqrt{\widehat{\text{Var}}\,(X)\,\widehat{\text{Var}}\,(Y)}} \qquad (2.12)$$

Why focus our attention on the concept of covariance between two random variables? The answer is that econometrics involves the study of relationships between variables. Since covariance tells us whether and to what extent two variables are related, it serves as one of the underpinnings of applied econometrics. A positive covariance implies that when X lies above its mean, so will Y, and when X lies below its mean, so will Y. This suggests (see Fig. 2.2) that the best-fitting line through a set of points with negative covariance will have a negative slope. Of course, in the special case of X and Y being uncorrelated, and thus having zero covariance, the best-fitting line will have zero slope.

We can see this more clearly if we relate the measure of sample covariance to the least-squares slope estimator given in Chapter 1. Rewriting the sample covariance estimator in deviations form, with $x_i = X_i - \bar{X}$ and $y_i = Y_i - \bar{Y}$,

$$\widehat{\text{Cov}}\,(X,\,Y) = \frac{1}{N-1} \Sigma x_i y_i \qquad (2.13)$$

Note that we have dropped the index $i = 1, 2, \ldots, N$ for convenience. Recall also that our sample estimator of the variance of X, sometimes denoted s_X^2, is given by

$$\widehat{\text{Var}}(X) = \frac{1}{N-1}\Sigma x_i^2$$

Now, consider the expression obtained by dividing the sample covariance by the sample variance

$$\frac{\widehat{\text{Cov}}(X, Y)}{\widehat{\text{Var}}(X)} = \frac{[1/(N-1)]\Sigma x_i y_i}{[1/(N-1)]\Sigma x_i^2} = \frac{\Sigma x_i y_i}{\Sigma x_i^2} \qquad (2.14)$$

This ratio is identically equal to the estimate of this slope obtained in Eq. (1.6) for a particular sample of N points. For any sample of data points, the least-squares slope estimator can be measured by the ratio of covariance, which takes the direction of the line, and the variance, a positive number which serves to normalize or adjust the units in which the data are measured. To apply this concept let us return to some of the numerical results used in the first chapter.

In the grade-point-average example described in Example 1.1, our calculations for the least-squares slope estimate can be used to calculate sample means, variance, and covariance. With the data presented in deviations form, i.e., measured as deviations about means, we find that $\bar{x}$ and $\bar{y} = 0$. The covariance between X and Y is given by

$$\frac{1}{N-1}\Sigma x_i y_i = \frac{19.50}{7} = 2.71$$

while the variance of X is given by

$$\frac{1}{N-1}\Sigma x_i^2 = \frac{162.00}{7} = 23.14$$

The covariance is positive, indicating a positive slope, and the ratio of sample covariance to sample variance, 2.71/23.14, yields the slope estimate, .12.

2.3 DESIRABLE PROPERTIES OF ESTIMATORS

We have previously argued that one useful property of a statistical estimator is for the estimator to be unbiased. Since the search for estimators is the heart of the science of econometrics, we will pause here to consider a broad set of properties that might be viewed as desirable. In order to tie our discussion in with the analysis of the regression model we will drop our discussion of specific parameters, such as mean, variance, and covariance, and simply ask what properties we ought to look for when choosing an estimator for an arbitrary parameter β. β is chosen here to apply to the slope estimator of a straight line, but that is irrelevant for our present discussion. Now consider four properties of estimators which are worthy of serious attention.

2.3.1 Lack of Bias

One very desirable property associated with an estimated regression parameter is for the distribution of the estimator to have the parameter as its mean value. Then if we could repeat the experiment many times for new sets of observations on Y, we would be assured of being right on average. We will say that $\hat{\beta}$ is an *unbiased* estimator if the mean or expected value of $\hat{\beta}$ is equal to the true value; that is, $E(\hat{\beta}) = \beta$. The difference between a biased and an unbiased estimator can be seen in Fig. 2.3. The reader should recall that for a sample of size N, $\Sigma X_i / N$ is an unbiased estimator of the true mean of a population, while $\Sigma(X_i - \bar{X})^2 / (N - 1)$ is an unbiased estimator of the true variance of the population. To clarify the exposition we shall define the bias associated with an estimated parameter as *follows*:

$$\text{Bias} = E(\hat{\beta}) - \beta$$

It is important to realize that while lack of bias in an estimator is a desirable property, lack of bias implies nothing about the dispersion of the estimator about the true parameter. In general, one would like the estimator to be unbiased and also to have a very small dispersion about the mean. This suggests that one should define a second criterion that allows one to choose among alternative unbiased estimators.

2.3.2 Efficiency

We say that $\hat{\beta}$ is an *efficient* unbiased estimator if for a given sample size the variance of $\hat{\beta}$ is smaller than the variance of any other unbiased estimators. In practice it is sometimes difficult to tell whether an estimator is efficient, so that it is natural to describe estimators in terms of their relative efficiency. One estimator is more efficient than another if it has smaller variance. A relatively efficient and a relatively inefficient estimator are shown graphically in Fig. 2.4.

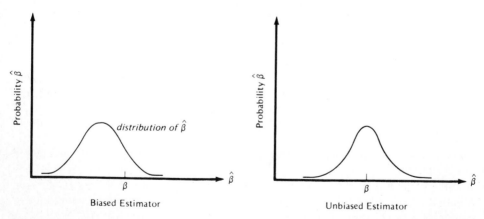

Figure 2.3 Bias.

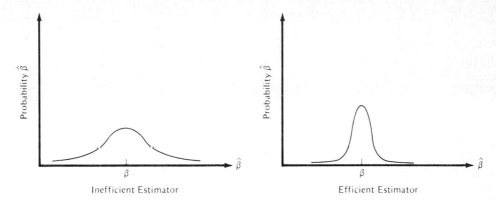

Figure 2.4 Efficiency.

Efficiency is a desirable objective because the greater the efficiency associated with an estimation process, the stronger the *statistical* statements that one can make about the estimated parameters. Thus, in the extreme case of an (unbiased) estimator with *zero* variance, we can state with certainty the numerical value of the true regression parameter.

2.3.3 Minimum Mean Square Error

There are many circumstances in which one is forced to trade off bias and variance of estimators. When the goal of a model is to maximize the precision of predictions, for example, an estimator with very low variance and some bias may be more desirable than an unbiased estimator with high variance. One criterion which is useful in this regard is the goal of minimizing *mean square error*, defined as

$$\text{Mean square error } (\hat{\beta}) = E(\hat{\beta} - \beta)^2$$

It is not difficult to show that this definition is equivalent to†

$$\text{Mean square error} = \left[\text{Bias } (\hat{\beta})\right]^2 + \text{Var } (\hat{\beta})$$

Thus, the criterion of minimizing mean square error takes into account the variance and the square of the bias of the estimator. When $\hat{\beta}$ is unbiased, the mean square error and variance of $\hat{\beta}$ are equal.

---

† If $\bar{\beta}$ is the expected value of the estimated regression coefficient,

$$E(\hat{\beta} - \beta)^2 = E\left[(\hat{\beta} - \bar{\beta}) + (\bar{\beta} - \beta)\right]^2 = E(\hat{\beta} - \bar{\beta})^2 + E(\bar{\beta} - \beta)^2 + 2(\bar{\beta} - \beta)E(\hat{\beta} - \bar{\beta})$$

$$= \text{Var } (\hat{\beta}) + \left[\text{Bias } (\hat{\beta})\right]^2 \quad \left[\text{This follows, since } \bar{\beta} = E(\hat{\beta}) \text{ by definition.}\right]$$

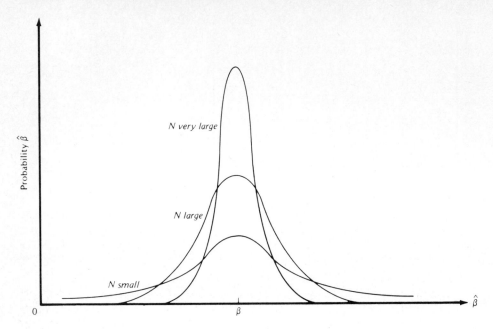

Figure 2.5 Consistency.

2.3.4 Consistency

To complete our discussion we consider the properties of estimators as the sample size gets very large, i.e., the *asymptotic*, or large-sample, properties. In this respect, we would like our estimator $\hat{\beta}$ to get close in some sense to the true β as the sample size increases; i.e., we would like the distribution of $\hat{\beta}$ to converge to β. More specifically, we hope that as the sample size gets infinitely large, the probability that $\hat{\beta}$ will differ from β will get very small. To apply this probabilistic concept to the choice of estimator, we define the probability limit of $\hat{\beta}$ (plim $\hat{\beta}$) as follows: plim $\hat{\beta}$ is equal to β if as N approaches infinity, the probability that $|\beta - \hat{\beta}|$ will be less than any arbitrarily small positive number will approach 1. With this concept it is natural to define the criterion of *consistency* as follows: $\hat{\beta}$ is a *consistent* estimator of β if the *probability limit* of $\hat{\beta}$ is β.† Roughly speaking, an estimator is consistent if the probability distribution of the estimator collapses to a single point (the true parameter) as the sample size gets arbitrarily large. This is described graphically in Fig. 2.5.

As a rule, econometricians tend to be more concerned with consistency than with lack of bias as an estimation criterion. A biased yet consistent estimator may not equal the true parameter on average, but will approximate the true parameter as the sample information grows larger. This is more reassuring from a practical point of view than the alternative of finding a parameter estimate

---

† Strictly speaking $\hat{\beta}$ converges to β in the probability limit if for any $\delta > 0$,

$$\lim_{N \to \infty} \text{Prob} \left(|\beta - \hat{\beta}| < \delta \right) = 1$$

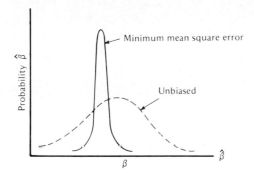

Figure 2.6 Mean square error.

which is unbiased yet which continues to deviate substantially from the true parameter as the sample size gets larger. Figure 2.6 illustrates two parameter estimators, one of which is unbiased with large variance. Because of the large tails, the second estimator, although biased, has sufficiently small variance to have on net a smaller mean square error.

It is natural to consider as an alternative criterion to consistency the objective that the *mean square error of the estimator approach zero as the sample increases.* The mean-square-error criterion implies that the estimator is *unbiased asymptotically* and that its variance goes to zero as the sample size gets very large. It turns out that an estimator with a mean square error that approaches zero will be consistent estimator but that the reverse need not be true. In most applications consistent estimators have mean square errors approaching zero, and the two criteria are used interchangeably.

2.4 PROBABILITY DISTRIBUTIONS

There are a number of specific probability distributions which will be of use at one or more places in the book. Since each of the distributions is related to the others, we have chosen to introduce them as a group, rather than when the occasion for using each specific distribution arises. The four distributions covered here are the normal, chi-square, t, and F distributions. Each has some relevance for each of three parts of the book, but as the reader will see, the t and F distributions receive the most use in Part One while the chi square appears more frequently in Part Three. The normal distribution does not receive as much use as one might expect in econometrics, but it appears first because it is most familiar to students of statistics and because it serves as the building block upon which the other distributions are based. The discussion which follows is meant to be descriptive and not rigorous.

2.4.1 Normal Distributions

The normal distribution is a continuous bell-shaped probability distribution, which appears as shown in Fig. 2.7. A normal distribution can be fully described

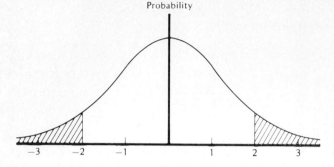

Figure 2.7 Standard normal distribution.

by its mean and its variance, so that if X were normally distributed, we would write $X \sim N(\mu_X, \sigma_X^2)$, which is read "$X$ is distributed as a normal variable with mean μ_X and variance σ_X^2."

It is useful to know that†

$$\text{Prob}\,(\mu_X - 1.96\sigma_X < X_i < \mu_X + 1.96\sigma_X) \approx .95 \tag{2.15}$$

$$\text{Prob}\,(\mu_X - 2.57\sigma_X < X_i < \mu_X + 2.57\sigma_X) \approx .99 \tag{2.16}$$

where μ_X and σ_X are the mean and standard deviations of the normal random variable X. The probability that a single observation of a normally distributed variable X will lie within about 2 standard deviations of its mean is approximately .95. The probability of being within about $2\frac{1}{2}$ standard deviations is about .99. Conversely, the probability that a single observation will be more than 2 $(2\frac{1}{2})$ standard deviations away from the mean is .05 (.01). Figure 2.7 contains an illustration of a normal variable with mean 0 and standard deviation 1. The probability that an observation of the random variable X will be in one or the other of the shaded areas is equal to .05.

Why study the normal distribution? We will see the answer in greater detail a little farther on, but for the moment consider that fact that in practice we can never be sure of the exact form of the probability distribution that underlies any variable. The normal distribution is a frequent choice of probability distribution for at least three reasons:

1. It is symmetric and bell-shaped, a reasonable way for us to describe (we hope) the distribution (not of the underlying variables in our model but) of the parameters, such as slope and intercept, that we hope to estimate.
2. The distribution is fully described by its mean and variance, so that we need not worry about the properties of the third moment (skewness), fourth moment (kurtosis), and higher moments of probability distributions.

---

† If X is normally distributed,

$$p(X = X_i) = \frac{1}{\sqrt{2\pi}\,\sigma_X} \exp\left[-\frac{1}{2}\left(\frac{X - \mu_X}{\sigma_X}\right)^2 \right] dX$$

Note that $\exp A = e^A$.

3. The following result, which holds for normal variables, helps us develop many of the statistical tests used in econometrics.

Result 10 If two (or more) random variables are normally distributed with identical means and variances, any weighted sum of these variables will be normally distributed.

2.4.2 Chi-Square Distribution

The chi square is useful for testing hypotheses that deal with *variances* of random variables. Its application is derived from Result 11.

Result 11 The sum of the *squares* of N independently distributed *normal* random variables (with mean 0 and variance 1) is distributed as *chi square* with N degrees of freedom.

Assume, for example, that we calculate the sample variances s^2 of N observations drawn from a normal distribution with variance σ^2. Then it is not difficult to show that $(N - 1)s^2/\sigma^2$ will be distributed as chi square with $N - 1$ degrees of freedom.† By examining critical values of the chi-square distribution with the appropriate number of degrees of freedom, we can decide whether or not to reject the null hypothesis that the variance of the random variable equals a given number.

The chi square starts at the origin, is skewed to the right, and has a tail which extends infinitely far to the right (as shown in Fig. 2.8). The exact shape of the distribution depends upon the number of degrees of freedom, the distribution becoming more and more symmetric as the number of degrees of freedom gets larger. When the number of degrees of freedom gets very large, the chi-square distribution approximates the normal. A table of the chi square is given at the back of the book (Table 2).

2.4.3 The t distribution

In statistics the assumption is sometimes made that the variance of a random variable is known. This simplifies the analysis but is clearly not realistic. How do we test hypotheses when the variance is not known? The answer lies in the t distribution. The central result which allows us to use the t distribution is as follows.

Result 12 Assume that X is normally distributed with mean 0 and variance 1 and Z is distributed as chi square with N degrees of freedom. Then if X

---

† See, for example, R. E. Beals, *Statistics for Economists* (Chicago: Rand McNally, 1972); A. M. Mood and F. A. Graybill, *Introduction to the Theory of Statistics*, 2d ed. (New York: McGraw-Hill, 1963); and J. E. Freund, *Mathematical Statistics* (Englewood Cliffs, NJ: Prentice-Hall, 1962).

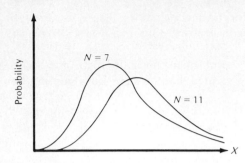

Figure 2.8 Chi-square distribution.

and Z are independent, $X/\sqrt{Z/N}$ has a t distribution with N degrees of freedom.

Figure 2.9 illustrates the t distribution. Like the normal, the t is symmetric, and it approximates the normal for large sample sizes. But the t has fatter tails than the normal, an occurrence which is especially pronounced for sample sizes of roughly 30 or less. To see how Result 12 aids us, recall that for X normal $(X - \mu_X)/(\sigma/\sqrt{N})$ is normally distributed with 0 mean and unit variance. But if σ is not known, we must replace σ^2 by the sample variance s^2. Since $(N - 1)s^2/\sigma^2$ follows a chi-square distribution and $(\overline{X} - \mu_X)/(\sigma/\sqrt{N})$ is unit normal, Result 12 tells us that

$$\frac{(\overline{X} - \mu_X)/(\sigma/\sqrt{N})}{\sqrt{(N-1)s^2/\sigma^2}} \sqrt{N-1} = \frac{(\overline{X} - \mu_X)\sqrt{N}}{s} \tag{2.17}$$

The chi square starts at the origin, is skewed to the right, and has a tail which extends infinitely far to the right (as shown in Fig. 2.8). The exact shape of the distribution depends upon the number of degrees of freedom, the distribution becoming more and more symmetric as the number of degrees of freedom gets larger. When the number of degrees of freedom gets very large, the chi-square distribution approximates the normal. A table of the chi square is given at the back of the book (Table 2).

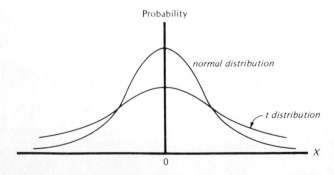

Figure 2.9 t distribution.

2.4.4 The F distribution

There are likely to be occasions when we wish to test joint hypotheses involving two or more regression parameters. For example, we may wish to test the hypothesis that the regression and slope are both zero against the alternative that one or the other or both are nonzero. The proper test statistic is based on the F distribution and is characterized by two parameters, the first being associated with the number of unconstrained degrees of freedom. The F distribution, like the chi square, has a skewed shape and ranges in value from 0 to infinity (see Fig. 2.10).

More generally, the F distribution is used to do tests involving the equality of two variances. Its usefulness derives from Result 13.

Result 13 If X and Z are independent and distributed as chi square with N_1 and N_2 degrees of freedom, respectively, then $(X/N_1)/(Z/N_2)$ is distributed according to an F distribution with N_1 and N_2 degrees of freedom.

To see the usefulness of Result 13, assume that we have obtained samples of size N_1 and N_2 from two different normal distributions X and Z. The variance of X is *estimated* as

$$s_X^2 = \frac{1}{N_1 - 1} \sum_{i=1}^{N_1} (X_i - \bar{X})^2$$

and the variance of Z is

$$s_Z^2 = \frac{1}{N_2 - 1} \sum_{i=1}^{N_2} (Z_i - Z)^2$$

If we wish to test whether $\sigma_X^2 = \sigma_Z^2$, we can calculate the statistic s_X^2/s_Z^2. If X and Z are independent, then $(N_1 - 1)s_X^2/\sigma_X^2$ is distributed as chi square with $N_1 - 1$ degrees of freedom and $(N_2 - 1)s_Z^2/\sigma_Z^2$ is distributed as chi square with $N_2 - 1$ degrees of freedom. Then

$$\frac{\left[(N_1 - 1)s_X^2/\sigma_X^2\right]}{(N_1 - 1)}$$

$$\frac{\left[(N_2 - 1)s_Z^2/\sigma_Z^2\right]}{(N_2 - 1)}$$

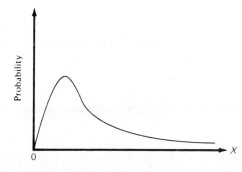

Figure 2.10 F distribution.

will be distributed as an F distribution. Note that if $\sigma_X^2 = \sigma_Z^2$, this reduces to s_X^2/s_Z^2 and the ratio of the estimated variances follows an F distribution with $N_1 - 1$ and $N_2 - 1$ degrees of freedom.

To avoid difficulties, the F statistic is calculated with the larger estimate of variance in the numerator and the smaller estimate in the denominator. The greater the difference between the two variances the greater the F statistic. Thus, with a sufficiently large value of F we may reject the null hypothesis. In practice, hypothesis testing is accomplished by choosing a level of significance and then looking up the critical value of the F distribution in a standard F table.

2.5 HYPOTHESIS TESTING AND CONFIDENCE INTERVALS

In this section we review the problem of testing hypotheses of a statistical nature. Hypotheses that occur most often in econometrics involve slopes and intercepts of regression lines but may also involve variances or covariances of probability distributions. For a simple example, reconsider the grade-point-average example of Chap. 1. The slope of .12 gives us a good guess for the impact of family income on grade, but how reliable is that guess? Specifically, how can we be sure that the slope is not really zero, so that income and grade-point average are unrelated? This is a hypothesis-testing problem. Related to hypothesis testing is the concept of a confidence interval. While .12 is a good guess or estimate of the slope, we certainly would not be prepared to argue that .12 measures the slope of the relationship between income and grades of all students. To show how reliable our results are, we need to use available data to make probabilistic statements about our slope estimate. Specifically, we might find that we can state that with probability .95 the interval .06 to .18 contains the true slope relating income to grade-point average. The .06 to .18 interval is called a 95 percent confidence interval for the slope.

The relationship between hypothesis testing and confidence intervals is a close one. To see this assume that we wish to test the hypothesis that the slope is 0. We say that the *null hypothesis* is that the slope is 0. However, since we know that 0 lies outside the 95 percent confidence interval, we conclude (with 95 percent confidence) that we *reject* the null hypothesis of a zero slope.

To continue our review in further detail, let us consider how the concepts of hypothesis testing and confidence intervals apply when we are concerned with the determination of the mean of a random variable. Specifically, we assume for the moment that we know the variance of a random variable X (which is normally distributed) but that the true mean is unknown. It is not surprising that the sample mean $\overline{X}$ will provide a reasonable guess at the true value of the mean, but we wish to make statements about the accuracy with which we feel we have estimated the unknown mean value. Since confidence statements are difficult to make about individual point estimates such as the sample mean, we make use of *confidence intervals*. Assume, for example, that we wish to obtain a 95 percent confidence interval about the sample mean (this is said to be associated with a 5 percent level of significance). We obtain the interval by utilizing the fact that $\overline{X}$ will be normally distributed with standard deviation $\sigma_X/\sqrt{N}$, where N is the number of observations. In particular, the 95 percent confidence interval will be

$$\overline{X} - \frac{1.96\sigma_X}{\sqrt{N}} \le \mu_X \le \overline{X} + \frac{1.96\sigma_X}{\sqrt{N}}$$

Suppose, for example, that $N = 100$ and $\sigma_X = 10$. Then $\overline{X}$ is normally distributed with a standard deviation of 1. If the point estimate of μ_X is $\overline{X} = 3$, the 95 percent confidence interval will be $1 \le \mu_X \le 5$. The 95 percent confidence interval suggests to us that it is very likely that the (1, 5) interval will contain the true mean μ_X.

The interpretation of the statement that "with 95 percent confidence $1 \le \mu_X \le 5$" is as following. If we could obtain a large number of samples each of size $N = 100$, we would obtain many different point estimates of μ_X. If we calculated the interval $\overline{X} \pm 2\sigma_X/\sqrt{N}$ corresponding to each sample's estimate of μ_X, we would have a number of interval statements such as

i $\qquad\qquad\qquad 1 \le \mu_X \le 5 \qquad$ if $\overline{X} = 3$

ii $\qquad\qquad\qquad 1.5 \le \mu_X \le 5.5 \qquad$ if $\overline{X} = 3.5$

iii $\qquad\qquad\qquad .7 \le \mu_X \le 4.7 \qquad$ if $\overline{X} = 2.7$

Some of these intervals can be expected to be false, i.e., to exclude the true mean. But over a large number of such calculations, 95 percent of the intervals obtained can be expected to be true, i.e., to contain the true mean.

We are now in a position to utilize the notion of confidence interval to test hypotheses. Consider the null hypothesis that the true mean is equal to zero. For the sample mean of 3 in the above example, we see that the null hypothesis is unlikely to be true, and we reject the null hypothesis (at the 5 percent level of significance) in preference to the alternative—rather vague—hypothesis that the mean is not 0. Note that the null hypothesis has been rejected because it is highly unlikely (although possible) that we would have obtained a sample mean of 3 had the true mean been 0. As a shortcut for testing the null hypothesis that the mean is 0, we can calculate the statistic $Z = \overline{X}/(\sigma_X/\sqrt{N})$. This statistic will be normally distributed with a variance of 1 and, if the null hypothesis is true, a mean of 0. If the statistic is greater than 1.96 in absolute value, we can reject the null hypothesis at the 5 percent level, while if it is greater than 2.57, we can reject it at the 1 percent level (a more powerful statement statistically). Suppose, for example the we knew that for a given sample the Z value was 2.13. By looking at Table 1,† under the .03 column and on the 2.1 row, we would find that the probability that Z is greater than or equal to 2.13 is equal to .0166. Likewise the probability that Z is less than or equal to -2.13 is also .0166.

---

† Single-numbered tables appear at the end of the book.

Taking both into account we would associate a .0332 or 3.32 percent significance level with Z. Since Z is greater than 1.96, we can reject the null hypothesis that the true mean of the distribution is zero at the 5 percent (or the 4 percent for that matter) level.

Up to this point we have assumed that the variance of X is known, but it is more likely (in the context of econometric models especially) that the variance will not be known. We therefore need to replace the unknown variance σ_X^2 with the estimated sample variance $\hat{s}_X^2$. (In the text we will be referring to the true error variance as estimated by s^2.) The appropriate test statistic for null hypotheses concerning the mean of X is obtained from the standardized variable obtained by subtracting the true mean from the sample mean and dividing the difference by the sample standard deviation

$$\frac{\overline{X} - \mu_X}{s_X / \sqrt{N}}$$

When we wish to test the null hypothesis that $\mu_X = 0$, this simplifies to

$$\frac{\overline{X}}{s_X / \sqrt{N}} \tag{2.18}$$

Since this statistic follows a t distribution, we shall call it a t statistic. The t statistic can be used to construct confidence intervals in a manner analogous to the normal distribution. A 95 percent confidence interval would be

$$\overline{X} \pm \frac{t_c s_X}{\sqrt{N}} \tag{2.19}$$

where t_c is the critical value of the t distribution determined from a statistical table based on the number of degrees of freedom in the data and the desired level of significance. The number of degrees of freedom equals the number of data points minus the number of constraints or restrictions placed on the data by the statistical procedure being used. As an example of how to calculate t_c, we must select a value from the table of the t distribution, so that 2.5 percent of the t distribution lies outside either end of the corresponding interval. This is shown in Fig. 2.11 for a t distribution with 60 degrees of freedom. Since we wish 2.5 percent to be in each tail, we select $t_c = 2.00$ reading in the column labeled .05.

To carry out a test of the hypothesis that the true mean equals a given value μ_X^*, we must first clarify what the alternative hypothesis is. We do this by specifying the null hypothesis $\mu_X = \mu_X^*$ and the alternative hypothesis that $\mu_X \neq \mu_X^*$, as well as a level of significance such as 5 percent or 1 percent. Using the critical value of the t distribution, we calculate the appropriate confidence interval. If the hypothesized mean μ_X^* lies outside the confidence interval, we reject the null hypothesis. If it lies inside, we fail to reject. We should note in passing that alternative hypotheses need not be of the two-tailed variety, in which the true mean may be negative or positive. There are frequent occasions in econometrics when *one-tailed tests* will be desirable. This involves

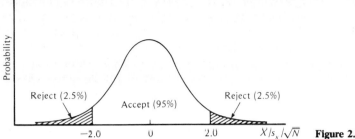

Figure 2.11 Two-tailed test.

only minor adjustments in the construction of the confidence intervals described previously. For example, suppose that we wish to test the hypotheses that $\mu_X = 0$ but have strong reasons *a priori* to believe that if μ_X is not equal to 0, then it is positive. Then, a one-tailed test is appropriate. The test is as before, but the critical value t_c is chosen so that 5 percent of the distribution lies in one tail, as shown in Fig. 2.12. In the case where the number of degrees of freedom is 60, we read the critical value to be 1.671 from the column of the t table labeled .10.

2.5.1 Type I and Type II Errors

The choice of level of significance, usually 1 or 5 percent, or corresponding to the choice of the size of confidence interval, is best understood by considering what kinds of errors might be made when hypothesis tests are made. Suppose we test the null hypothesis that $\beta = 0$ and at a 5 percent level of significance choose to *reject* the null hypothesis. It is certainly possible that we will incorrectly reject the null hypothesis. This mistake is called a *Type I error*, and the probability of its occurrence is .05, associated with the 5 percent level of significance. Now suppose that we collect a different data set and find a 95 percent confidence interval to lie between $-.02$ and .26. In this case we would fail to reject the null hypothesis that $\beta = 0$ and thus implicitly accept it as true. However, it is also possible that we would make a mistake in this case. The true value of β might well be .05, in which case we would have accepted the null hypothesis $\beta = 0$ when it was, in fact, false. This kind of mistake, called a *Type II error*, is a likely

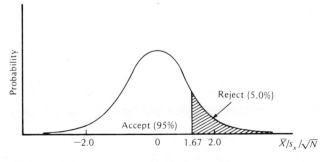

Figure 2.12 One-tailed test.

possibility since the confidence interval contains a large number of points. Although we will not be concerned with the problem of measuring the "size" of the Type II error, one result is useful.

Suppose we change the level of significance from 5 percent to 1 percent. Then the 95 percent confidence for β will be larger. This implies that the probability of incorrectly rejecting the null hypothesis (Type I error) falls from 5 percent to 1 percent, but at the same time the probability of a Type II error increases with the size of the confidence interval. Thus, in selecting a level of significance, one faces a tradeoff: as we lower the probability of Type I error, we increase the probability of Type II error. The choice to be made depends heavily on the problem at hand and the goals of the researcher, but it is usually the case in econometrics that one chooses a rather low level of significance and therefore a low probability of Type I error.

APPENDIX 2.1 THE PROPERTIES OF THE EXPECTATIONS OPERATOR

This appendix briefly reviews some of the properties of the expectations operator that will be useful in the text.

Result 1

$$E(aX + b) = aE(X) + b \qquad (A2.1)$$

where X is a random variable, and a and b are constants.

Result 2†

$$E\left[(aX)^2\right] = a^2 E(X^2) \qquad (A2.2)$$

Result 3

$$\text{Var}\,(aX + b) = a^2\,\text{Var}\,(X) \qquad (A2.3)$$

PROOF By definition

$$\text{Var}\,(aX + b) = E\left[(aX + b) - E(aX + b)\right]^2$$

---

† Note, however, that it is *not true* that $E(X^2) = [E(X)]^2$. To see this in the simplest case, let $X = 1$ when a coin appears heads and $X = 0$ when the coin appears tails. Then for a fair coin, $p_1 = \frac{1}{2}$ and $p_0 = \frac{1}{2}$, so that $E(X^2) = \frac{1}{2}(1^2) + \frac{1}{2}(0^2) = \frac{1}{2}(1) = \frac{1}{2}$. However $E(X) = \frac{1}{2}(1) + \frac{1}{2}(0) = \frac{1}{2}$, and $[E(X)]^2 = \frac{1}{4}$. Thus, one must be very careful to apply Results 1 and 2 only when a and b are constants, not when they are random variables or functions of random variables.

But $E(aX + b) = aE(X) + b$, using Result 1. Therefore,

$$\text{Var}\,(aX + b) = E[\,aX - E(aX)\,]^2 = E[\,aX - aE(X)\,]^2$$
$$= E[\,a(X - E(X))\,]^2 = a^2E[\,X - E(X)\,]^2 \qquad \text{by Result 2}$$
$$= a^2\,\text{Var}\,(X)$$

Now, we can extend our use of the expectations operator to prove some useful results concerning the covariance between two random variables. First a preliminary result.

Result 4 If X and Y are random variables, then
$$E(X + Y) = E(X) + E(Y) \tag{A2.4}$$

Result 5
$$\text{Var}\,(X + Y) = \text{Var}\,(X) + \text{Var}\,(Y) + 2\,\text{Cov}\,(X, Y) \tag{A2.5}$$

PROOF

$$\text{Var}\,(X + Y) = E[\,(X + Y) - E(X + Y)\,]^2$$
$$= E[\,(X + Y) - E(X) - E(Y)\,]^2 \qquad \text{by Result 4}$$
$$= E[\,(X - E(X)) + (Y - E(Y))\,]^2$$
$$= E[\,(X - E(X))^2 + (Y - E(Y))^2$$
$$+ 2(X - E(X))(Y - E(Y))\,]$$
$$= E[\,X - E(X)\,]^2 + E[\,Y - E(Y)\,]^2$$
$$+ 2E[\,(X - E(X))(Y - E(Y))\,]$$
$$= \text{Var}\,(X) + \text{Var}\,(Y) + 2\,\text{Cov}\,(X, Y)$$

Result 6 If X and Y are independent, then
$$E(XY) = E(X)E(Y)$$

Result 7 If X and Y are independent, then
$$\text{Cov}\,(X, Y) = 0 \qquad [\,\text{and} \qquad \text{Var}\,(X + Y) = \text{Var}\,(X) + \text{Var}\,(Y)\,]$$

PROOF
$$\text{Cov}\,(X, Y) = E[\,X - E(X)\,][\,Y - E(Y)\,]$$
$$= E[\,XY - E(X)Y - XE(Y) + E(X)E(Y)\,]$$
$$= E(XY) - E(X)E(Y)$$
$$= 0 \qquad \text{by Result 6}$$

Result 8

$$\text{Var}\,(\overline{X}) = \frac{\sigma^2}{N}$$

where $\overline{X}$ is the sample mean of a random variable with mean μ and variance σ^2.

PROOF

$$\text{Var}\,(\overline{X}) = \text{Var}\,\left(\frac{1}{N}\sum_{i=1}^{N} X_i\right) \qquad \text{by definition of } \overline{X}$$

$$= \left(\frac{1}{N}\right)^2 \text{Var}\,\left(\sum_{i=1}^{N} X_i\right) \qquad \text{by Result 3}$$

$$= \left(\frac{1}{N}\right)^2 \sum_{i=1}^{N} \text{Var}\,(X_i) \qquad \begin{array}{l}\text{by Results 5 and 7 and the assumption}\\ \text{that each } X_i \text{ is independent of each other } X_i\end{array}$$

$$= \left(\frac{1}{N}\right)^2 \sum_{i=1}^{N} \sigma^2 = \left(\frac{1}{N}\right)^2 (N\sigma^2) = \frac{\sigma^2}{N}$$

Result 8 shows that the variance of the estimator of the mean $\overline{X}$ falls as the sample size increases. Thus, with more and more information in the form of a larger sample size, we can get more and more accuracy in our estimates of the true mean μ.

Result 9

$$E\left[\frac{1}{N-1}\sum_{i=1}^{N}\left(X_i - \overline{X}\right)^2\right] = \sigma^2$$

PROOF First, consider the term involving the summation operator

$$\sum_{i=1}^{N}\left(X_i - \overline{X}\right)^2 = \sum_{i=1}^{N}\left[(X_i - \mu) - (\overline{X} - \mu)\right]^2$$

$$= \sum_{i=1}^{N}\left[(X_i - \mu)^2 + (\overline{X} - \mu)^2 - 2(X_i - \mu)(\overline{X} - \mu)\right]$$

$$= \sum_{i=1}^{N}(X_i - \mu)^2 + \sum_{i=1}^{N}(\overline{X} - \mu)^2 - 2(\overline{X} - \mu)\sum_{i=1}^{N}(X_i - \mu)$$

$$= \sum_{i=1}^{N}(X_i - \mu)^2 + N(\overline{X} - \mu)^2 - 2(\overline{X} - \mu)N(\overline{X} - \mu)$$

$$\text{since } \sum_{i=1}^{N} (X_i - \mu) = \sum_{i=1}^{N} X_i - N\mu = N(\bar{X} - \mu)$$

$$= \sum_{i=1}^{N} (X_i - \mu)^2 - N(\bar{X} - \mu)^2$$

Therefore, taking expected values gives

$$E\left[\frac{1}{N-1} \sum_{i=1}^{N} (X_i - \bar{X})^2 \right] = E\left[\frac{1}{N-1} \sum_{i=1}^{N} (X_i - \mu)^2 - \frac{N}{N-1} (\bar{X} - \mu)^2 \right]$$

$$= \frac{1}{N-1} E\left[\sum_{i=1}^{N} (X_i - \mu)^2 \right] - \frac{N}{N-1} E\left[(\bar{X} - \mu)^2 \right]$$

$$= \frac{1}{N-1} \sum_{i=1}^{N} E\left[(X_i - \mu)^2 \right] - \frac{N}{N-1} \frac{\sigma^2}{N} \quad \text{by Results 3 and 8}$$

$$= \frac{1}{N-1} N\sigma^2 - \frac{N}{N-1} \frac{\sigma^2}{N} \quad \text{by the definition of variance}$$

$$= \frac{N}{N-1} \sigma^2 - \frac{1}{N-1} \sigma^2 = \sigma^2$$

EXERCISES

A number of the following questions pertain to the data set in Table 2.1. Data were collected from a survey of econometrics students, all of whom responded. The variables are defined as

$$\text{RENT} = \text{total monthly rent in dollars}$$
$$\text{NO} = \text{number of persons in apartment}$$
$$\text{RM} = \text{number of rooms}$$
$$\text{SEX} = \begin{cases} 1 & \text{if female} \\ 0 & \text{if male} \end{cases}$$
$$\text{DIST} = \text{distance from center of campus, blocks}$$
$$\text{RPP} = \frac{\text{RENT}}{\text{NO}} = \text{rent per person}$$

2.1 RPP is a measure of rent paid per person. Show that $\overline{(\text{RENT}/\text{NO})} = \overline{\text{RPP}}$ is not equal to $\overline{\text{RENT}}/\overline{\text{NO}}$.

2.2 The results from Exercise 2.1 suggest that, in general, $E(Y/X) \neq E(Y)/E(X)$. Show that for the following example $E(Y/X)$ is positive and $E(Y)/E(X)$ is negative:

$$X = -4 \qquad Y = -8 \qquad \text{Prob} = \tfrac{1}{2}$$
$$X = 2 \qquad Y = 60 \qquad \text{Prob} = \tfrac{1}{2}$$

2.3 Assume that RPP is distributed normally with mean μ_{RPP} and variance σ^2_{RPP}. Test the hypothesis that $\mu_{\text{RPP}} = \$135$ at the 5 percent level of significance if (a) $\sigma^2_{\text{RPP}} = 2,150$; (b) σ^2_{RPP} is unknown. Pay particular attention to your choice of test statistics.

Table 2.1 Rental data

RENT	NO	RM	SEX	DIST	RPP = RENT/NO
$230	2	2	1	7	$115.00
245	2	2	0	24	122.50
190	1	1	1	0	190.00
203	4	2	0	24	50.75
450	3	2	1	4	150.00
280	2	2	1	6	140.00
310	2	2	0	8	155.00
185	2	1	0	8	92.50
218	2	2	0	42	109.00
185	1	1	1	8	185.00
340	2	2	1	3	170.00
230	2	2	0	60	115.00
245	1	1	1	24	245.00
200	2	2	0	36	100.00
125	1	1	0	3	125.00
300	3	3	0	9	100.00
350	2	2	0	16	175.00
100	1	1	0	5	100.00
280	2	2	1	6	140.00
175	2	1	0	4	87.50
310	2	2	0	10	155.00
450	3	2	0	5	150.00
160	2	1	0	12	80.00
285	1	1	0	4	285.00
255	2	2	0	8	127.50
340	4	2	0	3	85.00
300	2	2	0	11	150.00
880	6	6	1	6	146.67
800	5	5	1	10	160.00
450	3	3	0	5	150.00
630	6	6	0	24	105.00
480	3	3	0	24	160.00

2.4 Now assume that RPP among males is distributed normally with mean μ_{RPP}^m and variance σ_{RPP}^{2m}. RPP among females is also assumed to be distributed normally with mean μ_{RPP}^f and the variance σ_{RPP}^{2f}. Test the hypothesis that $\mu_{RPP}^m = \mu_{RPP}^f$ at the 5 percent level of significance when you are given that $\sigma_{RPP}^{2f} = \sigma_{RPP}^{2m} = 1,681$.

2.5 (Difficult)† Repeat Exercise 2.5 assuming $\sigma_{RPP}^{2f} = \sigma_{RPP}^{2m}$ but that their common value is unknown.

2.6 In part (a) of Exercise 2.3 we assumed that RPP was distributed normally with unknown mean μ_{RPP} and known variance $\sigma_{RPP}^2 = 2,150$. Assuming, as we do in part (b), that σ_{RPP}^2 is unknown, test at the 5 percent level of significance that $\sigma_{RPP}^2 = 2,150$. *Hint:* Under the hypothesis that $\sigma_{RPP}^2 = 2,150$, find the distribution of $(N - 1)s^2/2,150$, where

$$s^2 = \frac{1}{N - 1} \sum_{i=1}^{N} (RPP_i - \overline{RPP})^2$$

† See, for example, H. M. Blalock, Jr., *Social Statistics* (New York: McGraw-Hill, 1972), pp. 223–226.

2.7 In Exercise 2.6 we assumed that $\sigma_{RPP}^{2m} = \sigma_{RPP}^{2f}$. Test, at the 5 percent level of significance, that $\sigma_{RPP}^{2f} = \sigma_{RPP}^{2m}$.

2.8 Assume that X is a normally distributed random variable with mean μ_X and variance σ_X^2. Let $Z = (\bar{X} - \mu_X)/\sigma_X$ be a new random variable. Prove that Z is normally distributed with mean 0 and a variance of 1.

2.9 Assume that X is normally distributed with mean 10 and variance 625. Find the probability that $X \geq 30$.

2.10 A coin is flipped 6 times. You wish to test the hypothesis that probability of heads = probability of tails = $\frac{1}{2}$. How do you proceed?

2.11 The sample correlation coefficient between two variables X and Y is denoted (X, Y) and is given by

$$\hat{\rho}(X, Y) = \frac{\frac{1}{N} \sum_{i=1}^{N} (X_i - \bar{X})(Y_i - \bar{Y})}{\sqrt{\frac{1}{N} \sum_{i=1}^{N} (X_i - \bar{X})^2} \sqrt{\frac{1}{N} \sum_{i=1}^{N} (Y_i - \bar{Y})^2}} \qquad \text{where } \bar{X} = \frac{1}{N}\Sigma X_i$$

$$\bar{Y} = \frac{1}{N}\Sigma Y_i$$

Show that if one estimates the regressions

$$Y = a + bX$$
$$X = A + BY$$

the product of the estimates for b and B will equal $[\hat{\rho}(X, Y)]^2$.

2.12 If X is normally distributed with mean μ and variance σ^2, find a transformation of X that has the chi-square distribution with 1 degree of freedom.

2.13 Show that $E(X)^2 = (E(X))^2$ occurs only if X takes on only one value with probability 1.

THREE

THE TWO-VARIABLE REGRESSION MODEL

In Chapter 1 we introduced the process of building and testing models by describing the method of least squares as one of a number of possible means by which a curve can be fitted to data. Our concern was directed toward the algebra of parameter estimation rather than the statistics of model testing. In this chapter we will discuss the statistical testing of the least-squares regression model that contains one dependent and one independent variable. First we describe the assumptions underlying the two-variable model and then we analyze the statistical properties of the least-squares parameter estimates. We will see that under certain assumptions least-squares estimates are unbiased, consistent, and efficient. The distribution of the estimated parameters will then be used to construct confidence intervals and to test hypotheses about the model. To complete the chapter we introduce the concept of R^2, a measure of the goodness of fit of the regression model. We will defer to Chapter 4 a discussion of the regression model with more than two variables.

3.1 THE MODEL

Our objective is to understand the probabilistic nature of the regression model. To do this we expand the analysis to allow for the fact that for a given observed value of X (the independent variable), we may observe many possible values of Y (the dependent variable). As an example consider the consumption pattern of an individual who receives an income of \$10,000 each year. The portion of this money expended on food is likely to vary each year because of changes in the environment facing the individual. Unless additional knowledge is available, we presume that for each observation X (income) observations on Y (food purchases) will differ in a random fashion. To describe this situation formally, we add a random "error" component to the model, writing it as

$$Y_i = \alpha + \beta X_i + \varepsilon_i \tag{3.1}$$

where for each observation Y is a *random variable*, X is fixed or *nonstochastic* (known by the experimenter), and ε is a *random error term*, whose values are based on an underlying probability distribution. Notice that we have switched our notation to use Greek letters to represent the intercept and slope of the line, i.e., the regression parameters, since our model now contains a random error term.†

The error term may arise through the interplay of several forces.‡ First, errors appear because the model is a simplification of reality.§ We assume, for example, that price is the sole determinant of the demand for a product. In fact, several omitted variables related to demand, e.g., individual tastes, population, income, and weather, may be included in the error term. If these omitted effects are small, it is reasonable to assume that the error term is random. A second source of error is associated with the collection and measurement of the data. Economic and business data will frequently be difficult to measure. For example, an individual firm may not be willing to relinquish explicit cost data, so that error-free estimates of costs will not be obtained. Given these sources of error, our decision to represent the relationship in Eq. (3.1) as a *stochastic* one should be clear. For every value X there exists a probability distribution of ε and therefore a probability distribution of the Y's. This is depicted graphically in Fig. 3.1.

We are now in a position to specify fully the two-variable linear regression model by listing its important assumptions.

i. The relationship between Y and X is linear, as described in Eq. (3.1).
ii. The X_i's are nonstochastic variables whose values are fixed.¶
iii. *a.* The error term has zero expected value and constant variance for all observations; that is, $E(\varepsilon_i) = 0$ and $E(\varepsilon_i^2) = \sigma^2$.
  b. The random variables ε_i are uncorrelated in a statistical sense; i.e., errors corresponding to different observations have zero correlation. Thus, $E(\varepsilon_i \varepsilon_j) = 0$, for $i \neq j$.
  c. The error term is normally distributed.

---

† Parameters are constant in each individual problem but may change from problem to problem.
‡ The error term must be distinguished from the *residual* ($\hat{\varepsilon}_i = Y_i - \hat{Y}_i$) or deviation of the dependent variable observation from its fitted value. Errors are associated with the *true* regression model, while residuals arise from the *estimation* process.
§ We have chosen to postpone a discussion of sources of error until Chapters 8 and 9.
¶ To be complete we should add to our stated assumption a further assumption that the variance of X is nonzero, and it is finite for any sample size.

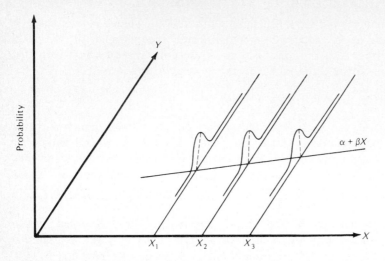

Figure 3.1 Two-variable regression model.

This list of assumptions, excluding iiic, constitutes the *classical linear regression model*.

Equation (3.1) is often termed the *specification* of the model. Note that we have presumed that Y is related to X, rather than vice versa. The statistical implications of this choice are discussed in Section 3.4.2. Also, we have restricted ourselves to one right-hand variable. The implications of omitting other "relevant" variables are discussed in Section 4.6.

The assumption that the X's are fixed is equivalent to the assumption that the independent variable in question is perfectly controlled by the researcher, who can change its value in accordance with experimental objectives. Such an assumption of nonrandomness in the X variable is highly unrealistic in the study of most business and economic problems. It has been made here solely for expositional purposes. Most of the results of least-squares regression analysis hold under more general assumptions than this, but are substantially more difficult to prove. The fixed X assumption will be relaxed in Chapter 5.

The assumption that the error term has zero expected value is made in part as a matter of convenience. To see this, assume that the average effect of the omitted errors is equal to α'; that is, $E(\varepsilon_i) = \alpha'$. Then we can write the two-variable model as

$$Y_i = \alpha + \beta X_i + \varepsilon_i + (\alpha' - \alpha') = (\alpha + \alpha') + \beta X_i + (\varepsilon_i - \alpha')$$
$$= \alpha^* + \beta X_i + \varepsilon_i^*$$

where

$$\alpha^* = (\alpha + \alpha') \qquad \varepsilon_i^* = (\varepsilon_i - \alpha')$$
$$E(\varepsilon_i^*) = E(\varepsilon_i - \alpha') = \alpha' - \alpha' = 0$$

Thus, if the error term did have nonzero mean, the original model would be

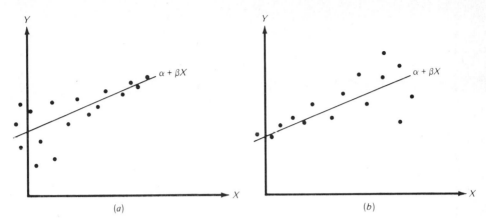

Figure 3.2 Heteroscedasticity.

equivalent to a new model with a different intercept but with an error term having zero mean.

If the error term has a constant variance (as assumed), we call it *homoscedastic*; but if the variance is changing, we call the error *heteroscedastic*. *Heteroscedasticity* (as opposed to *homoscedasticity*) might arise if one is examining a cross section of firms in an industry. There may be reason to believe that error terms associated with very large firms will have greater variance than those associated with small firms. Figure 3.2 illustrates two cases of heteroscedasticity. In Fig. 3.2*a* the variance of the error term decreases as the value of X increases, while in Fig. 3.2*b* the variance of the errors increases with X.

The assumption that errors corresponding to different observations are uncorrelated is important in both time-series and cross-section studies. When the error terms from different observations are correlated, we say that the error process is *serially correlated* or *autocorrelated*.† Figure 3.3 illustrates negative and positive serial correlation in a time-series study. In this case negative serial correlation means that negative errors in one time period are associated with positive errors in the next, and vice versa. Thus, in Fig. 3.3*a* the data points fluctuate above and below the true regression line with some regularity. When positive serial correlation occurs, on the other hand, a positive error in one period will tend to be associated with a positive error in the next period. Thus, in Fig. 3.3*b* the errors follow a pattern where first they are negative (low values of X) and then they are positive (high values of X).

We should note that as a corollary to assumptions ii and iii*a*, we are implicitly assuming that the error term is uncorrelated with the X's. This follows from the assumption that the X's are nonstochastic. Then

$$E(X_i\varepsilon_i) = X_i E(\varepsilon_i) = 0$$

We shall need this assumption explicitly when we expand our analysis to cover

---

† We shall use the terms *serial correlation* and *autocorrelation* interchangeably in this book.

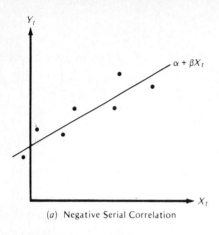
(a) Negative Serial Correlation

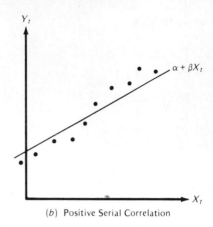
(b) Positive Serial Correlation

Figure 3.3 Serial correlation.

models in which the X's are stochastic, i.e., drawn randomly from a probability distribution. In addition, assumptions iii$a$ and iii$b$ allow us to conclude that the expected value of the sum of the errors in any sample will be identically zero; i.e.,

$$E(\Sigma \varepsilon_i) = \Sigma E(\varepsilon_i) = 0$$

This result follows from the statement of iii$a$, $E(\varepsilon_i) = 0$, which implies that the expected value of error terms associated with a *particular* X will be identically zero for repeated sampling of Y's associated with that X. To obtain this result we fix or keep constant each value of X; then we draw samples for the random errors from a population with a known probability distribution. It is the expected value of *each* of these samples of error terms that we assume to be identically zero.†

Before we consider the estimation procedure in the stochastic model, two observations are worthy of special note. First, we have described each disturbance, or error term, as having constant variance σ^2. The variance is, of course, an unknown parameter and must be estimated as part of the regression model. Thus, the stochastic regression model described here has three unknown parameters, while the curve-fitting model of Chapter 1 has only two. Second, we have described the assumptions of the model in terms of the error disturbance ε, but we could just as easily have written the assumptions in terms of the probability distribution of the variable Y. In this case the assumptions would

---

† Another way of saying this is that the probability distribution from which the ε samples are drawn has a mean of 0. In addition, it is the same probability distribution from which the ε samples are drawn for all values of X.

appear as follows:

iii. *a'.* The random variable Y has expected value $\alpha + \beta X$ and variance σ^2:

$$[E(Y_i) = E(\alpha + \beta X_i + \varepsilon_i) = \alpha + \beta X_i + E(\varepsilon_i) = \alpha + \beta X_i]$$

b'. The random variables Y_i are uncorrelated.

In order to perform statistical tests on the linear model, we need to specify the probability distribution of the error term. In the *classical normal linear regression model* we add assumption iiic that the error term is normally distributed. This assumption is important for the statistical testing of the model. If one is willing to believe that the individual errors due to measurement and to omission are small and independent of each other, the normality assumption is a reasonable one. Given the assumption that the error term ε is normally distributed, it follows that the dependent variable Y is also normally distributed (since Y_i is a constant but ε_i is normal).

3.2 BEST LINEAR UNBIASED ESTIMATION

Now let us examine the characteristics of the parameter estimates described in Chapter 1 associated with the least-squares procedure. Recall that these parameter estimates result from a specific sample of observations of the dependent and independent variables. Since the sample may vary, the estimates may vary as well and thus are associated with a random variable.† Because our model is stochastic, we have shown the formulas for the regression intercept and slope as $\hat{\alpha}$ and $\hat{\beta}$ (where the "hats" over α and β represent estimated values), but it is important to realize that the notation $\hat{\beta}$ serves a double purpose: it refers to the slope *estimate* resulting from a specific sample as well as to the *estimator* (a formula that applies to any sample) that follows a probability distribution.

We hope, of course, that the ordinary least-squares (OLS) estimators are unbiased and consistent. In fact, one of the nice properties of the ordinary least-squares estimator is that of all linear unbiased estimators, i.e., estimators which are linear in the independent variable and which yield unbiased estimates,

---

† To be more exact, recall that we are analyzing a model in which the N values of the independent variables are assumed fixed. If we select a single sample of Y observations associated with the values of the independent variable, we can obtain an "estimate" of the regression slope that is based on the particular observations on Y which happened to occur. If we then replicate or repeat the experiment with the same X values, we obtain a new set of observations on Y (because the ε's will differ in the new sample) and thus a new estimate of the slope parameter. If we were to draw sufficient samples of the Y variable, we would obtain a distribution of estimates of the intercept and slope parameters. Since each observed sample of Y produces specific estimates of the intercept and slope, when we sample Y values it is equivalent to sampling estimates of α and β out of the distribution of sample estimates.

the estimates resulting from the OLS estimator have the minimum variance, i.e., are "best." This is the basis of the Gauss-Markov theorem.

> **Gauss-Markov theorem** Given assumptions i, ii, iii*a*, and iii*b*, the estimators $\hat{\alpha}$ and $\hat{\beta}$ are the best (most efficient) linear unbiased estimators of α and β in the sense that they have the minimum variance of all linear unbiased estimators.

To understand the import of the Gauss-Markov theorem, we must first note that $\hat{\beta}$ (and $\hat{\alpha}$) is a linear estimator, since $\hat{\beta}$ can be written as a weighted average of the individual observations on Y.† However, there are a large number of possible linear estimators that one might use to estimate the intercept and slope and a smaller number which are unbiased.‡ However, $\hat{\beta}$ has the additional property that its probability distribution has the smallest variance of all other linear estimators that are unbiased. The objective of finding the best linear estimator (BLUE) is one that will pop up again and again in the text. We will see that if certain of the assumptions of the Gauss-Markov theorem do not hold, the least-squares estimators will no longer be BLUE. Our goal will then be to obtain an estimator other than least-squares which is BLUE.

It is important to realize that the Gauss-Markov theorem does not apply to nonlinear estimators. It is possible that a nonlinear estimator might be unbiased and have lower variance than the least-squares linear estimator. More generally, an estimator may be biased and have a lower mean square error than the unbiased estimator. This suggests that there may be circumstances in which one wishes to utilize an objective other than "best linear unbiased" when selecting an estimation routine. For example, biased nonlinear estimators having minimum mean square error are being seriously studied and appear to have useful applications.

We shall not attempt to prove the Gauss-Markov theorem at this point, but we shall find expressions for the mean and variance of the least-squares estimators.§ To simplify matters we shall work with the data transformed to appear in the form of deviations about means; i.e., we use $x_i = X_i - \overline{X}$ and $y_i = Y_i - \overline{Y}$.

From Eq. (3.1), recall that $Y_i = \alpha + \beta X_i + \varepsilon_i$. Summing over all N observations and dividing by N, we find that

$$\overline{Y} = \alpha + \beta \overline{X} + \bar{\varepsilon} \tag{3.2}$$

where $\bar{\varepsilon}$ represents the *sample* mean of the error term. Subtracting (3.2) from

---

† The details follow momentarily. In general, $\hat{\beta}$ is said to be linear in y if $\hat{\beta}$ can be written as $\Sigma c_i y_i$, where each c_i is constant. However, if, for example, $\beta' = \Sigma c_i \log y_i$, then β' is a nonlinear estimator (in y).

‡ See Exercise 3.10 for an example.

§ See Appendix 4.1 for a proof of the Gauss-Markov theorem for the general linear model.

(3.1) and combining terms gives

$$Y_i - \bar{Y} = \beta(X_i - \bar{X}) + (\varepsilon_i - \bar{\varepsilon})$$

or
$$y_i = \beta x_i + \varepsilon_i - \bar{\varepsilon} \tag{3.3}$$

There is, of course, no reason that $\bar{\varepsilon}$ will equal 0 in the sample, even though $E(\varepsilon_i) = 0$. However, Eq. (3.3) will be used only when we derive results concerning the bias or lack of bias of estimators. Therefore, to simplify our presentation, we will make the implicit assumption that $\bar{\varepsilon} = 0$ and write the model in deviations form as

$$y_i = \beta x_i + \varepsilon_i \tag{3.4}$$

Now, recall (from Chapter 1) that the true regression line in such cases is $E(y_i) = \beta x_i$ and the estimated slope is

$$\hat{\beta} = \frac{\sum x_i y_i}{\sum x_i^2} \tag{3.5}$$

Because y_i is a random variable, $\hat{\beta}$ will also be random, so that it is natural to determine the properties of the distribution of $\hat{\beta}$. The details are relatively straightforward, but since they are somewhat tedious, we have relegated them to Appendix 3.1. The proofs rely primarily on the results involving the summation and expectations operators, as described in Appendixes 1.1 and 2.1, as well as the assumptions of the classical linear regression model. The first result is that†

$$E(\hat{\beta}) = \beta \tag{3.6}$$

so that $\hat{\beta}$ is an *unbiased estimator* of β.

The second result is that

$$\text{Var}(\hat{\beta}) = \frac{\sigma^2}{\sum x_i^2} \tag{3.7}$$

so that the variance of $\hat{\beta}$ depends solely on the error variance, the variance of the X's, and the number of observations. Using a similar derivation, we find that the mean and variance of the estimator of the intercept term are (see Exercise 3.11)

$$E(\hat{\alpha}) = \alpha \tag{3.8}$$

$$\text{Var}(\hat{\alpha}) = \sigma^2 \frac{\sum X_i^2}{N\sum(X_i - \bar{X})^2} \tag{3.9}$$

Finally, consider the covariance between $\hat{\alpha}$ and $\hat{\beta}$. Once again using a similar

† The properties of the expectations operator E are given in Appendix 2.1.

derivation, we can prove that

$$\text{Cov}\,(\hat{\alpha}, \hat{\beta}) = \frac{-\bar{X}\sigma^2}{\Sigma x_i^2} \tag{3.10}$$

Given this information about the means and variances of the least-squares estimators and their covariance, we are ready to discuss statistical testing of the linear model. First, it is important to note that since $\hat{\beta}$ is a weighted average of the y's, and the y_i's are normally distributed, *the estimator $\hat{\beta}$ will be normally distributed* (a linear combination of independent normally distributed variables will be normally distributed). Even if the y's are not normally distributed, the distribution of $\hat{\beta}$ can be shown to be asymptotically normal (under reasonable conditions) by appeal to the central-limit theorem of statistics.† Thus, our results will be approximately correct for large samples even without the assumption of normality. To sum up our conclusions to this point we can write‡

$$\hat{\beta} \sim N\left(\beta, \frac{\sigma^2}{\Sigma x_i^2}\right) \tag{3.11}$$

$$\hat{\alpha} \sim N\left(\alpha, \sigma^2 \frac{\Sigma X_i^2}{N \Sigma x_i^2}\right) \tag{3.12}$$

$$\text{Cov}\,(\hat{\alpha}, \hat{\beta}) = -\frac{\bar{X}\sigma^2}{\Sigma x_i^2} \tag{3.13}$$

Notice that the variance of $\hat{\beta}$ varies directly with the variance of ε. Thus, other things being equal, we are likely to obtain more precise parameter estimates of the slope when the variance of the error term is small. On the other hand, the variance of $\hat{\beta}$ varies inversely with Σx_i^2. Thus, the larger the variance of X_i, the better you are likely to do in estimating β. Put more simply, it will be difficult to determine the slope of the regression line accurately when all the sample data on the X's are limited to a small interval.

While the expression for the variance of $\hat{\alpha}$ looks quite complicated, we can note that the expression simplifies to σ^2/N when the mean of X is identically zero. In this case the variance of $\hat{\alpha}$ is at a minimum. This result is not likely to be of much interest in applications, because intercept parameters are usually not of primary concern. Notice also that the sign of the covariance of $\hat{\alpha}$ and $\hat{\beta}$ is opposite in sign to $\bar{X}$. If the mean of X is positive, for example, an overestimate of $\hat{\alpha}$ is likely to be associated with an underestimate of $\hat{\beta}$.

Our analysis is not yet complete, since we need to utilize the sample information to obtain an estimator of the true population variance σ^2. The

---

† Roughly speaking the central-limit theorem states that the distribution of the sample mean of an independently distributed variable will tend toward normality as the sample size gets infinitely large. It applies to $\hat{\beta}$ because $\hat{\beta}$ is a linear combination of the y_i's.

‡ Equation (3.11) reads that "$\hat{\beta}$ follows a normal distribution with mean β and variance $\sigma^2/\Sigma x_i^2$."

actual derivation of such an estimator involves maximum-likelihood estimation and will not be shown here.† On the basis of that result, we will use the following sample estimate of the true variance σ^2:

$$s^2 = \hat{\sigma}^2 = \frac{\Sigma \hat{\epsilon}_i^2}{N-2} = \frac{\Sigma (Y_i - \hat{\alpha} - \hat{\beta} X_i)^2}{N-2} \tag{3.14}$$

where $\hat{\epsilon}_i^2 = Y_i - \hat{Y}_i$ is the regression *residual*. The *residual variance* s^2 can be shown to be an unbiased as well as consistent estimator of the error variance.‡ The reader might wonder why the *sum of the squared residuals* $\Sigma \hat{\epsilon}_i^2$ was divided by $N-2$ in order to get an unbiased estimator of the true variance. The answer lies in the fact that there are N data points in the estimation process but the estimation of the slope and intercept puts two constraints on the data. This leaves $N-2$ unconstrained observations with which to estimate the residual variance. for this reason, the proper divisor of $N-2$ is referred to as the number of degrees of freedom.

With an estimate of σ^2, we can return to Eqs. (3.11) to (3.13) to obtain sample estimates of the variances associated with the estimated parameters $\hat{\alpha}$ and $\hat{\beta}$ as well as an estimate of the covariance between the two. Each of the three estimates is listed below:

$$s_{\hat{\beta}}^2 = \frac{s^2}{\Sigma x_i^2} \tag{3.15}$$

$$s_{\hat{\alpha}}^2 = s^2 \left(\frac{\Sigma X_i^2}{N \Sigma x_i^2} \right) \tag{3.16}$$

$$\widehat{\text{Cov}} \, (\hat{\alpha}, \hat{\beta}) = - \frac{\bar{X} s^2}{\Sigma x_i^2} \tag{3.17}$$

$s_{\hat{\beta}}$ and $s_{\hat{\alpha}}$, the *standard errors* of the estimated coefficients $\hat{\beta}$ and $\hat{\alpha}$, respectively, provide a measure of the dispersion of the estimates (as do the sample estimates of the variances) about their means. They should not be confused with the standard error of the regression s, which measures the dispersion of the error term associated with the regression line.

3.3 HYPOTHESIS TESTING AND CONFIDENCE INTERVALS

Given the knowledge of the distributions of $\hat{\alpha}$ and $\hat{\beta}$, it is possible to construct confidence intervals and to test hypotheses concerning the regression parameters. Confidence intervals, or *interval estimates*, provide a range of values which

---

† See Appendix 3.2 for further details.
‡ s is called the *standard error of the regression*. (SER, SE, and SEE are also occasionally used to represent s. The latter is short for standard error of estimate.) For a proof that s^2 is unbiased, see Appendix 3.3.

are likely to contain the true regression parameters. With every confidence interval we associate a *level of statistical significance*. Given the level of significance, the confidence intervals are constructed so that the probability that the interval contains the true regression parameter is 1 minus the level of significance. Confidence intervals are particularly useful for testing statistical hypotheses about the estimated regression parameters. The most common test relates to the *null hypothesis*. In general a null hypothesis is a statement or hypothesis that assumes that a certain effect is not present. Because researchers hope to accept the model, the null hypothesis is often constructed so as to make its rejection possible. As as example, consider an attempt to explain aggregate consumption expenditures C in terms of aggregate disposable income DI. A reasonable specification of the model might be that $E(C) = \alpha + \beta(DI)$. We would expect consumption and disposable income to be positively related, so that β should be positive. However, to test the validity of the model we set up the null hypothesis that β equals 0. We hope to reject the null hypothesis by obtaining a value of $\hat{\beta}$ which is sufficiently greater than 0 to cast significant doubt on the hypothesis that β equals 0. Assume, for example, that $\hat{\beta}$ is estimated to be .9. If we choose a level of significance of 10 percent, the 90 percent confidence interval for β might be

$$.6 < \beta < 1.2$$

This means that the probability that β is within the range .6 to 1.2 is .90. In addition it means that we can reject the null hypothesis that β equals 0 with greater than 90 percent confidence.

One of our prime objectives in econometrics is to analyze data in a manner that permits us to test and evaluate our models. In practice a researcher may have several plausible models from which to choose, and although the choice will depend partly on the purpose of the model, it will also depend on empirical information, i.e., the data. The simultaneous comparison of many models is methodologically difficult. Usually we examine models sequentially, attempting to validate each model as it is brought under study. This means that each model must be specified in a form which yields empirically testable hypotheses. If the data are inconsistent with the model, the model is rejected and an alternative is considered. If the data are consistent with the model, the model is implicitly accepted—until new testable hypotheses or new data are available. Thus, hypothesis testing pertains to a *single* model and will result in model rejection or model acceptance.

In hypothesis testing a rule for acceptance and rejection must be chosen before the data are examined. One frequently used rule involves the 5 percent level of significance, which sets up a criterion that the rejection of the null hypothesis when it is in fact true should occur less than 5 percent of the time. The choice of significance level is arbitrary and depends in practice on the types of conclusions to be reached from the model. It is important to realize, however, that hypothesis testing in classical econometrics deals almost solely with the problem of incorrectly rejecting a true hypothesis (Type I error). Because of the nature of testable hypotheses which are specified, alternative hypotheses are most frequently ill defined, making it impossible to judge the number of times one will accept the null hypothesis when it is in fact false (Type II error). For this reason, in applied work we tend to distinguish between rejection of a null hypothesis and its acceptance. Thus, we will often state that a null hypothesis has been rejected at a 5 percent level of significance, while leaving implicit the acceptance of the alternative hypothesis.

For example, with our consumption model we tested the null hypothesis that β equals 0. On the basis of our estimated slope parameter we rejected the null hypothesis in favor of the alternative hypothesis that the slope is nonzero. However, we could have chosen to begin our analysis with a more specific alternative hypothesis, e.g., that the slope parameter is positive. This would slightly alter the statistical testing involved and would add additional information if the null hypothesis were rejected.

It is standard practice in applied econometric work to examine the test statistics and the standard errors of the coefficients carefully. When rejection of the null hypothesis is valid, the model is usually accepted, at least until further information to the contrary becomes available. The level of significance necessary for model acceptance varies substantially between researchers and between types of model being investigated. For example, a model estimated with a large number of observations may allow one to reject null hypotheses of zero coefficients for many explanatory variables. Thus, we might choose to select a somewhat lower significance level to make rejection of the null hypothesis more difficult.

The statistical test for rejecting the null hypothesis associated with a regression coefficient is usually based upon the t distribution. The t distribution is relevant because for statistical testing we need to utilize a sample estimate of the error variance rather than its true value. To use the t distribution to construct 95 percent confidence intervals for the estimated parameters, we first standardize the estimated regression parameter, say $\hat{\beta}$, by subtracting its hypothesized true value β_0 and dividing by the estimate of its standard error [see Eq. (3.15)].

$$t_{N-2} = \frac{\hat{\beta} - \beta_0}{s_{\hat{\beta}}} = \frac{\hat{\beta} - \beta_0}{s \Big/ \sqrt{\sum x_i^2}} \tag{3.18}$$

The standardized variable t_{N-2} will follow the t distribution with $N - 2$ degrees of freedom. Now, we select an appropriate value t_c, called the *critical value*, which assures that 2.5 percent of the t distribution lies in each of its tails, i.e.,

$$\text{Prob}\,(-t_c < t_{N-2} < t_c) = .95 \tag{3.19}$$

where Prob denotes probability. The critical value of the distribution varies with the number of degrees of freedom, but will equal 1.96, the critical value for the normal distribution when the number of observations is large.

Now, by substituting from (3.18) we obtain

$$\text{Prob}\left(-t_c < \frac{\hat{\beta} - \beta_0}{s_{\hat{\beta}}} < t_c\right) = .95 \tag{3.20}$$

The critical value of the t statistic in Eq. (3.18) will be central to our decision of whether or not to reject null hypotheses concerning specific values of the true slope parameter β. However, it is of more immediate importance to rewrite Eq. (3.20) slightly to obtain

$$\text{Prob}\left(\hat{\beta} - t_c s_{\hat{\beta}} < \beta_0 < \hat{\beta} + t_c s_{\hat{\beta}}\right) = .95 \tag{3.21}$$

from which we obtain a 95 percent confidence interval for β equal to

$$\hat{\beta} \pm t_c s_{\hat{\beta}} = \hat{\beta} \pm t_c \frac{s}{\sqrt{\Sigma x_i^2}} \tag{3.22}$$

Using a similar procedure, we obtain a 95 percent confidence interval for α

$$\hat{\alpha} \pm t_c s_{\hat{\alpha}} = \hat{\alpha} \pm t_c s \frac{\sqrt{\Sigma X_i^2}}{\sqrt{N \Sigma x_i^2}} \tag{3.23}$$

Of course, it is possible to determine confidence intervals for any level of significance as long as the critical value of the t distribution is correctly chosen. Confidence intervals for the unknown parameters provide us with a statistical statement about the range of values likely to contain the true parameter. Thus, Eq. (3.22) tells us that an interval of t_c standard deviations on either side of the estimated slope parameter has a probability of .95 of containing the true parameter. [We already know that if forced to make a single guess at the true parameter in the correctly specified model $Y = \alpha + \beta X + \varepsilon$, we would select the estimated parameter $\hat{\beta}$, because $\hat{\beta}$ is an (efficient) unbiased estimator of β.]

The most usual hypothesis which is tested in the two-variable regression model is that there is no relationship between the variables X and Y. This test is accomplished by considering the following hypotheses:

Null hypothesis: $\qquad\qquad\qquad\beta = 0$

Alternative hypothesis: $\qquad\quad\;\beta \neq 0$

According to the null hypothesis, β equals 0, so that the appropriate test statistic becomes $\hat{\beta}/s_{\hat{\beta}}$. If the ratio of the estimated parameter to its (estimated) standard error is greater than or equal to t_c *in absolute value*, we reject the null hypothesis. Since $t_c = 1.96$ for a large sample size and a 5 percent level of significance, we can often apply the rule of thumb that if the value of the test statistic is greater than 2 in absolute value, we reject the null hypothesis. Another way of looking at this is in terms of the confidence interval about $\hat{\beta}$. If 0 lies within the confidence interval, we cannot reject the null hypothesis, but if it lies outside we do reject it. It is important to stress again that failure to reject the null hypothesis does not necessarily imply its truth. Our hypothesis and confidence interval has been constructed in such a manner that if the null hypothesis is true, we will reject it falsely only 5 percent of the time. The testing procedure tells us little about the situation in which we will accept the null hypothesis when it is in fact false. Acceptance of the alternative hypothesis must be done with this in mind.

Table 3.1 Calculation of s^2

Grade-point average calculations

(1)	(2)	(3)	(4)	(5)
x_i	y_i	$\hat{y}_i = \hat{\beta} x_i$	$\hat{\epsilon}_i = y_i - \hat{y}_i$	$\hat{\epsilon}_i^2$
7.5	1.0	.90	.10	.0100
1.5	.0	.18	− .18	.0324
1.5	.5	.18	.32	.1024
− 4.5	− 1.0	− .54	− .46	.2116
− 1.5	.0	− .18	.18	.0324
4.5	.5	.54	− .04	.0016
− 7.5	− .5	− .90	.40	.1600
− 1.5	− .5	− .18	− .32	.1024
				$\Sigma \hat{\epsilon}_i^2 = .6528$

$$s^2 = \frac{\Sigma \hat{\epsilon}_i^2}{N - 2} = \frac{.6528}{6} = .109 \qquad s = .33$$

Example 3.1 Grade-point average Reconsider the grade-point-average example from Chapter 1. The estimated relationship between grade-point average Y and family income X was

$$\hat{Y} = 1.38 + .12X$$

The calculations that allow us to determine s^2 are given in Table 3.1 (see Table 1.2 for preliminary details). To test the estimated regression parameters, we first select a level of significance—in this case 5 percent. Then we find the critical value of the t distribution (from Table 3) associated with a probabililty of .05 and 6 degrees of freedom (recall that there are eight observations and two estimated parameters). In this case
mated parameters). In this case

$$t_c(5\% \text{ significance}) = 2.447$$

Then a 95 percent confidence interval for the estimated slope parameter would be

$$\beta = \hat{\beta} \pm t_c \frac{s}{\sqrt{\Sigma x_i^2}} = .12 \pm \frac{2.45 \times .33}{\sqrt{162}} = .12 \pm .06$$

or $$.06 < \beta < .18$$

In addition, $$t = \frac{\hat{\beta}}{\sqrt{s^2 / \Sigma x_i^2}} = \frac{.12}{\sqrt{.111/162}} = 4.6$$

We observe that 0 lies *outside* the 95 percent confidence interval for β, allowing us to reject at the 5 percent level of significance the hypothesis that $\beta = 0$. Equivalently, we can observe that the calculated value of $t(4.6)$ is greater than the critical t value of 2.45. Once again we are able to reject the null hypothesis.

Example 3.2   Consumption expenditures† For illustrative purposes we will consider several attempts to build a two-variable model that explains the dollar value of aggregate consumption expenditures C. As a first attempt we ran a regression in which consumption is the dependent variable and a random time series X is the independent variable.‡ Data were quarterly from the first quarter of 1959 to the fourth quarter of 1978. A typical estimated regression is

$$\hat{C} = 623.28 + .402X$$

The standard error of the intercept term is 147.54, and thus the t statistic is $623.28/147.54 = 4.22$. Since the regression involves 80 observations and 2 estimated parameters, we find (see Table 3) that the critical value of the t distribution at the 5 percent significance level is 2. Thus, we can reject the null hypothesis that the intercept is 0. However, the standard error for the coefficient of X is 2.91, and the t statistic is 0.14. We therefore cannot reject the null hypothesis of a zero slope at the 5 percent (or the 10 percent) level. For this reason, we conclude that consumer spending is not randomly determined and reject the model in order to search for a better alternative.

Before proceeding we decided to see what happened when we regressed C on a new random variable, drawn from the same probability distribution as X. Assuming that the assumptions of the classical *normal* regression model hold, we would expect that approximately 1 time in 20 the coefficient on the X variable would be significantly different from zero (we are using a 5 percent significance level). In other words, we will incorrectly reject the null hypothesis about 5 percent of the time. Much to our surprise the new regression that we ran yielded a significant t statistic! This just serves to reiterate the point that all regression results must be interpreted in the light of the statistical properties of the estimators. No matter how reliable the estimator, there is always a statistical chance that one will make incorrect inferences from the results.

A more reasonable choice for an explanatory variable is aggregate disposable income YD. When consumption is regressed on disposable income, the result is

$$\hat{C} = -7.37 + .90\text{YD}$$

In this case the intercept is significant at the 5 percent level (with a t statistic of 2.44), but, more important, the t statistic associated with the coefficient of the disposable income variable is 201.23. Thus, we can reject the null hypothesis of a zero slope in favor of the alternative hypothesis that the slope is nonzero. Rejection of the null hypothesis allows us to accept—at least provisionally—the two-variable regression model. Of course, further research might allow us to find a model of aggregate consumption which is more suitable than the one just described.

---

† The data underlying this example are listed in the Instructor's manual.
‡ The data for X were drawn randomly from a normal distribution with mean 50 and variance 25.

3.4 ANALYSIS OF VARIANCE AND CORRELATION

3.4.1 Goodness of Fit

The residuals of a regression can help to provide a useful measure of the extent to which the estimated regression line fits the sample data points. Roughly speaking, a good regression equation is one which helps to explain or account for a large proportion of the variance of Y. Large residuals imply a poor fit, while small residuals imply a good fit. The problem with using the residual (or an estimate of the variance of the error term) as a measure of goodness of fit is that the value of the residual depends upon the units of measure of the dependent variable. We would like to find a measure of goodness of fit which is unit-free and for which certain statistical tests can be of value. Intuitively, it seems reasonable that the residual variable divided by the variance of Y will provide the kind of comparison which is sought.

We begin by defining the *variation* of Y about its mean (not the variance) as

$$\text{Variation}(Y) = \Sigma(Y_i - \overline{Y})^2$$

Our goal is to divide the variation of Y into two distinct parts, the first accounted for by the regression equation and the second associated with the unexplained portion (the error term) of the model. Assume first that the slope of the linear regression model is known to be 0, and we fit a regression estimating only an intercept. Then the best prediction for Y_i associated with any value of X is given by the sample mean of Y:

$$\hat{Y}_i = \hat{\alpha} + 0 \cdot X_i = \hat{\alpha} = \overline{Y}$$

In this special case, we can conclude that the variation of Y measures the square of the difference between the observed values Y_i and the predicted values $\hat{Y}_i = \overline{Y}$. More generally, when the slope may be nonzero we can improve our predictions by accounting for the fact that the fitted or predicted values of Y_i are dependent upon the observations on X_i; that is,

$$\hat{Y}_i = \hat{\alpha} + \hat{\beta}X_i$$

The additional information will allow us to improve our prediction and to reduce the unexplained portion of the variation in Y. To see this, consider the following identity, which holds for all sample observations:

$$Y_i - \overline{Y} = (Y_i - \hat{Y}_i) + (\hat{Y}_i - \overline{Y}) \tag{3.24}$$

The term on the left of the equals sign denotes the difference between the sample value of Y and the mean of Y, the first right-hand term the residual $\hat{\varepsilon}_i$, and the second right-hand term the difference between the predicted value of Y and the mean of Y. This is depicted graphically in Fig. 3.4.

The analysis to this point depends solely upon one sample point. To expand the analysis to cover all sample points and to measure variation, we square both

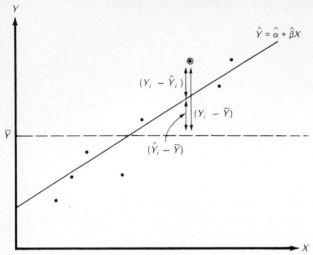

Figure 3.4 Decomposition of Y_i.

sides of Eq. (3.24) and then sum over all observations $i = 1, 2, \ldots, N$:

$$\Sigma(Y_i - \overline{Y})^2 = \Sigma(Y_i - \hat{Y}_i)^2 + \Sigma(\hat{Y}_i - \overline{Y})^2 + 2\Sigma(Y_i - \hat{Y}_i)(\hat{Y}_i - \overline{Y})$$

(3.25)

The last term of the expression can be shown to be identically 0 by using two properties of the least-squares residuals, $\Sigma\hat{\varepsilon}_i = 0$ and $\Sigma\hat{\varepsilon}_i X_i = 0$. All the derivations appear in Appendix 3.3. Therefore,

$$\underset{\substack{\text{Total variation of}\\ Y \text{ (or total sum of}\\ \text{squares)}}}{\Sigma(Y_i - \overline{Y})^2} = \underset{\substack{\text{Residual variation of}\\ Y \text{ (or error sum of}\\ \text{squares)}}}{\Sigma(Y_i - \hat{Y}_i)^2} + \underset{\substack{\text{Explained variation}\\ \text{of } Y \text{ (or regression}\\ \text{sum of squares)}}}{\Sigma(\hat{Y}_i - \overline{Y})^2}$$

$$\text{TSS} \quad = \quad \text{ESS} \quad + \quad \text{RSS} \qquad (3.26)$$

To normalize the breakdown of the variation in Y, we divide both sides of the equation by the total sum of squares to get

$$1 = \frac{\text{ESS}}{\text{TSS}} + \frac{\text{RSS}}{\text{TSS}}$$

We define the *R squared* (R^2) of the regression equation as

$$R^2 = 1 - \frac{\text{ESS}}{\text{TSS}} = \frac{\text{RSS}}{\text{TSS}} \qquad (3.27)$$

R^2 is the proportion of the total variation in Y explained by the regression of Y on X. Since the error sum of squares ranges in values between 0 and the total sum of squares, it is easy to see the R^2 ranges in value between 0 and 1. An R^2 of 0 occurs when the linear regression model does nothing to help explain the variation in Y. This might occur when the values of Y lie randomly around the horizontal line $Y = \overline{Y}$ or when the sample points lie on a circle (Fig. 3.5b). An R^2 of 1 can occur only when all sample points lie on the estimated regression line, i.e., the case of a perfect fit (Fig. 3.5a).

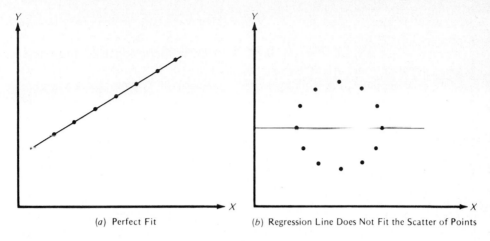

(a) Perfect Fit   (b) Regression Line Does Not Fit the Scatter of Points

Figure 3.5 Measuring R-squared.

It would be useful at this point to relate the notion of R^2 to the regression parameters estimated earlier in this chapter. To do so we write variables measured as deviations from their means, representing them in lowercase letters:

$$y_i = Y_i - \overline{Y} \qquad x_i = X_i - \overline{X}$$

The predicted values of y_i are

$$\hat{y}_i = \hat{\beta} x_i$$

and each dependent variable observation can be subdivided as

$$y_i = \hat{y}_i + \hat{\varepsilon}_i$$

where $\hat{\varepsilon}_i$ is the regression residual. Then

$$\Sigma y_i^2 = \Sigma \hat{y}_i^2 + \Sigma \hat{\varepsilon}_i^2 \qquad \text{since } \Sigma \hat{y}_i \hat{\varepsilon}_i = \hat{\beta} \Sigma x_i \hat{\varepsilon}_i = 0$$

$$= \hat{\beta}^2 \Sigma x_i^2 + \Sigma \hat{\varepsilon}_i^2$$

from which it follows that

$$R^2 = \frac{\text{RSS}}{\text{TSS}} = \frac{\Sigma \hat{y}_i^2}{\Sigma y_i^2} = \hat{\beta}^2 \frac{\Sigma x_i^2}{\Sigma y_i^2}$$

or

$$R^2 = 1 - \frac{\Sigma \hat{\varepsilon}_i^2}{\Sigma y_i^2} \tag{3.28}$$

Equation (3.28) provides a simple formula for calculating R^2.

Note that in the context of our discussion R^2 is only a descriptive statistic. Roughly speaking, we associate a high value of R^2 with a good fit of the regression line and a low value of R^2 with a poor fit. We must realize, however, that a low value of R^2 can occur for one or several related reasons. In certain cases the X variable may not be a good explanatory variable in the equation. Even though there is reason to believe that X does help in the prediction of Y, there might remain a good deal of unexplained variation in Y even after the variable X has appeared in the equation. In other words, the explanatory power of X might be poor relative to the total variation in the residual. In time-series studies, however, one often obtains high values of R^2 simply because any variable growing over time is likely to do a good job of explaining the variation of any other variable growing over time. In cross-section studies, on the other hand, a lower R^2 may occur even if the model is a satisfactory one, because of the large variation across individual units of observation which is inherently present in the data.†

It is occasionally useful to summarize the breakdown of the variation in Y in terms of an *analysis of variance*. In such a case, the total unexplained and explained variations in Y are converted into *variances* by dividing by the appropriate number of degrees of freedom.‡ Thus, the variance in Y is the total variation divided by $N - 1$, the explained variance is equal to the explained variation (since the regression involves only one additional constraint above the one used to estimate the mean of Y), and the residual variance is the residual variation divided by $N - 2$.

3.4.2 Correlation

The R^2 is usually of value in analyzing a regression model in which a causal relationship between the dependent variable Y and the independent variable X has been specified. Thus, R^2 is interpreted as more than a measure of correlation between several variables. Regression and correlation techniques differ in that correlation techniques do not involve an implicit assumption of causality, while regression techniques do. We have seen in Chapter 1 that the choice of dependent and independent variables in a regression model is a crucial one. The dependent variable is the variable to be explained or predicted, while the independent variable is the moving force or causal variable. The least-squares technique is appropriate only if the causal structure of the model can be determined before the data are examined. Least-squares regression techniques serve the purpose of *validating* the previously developed model. If a model $Y = \alpha + \beta X$ is specified, one may interpret a significant t statistic on the regression slope parameter as evidence tending to validate the model. On the other hand, an insignificant statistic would lead toward invalidation of the model.

---

† This suggests quite properly that R^2 alone may not be a suitable measure of the extent to which a model is satisfactory. A better overall measure might be a statistic which describes the predictive power of the model in the face of new data.

‡ The number of degrees of freedom associated with a calculated statistic is the number of available observations minus the number of constraints placed on the data by the calculation procedure. Thus an estimate of the variation in Y involves $N - 1$ degrees of freedom because one constraint is placed on the data (1 degree of freedom is used up) when deviations are measured about the sample mean which must in itself be calculated. An additional degree of freedom is used up in the calculation of the slope parameter, leaving $N - 2$ degrees of freedom associated with the unexplained variation in the problem.

As an example of correlation without causality, consider a series of observations over time that might have been obtained in a nineteenth-century study of medicine in Africa. One might find a high correlation between the number of doctors present in a region and the prevalence of disease in that same region, but it would be wrong to infer that the presence of doctors is in fact a cause of the spreading disease.

Thus, high correlations do not provide for an inference of causality. One must specify *a priori* (based on previous information) that the number of doctors in a region is a function of the prevalence of disease and test statistically whether such a relationship holds if one is to use regression techniques correctly.

Notice that regression techniques *assume* but do not prove causality. Correlation techniques are often used by researchers to suggest hypotheses or to confirm previously held suspicions. Such procedures are acceptable as long as the researcher is careful not to infer causality directly from the data analysis. There are numerous cases in economics, business, and other fields in which two variables are highly correlated but both are determined by a third underlying variable. If such is the case, the underlying variable should appear in the regression model as the independent variable.

It is natural to ask what happens to the regression slope parameter when an incorrect causal specification is made. Let us refer back to our discussion at the end of Chapter 1, and compare the slope parameters associated with the following regression models:

i $\qquad\qquad\qquad Y = a + bX + e$

ii $\qquad\qquad\qquad X = A + BY + e'$

The least-squares estimators of b and B are

$$\hat{b} = \frac{\Sigma x_i y_i}{\Sigma x_i^2} \qquad \hat{B} = \frac{\Sigma x_i y_i}{\Sigma y_i^2}$$

The two regression slopes will yield identical conclusions about the relationship between movement in X and movement in Y *only if* $\hat{b} = 1/\hat{B}$ or equivalently if $R^2 = 1$ (see Exercise 3.4). Thus, the choice of specification of the regression model will affect our parameter estimates and our predictions.

3.4.3 Testing the Regression Equation

The procedure of subdividing the variation in Y into two components suggests a statistical test of the existence of a linear relationship between Y and X. Consider the ratio

$$F_{1,\,N-2} = \frac{\text{explained variance}}{\text{unexplained variance}} = \frac{\text{RSS}/1}{\text{ESS}/(N-2)} = \frac{\hat{\beta}^2 \Sigma x_i^2}{s^2}$$

Other things being equal, we would expect a strong statistical relationship between X and Y to result in a large ratio of explained to unexplained variance. This test can be applied directly because $F_{1,\,N-2}$ follows a known distribution (the F distribution) with 1 and $N - 2$ degrees of freedom. The subscripts on F

are used to denote the number of degrees of freedom in the numerator and denominator, respectively. The value of the F statistic will be 0 only when the explained variance in the regression is 0. One would associate a low value with a weak (linear) relationship between X and Y and a high value with a strong (linear) relationship. Fortunately, the exact numerical distribution of the F statistic is known (see Table 4 of the F distribution). For example, one would reject the null hypothesis of no relationship between Y and X at the 5 percent significance level by looking up the appropriate critical value of the F distribution (5 percent significance) with 1 and $N - 2$ degrees of freedom. If the value of $F_{1, N-2}$ calculated from the regression is larger than the critical value, we reject the null hypothesis at the 5 percent level. If the value of $F_{1, N-2}$ is lower than the critical value, we cannot reject the null hypothesis.

A careful reading should lead us to suspect that the F test just described bears a close relationship to the t test associated with the null hypothesis that $\beta = 0$. In fact, we can state quite generally that $F_{1, N-2} = t_{N-2}^2$ for the same level of significance. The F test has been introduced explicitly here because it will be useful for joint tests of hypotheses including a test of the significance of a multiple regression equation. We will make use of the F test for this purpose in Chapter 4.

Example 3.3 Retail auto sales A study was made of the relationship between retail auto sales (dependent variable) and the level of aggregate wages and salaries in the economy (independent variable). One would expect a higher level of wages and salaries to lead to an increase in auto sales. The following is a summary of the regression of retail sales on wages and salaries using monthly time-series data. The equation to be estimated is

$$S = \alpha + \beta W + \varepsilon$$

where S is the monthly retail auto sales from January 1963 to April 1970 in *millions* of dollars and, W is the monthly wages from January 1963 to April 1970 in *billions* of dollars. The fitted regression line is listed below. We have included the t statistics in parentheses below the estimated coefficients. We have placed a hat above the dependent variable as a reminder that the equation is used to calculate estimated values of the dependent variable.

$$\hat{S} = \underset{(7.4)}{1{,}767.61} + \underset{(18.5)}{7.48\ W} \qquad R^2 = .80 \qquad F_{1, 86} = 344.0$$

The positive constant (representing the intercept term) implies that hypothetically if there were no wages in a given month, individuals would still purchase automobiles. The coefficient of the wage variable can be interpreted to mean that a $1 billion increase in wages and salaries will lead to a $7.48 million increase in auto sales. (The model could be used to predict the future level of auto sales conditional on future salaries.) Notice that the slope coefficient is usually interpreted to measure the change in the dependent variable associated with a *small* change in the independent variable. (In fact in the linear model $\hat{\beta} = \partial S / \partial W$ holds for all changes in W.) The estimated coefficient is not unit-free. Its value is directly related to the units of measurement of the dependent variable S (millions of dollars) and the independent variable W (billions of dollars). In this example we have chosen to write the t statistics, rather than the estimated standard errors, in parentheses. Using the t statistics we can reject the null hypothesis that the intercept and the slope are 0 (taken individually) at the 1 percent as well as the 5 percent level of significance. The R^2 of .80 implies that the regression equation explains 80 percent of the variation in the dependent variable. The $F_{1,86}$ value of 344 allows one to reject the null hypothesis that there is no relationship between auto sales and wages and salaries (at the 1 percent level).

If one had reason to believe quite strongly that the graph of auto sales versus wages and salaries should pass through the origin, despite the fact that we have rejected the null hypothesis of a 0 intercept, it would be natural to run the regression without a constant term (we leave the derivation of the slope estimator as an exercise for the reader). The results for the identical sample are

$$\hat{S} = 11.71 \, W \qquad R^2 = .54$$
$$(10.2)$$

While the t test allows one to reject the null hypothesis, it seems clear that the suppression of the constant term has lowered the explanatory power of the equation.† Thus, one will estimate the regression model with an intercept. Only if there is strong reason to force the equation through the origin should the intercept be equated to 0.

Example 3.4 In the grade-point-average problem (Example 1.1) we calculated the following additional statistics:

$$R^2 = .77 \qquad F_{1,6} = 21.2$$

The R^2 of .77 allows us to conclude that the family income variable helps to explain 77 percent of the variation in grade-point average for the sample of eight individuals. The F statistic allows us to test the null hypothesis of no relationship between grade-point average and family income. To do so, we use a table of the F distribution to determine the critical value associated with a 5 percent level of significance and 1 and 6 degrees of freedom in the numerator and denominator, respectively. (The 1 degree of freedom is used because the model includes a single explanatory variable, while the 6 degrees of freedom result from the fact that there are eight observations and two parameters to be estimated.) In this case the critical value of F at the 5 percent level is 5.99. Since the calculated F of 21.2 is greater than the critical value, we reject the null hypothesis at the 5 percent level of significance.

---

† In actuality the R^2 associated with an equation containing no constant term must be interpreted with great care. When the constant is dropped, the derivation in the test must be modified. Of particular importance is the fact that R^2 as defined in Chapter 1 lies within the 0 to 1 range. In this case, a comparison of the predicted or fitted values of the dependent variables made it clear that the explanatory power of the equation had declined.

APPENDIX 3.1 VARIANCE OF THE LEAST-SQUARES SLOPE ESTIMATOR

Result 1

$$E(\hat{\beta}) = \beta$$

PROOF Recall that $\hat{\beta} = \Sigma x_i y_i / \Sigma x_i^2$. To simplify the derivation which follows, let

$$c_i = \frac{x_i}{\Sigma x_i^2} \qquad (A3.1)$$

Each c_i is a constant, i.e., nonrandom, since the x's are fixed in the sample. Substituting into the equation for $\hat{\beta}$, we get

$$\hat{\beta} = \Sigma c_i y_i \qquad (A3.2)$$

which expresses the estimated slope parameter as a weighted sum of the observation on the dependent variable. We shall use this expression to derive the variance of $\hat{\beta}$ explicitly. (All summations are implicitly assumed to involve observations $i = 1, 2, \ldots, N$.) First, in our notation

$$\hat{\beta} = \Sigma c_i y_i = \Sigma c_i (\beta x_i + \varepsilon_i) \qquad \text{since } y_i = \beta x_i + \varepsilon_i$$

$$= \beta \Sigma c_i x_i + \Sigma c_i \varepsilon_i \qquad \text{from Appendix 1.1} \qquad (A3.3)$$

Therefore,

$$E(\hat{\beta}) = \beta \Sigma c_i x_i + E(\Sigma c_i \varepsilon_i)$$

$$= \beta \Sigma c_i x_i + \Sigma c_i E(\varepsilon_i) \qquad \text{from Appendix 2.1}$$

But $E(\varepsilon_i) = 0$, so that

$$E(\hat{\beta}) = \beta \Sigma c_i x_i = \beta$$

The fact that $\Sigma c_i x_i = 1$ follows directly from the definition of c_i:

$$\Sigma c_i x_i = \Sigma \left(\frac{x_i}{\Sigma x_i^2} \right) x_i = \Sigma \frac{x_i^2}{\Sigma x_i^2} = \frac{\Sigma x_i^2}{\Sigma x_i^2} = 1$$

Result 2

$$\text{Var}(\hat{\beta}) = \frac{\sigma^2}{\Sigma x_i^2}$$

PROOF

$$\text{Var}(\hat{\beta}) = E(\hat{\beta} - \beta)^2$$

But

$$(\hat{\beta} - \beta) = \beta \Sigma c_i x_i + \Sigma c_i \varepsilon_i - \beta \qquad \text{from Eq. (A3.3)}$$
$$= \beta(\Sigma c_i x_i - 1) + \Sigma c_i \varepsilon_i$$
$$= \Sigma c_i \varepsilon_i \qquad \text{from derivation in Result 1}$$

Therefore,

$$(\hat{\beta} - \beta)^2 = (\Sigma c_i \varepsilon_i)^2 \qquad (A3.4)$$

and $\quad \mathrm{Var}\,(\hat{\beta}) = E(\Sigma c_i \varepsilon_i)^2 = E\left[(c_1 \varepsilon_1)^2 + 2(c_1 c_2 \varepsilon_1 \varepsilon_2) + (c_2 \varepsilon_2)^2 + (c_N \varepsilon_N)^2\right]$

But, by assumption the ε_i are uncorrelated; that is, $E(\varepsilon_i \varepsilon_j) = 0$ for $i \neq j$. Therefore,

$$\mathrm{Var}\,(\hat{\beta}) = E(c_1 \varepsilon_1)^2 + E(c_2 \varepsilon_2)^2 + E(c_N \varepsilon_N)^2 = c_1^2 E(\varepsilon_1^2) + c_2^2 E(\varepsilon_2^2) + c_N^2 E(\varepsilon_N^2)$$
$$= \Sigma c_i^2 E(\varepsilon_i^2) = \sigma^2 \Sigma c_i^2$$

But

$$\Sigma c_i^2 = \frac{\Sigma x_i^2}{(\Sigma x_i^2)^2} = \frac{1}{\Sigma x_i^2}$$

Therefore,

$$\mathrm{Var}\,(\hat{\beta}) = \frac{\sigma^2}{\Sigma x_i^2} \qquad (A3.5)$$

APPENDIX 3.2 MAXIMUM-LIKELIHOOD ESTIMATION

A concept frequently used in econometrics is that of *maximum likelihood.* Crucial to the concept of maximum likelihood is the fact that different statistical populations generate different samples; any one sample being scrutinized is more likely to have come from some populations than from others. For example, if one were sampling coin tosses and a sample mean of .5 were obtained (representing half heads and half tails), it would be clear that the most likely population from which the sample was drawn would be a population with a true mean of .5. Figure A3.1 illustrates a more general case in which a sample $(X_1, X_2, \ldots, X_8)$ is known to be drawn from a normal population with given variance but unknown mean. Assume that it is known that observations come from either distribution A or distribution B. It should be immediately clear that if the true population were B, the probability that we would have obtained the sample shown would be quite small. However, if the true population were A, the probability that we would have drawn the sample would be substantially larger. In that sense, the observations "select" the population A as the most likely to have yielded the observed data.

We define the maximum-likelihood estimator of a parameter β as the value of $\hat{\beta}$ which would most likely generate the observed sample observations

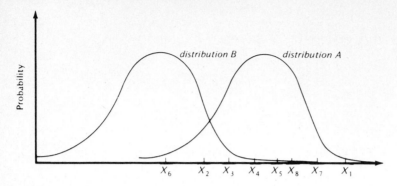

Figure A3.1 Maximum-likelihood estimation.

$Y_1, Y_2, \ldots, Y_N$. In general, if Y_i is normally distributed and each of the Y's is drawn independently, the maximum-likelihood estimator maximizes

$$p(Y_1)p(Y_2) \cdots p(Y_N)$$

where each p represents a probability associated with the normal distribution.

Before applying our definition directly to the linear regression model, two points should be stressed:

1. The calculated maximum-likelihood estimate is a function of the *particular* sample of Y's chosen. A different sample would result in a different maximum-likelihood estimator.
2. $p(Y_1)p(Y_2) \cdots p(Y_N)$ is often referred to as the *likelihood function*. The likelihood function depends not only on the sample values but also on the unknown parameters of the problem. In describing the likelihood function, we often think of the unknown parameters as varying while the Y's are fixed. This seems reasonable, because finding the maximum-likelihood estimator involves a search over alternative parameter estimators to find those estimators which would be most likely to generate the given sample. For this reason, the likelihood function must be interpreted differently from the joint probability distribution. In the joint probability distribution, the Y's vary and the underlying parameters are fixed.

Now we are in a position to search for the maximum-likelihood estimators of the parameters of the two-variable linear regression model $Y_i = \alpha + \beta X_i + \varepsilon_i$. We know from our initial assumptions that each Y_i is normally distributed with mean $\alpha + \beta X_i$ and variance σ^2. The probability distribution can be written explicitly as†:

$$p(Y_i) = \frac{1}{\sqrt{2\pi\sigma^2}} \exp\left[-\frac{1}{2\sigma^2}(Y_i - \alpha - \beta X_i)^2 \right] \tag{A3.6}$$

† See A. M. Mood and F. A. Graybill, *Introduction to the Theory of Statistics* (New York: McGraw-Hill, 1963), for details.

Then the likelihood function is

$$L(Y_1, Y_2, \ldots, Y_N, \alpha, \beta, \sigma^2) = p(Y_1)p(Y_2) \cdots p(Y_N)$$

$$= \prod_{i=1}^{N} \frac{1}{\sqrt{2\pi\sigma^2}} \exp\left[-\frac{1}{2\sigma^2}(Y_i - \alpha - \beta X_i)^2 \right]$$

$$(A3.7)$$

where $\prod$ denotes the product of N factors.

We wish to maximize the likelihood function with respect to the parameters α, β, and σ^2. To find the optimum it is necessary to differentiate the likelihood function with respect to each of the three unknown parameters, equate the derivatives to zero, and solve. In fact, it is easier to work with the (natural) logarithm of L rather than L itself, an acceptable procedure because L is always nonnegative and the logarithmic function is monotonic; i.e., it preserves ordering. Differentiating (A3.7) partially with respect to α, β, and σ^2 yields

$$\frac{\partial(\log L)}{\partial \alpha} = \frac{1}{\sigma^2}\Sigma(Y_i - \alpha - \beta X_i) = 0 \qquad (A3.8)$$

$$\frac{\partial(\log L)}{\partial \beta} = \frac{1}{\sigma^2}\Sigma[X_i(Y_i - \alpha - \beta X_i)] = 0 \qquad (A3.9)$$

$$\frac{\partial(\log L)}{\partial \sigma^2} = \frac{-N}{2\sigma^2} + \frac{1}{2\sigma^4}\Sigma(Y_i - \alpha - \beta X_i)^2 = 0 \qquad (A3.10)$$

The solution to Eqs. (A3.8) to (A3.10) yields the following maximum-likelihood estimators:

$$\alpha' = \bar{Y} - \beta'\bar{X} \qquad \beta' = \frac{\Sigma(X_i - \bar{X})(Y_i - \bar{Y})}{\Sigma(X_i - \bar{X})^2} \qquad \sigma^{2'} = \frac{\Sigma(Y_i - \alpha' - \beta'X_i)^2}{N}$$

It is now apparent that the maximum-likelihood estimators of α and β are identically equal to the least-squares estimators. It follows therefore that α' and β' are BLUE (best linear unbiased estimators). $\sigma^{2'}$, however, is a biased (although consistent) estimator of σ^2.

APPENDIX 3.3 SOME PROPERTIES RELATING TO THE LEAST-SQUARES RESIDUALS

The first two properties hold for the least-squares residuals in both the two-variable model and the multiple regression model which follows. Note that neither result depends on the normality of the error process or on the assumption that the least-squares estimators are BLUE.

Property 1

$$\Sigma \hat{\epsilon}_i = 0 \qquad\qquad\qquad (A3.11)$$

PROOF In the two-variable model, $Y_i = \hat{\alpha} + \hat{\beta} X_i$, or with the data in derivations form, $\hat{y}_i = \hat{\beta} x_i$. By definition

$$\hat{\epsilon}_i = y_i - \hat{y}_i = y_i - \hat{\beta} x_i$$

Then,

$$\Sigma \hat{\epsilon}_i = \Sigma y_i - \hat{\beta} \Sigma x_i = N\bar{y} - \hat{\beta} N\bar{x} = 0$$

since $\bar{x} = \bar{y} = 0$ when the data are in deviations form.

Property 2

$$\Sigma \hat{\epsilon}_i X_i = 0$$

PROOF Again, using the two-variable model when the data are in deviations form, we have

$$\Sigma \hat{\epsilon}_i X_i = \Sigma \hat{\epsilon}_i x_i + \Sigma \hat{\epsilon}_i \bar{X} = \Sigma \hat{\epsilon}_i x_i$$

(using Property 1). Then

$$\Sigma \hat{\epsilon}_i x_i = \Sigma(y_i - \hat{\beta} x_i) x_i = \Sigma x_i y_i - \hat{\beta} \Sigma x_i^2$$

But $\hat{\beta}$ is the least-squares estimator, and $\hat{\beta} = \Sigma x_i y_i / \Sigma x_i^2$. Therefore

$$\Sigma \hat{\epsilon}_i x_i = \Sigma x_i y_i - \frac{\Sigma x_i y_i}{\Sigma x_i^2} \Sigma x_i^2 = 0$$

Property 3

$$\Sigma(Y_i - \hat{Y}_i)(\hat{Y}_i - \bar{Y}) = 0 \qquad \text{from Eq. (3.25)}$$

PROOF

$$\Sigma(Y_i - \hat{Y}_i)(\hat{Y}_i - Y) = \Sigma \hat{\epsilon}_i(\hat{Y}_i - \bar{Y})$$

$$= \Sigma \hat{\epsilon}_i \hat{Y}_i - \bar{Y} \Sigma \hat{\epsilon}_i$$

$$= \Sigma \hat{\epsilon}_i(\hat{\alpha} + \hat{\beta} X_i) - \bar{Y} \Sigma \hat{\epsilon}_i$$

$$= \hat{\alpha} \Sigma \hat{\epsilon}_i + \hat{\beta} \Sigma \hat{\epsilon}_i X_i - \bar{Y} \Sigma \hat{\epsilon}_i$$

$$= 0 \qquad \text{using Properties 1 and 2}$$

Property 4 s^2 is an unbiased estimator of σ^2.

PROOF Recall that $\hat{\epsilon}_i = y_i - \hat{\beta} x_i$ when the model is written in deviations form. But $y_i = \beta x_i + \varepsilon_i$. Therefore,

$$\hat{\varepsilon}_i = \beta x_i + \varepsilon_i - \hat{\beta} x_i = (\beta - \hat{\beta}) x_i + \varepsilon_i$$

(As in the text we have implicitly assumed that the errors ε_i have a sample mean of zero.) Squaring and summing over all N observations, we find that

$$\Sigma \hat{\varepsilon}_i^2 = (\hat{\beta} - \beta)^2 \Sigma x_i^2 + \Sigma \varepsilon_i^2 - 2(\hat{\beta} - \beta)\Sigma x_i \varepsilon_i$$

Now, taking the expectation of both sides, we get

$$E(\Sigma \hat{\varepsilon}_i^2) = E(\hat{\beta} - \beta)^2 \Sigma x_i^2 + E(\Sigma \varepsilon_i^2) - 2E\left[(\hat{\beta} - \beta)\Sigma x_i \varepsilon_i\right]$$

But

$$\text{Var}(\hat{\beta}) = E(\hat{\beta} - \beta)^2 = \frac{\sigma^2}{\Sigma x_i^2} \qquad \text{see Eq. (A3.5)}$$

$$\text{Var}(\varepsilon_i) = E(\Sigma \varepsilon_i^2) = (N - 1)\sigma^2 \qquad \text{see Result 9, Appendix 2.1}$$

In addition $\hat{\beta} - \beta = \Sigma x_i \varepsilon_i / \Sigma x_i^2$ [this follows from (A3.3) and the fact that $\Sigma c_i x_i = 1$ so that $\Sigma x_i \varepsilon_i = (\hat{\beta} - \beta)\Sigma x_i^2$, and the last term equals

$$-2E\left[(\hat{\beta} - \beta)^2\right]\Sigma x_i^2 = -2\sigma^2$$

Combining these three results, we find

$$E(\Sigma \hat{\varepsilon}_i^2) = \sigma^2 + (N - 1)\sigma^2 - 2\sigma^2 = (N - 2)\sigma^2$$

or

$$E(s^2) = \frac{E(\Sigma \hat{\varepsilon}_i^2)}{N - 2} = \sigma^2$$

EXERCISES

3.1 Construct 95 percent confidence intervals for the estimated parameters for Exercise 1.1. Can you reject the null hypothesis that $\beta = 0$? $\beta = 1$?

3.2 Discuss the differences in statistical tests associated with the estimated parameters of a regression when:
    (*a*) The error variance is known or not known.
    (*b*) The sample size is finite or infinite.

3.3 Since the standard error of the regression coefficient $\hat{\beta}$ varies inversely with the variance of X, one can improve the significance of the estimated parameter by selecting values of X at the endpoints of the range of possible values. Explain why this is true, and discuss whether such a procedure is desirable.

3.4 Prove that the estimated slope of the regression of Y on X will equal the reciprocal of the estimated slope of the regression of X on Y only if $R^2 = 1$.

3.5 Can you give an example of an estimator which is asymptotically unbiased but not consistent?

3.6 When the mean of X is identically 0, the covariance between the estimated slope and intercept is 0. Can you explain intuitively why this is true?

3.7 Suppose that you are attempting to build a model that explains aggregate savings behavior as a function of the level of interest rates. Would you rather sample during a period of fluctuating interest rates or a period in which interest rates were relatively constant? Explain.

3.8 Prove that the estimated residuals from the linear regression and the corresponding sample values of X are uncorrelated; that is, $\Sigma X_i \hat{\epsilon}_i = 0$. *Hint:* The problem will be easier if you work with the data in deviations form.

3.9 Prove that R^2 for the two-variable regression is unchanged if a linear transformation is made on both variables; that is, $Y^* = a_1 + a_2 Y$, $X^* = b_1 + b_2 X$.

3.10 Return once again to the data in Exercise 1.1. Break the data down into two groups of five observations each, according to the order of magnitude of the independent variable (money supply). In other words the first group should contain the five sample points associated with the five smallest values of the money supply. Calculate the following parameter:

$$ B = \frac{\bar{Y}_2 - \bar{Y}_1}{\bar{X}_2 - \bar{X}_1} $$

where the subscript refers to the group number. ($\bar{Y}_2$ is the mean of all Y's in the second group.)

(a) Describe the foregoing process geometrically. In what sense is B an estimated slope parameter?

(b) Compare your estimated parameter to the least-squares slope estimate. Can you prove that B is an unbiased estimator of the true regression slope parameter?

(c) Prove that the variance of the parameter B must be greater than or equal to the variance of the least-squares estimator.

3.11 Prove that

$$ E(\hat{\alpha}) = \alpha \quad \text{and} \quad \text{Var}(\hat{\alpha}) = \sigma^2 \frac{\Sigma X_i^2}{N \Sigma (X_i - \bar{X})^2} $$

where $\hat{\alpha}$ is the least-squares intercept estimator.

3.12 Prove that

$$ \text{Cov}(\hat{\alpha}, \hat{\beta}) = \frac{-\bar{X}\sigma^2}{\Sigma x_i^2} $$

where $\hat{\alpha}$ is the intercept estimator and $\hat{\beta}$ is the slope estimator.

THE MULTIPLE REGRESSION MODEL

In this chapter we discuss regression models which contain two or more independent variables (in addition to the constant term), i.e., the *multiple* regression model. We begin by describing the assumptions underlying the classical multiple regression model and by showing how the least-squares parameter estimates can be obtained in a model with two explanatory variables. We then discuss the interpretation of regression coefficients and statistics in the multiple regression model. As we will see, problems may arise because of the interaction between the explanatory variables in the regression equation. The problem of multicollinearity, for example (involving highly correlated explanatory variables), can be considerably important in the multiple regression model. We place particular emphasis in this chapter on the various regression statistics which aid in the interpretation of the model, including partial correlation coefficients, beta coefficients, and elasticities. Throughout the chapter examples are used to illustrate the general discussion in the text.

4.1 THE MODEL

We extend the two-variable model by assuming that the dependent variable Y is a linear function of a series of independent variables $X_1, X_2, \ldots, X_k$, and an error term. This model is a natural extension of the two-variable model, so that it will be unnecessary to derive all our earlier results in full detail.

We write the multiple regression model as

$$Y_i = \beta_1 + \beta_2 X_{2i} + \beta_3 X_{3i} + \cdots + \beta_k X_{ki} + \varepsilon_i \tag{4.1}$$

where Y = the dependent variable,

X's = independent or explanatory variables,

ε = error term.

X_{2i} represents, for example, the ith observation on explanatory variable X_2. β_1 is the constant term, or intercept, of the equation. It is sometimes helpful to rewrite Eq. (4.1) as

$$Y_i = \beta_1 X_{1i} + \beta_2 X_{2i} + \beta_3 X_{3i} + \cdots + \beta_k X_{ki} + \varepsilon_i \tag{4.2}$$

where $X_{1i} = 1$ for all observations $i = 1, 2, \ldots, N$. The model in Eq. (4.2) is identical to that of (4.1), but it is more useful for the matrix development of the multiple regression model presented in Appendix 4.3.

The assumptions of the multiple regression model are quite similar to those of the two-variable model:

i. The model specification is given by Eq. (4.1).

ii. The X's are nonstochastic. In addition, *no exact linear relationship exists between two or more of the independent variables.*

iii. *a.* The error term has 0 expected value and constant variance for all observations.

b. Errors corresponding to different observations are uncorrelated.

c. The error variable is normally distributed.

Assumptions i, ii, and iii, which make up the *classical multiple regression model*, could also be restated in terms of the distribution of the Y's rather than the errors.† The only new assumption, concerning the possibility of a linear relationship between the X's, will be discussed when we examine multicollinearity.

For simplicity we shall often consider a special case of the multiple regression model, the three-variable model

$$Y_i = \beta_1 + \beta_2 X_{2i} + \beta_3 X_{3i} + \varepsilon_i$$

The least-squares procedure is equivalent to searching for parameter estimates which minimize the residual (or error) sum of squares, defined as

$$\text{ESS} = \Sigma \hat{\varepsilon}_i^2 = \Sigma (Y_i - \hat{Y}_i)^2 \qquad \text{where } \hat{Y}_i = \hat{\beta}_1 + \hat{\beta}_2 X_{2i} + \hat{\beta}_3 X_{3i}$$

Just as we did in Chapter 1, we can use the calculus to find the values of β_1, β_2, and β_3 which minimize ESS. Assuming that there are more than three observations and that the underlying equations are independent, the solution (see Appendix 4.1 for details) is

$$\hat{\beta}_1 = \overline{Y} - \hat{\beta}_2 \overline{X}_2 - \hat{\beta}_3 \overline{X}_3 \tag{4.3}$$

† In terms of the Y variable, iii*a* and *c* are equivalent to the assumption that the Y_i's are independent normally distributed variables with mean $E(Y_i) = \beta_1 + \beta_2 X_{2i} + \beta_3 X_{3i} + \cdots + \beta_k X_{ki}$ and with variance σ^2.

where

$$\bar{X}_2 = \Sigma X_{2i}/N$$

$$\bar{X}_3 = \Sigma X_{3i}/N$$

$$\hat{\beta}_2 = \frac{(\Sigma x_{2i} y_i)(\Sigma x_{3i}^2) - (\Sigma x_{3i} y_i)(\Sigma x_{2i} x_{3i})}{(\Sigma x_{2i}^2)(\Sigma x_{3i}^2) - (\Sigma x_{2i} x_{3i})^2} \tag{4.4}$$

$$\hat{\beta}_3 = \frac{(\Sigma x_{3i} y_i)(\Sigma x_{2i}^2) - (\Sigma x_{2i} y_i)(\Sigma x_{2i} x_{3i})}{(\Sigma x_{2i}^2)(\Sigma x_{3i}^2) - (\Sigma x_{2i} x_{3i})^2} \tag{4.5}$$

4.2 REGRESSION INTERPRETATION AND STATISTICS

Interpretation of regression coefficients requires an expansion of our analysis in the two-variable model. For example, in the three-variable model

$$Y_i = \beta_1 + \beta_2 X_{2i} + \beta_3 X_{3i} + \varepsilon_i$$

the coefficient β_2 measures the change in Y associated with a unit change in X_2 on the assumption that all other values for the remaining explanatory variables are held constant. Likewise the coefficient β_3 measures the change in Y associated with a unit change in X_3. In both cases the assumption that the values of the remaining explanatory variables are constant is crucial to our interpretation of the coefficients. We show in more detail exactly how one holds other variables constant in Appendix 4.2 and encourage the reader to follow the details. To signify that other variables are held constant, we call the unknown slope parameters *partial regression coefficients* (they correspond to the values of the *partial derivatives* of Y with respect to X_2 and X_3).

In order to test the significance of individual regression coefficients, it is natural to ask whether the Gauss-Markov theorem (discussed in Chapter 3) extends to the multiple regression model and whether one can obtain an unbiased estimate of the variance σ^2 as well as information about the distribution of the estimated regression parameters. The derivations of the statistical properties of the multiple regression model are cumbersome without the use of matrix algebra, and so we simply provide a summary of the important results:†

1. Given assumptions i, ii, iii*a* and iii*b*, the Gauss-Markov theorem applies; i.e., the ordinary least-squares estimator of each coefficient β_j, $j = 1, 2, \ldots, k$, is BLUE. (When the error term is normally distributed, it is equivalent to the *maximum-likelihood estimator* as well; see Appendix 3.2.)
2. An unbiased and consistent estimate of σ^2 is provided by

$$s^2 = \frac{\Sigma \hat{\varepsilon}_i^2}{N - k}$$

† The multiple regression model is presented in matrix form in Appendix 4.3.

3. When the error is normally distributed, t tests can be applied to test the regression coefficients because

$$\frac{\hat{\beta}_j - \beta_j}{s_{\hat{\beta}_j}} \sim t_{N-k} \qquad \text{for } j = 1, 2, \ldots, k$$

In other words, the estimated regression parameters, normalized by subtracting the mean and dividing by the *estimated* standard error, follow the t distribution with $N - k$ degrees of freedom. Finally, the *standard errors* of each of the coefficients $s_{\hat{\beta}_1}, s_{\hat{\beta}_2}, \ldots, s_{\hat{\beta}_k}$ are derived in Appendix 4.3 because their calculation involves matrix inversion. Since we will occasionally use the three-variable model for examples, we will reproduce three formulas here; the first two calculate the estimated *variance* of each coefficient and the third, the covariance between the two

$$\widehat{\text{Var}}\left(\hat{\beta}_2\right) = \frac{s^2}{\Sigma x_{2i}^2 (1 - r^2)} \tag{4.6}$$

$$\widehat{\text{Var}}\left(\hat{\beta}_3\right) = \frac{s^2}{\Sigma x_{3i}^2 (1 - r^2)} \tag{4.7}$$

$$\widehat{\text{Cov}}\left(\hat{\beta}_2, \hat{\beta}_3\right) = \frac{-s^2 r}{(1 - r^2)\sqrt{\Sigma x_{2i}^2 \Sigma x_{3i}^2}} \tag{4.8}$$

where $r = \Sigma x_{2i} x_{3i} / \sqrt{\Sigma x_{2i}^2 \Sigma x_{3i}^2}$ is the simple correlation between x_2 and x_3.

4.3 F TESTS, R^2, AND CORRECTED R^2

To extend the notion of R^2 as a measure of goodness of fit to the multiple regression model, we repeat and extend some of the earlier discussion (Section 3.4) about the decomposition of the variation in the dependent variable Y. Recall that the model with k variables is

$$Y_i = \beta_1 + \beta_2 X_{2i} + \cdots + \beta_k X_{ki} + \varepsilon_i \tag{4.9}$$

We can break down the difference between Y_i and its mean $\bar{Y}_i$ as follows:

$$\left(Y_i - \bar{Y}\right) = (Y_i - \hat{Y}_i) + \left(\hat{Y}_i - \bar{Y}\right) \tag{4.10}$$

Squaring both sides and summing over all observations (1 to N), we obtain†

$$\Sigma(Y_i - \overline{Y})^2 = \Sigma(Y_i - \hat{Y}_i)^2 + \Sigma(\hat{Y}_i - \overline{Y})^2 \qquad (4.11)$$

$$\underset{\substack{\text{Variation} \\ \text{in } Y}}{} \qquad \underset{\substack{\text{Residual} \\ \text{variation}}}{} \qquad \underset{\substack{\text{Explained} \\ \text{variation}}}{}$$

or, using the terminology introduced in Chapter 3,

$$\underset{\substack{\text{Total sum} \\ \text{of squares}}}{\text{TSS}} = \underset{\substack{\text{Residual sum} \\ \text{of squares}}}{\text{ESS}} + \underset{\substack{\text{Regression sum} \\ \text{of squares}}}{\text{RSS}} \qquad (4.12)$$

Then, we define R^2 as

$$R^2 = \frac{\text{RSS}}{\text{TSS}} = \frac{\Sigma(\hat{Y}_i - \overline{Y})^2}{\Sigma(Y_i - \overline{Y})^2} = 1 - \frac{\Sigma\hat{\varepsilon}_i^2}{\Sigma(Y_i - \overline{Y})^2} \qquad (4.13)$$

R^2 measures the proportion of the variation in Y which is "explained" by the multiple regression equation. R^2 is often informally used as a goodness-of-fit statistic and to compare the validity of regression results under alternative specifications of the independent variables in the model. There are several problems with the use of R^2. In the first place, *all our statistical results follow from the initial assumption that the model is correct*, and we have no statistical procedure to compare alternative specifications. Second, R^2 is sensitive to the number of independent variables included in the regression model. The addition of more independent variables to the regression equation can never lower R^2 and is likely to raise it (the addition of a new explanatory variable does not alter TSS but is likely to increase RSS). Thus, one would simply add more variables to an equation if one wished only to maximize R^2. Finally, the interpretation and use of R^2 become difficult when a model is formulated which has a 0 intercept. In such a case the ratio of the regression sum of squares to the total sum of squares need not lie within the 0 to 1 range.‡

The difficulty with R^2 as a measure of goodness of fit is that R^2 pertains to explained and unexplained *variation* in Y and therefore does not account for the number of degrees of freedom in the problem. A natural solution is to concern oneself with *variances*, not variations, thus eliminating the dependence of

---

† $\Sigma(Y_i - \overline{Y})^2 = \Sigma(Y_i - \hat{Y}_i)^2 + \Sigma(\hat{Y}_i - \overline{Y})^2 + 2\Sigma(Y_i - \hat{Y}_i)(\hat{Y}_i - \overline{Y})$. But the last term is identically zero, since

$$\Sigma(Y_i - \hat{Y}_i)(\hat{Y}_i - \overline{Y}) = \Sigma\hat{\varepsilon}_i(\hat{Y}_i - \overline{Y}) = \Sigma\hat{\varepsilon}_i\hat{Y}_i - \Sigma\hat{\varepsilon}_i\overline{Y}$$

$$= \Sigma\hat{\varepsilon}_i(\hat{\beta}_1 + \hat{\beta}_2 X_{2i} + \cdots + \hat{\beta}_k X_{ki}) - \overline{Y}\Sigma\hat{\varepsilon}_i$$

$$= \hat{\beta}_1\Sigma\hat{\varepsilon}_i + \hat{\beta}_2\Sigma\hat{\varepsilon}_i X_{2i} + \cdots + \hat{\beta}_k\Sigma\hat{\varepsilon}_i X_{ki} - \overline{Y}\Sigma\hat{\varepsilon}_i$$

$$= 0 \quad \text{since } \Sigma\hat{\varepsilon}_i = 0 \text{ and } \Sigma\hat{\varepsilon}_i X_{ji} = 0 \text{ for } j = 2, 3, \ldots, k$$

Note that the proof is analogous to the derivation given in Section 3.4 and Appendix 3.3.

‡ The use of R^2 in a model with zero intercept is discussed in detail in D. Aigner, *Basic Econometrics* (Englewood Cliffs, N.J.: Prentice-Hall, 1971), pp. 85–90.

goodness of fit on the number of independent variables in the model. (Recall that variance equals variation divided by degrees of freedom.) We define $\bar{R}^2$, or *corrected* R^2, as

$$\bar{R}^2 = 1 - \frac{\text{Var}(\hat{\varepsilon})}{\text{Var}(Y)}$$

where the sample variances of $\hat{\varepsilon}$ and Y are calculated as follows:†

$$\text{Var}(\hat{\varepsilon}) = s^2 = \frac{\Sigma\hat{\varepsilon}_i^2}{N-k} \qquad \text{Var}(Y) = \frac{\Sigma(Y_i - \bar{Y})^2}{N-1}$$

where k is the number of independent variables. Even though the error sum of squares will decrease (or remain the same) as new explanatory variables are added, the residual variance need not. Notice that both the numerator and denominator in the definition of Var $(\hat{\varepsilon})$ change when an additional variable is added to the model. In addition, by noting that (from (4.13))

$$R^2 = 1 - \frac{s^2}{\text{Var}(Y)}\frac{N-k}{N-1} \tag{4.14}$$

it is easy to derive a formula‡ for the relationship between R^2 and $\bar{R}^2$:

$$\bar{R}^2 = 1 - (1 - R^2)\frac{N-1}{N-k} \tag{4.15}$$

Upon examination of Eq. (4.15), it becomes immediately apparent that:

1. If $k = 1$, then $R^2 = \bar{R}^2$.
2. If k is greater than 1, then $R^2 \geq \bar{R}^2$.
3. $\bar{R}^2$ can be negative.

$\bar{R}^2$ thus has a number of properties which make it a more desirable goodness-of-fit measure than R^2. When new variables are added to a regression model, R^2 always increases, while $\bar{R}^2$ may rise or fall.§ The use of $\bar{R}^2$ eliminates at least some of the incentive for researchers to include numerous variables in a model without much thought about why they should appear. To give a simple but true

---

† We divide by $N - 1$ in calculating the variance of Y because 1 degree of freedom is used when the mean of Y is calculated. However, we divide by $N - k$ when calculating the variance of $\hat{\varepsilon}$ because k parameters of the regression model must be estimated before $\hat{\varepsilon}$ can be calculated (and thus the loss of k degrees of freedom from the original N).

‡ From Eq. (4.14) it follows that $1 - R^2 = [s^2/\text{Var}(Y)][(N-k)/(N-1)]$. But $1 - \bar{R}^2 = s^2/\text{Var}(Y)$. Therefore $1 - R^2 = (1 - \bar{R}^2)[(N-k)/(N-1)]$. Solving, we get $\bar{R}^2 = 1 - (1 - R^2)[(N-1)/(N-k)]$.

§ It is interesting to note that a simple general rule does exist for the individual wishing to maximize corrected R^2. If independent variables are left in the regression equation when their t statistic is greater than 1 and dropped otherwise, then corrected R^2 will be maximized with respect to the set of independent variables under consideration. For details, see P. J. Dhrymes, "On the Game of Maximizing $\bar{R}^2$," *Australian Economic Papers*, vol. 9, December 1970.

example, consider a model in which 25 observations were obtained and used to test a model. The reported R^2 was .8. However, this value resulted only after 17 independent variables were included in the model. The value of $\overline{R}^2$ associated with the same model would be [from Eq. (4.15)] only .4. Clearly the value of corrected R^2 gives a more accurate picture of the limitations of this particular model. However, one should not conclude that the corrected R^2 solves all the difficulties associated with using R^2 as a measure of goodness of fit. The decision about whether or not variables should be included in the model should still depend largely upon *a priori* theoretical considerations. And in any case the numerical value of corrected R^2 will be sensitive to the kind of data being used.

The F statistic printed out by most regression programs can be used in the multiple regression model to test the significance of the R^2 statistic. Strictly speaking, the F statistic with $k - 1$ and $N - k$ degrees of freedom allows us to test the hypothesis that *none* of the explanatory variables helps to explain the variation of Y about its mean. In other words, the F statistic tests the joint hypothesis that $\beta_2 = \beta_3 = \cdots = \beta_k = 0$. It can be shown that

$$F_{k-1, N-k} = \frac{R^2}{1 - R^2} \frac{N - k}{k - 1}$$

If the null hypothesis is true, then we would expect R^2, and therefore F, to be close to 0. Thus, we use a high value of the F statistic as a rationale for rejecting the null hypothesis. (See Chapters 2 and 3 for details.) In the two-variable model, for example, the F statistic tests whether the regression line is horizontal. In such a case, $R^2 = 0$ (see Chapter 3) and the regression explains none of the variation in the dependent variable. Notice that we do not test whether the regression passes through the origin ($\beta_1 = 0$); our objective is simply to see whether we can explain any variation around the mean of Y. As a practical matter, the F test of the significance of a regression equation is of limited use because it is likely that the F statistic will allow for rejection of the null hypothesis, whether or not the model explains the structure under study. In fact, it is possible for the R^2 to be significant at a given level, even though none of the regression coefficients are found to be significant according to individual t tests.† If the value of the F statistic is not significantly different from 0, we must conclude that the explanatory variables do little to explain the variation of Y about its mean. We will show some more valuable applications of the F test in Chapter 5.

What if we were to use R^2 to compare the validity of alternative regression models when the dependent variable varies from regression to regression? Such a problem occurs frequently in econometric model building when the researcher has little prior information about what functional form the dependent variable

---

† This situation might arise, for example, if the independent variables are highly correlated with each other. The result may be high standard errors for the coefficients and low t values; yet the model as a whole might fit the data very well. See Section 4.4 for further details relating to the problem of multicollinearity.

in the model ought to take. Consider the two models

I
$$Y_i = \beta_1 + \beta_2 X_{2i} + \beta_3 X_{3i} + \varepsilon_i \qquad (4.16)$$

II
$$Y_i - X_{2i} = \beta_1' + \beta_2' X_{2i} + \beta_3' X_{3i} + \varepsilon_i' \qquad (4.17)$$

Model I differs from II only in that the dependent variables differ. (Y might be total local government expenditures, including federal grants, and X_2 might be grants, making the second dependent variable expenditures paid for by locally raised revenues.) It can be shown (see Exercise 4.1) that

1. The R^2 and $\bar{R}^2$ measures associated with models 1 and 2 will differ.
2. $\hat{\beta}_1' = \hat{\beta}_1$, $\hat{\beta}_2' = \hat{\beta}_2 - 1$, and $\hat{\beta}_3' = \hat{\beta}_3$.
3. The true errors as well as the least-squares residuals and the residual variance will be identical in the two models.

Thus, both versions of the model use identical information about the process under study, yet the measures of goodness of fit will vary considerably from one case to the other. The result is that R^2 cannot be used *directly* to compare models with different dependent variables.

Example 4.1 Auto sales† In order to predict quarterly auto sales using a single-equation model, three explanatory variables are likely to be of value. One would expect that sales would move in the same direction as disposable income but that they would be inversely related to the recent price of autos and to the cost of borrowing money to finance the purchase. We therefore use the following data for our model (for the period 1959 through 1978):

   S = quarterly auto sales, billions of current dollars
   YP = quarterly personal income, billions of current dollars
   R = 3-month Treasury bill rate in percentage terms for same time period
   CPI = quarterly Consumer Price Index of new cars (1957 to 1959 = 100) for same time period

   The equation to be estimated is

$$S_t = \beta_1 + \beta_2 \text{YP}_t + \beta_3 R_t + \beta_4 \text{CPI}_t + \varepsilon_t$$

   where t denotes that the data are measured at time t. The regression results (as they may be printed out by a standard computer program) are listed as

---

† The data used in this example are listed in the instructor's manual.

follows:

Coefficient	Value	Standard error	t statistic
β_1	56.36	6.70	8.4
β_2	.036	.003	10.7
β_3	− .508	.073	−7.0
β_4	− .088	.035	−2.5

Number of variables = 4 (including the constant)

Number of observations = 80   Degrees of freedom = 76

$R^2 = .841$ $\bar{R}^2 = .835$

$F(3,76) = F_{3,76} = 133.8$

Standard error of regression(s) = 2.97

Sum of squared residuals ESS = 668.7

All estimated coefficients are significant at the 5 percent level, since all t statistics are greater than 2 in absolute value and there are 84 degrees of freedom. For this reason, none of the variables should be dropped from the regression. As expected, the monthly income coefficient is positive. It can be interpreted to mean that an increase of $1 billion in disposable income will lead to a $36 *million* increase in auto sales, with the effects of all other variables held constant. Also, if the interest rate rises by 1 percentage point, auto sales will drop by $508 million in the following quarter. Finally, the estimated price-index coefficient tells us that if the Consumer Price Index for new cars goes up by 1 point (other things being equal), auto sales will drop by $88 million.

The R^2 and $\bar{R}^2$ statistics are very close in magnitude as expected, since there are a large number of degrees of freedom in the model. The F statistic with 3 and 76 degrees of freedom is highly significant, allowing us to reject the null hypothesis that all explanatory variable coefficients are jointly 0. Finally, the reader should check that the sum of squared residuals is closely related to the standard error of the regression, since $s^2 = \text{ESS}/76$.

Example 4.2 Interest-rate determination In this example we build a single-equation model whose purpose is to forecast short-term interest rates. We restrict our attention to the least-squares estimation of the model, although we consider a more sophisticated estimation of this same model in Chapter 6 when we deal with the problem of serially correlated errors. Finally, we use the least-squares model to forecast short-term interest rates in Example 8.2. Throughout our discussion the reader will find it valuable to examine Table 4.1, which summarizes six of the regression results obtained during the process of building the single-equation model. The model is estimated

Table 4.1 Selected regression results

t statistics in parentheses

Independent variables	(1)	(2)	(3)	(4)	(5)	(6)
YD_t	.032	.037	.030	.054	.050	.053
	(6.67)	(7.01)	(7.00)	(23.22)	(14.55)	(14.76)
ΔYD_t	− .109	− .172				
	(−.69)	(−1.00)				
$\Delta M_t + \Delta M_{t-1} + \Delta M_{t-2}$	− .197	− .303	− .208	− .305	− .294	− .280
	(−3.36)	(−4.73)	(−3.71)	(−7.38)	(−5.93)	(−6.13)
$\Delta P_t / P_t$	372.922					
	(5.91)					
$\Delta P_t / P_t + \Delta P_{t-1} / P_{t-1}$		249.970	218.17			
		(6.96)	(7.26)			
$\Delta P_t / P_t + \Delta P_{t-1} / P_{t-1} + \Delta P_{t-2} / P_{t-2}$				99.651	41.54	104.37
				(7.83)	(1.89)	(5.23)
Constant	− 1.072	− 1.086	− .924	− 3.750	− 3.011	− 3.662
	(−1.99)	(−1.85)	(−1.83)	(−14.90)	(−7.87)	(−9.45)
N	157	157	157	181	121	145
R^2	.649	.672	.665	.863	.739	.853
$\bar{R}^2$	.640	.664	.658	.860	.732	.849
Time bounds	1960–73	1960–73	1960–73	1955–70	1958–68	1958–70
s	.816	.788	.794	.524	.509	.552
F	70.29	77.93	101.27	370.93	110.29	271.88

using monthly time-series data running from January of the initial year through January of the final year of observation. The variables used in the estimation process are as follows:

R = interest rate on 3-month Treasury bills (dependent variable)
YD = aggregate disposable income, billions of 1958 dollars
M = aggregate money supply (currency plus demand deposits), billions of current dollars
P = Consumer Price Index (1958 = 100)

The symbol Δ is used to denote the process of differencing, i.e.,

$$\Delta YD_t = YD_t - YD_{t-1}$$

The first equation (column 1) includes four explanatory variables. Disposable income is expected to have a strong positive effect on interest rates, since increases in disposable income imply increases in the demand for liquid assets. As expected, the YD coefficient is positive and statistically significant (at the 1 percent and 5 percent levels). The change in disposable income is added in an attempt to include (in a detailed manner) the time process involved as interest rates adjust to disposable income changes.

Because this variable is statistically insignificant, no serious attempt is made to evaluate the sign of its coefficient. The third variable included in the model is a *moving sum* of *changes* in the money supply. The moving sum (in this case) is a simple sum of money changes over a 3-month period. It is expected that, other things being equal, increases in the average of past changes in the money *supply* will lead to lower interest rates. The results are consistent with this notion, since the regression coefficient is negative and significant at the 5 percent level. Finally, a variable is entered to account for the effect of the rate of change of prices. One would expect (as is borne out) that an increase in the rate of price change will lead to an increase in interest rates. While the results are generally good (three significant t values and an R^2 of .649), the standard error of the regression is unsatisfactorily high. The standard error of .816 is best interpreted in relation to the mean value of the dependent variable, in this case 3.78. The standard error is approximately 22 percent of the dependent variable mean; from experience we would hope for a *percentage standard error* closer to 10 or 15 percent.†

In the second regression equation (column 2), the inflation variable is changed from a 1-month rate of change to a 2-month moving-sum rate of change. As in the case of the money supply, it is suspected that inflation affects interest rates with a lag. The results suggest that some improvement has taken place. R^2 has increased (as well as $\bar{R}^2$), as has the F statistic. The fact that the standard error of the equation has decreased is also indicative of a gain in predictive power. In the third regression equation (column 3), the previously insignificant ΔYD term is dropped from the equation. This leaves all individual regression coefficients significant and results in a very small increase in the standard error of the regression (since the residual sum of squares has increased more than has the number of degrees of freedom).

As a final attempt to improve the regression model, the moving-sum rate of inflation variable is increased from a 2- to a 3-month average. The results of the regressions are listed in columns 4 to 6, each regression being associated with a different set of time bounds. The alteration in the moving-sum inflation term has substantially increased the explanatory power of the equation in all three cases. In regression 6, for example, R^2 has increased to .853, while the standard error of the regression has diminished to .552. This is slightly less than 15 percent of the mean of the dependent variable. At the same time each of the t statistics has increased somewhat in magnitude (in absolute value). For these reasons the final model specification is chosen to be the specification implicit in regressions 4 to 6. The specific set of time bounds chosen should depend not upon an analysis of minor changes in regression statistics but upon the specific purposes for which the regression equation is to be used. In most actual applications, for example, the model will be estimated using all recent data, so that complete information can be used in the forecasting process.

---

† Since there is no useful test for evaluating the magnitude of the standard error, we must rely on qualitative judgments about how low a percentage standard error is desirable.

Example 4.3   Consumption function Three separate regression equations were used to describe some of the econometric issues involved with the estimation of a simple aggregative consumption function. The three models are as follows (data are quarterly, from 1954–1 to 1971–4, in current dollars):

I $$C_t = \alpha_1 + \beta_1 Y_t + \varepsilon_{1t}$$

II $$C_t = \alpha_2 + \beta_2 Y_t + \gamma_2 C_{t-1} + \varepsilon_{2t}$$

III $$S_t = \alpha_3 + \beta_3 Y_t + \varepsilon_{3t} \qquad S_t \equiv Y_t - C_t$$

The regression results are listed in the following table:

Model	Coefficient	Value	t statistic
I	$\hat{\alpha}_1$	14.51	7.03
	$\hat{\beta}_1$	0.88	173.06
	$R^2 = .9977$	ESS = 966.5	SER = 3.72
II	$\hat{\alpha}_2$	5.52	3.06
	$\hat{\beta}_2$	0.31	4.85
	$\hat{\gamma}_2$	0.65	8.78
	$R^2 = .9989$	ESS = 440.70	SER = 2.55
III	$\hat{\alpha}_3$	−14.51	−7.03
	$\hat{\beta}_3$	0.12	24.57
	$R^2 = .8961$	ESS = 966.5	SER = 3.72

Model I describes the simplest form of the consumption function, in which consumption is determined purely from disposable income Y in the same time period. The coefficient of the disposable income variable measures the marginal propensity to consume. In model II a term is added to include the effect of lagged consumption on present consumption. The term is included to allow for current consumption to be closely dependent upon its own recent behavior as well as on income. The coefficient of the disposable-income term must be interpreted differently in model II and model I. The value of .31 refers to the change in consumption associated with a 1-unit change in disposable income, assuming that consumption in the previous period has remained unchanged. The reader should note that the total effect of a change in disposable income on consumption will take place over time and can be measured only by calculating the long-run marginal propensity to consume under the assumption that consumption patterns are equal over time.† Solving for $C_t = C_{t-1}$, we find that the long-run marginal propensity to consume implied by model II is .31/(1 − .65) = .88.

† A detailed analysis of model II is presented in Chapter 9 when distributed lags are discussed.

The reader should notice the slight increase in R^2 from model I to model II. R^2 will always increase when additional variables are added to the model, as long as those variables are correlated with the dependent variable and not collinear with the other independent variables. Since the R^2 for the original equation is already quite high, it is tempting to assume that adding additional variables cannot add much to the explanatory power of the model, but the significant t statistic on the lagged consumption term in model II shows that this is not the case.

Model III represents a savings function, not a consumption function, but a quick examination of the regression results shows the two to be quite closely related. This is not surprising, since savings is defined to be the difference between disposable income and consumption for all observations of the data. Notice that the estimated coefficients are very closely related to each other. The intercepts differ only by sign, and the sum of the two slope coefficients is identically 1. The reader can see why this is true by substituting $Y_t - C_t$ for S_t in model III and comparing the results with model I. In addition, the regression sum of squares and standard error of the regressions are identical in both models. In fact, it is not difficult to show that the estimated residuals are identical in both cases. What appears surprising at first is that the R^2 falls substantially when moving from model I to model III. The reason for this drop can be seen by recalling the definition of R^2:

$$R^2 = 1 - \frac{\text{ESS}}{\text{TSS}}$$

Since the estimated residuals are identical in both equations, the error sum of squares is also identical. However, the total sum of squares is different in the two models because the dependent variables are different. The point of this example is that models can be alike in almost all respects (including the ability to forecast or predict) and yet differ substantially in R^2. To depend solely on the use of R^2 as a measure of the explanatory power of a regression equation can be misleading because of the sensitivity of R^2 to the choice of dependent variable. We shall see in Chapter 8 that the standard error of the regression is often more useful as a measure of predictive power of a regression equation than R^2.

4.4 MULTICOLLINEARITY

One of the assumptions of the classical multiple regression model is that there exists no exact linear relationship between the independent variables in the model. If such a linear relationship does exist, we say that the independent variables are perfectly *collinear* or that perfect *collinearity* exists. Assume, for example, that the grade-point-average model (from Chapter 1) consisted of the following three independent variables:

X_2 = family income, thousands of dollars
X_3 = average hours of study per day
X_4 = average hours of study per week

Variables X_3 and X_4 are collinear because $X_4 = 7X_3$ for *each and every* student being surveyed. If regression results were somehow obtained, it would be impossible to interpret the coefficient of the X_3 variable without simultaneously examining the coefficient of the X_4 variable.† Each parameter makes perfect sense if only one of the collinear variables appears in the model. When both appear, we are faced with an impossible problem. The coefficient of the X_3 variable is a partial regression coefficient measuring the change in Y associated with a unit change in X_3 *with all other variables constant*. Since it is impossible to keep all other variables constant, we are not able to interpret (or even define) the regression coefficient. The example is so obvious as to suggest that perfect collinearity cannot arise in a realistic setting. There are instances, however, where more complex linear relationships between the independent variables can appear in a model if proper care is not taken. Pure or perfect collinearity is easy to discover because it will be impossible for the computer (or the individual) to calculate least-squares estimates of the parameters. (With collinearity, the system of equations to be solved contains two or more equations which are not independent.) Collinearity presents no particular problem if the linear relationship is known to the researcher. In the grade-point example, one need simply eliminate one of the variables X_3 and X_4 without any loss of predictive or explanatory power.

In practice, we are often faced with the more difficult problem of having independent variables with a high degree of *multicollinearity*. Multicollinearity arises when two or more variables (or combinations of variables) are highly (but not perfectly) correlated with each other. It may be a sample problem, in which case new data may cause the problem to disappear. However, multicollinearity may not be peculiar to a specific sample. In this case the model can be used with all its variables if sufficient care is given to the interpretation of the regression results.

Suppose, for example, that two variables are highly positively correlated (but not perfectly collinear). Then, it will be possible to obtain least-squares estimates of the regression coefficients, but *interpretation* of the coefficients will be quite difficult. The partial regression coefficient of the first of the two highly correlated variables is interpreted to measure the change in Y due to a change in the variable in question, *other things being equal*. But, the presence of multicollinearity implies that there will be very few data in the sample to give one confidence about such an interpretation. Any time a given change in one

---

† With perfect collinearity, we cannot calculate the least-squares parameter estimates. To see this, reconsider Eqs. (4.3) to (4.5) when X_2 and X_3 are perfectly collinear. In this case, Eqs. (4.4) and (4.5) will not be independent, and no solution will exist.

variable occurs, the corresponding observation on its highly correlated partner is likely to change predictably. Not surprisingly, the distributions of the estimated regression parameters are quite sensitive to multicollinearity. These distributions are sensitive not only to the correlation between independent variables but also to the magnitude of the standard error of the regression. (Recall that in the two-variable model, the estimated variance of $\hat{\beta}$ is $s^2/\sum x_i^2$.) In practice, this sensitivity shows up in the form of very high standard errors for the regression parameter.

All this can be seen clearly if we examine the formulas for the variances of the estimated parameters given in Eqs. (4.6) and (4.7), especially in the light of the estimated variance for the two-variable model. Both denominators here include the term $1 - r^2$, which does not appear in the corresponding formula in Chapter 3. When X_2 and X_3 are uncorrelated in the sample, $r = 0$ and the formulas are essentially identical. However, when r becomes high (close to 1) in absolute value, multicollinearity is present, with the result that the estimated variances of both $\hat{\beta}_2$ and $\hat{\beta}_3$ get very large. This tells us that while $\hat{\beta}_2$ and $\hat{\beta}_3$ will remain unbiased estimators, the reliance that we can place on the value of one or the other will be small when multicollinearity is present. This can present a problem if we believe that one or both of two variables ought to be in a model, but we cannot reject the null hypothesis because of the large estimated standard errors. It may be reasonable in such cases to drop one of the two variables from the equation and to reestimate it. We shall see in Chapter 5 that this can cause bias in the reestimated model, but it will help us to be aware of the effect of the multicollinearity in the original model.†

A rule of thumb states that multicollinearity is likely to be a problem if the simple correlation between two variables is larger than the correlation of either or both variables with the dependent variable. Such a rule may be quite reasonable if there are only two independent variables in the model but can be unreliable in the general case. The principal reason is that simple correlations do not give any information about the possibility of more complicated linear relationships between the independent variables.‡

Because multicollinearity is dependent directly upon the sample of observations, little can be done to resolve it unless more information about the process in question is available. The easiest way to tell whether multicollinearity is

---

† As described in Chapter 5 (under the subject of specification error), the gain in the reduction in the standard error of one variable when a second variable is dropped from the equation must be traded off against the possible introduction of bias due to misspecification of the equation. For a more detailed discussion of this issue and some related tests, see C. Toro-Vizcarrondo and T. D. Wallace, "A Test of the Mean Square Error Criterion for Restrictions in Linear Regression," *Journal of the American Statistical Association*, vol. 63, pp. 558–572, 1968, and "Tables for the Mean Square Error Test for Exact Linear Restrictions in Regression," *Journal of the American Statistical Association*, vol. 64, pp. 1649–1663, 1969.

‡ For an additional treatment of tests for multicollinearity see D. E. Farrar and R. R. Glauber, "Multicollinearity in Regression Analysis: The Problem Re-visited," *Review of Economics and Statistics*, vol. 49, pp. 92–107, 1967. See also D. A. Belsley, E. Kuh, and R. E. Welsch, *Regression Diagnostics: Identifying Influential Data and Sources of Collinearity* (New York: Wiley, 1980).

causing problems is to examine the standard errors of the coefficients. If several coefficients have high standard errors and dropping one or more variables from the equation lowers the standard errors of the remaining variables, multicollinearity will usually be the source of the problem. A more sophisticated analysis would take into account the fact that the *covariance* between estimated parameters (as well as the individual standard errors) may be sensitive to multicollinearity. As Eq. (4.8) shows, a high degree of collinearity will be associated with a relatively high (in absolute value) covariance between estimated parameters.† This suggests that if one estimated parameter $\hat{\beta}_i$ overestimates the true parameter β_i, a second parameter estimate $\hat{\beta}_j$ is likely to underestimate β_j, and vice versa.‡

4.5 BETA COEFFICIENTS AND ELASTICITIES

4.5.1 Beta Coefficients

Beta coefficients are occasionally used to make statements about the relative importance of the independent variables in a multiple regression model. To determine beta coefficients, one simply performs a linear regression in which each variable is *normalized* by subtracting its mean and dividing by its estimated standard deviation. The normalized regression model looks as follows:

$$\frac{Y_i - \overline{Y}}{s_Y} = \beta_2^* \frac{X_{2i} - \overline{X}_2}{s_{X_2}} = \beta_3^* \frac{X_{3i} - \overline{X}_3}{s_{X_3}} + \cdots + \beta_k^* \frac{X_{ki} - \overline{X}_k}{s_{X_k}} + \varepsilon_i$$

$$(4.18)$$

The beta coefficients bear a close relationship to the estimated coefficients of the original unnormalized multiple regression model. It is not difficult to prove that§

$$\hat{\beta}_j^* = \hat{\beta}_j \frac{s_{X_j}}{s_Y} \qquad j = 2, 3, \ldots, k \tag{4.19}$$

In other words, the beta coefficient adjusts the estimated slope parameter by the ratio of the standard deviation of the independent variable to the standard deviation of the dependent variable. A beta coefficient of .7 can be interpreted to mean that a 1 standard deviation change in the independent variable will lead

---

† An example of this is given in J. Johnson, *Econometric Methods*, 2d ed. (New York: McGraw-Hill, 1972), pp. 160–163.

‡ One way of improving parameter estimates without the availability of new data involves the use of *ridge regression*. For some details relating to this estimation process, see B. T. McCallum, "Artificial Orthogonalization in Regression Analysis," *Review of Economics and Statistics*, vol. 52, pp. 110–113, 1970, and H. D. Vinod, "A Survey of Ridge Regression and Related Techniques for Improvements over Ordinary Least Squares," *Review of Economics and Statistics*, vol. 60, pp. 121–131, 1978.

§ Writing Eq. (4.18) in deviations form and multiplying both sides by s_Y, we get $y_i = \beta_2^*(s_Y/s_{X_2})x_{2i} + \beta_3^*(s_Y/s_{X_3})x_{3i} + \cdots + \beta_k^*(s_Y/s_{X_k})x_{ki} + \varepsilon_i^*$, from which our result follows directly.

to a .7 standard deviation change in the dependent variable. Both beta coefficients and partial correlation coefficients are connected with the variance of Y, the dependent variable. However, the rescaling associated with the normalized regression makes it possible to compare beta coefficients directly. This cannot be done with the original X's because the dependent variables are in different units with different variances. It is interesting to note that the beta coefficient of the independent variable in the two-variable model is identically equal to the simple correlation between the two variables. The beta coefficient of the constant term is undefined since the constant term drops out as a result of the normalization process.†

4.5.2 Elasticity

Quite frequently in economics and business one may be interested in interpreting the effect of a percentage change of an independent variable on the dependent variable. The notion of the *elasticity* of a variable is used for this purpose. The elasticity of Y with respect to X_2, for example, can be defined as the percentage change in Y divided by the percentage change in X_2. In general, elasticities are not constant but change when measured at different points along the regression line. The elasticities which are usually printed out by computer programs are calculated *at the point of the means of each of the independent variables*. For the jth coefficient the elasticity is evaluated as

$$E_j = \hat{\beta}_j \frac{\overline{X_j}}{\overline{Y}} \approx \frac{\partial Y}{\overline{Y}} \Big/ \frac{\partial X}{\overline{X}} \tag{4.20}$$

The values of the elasticity are unbounded and may be positive or negative. Elasticities turn out to be particularly useful because they are unit-free; i.e., their values are independent of the units in which the variables are measured. For example, if $E_j = 2.0$, we can say that about the mean of the variables a 1 percent increase in X_j will lead to a 2 percent increase in Y. If $E_j = -.5$, a 1 percent increase in X_j will lead to a .5 percent decrease in Y. In general, large elasticities imply that the dependent variable is very responsive to changes in the independent variable. Note finally that in forecasting, elasticities are likely to be more valuable if they are evaluated at the most recent point, rather than at the point of means.

4.6 PARTIAL CORRELATION AND STEPWISE REGRESSION

In the multiple regression model, it is natural to look for an extension of the notion of simple correlation to account for the fact that other variables are kept constant when a given regression parameter is examined. Specifically, we wish to

† Beta coefficients, or *standardized regression coefficients*, are discussed in more detail in Aigner, op. cit., pp. 72–80.

see whether the dependent variable and one independent variable are related after netting out the effect of any other independent variables in the model. To do so, we consider the model

$$Y_i = \beta_1 + \beta_2 X_{2i} + \beta_3 X_{3i} + \varepsilon_i$$

The *partial correlation coefficient* between Y and X_2 must be defined in such a way that it measures the effect of X_2 on Y *which is not accounted for by the other variable in the model*. More specifically, the partial correlation coefficient is calculated by eliminating the linear effect of X_3 on Y (as well as the linear effect of X_3 on X_2) and then running the appropriate regression. The steps are as follows:

1. Run the regression of Y on X_3 and obtain fitted values

$$\hat{Y} = \hat{\alpha}_1 + \hat{\alpha}_2 X_3$$

2. Run the regression of X_2 on X_3 and obtain fitted values

$$\hat{X}_2 = \hat{\gamma}_1 + \hat{\gamma}_2 X_3$$

3. Remove the influence of X_3 on both Y and X_2. Let

$$Y^* = Y - \hat{Y} \qquad X_2^* = X_2 - \hat{X}_2$$

4. The partial correlation between X_2 and Y is then the simple correlation between Y^* and X_2^* (see Chapter 2).

To see why the regression of Y^* on X_2^* gives us our desired partial correlation coefficient, notice that Y^* and X_2^* are both uncorrelated with X_3 by construction.† Then, the regression of Y^* on X_2^* relates the part of Y which is uncorrelated with X_3 to the part of X_2 which is uncorrelated with X_3. We shall denote the partial correlation coefficient and simple correlations as follows:

$r_{YX_2 \cdot X_3} =$ partial correlation of Y and X_2 (controlling for X_3)
$\phantom{r_{YX_2 \cdot X_3}}r_{YX_2} =$ simple correlation between Y and X_2
$\phantom{r_{YX_2 \cdot X_3}}r_{X_2 X_3} =$ simple correlation between X_2 and X_3

Given the definition of partial correlation, it is not difficult (although somewhat tedious) to derive the relationship between partial correlation and simple correlation among the relevant variables. We shall state the result without proof, since the details are messy but not very insightful:‡

$$r_{YX_2 \cdot X_3} = \frac{r_{YX_2} - r_{YX_3} r_{X_2 X_3}}{\sqrt{1 - r_{X_2 X_3}^2}\ \sqrt{1 - r_{YX_3}^2}} \tag{4.21}$$

$$r_{YX_3 \cdot X_2} = \frac{r_{YX_3} - r_{YX_2} r_{X_2 X_3}}{\sqrt{1 - r_{X_2 X_3}^2}\ \sqrt{1 - r_{YX_2}^2}} \tag{4.22}$$

---

† The fact that Y^* and X_3 (for example) are uncorrelated follows directly from the fact that Y^* represents the residual of the regression of Y on X_3. We have seen in the previous chapter that regression residuals are uncorrelated with explanatory variables.

‡ See A. Koutsoyiannis, *Theory of Econometrics* (London: Macmillan, 1973), pp. 126–129, for details.

Several observations about partial correlation coefficients can be made directly by examination of Eqs. (4.21) and (4.22). First, partial correlations must range in value from -1 to $+1$, just like simple correlations (recall the derivation of simple correlation). A zero partial correlation between Y and X_2 indicates that there is no linear relationship between Y and X_2 *after the linear effect of X_3 on each has been accounted for*. In such a case we would conclude that X_2 does not have a *direct* effect on Y in the model. In fact, partial correlation coefficients are often used to determine the relative importance of different variables in multiple regression models.

It is interesting to note the relationship between partial correlation and multicollinearity. If X_2 and X_3 are uncorrelated, that is, $r_{X_2X_3} = 0$, and X_3 and Y are uncorrelated as well ($r_{YX_3} = 0$), the partial correlation between X_2 and Y reduces to the simple correlation between the two variables. If, on the other hand, X_2 and X_3 are perfectly correlated, that is, $r_{X_2X_3} = 1$, the partial correlation cannot be determined.

It is now useful to look at the relationship between partial correlation and R^2. In the two-variable model it is not difficult to show that it is possible to interpret R^2 as the square of the simple correlation between the dependent and independent variables. It is also possible to interpret the partial correlation between Y and X_2 as measuring the square root of the percentage of variance in Y which is not accounted for by X_3 but which is accounted for by the part of X_2 which is uncorrelated with X_3. Given this fact, it is possible to factor the multiple correlation coefficient into distinct components, each of which serves to explain a proportion of the regression sum of squares in the model. Indeed it is possible to derive the following relationship between multiple and partial correlation:

$$r_{YX_2 \cdot X_3}^2 = \frac{R^2 - r_{YX_3}^2}{1 - r_{YX_3}^2} \tag{4.23}$$

or

$$1 - R^2 = \left(1 - r_{YX_3}^2\right)\left(1 - r_{YX_2 \cdot X_3}^2\right) \tag{4.24}$$

The relationships described in Eqs. (4.23) and (4.24) are not easy to interpret. Equation (4.23) describes the fact (taking square roots of both sides) that the partial correlation coefficient can be determined by taking the square root of the percentage of the variance in Y explained by X_2 (with both variables adjusted to eliminate the effect of X_3).

Perhaps the most frequent use of partial correlation comes in the *stepwise regression* procedure. In stepwise regression one adds variables to a model to maximize the R^2 or equivalently to minimize the error sum of squares (ESS). The partial correlation between each explanatory variable and the dependent variable is useful in determining which variable to add because it tells us whether a given variable affects the dependent variable after the impact of all variables previously included in the model has been eliminated. While stepwise regression can be useful in helping one to look at data when there are a large number of possible explanatory variables to include, it is of little or no value when one is attempting to analyze a model statistically.† The reason is that t and F tests consider the test of a null hypothesis under the assumption that the model is given correctly, i.e., correctly specified. If we have searched over a large set of variables, selecting those that fit well, we are likely to get significant t tests with great frequency. As a result, the large t statistics do not allow us to reject the null hypothesis at a given level of significance.

Example 4.4 Sales of durable goods In order to predict the monthly sales of durable goods via a linear regression model, the following data are used:

1. Dependent variable
   SD = monthly retail sales of durable goods
2. Independent variables
   DI = retail inventory of department stores in durable goods
   IS = inventory sales ratios for all durable goods, retail stores
   I = open market rate on prime 4- to 6-month commercial paper
   E = average hourly gross earnings of workers
   P = Consumer Price Index for durable goods

The model is specified to be

$$SD_t = \beta_1 + \beta_2 DI_{t-6} + \beta_3 IS_{t-1} + \beta_4 I_{t-1} + \beta_5 E_{t-1} + \beta_6 P_{t-1} + \varepsilon_t$$

The regression results are

Range of data = January 1963 to April 1970

Degrees of freedom = 82 $R^2 = .93$

Standard error of the regression(s) = 263.4 $\bar{R}^2 = .92$

Sum of squared residuals = 5.7×10^6 $F(5/82) = 220.6$

Coefficient	Value	Standard error	t statistic	Mean
$\hat{\beta}_1$	12,091.0	2,321.1	5.2	1.0
$\hat{\beta}_2$	.109	.06	1.8	15,507.9
$\hat{\beta}_3$	$-1,690.3$	483.6	-3.5	1.96
$\hat{\beta}_4$	-76.2	65.6	-1.2	5.28
$\hat{\beta}_5$	5,585.6	974.4	5.7	2.96
$\hat{\beta}_6$	-175.6	34.4	-5.1	105.1

† For details, see N. Draper and H. Smith, *Applied Regression Analysis* (New York: Wiley, 1966), chap. 6.

Coefficient	Partial	Beta	Elasticity
$\hat{\beta}_2$	.19373	.30787	.20864
$\hat{\beta}_3$	− .36010	− .22599	− .40806
$\hat{\beta}_4$	− .12719	− .11866	− .04942
$\hat{\beta}_5$	.53486	1.55429	2.03112
$\hat{\beta}_6$	− .49147	− .67094	−2.26809

Covariance matrix

$$
\begin{array}{l}
\hat{\beta}_1 \\
\hat{\beta}_2 \\
\hat{\beta}_3 \\
\hat{\beta}_4 \\
\hat{\beta}_5 \\
\hat{\beta}_6
\end{array}
\left[
\begin{array}{cccccc}
5.39 \times 10^6 & & & & & \\
-45.5 & .0037 & & & & \\
-5.9 \times 10^5 & -4.83 & 2.3 \times 10^5 & & & \\
9.1 \times 10^4 & -.056 & -1.4 \times 10^4 & 4{,}307 & & \\
1.04 \times 10^6 & -53.3 & -1.4 \times 10^4 & -9{,}869 & 9.5 \times 10^5 & \\
-6.7 \times 10^4 & 1.5 & 3.05 & -531 & -2.3 \times 10^4 & 1{,}181
\end{array}
\right]
$$

Correlation matrix

	SD_t	DI_{t-6}	IS_{t-1}	I_{t-1}	E_{t-1}	P_{t-1}
SD_t	1.000					
DI_{t-6}	.943	1.000				
IS_{t-1}	.759	.865	1.000			
I_{t-1}	.831	.910	.860	1.000		
E_{t-1}	.920	.966	.843	.947	1.000	
P_{t-1}	.773	.838	.728	.906	.938	1.000

It is not a coincidence that all independent variables have been chosen to be lagged at least one time period. This accounts for lags in response, while at the same time making the prediction or forecasting problem much easier. If one wished to predict monthly retail sales of durable goods at time t, one need simply use the regression equation

$$\widehat{SD}_t = 12{,}091.0 + .109DI_{t-6} - 1{,}690.3IS_{t-1} - 76.2I_{t-1}$$
$$+ 5{,}595.6E_{t-1} - 175.6P_{t-1}$$

To evaluate SD in period $t + 1$, we substitute values for DI given 6 months previously, IS given 1 month previously, etc. If the independent variables were not lagged, some sort of extrapolation process would be needed to forecast their values before a prediction for the dependent variable could be made.†

† This forecasting problem, in the context of a single-equation regression model, is discussed in Chapter 8.

It is instructive to examine the complete regression output carefully. Notice that all diagonal elements of the covariance matrix are positive. These are the variances of the estimated coefficients and are equal to the square of the standard errors of the coefficients. The off-diagonal terms are covariances, which are useful in performing tests involving combinations of the coefficients of the independent variables. The correlation matrix includes the simple correlation coefficients between all combinations of the dependent and independent variables. As expected, the correlation between each variable and itself is identically equal to 1. All other correlation coefficients are positive and close to 1, which is a typical result when one is working with highly trended time-series data. The high correlations are an indication that multicollinearity may be a problem in the model, but the problem does not seem to be important in light of the significant t statistics associated with the regression results. The column labeled *partial* contains the list of partial correlation coefficients, while the column labeled *beta* includes all the beta coefficients. In this particular example, the independent variable coefficients with the largest t statistics in absolute value tend to have the largest beta and partial correlation coefficients (this is always true for betas and partial correlations). The beta of 1.55 on lagged earnings can be interpreted to mean that a 1 standard deviation increase in lagged earnings will lead to a 1.55 standard deviation increase in the retail sales of durable goods. The partial correlation coefficient of .53 on the earnings variable, on the other hand, implies that 28 percent ($.53^2$) of the variance of SD not accounted for by the other independent variables is accounted for by earnings. By examining the elasticities, we see that retail sales of durable goods are very sensitive to changes in gross earnings of workers and to the Consumer Price Index for durable goods. If earnings were to rise by 1 percent, then we might expect retail sales to increase slightly more than 2 percent. On the other hand, if the Consumer Price Index were to rise by 1 percent, retail sales would be expected to fall about 2.3 percent.

APPENDIX 4.1 LEAST-SQUARES PARAMETER ESTIMATION

Our goal is to minimize ESS $= \Sigma(Y_i - \hat{\beta}_1 - \hat{\beta}_2 X_{2i} - \hat{\beta}_3 X_{3i})^2$. We can do so by calculating the partial derivatives with respect to the three unknown parameters β_1, β_2, and β_3, equating each to 0 and solving. To simplify we do this with the model in derivations form, so that

$$\text{ESS} = \Sigma\left(y_i - \hat{\beta}_2 x_{2i} - \hat{\beta}_3 x_{3i}\right)^2$$

Then

$$\frac{\partial ESS}{\partial \beta_2} = 0 \quad \text{or} \quad \Sigma x_{2i} y_i = \beta_2 \Sigma x_{2i}^2 + \beta_3 \Sigma x_{2i} x_{3i} \qquad (A4.1)$$

$$\frac{\partial ESS}{\partial \beta_3} = 0 \quad \text{or} \quad \Sigma x_{3i} y_i = \beta_2 \Sigma x_{2i} x_{3i} + \beta_3 \Sigma x_{3i}^2 \qquad (A4.2)$$

To solve, we multiply (A4.1) by Σx_{3i}^2 and (A4.2) by $\Sigma x_{2i} x_{3i}$ and subtract the latter from the former:

$$\Sigma x_{2i} y_i \Sigma x_{3i}^2 - \Sigma x_{3i} y_i \Sigma x_{2i} x_{3i} = \beta_2 \left[\Sigma x_{2i}^2 x_{3i}^2 - (\Sigma x_{2i} x_{3i})^2 \right]$$

or

$$\hat{\beta}_2 = \frac{(\Sigma x_{2i} y_i)(\Sigma x_{3i}^2) - (\Sigma x_{3i} y_i)(\Sigma x_{2i} x_{3i})}{(\Sigma x_{2i}^2)(\Sigma x_{3i}^2) - (\Sigma x_{2i} x_{3i})^2}$$

It follows that

$$\hat{\beta}_3 = \frac{(\Sigma x_{3i} y_i)(\Sigma x_{2i}^2) - (\Sigma x_{2i} y_i)(\Sigma x_{2i} x_{3i})}{(\Sigma x_{2i}^2)(\Sigma x_{3i}^2) - (\Sigma x_{2i} x_{3i})^2}$$

Finally, if we set the derivative of ESS with respect to β_1 equal to zero when the data are not in deviations form, we find that

$$\hat{\beta}_1 = \bar{Y} - \hat{\beta}_2 \bar{X}_2 - \hat{\beta}_3 \bar{X}_3$$

APPENDIX 4.2 PARTIAL REGRESSION COEFFICIENTS

Consider the three-variable multiple regression model

$$Y_i = \beta_1 + \beta_2 X_{2i} + \beta_3 X_{3i} + e_i \qquad (A4.3)$$

Our task here is to discuss in some detail how one might interpret the partial regression coefficient, say β_2, in Eq. (A4.3). We argued in the text that β_2 measures the effect of X_2 on Y, with the effect of X_3 controlled or held constant. In theory it makes sense to hold X_3 constant while increasing X_2, but how is this concept actually applied when we obtain least-squares estimates for β_2 (as well as β_3)? The answer lies in the realization that the estimated coefficient in the three-variable regression model can be calculated by performing two two-variable regressions. (This result generalizes to any multiple regression model.) The first regression adjusts the variable X_2 to "hold X_3 constant," while the second regression estimates the effect of this adjusted variable on Y. The procedure occurs in the following steps.

Step 1 Regress X_2 on X_3. When the equation has been estimated, we can calculate the fitted values and residuals of the model. To simplify we will work with the data in deviations form, so that the model is

$$x_{2i} = \hat{\alpha} x_{3i} + \hat{u}_i \qquad \text{and} \qquad x_{2i} = \hat{x}_{2i} + \hat{u}_i$$

where $\quad \hat{x}_{2i} = \hat{\alpha} x_{3i} \qquad \hat{u}_i = x_{2i} - \hat{\alpha} x_{3i} = x_{2i} - \hat{x}_{2i} \qquad$ and $\qquad \hat{\alpha} = \dfrac{\Sigma x_{2i} x_{3i}}{\Sigma x_{3i}^2}$

Our interest lies in $\hat{u}_i$, the residuals, since $\hat{u}_i$ represents that portion of X_2 which is uncorrelated with X_3. (Recall that the regression residuals are uncorrelated with the right-hand variable.) In fact, holding X_3 constant means eliminating from X_2 that component that is correlated with X_3.

Step 2 Regress Y on $\hat{u}$. If we work with the data in deviations form, the model is

$$y_i = \gamma \hat{u}_i + v_i$$

When it is estimated, we find that

$$\hat{\gamma} = \frac{\Sigma y_i \hat{u}_i}{\Sigma \hat{u}_i^2}$$

$\hat{\gamma}$ represents the effect of "adjusted X_2" on Y and according to our argument should measure the effect on X_2 on Y holding X_3 constant. If we are correct, it must be true that $\hat{\gamma} = \hat{\beta}_2$. To see this we need only perform a few algebraic calculations:

$$\hat{\gamma} = \frac{\Sigma y_i \hat{u}_i}{\Sigma \hat{u}_i^2}$$

But

$$\hat{u}_i = x_{2i} - \hat{\alpha} x_{3i} = x_{2i} - \frac{\Sigma x_{2i} x_{3i}}{\Sigma x_{3i}^2} x_{3i}$$

Therefore

$$\frac{\Sigma y_i \hat{u}_i}{\Sigma \hat{u}_i^2} = \frac{\Sigma x_{2i} y_i - \dfrac{\Sigma x_{2i} x_{3i}}{\Sigma x_{3i}^2} \Sigma x_{3i} y_i}{\Sigma x_{2i}^2 + \left(\dfrac{\Sigma x_{2i} x_{3i}}{\Sigma x_{3i}^2}\right)^2 \Sigma x_{3i}^2 - 2 \dfrac{\Sigma x_{2i} x_{3i}}{\Sigma x_{3i}^2} \Sigma x_{2i} x_{3i}}$$

Now, multiplying both sides of the ratio by Σx_{2i}^2 and simplifying, we get

$$\hat{\gamma} = \frac{\Sigma x_{2i} y_i \Sigma x_{3i}^2 - \Sigma x_{2i} x_{3i} \Sigma x_{3i} y_i}{\Sigma x_{2i}^2 \Sigma x_{3i}^2 - (\Sigma x_{2i} x_{3i})^2} = \hat{\beta}_2$$

APPENDIX 4.3 THE MULTIPLE REGRESSION MODEL IN MATRIX FORM

Representation of the Multiple Regression Model

The purpose of this appendix, like that of the appendixes to other chapters, is to present generalizations of important textual items. It would be difficult to accomplish this in a compact form without using matrix algebra. Matrix algebra provides a clear and concise means of describing the techniques of econometrics. We presume that the reader of these appendixes has a prior knowledge of matrix algebra and make no attempt to describe or prove its basic theorems. These materials are clearly presented in other textbooks, which should provide an ample review for the interested reader.†

We begin by representing the linear model in matrix form. Recall from the text that the regression model includes $k + 1$ variables—a dependent variable and k independent variables (including the constant term). Since there are N observations, we can summarize the regression model by writing a series of N equations, as follows:

$$Y_1 = \beta_1 + \beta_2 X_{21} + \beta_3 X_{31} + \cdots + \beta_k X_{k1} + \varepsilon_1$$
$$Y_2 = \beta_1 + \beta_2 X_{22} + \beta_3 X_{32} + \cdots + \beta_k X_{k2} + \varepsilon_2 \qquad (A4.4)$$

$$\cdots \cdots \cdots \cdots \cdots \cdots \cdots \cdots \cdots \cdots \cdots$$

$$Y_N = \beta_1 + \beta_2 X_{2N} + \beta_3 X_{3N} + \cdots + \beta_k X_{kN} + \varepsilon_N$$

The corresponding matrix formulation of the model is

$$\mathbf{Y} = \mathbf{X}\boldsymbol{\beta} + \boldsymbol{\varepsilon} \qquad (A4.5)$$

in which

$$\mathbf{Y} = \begin{bmatrix} Y_1 \\ Y_2 \\ \vdots \\ Y_N \end{bmatrix} \quad \mathbf{X} = \begin{bmatrix} 1 & X_{21} & \cdots & X_{k1} \\ 1 & X_{22} & \cdots & X_{k2} \\ \vdots & \vdots & & \vdots \\ 1 & X_{2N} & \cdots & X_{kN} \end{bmatrix} \quad \boldsymbol{\beta} = \begin{bmatrix} \beta_1 \\ \beta_2 \\ \vdots \\ \beta_k \end{bmatrix} \quad \boldsymbol{\varepsilon} = \begin{bmatrix} \varepsilon_1 \\ \varepsilon_2 \\ \vdots \\ \varepsilon_N \end{bmatrix} \quad (A4.6)$$

where $\mathbf{Y} = N \times 1$ column vector of dependent variable observations
$\mathbf{X} = N \times k$ matrix of independent variable observations
$\boldsymbol{\beta} = k \times 1$ column vector of unknown parameters
$\boldsymbol{\varepsilon} = N \times 1$ column vector of errors

In our representation of the matrix $\mathbf{X}$, each component $\mathbf{X}_{ji}$ has two subscripts, the first signifying the appropriate column (variable) and the second the appropriate row (observation). Each column of $\mathbf{X}$ represents a vector of N observations on a given variable, with all observations associated with the intercept equal to 1.

† See, for example, Johnson, op. cit., chap. 4; and A. Goldberger, *Econometric Theory* (New York: Wiley, 1964), chap. 2.

The assumptions of the classical linear regression model can be represented as follows:

i. The model specification is given by Eq. (A4.4).
ii. The elements of $\mathbf{X}$ are fixed and have finite variance. In addition, $\mathbf{X}$ has rank k, which is less than the number of observations N.
iii. ε is normally distributed with $E(\varepsilon) = \mathbf{0}$ and $E(\varepsilon\varepsilon') = \sigma^2\mathbf{I}$, where $\mathbf{I}$ is an $N \times N$ identity matrix.

The assumption that $\mathbf{X}$ has rank k guarantees that perfect collinearity will not be present. With perfect collinearity, one of the columns of $\mathbf{X}$ would be a linear combination of the remaining columns and the rank of $\mathbf{X}$ would be less than k. The error assumptions are the strongest possible, since they guarantee the statistical as well as arithmetic properties of the ordinary least-squares estimation process. In addition to normality we assume that each error term has mean 0, all variances are constant, and all covariances are 0. The *variance-covariance matrix* $\sigma^2\mathbf{I}$ appears as follows:

$$E(\varepsilon\varepsilon') = E\left\{ \begin{bmatrix} \varepsilon_1 \\ \varepsilon_2 \\ \vdots \\ \varepsilon_N \end{bmatrix} \begin{bmatrix} \varepsilon_1 & \varepsilon_2 & \cdots & \varepsilon_N \end{bmatrix} \right\}$$

$$= \begin{bmatrix} E(\varepsilon_1^2) & E(\varepsilon_1\varepsilon_2) & \cdots & E(\varepsilon_1\varepsilon_N) \\ E(\varepsilon_2\varepsilon_1) & E(\varepsilon_2^2) & \cdots & E(\varepsilon_2\varepsilon_N) \\ \cdots & \cdots & \cdots & \cdots \\ E(\varepsilon_N\varepsilon_1) & E(\varepsilon_N\varepsilon_2) & \cdots & E(\varepsilon_N^2) \end{bmatrix}$$

$$= \begin{bmatrix} \text{Var}(\varepsilon_1) & \text{Cov}(\varepsilon_1, \varepsilon_2) & \cdots & \text{Cov}(\varepsilon_1, \varepsilon_N) \\ \text{Cov}(\varepsilon_1, \varepsilon_2) & \text{Var}(\varepsilon_2) & \cdots & \text{Cov}(\varepsilon_2, \varepsilon_N) \\ \cdots & \cdots & \cdots & \cdots \\ \text{Cov}(\varepsilon_1, \varepsilon_N) & \text{Cov}(\varepsilon_2, \varepsilon_N) & \cdots & \text{Var}(\varepsilon_N) \end{bmatrix} \quad \text{(A4.7)}$$

where ε' is the $1 \times N$ vector transpose of ε. If we had chosen to represent assumption iii in terms of the distribution of $\mathbf{Y}$, we would write

iii'. $\mathbf{Y}$ is normally distributed, $E(\mathbf{Y}) = \mathbf{Y}\beta$, and $E\{[\mathbf{Y} - E(\mathbf{Y})][\mathbf{Y} - E(\mathbf{Y})]'\} = \sigma^2\mathbf{I}$.

Least-Squares Estimation

Our objective is to find a vector of parameters $\hat{\beta}$ which minimize the sum of the squared residuals

$$ESS = \sum_{i=1}^{N} \hat{\varepsilon}_i^2 = \hat{\varepsilon}'\hat{\varepsilon} \quad \text{(A4.8)}$$

where

$$\hat{\varepsilon} = \mathbf{Y} - \hat{\mathbf{Y}} \quad \text{(A4.9)}$$

and

$$\hat{\mathbf{Y}} = \mathbf{X}\hat{\boldsymbol{\beta}} \tag{A4.10}$$

$\hat{\varepsilon}$ represents the $N \times 1$ vector of regression residuals, while $\hat{\mathbf{Y}}$ represents the $N \times 1$ vector of fitted values for $\mathbf{Y}$. Substituting (A4.9) and (A4.10) into (A4.8), we get

$$\hat{\varepsilon}'\hat{\varepsilon} = (\mathbf{Y} - \mathbf{X}\hat{\boldsymbol{\beta}})'(\mathbf{Y} - \mathbf{X}\hat{\boldsymbol{\beta}}) = \mathbf{Y}'\mathbf{Y} - \hat{\boldsymbol{\beta}}'\mathbf{X}'\mathbf{Y} - \mathbf{Y}'\mathbf{X}\hat{\boldsymbol{\beta}} + \hat{\boldsymbol{\beta}}'\mathbf{X}'\mathbf{X}\hat{\boldsymbol{\beta}}$$

$$= \mathbf{Y}'\mathbf{Y} - 2\hat{\boldsymbol{\beta}}'\mathbf{X}'\mathbf{Y} + \hat{\boldsymbol{\beta}}'\mathbf{X}'\mathbf{X}\hat{\boldsymbol{\beta}} \tag{A4.11}$$

The last step follows because $\hat{\boldsymbol{\beta}}'\mathbf{X}'\mathbf{Y}$ and $\mathbf{Y}'\mathbf{X}\hat{\boldsymbol{\beta}}$ are both scalars and are thus equal to each other. To determine the least-squares estimators, we minimize the error sum of squares ESS as follows,

$$\frac{\partial \text{ESS}}{\partial \hat{\boldsymbol{\beta}}} = -2\mathbf{X}'\mathbf{Y} + 2\mathbf{X}'\mathbf{X}\hat{\boldsymbol{\beta}} = 0$$

$$\hat{\boldsymbol{\beta}} = (\mathbf{X}'\mathbf{X})^{-1}(\mathbf{X}'\mathbf{Y}) \tag{A4.12}$$

The matrix $\mathbf{X}'\mathbf{X}$, called the *cross-product matrix*, is guaranteed to have an inverse because our assumption that $\mathbf{X}$ has rank k leads directly to the nonsingularity of $\mathbf{X}'\mathbf{X}$.† The reader should check that the matrix generalization of the least-squares estimation process reduces to the results derived in the text for both the two- and three-variable regression models.

Two results concerning the least-squares residuals may be useful in some of the derivations which follow:

$$\mathbf{X}'\hat{\varepsilon} = \mathbf{X}'(\mathbf{Y} - \mathbf{X}\hat{\boldsymbol{\beta}}) = \mathbf{X}'\mathbf{Y} - \mathbf{X}'\mathbf{X}\hat{\boldsymbol{\beta}} = 0 \tag{A4.13}$$

$$\hat{\varepsilon}'\hat{\varepsilon} = \mathbf{Y}'\mathbf{Y} - \hat{\boldsymbol{\beta}}'\mathbf{X}'\mathbf{Y} \qquad \text{from (A4.11) and (A4.12)} \tag{A4.14}$$

The first result proves that the sum of the cross-products of the independent variables and the residuals is 0. This is the sample analog of the assumption (since the X's are fixed) that $E(\mathbf{X}'\varepsilon) = \mathbf{0}$.

Now consider the properties of the least-squares estimator $\hat{\boldsymbol{\beta}}$. First, we can prove that $\hat{\boldsymbol{\beta}}$ is an unbiased estimator of $\boldsymbol{\beta}$:

$$\hat{\boldsymbol{\beta}} = (\mathbf{X}'\mathbf{X})^{-1}\mathbf{X}'\mathbf{Y} = (\mathbf{X}'\mathbf{X})^{-1}\mathbf{X}'(\mathbf{X}\boldsymbol{\beta} + \varepsilon) = (\mathbf{X}'\mathbf{X})^{-1}(\mathbf{X}'\mathbf{X})\boldsymbol{\beta} + (\mathbf{X}'\mathbf{X})^{-1}\mathbf{X}'\varepsilon$$

$$= \boldsymbol{\beta} + (\mathbf{X}'\mathbf{X})^{-1}\mathbf{X}'\varepsilon = \boldsymbol{\beta} + \mathbf{A}\varepsilon \qquad \text{where } \mathbf{A} = (\mathbf{X}'\mathbf{X})^{-1}\mathbf{X}' \tag{A4.15}$$

$$E(\hat{\boldsymbol{\beta}}) = \boldsymbol{\beta} + E(\mathbf{A}\varepsilon) = \boldsymbol{\beta} + \mathbf{A}E(\varepsilon) = \boldsymbol{\beta}$$

since $\mathbf{A}$ is fixed in repeated samples.

Looking at Eq. (A4.15), we notice that $\mathbf{A}\varepsilon = (\mathbf{X}'\mathbf{X})^{-1}\mathbf{X}'\varepsilon$ represents the regression of ε, the unknown error term on $\mathbf{X}$. As long as the effects of missing variables are randomly distributed, are independent of $\mathbf{X}$, and have 0 mean, the least-squares parameter estimates will be unbiased.

---

† The second-order conditions for the minimization of ESS follow from the fact that $\mathbf{X}'\mathbf{X}$ is a positive definite matrix.

The least-squares estimator will be normally distributed since $\hat{\beta}$ is a linear function of Y and Y is normally distributed. The properties of the variances of the individual $\hat{\beta}_i$'s and their covariances are determined as follows:

$$V = E\left[(\hat{\beta} - \beta)(\hat{\beta} - \beta)'\right]$$

$$= \begin{bmatrix} E(\hat{\beta}_1 - \beta_1)^2 & \cdots & E\left[(\hat{\beta}_1 - \beta_1)(\hat{\beta}_k - \beta_k)\right] \\ \cdots & & \cdots \\ E\left[(\hat{\beta}_k - \beta_k)(\hat{\beta}_1 - \beta_1)\right] & \cdots & E(\hat{\beta}_k - \beta_k)^2 \end{bmatrix}$$

$$= \begin{bmatrix} \text{Var}(\hat{\beta}_1) & \cdots & \text{Cov}(\hat{\beta}_1, \hat{\beta}_k) \\ \cdots & & \cdots \\ \text{Cov}(\hat{\beta}_1, \hat{\beta}_k) & \cdots & \text{Var}(\hat{\beta}_k) \end{bmatrix} \tag{A4.16}$$

The diagonal elements of V represent the variances of the estimated parameters, while the off-diagonal terms represent the covariances. For purposes of notational simplicity, we shall sometimes write $V = \text{Var}(\hat{\beta})$. Then

$$\text{Var}(\hat{\beta}) = E\left[(\hat{\beta} - \beta)(\hat{\beta} - \beta)'\right] = E\left[(A\varepsilon)(A\varepsilon)'\right] = E(A\varepsilon\varepsilon'A')$$

$$= AE(\varepsilon\varepsilon')A' = A(\sigma^2 I)A' = \sigma^2 AA'$$

since A and A' are matrices of fixed numbers. But

$$AA' = \left[(X'X)^{-1}X'\right]\left[(X'X)^{-1}X'\right]' = \left[(X'X)^{-1}X'\right]\left[X(X'X)^{-1}\right]$$

$$= (X'X)^{-1}(X'X)(X'X)^{-1} = (X'X)^{-1}$$

Therefore, $$E\left[(\hat{\beta} - \beta)(\hat{\beta} - \beta)'\right] = \sigma^2(X'X)^{-1} \tag{A4.17}$$

We have already proved that the least-squares estimator is linear and unbiased. In fact, $\hat{\beta}$ is the best linear unbiased estimator of β in the sense that it has the minimum variance of all unbiased estimators. To complete the proof of the *Gauss-Markov theorem*, we need to show that any other unbiased linear estimator b has greater variance than $\hat{\beta}$. Recall that $\hat{\beta} = AY$. Without loss of generality, we can write (the matrix C is assumed to be arbitrary)

$$b = (A + C)Y = AY + CY = \hat{\beta} + CY = (A + C)X\beta + (A + C)\varepsilon$$

If b is unbiased, then

$$E(b) = (X'X)^{-1}X'X\beta + CX\beta = (I + CX)\beta = \beta \tag{A4.18}$$

A necessary and sufficient condition for this to hold for all β is for

$$CX = 0$$

Now examine the matrix $\text{Var}(b)$. Since $b - \beta = (A + C)\varepsilon$,†

$$\text{Var}(b) = E\left[(b - \beta)(b - \beta)'\right] = E\left\{\left[(A + C)\varepsilon\right]\left[(A + C)\varepsilon\right]'\right\}$$

$$= E\left[(A + C)\varepsilon\varepsilon'(A + C)'\right] = (A + C)E(\varepsilon\varepsilon')(A + C)'$$

$$= \sigma^2(A + C)(A + C)'$$

† Since $AX = (X'X)^{-1}X'X = I$, $b - \beta = (A + C)X\beta + (A + C)\varepsilon - \beta = AX\beta - \beta + CX\beta + (A + C)\varepsilon = (A + C)\varepsilon$

But

$$(\mathbf{A} + \mathbf{C})(\mathbf{A} + \mathbf{C})' = \mathbf{AA'} + \mathbf{CA'} + \mathbf{AC'} + \mathbf{CC'}$$

$$= (\mathbf{X'X})^{-1}\mathbf{X'X}(\mathbf{X'X})^{-1} + \mathbf{CX}(\mathbf{X'X})^{-1} + (\mathbf{X'X})^{-1}\mathbf{X'C'} + \mathbf{CC'}$$

$$= (\mathbf{X'X})^{-1} + \mathbf{CC'} \quad \text{since } \mathbf{CX} = \mathbf{X'C'} = \mathbf{0}$$

Therefore,

$$\text{Var (b)} = \sigma^2[(\mathbf{X'X})^{-1} + \mathbf{CC'}] = \text{Var } (\hat{\boldsymbol{\beta}}) + \sigma^2\mathbf{CC'} \tag{A4.19}$$

We can observe that $\mathbf{CC'}$ is a positive semidefinite matrix. The only case in which the quadratic form associated with this matrix will be 0 is when $\mathbf{C} = \mathbf{0}$ (all elements are 0). When $\mathbf{C} = \mathbf{0}$, our alternative estimator becomes the ordinary least-squares estimator $\hat{\boldsymbol{\beta}}$ and our theorem is proved.

Estimating σ^2, t Tests

In order to calculate the variance-covariance matrix of the estimated parameters, we need to determine an estimate for the scalar σ^2. A natural choice for such an estimator is

$$s^2 = \frac{\hat{\varepsilon}'\hat{\varepsilon}}{N - k} \tag{A4.20}$$

It is tedious, but not difficult, to prove that s^2 provides an unbiased estimator of σ^2. It follows that $s^2(\mathbf{X'X})^{-1}$ yields an unbiased estimator of Var $(\hat{\boldsymbol{\beta}})$. While normal distribution hypothesis tests are possible when σ^2 is known, we are forced to rely on the use of the t test when s^2 is used to approximate σ^2. To do so, we use the following statistical results:

1. $\hat{\varepsilon}'\hat{\varepsilon}/\sigma^2$ is distributed as chi square with $N - k$ degrees of freedom.
2. $(N - k)s^2/\sigma^2$ is distributed as chi square with $N - k$ degrees of freedom.
3. $(\hat{\beta}_i - \beta_i)$, for $i = 1, 2, \ldots, k$, is normally distributed with mean 0 and variance $\sigma^2 V_i$, where V_i is the ith diagonal element of $(\mathbf{X'X})^{-1}$.
4. $(N - k)s^2/\sigma^2$ and $\hat{\beta}_i - \beta_i$ are independently distributed.

It follows that

$$t_{N-k} = \frac{\hat{\beta}_i - \beta_i}{s\sqrt{V_i}} \tag{A4.21}$$

is t-distributed with $N - k$ degrees of freedom. This allows us to construct confidence intervals for individual regression parameters in a manner analogous to the procedure described in Chapter 2. To test a hypothesis about a particular value of β_i, we substitute that value into Eq. (A4.21). If the t value is great enough in absolute value, we reject the null hypothesis at the appropriately chosen level of confidence. A 95 percent confidence interval for the individual parameter β_i is given by

$$\hat{\beta}_i \pm t_c \left(s\sqrt{V_i} \right) \tag{A4.22}$$

where t_c is the critical value of the t distribution associated with a 5 percent level of significance.

R^2, F Test

As in the text, we can break down the total variation of Y into two portions, one representing the explained variation and the second the unexplained. First assume that the Y variable has a 0 mean. In matrix notation, the derivation follows from the fact that we can write the vector $\mathbf{Y}$ as the sum of its predicted values $\hat{\mathbf{Y}} = \mathbf{X}\hat{\boldsymbol{\beta}}$ and the residual vector $\hat{\boldsymbol{\varepsilon}}$:

$$\mathbf{Y} = \mathbf{X}\hat{\boldsymbol{\beta}} + \hat{\boldsymbol{\varepsilon}}$$

Then

$$\mathbf{Y'Y} = (\mathbf{X}\hat{\boldsymbol{\beta}} + \hat{\boldsymbol{\varepsilon}})'(\mathbf{X}\hat{\boldsymbol{\beta}} + \hat{\boldsymbol{\varepsilon}}) = \hat{\boldsymbol{\beta}}'\mathbf{X'X}\hat{\boldsymbol{\beta}} + \hat{\boldsymbol{\varepsilon}}'\mathbf{X}\hat{\boldsymbol{\beta}} + \hat{\boldsymbol{\beta}}'\mathbf{X'}\hat{\boldsymbol{\varepsilon}} + \hat{\boldsymbol{\varepsilon}}'\hat{\boldsymbol{\varepsilon}}$$

$$= \hat{\boldsymbol{\beta}}'\mathbf{X'X}\hat{\boldsymbol{\beta}} + \hat{\boldsymbol{\varepsilon}}'\hat{\boldsymbol{\varepsilon}} \qquad \text{since } \mathbf{X'}\hat{\boldsymbol{\varepsilon}} = \mathbf{0} \text{ and } \hat{\boldsymbol{\varepsilon}}'\mathbf{X} = \mathbf{0} \tag{A4.23}$$

or $\qquad$ TSS = RSS + ESS

where TSS = total sum of squares
$\qquad$ RSS = regression (explained) sum of squares
$\qquad$ ESS = residual (unexplained) sum of squares

Then

$$R^2 = 1 - \frac{\text{ESS}}{\text{TSS}} = 1 - \frac{\hat{\boldsymbol{\varepsilon}}'\hat{\boldsymbol{\varepsilon}}}{\mathbf{Y'Y}} = \frac{\hat{\boldsymbol{\beta}}'\mathbf{X'X}\hat{\boldsymbol{\beta}}}{\mathbf{Y'Y}} \tag{A4.24}$$

When the dependent variable does not have 0 mean, we must modify our definition of R^2 somewhat. Then

$$y_i = Y_i - \frac{\sum\limits_{i=1}^{N} Y_i}{N}$$

from which it follows that

$$\mathbf{y'y} = \mathbf{Y'Y} - N\left[\frac{\sum\limits_{i=1}^{N} Y_i}{N}\right]^2$$

and

$$R^2 = \frac{\text{RSS}}{\text{TSS}} = \frac{\hat{\boldsymbol{\beta}}'\mathbf{X'X}\hat{\boldsymbol{\beta}} - N(\sum Y_i / N)^2}{\mathbf{y'y}} \tag{A4.25}$$

In order to correct for the dependence of goodness of fit on degrees of freedom, we define $\bar{R}^2$, or corrected R^2, as

$$\bar{R}^2 = 1 - \frac{\hat{\varepsilon}'\hat{\varepsilon}/(N-k)}{\mathbf{y}'\mathbf{y}/(N-1)} = 1 - \left(\frac{\hat{\varepsilon}'\hat{\varepsilon}}{\mathbf{y}'\mathbf{y}}\right)\left(\frac{N-1}{N-k}\right) \qquad \text{(A4.26)}$$

Now it is appropriate to consider statistical tests on sets of regression coefficients. The most frequently used test involves the test of the joint hypothesis that $\beta_2 = \beta_3 = \cdots = \beta_k = 0$. The appropriate F statistic (obeying the F distribution) is

$$F_{k-1,N-k} = \frac{R^2}{1-R^2}\frac{N-k}{k-1}$$

Other tests involving combinations of the regression parameters are sometimes used. Again, assume that Y has a 0 mean. In this case, we can use the result that

$$F = \frac{(\hat{\beta}-\beta)'\mathbf{X}'\mathbf{X}(\hat{\beta}-\beta)}{\hat{\varepsilon}'\hat{\varepsilon}}\frac{N-k}{k-1}$$

is F-distributed with $k-1$ and $N-k$ degrees of freedom. To test joint hypotheses involving the individual regression parameters, we simply substitute the appropriate test values for β and evaluate the F statistic. A sufficiently large value of F allows us to reject the null hypothesis.

EXERCISES

4.1 Consider the following two models:

I
$$Y_i = \beta_1 + \beta_2 X_{2i} + \beta_3 X_{3i} + \varepsilon_i$$

II
$$(Y_i - X_{2i}) = \beta_1' + \beta_2' X_{2i} + \beta_3' X_{3i} + \varepsilon_i'$$

(a) Prove that $\hat{\beta}_2' = \hat{\beta}_2 - 1$, $\hat{\beta}_1' = \hat{\beta}_1$, and $\hat{\beta}_3' = \hat{\beta}_3$.
(b) Prove that the least-squares residuals are identical, that is, $\hat{\varepsilon}_i = \hat{\varepsilon}_i'$ for $i = 1, 2, \ldots, N$.
(c) Under what conditions will the R^2 associated with model II be less than the R^2 associated with model I?

4.2 Consider the following two experimental procedures:

1. Run the regression $Y_i = \beta_1 + \beta_2 X_{2i} + \beta_3 X_{3i} + \varepsilon_i$.
2. Run the regression $X_{2i} = \alpha_1 + \alpha_2 X_{3i} + \varepsilon_i'$, calculate the regresison residuals $\hat{\varepsilon}_i'$, and finally run the regression

$$Y_i = \beta_1' + \beta_2'\hat{\varepsilon}_i + \beta_3' X_{3i} + \varepsilon_i^*$$

Can you prove that $\hat{\beta}_2' = \hat{\beta}_2$? Can you explain intuitively why this result is true?

4.3 A somewhat naive researcher attempts to estimate an aggregate consumption function for the United States economy by regressing a consumption variable C on disposable income Y and savings S. The model is

$$C = \beta_1 + \beta_2 Y + \beta_3 S + \varepsilon$$

How good a fit is this researcher likely to get when this equation is run? Can you generalize your conclusion? *Hint:* Notice that $C = Y - S$ identically for all observations.

4.4 Assume that the sample variances (and standard deviations) of all the variables in a multiple regression model are identically the same. In this case what is the relationship between the estimated beta coefficients and the standard regression parameters?

4.5 "Estimated regression parameters, elasticities, beta coefficients, and partial correlation coefficients will always have the same sign." True or false? Explain.

4.6 Explain the differences between the concepts of simple correlation, partial correlation, and multiple correlation. Why is each useful?

USING THE MULTIPLE REGRESSION MODEL

We introduced the multiple regression model in the previous chapter, emphasizing how one interprets the estimated coefficients, measures goodness of fit, and performs statistical tests. In this chapter we continue our analysis of the multiple regression model by discussing some important but more advanced topics. We begin by considering the functional form of the regression model, concentrating on the distinction between linear and nonlinear models. We then consider how the regression model can be applied when one or more of the explanatory variables is a dummy variable. We also consider the appropriate t and F statistics to be applied when performing hypothesis tests involving dummy variables or groups of independent variables in general. Finally, we consider the problem of specification error i.e., what happens when the model that is estimated is incorrect, in including too many variables, excluding a variable, or having the wrong functional form. This serves as a basis for a brief treatment of the trade-offs involved in building econometric models.

5.1 THE GENERAL LINEAR MODEL

We have been dealing with equations which are strictly linear combinations of the X's. Such a restriction in specification is not as limiting as it might seem, because the linear regression model can be applied to a more general class of equations which are still *inherently linear*. Inherently linear models are models which can be expressed in a linear form by a proper transformation of the variables. *Inherently nonlinear* models, on the other hand, cannot be transformed to the linear form. Assume that we begin with a (nonlinear) model represented as

$$Y = F(X_2, X_3, \ldots, X_k, \varepsilon)$$

We can conclude that the model is inherently linear if it can be transformed into

$$f(Y) = \beta_1 + \beta_2 g_2(X_2, \ldots, X_k) + \cdots + \beta_k g_k(X_2, \ldots, X_k) + \varepsilon$$

or

$$Y^* = \beta_1 + \beta_2 X_2^* + \beta_3 X_3^* + \cdots + \beta_k X_k^* + \varepsilon \tag{5.1}$$

The functions f and g_2 through g_k must be known in order to estimate the coefficients. Notice that the relationship in Eq. (5.1) is inherently linear because it is linear with respect to the coefficients $\beta_1, \beta_2, \beta_3, \ldots, \beta_k$. We shall turn our attention to the estimation of inherently nonlinear models in Chapter 9. For the moment, however, it will be instructive to consider the possibility of finding suitable transformations in special cases. Consider the following econometric models:

I
$$Y = \beta_1 + \beta_2 X_2 + \beta_3 X_2^2 + \varepsilon \tag{5.2}$$

II
$$\log Y = \alpha_1 + \alpha_2 \log X_2 + \alpha_3 \log X_3 + \varepsilon \tag{5.3}$$

III
$$Y = \gamma_1 X_2^{\gamma_2} X_3^{\gamma_3} \varepsilon^* \tag{5.4}$$

IV
$$Y = \gamma_1 X_2^{\gamma_2} X_3^{\gamma_3} + \varepsilon' \tag{5.5}$$

Model I (the *polynomial model*) provides a means of testing to see whether the relationship between Y and X_2 is nonlinear (although the model itself is linear in the coefficients). Choosing regression parameters is equivalent to finding the best parabola which fits the points on a two-dimensional graph of Y and X_2, that is, Y is specified to be a *quadratic* function of X_2 (one is shown in Fig. 5.1a).

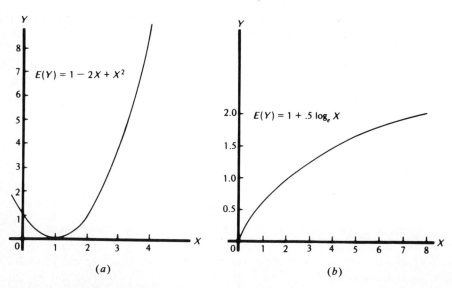

Figure 5.1 Nonlinear functional forms.

The quadratic form is often used when testing for nonlinearities, since one is provided by a standard t test of the null hypothesis that $\beta_3 = 0$.

Model II is also linear in the parameters and uses the logarithm of each variable to form the nonlinear function.† While the choice of the base of logarithms does not matter substantially (it affects only the constant term in the model) we will typically use natural logarithms to the base e in our analysis.‡ A simple example of the logarithmic function is illustrated in Fig. 5.1*b*. The function $Y = \log X$ is similar to the line $Y = X - 1$ when X is close to 1 and for most values of X can be closely approximated by the quadratic equation $Y = (X - 1) - (X - 1)^2/2$, so that the logarithmic function can be seen as a possible alternative to the quadratic function when one is specifying nonlinear equations.§ Model II can be used if one has reason to believe that variables enter multiplicatively rather than additively into the equation. This can most easily be seen by noticing that model II can be obtained from model III (the *multiplicative model*) by taking the logarithms of both sides.¶

The equivalence of the two models is seen by noting that

$$\alpha_1 = \log \gamma_1 \qquad \alpha_2 = \gamma_2 \qquad \alpha_3 = \gamma_3 \qquad \varepsilon = \log \varepsilon^*$$

Model IV appears to be quite similar to model III, but the similarity is deceptive because no transformation of model IV will provide a new model which is linear in the parameters.

The reader should not be lulled into a trap when considering transformations which make models linear in the parameters. Something is often lost in the process. For example, consider the transformation from model II to model III. If we assume that the error process ε is normally distributed, the error process in model III (ε^*) will not be normal. We usually assume that ε^* follows a distribution whose logarithm is itself normally distributed; i.e., it will be *lognormal*.‖

To conclude this section, let us consider some additional linear model specifications which are occasionally useful in applied work:

V   Exponential model: $Y = \exp\left[(\beta_1 + \beta_2 X_2 + \beta_3 X_3)\right]\varepsilon$ (5.6)

By taking logarithms of both sides this model can be transformed into

$$\log Y = \beta_1 + \beta_2 X_2 + \beta_3 X_3 + \log \varepsilon$$

VI   Reciprocal model: $Y = \dfrac{1}{\beta_1 + \beta_2 X_2 + \beta_3 X_3 + \varepsilon}$ (5.7)

---

† Readers familiar with calculus will recall that $\log Y$ has the property that $\log 1 = 0$ and that $d \log Y/dY = 1/Y$. This serves as the basis for our elasticity calculations, discussed in the previous chapter.

‡ e is approximately equal to 2.718; since $\log Y = (\log_{10} Y)(2.3026)$, a direct transformation between the two bases is possible.

§ This can be shown using a Taylor series expansion, developed in most calculus texts.

¶ Note that $\log A^b = b \log A$ and $\log AB = \log A + \log B$ for any A, B, and b.

‖ On the other hand, if ε^* is normal, tests of significance will be invalid when applied to model II since $\log \varepsilon^*$ will not follow the normal distribution.

This model can be transformed into

$$\frac{1}{Y} = \beta_1 + \beta_2 X_2 + \beta_3 X_3 + \varepsilon$$

VII Semilog model: $Y = \beta_1 + \beta_2 \log X_2 + \varepsilon$ (5.8)

VIII Interaction model: $Y = \beta_1 + \beta_2 X_2 + \beta_3 X_3 + \beta_4(X_2 X_3) + \varepsilon$ (5.9)

Model VIII is worthy of special attention because of the presence of the third right-hand variable, the product of variables X_2 and X_3. Such a term in an equation is called an *interaction term* or *interaction variable*. To see how interaction terms affect one's interpretation of the regression results (and thus why such terms are valuable), consider the impact of a change in X_2 on Y. Were the interaction term to be omitted, the effect would be measured by β_2. However, with the interaction, the effect is $\beta_2 + \beta_4 X_3$ [we get this by differentiating (5.9) with respect to X_2]. Thus, the effect of X_2 on Y depends upon the level of the variable X_3. If β_4 is positive, the effect of X_2 on Y will increase as the value of X_3 increases. As a result, interaction terms are often included in models in which one does not believe that right-hand explanatory variables have the same effect on Y, whatever the values of the other right-hand variables. Of course, this can be accomplished with other forms of equations, but the interaction term is a simple and direct option.†

Example 5.1 Estimation of cost functions Nonlinear equations which can be transformed to be linear in the parameters have been used to study cost functions for leather belt shops and for hosiery mills.† In the leather belt case, cost records were examined during the period 1935–1938 by 4-week accounting periods. The objective was to see whether or not costs were a nonlinear function of material inputs to the production process. The following regression was run (with all coefficients significant at the 5 percent level):

$$C = -60.178 + .77X + 70.18W$$

where C = total cost, thousands of dollars
    X = single-ply equivalent belting, thousands of square feet
    W = weight, pounds per square foot

No higher degree term of X was found to be significant, implying that the cost function was essentially linear.

---

† Interaction terms can be combined with quadratic terms to yield expressions such as $Y = \beta_1 + \beta_2 X_2 + \beta_3 X_3 + \beta_4 X_2 X_3 + \beta_5 X_2^2 + \beta_6 X_3^2 + \varepsilon$. Testing the null hypothesis that $\beta_4 = 0$ provides a test for interaction, and testing the joint hypothesis that $\beta_4 = \beta_5 = \beta_6 = 0$ provides a test of whether any nonlinearities are present. These tests are described in the Section 5.3.

† J. Dean, *Statistical Cost Functions of a Hosiery Mill* (Chicago: University of Chicago Press, 1940), and *The Relation of Cost to Output for a Leather Belt Shop* (New York: National Bureau of Economic Research, 1941), Technical Paper no. 2.

On the other hand, using monthly data (1935–1939) for hosiery mills, a nonlinear relationship between cost and time was found:

$$C = 13.635 + 2.068X + 1.308t - .022t^2$$

where C = total cost, thousands of dollars
  X = output, thousands of dozen pairs
  t = time, chronological months

5.2 USE OF DUMMY VARIABLES

The variables used in regression equations usually take values over some continuous range. This need not be the case, however, and at times we may wish to use one or more *independent* variables that are restricted to taking on two or more distinct values. (Estimation when the *dependent* variable is a dummy variable is discussed in Chapter 10.) For example, we may wish to account for the fact that some individuals go to college and others do not. To do so, we create a dummy variable, which takes on the value of 1 if the individual goes to college and 0 if not. Dummy variables are particularly useful when dealing with qualitative data. We also show how dummy variables can be used in the regression context to account for the fact that observations within a given category are associated with one set of regression parameters while observations in a second (or third) category are associated with different regression parameters.

Suppose that a firm uses two types of production processes to obtain its output. Upon the assumption that the output obtained from each process is normally distributed with different expected values but identical variances, we can represent the production process as a regression equation:

$$Y_i - \beta_1 + \beta_2 X_i + \varepsilon_i \tag{5.10}$$

where Y_i is the output associated with the ith input process and X_i is a dummy variable

$$X_i = \begin{cases} 1 & \text{if output obtained from machine A} \\ 0 & \text{if output obtained from machine B} \end{cases}$$

In this rather simple example, the intercept of the regression line measures the expected output associated with machine B, while the slope measures the difference in output associated with a change from machine B to machine A. This can be seen by taking expected values on both sides of Eq. (5.10) for $X_i = 0$ and $X_i = 1$:

$$E(Y_i) = \begin{cases} \beta_1 & X_i = 0 \\ \beta_1 + \beta_2 & X_i = 1 \end{cases}$$

It should immediately be clear that a test of the null hypothesis that $\beta_2 = 0$ provides a test of the hypothesis that there is no difference in the output associated with machines A and B. The reader should check that the actual least-squares estimates of the regression parameters are the mean output associated with machine B and the difference between mean outputs of A and B.

The dummy variable procedure can easily be modified if more than two distinct values are involved. For example, assume that in the above example three different processes may be employed and one wishes to account for the fact that the output produced by each of the three processes may not be identical. Two dummy variables can be constructed to account for this. (In general, if one needs to differentiate N items, $N - 1$ dummy variables will suffice.) Consider the model

$$Y_i = \beta_1 + \beta_2 X_{2i} + \beta_3 X_{3i} + \varepsilon_i \qquad (5.11)$$

where
$$X_{2i} = \begin{cases} 1 & \text{if output obtained from machine A} \\ 0 & \text{otherwise} \end{cases}$$

$$X_{3i} = \begin{cases} 1 & \text{if output obtained from machine B} \\ 0 & \text{otherwise} \end{cases}$$

Thus, the three production processes are represented by the following combination of values taken by the dummy variables:

Machine	X_2	X_3
A	1	0
B	0	1
C	0	0

By taking expected values for each of these three cases, we can interpret the regression results:

$$E(Y_i) = \begin{cases} \beta_1 + \beta_2 & X_{2i} = 1, \quad X_{3i} = 0 \\ \beta_1 + \beta_3 & X_{2i} = 0, \quad X_{3i} = 1 \\ \beta_1 & X_{2i} = 0, \quad X_{3i} = 0 \end{cases}$$

The regression intercept represents the expected value of output associated with machine C. The first slope coefficient represents the difference in output associated with a change from machine C to machine A, and the second slope coefficient measures the average change in output associated with a change from machine C to machine B. A test of the null hypothesis that $\beta_2 = 0$ provides a test of the hypothesis that there is no difference between the production process associated with machine A and that associated with machine C, while an analogous test comparing B to C is provided by a t test on the coefficient β_3.

Several comments are worthy of attention before the subject of dummy variables is pursued further.

1. The three alternative production processes were represented by two dummy variables (with the third implicit). Representing such a phenomenon by one

variable taking on three values, e.g., machine A = 2, machine B = 1, machine C = 0, is not equivalent to the dummy-variable technique unless the differences between outputs associated with the machine C-to-A and machine C-to-B comparisons are identical. In general, there is no reason to make such an interval assumption.

2. The dummy-variable process cannot be represented by three two-way variables X_2, X_3, and X_4, where X_4 takes on the value 1 when machine C is used and the value 0 otherwise. The introduction of the variable X_4 adds no additional information but does add a nonindependent equation in the derivation of the least-squares estimators. For this reason, it is impossible to obtain least-squares estimates of the regression parameters. This is perhaps best seen by noting the presence of *perfect collinearity* in the model. Collinearity exists because

$$X_{4i} = 1 - X_{2i} - X_{3i} \qquad \text{for each observation } i$$

3. Assume that one wishes to test the null hypothesis that there is no change in output associated with a movement from machine A to machine B. Such a test is provided by an F test of the null hypothesis that the regression coefficients β_2 and β_3 are equal (see Section 5.3). However, by rewriting the regression equation, the researcher can do the same test using the t statistic provided by the standard regression output. Write the regression model as

$$Y_i = \alpha_1 + \alpha_2 X_{2i} + \alpha_3(X_{3i} + X_{2i}) + \varepsilon_i$$

Then consider the three cases:

$$E(Y_i) = \begin{cases} \alpha_1 + \alpha_2 + \alpha_3 & X_{2i} = 1, \quad X_{3i} = 0 \\ \alpha_1 + \alpha_3 & X_{2i} = 0, \quad X_{3i} = 1 \\ \alpha_1 & X_{2i} = 0, \quad X_{3i} = 0 \end{cases}$$

A test of the desired hypothesis is then provided by a test of the null hypothesis that $\alpha_2 = 0$.

It is now natural to extend the notion of dummy variables to the more general case in which some of the independent variables are continuous while others are dummies. The classic example is the case of the aggregate consumption function, in which rationing, saving campaigns, etc., make wartime consumption behavior different from peacetime behavior. We shall distinguish between five different cases of a simple aggregate consumption function in which we assume that aggregate consumption is determined by aggregate disposable income with no lags involved (this simplification is purely for expositional purposes).

Case I:
$$C_t = \beta_1 + \beta_2 Y_t + \varepsilon_t \tag{5.12}$$

This is the case in which peacetime and wartime consumption behavior are assumed to be identical in all respects. There is no need for the use of a dummy variable if one has such knowledge *a priori*.

Case II:
$$C_t = \beta_1 + \beta_2 Y_t + \alpha D_t + \varepsilon_t \tag{5.13}$$

where D_t equals 1 if it is wartime and 0 otherwise. Noticing that $E(C_t)$ is equal to $\beta_1 + \beta_2 E(Y_t)$ in peacetime and $(\beta_1 + \alpha) + \beta_2 E(Y_t)$ in wartime, we see that case II corresponds to the assumption that the intercept of the consumption function changes during wartime but the slope parameter stays the same. A test of whether such a change is statistically significant is provided by a test of the null hypothesis that $\alpha = 0$.

Case III:
$$C_t = \beta_1 + \beta_2 Y_t + \gamma(D_t Y_t) + \varepsilon_t \tag{5.14}$$

Note that $E(C_t) = \beta_1 + \beta_2 E(Y_t)$ in peacetime and $E(C_t) = \beta_1 + (\beta_2 + \gamma)E(Y_t)$ in wartime, so that case III corresponds to the assumption that the intercept has remained constant but the slope parameter has changed. In other words, the model in case III assumes that the war brought about a change in the aggregate marginal propensity to consume. A test of whether this change is significant is provided by a test of the null hypothesis that the coefficient of $D_t Y_t$ is 0.

Case IV:
$$C_t = \beta_1 + \beta_2 Y_t + \alpha D_t + \gamma(D_t Y_t) + \varepsilon_t \tag{5.15}$$

This case corresponds to the situation in which both the slope and the intercept are allowed to change. The reader should note, however, that the model has still been expressed as a single equation in which the variance of the error term is assumed to be the same in war and peace years. Least-squares estimation yields *unique* estimates of the standard error of the regression and of the distributions of the estimated regression parameters.

Case V:
$$C_t = \begin{cases} \beta_1^* + \beta_2^* Y_t + \varepsilon_t^* & \text{war years} \\ \beta_1' + \beta_2' Y_t + \varepsilon_t' & \text{peace years} \end{cases} \tag{5.16}$$

In this case we have allowed the error variance to vary from war years to peace years. Case V corresponds, of course, to running two separate regressions and obtaining two separate estimates of the standard errors of the regression. The reader can check to see that the estimated regression parameters in case IV and case V are essentially equivalent ($\hat{\beta}_1' = \hat{\beta}_1$, $\hat{\beta}_1^* = \hat{\beta}_1 + \hat{\alpha}$, $\hat{\beta}_2' = \hat{\beta}_2$, $\hat{\beta}_2^* = \hat{\beta}_2 + \hat{\gamma}$). The choice of model IV or model V depends upon whether the researcher is willing to believe (before examining the data) that the error variance is constant over all model years.†

Example 5.2   Labor force participation In a study of labor-force participation and unemployment, Bowen and Finegan were concerned with the determinants of intercity differences in labor force participation rates for males 25 to 54 years old during the census week of 1950.‡ The variables

---

† It is, of course, possible to test the null hypothesis that the error variance is constant between war and peace years, or more generally to decide when it is reasonable to assume that regression models actually switch from one time period to another. See, for example, R. E. Quandt, "The Estimation of the Parameters of a Linear Regression Obeying Two Separate Regimes," *Journal of the American Statistical Association*, vol. 53, pp. 873–880, 1958, and "Test of the Hypothesis That a Linear Regression System Obeys Two Separate Regimes," *Journal of the American Statistical Association*, vol. 55, pp. 324–330, 1960.

‡ W. G. Bowen and T. A. Finegan, "Labor Force Participation and Unemployment," in Arthur M. Ross (ed.), *Employment Policy and Labor Markets* (Berkeley: University of California Press, 1965), table 4-2.

utilized were

   L = labor-force participation rate for males 25 to 54, percent
   U = unemployment rate, percent
   E = earnings, hundreds of dollars per year
OI = other income, hundreds of dollars per year
   S = schooling completed, years
   C = color, percentage nonwhite
   D = dummy variable, with a 1 assigned to each city in the South and a 0 to
      all other cities

The regression results for a sample of 78 cities were

$$\hat{L} = 94.2 - .24U - .20E - .69OI - .06S + .002C - .80D$$

The dummy variable was significant at the 10 percent level. One can conclude that in 1950 regional differences in customs or mixes of industry did have an effect on labor-force participation for prime-age males, with participation being .80 percent lower in the South than in the rest of the nation. The effect measured by the dummy variable appeared *not* to be stable over time because a similar regression model estimated for 1960 yielded an insignificant dummy-variable coefficient.

Example 5.3 Certificates of deposit In this example an equation is estimated that predicts the total volume of negotiable certificates of deposit (CD) held by the public on a monthly basis.† Our equation is a demand relationship, and one would therefore expect that the dependent variable should depend on total personal wealth and on the interest rate that individuals would receive when part of that wealth is invested in a certificate of deposit. The primary interest rate on certificates of deposit (RCDP) was therefore chosen as an explanatory variable. However, certificates of deposit must compete with other interest-bearing assets, such as Treasury bills and corporate bonds. Thus, the interest rates on Treasury bills (RTB) and corporate bonds (RBaa) are also explanatory variables; when these variables increase, the total demand for certificates of deposit should decrease. These interest-rate variables are multiplied by personal income (PI), this last variable serving as a proxy for personal wealth. The difference between the corporate bond interest rate and the interest rate on prime commercial paper (RCP) is also an explanatory variable, and represents the difference between long- and short-term interest rates; when this difference increases, a long-term investment (such as a certificate of deposit) becomes more attractive. Finally, the lagged dependent variable is also introduced.

    It has been shown that the volume of certificates of deposit, as well as many other financial variables, displays a definite seasonal behavior; i.e., there are certain periods during the year when the volume increases and

† This example has been adapted from R. Pindyck and S. Roberts, "Optimal Policies for Monetary Control," *Annals of Economic and Social Measurement*, January 1974.

other periods when it decreases, regardless of the behavior of the explanatory variables. For this reason a set of seasonal dummy variables is introduced to explain as much of this seasonal behavior as possible. The seasonal variables (denoted $S3$) take the form of monthly dummy variables multiplied by personal income. Thus, the first seasonal dummy takes on the value 1 when the observation occurs in the month of January and 0 otherwise. The first seasonal variable takes on the value of personal income in the month of January and 0 otherwise. There are a total of 12 seasonal variables in the model, but the constant term has been dropped to eliminate the collinearity problem. The equation was estimated using ordinary least squares with the following results (t statistics in parentheses):

$$\widehat{CD}_t = \underset{(14.61)}{.72947\,CD_{t-1}} - \underset{(-2.667)}{(.00150\,RTB_t)(PI_t)} + \underset{(6.903)}{(.00225\,RCDP_t)(PI_t)}$$

$$- \underset{(-2.453)}{(.00128\,RBaa_t)(PI_t)} + \underset{(2.929)}{.00154\,(RBaa_t - RCP_t)(PI_t)} + S3_t$$

$$R^2 = .9995 \qquad S3_t = \text{seasonal coefficient}_t \times PI_t$$

Seasonal coefficients

Month	Coefficient	t statistic	Month	Coefficient	t statistic	Month	Coefficient	t statistic
Jan.	.01057	2.886	May	.00952	2.656	Sept.	.01113	2.986
Feb.	.00977	2.768	June	.00971	2.659	Oct.	.01179	3.167
Mar.	.00974	2.279	July	.00163	3.137	Nov.	.01117	3.016
Apr.	.00916	2.607	Aug.	.01208	3.265	Dec.	.01147	3.086

The seasonal coefficients are all significant at the 5 percent level, suggesting that seasonal variations in the volume of certificates of deposit are quite important. The results suggest that August to January are the peak months for public holdings of CDs, while from February to July holdings are relatively lower.

5.3 THE USE OF t AND F-TESTS FOR HYPOTHESES INVOLVING MORE THAN ONE PARAMETER

We have already seen that the F distribution can be useful for testing hypotheses in the context of the multiple regression model. The most important example occurs when we wish to test the null hypothesis that a single regression coefficient is equal to zero (or any other number). In this case, the F test reduces to a t test, with the relevant t statistic calculated as the ratio of the estimated coefficient to the estimated standard error. The second use of the F test, seen previously, occurs when we wish to test the null hypothesis that all regression coefficients are equal to zero. While these two situations occur most frequently in econometrics, there are a number of other instances in which hypothesis testing can be important, and in each case the t and/or F distribution can be useful. Our plan, in this section, is to outline and give examples of these situations. The tests include the following:

1. Joint tests on several regression coefficients
2. Tests involving linear functions of the regression coefficients
3. Tests involving the equality of coefficients of different regressions

5.3.1 Joint Tests on Several Regression Coefficients

The F test on R^2 provides a test of the null hypothesis that all regression coefficients are zero, but there are circumstances in which we might want to test the joint significance of a subset of all of the regression coefficients. One case is provided in the discussion of dummy variables. Recall that in case IV we included a dummy variable and a dummy interaction term to allow for a shift in both the slope and the intercept of the consumption function during war years. If we wish to test whether the slope has changed or whether the intercept has changed, the t test is appropriate. However, it is also reasonable to test whether both the slope and intercept have changed. A second use of the joint test occurs when groups of variables appear in an econometric model and one wishes to see whether the group as a whole helps to explain the variation in the dependent variable. This is often the case for models which include sets of dummy variables, but it applies much more generally.

To see how the joint test works, reconsider the multiple regression model

$$Y = \beta_1 + \beta_2 X_2 + \cdots + \beta_k X_k + \varepsilon \qquad (5.17)$$

(We have dropped the index, which denotes the observation number, to simplify things.) We shall call this model the *unrestricted model UR*, since no assumptions have been made about any of the regression coefficients. Now assume that we wish to test whether a subset of the regression coefficients is jointly equal to zero. To do so it is useful to rewrite (5.17), dividing the variables into two groups, the first containing $k - q$ variables (including the constant) and the second including q variables:

$$Y = \beta_1 + \beta_2 X_2 + \cdots + \beta_{k-q} X_{k-q} + \beta_{k-q+1} X_{k-q+1} + \cdots + \beta_k X_k + \varepsilon$$
$$(5.18)$$

Now, assume that we wish to test the null hypothesis that the last q coefficients are jointly equal to zero. If all the last q coefficients equal zero, the correct model will be the *restricted* (by the zero coefficients) *model*, denoted R:

$$Y = \beta_1 + \beta_2 X_2 + \cdots + \beta_{k-q} X_{k-q} + \varepsilon \qquad (5.19)$$

The null hypothesis, then, is that $\beta_{k-q+1} = \cdots = \beta_k = 0$.

The construction of the test of the null hypothesis is rather straightforward. When we drop the q variables from the model and estimate Eq. (5.19), the restricted model, the residual or error sum of squares ESS_R must be larger than the error sum of squares associated with the unrestricted model ESS_{UR}. This is equivalent to the result that R^2 always increases (or remains constant) when additional variables are added to the regression model. If the null hypothesis is correct, dropping the q variables will have little or no effect on the explanatory power of the equation and ESS_R will be only slightly higher than ESS_{UR}. Of course, the magnitude of the increased error sum of squares must be interpreted in the context of the problem in question, so that any test of the null hypothesis must account for the number of restrictions, i.e., coefficients set equal to zero, and the number of degrees of freedom available in the unrestricted regression model.

The correct test statistic is

$$\frac{(ESS_R - ESS_{UR})/q}{ESS_{UR}/(N - k)} \tag{5.20}$$

Here, the numerator is the increase in the sum of squared residuals divided by the number of parameter restrictions implicit in the null hypothesis, and the denominator is the error sum of squares in the original unrestricted model divided by the number of degrees of freedom in the unrestricted model. If the null hypothesis is true, the test statistic given in (5.20) will have an F distribution, with q degrees of freedom in the numerator and $N - k$ in the denominator.

Readers with an interest in the underlying statistics might see that the F distribution results because (under the null hypothesis) both the numerator and denominator represent sums of squared variables and are distributed (independently) as chi square. In any case, the F test on the subset of regression coefficients is carried out just like the F test on the entire regression equation. We choose a level of significance, say 1 or 5 percent, and then compare the test statistic with the critical value of the F distribution. If the test statistic is larger than the critical value, we reject the null hypothesis and conclude that the subset of variables is statistically significant. Note that as a general rule two separate regression equations must be estimated to apply the test correctly. Only in special cases can the test be accomplished by estimating a single regression.

It is also important to realize that this F test is not the same as doing a set of individual t tests on each of the variables in the subset. It is not unlikely that all t tests will be insignificant, and yet when tested jointly, the F test will be significant. We are testing whether the *group* of variables is significant, not individual variables in that group. (We treat the special problem of testing when groups of dummy variables are involved in Appendix 5.1.)

It should be apparent that the F test just described is a generalization of the F test on R^2 discussed in Chapter 4. This result is not immediately apparent because the form of (5.20) differs from that appearing in Section 4.3. To check to see how the two relate, we might note first that the F test on a subset of coefficients can be written, not in terms of residual sums of squares but in terms of the R^2's from the two regression equations. This latter view is sometimes more useful for testing purposes because R^2's are reported (in published work, at least) more often than the residual sums of squares. To make the comparison, recall that $R^2 = 1 - ESS/TSS$, where TSS is the total sum of squares in the regression. Then

$$R_{UR}^2 = 1 - \frac{\text{ESS}_{UR}}{\text{TSS}_{UR}} \quad \text{and} \quad R_R^2 = 1 - \frac{\text{ESS}_R}{\text{TSS}_R}$$

Note that both regression equations have the same dependent variable and thus the same total sum of squares, that is, $\text{TSS}_{UR} = \text{TSS}_R$. By substituting the two equations above into (5.20) we find (with only a little manipulation) that the test statistic can also be written as

$$F_{q, N-k} = \frac{(R_{UR}^2 - R_R^2)/q}{(1 - R_{UR}^2)/(N - k)} \tag{5.21}$$

Now the fact that the F test on R^2 is a special case can readily be seen. For the test on R^2, the null hypothesis is that all $k - 1$ variables other than the constant are jointly equal to zero. In this case, the number of parameter restrictions becomes $q = k - 1$. In addition, the restricted model is simply the regression of Y on a constant. Since R^2 is a measure of the explained variation about the mean, R^2 is identically zero in the restricted case, that is, $R_R^2 = 0$. Substituting both of these pieces of information into (5.21) gives our desired result ($R_{UR}^2 = R^2$, of course).

Example 5.4   Demand for housing In an attempt to study the demand for housing,† the following regression model was specified:

$$\log Q = \beta_1 + \beta_2 \log P + \beta_3 \log Y + \varepsilon \tag{5.22}$$

where Q = measure of quantity of housing consumed by each of N families per year
P = price of unit of housing in family's locality
Y = measure of family income

The estimation results were (standard errors are in parentheses):

$$\widehat{\log Q} = 4.17 - \underset{(.11)}{} \underset{(.017)}{.247} \log P + \underset{(.026)}{.96} \log Y \qquad R^2 = .371 \qquad N = 3,120$$

$$\tag{5.23}$$

The results suggest a price elasticity of demand of $-.247$ and an income elasticity of .96.‡ Both elasticities are clearly significantly different from zero, since the t ratios are roughly 14 and 37 in absolute value. However, it is more interesting to ask whether the income elasticity .96 is significantly

---

† We wish to thank George Johnson for providing the materials constituting the examples in this section.

‡ Recall from Chapter 4 that the coefficients in a log-log equation are elasticities, since $(d \log Y)/(d \log X) = (dY/Y)/(dX/X)$.

different from 1. The correct statistic is

$$t_{N-k} = \frac{\hat{\beta}_3 - \beta_3}{s_{\hat{\beta}_3}}$$

or, in this case,

$$t_{3,117} = \frac{.96 - 1}{.026} = -1.54$$

Since the critical value of the t distribution at the 5 percent level is 1.96, we cannot reject the null hypothesis that the income elasticity of demand is 1.

Now, assume that we are concerned that the demand for housing of blacks might be different from for whites, so that the model specification is expanded to allow for different slopes and intercept. If we let D represent a dummy variable equal to 1 for black households and 0 otherwise, the expanded model is

$$\log Q = \beta_1 + \alpha_1 D + \beta_2 \log P + \alpha_2 D \log P + \beta_3 \log Y + \alpha_3 D \log Y + \varepsilon$$
$$(5.24)$$

When this expanded model was estimated, the results were

$$\widehat{\log Q} = 4.17 - \underset{(.02)}{.221} \log P + \underset{(.031)}{.920} \log Y + \underset{(.042)}{.006}\, D - \underset{(.061)}{.114}\, D \log P$$
$$+ \underset{(.120)}{.341}\, D \log Y \qquad R^2 = .380 \qquad (5.25)$$

If we were to perform t tests on the individual coefficients of the terms involving the dummy variables, we would find the first insignificant (at the 5 percent level), the second barely insignificant, and the third significant. However, we wish to test the null hypothesis that the dummy coefficients are all jointly equal to zero, i.e.,

$$\alpha_1 = \alpha_2 = \alpha_3 = 0$$

Because our information is given in terms of R^2 and not residual sums of squares, we need simply apply the formulation given in Eq. (5.21). In terms of that notation, $R^2_{UR} = .380$, $R^2_R = .371$, $N = 3,120$, $k = 6$, and $q = 3$. The appropriate F statistic is

$$\frac{(R^2_{UR} - R^2_R)/q}{(1 - R^2_{UR})/N - k} = \frac{(.380 - .371)/3}{(1 - .380)/3,114} = 15.1$$

This clearly exceeds the critical value of the F distribution at either the 1 or the 5 percent level, and so we reject the null hypothesis of identical housing demands for blacks and whites. Note that with a sufficiently large data set, it does not take much of an increase in R^2 to allow us to reject the null hypothesis of equality among a subset of coefficients.

5.3.2 Tests Involving Linear Functions of the Regression Coefficients

There are a number of occasions in which one might want to test hypotheses concerning linear combinations of regression coefficients. For example, if one estimated a consumption function $C = \beta_1 + \beta_2 Y_L + \beta_3 Y_{NL} + \varepsilon$, where Y_L represents labor income and Y_{NL} represents nonlabor income, one might wish to test the null hypothesis that the marginal propensity of consumption out of all income is 1; that is, $\beta_2 + \beta_3 = 1$. Or one might wish to test the hypothesis that two regression coefficients are equal, in this case, that $\beta_2 = \beta_3$. This latter hypothesis is a special case of a linear function on the coefficients because it can be rewritten as $\beta_2 - \beta_3 = 0$.

Since the tests are somewhat difficult to follow when given in full generality, we shall consider the two special cases listed above. The generalization is left to the reader as an exercise. Consider first the null hypothesis that the two regression coefficients sum to 1. We will call them β_2 and β_3 to simplify but will generalize by assuming that the model contains k variables and $N - k$ degrees of freedom. To construct the test, let $\beta^* = \hat{\beta}_2 + \hat{\beta}_3$. If the model has been specified correctly, each of the parameter estimators will be unbiased, so that β^* has expected value $\beta_2 + \beta_3 = 1$. If we knew the variance of β^*, we could easily construct our test because β^* is the sum of two normally distributed random variables and therefore normal. The appropriate test statistic would be $(\beta^* - 1)/\sigma_{\beta^*}$. However, we do not know the variance of β^*, so just as in the usual case, we must estimate the variance and use a t test to test the null hypothesis. The appropriate t statistic is given by

$$\frac{\beta^* - 1}{s_{\beta^*}}$$

where s_{β^*} is the estimated standard deviation of β^*.

To calculate s_{β^*} we need simply to recall our result from Chapter 2 that

$$\text{Var}(X + Y) = \text{Var}(X) + \text{Var}(Y) + 2\,\text{Cov}(X, Y)$$

Here we replace X and Y by the parameter estimators, to get

$$\text{Var}(\hat{\beta}^*) = \text{Var}(\hat{\beta}_2) + \text{Var}(\hat{\beta}_3) + 2\,\text{Cov}(\hat{\beta}_2, \hat{\beta}_3)$$

The standard deviation is, of course, the square root of the estimated variance. Also, the estimated variances of the individual coefficients are readily available, since they are simply the squares of the standard errors associated with each coefficient. However, the covariance must be obtained from the calculated variance-covariance matrix of the estimated parameters, usually an optional output on most computational systems. Note that the required covariance is between the coefficients and not the variables. There is no way to get such information from a matrix of covariances or correlations between the variables in the model (without matrix inversion).

Now consider the second test, a test of the null hypothesis that $\beta_2 = \beta_3$. If we were to proceed as before, we would calculate the test statistic β^*/s_{β^*}, where

$\beta^* = \hat{\beta}_2 - \hat{\beta}_3$. In this case

$$s_{\beta^*} = \left[\text{Var}\,(\hat{\beta}_2) + \text{Var}\,(\hat{\beta}_3) - 2\,\text{Cov}\,(\hat{\beta}_2, \hat{\beta}_3) \right]^{1/2}$$

Once again, the test statistic will follow a t distribution, and the application of the test is straightforward.

For many analyses, the only difficulty with both the previous tests is that of obtaining the covariances between the estimated parameters. In this case, there is an alternative way of doing the identical tests, using the material developed in the previous section. As an example, consider the test of equality of two coefficients. To do the test, we propose to estimate the equation

$$\begin{aligned} Y_i &= \beta_1 + \beta_2(X_{2i} + X_{3i}) + \gamma X_{3i} + \cdots + \beta_k X_{ki} + \varepsilon_i \\ &= \beta_1 + \beta_2 X_{2i} + (\beta_2 + \gamma)X_{3i} + \cdots + \beta_k X_{ki} + \varepsilon_i \end{aligned} \qquad (5.26)$$

If the null hypothesis is true, $\gamma = 0$, which can be tested by a standard t test of the estimated coefficient of X_3 in Eq. (5.26). Thus, tests of functions of parameters can be kept simple by suitable transformations of the original model. We leave the somewhat more difficult test of the hypothesis $\beta_2 + \beta_3 = 1$ to the reader.

Example 5.5 Demand for housing Assume that we have estimated the unrestricted model in Eq. (5.24) of Example 5.4 and wish to test the null hypothesis that the income elasticity of demand for housing of blacks is equal to that of whites. From the specification of the model we know that

$$\beta_3 = \text{income elasticity of demand for whites}$$

$$\beta_3 + \alpha_3 = \text{income elasticity of demand for blacks}$$

(The latter result holds because $D = 1$ for black households.) The null hypothesis of equal elasticities is therefore $\alpha_3 = 0$. To test the null hypothesis, we need to calculate an estimate of α_3 and its estimated standard error and then apply the fact that the ratio of the estimated coefficient to its standard error will follow a t distribution. In this case, $\hat{\alpha}_3 = .341$ and $s_{\hat{\alpha}_3} = .120$. Therefore, under the null hypothesis, $\hat{\alpha}_3/s_{\hat{\alpha}_3} = .341/.120 = 2.84$ follows a t distribution with 3,114 degrees of freedom. Since 2.84 is greater than the critical value (1.96) at the 5 percent level, we reject the null hypothesis that the income elasticities of demand for housing are equal.

Now assume that we wish to test the null hypothesis that the elasticity of demand for housing by blacks is equal to 1. In this case, the null hypothesis is $\beta_3 + \alpha_3 = 1$ or $\beta_3 + \alpha_3 - 1 = 0$, which suggests a test involving a linear function of two of the regression coefficients. Using our analysis in the text, we need simply apply a t test, since (under the null hypothesis) $(\beta^* - 1)/s_{\beta^*}$ follows a t distribution, where $\beta^* = \hat{\beta}_3 + \hat{\alpha}_3$. Clearly, $\hat{\beta}_3 + \hat{\alpha}_3 = .920 + .341 = 1.261$. To calculate s_{β^*} we use the fact that

$$\text{Var}\,(\hat{\beta}_3 + \hat{\alpha}_3) = \text{Var}\,(\hat{\beta}_3) + \text{Var}\,(\hat{\alpha}_3) + 2\,\text{Cov}\,(\hat{\alpha}_3, \hat{\beta}_3)$$

$\text{Var}\,(\hat{\beta}_3)$ is the square of $s_{\hat{\beta}_3}$, and therefore $\text{Var}\,(\hat{\beta}_3) = (.031)^2 = .00096$.

Likewise, Var $(\hat{\alpha}_3) = (.120)^2 = .0144$. However, Cov $(\hat{\beta}_3, \hat{\alpha}_3)$ must be obtained from the printed variance-covariance matrix of the estimated parameters. In this case, we found that 2 Cov $(\hat{\beta}_3, \hat{\alpha}_3) = -.00317$. Therefore,

$$\text{Var}\left(\hat{\beta}_3 + \hat{\alpha}_3\right) = .00096 + .0144 - .00317 = .00902$$

and
$$s_{\beta^*} = (.00902)^{1/2} = .095$$

Finally,

$$\frac{\beta^* - 1}{s_{\beta^*}} = \frac{1.261 - 1}{.095} = \frac{.261}{.095} = 2.75$$

Since 2.75 is greater than the critical value of the t distribution at the 5 percent level, we reject the null hypothesis that the black income elasticity of demand is equal to 1.

One final note: if one does not want to rely on the information from the variance-covariance matrix, the null hypothesis of a unitary black income elasticity of demand can be tested in another way. We simply rewrite the original unrestricted model, defining D to be equal to 1 for whites and 0 elsewhere. When this model is reestimated, the newly estimated parameter β_3 will now measure black income elasticity of demand and a direct t test can be used.

5.3.3 Tests Involving the Equality of Coefficients of Different Regressions

All the tests so far have involved a single linear regression model and a single data set. There are times, however, when one is not sure whether a given model applies to two different data sets. Take, for example, the consumption-function example used in the earlier discussion of dummy variables. Case V illustrates the most general formulation of the model, in which it is assumed that one regression model applies in war years and a second model applies in years of peace. Note that it differs from case IV since we are assuming not only that the slope and intercept parameters are distinct but also the error structures are different as well. In fact, one common use of this test occurs when one is deciding whether or not it is suitable to pool time-series and cross-section data. This specific issue is discussed in some detail in Chapter 9.

To test whether the assumption of two different regression models is correct we usually start with the null hypothesis that the regressions are identical and see whether or not we can reject the null hypothesis.[†] Consider the regression models

$$Y_i = \beta_1 + \beta_2 X_{2i} + \cdots + \beta_k X_{ki} + \varepsilon_i \tag{5.27a}$$

$$Y_j = \alpha_1 + \alpha_2 X_{2j} + \cdots + \alpha_k X_{kj} + \varepsilon_j \tag{5.27b}$$

[†] This test was devised by Gregory C. Chow in "Tests of Equality between Sets of Coefficients in Two Linear Regressions," *Econometrica*, vol. 28, pp. 591–605, July 1960. See also Franklin M. Fisher, "Tests of Equality between Sets of Coefficients in Two Linear Regressions: An Expository Note," *Econometrica* pp. 361–366, March 1970.

In the first equation, we assume that there are N observations, and we subscript the variables with i to denote observations running from 1 to N. In the second equation, we subscript the variables with j to allow the number of observations to differ. In this case, we will assume that j runs from 1 to M. Of course we have allowed all regression coefficients to differ from Eq. (5.27a) to Eq. (5.27b). Suppose we estimate the model implied by the two equations. This is done, of course, by applying ordinary least squares to each equation individually. Since no restrictions have been placed on the parameters of the model, we can calculate what is essentially equivalent to the unrestricted sum of squares as the sum of the residual sums of squares of the individual equations, that is, $\text{ESS}_{UR} = \text{ESS}_1 + \text{ESS}_2$. The number of degrees of freedom involved is the sum of the number of degrees of freedom in each individual regression, that is, $(N - k) + (M - k) = N + M - 2k$.

Now assume that the null hypothesis is true, that is, $\alpha_1 = \beta_1$, $\alpha_2 = \beta_2, \ldots, \alpha_k = \beta_k$. Then the regression model can be written as a single equation

$$Y_i = \beta_1 + \beta_2 X_{2i} + \cdots + \beta_k X_{ki} + \varepsilon_i \tag{5.28}$$

where the subscript i now runs from observation 1 to observation $N + M$. Now we estimate (5.28) using ordinary least squares and calculate the restricted residual sum of squares ESS_R. If the null hypothesis is true, the restrictions will not hurt the explanatory power of the model and ESS_R will not be much larger than ESS_{UR}. As before, we can perform an F test to see whether the difference between the two residual sums of squares is significant. Since there are $N + M - 2k$ degrees of freedom in the unrestricted regression and there are k restrictions, the appropriate F statistic is†

$$F_{k, N+M-2k} = \frac{(\text{ESS}_R - \text{ESS}_{UR})/k}{\text{ESS}_{UR}/(N + M - 2k)} \tag{5.29}$$

If the F statistic is larger than the critical value of the F distribution with k and $N + M - 2k$ degrees of freedom, we can reject the null hypothesis. Here rejection implies that two separate regressions must be estimated: the data cannot be pooled.‡

Example 5.6 Demand for housing Suppose that we had reason to believe that it was proper to estimate a housing-demand model that consisted of two equations, one describing black housing demand and the other white housing demand. (This is equivalent to case V in the section on dummy variables.) The model is

$$\log Q = \begin{cases} \beta_1 + \beta_2 \log P + \beta_3 \log Y + \varepsilon & \text{for all white households} \\ \gamma_1 + \gamma_2 \log P + \gamma_3 \log Y + u & \text{for all black households} \end{cases}$$

---

† The statistic follows an F distribution because each error sum of squares can be shown to follow a chi-square distribution, the numerator with k degrees of freedom and the denominator with $N + M - 2k$. Since the two distributions are independent, the ratio follows an F distribution.

‡ This test can also be applied to tests involving subsets of coefficients and in cases where there is insufficient data to estimate two individual regression equations separately. For details, see Chow, op. cit., and Fisher, op. cit.

We wish to test the null hypothesis that the set of coefficients in the black demand equation are equal to the set of coefficients in the white demand equation. The null hypothesis is that (jointly)

$$\beta_1 = \gamma_1 \qquad \beta_2 = \gamma_2 \qquad \beta_3 = \gamma_3$$

To perform the test we first estimated the model above and added the residual sum of squares in each of the equations. We found that $ESS_{UR} = 13{,}640$. Now assume that the null hypothesis of equality is true, in this case the model reduces to

$$\log Q = \beta_1 + \beta_2 \log P + \beta_3 \log Y + \varepsilon \qquad \text{for all households}$$

When we estimated this restricted model, we found the error sum of squares to be $ESS_R = 13{,}838$. Since there are $k = 3$ restrictions, and $N + M - 2k = 3{,}120 - 6 = 3{,}114$ degrees of freedom, the appropriate F statistic with 3 restrictions and 3,114 degrees of freedom is

$$F_{3,\,3,114} = \frac{(13{,}838 - 13{,}640)/3}{13{,}640/3{,}114} = 15.1$$

Since the value of the F statistic is greater than the critical value of the F distribution at the 5 percent level, we reject the null hypothesis. It is incorrect to assume equal coefficients.

The conclusion of Example 5.6 is not surprising in the light of the earlier test results in Examples 5.4 and 5.5. What might seem surprising is that the test statistic here is identical to the F statistic calculated in Example 5.4. This is not a coincidence. In the unrestricted model in Example 5.4 we allowed the intercept and all slope coefficients to vary, just as we have done here, by specifying two different demand equations. When estimated using ordinary least-squares estimation, both parameter estimates will be identical. The reason is that both models are analytically equivalent. They allow for the same parameter shifts, they have the same number of degrees of freedom, and they will yield the same residuals and residual sum of squares. Of course, the residual sum of squares in the two-equation specification is the sum of the ESSs for each equation. Thus, while testing subsets of coefficients will not in general be the same as testing for the equality of coefficients between equations, the two are identical when one introduces dummy variables so that *all* parameters in the model shift between the two sets of data being analyzed.

One note of warning. The fact that the two statistical tests are identical in this case does not imply that the models described as case IV and case V in the section on dummy variables are identical. Case V is more general than case IV because it allows for error structures to differ between the two equations. This might involve different variances or more complicated differences in error structure. In such cases ordinary least squares does not yield efficient parameter estimates, nor does it yield unbiased estimates of regression statistics. If we reject the null hypothesis of equality between coefficients, we should view case V, in which two equations are used, i.e., the data are stratified, as the appropriate choice. Only if we conclude that the error structures are identical is case IV correct. These issues and the appropriate statistical tests are discussed in Chapter 6.

5.4 PIECEWISE LINEAR REGRESSION

Most of the econometric models we have studied to this point have been continuous models in the sense that both dependent and independent variables take on a large number of values and small changes in one variable have a measurable impact on another variable. This framework was modified somewhat when we used dummy variables to account for shifts in either slope or intercept or both. It is therefore reasonable to extend the analysis one further step: to allow for changes in slope, with the restriction that the line being estimated not be discontinuous. A simple example is drawn in Fig. 5.2. The true model is a continuous one, with a structural break. If we were explaining consumption as a function of income, for example, the structural break might occur sometime during World War II (or there might be two breaks, one at the beginning and one at the end). We stress that this model is different from the previous dummy-variable models because we have assumed that there is no discontinuity or shift in the consumption level from year to year. Such a model is called a *piecewise linear model*, and in this case it consists of two straight line segments.

We shall see in a moment that such a model can be estimated using ordinary least-squares with the appropriate use of dummy variables. However, we should mention that piecewise linear models are really special cases of a much larger set of models or relationships, called *spline functions*. Spline functions are functions with distinct pieces, as in our example, but the relationship or curve representing each piece is a continuous function and not necessarily a straight line. In the most usual case, the spline is chosen to be a polynomial of the third degree or so, and the procedure guarantees that the first and second derivatives will be continuous.†

To estimate the model given in Fig. 5.2 consider the expression

$$C_t = \beta_1 + \beta_2 Y_t + \beta_3 (Y_t - Y_{t_0}) D_t + \varepsilon_t \tag{5.30}$$

where C_t = consumption
   Y_t = income
   Y_{t_0} = income in year in which structural break occurs

and
$$D_t = \begin{cases} 1 & \text{if } t > t_0 \\ 0 & \text{otherwise} \end{cases}$$

---

† For a more serious and extended discussion of spline functions, see D. J. Poirier, *The Econometrics of Structural Change* (Amsterdam: North-Holland, 1976). For a more elementary description of the estimation of spline functions, see D. Suits, A. Mason, and L. Chan, "Spline Functions Fitted by Standard Regression Methods," *Review of Economics and Statistics*, vol. LX, pp. 132–139, February 1978. An interesting example appears in J. Barth, A. Kraft, and J. Kraft, "Estimation of the Liquidity Trap Using Spline Functions," *Review of Economics and Statistics*, vol. LVII, pp. 218–222, May 1976.

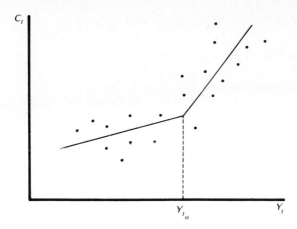

Figure 5.2 Piecewise-linear-regression model.

For years before and including the break, $D_t = 0$, so that

$$E(C_t) = \beta_1 + \beta_2 Y_t \tag{5.31}$$

However, after the break, $D_t = 1$, so that

$$E(C_t) = \beta_1 + \beta_2 Y_t + \beta_3 Y_t - \beta_3 Y_{t_0}$$

or
$$E(C_t) = (\beta_1 - \beta_3 Y_{t_0}) + (\beta_2 + \beta_3) Y_t \tag{5.32}$$

Before the break, the line has slope β_2, but the slope changes to $\beta_2 + \beta_3$ afterward (and the intercept changes as well). Note, however, that there is no discontinuity in the relationship, since

$$E(C_{t_0}) = \beta_1 + \beta_2 Y_{t_0} \qquad \text{from (5.31)}$$

$$= (\beta_1 - \beta_3 Y_{t_0}) + (\beta_2 + \beta_3) Y_{t_0} = \beta_1 + \beta_2 Y_{t_0} \qquad \text{from (5.32)}.$$

Note also that when $\beta_3 = 0$, the consumption equation reduces to a single straight-line segment, so that a t test using $\hat{\beta}_3$ provides a simple test for structural change.

What if there were two structural breaks, rather than one, occurring at times t_0 and t_1? The appropriate model would then be

$$C_t = \beta_1 + \beta_2 Y_t + \beta_3 (Y_t - Y_{t_0}) D + \beta_4 (Y_t - Y_{t_1}) D' + \varepsilon_t \tag{5.33}$$

where Y_{t_1} represents the income at which a second structural break occurs

$$D' = \begin{cases} 1 & \text{if } t > t_1 \\ 0 & \text{otherwise} \end{cases}$$

The equations of each of the three line segments are then

$$E(C_t) = \begin{cases} \beta_1 + \beta_2 Y_t & 0 < t \leq t_0 \\ (\beta_1 - \beta_3 Y_{t_0}) + (\beta_2 + \beta_3) Y_t & t_1 \leq t \leq t_2 \\ (\beta_1 - \beta_3 Y_{t_0} - \beta_4 Y_{t_1}) + (\beta_2 + \beta_3 + \beta_4) Y_t & t \geq t_1 \end{cases}$$

The reader should check that, as before, no discontinuities occur at the point of structural break.

5.5 SPECIFICATION ERROR

Much of our discussion of econometrics has relied heavily upon the assumption that the model to be estimated is correctly specified, i.e., that it represents the underlying process. Once the correct specification of the model is assumed, model estimation and model testing become relatively straightforward. In reality, however, we can never be sure that a given model is correctly specified. In fact, applied researchers usually examine more than one possible specification, attempting to find the specification which best describes the process under study. We attempt to give the reader a feeling for the hazards involved in searching for a model by discussing the costs associated with the model misspecification. We concern ourselves with two types of misspecification, the first occurring when relevant variables are omitted from the linear regression, and the second occurring when irrelevant variables are added to the equation. We do not consider misspecification errors associated with the disturbance term, since much of this material is discussed in Chapters 6 and 7. Finally, we pause only briefly to discuss misspecifications associated with the incorrect choice of functional form, since much of that material will be implicitly covered in Section 9.4 on nonlinear estimation. Once again, we use special cases to illustrate our major arguments, although most results can be generalized using the tools of matrix algebra.†

5.5.1 Omitted Variables

Consider first the case in which a variable is unknowingly omitted from a "true" or correct model specification.‡ Assume that the true model is given by Eq. (5.34),

$$y_i = \beta_2 x_{2i} + \beta_3 x_{3i} + \varepsilon_i \tag{5.34}$$

while the regression model is given by§

$$y_i = \beta_2^* x_{2i} + \varepsilon_i^* \tag{5.35}$$

All the assumptions of the classical linear model hold for Eq. (5.34).

As was derived in Chapter 1, the estimated slope parameter is

$$\hat{\beta}_2^* = \frac{\sum x_{2i} y_i}{\sum x_{2i}^2} \tag{5.36}$$

---

† The material used in this section is discussed in more detail in two excellent discussions of model misspecification, P. Rao and R. L. Miller, *Applied Econometrics* (Belmont, Calif.: Wadsworth, 1971); and J. Kmenta, *Elements of Econometrics* (New York: Macmillan, 1971), pp. 391–406. The original source material is H. Theil, "Specification Errors and the Estimation of Economic Relationships," *Review of the International Statistical Institute*, vol. 25, pp. 41–51, 1957.

‡ Such a variable might be omitted by choice if sufficiently accurate data are not available to the researcher.

§ We shall work with data in deviations form and assume $\bar{\varepsilon} = 0$ to simplify the derivations. Most, but not all, of the results hold for the intercept of the equation. Since the effect of model misspecification on the intercept is not usually of paramount importance, we leave the details to the reader (see Exercise 5.1).

Substituting y_i, defined as in Eq. (5.34), into Eq. (5.36) and solving, we get

$$\hat{\beta}_2^* = \frac{\sum x_{2i}\beta_2 x_{2i} + \sum x_{2i}\beta_3 x_{3i} + \sum x_{2i}\epsilon_i}{\sum x_{2i}^2}$$

$$= \frac{\beta_2\sum x_{2i}^2 + \beta_3\sum x_{2i}x_{3i} + \sum x_{2i}\epsilon_i}{\sum x_{2i}^2}$$

$$= \beta_2 + \beta_3\frac{\sum x_{2i}x_{3i}}{\sum x_{2i}^2} + \frac{\sum x_{2i}\epsilon_i}{\sum x_{2i}^2}$$

Since, X_2 is fixed and $E(\epsilon_i) = 0$, the last term has expectation zero, so that

$$E(\hat{\beta}_2^*) = \beta_2 + \beta_3\frac{\sum x_{2i}x_{3i}}{\sum x_{2i}^2} = \beta_2 + \beta_3\frac{\text{Cov}(x_2, x_3)}{\text{Var}(x_2)} \tag{5.37}$$

Since there is no guarantee that the second term will be 0, the least-squares slope estimate of Eq. (5.35) will yield a biased estimate of the true slope parameter β_2. This bias will not disappear as the sample size grows large, so that the omission of a variable from the true model yields inconsistent parameter estimates as well. The only case in which the bias (and inconsistency) will completely disappear occurs when $\text{Cov}(x_2, x_3) = 0$, that is, when x_2 and x_3 are uncorrelated in the sample.† This result generalizes if there are numerous independent variables. Only when the omitted variable is uncorrelated with all the included independent variables does the bias disappear, and this is extremely unlikely with business and economic data.

The formula in Eq. (5.37) is useful because it tells that the direction of any bias which might occur depends upon the correlation between the omitted variable and all included variables, as well as on the sign of the true slope coefficient β_3. To the extent that x_2 and r_3 are highly correlated, the coefficient of x_2 will include the effect of the x_3 variable and will be biased.‡ When x_2 and x_3 are uncorrelated, x_2 picks up none of the effect of x_3 and no bias occurs. As a practical matter, it is the *extent* of the specification bias which is important. This suggests that a careful researcher will consider not only the question of missing variables but their possible correlation with included model variables as well.

To be complete, we should pause to consider the effect of variable omission on the error variance and its estimator. First consider the case in which x_2 and x_3 are uncorrelated. Then $\hat{\beta}_2^*$ will be an unbiased estimator of β_2 and will have an identical variance with $\hat{\beta}_2$. The only difficulty with model misspecification arises because the usual *estimator* of the variance of $\hat{\beta}_2^*$ will be biased.§ However, in the more general case when x_2 and x_3 are correlated, the two

---

† A high variance for x_2 will lower the amount of bias, but the bias will never reach zero, since we have assumed a finite variance for all sample x's.

‡ It is interesting (and useful when generalizations are made) to note that the correlation in question is simply the regression coefficient associated with the auxiliary regression of x_3 on x_2.

§ It is cumbersome but not difficult to show that the estimated variance of $\hat{\beta}_2^*$ will be biased upward.

estimators will not have identical variances. In the two-variable model, the actual variance of $\hat{\beta}_2^*$ will be less than the actual variance of $\hat{\beta}_2$, even though the model is misspecified.† If one is willing to give up lack of bias as an important objective, the omitted-variable specification has some merit. This is particularly true when omitted variables are thought to be uncorrelated with included variables.

5.5.2 Presence of an Irrelevant Variable

Now consider the case in which an irrelevant variable is added to the equation. Assume that the true model is given by

$$y_i = \beta_2 x_{2i} + \varepsilon_i \tag{5.38}$$

and the regression model is given by

$$y_i = \beta_2^* x_{2i} + \beta_3^* x_{3i} + \varepsilon_i^* \tag{5.39}$$

The effects of adding an irrelevant variable are quite different from the effects of omitting a variable. The addition of the irrelevant variable x_3 implies that we are not taking into account the true parameter restriction $\beta_3^* = 0$. We would expect that not taking into account all the information available about the model (the zero restriction) would lead to a loss of degrees of freedom and therefore to a loss of efficiency, but no loss of consistency and no bias. To see that this is the case, we calculate the estimated coefficient of the variable x_2 in Eq. (5.39). Using the derivation described in Chapter 4 [Eq. (4.4)], we find that

$$\hat{\beta}_2^* = \frac{(\sum x_{3i}^2)(\sum x_{2i} y_i) - (\sum x_{2i} x_{3i})(\sum x_{3i} y_i)}{(\sum x_{2i}^2)(\sum x_{3i}^2) - (\sum x_{2i} x_{3i})^2} \tag{5.40}$$

Substituting for y_i from Eq. (5.38) and solving, we get

$$\hat{\beta}_2^* = \beta_2 + \frac{(\sum x_{3i}^2)(\sum x_{2i} \varepsilon_i) - (\sum x_{2i} x_{3i})(\sum x_{3i} \varepsilon_i)}{(\sum x_{2i}^2)(\sum x_{3i}^2) - (\sum x_{2i} x_{3i})^2}$$

from which it follows that (taking expected values with x_2 and x_3 fixed)

$$E(\hat{\beta}_2^*) = \beta_2$$

Thus, the inclusion of an irrelevant variable does not bias the slope parameter estimates of any of the slope variables which appear in the "true" model. It is not difficult to show that the intercept of the equation is unbiased as well and that the estimate of the coefficient of x_3 will have an expected value of 0. We leave both of these proofs to the reader (see Exercises 5.3 and 5.4).

The inclusion of irrelevant variables does affect the efficiency of the least-squares estimator, since the variance of the estimated slope coefficient $\hat{\beta}_2^*$ will,‡ in general, be larger than the variance of the coefficient $\hat{\beta}_2$. (The only case

---

† This is shown in Rao and Miller, op. cit.

‡ For further details, see Kmenta, op.cit., pp. 396–399.

in which a loss of efficiency will not occur is the special case when x_2 and x_3 are uncorrelated, again an unlikely possibility.) This loss of efficiency makes it more difficult to reject the null hypothesis of a zero slope parameter. However, the estimated variance of $\hat{\beta}_2^*$ will be an unbiased estimator of the true variance of $\hat{\beta}_2^*$. This suggests that the loss of efficiency will be accounted for when the standard error of the regression is calculated. Thus, we can be quite confident in rejecting the zero-slope null hypothesis when some irrelevant variables are included in the model.

5.5.3 Nonlinearities

Another specification error can occur when the researcher chooses to estimate a linear regression model that is linear in the explanatory variables when the true regression model is nonlinear in the explanatory variables. A simple example of such a specification error occurs when the true model is of the polynomial form described in

$$y_i = \beta_2 x_{2i} + \beta_3 x_{2i}^2 + \beta_4 x_{2i}^3 + \varepsilon_i \tag{5.41}$$

while the estimated model is†

$$y_i = \beta_2^* x_{2i} + \varepsilon_i^* \tag{5.42}$$

The choice of the model in Eq. (5.42) is a special case of omitted variables, as described earlier. This suggests that specification of a linear model when the true model is nonlinear can lead to biased and inconsistent parameter estimates. The same conclusion holds when a polynomial approximation to an inherently nonlinear equation is used (see Section 9.4).

5.5.4 Costs of Model Building

The previous analysis of specification error suggests some of the serious difficulties involved with the model-building process. If we are unsure of which explanatory variables ought to appear in a model, we face several trade-offs. The analysis shows that the cost of excluding a variable which should appear in the model is bias and inconsistency. The cost of adding one or more irrelevant variables, on the other hand, is loss of efficiency. If the number of observations available is rather large, it seems reasonable to opt for the risk of adding irrelevant variables because the loss of degrees of freedom associated with the addition of several independent variables to the model is unlikely to be serious. If the number of observations is not large, however, loss of efficiency becomes a serious matter. If all potential model variables are known, the choice of model form must be made in terms of the bias-efficiency trade-off, with the result dependent upon our objectives. If accurate forecasting is the goal, minimizing

---

† We often estimate polynomial equations such as that given in Eq. (5.41) as a test for nonlinearity in the independent variables.

mean square error appears to be one reasonable objective, since it accounts for both bias and efficiency.† Thus, we might estimate each of several alternative models over a given time period and compare the mean square errors associated with each model.‡ This notion of validating models, or of choosing among model forms by means of simulation, is described in detail in Part Two.

In terms of classical statistics, it is not difficult to test whether irrelevant variables are present. Since the coefficients of irrelevant variables have expected values of 0, we need simply apply standard t tests if we wish to evaluate the relevancy of individual variables and an F test if we wish to test the relevancy of a group of variables. Such testing is feasible if we know the set of variables which might conceivably appear in the model, but it fails completely when we are unsure which variables ought to appear in the model. As a rule, standard statistical testing is inappropriate when two essentially unrelated models are to be compared. Once again, we must rely upon the use of simulation techniques to make such comparisons.§ In the case of omitted variables, simple statistical tests are also unlikely to be available, since we usually cannot measure or do not have any knowledge of the omitted variable; t tests and F tests are appropriate only when the omitted variables are known.

Example 5.7 Demand for money In a study of the long- and short-run demand for money, Chow estimated the following demand equation (standard errors are in parentheses, and all data are quarterly):¶

$$\hat{M}_t = .1365 + \underset{(.148)}{1.069}\, Y_{pt} - \underset{(.13897)}{.01321}\, Y_t - \underset{(.0540)}{.7476}\, R_t \qquad R^2 = .9965$$

where M = natural logarithm of total money stock
Y_p = natural logarithm of permanent income
Y = natural logarithm of current income
R = natural logarithm of rate of interest

Since Chow views the estimated equation as a long-run equation for the demand for money, he concludes that permanent income is more important than current income as the long-run constraint on individual assets. (The Y

---

† Recall from Chapter 2 that mean square error = variance + bias².
‡ One of the difficulties with such a procedure is that knowledge of mean square error does not give us independent knowledge of bias (and variance).
§ Bayesian econometrics provides a suitable framework in which the limitations of the classical methods of model construction and model testing can be seen. See, for example, A. Zellner, *An Introduction to Bayesian Inference in Econometrics* (New York: Wiley, 1971), and E. Leamer, *Specification Searches in Econometrics* (New York: Wiley, 1979). For further reading about a different error-estimation procedure see A. C. Harvey and P. Collier, "Testing for Functional Misspecification in Regression Analysis," *Journal of Econometrics*, vol. 6, pp. 103–119, 1977; and Y. P. Gupta and E. Maasoumi, "Omitted Variables, Variability of Estimated Parameters and the Appearance of Autocorrelated Disturbances," *Journal of Econometrics*, vol. 9, pp. 387–389, 1979.
¶ G. C. Chow, "On the Long-Run and Short-Run Demand for Money," *Journal of Political Economy*, vol. 74, pp. 111–131, April 1966.

variable is insignificant, while the Y_p variable is highly significant.) However, it is possible to argue that the estimated equation is in fact a misspecification of the correct long-run demand-for-money equation. Taylor and Newhouse argue that the correct specification is[†]

$$M_t = \beta_1 + \beta_2 Y_{pt} + \beta_3 Y_t + \beta_4 R_t + \beta_5 M_{t-1} + \varepsilon_t$$

If this specification is correct, we would expect the coefficients of the estimated equation to be biased. We can approximate the extent of this bias by using our results on the effects of omitted-variable specification error. Consider the estimated permanent income coefficient, since it is crucial to the policy conclusion which was reached. If the correct model had been

$$M_t = \alpha_1 + \alpha_2 Y_{pt} + \alpha_3 M_{t-1} + u_t$$

then from Eq. (5.37) we could conclude that the bias in the estimated coefficient $\hat{\alpha}_2$ of the equation $M_t = \alpha_1 + \alpha_2 Y_{pt}$ would be

$$E(\hat{\alpha}_2) - \alpha_2 = \alpha_3 \frac{\text{Cov}(Y_{pt}, M_{t-1})}{\text{Var}(Y_{pt})}$$

While we have not done so in the text, it is possible to extend the formula for specification bias to apply to equations with numerous explanatory variables. In our case the bias in the permanent income term is estimated by

$$E(\hat{\beta}_2) - \beta_2 = \beta_5 d_2$$

where d_2 is the coefficient of Y_{pt} in the auxiliary regression of M_{t-1} on Y_{pt}, Y_t, and R_t, that is,

$$M_{t-1} = d_1 + d_2 Y_{pt} + d_3 Y_t + d_4 R_t + v_t$$

If the variable M_{t-1} is unavailable, we would have to speculate about the extent of any specification bias present. However, in this particular example M_{t-1} is available, since it involves a one-period lag of a variable present in the misspecified equation. Since M_{t-1} and Y_{pt} are known to be highly correlated and we expect the sign of M_{t-1} to be positive when the correctly specified equation is run, we would predict that the bias is positive and substantial. In other words, the extent of the importance of permanent income is overstated because of the specification error. This guess is borne out when the correctly specified model is estimated. The results are:

$$\hat{M}_t = .3067 + \underset{(.14284)}{.06158}\, Y_{pt} + \underset{(.0940)}{.3274}\, Y_t - \underset{(.0597)}{.3325}\, R_t + \underset{(.0669)}{.5878}\, M_{t-1} \qquad R^2 = .9988$$

The M_{t-1} coefficient is positive and significant, while the Y_{pt} coefficient is positive but is insignificant at the 5 percent level. Thus, the original conclusion ought to be revised to state that current income is more important than permanent income in explaining the demand for money.

[†] L. D. Taylor and J. P. Newhouse, "On the Long-Run and Short-Run Demand for Money: A Comment," *Journal of Political Economy*, vol. 77, pp. 851–856, 1969.

5.6 THE MULTIPLE REGRESSION MODEL WITH STOCHASTIC EXPLANATORY VARIABLES

To this point we have assumed that the independent variables in the multiple regression model were fixed in repeated samples, i.e., nonstochastic. In practice, such an assumption is likely to be unreasonable, given that we infrequently have the opportunity to repeat an experiment a second time. The analysis of economic and social science behavior usually consists of looking at past occurrences, which are not likely to be repeated. Fortunately for most of the work completed to this point, it is possible to assume that the X's are drawn at random from a probability distribution and still maintain most of the previous results. In this spirit we will make the following assumptions:

i. The distribution of each of the explanatory variables is independent of the true regression parameters.
ii. Each of the explanatory variables is distributed independently of the true errors in the model.

In interpreting the multiple regression problem, we might think of the set of N observations on Y being drawn simultaneously with the set of N observations on each of the independent variables. In theory many such N observation drawings of Y's and X's could be made. But, it is useful to focus on the estimated parameters associated with a *given* drawing of the X's. Then the previous results for the multiple regression model apply, and we may think of the estimated regression parameters as being estimated *conditional* on the given values of the X's. From this perspective, least-squares estimators will remain unbiased in the sample. However, if we examine the unconditional properties of the OLS estimator, lack of bias is no longer guaranteed. In particular, if we drop assumption ii and replace it with the assumption that each of the explanatory variables is *uncorrelated* with the error term, *least squares* becomes biased. Fortunately it is still possible to show that OLS is consistent and for large samples (asymptotically) efficient. Finally it is also true that least-squares estimators are the maximum-likelihood estimators of the true regression parameters.

Because of the preceding results concerning stochastic explanatory variables (and the fact that estimators are often biased for other reasons), econometricians tend to focus on the large sample properties of estimators such as consistency. We will tend to do the same, especially in Chapters 7 and 11, where simultaneous-equation models are discussed.†

---

† In fact we will occasionally use the plim (probability limit) notation introduced briefly in Chapter 2 to define consistency. For a more detailed discussion of this subject, including a further analysis of the properties of OLS and other estimators, see A. Goldberger, *Topics in Regression Analysis* (New York: Macmillan, 1968), chap. 7.

APPENDIX 5.1 TESTS INVOLVING
DUMMY VARIABLE COEFFICIENTS

As normally used in multiple regression analysis, the coefficients on each dummy variable measure the differential impact between the indicated category (receiving a value of 1) and the category or dummy which has been dropped from the regression. As a result, the t test tests the null hypothesis that membership in the included and excluded categories have identical impacts. When there are two or more *sets* of dummy variables, this can make the regression results somewhat difficult to interpret and the t test is inappropriate. The difficulty can best be seen if we consider an example. Assume that we are predicting total expenditures on housing for homeowners as a function of income and number of children, each of which has been classified into a number of classes or categories. To be specific, let

H = annual expenditures on housing

$$I_1 = \begin{cases} 1 & \text{if income} < \$10,000 \text{ (low income)} \\ 0 & \text{otherwise} \end{cases}$$

$$I_2 = \begin{cases} 1 & \text{if income} > \$10,000 \text{ but} < \$20,000 \text{ (middle income)} \\ 0 & \text{otherwise} \end{cases}$$

$$I_3 = \begin{cases} 1 & \text{if income} > \$20,000 \text{ (high income)} \\ 0 & \text{otherwise} \end{cases}$$

$$C_1 = \begin{cases} 1 & \text{if no children} \\ 0 & \text{otherwise} \end{cases}$$

$$C_2 = \begin{cases} 1 & \text{if 1 or 2 children} \\ 0 & \text{otherwise} \end{cases}$$

$$C_3 = \begin{cases} 1 & \text{if more than 2 children} \\ 0 & \text{otherwise} \end{cases}$$

When we drop the first dummy variable in each category but include a constant term, the model specification is

$$H = \alpha + \beta_2 I_2 + \beta_3 I_3 + \gamma_2 C_2 + \gamma_3 C_3 + \varepsilon$$

With this specification β_2 measures the differential expenditures on housing for an individual with no children and a \$10,000 to \$20,000 income relative to an individual with no children and less than \$10,000 in income. The t test on $\hat{\beta}_2$ tests the null hypothesis that housing expenditures are equal for both groups. The comparison is thus made relative to *all* categories represented by dummies which have been dropped from the model. Frequently this comparison will not be a particularly useful one for the researcher. A more constructive analysis might involve the measurement of the differential expenditures on housing of a middle-income individual relative to a low-income individual, both of whom have the *average* number of children of all individuals in the sample.† The corresponding t test would not depend on the characteristics of all omitted dummies. In this way each set of dummy variable coefficients has intuitive meaning independent of the categories of the remaining dummy variables in the model.

To see how the same data can be used to yield a multiple regression whose coefficients can be interpreted in this manner, consider the following list of variables and revised specification of the original model:

$$J_1 = \begin{cases} 1 & \text{if low income} \\ 0 & \text{if middle income} \\ -1 & \text{if high income} \end{cases} \qquad J_2 = \begin{cases} 1 & \text{if middle income} \\ 0 & \text{if low income} \\ -1 & \text{if high income} \end{cases}$$

$$D_1 = \begin{cases} 1 & \text{if no children} \\ 0 & \text{if 1 or 2} \\ -1 & \text{if more than 2} \end{cases} \qquad D_2 = \begin{cases} 1 & \text{if 1 or 2 children} \\ 0 & \text{if none} \\ -1 & \text{if more than 2} \end{cases}$$

$$H = a + b_1 J_1 + b_2 J_2 + c_1 D_1 + c_2 D_2 + \varepsilon$$

We can see how the coefficients are interpreted by doing some simple arithmetic. For all possible combinations of family characteristics, we calculate the expected value of the dependent variable:

Category	Expected value $E(H)$
Low income, 0 children	$a + b_1 + c_1$
Middle income, 0 children	$a + b_2 + c_1$
High income, 0 children	$a - b_1 - b_2 + c_2$
Low income, 1 or 2 children	$a + b_1 + c_2$
Middle income, 1 or 2 children	$a + b_2 + c_2$
High income, 1 or 2 children	$a - b_1 - b_2 + c_2$
Low income, more than 2 children	$a + b_1 - c_1 - c_2$
Middle income, more than 2 children	$a + b_2 - c_1 - c_2$
High income, more than 2 children	$a - b_1 - b_2 - c_1 - c_2$

If we then sum over all nine categories we find that the overall expected value or average effect is equal to a, the constant term. If we sum all categories taken in combinations of three (for example, 0 children, 1 or 2 children, more than 2 children), we find that the average effect for each category or group is also a.

With this background the interpretation of the coefficients becomes straightforward. For example, b_1 measures the extent to which low-income individuals spend differentially on housing *relative to the average individual in the sample.* c_1 measures the differential spending associated with having no children. For individuals with no children and low incomes, the differential is $b_1 + c_1$. The t test associated with b_1 then provides a test of the null hypothesis that the spending of low-income individuals is different from the average, while

† Much of the motivation for this discussion comes from F. Andrews, J. Morgan, and S. Sonquist, *Multiple Classification Analysis* (Ann Arbor: The Institute for Social Research, 1973).

the t test associated with c_1 tests whether families with no children spend differently from the average.

There is, of course, a close relationship between the coefficients in both models since the information contained in both is identical.

$$\beta_2 = b_2 - b_1 \qquad \beta_3 = -2b_1 - b_2$$

$$\gamma_2 = c_2 - c_1 \qquad \gamma_3 = -2c_1 - c_2 \qquad \alpha = a + b_1 + c_1$$

Which alternative specification of the form for dummy variables should one choose? The answer depends upon the use to which the results are to be put. Our new suggestion about specification is somewhat more complicated from a computational point of view, and the t tests which result are different from those arising directly from the usual specification; the choice therefore depends in part upon which null hypotheses one would like to test easily and directly. In many cases the null hypotheses associated with the alternative specification are more appropriate than the ones arising directly from the usual dummy-variable specification. Since these hypotheses involve linear relationships between coefficients, they can be calculated from the original results using the variance-covariance matrix, but these calculations are quite tedious. Finally, the newer specification can be especially useful when there are large sets of dummy-variable predictors because it makes their interpretation quite straightforward. However, when one or more of the predictors is a continuous variable, the interpretation becomes more difficult and the advantage of the procedure begins to disappear.

EXERCISES

5.1 Prove that the omission of a variable from a "true" regression model will lead in general to a biased estimate of the regression intercept. Under what special conditions will the bias become zero?

5.2 Assume that the true regression model is of the form

$$y_i = \beta_2 x_{2i} + \beta_3 x_{2i}^2 + \varepsilon_i$$

If the regression $y_i = \beta_2^* x_{2i} + \varepsilon_i^*$ is run, what can you say about the direction of the bias of the slope coefficient?

5.3 Prove that the coefficient of an irrelevant variable will have expected value of 0. *Hint:* Using the analog of Eq. (5.40), solve for the estimated parameter $\hat{\beta}_3^*$ and then take expected values.

5.4 Prove that the inclusion of an irrelevant variable does not bias the estimated intercept parameter.

5.5 Suppose that you believe that the true model is given by $Y = \beta_2 X_2 + \beta_3 X_3 \ldots \beta_k X_k + \varepsilon$. What is gained or lost by running the regression on the model $Y = \beta_1 + \beta_2 X_2 + \beta_3 X_3 \ldots \beta_k X_k + \varepsilon$?

5.6 Given the model

$$\log Y = \beta_1 + \beta_2 \log X_2 + \beta_3 \log X_3 + \varepsilon$$

prove that the estimated regression coefficients are the elasticities associated with Y and each of the X's and that these elasticities are constant over the regression line.

5.7 We wish to analyze student housing demand in the Ann Arbor campus area from the rental data given in Table 2.1. As a measure of the demand for a unit's services, construct the variables RENT PER and ROOM PER, defined as follows: RENT PER = RENT (per unit)/NO (number of persons in unit). (RENT PER is listed as RPP in Chap. 2.) ROOM PER = rooms (RM)/NO (number of persons). Then estimate the models:

I $\qquad$ RENT PER $= \beta_1 + \beta_2(SEX) + \beta_3(ROOM\ PER) + \beta_4(DIST) + \varepsilon$

II $\qquad$ RENT PER $= \beta_1 + \beta_3(ROOM\ PER) + \beta_4(DIST) + \varepsilon$

(In model II, β_2 is constrained to be zero.)

(a) In model I, test the hypothesis that $\beta_3 = 0$ (as opposed to $\beta_3 > 0$). Is this what you would expect?

(b) In model I, test the hypothesis that $\beta_4 = 0$ (as opposed to $\beta_4 < 0$). Is this what you would expect?

(c) In model I, use a t test to test the hypothesis that $\beta_2 = 0$. Now using the sum of squared residuals from the estimates of models I and II, do an F test to test the hypothesis that $\beta_2 = 0$. You should recall that if $X = (ESS_{II} - ESS_I)/(ESS_I/32 - 4)$, X follows an F distribution with $(1, 28)$ degrees of freedom. How are the two tests in part (c) related?

5.8 It is suggested that men and women may not have the same appreciation for spaciousness (as measured by ROOM PER) or for proximity to campus (as measured by DIST). Estimate model III.

III $\quad$ RENT PER $= \beta_1 + \beta_2(SEX) + \beta_3(ROOM\ PER) + \beta_4(DIST) + \beta_5[(ROOM\ PER(SEX)]$

$$+ \beta_6[(DIST(SEX)] + \varepsilon$$

(a) Test separately the hypotheses that $\beta_5 = 0$ and that $\beta_6 = 0$.
(b) Use an F test to test the joint hypothesis that $\beta_5 = \beta_6 = 0$.
(c) Compute $\bar{R}^2$ for models I, II, and III.

5.9 The results from Exercise 5.8 suggest that the demand for housing by men and women is fundamentally different. To see just how different it is, do the following. Divide the data into two groups according to sex and estimate the models:

IV $\qquad$ RENT PER $= \alpha_0 + \alpha_1(ROOM\ PER) + \alpha_2(DIST) + \varepsilon$ $\quad$ males only

V $\qquad$ RENT PER $= \gamma_0 + \gamma_1(ROOM\ PER) + \gamma_2(DIST) + \varepsilon$ $\quad$ females only

(a) Test separately the hypotheses that $\gamma_1 = 0$ and that $\gamma_2 = 0$.
(b) Test the joint hypothesis that $\gamma_1 = \gamma_2 = 0$.

5.10 How can you recover the estimates of $\gamma_0, \gamma_1, \gamma_2$ (Exercise 5.9) from the estimates of $\beta_1, \beta_2, \beta_3, \beta_4, \beta_5,$ and β_6 in model III?

5.11 How would you interpret (economically) the coefficients γ_1 and γ_2 (from Exercise 5.10)? Why might γ_2 be positive?

5.12 In Model I (Exercise 5.7), compute the beta coefficients associated with each explanatory variable.

SERIAL CORRELATION AND HETEROSCEDASTICITY

Having completed a discussion of the classical normal linear regression model, it seems natural to review each of the model's assumptions in turn. Our goal is to determine those situations in which the assumptions are violated and to find estimation procedures which improve upon the ordinary least-squares procedure when such violations occur. The assumptions are listed below to refresh the reader's memory:

1. The model is specified as

$$Y_i = \beta_1 + \beta_2 X_{2i} + \beta_3 X_{3i} + \cdots + \beta_k X_{ki} + \varepsilon_i \qquad (6.1)$$

2. The X's have finite mean and variance and are uncorrelated with the errors in the model. No linear relationship exists between two or more of the independent variables (no collinearity).
3. The errors are independently distributed from a normal population with 0 expected value and constant variance.

We have seen from the previous chapter that the assumption that the model is correct as specified in Eq. (6.1) is an important one. In practice one usually does not have sufficient knowledge to specify accurately both the relevant functional form and the variables which should appear in the model. The problem of collinearity has been detailed in Chapter 4 and will not be pursued further here. The problem arising when the X's and the error term are correlated will be treated separately in the following chapter.

The third assumption consists of several important parts. The assumption of normality was discussed in Chapter 3. Even without the normality assumption, it is possible to prove that least-squares regression estimates of the true underlying parameters are unbiased as well as consistent. In fact, least-squares estimates remain BLUE. However, without the normality assumption one cannot use the standard formulas for the t and F distributions to perform statistical tests.†️ Fortunately, the central-limit theorem (see Chapter 2) provides a rationale for using standard statistical tests as approximately correct for reasonably large sample sizes.

There are statistical methods which allow one to test for normality, but these tests are seldom used by econometricians.‡️ The primary reason is that the tests are not statistically powerful, in the sense that one may often fail to reject the null hypothesis of normality even when the error distribution is nonnormal.§️ In addition, were we to decide that the normality assumption was invalid, alternative estimation procedures and statistical tests would be substantially more complicated than those associated with the normal classical regression model.

The assumption that the error term has a zero expected value is usually not seriously considered by econometricians. The reason is that if the error has a nonzero expected value, the estimated regression slope parameters will remain unchanged while the intercept will pick up the effect of the nonzero expected value. It will, of course, be impossible to differentiate between the true intercept and the nonzero expected value in the error term, but in most econometric applications the intercept term is not of central concern. The assumption of the independence of the errors i.e., no serial correlation, will be considered in Section 6.2, while Section 6.1 will focus on the assumption that the errors have constant variance.

6.1 HETEROSCEDASTICITY

There are occasions in econometric modeling when the assumption of constant error variance, or *homoscedasticity*, will be unreasonable. For example, if one is examining a cross section of firms in one industry, there may be reason to

---

† In addition, it is impossible to prove that ordinary least-squares estimates are maximum likelihood, since the maximum-likelihood approach depends critically upon the assumption of normality. However, it is possible to show that even in small samples, t and F tests are likely to be approximately valid when the error distribution deviates from normality. For details, see, for example, H. Theil, *Principles of Econometrics* (New York: Wiley, 1971), chap. 8.

‡ One direct test would proceed as follows. Calculate the standardized residuals from a multiple regression by dividing each residual by the standard error of the regression. If the errors are normal, the distribution of standardized residuals should be unit-normal. A nonparametric (no assumption is made about probability distributions) test can then be used to see whether the distribution of standardized residuals is statistically different from the unit-normal distribution. (The use of the Kolmogorov-Smirnov test is described in H. D. Brunk, *An Introduction to Mathematical Statistics* (New York: Blaisdell, 1965), p. 363. For a discussion of other statistical tests, see G. S. Maddala, *Econometrics* (New York: McGraw-Hill, 1977), pp. 305–307.

§ For further discussion of this issue see F. J. Anscombe and J. W. Tukey, "The Examination and Analysis of Residuals," *Technometrics*, vol. 5, pp. 141–162, 1963.

believe that error terms associated with very large firms have larger variances than error terms associated with smaller firms; sales of larger firms might be more volatile than sales of smaller firms. Or consider a cross-section study of family income and expenditures.† It seems plausible to expect that low-income individuals would spend at a rather steady rate, while the spending patterns of high-income families would be relatively volatile. The regularity of low-income spending occurs because most expenditures are on the necessities of life, making large fluctuations a physical impossibility. This suggests that in a model where expenditures are the dependent variable, error variances associated with high-income families would be greater than their low-income counterparts. *Heteroscedasticity*, or unequal variances, does not usually occur in time-series studies, because changes in the dependent variable and changes in one or more of the independent variables are likely to be of the same order of magnitude.‡ For example, in the aggregate-consumption-function examples of Chapter 3, both consumption and disposable income grow at about the same rate over time.

For a model with heteroscedastic error disturbances we will assume that each error term ε_i is normally distributed with variance σ_i^2, where the variance Var $(\varepsilon_i) = E(\varepsilon_i^2) = \sigma_i^2$ is not constant over observations. When heteroscedasticity is present, ordinary least-squares estimation places more weight on the observations which have large error variances than on those with small error variances. The implicit weighting of ordinary least squares occurs because the sum of squared residuals associated with large variance error terms is likely to be substantially greater than the sum of squared residuals associated with low variance errors. The regression line will be adjusted to minimize the total sum of squared residuals, and this can best be accomplished by guaranteeing a very good fit in the large variance portion of the data. Because of this implicit weighting, ordinary least-squares parameter estimates are unbiased and consistent, but they are not *efficient*; i.e., the variances of the estimated parameters are not the minimum variances. In addition, the *estimated variances* of the estimated parameters will be biased estimators of the true variance of the estimated parameters.

The fact that the parameter estimates are unbiased can be seen in the context of the two-variable model with variables measured as deviations about their means. Then

$$\hat{\beta} = \frac{\sum x_i y_i}{\sum x_i^2} = \frac{\sum x_i(\beta x_i + \varepsilon_i)}{\sum x_i^2} = \beta + \frac{\sum x_i \varepsilon_i}{\sum x_i^2}$$

and

$$E(\hat{\beta}) = \beta + \frac{E(\sum x_i \varepsilon_i)}{\sum x_i^2} = \beta$$

Notice that variances of the error terms play no role in the proof that least-squares estimates are unbiased.

---

† This example is studied in detail in S. J. Prais and H. S. Houthakker, *The Analysis of Family Budgets* (Cambridge: Cambridge University Press, 1955).

‡ Of course variances might fall over time as measurement techniques improved.

The difficulty with the variances of the estimated parameters can also be seen in the two-variable case. Then, from Chapter 3 we know that

$$\text{Var}\,(\hat{\beta}) = \frac{\sigma^2}{\Sigma x_i^2} \tag{6.2}$$

The variance of the error was taken out of the summation sign during the derivation because the variance was assumed constant. However, when heteroscedasticity is present, the variance is not constant and the derivation does not hold. The result is that the standard formula (6.2) will lead to biased estimates of the variances of each of the estimated parameters. If these biased estimates are used, statistical tests and confidence intervals will be incorrect.

The inefficiency of the least-squares estimator arises even if the variances of the parameter estimates are *correctly* determined. In this case, the variances will be larger than the variances associated with an alternative linear unbiased estimator, discussed in the following pages.†

6.1.1 Corrections for Heteroscedasticity

We discuss the appropriate estimation technique (which is unbiased, consistent, and efficient) in each of three conceptually separate cases. Each case relies to a different degree upon prior and sample information, but all involve relatively simple estimation procedures.

Case I: Known variances We first assume that sufficient prior knowledge is available for values of each of the error variances to be known; that is, $\text{Var}\,(\varepsilon_i) = \sigma_i^2$ is known *a priori*. The case of known variances occurs occasionally in econometric work but is especially important here in illustrating how to correct for heteroscedasticity. The appropriate technique, called *weighted least squares*, is a special case of a more general econometric technique, known as *generalized least squares*. A matrix derivation of the generalized least-squares procedure appears in Appendix 6.1.

The weighted least-squares estimation procedure, which can be derived from the maximum-likelihood function (see Appendix 3.2), is best illustrated in the two-variable model. The appropriate estimator is obtained by minimizing the expression

$$\Sigma \left(\frac{Y_i - \hat{\alpha} - \hat{\beta} X_i}{\sigma_i} \right)^2$$

$\hat{\alpha}$ and $\hat{\beta}$ are, of course, the desired parameter estimates. When the original variables are written in deviations form, the original objective is modified to that

† For a discussion of the consistency of estimators and further details about efficiency, see J. Kmenta, *Elements of Econometrics* (New York: Macmillan, 1971), sec. 8-1.

of minimizing the expression†

$$\sum \left(\frac{y_i - \hat{\beta} x_i}{\sigma_i} \right)^2$$

Solving for the least-squares parameter estimates (as in Chapter 1), we find that

$$\hat{\beta} = \frac{\sum x_i y_i / \sigma_i^2}{\sum x_i^2 / \sigma_i^2} = \frac{\sum (x_i / \sigma_i)(y_i / \sigma_i)}{\sum (x_i / \sigma_i)^2} = \frac{\sum x_i^* y_i^*}{\sum (x_i^*)^2} \qquad \text{where } x_i^* = x_i / \sigma_i$$

$$y_i^* = y_i / \sigma_i$$

Thus, the desired estimation procedure is accomplished by weighting the original data and then performing ordinary least-squares estimation upon the transformed model.

To use weighted least squares in the multiple-regression case, we redefine the variables in the original regression model of Eq. (6.1) as

$$Y_i^* = \frac{Y_i}{\sigma_i} \qquad X_{ji}^* = \frac{X_{ji}}{\sigma_i} \qquad j = 1, 2, \ldots, k \qquad \varepsilon_i^* = \frac{\varepsilon_i}{\sigma_i}$$

In place of the original linear model (6.1) we use the transformed model

$$Y_i^* = \beta_1 X_{1i}^* + \beta_2 X_{2i}^* + \cdots + \beta_k X_{ki}^* + \varepsilon_i^* \qquad (6.3)$$

or, equivalently, $\quad \dfrac{Y_i}{\sigma_i} = \beta_1 \dfrac{1}{\sigma_i} + \beta_2 \dfrac{X_{2i}}{\sigma_i} + \cdots + \beta_k \dfrac{X_{ki}}{\sigma_i} + \dfrac{\varepsilon_i}{\sigma_i}$

Note that the transformed error term is homoscedastic (has constant variance)‡

$$\text{Var}(\varepsilon_i^*) = \text{Var}\left(\frac{\varepsilon_i}{\sigma_i} \right) = \frac{1}{\sigma_i^2} \text{Var}(\varepsilon_i) = \frac{\sigma_i^2}{\sigma_i^2} = 1$$

Why does this procedure yield efficient parameter estimators? The reason is that by construction, the transformed model satisfies all the assumptions of the classical linear regression model (including constant error variance). We know therefore (according to the Gauss-Markov theorem) that the estimators must be efficient.

Unfortunately the analysis just completed is limited in its applicability because the individual error variances are not always known. In fact the necessary information for the application of weighted least squares is the *relative* magnitude of the error variances. Such information may be available, particularly in cross-section studies for which substantial prior empirical evidence is available, but there are many situations in which the relative magnitude of the error variances is not known in advance. This suggests that one might consider

† To be correct, the deviations form must be obtained by transforming the model (dividing by σ_i) and then subtracting variable means.

‡ In addition it is worth noting that in the transformed equation the intercept is multiplied by a variable which varies over time. For many regression programs this means that the usual constant term must be suppressed.

special cases in which sufficient sample information is available to make reasonable guesses of the true error variances.

Case II: Unknown variances to be estimated from the sample In most econometric models only one value of the dependent variable is associated with each given set of independent variable observations. In this case, if no prior information is available, it will be impossible to obtain estimates of the variances of the individual error terms. However, if several observations are available (at least two) for each set of observations on the independent variables, then a solution to the problem does exist. Since such a situation occurs infrequently in actual economic and business applications, we shall not describe the proper estimation procedure in detail. Instead, we consider a simple example which makes use of the presence of multiple observations on each dependent variable (associated with *each* set of independent variables).† Note that in models with several independent variables this case would be unlikely simply because the number of combinations of observations on the independent variables would itself be large.

Example 6.1 Housing expenditures In this example we consider a cross-section study of annual housing expenditures and annual income of a group of families. The sample consists of 20 observations, divided into four groups of five each. The sample within each group was obtained (hypothetically) by determining housing expenditures of five families with the identical income. The data are listed below:

Group	Housing expenditures, $000					Income, $000
1	1.8	2.0	2.0	2.0	2.1	5.0
2	3.0	3.2	3.5	3.5	3.6	10.0
3	4.2	4.2	4.5	4.8	5.0	15.0
4	4.8	5.0	5.7	6.0	6.2	20.0

The housing-expenditure model is hypothesized to be

$$Y_i = \alpha + \beta X_i + \varepsilon_i$$

where Y_i is housing expenditures and X_i is income. An ordinary least-squares regression yields the following regression estimates (t statistics in parentheses):

$$Y_i = 890.0 + .237 \, X_i \qquad R^2 = .93 \qquad F = 252.7$$
$$\quad\;\; (4.4) \quad\;\; (15.9)$$

A graphical examination of both the data and knowledge of prior expenditure studies suggested that heteroscedasticity is present in the model.

---

† For details concerning this procedure see Kmenta, op. cit., pp. 264–267.

(We shall discuss the correct statistical tests later in the chapter.) Given that data are available by *groups* of the dependent variable, correcting for heteroscedasticity using the principles of case II is possible. Independent estimates of the error variances associated *within each group* are approximated by calculating the sample variance of housing expenditures Y. These estimated variances are 9,800, 50,400, 102,400, and 302,400 for groups 1 to 4, respectively. When the corrected case II procedure is used, a slightly higher estimate of the income regression coefficient is obtained and all coefficients are significant at the 5 percent level.

Case III: Error variances vary directly with an independent variable When the error variance is not known and it is impossible to estimate error variances using grouped data, we must search for another source of information. One possibility is the existence of a relationship between the error variances and the values of one of the explanatory variables in the regression model. Specifically we assume that

$$\text{Var}(\varepsilon_i) = CX_i^2$$

where C is a nonzero constant and X_i is an observation on one of the independent variables. This type of information about error variances is likely to occur quite frequently in both macroeconomic and microeconomic empirical studies. For example, in the housing-expenditure example (Example 6.1) it may be reasonable to assume that the error variance is proportional to the square of the income variable. To illustrate the use of weighted least squares in case III, assume, for example, that $\text{Var}(\varepsilon_i) = CX_{2i}^2$ in the general linear regression model

$$Y_i = \beta_1 + \beta_2 X_{2i} + \cdots + \beta_k X_{ki} + \varepsilon_i$$

Then, proceeding as in case I, we use weighted least squares as the correct estimation procedure. To do so, we redefine the variables in the above equation as follows (the value of the constant C does not affect the weighted least-squares procedure):

$$Y_i^* = \frac{Y_i}{X_{2i}} \qquad X_{ji}^* = \frac{X_{ji}}{X_{2i}} \qquad j = 1, 2, \ldots, k \qquad \varepsilon_i^* = \frac{\varepsilon_i}{X_{2i}}$$

The transformed regression equation is

$$\frac{Y_i}{X_{2i}} = \beta_1 \frac{1}{X_{2i}} + \beta_2 + \beta_3 \frac{X_{3i}}{X_{2i}} + \cdots + \beta_k \frac{X_{ki}}{X_{2i}} + \frac{\varepsilon_i}{X_{2i}} \tag{6.4}$$

We can see that the transformed error term is homoscedastic, since

$$\text{Var}(\varepsilon_i^*) = \text{Var}\left(\frac{\varepsilon_i}{X_{2i}}\right) = \frac{1}{X_{2i}^2}\text{Var}(\varepsilon_i) = C$$

In this particular case the original intercept term has become a variable term, while the slope parameter associated with the variable X_2 has become the new intercept term. Ordinary least-squares regression estimates of the parameters in

Eq. (6.4) will yield the appropriate (efficient) parameter estimates, since the errors in the transformed equation are homoscedastic.†

Example 6.2   Housing expenditures The housing-expenditure model (Example 6.1) can be estimated with a correction for heteroscedasticity as suggested by case III. The transformed model is

$$\frac{Y_i}{X_i} = \beta^* + \alpha^* \frac{1}{X_i} + \varepsilon_i^*$$

and the regression results are

$$\frac{\hat{Y}_i}{X_i} = \underset{(21.3)}{.249} + \underset{(7.7)}{752.9} \frac{1}{X_i} \qquad R^2 = .76 \qquad F = 58.7$$

Notice that the revised estimate of the regression coefficient associated with income is .249, an increase over the ordinary least-squares estimate. As expected, the correct use of t and F statistics still allows one to conclude that all regression coefficients are significant at the 5 percent level. Note that the R^2 measure associated with the weighted least-squares procedure is lower than the R^2 associated with the unweighted procedure. The decline in R^2 should not be taken as an indication that the heteroscedasticity correction was incorrect, since the weighted least-squares procedure involves the use of a transformed dependent variable.

The reported R^2 therefore fails to provide a useful measure of goodness of fit for the original (unweighted model). A better measure would be to use the original equation and the efficient parameter estimates to calculate regression residuals. In this case the residuals $\hat{\varepsilon}_i$ would be calculated from $\hat{\varepsilon}_i = Y_i - 752.9 - .249X_i$. We then have two choices for measuring goodness of fit. First, we can use the standard R^2 formula to calculate $1 - \text{ESS/TSS}$. This R^2 calculation is always less than the ordinary least-squares measure of R^2 (why?) and has the undesirable property of not necessarily being between 0 and 1. For that reason we suggest a second alternative. We use the efficiently estimated parameters to estimate fitted values $\hat{Y}_i = 752.9 + .249X_i$ and use as our measure of goodness of fit the square of the simple correlation between Y_i and $\hat{Y}_i$. In this particular example both choices yielded measures of fit to be .92. In other cases the two goodness-of-fit measures could differ substantially from each other. Econometricians tend not to use either method of goodness of fit, in part because of computational problems and in part because their focus of interest is not on goodness of fit in the first place.

6.1.2   Tests for Heteroscedasticity

Having discussed modifications of the least-squares procedure in three separate cases, it is natural to consider whether appropriate statistical procedures can be

† For additional details see ibid., pp. 257–264.

found to test for heteroscedasticity. In each case we wish to find a test of the null hypothesis of *homoscedasticity*, that is, $\sigma_1^2 = \sigma_2^2 = \sigma_3^2 = \cdots = \sigma_N^2$, where N is the number of observations. The specific alternative hypothesis against which the null hypothesis is to be tested depends upon the estimation procedure considered to yield the most desirable correction for heteroscedasticity. Recall that two of the three cases of heteroscedasticity involved corrective techniques which were dependent upon the sample data collected. We will therefore discuss three statistical tests, each using the data to test homoscedasticity against an alternative hypothesis of heteroscedasticity. The first test (case II) does not involve a specific assumption about the nature of the heteroscedasticity, but it does depend heavily upon the data being grouped in the appropriate manner and is of limited value. The second test procedure involves a very specific alternative hypothesis, which is consistent with the model described in case III. The final test allows for somewhat more general alternative hypotheses and is also consistent with case III.

Case II: Bartlett's test† Assume that there are N observations available for a regression model in which the data are associated with G groups, each of which has a distinct set of independent variable observations. Let N_1 be the number of observations associated with the first group, N_2 the number associated with the second group, and in general N_g the number of observations associated with the gth group, $g = 1, 2 \ldots G$. Also let $\bar{Y}_g$ be the mean of the sample values of Y within the gth group. The assumption of repeated experimental situations may be valid in practice, but even if not, it is possible to make the test an approximate one. The test procedure appears quite complex, but it is quite easy to apply in practice. It involves the calculation of a test statistic (with a known probability distribution) which is based on estimates of the error variances as provided by estimates of the variances of the dependent variable associated with each set of independent variable observations. More specifically, the test procedure is as follows:

1. Estimate $s_g^2 = (1/N_g) \sum_{i=1}^{N_g} (Y_i - \bar{Y}_g)^2$ for each group of observations, $g = 1, 2, \ldots, G$. s_g^2 can be shown‡ to provide a consistent estimate of σ_g^2.
2. Calculate the test statistic S:

$$S = - \frac{N \log \left(\sum_{g=1}^{G} \frac{N_g}{N} s_g^2 \right) - \sum_{g=1}^{G} N_g \log s_g^2}{1 + \frac{1}{3(G-1)} \left(\sum_{g=1}^{G} \frac{1}{N_g} - \frac{1}{N} \right)}$$

† See A. M. Mood, *Introduction to the Theory of Statistics* (New York: McGraw-Hill, 1950), pp. 269–270; or Edward J. Kane, *Economic Statistics and Econometrics* (New York: Harper & Row, 1968), pp. 373–374.

‡ For further details see Mood, op. cit.; and J. B. Ramsey, "Tests for Specification Errors in Classical Linear Least-Squares Regression Analysis," *Journal of the Royal Statistical Society*, ser. B, vol. 31, pp. 350–371, 1969.

3. Under the assumption of homoscedasticity, it is possible to show that S will be distributed as a chi-square statistic with $G - 1$ degrees of freedom.† Using a chi-square statistical table, we reject the null hypothesis of equal variances in all groups if S is greater than the critical value of the chi-square distribution at the chosen level of significance.
4. If the null hypothesis is rejected, we apply the modification of least squares as described previously.

Example 6.3 Bartlett's test Bartlett's test can be applied to the housing-expenditure example described in Examples 6.1 and 6.2. Recall that the model is $Y_i = \alpha + \beta X_i + \varepsilon_i$, where Y represents housing expenditure and X represents income. The data are divided into four groups of five observations each. The estimated values of s_g^2 (9,800, 50,400, 102,400, and 302,400) are used in the calculation of the test statistic S, for which a value of 10.7 is obtained. Under the null hypothesis that σ_g^2 is constant, the test statistic S will follow the chi-square distribution with 3 degrees of freedom (the number of groups minus 1). At the 5 percent level the critical value of the chi-square distribution is 7.81. Thus, we can reject the null hypothesis of homoscedasticity at the 5 percent level of significance.

Case III: Goldfeld-Quandt test‡ Assume that we are considering a two-variable model and wish to test the null hypothesis of homoscedasticity against the alternative hypothesis that $\sigma_i^2 = CX_i^2$, as described in case III of the previous section. The Goldfeld-Quandt test procedure is quite simple to apply. It involves the calculation of two least-squares regression lines, one using data thought to be associated with low variance errors and the other using data thought to be associated with high variance errors. If the residual variances associated with each regression line are approximately equal, the homoscedasticity assumption cannot be rejected, but if the residual variance increases substantially, it is possible to reject the null hypothesis. The Goldfeld-Quandt test can be carried out in the following manner:

1. Order the data by the magnitude of the independent variable X, which is thought to be related to the error variance.
2. Omit the middle d observations. d might be chosen, for example, to be approximately one-fifth of the total sample size.
3. Fit two separate regressions, the first (indicated by subscript 1) for the portion of the data associated with low values of X, and the second (indicated by subscript 2) associated with high values of X. Each regression will involve $(N - d)/2$ pieces of data and $[(N - d)/2] - 2$ degrees of freedom. d must

---

† See P. G. Hoel, *Introduction to Mathematical Statistics*, 2d ed. (New York: Wiley, 1955), p. 195.
‡ S. M. Goldfeld and R. E. Quandt, "Some Tests for Homoscedasticity," *Journal of the American Statistical Society*, vol. 60, pp. 539–547, 1965.

be small enough to ensure that enough degrees of freedom are available to allow for the proper estimation of each of the separate regressions.

4. Calculate the residual sum of squares associated with each regression, ESS_1, associated with low X's, and ESS_2, associated with high X's. (ESS is described in Chapter 3.)

5. Assuming that the error process is normally distributed (and no serial correlation is present), the statistic ESS_2/ESS_1 will be distributed as an F statistic with $(N - d - 4)/2$ degrees of freedom in both the numerator and the denominator. We can reject the null hypothesis at a chosen level of significance if the calculated statistic is greater than the critical value of the F distribution as determined from an F table.

The Goldfeld-Quandt test can easily be applied to the general linear model by ordering the observations by the magnitude of one of the independent variables. The number of degrees of freedom in the F statistic will be $(N - d - 2k)/2$, where k is the number of independent variables (including a constant term) in the model. The Goldfeld-Quandt test works because it allows for the independent regression estimation of high and low observation data. However, there is an important cost involved. Because no restrictions are made on the regression parameters (as well as the error variances) in each of the two regressions run, statistical power is lost. A more powerful test would take into account the information that the regression parameters are identical for both sets of data and that only the error variance has changed. Finally, the choice of the number of middle observations to eliminate from the test is somewhat arbitrary. If no middle observations are eliminated, the test is still correct, but experience shows that elimination of observations associated with errors of almost equal variance from the test procedure improves the power of the test.†

Example 6.1 Goldfeld-Quandt test The Goldfeld-Quandt test can be applied to the housing-expenditure example used previously. The data are divided into two samples, the first including those with incomes of $5,000 and $10,000 and the second including higher-income families ($15,000 and $20,000). No middle observations are dropped from the sample because a natural break in the data is available without observations begin omitted. The output associated with the two separate regression equations is as follows (t statistics in parentheses):

I   Low-income families:

$$Y_i = \underset{(3.1)}{600.0} + \underset{(11.3)}{.276}\, X_i \qquad R^2 = .94 \qquad ESS_1 = 3.0 \times 10^5$$

II   High-income families:

$$Y_i = \underset{(1.4)}{1,540.0} + \underset{(3.1)}{.20}\, X_i \qquad R^2 = .55 \qquad ESS_2 = 20.2 \times 10^5$$

† See ibid.

The F statistic used to test the homoscedasticity assumption is $\text{ESS}_2/\text{ESS}_1$ = 6.7. Under the null hypothesis this will be distributed as F with 8 degrees of freedom in the numerator and the denominator. Examination of the table of the F distribution shows that the critical value of the F at the 1 percent level of significance is 3.44. We conclude that we can reject the null hypothesis in favor of the alternative hypothesis of heteroscedasticity.

Case III: Park-Glejser test† One of the difficulties with the Goldfeld-Quandt test and other tests for heteroscedasticity is that the test itself does not help one to compare a series of alternative hypotheses about the form that heteroscedasticity might take, and it does not provide a constructive means by which such adjustments might be made. On the other hand, an examination of the residual pattern does not allow one to test hypotheses about heteroscedasticity statistically. The following proposed tests are based directly on the work of Glejser and Park. While there are some serious problems associated with the tests, they have the advantage of being easy to use and constructive. Consider the following model, which includes an assumption about the relationship between the true error variance and an independent variable X (this is Park's suggestion):

$$Y_i = \alpha + \beta X_i + \varepsilon_i \tag{6.5}$$

$$\text{Var}\,(\varepsilon_i) = \sigma_i^2 = \sigma^2 X_i^\delta e^{u_i} \tag{6.6}$$

where e is the base of natural logarithms and u_i is a homoscedastic error term. Taking natural logarithms of both sides of (6.6), we find that

$$\log \sigma_i^2 = \log \sigma^2 + \delta \log X_i + u_i \tag{6.7}$$

or $$\log \sigma_i^2 = \gamma + \delta \log X_i + u_i \tag{6.8}$$

If we estimate (6.5) using ordinary least squares, we can use the regression residuals to estimate Eq. (6.8) as

$$\log \hat{\varepsilon}_i^2 = \gamma + \delta \log X_i + u_i \tag{6.9}$$

We then perform a t test on the slope coefficient. If it is insignificantly different from 0, we assume that the residuals are homoscedastic. However, if the coefficient is significant, we can use that information to adjust the original model for heteroscedasticity. To make the adjustment we simply transform the original model in (6.5) dividing by $X_i^{\hat{\delta}/2}$. The transformed model (note that the constant term is omitted) is

$$\frac{Y_i}{X_i^{\hat{\delta}/2}} = \alpha \frac{1}{X_i^{\hat{\delta}/2}} + \beta X_i^{1 - \hat{\delta}/2} + \frac{\varepsilon_i}{X_i^{\hat{\delta}/2}}$$

† See H. Glejser, "A New Test for Heteroscedasticity," *Journal of the American Statistical Association*, vol. 64, pp. 316–323, 1969; R. E. Park, "Estimation with Heteroscedastic Error Terms," *Econometrica*, vol. 34, no. 4, p. 888, October 1966; S. M. Goldfeld and R. E. Quandt, *Nonlinear Methods in Econometrics* (Amsterdam: North-Holland, 1972), Chap. 3.

This transformation reduces to the earlier case III example when $\hat{\delta} = 2$, so that Var (ε_i) is proportional to X_i^2. But whatever the value of $\hat{\delta}$, it should yield efficient results since

$$\text{Var}\left(\frac{\varepsilon_i}{X_i^{\hat{\delta}/2}}\right) = \frac{1}{X_i^{\hat{\delta}}}\text{Var}\ (\varepsilon_i) = \sigma^2 X_i^{(\delta-\hat{\delta})}e^{u_i}$$

Thus, as long as $\hat{\delta}$ provides a close estimate of δ, Var (ε_i) will be approximately constant and the Gauss-Markov theorem can be invoked.

The test and correction just discussed is appealing because it allows one to avoid making an arbitrary assumption about the exact form that the nonconstant error variance might take. However, a number of potentially serious problems limit the desirability of the test and must be considered when any application is made. First, the nature of the test causes the error term in (6.9) itself to be heteroscedastic. The result (as we have seen) is that the estimates of the standard errors and the corresponding t tests will be biased. Second, there is a one-stage estimation procedure for dealing with this sort of heteroscedasticity which is more complex technically (and thus not illustrated here) but which has the desirable outcome that all parameter estimators are maximum-likelihood estimators.†

We might conclude by pointing out that error specifications other than the one given in (6.6) are possible and have potentially different implications for estimation‡. For example, one can use the absolute value of the residuals $|\varepsilon_i|$ to estimate

$$|\hat{\varepsilon}_i| = a + bX_i + w_i \tag{6.10}$$

With this functional form, we must test the significance of both the intercept and the slope. If b is not different from zero, homoscedasticity is assumed to be the case. If b is significant but a is not, we can assume that Var $(\varepsilon_i) = b^2X_i^2$ and deflate each variable by X_i to adjust for heteroscedasticity. However, if both a and b are significantly different from zero, a more accurate model would be Var $(\varepsilon_i) = (a + bX_i)^2$, in which case it is appropriate to deflate by $\hat{a} + \hat{b}X_i$, rather than X_i itself. Of course, this correction procedure suffers from the same problems as the one described earlier.

Example 6.5 Park-Glejser test We applied two variations on the Park-Glejser test for heteroscedasticity to the housing-expenditure example. In both instances we used the residuals from the least-squares regression given in Example 6.1 to perform our tests. First, we regressed the natural logarithm of the square of the residuals on the natural logarithm of income, obtaining the following results (t statistics in parentheses):

$$\widehat{\log \hat{\varepsilon}_i^2} = \underset{(-1.4)}{-9.37} + \underset{(3.0)}{2.13} \log X_i \qquad R^2 = .33$$

---

† This procedure is discussed in Kmenta, op. cit.
‡ See Glejser, op. cit.

Since the slope coefficient is significantly different from 0 at the 5 percent level, we conclude (as previously) that heteroscedasticity is present. To obtain efficient parameter estimates we transformed the original model, dividing each variable (including the constant term) by $X_i^* = X_i^{1.065}$. The regression results were

$$\frac{\hat{Y}_i}{X_i^*} = \underset{(7.8)}{747.0}\left(\frac{1}{X_i^*}\right) + \underset{(21.3)}{.250}\, X^{-.065} \qquad R^2 = .76$$

Not surprisingly the results were very similar to the results obtained in Example 6.2, in which we deflated by X_i. Of course, the two results would not have been similar had the coefficient on $\log X_i$ been substantially different from 2, and that is just the reason that a test such as the Park-Glejser is more satisfactory than an arbitrary decision about how to deflate to correct for heteroscedasticity.

Second, we tested for heteroscedasticity by regressing the absolute values of the residuals on income with the following outcome:

$$|\hat{\varepsilon}_i| = \underset{(-0.3)}{-27.20} + \underset{(3.4)}{.0245}\, X_i \qquad R^2 = .40$$

Once again the t test for significance of the slope coefficient allows us to conclude that heteroscedasticity is present. Since the intercept was insignificant, we adjusted to obtain efficient estimates by deflating by X_i and obtaining results identical to those given in Example 6.2. Had the intercept been statistically significant as well, the adjusted coefficient estimates might have been somewhat different.

We should note that our use of t tests to make statistical inferences about the efficiently estimated model parameters is not strictly correct. When the weights used in the estimation have themselves been estimated, the parameter estimator no longer follows a t distribution. However, the distribution does approach a normal distribution as the sample size gets large, so that the use of t statistics *seems* to be a reasonably conservative approach to testing.

6.2 SERIAL CORRELATION

The assumption that errors corresponding to different observations are uncorrelated often breaks down in time-series studies but can be a problem in some cross-section work as well. Recall that when the error terms from different (usually adjacent) time periods (or cross-section observations) are correlated, we say that the error term is *autocorrelated* or *serially correlated*. Serial correlation occurs in time-series studies when the errors associated with observations in a given time period carry over into future time periods. For example, if we are predicting the growth of stock dividends, an overestimate in one year is likely to lead to overestimates in succeeding years.

In this section we deal with the problem of *first-order serial correlation*, in which errors in one time period are correlated directly with errors in the ensuing time period.† While it is certainly possible that serial correlation can be negative as well as positive, we concern ourselves primarily with the case of positive serial correlation, in which errors in one time period are positively correlated with errors in the next time period. Positive serial correlation frequently occurs in time-series studies, either because of correlation in the measurement error component of the error term or more likely, because of the high degree of correlation over time present in the cumulative effects of the omitted variables in the regression model.

As a general rule, the presence of serial correlation will not affect the unbiasedness or consistency of the ordinary least-squares regression estimators, but it does affect their efficiency.‡ In the case of positive serial correlation, this loss of efficiency will be masked by the fact that the estimates of the standard errors obtained from the least-squares regression will be smaller than the true standard errors. In other words, the regression estimators will be unbiased, but the standard error of the regression will be biased downward.§ This will lead to the conclusion that the parameter estimates are more precise than they actually are. There will be a tendency to reject the null hypothesis when, in fact, it should not be rejected. We shall not prove these results in the chapter, but one can obtain an intuitive feeling for why they are true by examining Fig. 6.1a and b.¶

Both graphs illustrate the presence of positive serial correlation in a model with a single independent explanatory variable. In Fig. 6.1a, the error term associated with the first observation happens to be positive. This leads to a series of error terms, the first four of which are positive and the last two of which are negative. In Fig. 6.1b, the oppositive case has occurred, the first four errors being negative, and the last two being positive. In the first case the estimated regression slope is lower than the true slope, while in the second case it is higher. Since both cases are equally likely to occur, it seems reasonable that least-squares slope estimates will be correct on average; i.e., they will be unbiased. However, in both cases, the least-squares regression lines fit the observed sample data points more closely than the true regression line; this leads to an R^2 that gives an overly optimistic picture of the success of least-squares regression. More important, however, least squares will lead to an estimate of the error variance which is smaller than the true error variance.‖ Once again the success of the regression procedure will be overstated if the least-squares estimate of the error variance is used to do statistical tests.

---

† The more general case can be handled with the use of generalized least-squares estimation, as detailed in Appendix 6.1 and with time-series techniques discussed in Part Three.

‡ If the model includes a lagged dependent variable, the problems are much more severe. The lagged-dependent-variable case will be discussed briefly in Section 7.7.

§ This holds provided that the X's are not negatively serially correlated.

¶ Some of these assertions are proved in Appendix 6.1.

‖ For a discussion of the lack of bias and consistency of the parameter estimators as well as details concerning efficiency, see Kmenta, op. cit., sec. 8-2.

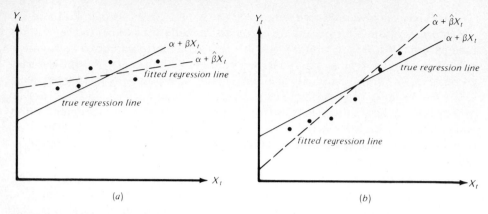

Figure 6.1 Positive serial correlation.

We proceed at this point to discuss several possible solutions to the problem of serial correlation and then suggest a means by which one might test for the presence of serial correlation. However, the reader should bear in mind that both the solutions to the serial-correlation problem and the tests themselves have certain shortcomings. There are cases, for example, when the use of alternative procedures to deal with the serial-correlation problem introduces inefficiencies which are greater than the inefficiency associated with serial correlation. Thus, judgment must be exercised in the choice of estimation techniques.

6.2.1 Corrections for Serial Correlation

We assume that each of the error terms in a linear regression model is drawn from a normal population with 0 expected value and constant variance but that the errors are not independent over time. Since serial correlation is usually present in time-series data, we use a subscript of t (in place of i) and assume that the total number of observations is T. The model is†

$$Y_t = \beta_1 + \beta_2 X_{2t} + \beta_3 X_{3t} + \cdots + \beta_k X_{kt} + \varepsilon_t \tag{6.11}$$

$$\varepsilon_t = \rho\varepsilon_{t-1} + v_t \qquad 0 \le \rho < 1 \tag{6.12}$$

where v_t is distributed as $N(0, \sigma_v^2)$ and is independent of other errors over time, as well as being independent of ε; and ε_t is distributed as $N(0, \sigma_\varepsilon^2)$ but is not independent of other errors over time. The error process as described in Eq. (6.12) is generated by a rule which says that the error in time period t is determined by diminishing the value of the error in the previous period (multiplying by ρ) and then adding the effect of a random variable with 0 expected value. It is the most elementary form of an *autoregressive* error process.‡

---

† X_{1t} is identically equal to 1 for all observations. Equation (6.12) is said to describe a first-order autoregressive process AR(1), as described in Chapter 15.

‡ We shall consider autoregressive error processes in full generality and in greater detail in Part Three.

It is easy to check that the effect of an error in any given time period is felt in all future time periods, with a magnitude which diminishes over time. We simply calculate the covariances of ε_t with all previous time periods:

$$\text{Var}\,(\varepsilon_t) = E(\varepsilon_t^2) = E\big[(\rho\varepsilon_{t-1} + v_t)^2\big] = E(\rho^2\varepsilon_{t-1}^2 + v_t^2 + 2\rho\varepsilon_{t-1}v_t)$$

$$= \rho^2 E(\varepsilon_{t-1}^2) + E(v_t^2) \qquad \text{since } \varepsilon \text{ and } v \text{ are independent}$$

$$= \rho^2\,\text{Var}\,(\varepsilon_t) + \sigma_v^2 \qquad \text{since } \varepsilon \text{ is homoscedastic}$$

Solving gives $\text{Var}\,(\varepsilon_t)(1 - \rho^2) = \text{Var}\,(v_t)$, or

$$\text{Var}\,(\varepsilon_t) = \sigma_\varepsilon^2 = \frac{\sigma_v^2}{1 - \rho^2} \tag{6.13}$$

$$\text{Cov}\,(\varepsilon_t, \varepsilon_{t-1}) = E(\varepsilon_t\varepsilon_{t-1}) = E\big[(\rho\varepsilon_{t-1} + v_t)\varepsilon_{t-1}\big] = E(\rho\varepsilon_{t-1}^2 + v_t\varepsilon_{t-1})$$

$$= \rho E(\varepsilon_{t-1}^2) = \rho\,\text{Var}\,(\varepsilon_t) = \rho\sigma_\varepsilon^2 \tag{6.14}$$

Likewise,
$$\text{Cov}\,(\varepsilon_t, \varepsilon_{t-2}) = E(\varepsilon_t\varepsilon_{t-2}) = \rho^2\sigma_\varepsilon^2 \tag{6.15}$$

$$\text{Cov}\,(\varepsilon_t, \varepsilon_{t-3}) = E(\varepsilon_t\varepsilon_{t-3}) = \rho^3\sigma_\varepsilon^2 \tag{6.16}$$

Before proceeding to discuss solutions to the problem of serial correlation, it will be useful to make two further observations about the error-generating process which will be of value when explicit estimation techniques are discussed:

1. Some difficulty arises when the error term for the first time period is considered. That error is a function of errors in the previous time period for which no data are available. The result of Eq. (6.13) suggests that we assume that ε_1 is normally distributed with mean 0 and variance $\sigma_v^2/(1 - \rho^2)$.
2. A useful formula for the first-order serial correlation coefficient ρ is

$$\rho = \frac{\text{Cov}\,(\varepsilon_t, \varepsilon_{t-1})}{v_\varepsilon^2} = \frac{\text{Cov}\,(\varepsilon_t, \varepsilon_{t-1})}{\big[\text{Var}\,(\varepsilon_t)\big]^{1/2}\big[\text{Var}\,(\varepsilon_{t-1})\big]^{1/2}} \tag{6.17}$$

since $\sigma_\varepsilon^2 = \text{Var}\,(\varepsilon_t) = \text{Var}\,(\varepsilon_{t-1})$. Thus, ρ measures the correlation coefficient between errors in time period t and errors in time period $t - 1$. When ρ equals 0, no first-order serial correlation is present, while a large value of ρ implies the existence of first-order serial correlation.

If ρ were known, it would be easy to adjust the ordinary least-squares regression procedure to obtain efficient parameter estimates. The procedure involves the use of *generalized differencing* to alter the linear model into one in which the errors are independent. To describe this procedure, we use the fact that the linear model in Eq. (6.11) holds *for all time periods*. In particular,

$$Y_{t-1} = \beta_1 + \beta_2 X_{2t-1} + \cdots + \beta_k X_{kt-1} + \varepsilon_{t-1} \tag{6.18}$$

Multiplying (6.18) by ρ and subtracting from Eq. (6.11), we obtain the desired transformation:

$$Y_t^* = \beta_1(1 - \rho) + \beta_2 X_{2t}^* + \cdots + \beta_k X_{kt}^* + v_t \tag{6.19}$$

where

$$Y_t^* = Y_t - \rho Y_{t-1} \qquad X_{2t}^* = X_{2t} - \rho X_{2t-1}$$
$$X_{kt}^* = X_{kt} - \rho X_{kt-1} \qquad v_t = \varepsilon_t - \rho \varepsilon_{t-1}$$

are *generalized differences* of Y_t, $X_{2t}, \ldots, X_{kt}$, and v_t. By construction the transformed equation has an error process which is independently distributed with 0 mean and constant variance [see Eq. (6.12)]. Thus, ordinary least-squares regression applied to Eq. (6.19) will yield efficient estimates of all the regression parameters. Of course, the intercept of the original model must be calculated from the estimated intercept associated with Eq. (6.19).†

We have restricted our discussion of serial correlation to the case in which ρ is strictly less than 1. However, the case in which ρ is identically equal to 1 is of particular interest because it leads to a commonly used estimation procedure.‡ The solution process, known as *first-differencing*, is applied if we estimate the transformed equation (by analogy to the generalized differencing procedure):

$$Y_t^* = \beta_2 X_{2t}^* + \beta_3 X_{3t}^* + \cdots + \beta_k X_{kt}^* + v_t \qquad \text{where } Y_t^* = Y_t - Y_{t-1} \qquad (6.20)$$
$$X_{2t}^* = X_{2t} - X_{2t-1}$$
$$X_{kt}^* = X_{kt} - X_{kt-1}$$
$$v_t = \varepsilon_t - \varepsilon_{t-1}$$

Note that first-differencing eliminates the need for a constant term in the transformed equation. The intercept of the original equation must be calculated by solving in the original equation when the variables are measured at their respective means.§ If a constant term were included, it would pick up the effect of any time trend present in the initial model.

The generalized differencing procedure would be very useful if the value of ρ were known *a priori*. Because this is usually not the case, we examine three alternative procedures for estimating ρ, each of which has certain computational advantages and disadvantages. All three of these procedures yield estimated parameters with the desired properties when the sample size is large, but little is known about their small-sample properties.

---

† There is only one serious difficulty associated with the generalized differencing process. As described, the transformed equation is defined only for the time period 2, 3, ... , T. Dropping the initial time period from the regression procedure seems plausible, but it results in the loss of important information. A better solution would take the first time period observations into account as follows:

$$Y_1^* = \sqrt{1 - \rho^2}\, Y_1 \qquad X_{21}^* = \sqrt{1 - \rho^2}\, X_{21} \qquad \cdots \qquad X_{k1}^* = \sqrt{1 - \rho^2}\, X_{k1}$$

This transformation works because it adjusts the variance of Y and the X's for the first time period, so that the corresponding error variance is equal to the error variance associated with all other time periods. By construction, $\varepsilon_1^* = (1 - \rho^2)^{1/2}\varepsilon_1$ and $\mathrm{Var}\,(\varepsilon_1^*) = (1 - \rho^2)\mathrm{Var}\,(\varepsilon_1) = \sigma_v^2$.

‡ Note, however, that as ρ approaches 1, the error variance in the original equation becomes infinitely large, so that the previous analysis does not follow.

§ In the two-variable model, for example, $Y_t^* = \beta X_t^*$. To obtain the intercept estimate, we estimate β and then substitute to obtain $\hat{\alpha} = \bar{Y} - \beta\bar{X}$.

The Cochrane-Orcutt procedure† This procedure involves a series of iterations, each of which produces a better estimate of ρ than the previous one. It uses the notion that ρ is a correlation coefficient associated with errors of adjacent time periods. In the first step, ordinary least squares is used to estimate the original model [Eq. (6.11)]. The residuals from this equation are then used to perform the regression

$$\hat{\varepsilon}_t = \rho \hat{\varepsilon}_{t-1} + v_t \tag{6.21}$$

The estimated value of ρ is used to perform the generalized differencing transformation process, and a new regression is run. The transformed equation is

$$Y_t^* = \beta_1(1 - \hat{\rho}) + \beta_2 X_{2t}^* + \cdots + \beta_k X_{kt}^* + v_t \qquad \text{where } \begin{aligned} Y_t^* &= Y_t - \hat{\rho}Y_{t-1} \\ X_{2t}^* &= X_{2t} - \hat{\rho}X_{2t-1} \\ X_{kt}^* &= X_{kt} - \hat{\rho}X_{kt-1} \end{aligned}$$

The estimated transformed equation yields parameter values for the original intercept $\hat{\beta}_1$ and all the slope parameters $\hat{\beta}_2, \ldots, \hat{\beta}_k$. These revised parameter estimates are substituted into the *original* equation, and new regression residuals are obtained. The new estimated residuals are

$$\hat{\hat{\varepsilon}}_t = Y_t - \hat{\beta}_1 - \hat{\beta}_2 X_{2t} - \cdots - \hat{\beta}_k X_{kt}$$

By running the regression

$$\hat{\hat{\varepsilon}}_t = \rho \hat{\hat{\varepsilon}}_{t-1} + v_t$$

these second-round residuals can be used to obtain a new estimate of ρ. The iterative process can be carried on for as many steps as the researcher desires. Standard procedure is to stop the iterations when the new estimates of ρ differ from the old ones by less than .01 or .005, or after 10 or 20 estimates of ρ have been obtained. The specific choice made depends upon the computational costs involved. The primary difficulty with the Cochrane-Orcutt procedure is that there is no guarantee that the final estimate of ρ will be the optimal estimate, in the sense of minimizing the sum of squared residuals. The difficulty arises because the iterative technique may lead to a local rather than a global minimum.

The Hildreth-Lu procedure‡ In this procedure, a set of grid values is specified for ρ. These are usually spaced values which are to serve as guesses for the value of ρ. If one knew that positive serial correlation were present, one might choose grid values of ρ equal to 0, .1, .2, .3, .4, .5, .6, .7, .8, .9, 1.0. For each value of ρ,

† D. Cochrane and G. H. Orcutt, "Application of Least Squares Regressions to Relationships Containing Autocorrelated Error Terms," *Journal of the American Statistical Association*, vol. 44, pp. 32–61, 1949.

‡ G. Hildreth and J. Y. Lu, "Demand Relations with Autocorrelated Disturbances," *Michigan State University Agricultural Experiment Station, Technical Bulletin 276*, November 1960.

the transformed equation

$$Y_t^* = \beta_1(1 - \rho) + \beta_2 X_{2t}^* + \cdots + \beta_k X_{kt}^* + v_t$$

is estimated. The procedure selects the equation with the lowest sum of squared residuals as the best equation. The procedure can be continued with new grid values chosen in the neighborhood of the ρ value that is first selected until the desired accuracy is attained. In using the Hildreth-Lu procedure, we may choose any limits and any spacing arrangement for the grid values. The technique is practical and if used with sufficient care, will make it likely that the maximum-likelihood estimate of ρ is approximated. Care should be exercised in the choice of grid values so that the minimum sum of squares obtained is global rather than local.

The Durbin procedure† The generalized difference form of the linear model is

$$Y_t - \rho Y_{t-1} = \beta_1(1 - \rho) + \beta_2(X_{2t} - \rho X_{2t-1}) + \cdots + \beta_k(X_{kt} - \rho X_{kt-1}) + v_t$$
(6.22)

Rewriting this equation slightly, we see that

$$Y_t = \beta_1(1 - \rho) + \rho Y_{t-1} + \beta_2 X_{2t} - \rho \beta_2 X_{2t-1} + \cdots + \beta_k X_{kt} - \rho \beta_k X_{kt-1} + v_t$$
(6.23)

This suggests that we obtain an estimate for ρ by treating the model in Eq. (6.23) directly as a linear regression model. The estimated coefficient of the Y_{t-1} variable will yield an estimate of ρ which is accurate in large samples, as well as parameter estimates of $\beta_1, \beta_2, \ldots, \beta_k$. However, these parameter estimates can be improved if we substitute the estimated serial correlation coefficient $\hat{\rho}$ into

$$Y_t - \hat{\rho} Y_{t-1} = \beta_1(1 - \hat{\rho}) + \beta_2(X_{2t} - \hat{\rho} X_{2t-1}) + \cdots + \beta_k(X_{kt} - \hat{\rho} X_{kt-1}) + v_t$$
(6.24)

Estimation of Eq. (6.24) yields a new, more efficient set of parameter estimates.

6.2.2 Tests for Serial Correlation

Durbin-Watson test We shall now consider a test of the null hypothesis that no serial correlation is present ($\rho = 0$). The alternative hypothesis can be that ρ is nonzero or, in the one-tailed case, that ρ is positive (or negative). By far the most popular test for serial correlation is the *Durbin-Watson test*.‡ We concentrate for the remainder of this section on its use and misuse. Alternative parametric and

---

† J. Durbin, "Estimation of Parameters in Time-Series Regression Models," *Journal of the Royal Statistical Society*, ser. B, vol. 22, pp. 139–153, 1960.

‡ J. Durbin and G. S. Watson, "Testing for Serial Correlation in Least Squares Regression," *Biometrika*, vol. 38, pp. 159–177, 1951. This test is not directly applicable if the regression does not contain a constant term.

nonparametric tests (which involve no distributional assumptions) are not discussed here.†

The Durbin-Watson test involves the calculation of a test statistic based on the residuals from the ordinary least-squares regression procedure. The statistic is defined as

$$\text{DW} = \frac{\sum_{t=2}^{T} (\hat{\varepsilon}_t - \hat{\varepsilon}_{t-1})^2}{\sum_{t=1}^{T} \hat{\varepsilon}_t^2} \tag{6.25}$$

Note that the numerator cannot include a difference for the first observation in the sample since no earlier observation is available. In addition, if any gaps occur in the data (when observations are missing), the number of entries in the numerator must be further reduced, once for each gap. When successive values of $\hat{\varepsilon}_t$ are close to each other, the DW statistic will be low, indicating the presence of positive serial correlation. The DW statistic will lie in the 0 to 4 range, with a value near 2 indicating no first-order serial correlation.‡ Exact interpretation of the DW statistic is difficult because the sequence of error terms depends not only on the sequence of ε's but also on the sequence of all the X values. For this reason, most tables include test statistics which vary with the number of independent variables and the number of observations. Two limits are given, usually labeled d_l and d_u. If one is investigating the possibility of positive serial correlation, a value for DW below d_l allows one to reject the null hypothesis of no serial correlation. If DW is greater than d_u, the null hypothesis is retained. The range between d_l and d_u leaves us with inconclusive results. For negative serial correlation we simply view matters from the endpoint of 4 instead of the endpoint of 0. The null hypothesis is rejected if the DW statistic is greater than $4 - d_l$, and the hypothesis is accepted if DW is less than $4 - d_u$ and greater than d_u. Within the range between $4 - d_u$ and $4 - d_l$ the test is inconclusive. (See Table 6.1 for a summary of the Durbin-Watson test.)

The region of indeterminacy of the statistical test is due to the fact that the sequence of residuals is influenced by the movement of the independent variables in the regression equation. In this region, it is possible that the seeming correlation of the errors is due to the autocorrelation of the independent variable and not to the serial correlation of the error terms.

We conclude this section by showing the range of the DW statistic and the range of indeterminacy explicitly in a two-variable example (with both variables

† Nonparametric tests are described in S. Siegel, *Nonparametric Statistics for the Behavioral Sciences* (New York: McGraw-Hill, 1956). Other tests are discussed in H. Theil, "The Analysis of Disturbances in Regression Analysis," *Journal of the American Statistical Association*, vol. 60, pp. 1067–1079, 1965.

‡ The DW statistic cannot be used if the regression equation contains a lagged dependent variable. This matter is pursued further in Section 7.7.

Table 6.1 Range of the Durbin-Watson statistic

Value of DW	Result
$4 - d_l < \text{DW} < 4$	Reject null hypothesis; negative serial correlation present
$4 - d_u < \text{DW} < 4 - d_l$	Result indeterminate
$2 < \text{DW} < 4 - d_u$	Accept null hypothesis
$d_u < \text{DW} < 2$	Accept null hypothesis
$d_l < \text{DW} < d_u$	Result indeterminate
$0 < \text{DW} < d_l$	Reject null hypothesis; positive serial correlation present

measured as deviations about means). We assume that

$$y_t = \beta x_t + \varepsilon_t \tag{6.26}$$

$$\varepsilon_t = \rho \varepsilon_{t-1} + v_t \qquad -1 < \rho < 1 \tag{6.27}$$

$$x_t = r x_{t-1} + w_t^* \qquad 0 \le r < 1 \tag{6.28}$$

where w_t^* is a random uncorrelated error term. The third assumption takes account of the fact that the independent variable is likely to be highly autocorrelated in time-series studies. The serial correlation coefficient r makes this assumption explicit. Expanding the definition of DW from Eq. (6.25), we find that

$$\text{DW} = \frac{\sum\limits_{t=2}^{T} \hat{\varepsilon}_t^2 - 2\sum\limits_{t=2}^{T} \hat{\varepsilon}_t \hat{\varepsilon}_{t-1} + \sum\limits_{t=2}^{T} \hat{\varepsilon}_{t-1}^2}{\sum\limits_{t=1}^{T} \hat{\varepsilon}_t^2}$$

Then, by making several approximations, we can determine that†

$$\text{DW} \approx 2(1 - \hat{\rho}) \tag{6.29}$$

It should now be clear that when there is no serial correlation ($\rho = 0$), the DW statistic will be close to 2. Positive serial correlation is clearly associated with DW values below 2 and negative serial correlation with DW values above 2. Now we can take into account the serially correlated nature of the independent variable. Since $\hat{\varepsilon}_i = y_i - \hat{\beta} x_i$ and $y_i = \beta x_i + \varepsilon_i$, it follows that $\hat{\varepsilon}_t = \varepsilon_t + (\beta -$

---

† We assume that

$$\sum_{t=2}^{T} \hat{\varepsilon}_t^2 \approx \sum_{t=1}^{T} \hat{\varepsilon}_t^2 \approx \sum_{t=2}^{T} \hat{\varepsilon}_{t-1}^2 \qquad \text{and} \qquad \sum_{t=2}^{T} \hat{\varepsilon}_t \hat{\varepsilon}_{t-1} \approx \sum_{t=1}^{T} \hat{\varepsilon}_t \hat{\varepsilon}_{t-1}$$

Then it follows by direct substitution that

$$\text{DW} \approx 2 - 2\frac{\sum\limits_{t=1}^{T} \hat{\varepsilon}_t \hat{\varepsilon}_{t-1}}{\sum\limits_{t=1}^{T} \hat{\varepsilon}_t^2} \approx 2 - 2\frac{\text{Cov}(\hat{\varepsilon}_t, \hat{\varepsilon}_{t-1})}{\text{Var}(\hat{\varepsilon}_t)} \approx 2 - 2\hat{\rho}$$

$\hat{\beta})x_t$. Then squaring, summing over all observations, and dividing by T we get:

$$\text{Var } (\hat{\varepsilon}_t) = \text{Var } (\varepsilon_t) + (\beta - \hat{\beta})^2 \text{ Var } (x_t) \tag{6.30}$$

Using a similar procedure, we can show that†

$$\text{Cov } (\hat{\varepsilon}_t, \hat{\varepsilon}_{t-1}) = \text{Cov } (\varepsilon_t, \varepsilon_{t-1}) + (\beta - \hat{\beta})^2 \text{ Cov } (x_t, x_{t-1}) \tag{6.31}$$

while Eq. (6.28) allows us to conclude that

$$\text{Cov } (x_t, x_{t-1}) = r \text{ Var } (x_t) \tag{6.32}$$

Substituting Eqs. (6.30) to (6.32) into Eq. (6.29), we can evaluate the DW statistic in terms of the distribution of the error term and the explanatory variable.

$$\text{DW} \approx 2 - 2\frac{\text{Cov } (\varepsilon_t, \varepsilon_{t-1}) + r(\beta - \hat{\beta})^2 \text{ Var } (x_t)}{\text{Var } (\varepsilon_t) + (\beta - \hat{\beta})^2 \text{ Var } (x_t)} \tag{6.33}$$

If the estimated slope parameter is identically equal to the true parameter, then the presence of serial correlation in the X variable is irrelevant to the calculation of the DW statistic. Despite the fact that $\hat{\beta}$ is an unbiased estimator of β, there will be sampling error involved in the estimation process, and so $\hat{\beta}$ will not be identically equal to β. It should be immediately clear from Eq. (6.33) that, other things being equal, a higher value of r will lead to a lower value of the DW statistic. In fact, a value of r close to 1 may push the DW statistic close to 0, even though the error terms may be uncorrelated themselves. The reason for the upper and lower limits associated with the DW test now becomes clear. If $r = 1$, the d_l limit is the proper one to apply. Anything below d_l indicates positive serial correlation. If $r = -1$, on the other hand, the d_u limit should be used. Anything above d_u indicates that positive serial correlation cannot be accepted. In working with time series, the X's are likely to be autocorrelated, so that the d_l limit may be the more accurate of the two.

Example 6.6   Bituminous coal‡ An attempt was made to explain the demand for bituminous coal (COAL) as a function of the Federal Reserve Board index of iron and steel production (FIS), the Federal Reserve Board index of electrical utility production (FEU), the wholesale price index for coal (PCOAL), and the wholesale price index for natural gas (PGAS). The quantity demanded of bituminous coal has been seasonally adjusted, and the adjusted series was used to perform a linear regression on the explanatory variables listed above. The time series run monthly from January 1965 to December 1972.

---

† As in the text, we can write $\hat{\varepsilon}_{t-1} = \varepsilon_{t-1} + (\beta - \hat{\beta})x_{t-1}$. Multiplying this term by $\hat{\varepsilon}_t = \varepsilon_t + (\beta - \hat{\beta})x_t$, summing over all observations, and eliminating all cross terms, we get the desired results.

‡ This example was constructed by Dynamics Associates, Cambridge, Mass., and is used by permission.

The output from the original regression is as follows (with t statistics in parentheses):

$$\widehat{COAL} = 12{,}262 + 92.34\,FIS + 118.57\,FEU - 48.90\,PCOAL$$
$$\phantom{\widehat{COAL} = } \underset{(3.51)}{} \quad \underset{(6.46)}{} \quad \underset{(7.14)}{} \quad \underset{(-3.82)}{}$$

$$+ 118.91\,PGAS$$
$$\underset{(3.18)}{}$$

$$R^2 = .692 \qquad F(4/91) = 51.0 \qquad DW = .95$$

Although all the t statistics are highly significant, the low DW statistic indicates that serial correlation is likely to be present in the estimated residuals.† In order to correct for the presence of positive first-order serial correlation, the Hildreth-Lu procedure was applied. A series of regressions was run, each with a different chosen value of ρ. The grid search is described by the following table:

ρ	Sum of squared residuals (ESS)	ρ	Sum of squared residuals (ESS)
− 1.0	3.8×10^8	.0	1.2×10^8
−.8	3.1×10^8	.2	1.0×10^8
−.6	2.5×10^8	.4	9.2×10^7
−.4	2.0×10^8	.6	9.0×10^7
−.2	1.5×10^8	.8	9.6×10^7
		1.0	1.1×10^8

The final value of ρ chosen was .6, the value associated with the smallest sum of squared residuals of the regressions run. When ρ was assigned the value of .6, the autoregressive transformation performed, and the final regression run, the results were

$$\widehat{COAL^*} = 16{,}245 + 75.29\,FIS^* + 100.26\,FEV^* - 38.98\,COAL^*$$
$$\phantom{\widehat{COAL^*} = } \underset{(3.3)}{} \quad \underset{(4.4)}{} \quad \underset{(3.7)}{} \quad \underset{(-2.0)}{}$$

$$+ 105.99\,PGAS^*$$
$$\underset{(2.0)}{}$$

where $COAL^* = COAL - .6COAL_{-1}$ $\qquad FEV^* = FEV - .6FEV_{-1}$

 $PGAS^* = PGAS - .6PGAS_{-1}$ $\qquad FIS^* = FIS - .6FIS_{-1}$

 $PCOAL^* = PCOAL - .6PCOAL$ $\qquad DW = 2.07$

Notice that the DW statistic is substantially higher than in the original regression and that all the estimated regression coefficients continue to be significant at the 5 percent level.

---

† The critical values of the DW statistic (at the 5 percent significance level) with 96 observations and 4 independent variables are $d_l = 1.58$ and $d_u = 1.75$.

Example 6.7 Interest-rate determination In this example we reconsider the attempt (see Example 4.2) to estimate a single-equation model which explains the time path of the 3-month Treasury bill rate R_t as a function of aggregate disposable income YD_t, a 3-month moving sum of changes in the money supply ($MAM_t = \Delta M_t + \Delta M_{t-1} + \Delta M_{t-2}$), and a 3-month moving sum of the rate of change of the price level ($MAP_t = \Delta P_t/P_t + \Delta P_{t-1}/P_{t-1} + \Delta P_{t-2}/P_{t-2}$). One of the final equations estimated using ordinary least squares, with t statistics in parentheses, is

$$\hat{R}_t = \underset{(-9.45)}{-3.662} + \underset{(14.76)}{.053}\, YD_t - \underset{(-6.13)}{.280}\, MAM_t + \underset{(5.23)}{104.37}\, MAP_t$$

$$R^2 = .853 \quad \bar{R}^2 = .849 \quad F(3/141) = 271.9 \quad s = SER = .552 \quad DW = .24$$

The low DW statistic of .24 strongly suggests the presence of positive first-order serial correlation. This is borne out when we examine a graph of the actual and fitted values of the ordinary least-squares regression in Fig. 6.2. While the R^2 for the equation is reasonably high, the fit, as shown graphically, leaves much to be desired. The existence of serial correlation can be seen graphically by noticing that regression residuals tend to be highly correlated. When the fitted value associated with one observation lies below the true value, it is very likely that neighboring fitted values will do the same. What is especially discouraging from the forecasting perspective is that the last seven fitted or predicted values lie below the actual values. This suggests that unless corrections are made for the presence of serial correlation, forecasts are likely to understate the actual interest-rate time series.

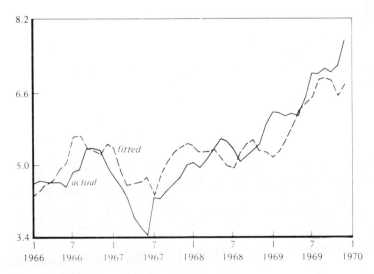

Figure 6.2 Interest-rate determination.

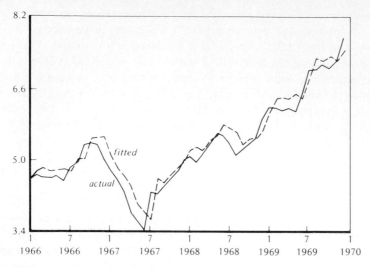

Figure 6.3 Interest-rate determination.

To improve our results, we reestimated the interest rate equation, using the Hildreth-Lu procedure to correct for serial correlation. The results are

$$\hat{R}_t^* = - \underset{(-2.70)}{5.155} + \underset{(4.81)}{.066}\,YD_t^* - \underset{(-1.14)}{.040}\,MAM_t^* + \underset{(1.74)}{37.78}\,MAP_t^*$$

where $R_t^* = R_t - .956R_{t-1}$ $YD_t^* = YD_t - .956YD_{t-1}$

$MAM_t^* = MAM_t - .956MAM_{t-1}$ $MAP_t^* = MAP_t - .956MAP_{t-1}$

$$R^2 = .177 \qquad F(3/174) = 10.1 \qquad DW = 1.42$$
$$\overline{R}^2 = .159 \qquad SER = .230 \qquad \hat{\rho} = .956$$

All the statistics listed above were obtained from the transformed equation which used the generalized differencing process. Since we are explaining differences in interest rates, rather than levels, the result is that R^2 has fallen, as have the t statistics. However, for our purposes what is important is the ability of the equation to forecast. In fact, the correction for serial correlation substantially improves the fit of the original equation, as seen by examining the plot of fitted and actual values in Fig. 6.3.

APPENDIX 6.1 GENERALIZED LEAST-SQUARES ESTIMATION

In Appendix 4.3 we discussed the matrix generalization of the multiple regression model. Among the assumptions of the classical linear model was the assumption that the error term was not autocorrelated and had constant variance. In matrix notation we wrote

$$E(\varepsilon\varepsilon') = \sigma^2\mathbf{I}$$

where $\mathbf{I}$ is an $N \times N$ identity matrix.

In this appendix we generalize the linear model to apply to cases where serial correlation and heteroscedasticity are present. We accomplish this by altering our assumption about the variance-covariance matrix of the error terms. We assume that

$$E(\varepsilon\varepsilon') = \sigma^2\Omega \tag{A6.1}$$

σ^2 is assumed to be unknown, but Ω is a known $N \times N$ matrix. This is equivalent to the assumption that the elements of Ω are known up to a multiplicative scalar. The only assumption we need to make about the matrix Ω is that it is positive definite.† This assumption is quite general, yet necessary for the derivations which follow. The generality of the assumed error structure is evidenced by the fact that heteroscedasticity and first-order serial correlation are special cases.

The most general form of the heteroscedasticity case occurs when the error structure is

$$\begin{bmatrix} \sigma_1^2 & 0 & \cdots & 0 \\ 0 & \sigma_2^2 & \cdots & 0 \\ \cdots & \cdots & \cdots & \cdots \\ 0 & 0 & \cdots & \sigma_N^2 \end{bmatrix}$$

Heteroscedasticity differs from the classical model only in the fact that the error variances differ between observations. All error covariances are assumed equal to 0. In the first-order serial correlation example, however, none of the elements of Ω are equal to 0. In this case, the variance-covariance matrix is

$$\sigma^2 \begin{bmatrix} 1 & \rho & \rho^2 & \cdots & \rho^{N-1} \\ \rho & 1 & \rho & \cdots & \rho^{N-2} \\ \rho^2 & \rho & 1 & \cdots & \rho^{N-3} \\ \cdots & \cdots & \cdots & \cdots & \cdots \\ \rho^{N-1} & \rho^{N-2} & \rho^{N-3} & \cdots & 1 \end{bmatrix}$$

The objective of generalized least-squares estimation is to find parameter estimates for the vector β in the most efficient manner possible, by accounting for the information provided by the knowledge of the form of the matrix Ω. Assuming that all other least-squares assumptions hold, we can get best linear unbiased parameter estimates if we transform the original data set so that the variance-covariance matrix of the transformed errors equals $\sigma^2\mathbf{I}$. Once this is done, application of the Gauss-Markov theorem will give us our desired result.

† A matrix $\mathbf{A}$ is positive definite if and only if $\mathbf{x'Ax}$ is greater than 0, for all $\mathbf{x}$ not equal to 0, where $\mathbf{x}$ is an $N \times 1$ vector. See Appendix 4.3 for references which describe the basic results of matrix algebra.

The assumption that Ω is a positive definite matrix is sufficient to guarantee that such a strategy will always succeed. We use a basic theorem of matrix algebra which states that there exists a nonsingular $N \times N$ matrix $\mathbf{H}$ such that

$$\mathbf{H}\Omega\mathbf{H}' = \mathbf{I} \tag{A6.2}$$

We will find it useful to rewrite (A6.2) in the form

$$\Omega = \mathbf{H}^{-1}(\mathbf{H}')^{-1} = (\mathbf{H}'\mathbf{H})^{-1} \tag{A6.3}$$

from which it follows that

$$\mathbf{H}'\mathbf{H} = \Omega^{-1} \tag{A6.4}$$

We use the matrix $\mathbf{H}$ to transform the original model as follows:

$$\mathbf{H}\mathbf{Y} = \mathbf{H}\mathbf{X}\beta + \mathbf{H}\varepsilon \tag{A6.5}$$

$$\text{or} \qquad \tilde{\mathbf{Y}} = \tilde{\mathbf{X}}\beta + \tilde{\varepsilon} \qquad\qquad \begin{aligned} \tilde{\mathbf{Y}} &= \mathbf{H}\mathbf{Y} \\ \text{where } \tilde{\mathbf{X}} &= \mathbf{H}\mathbf{X} \\ \tilde{\varepsilon} &= \mathbf{H}\varepsilon \end{aligned} \tag{A6.6}$$

The error term $\tilde{\varepsilon}$ is consistent with the classical linear model, since, from Eq. (A6.2),

$$E(\tilde{\varepsilon}\tilde{\varepsilon}') = E(\mathbf{H}\varepsilon\varepsilon'\mathbf{H}') = \sigma^2\mathbf{H}\Omega\mathbf{H}' = \sigma^2\mathbf{I}$$

Since (A6.6) obeys the classical assumptions, we know that the application of ordinary least squares will yield best unbiased parameter estimates. Hence the estimator

$$\tilde{\beta} = (\tilde{\mathbf{X}}'\tilde{\mathbf{X}})^{-1}\tilde{\mathbf{X}}'\tilde{\mathbf{Y}} \tag{A6.7}$$

will be efficient.†

In terms of our original data, the generalized least-squares estimator $\tilde{\beta}$ is

$$\tilde{\beta} = \left[(\mathbf{H}\mathbf{X})'(\mathbf{H}\mathbf{X})\right]^{-1}(\mathbf{H}\mathbf{X})'(\mathbf{H}\mathbf{Y}) = (\mathbf{X}'\mathbf{H}'\mathbf{H}\mathbf{X})^{-1}\mathbf{X}'\mathbf{H}'\mathbf{H}\mathbf{Y}$$

$$= (\mathbf{X}'\Omega^{-1}\mathbf{X})^{-1}\mathbf{X}'\Omega^{-1}\mathbf{Y} \tag{A6.8}$$

The variance-covariance matrix of the estimated parameter vector $\tilde{\beta}$ is

$$E\left[(\tilde{\beta} - \beta)(\tilde{\beta} - \beta)'\right] = \sigma^2(\tilde{\mathbf{X}}'\tilde{\mathbf{X}})^{-1} = \sigma^2(\mathbf{X}'\mathbf{H}'\mathbf{H}\mathbf{X})^{-1}$$

$$= \sigma^2(\mathbf{X}'\Omega^{-1}\mathbf{X})^{-1} \tag{A6.9}$$

It is worth checking to see that the generalized least-squares results coincide with those of ordinary least squares when $\Omega = \mathbf{I}$. The reader can do so by substituting for Ω in Eqs. (A6.8) and (A6.9) and solving.

In order to apply generalized least-squares (GLS) estimation, we need an estimate of Ω, and in order to perform statistical tests, we need to estimate σ^2. When Ω is known, we could estimate σ^2 from the residuals of the GLS regression. To do so, we use our knowledge of the classical linear model, in

---

† The Gauss-Markov theorem still applies here because all transformations of the data are *linear*.

which an unbiased estimate of σ^2 is given by

$$\hat{\sigma}^2 = \frac{1}{N-k}\tilde{u}'\tilde{u}$$

where $\tilde{u}$ is the vector of GLS residuals in this case. Substituting gives

$$\hat{\sigma}^2 = \frac{1}{N-k}(H\hat{\varepsilon})'(H\hat{\varepsilon}) = \frac{1}{N-k}(\hat{\varepsilon}'\Omega^{-1}\hat{\varepsilon})$$

so that an unbiased estimate of $E[(\tilde{\beta}-\beta)(\tilde{\beta}-\beta)']$ is given by

$$\frac{1}{N-k}(\hat{\varepsilon}'\Omega^{-1}\hat{\varepsilon})(X'\Omega^{-1}X)^{-1} \tag{A6.10}$$

If ε is assumed normal, it is possible to show that $\tilde{\beta}$ is normally distributed. Thus, statistical tests can be applied just as in the case of the classical model.

Our final problem is to find a consistent estimate of Ω. An obvious difficulty arises because Ω is an $N \times N$ matrix with $N(N+1)/2$ elements. It is impossible to estimate all elements of Ω from only N observations, so that if no other information is available, we must parameterize the form of Ω. The heteroscedasticity and first-order serial correlation assumptions provide two useful ways of parameterizing the model, although numerous alternatives are available.

Once a consistent estimator of Ω is used, our estimator will lose the property of being an unbiased estimator but will retain an appropriate large-sample property (something close to consistency). If Ω is estimated consistently by a matrix V, the GLS estimator and its variance-covariance matrix are

$$\hat{\beta} = (X'V^{-1}X)^{-1}X'V^{-1}Y \tag{A6.11}$$

$$E[(\hat{\beta}-\beta)(\hat{\beta}-\beta)'] = \frac{1}{N-k}(\hat{\varepsilon}'V^{-1}\hat{\varepsilon})(X'V^{-1}X)^{-1}$$

$$= \frac{1}{N-k}(\tilde{u}'\tilde{u})(X'V^{-1}X)^{-1} \tag{A6.12}$$

where $\hat{\varepsilon}$ are the ordinary least-squares residuals and $\tilde{u}$ are the generalized least-squares residuals.

In order to complete this appendix, it will be useful to describe the transformation matrix H in both the heteroscedasticity and the first-order serial-correlation cases. In the former it is quite easy to choose H so that $H'H = \Omega^{-1}$. The reader should check to see that

$$H = \begin{bmatrix} \dfrac{1}{\sigma_1} & 0 & \cdots & 0 \\ 0 & \dfrac{1}{\sigma_2} & \cdots & 0 \\ \cdots & \cdots & \cdots & \cdots \\ 0 & 0 & \cdots & \dfrac{1}{\sigma_N} \end{bmatrix}$$

is the correct choice. In addition, the reader should check that transforming the data according to the matrix **H** is equivalent to the weighted least-squares procedure described in the text.

The derivation of **H** in the first-order serial correlation case is somewhat more difficult. In this case,

$$
\mathbf{H} = \begin{bmatrix}
\sqrt{1 - \rho^2} & 0 & 0 & \cdots & 0 & 0 \\
-\rho & 1 & 0 & \cdots & 0 & 0 \\
0 & -\rho & 1 & \cdots & 0 & 0 \\
\cdots & & & & & \\
0 & 0 & 0 & \cdots & 1 & 0 \\
0 & 0 & 0 & \cdots & -\rho & 1
\end{bmatrix}
$$

The fact that **H** is the correct choice can be checked by evaluating $(\mathbf{H'H})^{-1} = \Omega$. The reader should verify that application of the transformation **H** to the data is equivalent to using the generalized differencing process and then applying ordinary least squares. In this sense, corrections for serial correlation involve the use of weighted least-squares estimation just as in the heteroscedasticity case.

What if ordinary least-squares estimation is used, even when GLS is appropriate? We know, first of all, that if Ω is known, OLS and GLS parameter estimates will be unbiased but OLS parameter estimates will have greater variance than their GLS counterparts. However, it is also true that the OLS estimate of the variance-covariance matrix will be biased. To see this, recall that the OLS variance-covariance matrix is

$$
\sigma^2(\mathbf{X'X})^{-1} \tag{A6.13}
$$

If the GLS model were in fact correct, the variance-covariance matrix of the parameter vector $\hat{\beta} = (\mathbf{X'X})^{-1}\mathbf{X'Y}$ would be

$$
E\big[(\hat{\beta} - \beta)(\hat{\beta} - \beta)'\big] = E\big\{\big[(\mathbf{X'X})^{-1}\mathbf{X'}\varepsilon\big]\big[(\mathbf{X'X})^{-1}\mathbf{X'}\varepsilon\big]'\big\}
$$

$$
\text{since } \hat{\beta} = \beta + (\mathbf{X'X})^{-1}\mathbf{X'}\varepsilon
$$

$$
= (\mathbf{X'X})^{-1}\mathbf{X'} E\big[(\varepsilon\varepsilon')\big]\mathbf{X}(\mathbf{X'X})^{-1}
$$

$$
= \sigma^2(\mathbf{X'X})^{-1}\mathbf{X'}\Omega\mathbf{X}(\mathbf{X'X})^{-1} \tag{A6.14}
$$

The reported variance-covariance matrix in (A6.13) may yield a rather poor estimate of the correct variance-covariance matrix for ordinary least-squares parameter estimates as given by (A6.14).

EXERCISES

6.1 Explain intuitively why weighted least squares yield more efficient parameter estimators than ordinary least squares when the error term is known to be heteroscedastic.

6.2 You are estimating a cross-section regression for a sample of 100 cities in the United States in which you hope to explain expenditures on education as a function of the median income in the community, the number of school-age children, and the level of state and federal grants received for educational purposes. Would you expect heteroscedasticity to be a problem in this case? If so, would you use Bartlett's test or the Goldfeld-Quandt test? Why?

6.3 You are estimating the relationship between a firm's sales and advertising expenditures in an industry. It becomes apparent to you that half the firms in the industry are large relative to the other half, and you are concerned about the proper estimation technique in such a situation. Assume that the error variances associated with the large firms are twice the error variances associated with the small firms.

(*a*) If you used ordinary least squares to estimate the regression of sales on advertising (assuming that advertising is an independent variable, uncorrelated with the error term), would your estimated parameters be unbiased? Consistent? Efficient?

(*b*) How might you revise the estimation procedure to eliminate or to resolve your difficulties?

(*c*) Can you test whether the original error-variance assumption is valid?

6.4 Why are the errors in cross-section studies unlikely to be serially correlated? Can you give an example in which serial correlation will be present?

6.5 Can ρ take on a value (in absolute value) which is greater than 1? What does this tell you about the stability of the model being studied?

6.6 Using the rental data in Table 2.1, Exercise 5.7, we estimated the model RENT PER $= \beta_1 + \beta_2(\text{SEX}) + \beta_3(\text{ROOM PER}) + \beta_4(\text{DIST}) + \varepsilon$. Using an F test, test the hypothesis that

$$\text{Variance } (\varepsilon_{\text{male}}) > \text{Variance } (\varepsilon_{\text{female}})$$

Hint: Run separate regressions of RENT PER $+ \beta_1 + \beta_3(\text{ROOM PER}) + \beta_4(\text{DIST}) + \varepsilon$ for males and females. Why did you drop the SEX variable for these regressions?)

6.7 Using the expenditure data set in Table 6.2, estimate the model

$$\text{EXP} = \beta_1 + \beta_2(\text{POP}) + \beta_3(\text{AID}) + \beta_4(\text{INC}) + \varepsilon$$

using ordinary least squares. Then use a Goldfeld-Quandt test to see if $V(\varepsilon) \sim \text{POP}^2$. If you reject the null hypothesis, reestimate the equation efficiently.

Table 6.2 Expenditure data set

E, N, S, W = dummy variable equal to 1 if state is in eastern, northern, southern, or western region, respectively; 0 otherwise

EXP	= total state and local government expenditures, millions of dollars
PCEXP	= per capita state and local government expenditures, dollars
POP	= population of state, thousands
DEN	= population density, thousands per square mile
DPOP	= percentage change in population from 1960 to 1970
URB	= percentage of population living in metropolitan areas (SMSAs)
PCINC	= per capita personal income, dollars
PS	= population attending primary or secondary public schools, thousands

State	E	N	S	W	EXP	PCEXP	PCAID	POP	DEN	DPOP	URB	PCINC	PS
Maine	1	0	0	0	704	686.16	186	1,026	.033182	2.50	21.6	3,664	251
N.H.	1	0	0	0	526	679.59	123	774	.085743	21.5	27.3	4,279	168
Vt.	1	0	0	0	411	893.48	235	460	.049639	14.1	0.	3,703	107
Mass.	1	0	0	0	5,166	891.30	190	5,796	.74061	10.5	84.7	4,825	1,203
R.I.	1	0	0	0	699	721.36	184	969	.92374	10.5	84.7	4,513	190
Conn.	1	0	0	0	2546	826.62	145	3,080	.63348	19.6	82.6	5,414	665
N.Y.	1	0	0	0	22,750	1,238.6	240	18,367	.38400	8.70	86.5	5,275	3,524
N.J.	1	0	0	0	5,911	804.33	141	7,349	.97713	18.2	76.9	5,379	1,513
Pa.	1	0	0	0	8,840	742.55	136	11,905	.26476	4.20	79.4	4,545	2,362
Ohio	0	1	0	0	6,867	640.46	112	10,722	.26167	9.70	77.7	4,572	2,422

SOURCE: U.S. Bureau of the Census, Census of Governments and Census of Population, 1970.

State	E	N	S	W	EXP	PCEXP	PCAID	POP	DEN	DPOP	URB	PCINC	PS
Ind.	0	1	0	0	3,457	653.99	103	5,286	.14644	11.4	61.9	4,364	1,221
Ill.	0	1	0	0	8,935	794,65	156	11,244	.20169	10.2	80.1	5,162	2,349
Mich.	0	1	0	0	7,799	865.31	147	9,013	.15863	13.4	76.7	4,982	2,197
Wisc.	0	1	0	0	3,757	830.09	116	4,526	.083101	11.8	57.6	4,279	995
Minn.	0	1	0	0	3,528	909.98	163	3,877	.048897	11.5	56.9	4,343	910
Iowa	0	1	0	0	2,108	730.93	113	2,884	.051554	2.40	35.6	4,316	647
Mo.	0	1	0	0	3,156	664.84	151	4,747	.068802	8.30	64.1	4,307	1,030
N. Dak.	0	1	0	0	475	749.21	201	634	.009152	−2.30	11.9	4,128	142
S. Dak.	0	1	0	0	521	766.18	195	680	.008953	−2.10	14.3	3,766	162
Neb.	0	1	0	0	1,052	688.48	134	1,528	.019978	5.10	42.8	4,451	330
Kans.	0	1	0	0	1,551	683.86	132	2,268	.027731	3.20	42.3	4,535	475
Del.	0	0	1	0	571	1,000.0	170	571	.28809	22.8	70.4	5,222	134
Md.	0	0	1	0	3,392	837.94	135	4,048	.40926	26.5	84.3	5,017	921
Va.	0	0	1	0	3,037	637.36	131	4,765	.11978	17.2	61.2	4,396	1,069
W. Va.	0	0	1	0	1,250	696.38	252	1,795	.074574	−6.20	31.3	3,624	410
N.C.	0	0	1	0	2,938	562.73	141	5,221	.10699	11.5	37.3	3,868	1.161
S.C.	0	0	1	0	1,512	562.50	153	2,688	.088933	8.70	39.3	3,500	624
Ga.	0	0	1	0	3,197	675.47	178	4,733	.081501	16.4	49.7	3,956	1,090
Fla.	0	0	1	0	4,771	649.38	114	7,347	.13583	37.1	68.6	4,450	1,514
Ky.	0	0	1	0	2,063	624.02	181	3,306	.083380	6.0	40.0	3,634	714
Tenn.	0	0	1	0	2,446	600.69	175	4,072	.098529	10.0	48.9	3,708	892
Ala.	0	0	1	0	2,104	597.56	193	3,521	.069437	5.40	52.3	3,476	784
Miss.	0	0	1	0	1,427	632.54	255	2,256	.047700	1.80	17.7	3,188	526
Ark.	0	0	1	0	1,014	504.98	199	2,008	.038656	7.70	30.9	3,345	462
La.	0	0	1	0	2,691	719.90	196	3,738	.083196	11.9	54.8	3,565	846
Okla.	0	0	1	0	1,767	671.10	190	2,633	.038280	9.90	50.1	3,837	607
Tex.	0	0	1	0	7,246	624.44	141	11,604	.044267	16.9	73.5	4,085	2,738
Mont.	0	0	0	1	587	819.83	252	716	.004918	2.90	24.4	4,083	178
Idaho	0	0	0	1	512	678.15	180	755	.009132	6.90	15.8	3,711	185
Wyo.	0	0	0	1	368	1,063.6	369	346	.003560	.700	0.	4,269	86
Colo.	0	0	0	1	1,920	812.18	183	2,364	.02782	25.8	71.7	4,600	575
N. Mex.	0	0	0	1	823	764.87	277	1,076	.008862	6.80	31.1	3,512	285
Ariz.	0	0	0	1	1,523	775.85	150	1,963	.017308	36.1	74.5	4,273	485
Utah	0	0	0	1	821	728.48	196	1,127	.013728	18.9	77.6	3,741	306
Nev.	0	0	0	1	543	1,018.8	180	533	.004850	71.3	80.7	5,209	131
Wash.	0	0	0	1	3,070	898.19	184	3,418	.051344	19.5	66.0	4,601	791
Oreg.	0	0	0	1	1,766	808.24	201	2,185	.022717	18.2	61.2	4,339	471
Calif.	0	0	0	1	20,052	982.41	200	20,411	.13054	27.0	92.7	5,087	4,501
Alaska	0	0	0	1	698	2,147.7	570	325	.000574	33.6	0.	5,222	85
Hawaii	0	0	0	1	940	1,152.0	202	816	.12700	21.7	81.9	5,153	182

6.8 (a) Using the residuals from the OLS estimation of EXP $= \beta_1 + \beta_2(\text{POP}) + \beta_3(\text{AID}) + \beta_4(\text{INC}) + \varepsilon$, perform a Park-Glejser test for heteroscedasticity by regressing $|\hat{\varepsilon}_i|$ on POP to test the hypothesis that Variance $(\hat{\varepsilon}_i) = C(\text{POP}_i)^2$.

(b) Regress $|\hat{\varepsilon}_i|$ on log $|\text{POP}_i|$ and test for heteroscedasticity. What would the difference be if you regressed log ε_i^2 on log POP_i?

(c) Using the results from the regression of log $|\varepsilon_i|$ on log $|\text{POP}_i|$, reestimate the model EXP $= \beta_1 + \beta_2(\text{POP}) + \beta_3(\text{AID}) + \beta_4(\text{INC}) + \varepsilon$.

6.9 This exercise uses the investment data set in Table 6.3.

(a) Define the new variable DEL by DEL = RAAA% − RCP%, and estimate by OLS the model
IRC = $\beta_1 + \beta_2(YD) + \beta_3(DEL) + \beta_4(PIRC) + \varepsilon$,

where
IRC = residential FIXED investment, 1972 dollars

YD = disposable personal income, 1972 dollars

RAAA% = corporate AAA bond interest rate

PIRC = deflator for investment in residential construction, 1972 = 100

(b) Using the residuals from the above regression, compute the DW statistic (or use the printed DW statistic) and test to see if there is positive serial correlation. (If possible, plot the residuals and see if you can tell whether serial correlation is present.)

(c) If the error term ε_t satisfies $\varepsilon_t = \rho\varepsilon_{t-1} + v_t$, a first-order serial-correlation model, what value of ρ is suggested by the computed DW statistic?

(d) Regress $\hat{\varepsilon}_t$ on $\hat{\varepsilon}_{t-1}$, suppressing the constant (step 1 in a Cochrane-Orcutt procedure). Estimate the model $\varepsilon_t = \rho\varepsilon_{t-1} + v_t$. Test at the 5 percent level of significance the hypothesis that $\rho = 1$.

(e) Derive the following variables:

$$IRC'_t = IRC_t - \hat{\rho}(IRC_{t-1}) \qquad YD'_t = YD_t - \hat{\rho}(YD_{t-1})$$

$$DEL'_t = DEL_t - \hat{\rho}(DEL_{t-1}) \qquad PIRC'_t = PIRC_t - \hat{\rho}(PIRC_{t-1})$$

where $\hat{\rho}$ is the estimated ρ from part (d) above. Regress IRC' on YD', DEL', and PIRC'. (*Hint:* The first observation in the sample is lost.) Use these estimates to obtain estimates of β_1, β_2, β_3, and β_4.

(f) Using an efficient estimation technique (such as Cochrane-Orcutt), estimate β_1, β_2, β_3, β_4, and ρ.

(g) Compare the estimates for β_1, β_2, β_3, and β_4 obtained in parts (a), (e), and (f). Should you expect them to be similar? Which procedure yields the highest R^2 where

$$R^2 = 1 - \frac{\Sigma(IRC_t - IRC_t^{pred})^2}{\Sigma(IRC_t - \overline{IRC})^2}.$$

Table 6.3 Investment data set†

Date	PIRC	IRC	YD	RCP%	RAAA%
1954-1	66.5	27.5	398.4	2.037	2.957
1954-2	66.8	29.3	396.4	1.633	2.877
1954-3	67.5	31.1	402.9	1.363	2.883
1954-4	67.5	33.0	410.7	1.310	2.887
1955-1	67.8	35.5	413.7	1.613	2.960
1955-2	68.5	36.0	422.6	1.967	3.033
1955-3	69.1	35.2	429.6	2.327	3.100
1955-4	69.3	33.7	436.6	2.833	3.117
1956-1	70.0	32.5	439.7	3.000	3.097
1956-2	71.2	32.3	443.1	3.263	3.260
1956-3	71.4	31.6	445.4	3.350	3.423
1956-4	71.2	31.1	451.0	3.630	3.677
1957-1	71.2	30.4	451.3	3.630	3.700
1957-2	71.4	29.6	454.0	3.683	3.773
1957-3	71.7	29.3	456.2	3.953	4.070
1957-4	71.1	29.5	454.8	3.993	3.997
1958-1	71.0	28.7	450.4	2.817	3.607
1958-2	71.2	28.7	453.2	1.717	3.580
1958-3	71.3	30.8	463.0	2.130	3.870
1958-4	71.3	34.1	469.5	3.213	4.093
1959-1	71.0	37.9	472.6	3.303	4.130
1959-2	71.0	39.2	480.0	3.603	4.353
1959-3	71.0	38.3	476.8	4.193	4.473
1959-4	71.1	36.9	480.7	4.760	4.570
1960-1	71.2	38.2	485.5	4.687	4.553
1960-2	71.4	34.8	488.4	4.073	4.453
1960-3	71.5	33.5	488.2	3.373	4.313
1960-4	71.4	33.4	486.3	3.270	4.320
1961-1	71.3	33.8	490.6	3.013	4.270
1961-2	71.3	34.0	497.6	2.860	4.283
1961-3	71.3	35.7	502.8	2.897	4.437
1961-4	71.3	37.0	511.9	3.057	4.410
1962-1	71.5	37.1	516.4	3.243	4.410
1962-2	71.6	38.6	521.1	3.203	4.297
1962-3	71.5	38.9	523.7	3.333	4.337
1962-4	71.4	38.8	526.1	3.263	4.257
1963-1	71.6	40.2	530.6	3.310	4.197
1963-2	71.1	43.3	535.5	3.317	4.220
1963-3	70.2	43.9	541.1	3.697	4.287
1963-4	70.6	45.6	549.1	3.907	4.333
1964-1	69.9	46.4	559.7	3.950	4.370
1964-2	70.8	44.1	575.8	3.933	4.407
1964-3	71.8	42.8	583.0	3.910	4.410
1964-4	72.2	41.9	589.7	4.063	4.430
1965-1	72.2	43.4	595.5	4.300	4.420
1965-2	71.5	44.1	603.4	4.380	4.443
1965-3	72.8	43.0	620.1	4.380	4.497
1965-4	72.9	42.3	631.3	4.470	4.613
1966-1	72.9	42.7	636.2	4.970	4.813
1966-2	75.2	40.1	639.0	5.427	5.003
1966-3	74.6	38.0	646.4	5.790	5.320
1966-4	75.9	33.3	652.6	6.000	5.383
1967-1	76.6	32.7	661.6	5.450	5.120
1967-2	76.6	36.3	667.5	4.717	5.263

Date	PIRC	IRC	YD	RCP%	RAAA%
1967-3	77.4	38.4	672.5	4.973	5.617
1967-4	77.4	41.4	677.7	5.303	6.027
1968-1	78.8	41.9	686.3	5.580	6.127
1968-2	80.0	42.9	696.6	6.080	6.253
1968-3	80.9	42.8	697.0	5.963	6.077
1968-4	83.1	43.6	700.7	5.963	6.243
1969-1	85.3	45.2	701.8	6.657	6.700
1969-2	86.8	44.7	707.2	7.540	6.887
1969-3	88.9	42.9	718.8	8.487	7.063
1969-4	90.0	40.1	723.0	8.620	7.467
1970-1	89.9	40.2	727.4	8.553	7.893
1970-2	91.0	38.3	742.6	8.167	8.140
1970-3	90.4	39.6	750.1	7.837	8.220
1970-4	90.9	43.4	745.6	6.293	7.907
1971-1	92.4	46.4	761.4	4.590	7.217
1971-2	94.4	51.3	769.9	5.040	7.473
1971-3	95.4	54.6	769.9	5.743	7.557
1971-4	97.1	56.4	775.9	5.067	7.300
1972-1	98.0	60.9	783.7	4.060	7.233
1972-2	98.4	61.6	790.7	4.577	7.277
1972-3	100.3	61.7	803.7	4.937	7.207
1972-4	103.3	63.8	827.1	5.333	7.137
1973-1	106.0	64.4	845.1	6.283	7.220
1973-2	109.8	62.0	852.7	7.467	7.307
1973-3	113.2	58.3	858.2	9.873	7.587
1973-4	115.0	54.0	862.1	8.980	7.650
1974-1	117.8	49.5	846.7	8.303	7.897
1974-2	120.8	46.8	843.1	10.457	8.363
1974-3	124.6	44.0	843.0	11.533	8.987
1974-4	127.0	39.7	835.1	9.050	9.017
1975-1	130.2	36.3	829.8	6.563	8.707
1975-2	131.8	37.0	874.1	5.920	8.873
1975-3	133.0	39.5	863.1	6.667	8.913
1975-4	135.6	42.3	871.7	6.120	8.810
1976-1	137.2	45.5	881.8	5.290	8.557
1976-2	140.7	46.8	886.3	5.570	8.533
1976-3	143.8	46.8	891.5	5.530	8.463
1976-4	147.6	52.3	900.9	4.990	8.183
1977-1	152.3	53.5	904.8	4.810	8.033
1977-2	157.6	58.0	918.6	5.237	8.013
1977-3	160.6	58.8	931.9	5.807	7.947
1977-4	166.1	60.3	946.6	6.593	8.103
1978-1	168.6	59.5	952.1	6.797	8.450
1978-2	175.7	59.9	960.3	7.200	8.670
1978-3	182.6	59.7	968.7	8.050	8.760
1978-4	188.2	60.3	983.2	9.900	9.030
1979-1	191.4	57.7	990.2	10.100	9.290

DATE　　　= quarterly date of observation
PIRC　　　= price index for residential construction
IRC　　　　= quarterly fixed investment in residential capital, billions of dollars
YD　　　　= disposable income, billions of dollars
RCP%　　　= interest rate on 4- to 6-month commercial paper, %
RAAA%　　= interest rate on AAA-rated corporate bonds, %

　† SOURCE: University of Michigan RSQE Macroeconomic Model, available also in the Survey of Current Business.

INSTRUMENTAL VARIABLES AND
TWO-STAGE LEAST SQUARES

To this point we have assumed that each of the independent variables in the linear regression model was uncorrelated with the true error term. We focus in this chapter on the possible failure of that assumption, placing particular emphasis on problems associated with simultaneous equation models. More generally, we see that there are three instances when independent variables may be correlated with the error term:

1. One or more of the independent variables is measured with error.
2. One or more of the independent variables is determined in part (through one or more separate equations) by the dependent variable.
3. One or more of the independent variables is a lagged dependent variable in a model in which the error term is serially correlated.

We begin the chapter with the problem of errors in variables. While important in itself, this topic also serves as a useful introduction to the simultaneous-equation model. We will see that the ordinary least-squares regression process loses some of its desirable properties when one or more of the right-hand variables in the equation is measured with error. Some of these lost properties can be regained if new variables, called *instruments*, replace the variables measured with error and a new instrumental-variables estimation technique is used to replace ordinary least squares.

While instrumental-variables estimation is relevant when dealing with errors in variables, it is even more useful when dealing with estimation problems in the context of simultaneous-equation models. For this reason we continue the chapter by introducing the notion of simultaneous-equation systems and discuss the identification problem in an intuitive manner. With this necessary background, we return to the estimation problem by describing the technique of two-stage least squares, a frequently used type of instrumental-variables estimator. Finally, we conclude the chapter by mentioning the serious difficulties which arise when we attempt to estimate an equation in which a lagged value of the left-hand variable appears as an explanatory variable at the same time that the error process is serially correlated.

7.1 CORRELATION BETWEEN AN INDEPENDENT VARIABLE AND THE ERROR TERM

The difficulties arising when the independent variables and the error are correlated can best be seen by taking a close look at the two-variable model, with both variables measured in deviations form. The least-squares slope estimator is

$$\hat{\beta} = \frac{\sum x_i y_i}{\sum x_i^2} \qquad \text{where } y_i = \beta x_i + \varepsilon_i$$

Substituting and expanding terms, we get

$$\hat{\beta} = \frac{\beta \sum x_i^2 + \sum x_i \varepsilon_i}{\sum x_i^2} = \beta + \frac{\sum x_i \varepsilon_i}{\sum x_i^2} \tag{7.1}$$

The estimator $\hat{\beta}$ has been proved to be an unbiased estimator of β when the X variable observations were assumed to be fixed in repeated samples. The proof depended heavily upon the fact that the expected value of the second term on the right-hand side of Eq. (7.1) was equal to 0. Unfortunately, if we generalize the model to one in which the X's are stochastic in nature, i.e., drawn from a probability distribution, the proof that $\hat{\beta}$ is an unbiased estimator of β does not necessarily follow. To resolve this difficulty, we give up the hope of proving that the expression $\sum x_i \varepsilon_i$ has an expected value of 0 and concentrate instead on its value as the sample size gets arbitrarily large. If we can prove that the expression approaches 0 as the sample size grows, we can prove the consistency of the estimated parameter.

As a general rule there is no guarantee that X and ε will be uncorrelated and therefore no guarantee that $\hat{\beta}$ will be a consistent estimator of β. To see this, consider the case in which X and ε are known to be positively correlated irrespective of the sample size. A quick examination of Eq. (7.1) makes it apparent that the term on the right-hand side of the equation will be positive and that $\hat{\beta}$ will overestimate the true parameter value no matter what the sample

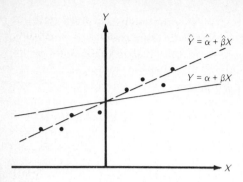

Figure 7.1 Correlations of x and e.

size. Thus, correlation between an independent variable and the error term leads, in general, to inconsistent ordinary least-squares parameter estimates. The particular example just used is depicted graphically in Fig. 7.1. The solid line represents the true regression line, while the dotted line represents the ordinary least-squares regression line. In achieving its objective of minimizing the sum of the squares of the estimated residuals, ordinary least squares yields biased and inconsistent estimates of the true regression slope parameter. In this case the slope has been overestimated. (The intercept estimate will be a biased and inconsistent estimator of the true intercept, while the estimated standard error of the regression and the standard errors of the coefficients will also be biased and inconsistent.)

7.2 ERRORS IN VARIABLES

We have assumed that all variables used in the regression calculation procedure were measured without error. In practice, measurement errors (as well as errors in misspecifying the model) are likely to occur, and, as we shall see, these errors can substantially alter the properties of the estimated regression parameters. We shall work through the problem of measurement error by considering several increasingly complex cases.

7.2.1 Case I: Y Is Measured with Error

Assume that the true regression model (written in deviations form) is

$$y_i = \beta x_i + \varepsilon_i \tag{7.2}$$

where ε_i represents errors associated with the specification of the model (the effects of omitted variables, etc.). Assume, in addition, that the variable y^*, rather than y, is obtained in the measurement process. We shall assume that

$$y_i^* = y_i + u_i \qquad \text{where Cov } (u_i, x_i) = 0 \tag{7.3}$$

The regression model is estimated with y^* as the dependent variable, with no account being taken of the fact that y^* is not an accurate measure of y. Adding the measurement error term u_i to each side of Eq. (7.2), we see that this is equivalent to running the regression

$$y_i^* = \beta x_i + (\varepsilon_i + u_i) \tag{7.4}$$

Note that if u_i did not have 0 mean, our estimated regression would need an intercept term. In any case, as long as u_i and x_i are uncorrelated, there is no problem associated with running the regression described in Eq. (7.4). The estimated slope parameter will be unbiased [since $E(u_i x_i) = 0$] and consistent. The only effect of the presence of measurement error in the dependent variable is to increase the error variance. However, the increased error variance will be accounted for in the estimate of s^2, the estimated residual variance, and all statistical tests will apply. (As a general rule, it is impossible to separate out the effects of errors associated with the regression model and measurement error, and no attempt is made to do so.) The situation is not so auspicious, however, when the X variable is also measured with error.

7.2.2 Case II: X Is Measured with Error

Assume that $x_i^* = x_i + v_i$, where x_i is the true value and x_i^* is the observed value. The true regression model is

$$y_i = \beta x_i + \varepsilon_i$$

while the actual regression run is

$$y_i = \beta x_i^* + (\varepsilon_i - \beta v_i) - \beta x_i^* + \varepsilon_i^* \tag{7.5}$$

Even if we assume that the measurement error in X is normally distributed with 0 mean, has no serial correlation, and is independent of the error in the true equation, problems arise when using ordinary least squares as a regression technique. This can be most easily seen by noting that the error ε^* and the variable x^* in Eq. (7.5) are correlated (or have a nonzero covariance). In particular,

$$\text{Cov}\,(\varepsilon_i^*, x_i^*) = E\big[(\varepsilon_i - \beta v_i)(x_i + v_i)\big] = -\beta \sigma_v^2$$

Thus, least-squares estimates of the regression parameters will be biased and inconsistent, the degree of bias and inconsistency being related to the variance of the measurement error.

7.2.3 Case III: X and Y Are Measured with Error†

This case contains no new conclusions compared with the previous case, but it will be instructive to examine it in some detail. The assumptions are as follows:

$$y_i^* = y_i + u_i \qquad u_i \sim N(0, \sigma_u^2) \qquad x_i^* = x_i + v_i \qquad v_i \sim N(0, \sigma_v^2) \qquad y_i = \beta x_i$$

† With no other error in the equation.

u_i and v_i are uncorrelated with each other as well as with x_i, and each error process itself involves no serial correlation. The estimated regression equation will be of the form

$$y_i^* = \beta x_i^* + (u_i - \beta v_i) \tag{7.6}$$

Now consider the ordinary least-squares estimator $\hat{\beta}$:

$$\hat{\beta} = \frac{\Sigma x_i^* y_i^*}{\Sigma x_i^{*2}} = \frac{\Sigma(x_i + v_i)(y_i + u_i)}{\Sigma(x_i + v_i)^2} = \frac{\Sigma(x_i + v_i)(\beta x_i + u_i)}{\Sigma(x_i + v_i)^2}$$

$$= \frac{\beta \Sigma x_i^2 + \beta \Sigma x_i v_i + \Sigma x_i u_i + \Sigma v_i u_i}{\Sigma x_i^2 + \Sigma v_i^2 + 2\Sigma x_i v_i}$$

Since x_i, u_i, and v_i are all stochastic, it is not easy to evaluate the bias of $\hat{\beta}$. The reason is that the expected value of the ratio of two random variables is not equal to the ratio of the expected value of the variables. However, we can evaluate the consistency of $\hat{\beta}$ by evaluating the expression for $\hat{\beta}$ in the limit as the sample size gets large. This calculation is denoted plim $\hat{\beta}$. Since u_i and v_i are uncorrelated with each other as well as x_i, it follows that†

$$\text{plim } \hat{\beta} = \text{plim} \frac{\beta \Sigma x_i^2}{\Sigma x_i^2 + \Sigma v_i^2} = \frac{\beta \text{ Var}(x)}{\text{Var}(x) + \sigma_v^2} = \frac{\beta}{1 + \sigma_v^2/\text{Var}(x)} \tag{7.7}$$

The derivation just completed suggests, under quite restrictive assumptions, that the presence of measurement error of the type in question will lead to an underestimate of the true regression parameter if ordinary least-squares techniques are used. It tells us in addition that if the variance in the error of measurement of X is known, one can obtain consistent parameter estimates. Unfortunately, it is difficult to imagine much information of this type being available.

As a final item, we should stress that case III has been developed under the assumption that no underlying equation error exists. This is, of course, unlikely to be the case, and makes further pursuit of solutions to the estimation problem in this context undesirable. In particular, we will not discuss the solution to the errors-in-variables problem in the unlikely situation that the ratio of the measurement error variances is known.‡

7.2.4 Instrumental-Variables Estimation

The problem of errors in measurement of regression variables is quite clearly an important one, and yet econometricians do not have much to offer in the way of

---

† We have utilized a result that for random variables Z_1 and Z_2, plim (Z_1/Z_2) = plim Z_1/plim Z_2. In this particular case we divide the numerator and denominator by N and use the fact that plim $\Sigma x_i^2/N = \text{Var}(x)$ and plim $\Sigma v_i^2/N = \sigma_v^2$.

‡ This case is discussed in detail in J. Johnston, *Econometric Methods*, 2d ed. (New York: McGraw-Hill, 1972), chap. 6, and in other standard texts. Alternative estimation techniques are discussed in J. Kmenta, *Elements of Econometrics* (New York: Macmillan, 1971), chap. 9.

useful solutions. As a general rule, we tend to pass over the problem of measurement error, hoping that the errors are too small and random to destroy the validity of the estimation procedure. One technique which is available and can solve (in principle) the measurement error problem is the technique of *instrumental-variables estimation*.† We shall briefly outline the concept of instrumental variables, in part because it is likely to be useful in error measurement and in part because it is an important estimation technique when one is dealing with models consisting of systems of simultaneous equations.

The method of instrumental variables involves the search for a new variable Z which is both highly correlated with the independent variable X and at the same time uncorrelated with the error term in the equation (as well as the errors of measurement of both variables). In practice, we are concerned with the consistency of parameter estimates and therefore concentrate on the relationship between the variable Z and the remaining model variables when the sample size gets large. We define the random variable Z to be an *instrument* if:

1. The correlations between Z and ε, u, and v in the equation approach zero as the sample size gets large.‡
2. The correlation between Z and X is nonzero as the sample size gets large.

In any given situation it is conceivable that no such instruments will exist or that many instruments will exist. If we are fortunate to be able to choose from several instruments, we simply select the one instrument (or combination of instruments) having the highest correlation with the X variable.

Assuming for the moment that such a variable can be found, we can alter the least-squares regression procedure to obtain estimated parameters which are consistent. Given the nature of the assumptions underlying the choice of instruments, there is unfortunately no guarantee that the estimation process will yield unbiased parameter estimates. To simplify matters, consider case II, in which $y_i = \beta x_i + \varepsilon_i$ and only x is measured with error (as $x^* = x + v$). The correct instrumental-variables estimator of the regression slope in the two-variable model is

$$\beta^* = \frac{\sum y_i z_i}{\sum x_i^* z_i} \tag{7.8}$$

The choice of this particular form of estimator is made so that the resulting estimates will be consistent. To see this, we can derive the relationship between the instrumental-variables estimator and the true slope parameter in a manner similar to the derivation in Eq. (7.1):

$$\beta^* = \frac{\sum y_i z_i}{\sum x_i^* z_i} = \frac{\beta \sum x_i^* z_i + \sum z_i \varepsilon_i^*}{\sum x_i^* z_i} = \beta + \frac{\sum z_i \varepsilon_i^*}{\sum x_i^* z_i} \tag{7.9}$$

---

† For a discussion of several alternative estimation procedures, see Johnston, op. cit., sec. 9-4.
‡Technically speaking, we need to refer to the properties of estimators in the probability limit.

Clearly, the choice of Z as an instrument guarantees that β^* will approach β as the sample size gets large (since $\sum z_i \varepsilon_i^* / N$ approaches 0) and will therefore be a consistent estimator of β. One might wonder why the variable x_i^* was not replaced by z_i in the denominator of the instrumental-variables estimator. The reader should check using the above procedure that the estimator $\beta^{**} = \sum y_i z_i / \sum z_i^2$ does not yield a consistent estimate of β (see Exercise 7.2).

The technique of instrumental variables appears to provide a simple solution to a difficult problem. We have defined an estimation technique which is guaranteed to yield consistent estimates if we can find an appropriate instrument. However, this is likely to be a very difficult problem when errors of measurement are present. The obvious instrument to choose is the true variable, but this is not available or it would have been chosen in the first place. In practice one must search for a suitable replacement which should be highly correlated with the original variable and uncorrelated with the error in the equation (as the sample size gets large).

Before considering simultaneous-equation models in the next section a few concluding comments may be instructive. First, the ordinary least-squares estimation technique is actually a special case of instrumental variables. This follows by definition, because in the classical regression model X is uncorrelated with the error term and because X is perfectly correlated with itself. Second, if we generalize the measurement error problem to errors in more than one independent variable, one instrument is needed to replace *each* of the designated independent variables. The parameter estimates obtained are, of course, sensitive to the specific choice of instruments made. Finally, we should note that instrumental-variables estimation guarantees consistent estimation, but it does not guarantee unbiased estimation. The loss of unbiasedness is not to be taken lightly. In time-series analysis, in particular, the existence of small samples limits the importance of the consistency criterion.

7.3 INTRODUCTION TO SIMULTANEOUS EQUATION MODELS

Quite frequently in business and economic modeling, the process or processes under study can best be represented by a series of simultaneous interdependent equations. The most common examples of such equations are supply-demand models, in which the price of a product is simultaneously determined by the interaction of producers and consumers in a market, and macroeconomic income determination models, in which aggregate consumption and aggregate disposable income are simultaneously determined. We shall use both these models to illustrate the fact that the ordinary least-squares estimation of individual equations in a simultaneous equation model can lead to biased and inconsistent parameter estimates. We shall then discuss in an elementary manner alternative single-equation estimation procedures which yield consistent parameter estimates. More advanced methods of estimating simultaneous equation systems and extensions of the techniques described here will be considered in Chapter 11.

From this point on we shall think of economic and business models as consisting of a series of equations, each equation serving to explain one variable which is determined in the model. For this reason, it will be useful to replace our former notions of independent and dependent variables with some new terminology. Consider a three-equation supply-demand model described as follows:

Supply: $Q_t^S = \alpha_1 + \alpha_2 P_t + \alpha_3 P_{t-1} + \varepsilon_t$

Demand: $Q_t^D = \beta_1 + \beta_2 P_t + \beta_3 Y_t + u_t$ (7.10)

Equilibrium: $Q_t^D = Q_t^S$

The supply equation, demand equation, and equilibrium condition will determine the market price and the quantity supplied (and demanded) when the market is in equilibrium. For this reason, the variables Q_t^D, Q_t^S, and P_t are often called *endogenous* variables; they are determined within the system of equations. On the other hand, the model contains two variables whose values are not determined directly within the system. These so-called *predetermined variables* help to cause the movement of the endogenous variables within the system. P_{t-1} and Y_t are both predetermined variables in the model summarized in Eq. (7.10). There is, of course, an important difference between the two predetermined variables. The first variable P_{t-1} is in fact determined within the system, but by past values of the variables. Thus, *lagged endogenous* variables are predetermined variables.† Finally, the variable Y_t is completely determined outside the model system and is called an *exogenous* variable.

We wish to consider whether bias or inconsistency will be introduced if (for example) the supply equation is estimated using ordinary least squares. In order to simplify matters, we shall rewrite the original model, eliminating the lagged price term from the supply equation and substituting for the equilibrium values of Q_t^S and Q_t^D (represented as Q_t). The theoretically specified model is:

Supply: $Q_t = \alpha_1 + \alpha_2 P_t + \varepsilon_t$

Demand: $Q_t = \beta_1 + \beta_2 P_t + \beta_3 Y_t + u_t$ (7.11)

To simplify our analysis, we will have occasion to use the model with all variables measured in deviations form, obtained by substituting $q_t = Q_t - \bar{Q}$, $y_t = Y_t - \bar{Y}$, and $p_t = P_t - \bar{P}$ into (7.11):

Supply: $q_t = \alpha_2 p_t + \varepsilon_t$

Demand: $q_t = \beta_2 p_t + \beta_3 y_t + u_t$ (7.12)

---

† In most of this chapter we shall consider all lagged endogenous variables as predetermined. This assumption is reasonable as long as there is no serial correlation associated with the error term in the equation containing the lagged endogenous equation. We discuss the specific problems associated with serial correlation and lagged endogenous variables in Section 7.7. For a more detailed discussion of lags, see Section 9.1.

Such a model is called a *structural model* because the form is given from the underlying theory. A structural model contains endogenous variables on the left-hand side and (if simultaneous) contains endogenous as well as predetermined variables on the right-hand side.

Our study of the properties of the equation system and derivations which follow will be aided if we solve the equations in (7.12) for each of the endogenous variables as a function solely of the predetermined variables in the model. The so-called *reduced-form solution* is listed below, first in terms of the original variables (7.13) and second when the variables are measured as deviations about their means (7.14).†

$$Q_t = \frac{\alpha_2 \beta_1 - \alpha_1 \beta_2}{\alpha_2 - \beta_2} + \frac{\alpha_2 \beta_3}{\alpha_2 - \beta_2} Y_t + \frac{\alpha_2 u_t - \beta_2 \varepsilon_t}{\alpha_2 - \beta_2}$$

$$P_t = \frac{\beta_1 - \alpha_1}{\alpha_2 - \beta_2} + \frac{\beta_3}{\alpha_2 - \beta_2} Y_t + \frac{u_t - \varepsilon_t}{\alpha_2 - \beta_2} \tag{7.13}$$

$$q_t = \frac{\alpha_2 \beta_3}{\alpha_2 - \beta_2} y_t + \frac{\alpha_2 u_t - \beta_2 \varepsilon_t}{\alpha_2 - \beta_2} = \pi_{12} y_t + v_{1t}$$

$$p_t = \frac{\beta_3}{\alpha_2 - \beta_2} y_t + \frac{u_t - \varepsilon_t}{\alpha_2 - \beta_2} = \pi_{22} y_t + v_{2t} \tag{7.14}$$

The reader should note that using variables measured in deviations form eliminates the constant term in each of the reduced-form equations but does not alter the other parameters in any way.

Let us assume that we wish to estimate the supply equation in (7.12) using ordinary least squares. The slope parameter estimate would be

$$\alpha_2 = \frac{\sum p_t q_t}{\sum p_t^2} \tag{7.15}$$

Substituting for q_t in equation system (7.12), we find that

$$\hat{\alpha}_2 = \frac{\sum p_t(\alpha_2 p_t + \varepsilon_t)}{\sum p_t^2} = \alpha_2 + \frac{\sum p_t \varepsilon_t}{\sum p_t^2} \tag{7.16}$$

If the summation $\sum p_t \varepsilon_t$ on the right-hand side equaled 0 on average, we would

---

† To get the reduced form in the latter case, for example, we set the right-hand side of both equations in (7.12) equal; that is, $\alpha_2 p_t + \varepsilon_t = \beta_2 p_t + \beta_3 y_t + u_t$. Solving for p_t, we obtain the second equation in (7.14). Then substituting this equation into $q_t = \alpha_2 p_t + \varepsilon_t$ in (7.12), we get the first equation in (7.14). When the reduced-form model contains lagged endogenous variables on the right-hand side of the equation, it is sometimes useful to solve the system further by repeated elimination to obtain a *final form*, in which current and lagged exogenous variables (and errors) appear on the right-hand side. The use of the final form is discussed in H. Theil, *Principles of Econometrics* (New York: Wiley, 1971), p. 464.

know that ordinary least squares was unbiased. Likewise, if the sum approached 0 as the sample size became large, we would know that ordinary least-squares estimation was consistent. Unfortunately, however, neither of the above is true in general. In simultaneous-equation models, where (endogenous) variables in one equation feed back into variables in another equation, the error terms are correlated with the endogenous variables and least squares is both biased and inconsistent. To see the existence of bias, we calculate the expected value of $\sum p_t \varepsilon_t$, while substituting for p_t in the reduced-form equation system (7.14):

$$E\left(\sum p_t \varepsilon_t\right) = \frac{\beta_3}{\alpha_2 - \beta_2} E\left(\sum y_t \varepsilon_t\right) + \frac{1}{\alpha_2 - \beta_2} E\left(\sum u_t \varepsilon_t\right) - \frac{1}{\alpha_2 - \beta_2} E\left(\sum \varepsilon_t^2\right)$$

$$= \frac{1}{\alpha_2 - \beta_2} E\left(\sum u_t \varepsilon_t\right) - \frac{1}{\alpha_2 - \beta_2} E\left(\sum \varepsilon_t^2\right) \qquad \text{since } y_t \text{ is exogenous}$$

$$= \frac{T \operatorname{Cov}(u_t, \varepsilon_t) - T \operatorname{Var}(\varepsilon_t)}{\alpha_2 - \beta_2} \qquad\qquad (7.17)$$

where T is the number of observations. The expression in Eq. (7.17) will equal 0 only when the errors from the two equations are uncorrelated and there is no error variance in the supply equation, or when the covariance and variance terms just happen to cancel out—both extremely unlikely occurrences. An analogous derivation would yield similar conclusions about the consistency properties of ordinary least squares.

In the case of the supply-demand model, it will not always be possible even to predict the direction of bias resulting from the use of least-squares estimation because the expression in (7.17) may be either positive or negative. In using least squares to estimate an aggregate-consumption function in a simple model of national income determination, however, the direction of bias is known. Written in deviations form, the structural model is

$$c_t = \beta y_t + \varepsilon_t \qquad y_t = c_t + i_t + g_t \qquad\qquad (7.18)$$

where c = aggregate consumption
  i = investment
  g = government spending
  y = national income
  β = marginal propensity to consume $(0 < \beta < 1)$
i_t and g_t are exogenous variables, and c_t and y_t are endogenous.

The reduced form of the model contains two equations with endogenous variables c_t and y_t on the left-hand side and exogenous variables i_t and g_t on the right. We solve by substituting for y_t in the consumption equation to get

$$c_t = \frac{\beta}{1-\beta} i_t + \frac{\beta}{1-\beta} g_t + \frac{\varepsilon_t}{1-\beta} \qquad y_t = \frac{1}{1-\beta} i_t + \frac{1}{1-\beta} g_t + \frac{\varepsilon_t}{1-\beta}$$

$$(7.19)$$

Thus, using ordinary least squares, we have

$$\hat{\beta} = \frac{\sum c_t y_t}{\sum y_t^2} \qquad \text{from Eq. (7.18)}$$

$$= \frac{\sum y_t(\beta y_t + \varepsilon_t)}{\sum y_t^2} = \beta + \frac{\sum y_t \varepsilon_t}{\sum y_t^2}$$

and

$$E\left(\sum y_t \varepsilon_t\right) = \frac{1}{1 - \beta}\left[E\left(\sum i_t \varepsilon_t\right) + E\left(\sum g_t \varepsilon_t\right) + E\left(\sum \varepsilon_t^2\right)\right]$$

$$= \frac{T}{1 - \beta} \text{Var}(\varepsilon_t)$$

Here, with only one structural equation containing an error term, the direction of bias is clear. Ordinary least squares will overestimate the true value of the marginal propensity to consume.

Before considering alternative estimation techniques which yield consistent parameter estimates, we should note that the reduced-form equations in (7.19) can be helpful if we wish to predict the long-run effects on C and Y of changes in government spending and investment. For example, a change of \$1 billion in exogenous government spending will lead, in the long run, to a change of $\beta/(1 - \beta)$ billion dollars in aggregate consumption and a change of $1/(1 - \beta)$ billion dollars in disposable income. The factor $1/(1 - \beta)$ is often called the *multiplier*, since the long-run effect is a multiple of the short-run effect.

7.4 CONSISTENT PARAMETER ESTIMATION

Let us return to the supply-demand example of Eqs. (7.11) and (7.12) and concentrate on the consistent estimation of the *supply parameters*. For convenience, the structural and reduced-form equation systems are reproduced below:

Structural model:

Supply: $\qquad\qquad q_t = \alpha_2 p_t + \varepsilon_t$

Demand: $\qquad\qquad q_t = \beta_2 p_t + \beta_3 y_t + u_t$ $\qquad\qquad$ (7.12)

Reduced-form model:

$$q_t = \pi_{12} y_t + v_{1t} \qquad p_t = \pi_{22} y_t + v_{2t} \qquad (7.14)$$

The discussion in Section 7.2 suggests one approach to the estimation problem —that of instrumental variables. In fact, instrumental-variables estimation is quite reasonable in the context of simultaneous-equation models, because the predetermined variables in the model serve as excellent instrumental variables. The fact that they are present in the model suggests that they are correlated with the endogenous variables, and the fact that they are predetermined guarantees (by assumption) that they are uncorrelated with the error term. In the supply-demand example the variable y_t would serve as a suitable instrument, yielding the following consistent estimate of the supply slope parameter:

$$\hat{\alpha}_2^* = \frac{\Sigma y_t q_t}{\Sigma p_t y_t}$$

As a rule, the selection of instruments need not be limited to the variables in the model, but such a limitation serves to simplify and regularize the search process.

   While the use of instrumental variables is a perfectly appropriate estimation process, we are often faced with the problem of choosing among several available instruments. Such a choice is often arbitrary and will affect the results of the estimation process. For this reason, we shall examine some alternative single-equation estimation techniques, each implicitly involving different assumptions about instrument choice. As a first step, consider the reduced-form equation system of Eq. (7.14). Since the reduced-form equations contain only exogenous variables on the right-hand side, it is clear that ordinary least squares will estimate the reduced form consistently and with lack of bias. Let us examine these estimated coefficients, $\hat{\pi}_{12}$ and $\hat{\pi}_{22}$, more closely. Notice that π_{12}/π_{22} is identically equal to α_2. This suggests that we can estimate α_2 consistently by solving for the reduced-form equations, estimating them using ordinary least squares, and then solving to get the estimates of the supply slope parameter, that is, $\hat{\alpha}_2^{**} = \hat{\pi}_{12}/\hat{\pi}_{22}$. In fact, such a procedure is quite legitimate for the supply-demand model and is called *indirect least-squares* estimation. The indirect least-squares estimation process can be used to obtain consistent parameter estimates.†

   When indirect least-squares estimation is possible and a unique estimate of the structural parameter is available, it is not difficult to show that indirect least-squares estimation is *identical* to instrumental-variables estimation with y_t being chosen as the instrument. To see this, substitute for $\hat{\pi}_{12}/\hat{\pi}_{22}$, using our knowledge about ordinary least-squares estimation:

$$\hat{\alpha}_2^{**} = \frac{\hat{\pi}_{12}}{\hat{\pi}_{22}} = \frac{\Sigma y_t q_t / \Sigma y_t^2}{\Sigma p_t y_t / \Sigma y_t^2} = \frac{\Sigma y_t q_t}{\Sigma p_t y_t} = \hat{\alpha}_2^*$$

   Unfortunately, the example above cannot be generalized. In some cases indirect least squares is not possible, and in other cases it leads to several distinct slope estimates. Consider first the same supply-demand example but assume that we wish to estimate the slope parameter of the *demand equation*. This would mean using the estimated parameters of the reduced form to obtain an estimate of the parameter β_2. But a brief glance at equation system (7.14) will show that this is impossible; there is no way that the structural parameter can be obtained through estimation of the reduced-form system.‡ On the other hand,

---

   † We cannot prove that indirect least-squares estimators are unbiased. The possible bias is introduced when the ratio of the two unbiased reduced-form estimated parameters is taken.

   ‡ The problem of structural equation is an important one. We will consider it in greater detail in the next section and in Chapter 11.

consider the supply-demand system when the demand equation has been modified to include a second exogenous variable W for wealth. The structural equations and reduced-form equations are listed below, with all variables measured in deviations form:

Structural model:
$$q_t = \alpha_2 p_t + \varepsilon_t$$
$$q_t = \beta_2 p_t + \beta_3 y_t + \beta_4 w_t + u_t \tag{7.20}$$

Reduced-form model:

$$q_t = \frac{\alpha_2 \beta_3}{\alpha_2 - \beta_2} y_t + \frac{\alpha_2 \beta_4}{\alpha_2 - \beta_2} w_t + \frac{\alpha_2 u_t - \beta_2 \varepsilon_t}{\alpha_2 - \beta_2} = \pi_{12} y_t + \pi_{13} w_t + v_{1t}$$

$$p_t = \frac{\beta_3}{\alpha_2 - \beta_2} y_t + \frac{\beta_4}{\alpha_2 - \beta_2} w_t + \frac{u_t - \varepsilon_t}{\alpha_2 - \beta_2} = \pi_{22} y_t + \pi_{23} w_t + v_{2t} \tag{7.21}$$

Once again, the reduced-form equations can be consistently estimated using ordinary least squares. However, we are faced with two choices of supply slope estimators when we attempt to use the indirect least-squares technique. The two estimators are $\hat{\pi}_{12}/\hat{\pi}_{22}$ (as before) and $\hat{\pi}_{13}/\hat{\pi}_{23}$. In general, both estimators will yield consistent estimates of the true parameter, but the estimates will not be identical in each sample. Thus, if we attempt to use indirect least squares, we are faced with two choices, either one of which may involve a loss of important information about the model being estimated.

We have seen that indirect least squares is impossible in some cases, yields a unique solution in other cases, and yields a surfeit of possible solutions in still a third case. Each of these three cases is important in its own right. To distinguish conceptually between the three cases, we shall pause to consider an important set of problems that arise when one is originally specifying the model to be studied.

7.5 THE IDENTIFICATION PROBLEM†

We have just seen that knowledge of the reduced form of a system of equations is not always sufficient to allow us to discern the value of the parameters in the original set of structural equations. The problem of whether we can determine the structural equations, given knowledge of the reduced form, is called the *identification problem*. However, we should note that knowledge of the structural parameters is not absolutely necessary if prediction or forecasting is our primary purpose, because forecasts can be obtained through the reduced-form equations directly.

The consideration of the identification problem comes before consideration of the estimation problem. Once a structural model has been specified, we must check immediately to see whether the equation or equations of interest are

---

† A more extensive discussion of the identification problem appears in Section 11.2.

identified, i.e., whether we can obtain knowledge of the structural parameters once the reduced form has been estimated. After the identification problem has been explicitly considered, we can then proceed to choose between alternative estimation techniques. As hinted in the previous section, the choice of estimation technique may be quite important in situations in which there is more than one way to estimate the structural parameters, given knowledge of the reduced form.

We shall say that an equation is *unidentified* if there is no way of estimating all the structural parameters from the reduced form. An equation is *identified* if it is possible to obtain values of the parameters from the reduced-form equation system. An equation is *exactly identified* if a unique parameter value exists and *overidentified* if more than one value is obtainable for some parameters. While we have concentrated on the identification of single equations in a structural system of equations, it is important to realize that within a given structural model, some equations may be identified while others may not. In fact, within a single equation, it is possible that some parameters may be identified while others may remain unidentified.

Let us continue with our discussion of the identification problem on a more practical level by considering the supply-demand models described previously. Consider first a supply-demand time-series model model in which there are no predetermined variables:

Supply: $$Q_t = \alpha_1 + \alpha_2 P_t + \varepsilon_t$$

Demand: $$Q_t = \beta_1 + \beta_2 P_t + u_t$$

(7.22)

We assume that the market is in equilibrium in each time period so that quantity demanded equals quantity supplied (we have already eliminated the equilibrium condition by substitution). The key to understanding the identification problem in the context of this model is to focus on the equilibrium condition. At each period of time, there is one value of the price P and one value for the quantity sold Q. In other words, the only data available to the econometrician are the market values (for each period of time) of P and Q. The errors in the equations will make it likely that the values of P and Q obtained will not be identical, but it is likely that all values will lie close to the equilibrium values of P and Q determined by the direct solution of the equations in the model. This situation is depicted in Fig. 7.2. When we try to estimate the separate supply and demand equations using the market data, we obtain meaningless results. There is no way to ascertain the true supply and demand slopes given only the equilibrium data. In fact, the only reason why estimation is possible is because errors appear in both equations.

The model we are describing is one in which both the supply curve and the demand curve are unidentified. Neither equation is identified, because there is no way to obtain the values of the structural parameters (the slopes and intercepts of the individual supply and demand curves) from the reduced-form equations. (The reader should check to see that the reduced form is simply the equation describing the point of intersection of the demand and supply curves

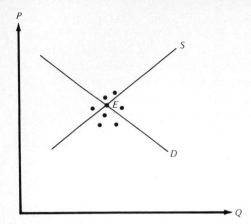

P

Q

Figure 7.2 Supply-demand model.

with errors attached.) The reduced-form equations for the deviations form are

$$p_t = \frac{u_t - \varepsilon_t}{\alpha_2 - \beta_2} \quad \text{and} \quad q_t = \frac{\alpha_2 u_t - \beta_2 \varepsilon_t}{\alpha_2 - \beta_2}$$

It should be apparent from examination of Fig. 7.2 that any pair of demand and supply curves intersecting at point E could just as easily have been the "true" demand and supply curves. In other words, there are an infinite number of structural models (demand and supply curves) which are consistent with the same reduced form (equilibrium value of P and Q). We stress that the problem here does not involve a lack of data. One could have an infinite number of data points for econometric analysis, but the best one could do would be to estimate the equilibrium values of P and Q with great accuracy; the demand and supply curves would still be unidentified.

It should be apparent that identification of equations in a model system necessitates further information of one sort or another. Consider, for example, the supply-demand system of Eq. (7.11) (reproduced here, for convenience):

Supply: $\qquad\qquad Q_t = \alpha_1 + \alpha_2 P_t + \varepsilon_t$

Demand: $\qquad\qquad Q_t = \beta_1 + \beta_2 P_t + \beta_3 Y_t + u_t$ $\qquad$ (7.23)

Under the assumption that $\beta_3 \neq 0$ and that Y_t does vary substantially over time, we cannot plot one demand curve and one supply curve for all time periods. Because income determines demand and income varies over time, we must account for the fact that the demand curve shifts over time. This situation is depicted in Fig. 7.3.

For each point in time, we obtain a set of values for P and Q, each of which describes the equilibrium (or an approximation thereof) of supply and demand. Because the demand curve shifts over time, the equilibrium values of P and Q also shift over time. It should be clear from Fig. 7.3 that the equilibrium values trace out the path of the underlying supply curve. Thus, the supply curve is

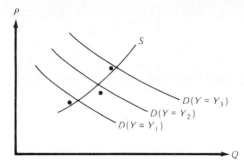

Figure 7.3 Supply curve identified.

identified because the supply parameters can be deduced from the reduced form (the movement of the equilibrium of P and Q). Notice that it is the movement of Y over time (or across observations in a cross-section analysis) that is necessary for the identification of the supply equation. The extent to which Y does move will have an effect on the confidence with which we can estimate the supply curve, but it is simply movement of Y that is important for purposes of identification.

We reiterate that identification is made possible by the existence of prior information about the exogenous variable Y. The supply equation is identified because the exogenous variable Y was excluded from the supply equation; i.e., the coefficient of Y in the supply equation was assumed to be 0. The demand equation is unidentified because prior information is not available which allows for the unique determination of the demand relationship. Were we to consider a model in which the supply relationship is determined by the temperature T in the region and the demand curve is not, then the prior information about the excluded exogenous variable (temperature) in the demand equation would allow the demand curve to be identified.

It is, of course, possible for both the demand and the supply curve to be identified. The following supply-demand model has just this property:

Supply: $Q_t = \alpha_1 + \alpha_2 P_t + \alpha_3 T_t + \varepsilon_t$

Demand: $Q_t = \beta_1 + \beta_2 P_t + \beta_3 Y_t + u_t$ (7.24)

In this case, it is not easy to depict the supply-demand relationship graphically. It should be clear, however, that if T and Y vary over time (and are not perfectly correlated), both the demand and supply relationships will shift. The movement of the equilibrium values of P and Q is quite complex, since it results from temperature and income changes, but if sufficient data are available, we can determine the structural values of the demand and supply parameters uniquely. The shifting of the supply curve associated with changes in T helps to plot out the demand curve at the same time that shifts in demand (changes in Y) plot out the supply curve. To reiterate, it is the prior (to estimation) knowledge that certain exogenous variables (known to appear in the structural system) are excluded from individual equations within that system that allows the equations to be identified.

While prior knowledge of the excluded variables in an equation is the most common type of information which allows for identification, it is not the only kind possible. To be more complete, we shall list some examples of the other kinds of prior knowledge which might be sufficient to allow for the identification of the parameters of the supply equation.

1. If the slope of the supply curve were known *a priori*, it would be easy to determine the supply intercept by choosing the straight line with the given slope which best fits the points in Fig. 7.2.
2. If the errors associated with the supply curve are zero (or close to zero relative to demand), then the supply curve can be identified. The (relatively) large variances associated with the demand curve cause the equilibria to shift over time and the supply curve is then traced out. This situation is depicted in Fig. 7.4.

As a final model, reconsider Eq. (7.20), in which the demand curve is a function not only of income but also of wealth (the two are assumed not to be highly correlated). In this case the demand curve shifts over time due to changes in two variables. The supply equation is overidentified because there are two exogenous variables in the supply-demand system of equations which are excluded from the supply equation.

Our discussion has implicitly involved a search for conditions which are necessary to guarantee the identification of one equation in a two-equation system. The conditions for identification can be generalized in two directions, the first involving a search for necessary and sufficient conditions for identification and the second involving problems which arise when a more complex system is studied. We shall deal in some detail with both these issues when the identification problem is reconsidered in Chapter 11.

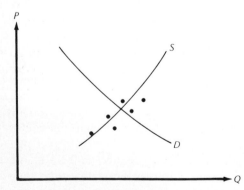

Figure 7.4 Supply curve identified.

7.6 TWO-STAGE LEAST SQUARES

Two-stage least squares (2SLS) provides a very useful estimation procedure for obtaining the values of structural parameters in overidentified equations. Two-stage least-squares estimation uses the information available from the specification of an equation system to obtain a unique estimate for each structural parameter. Intuitively speaking, the first stage of 2SLS involves the creation of an instrument, while the second stage involves a variant of instrumental-variables estimation. We describe very briefly the workings of two-stage least squares and outline some of its properties.†

Consider the supply-demand model described in Eq. (7.20). The structural model and the resulting reduced form are listed as follows (note that we are using deviations form, so that intercepts do not appear explicitly):

Structural model:

Supply: $\qquad\qquad q_t = \alpha_2 p_t + \varepsilon_t$

Demand: $\qquad\qquad q_t = \beta_2 p_t + \beta_3 y_t + \beta_4 w_t + u_t$ $\qquad\qquad$ (7.25)

Reduced form:

$$q_t = \pi_{12} y_t + \pi_{13} w_t + v_{1t} \qquad p_t = \pi_{22} y_t + \pi_{23} w_t + v_{2t} \qquad (7.26)$$

The supply equation of (7.25) is clearly overidentified so that neither indirect least squares nor instrumental variables (as described previously) would yield unique parameter estimates. The two-stage least-squares procedure works as follows:

1. In the first stage, the reduced-form equation for p_t is estimated using ordinary least squares. In general, this is accomplished by regressing p_t on all the predetermined variables in the equation system. From the first-stage regression, the fitted values of the dependent variable $\hat{p}_t$ are determined.‡ The fitted values $\hat{p}_t$ will by construction be independent of the error terms e_t and u_t (strictly speaking, this independence holds only in large samples, so that we are forced to rely on the consistency property of 2SLS). Thus, the first-stage process allows us to construct a variable which is linearly related to the predetermined model variables (through least-squares estimation) and which is purged of any correlation with the error term in the supply equation. It seems reasonable to view this newly created variable as an instrument to be used in the standard instrumental-variables estimation procedure.§ In order

---

† Two-stage least squares is described in more detail in Section 11.3.

‡ From (7.26), $\hat{p}_t = \hat{\pi}_{22} y_t + \hat{\pi}_{23} w_t$, where $\hat{\pi}_{22}$ and $\hat{\pi}_{23}$ are the ordinary least-squares parameter estimates.

§ It is possible to prove that two-stage least squares is an instrumental-variables estimator, whether the equation to be estimated is exactly identified or overidentified. For a proof, see, for example, Johnston, op cit., sec. 13-2.

to obtain more useful results, from a computational point of view, we shall proceed with the second stage of the estimation procedure in a slightly different manner.

2. In the second-stage regression, the supply equation of the structural model is estimated by replacing the variable p_t with the first-stage fitted variable $\hat{p}_t$. The use of ordinary least squares in this second stage will yield a consistent estimator of the supply parameter α_2. If additional predetermined variables appeared in the supply equation, two-stage least squares would also estimate those parameters consistently.

The 2SLS procedure is quite easy to use and is frequently employed when overidentified equations are present. By construction, 2SLS eliminates the problem of an oversupply of instruments by using combinations of the predetermined variables to create a new instrument. When an equation is exactly identified, 2SLS estimation is identical to indirect least-squares and instrumental-variables estimation. To see this, reexamine the model depicted in Eqs. (7.12) and (7.14). The 2SLS estimation would proceed as follows:

1. Use OLS to estimate the second part of Eq. (7.14). Then calculate the fitted values

$$\hat{p}_t = \hat{\pi}_{22}^* y_t \qquad \text{when } \hat{\pi}_{22}^* = \frac{\Sigma p_t y_t}{\Sigma y_t^2}$$

2. Use OLS to estimate the equation

$$q_t = \hat{\alpha}_2 \hat{p}_t + \varepsilon_t$$

Then,
$$\hat{\alpha}_2^{***} = \frac{\Sigma \hat{p}_t q_t}{\Sigma \hat{p}_t^2} = \frac{\Sigma y_t q_t (\Sigma p_t y_t / \Sigma y_t^2)}{\Sigma y_t^2 (\Sigma p_t y_t / \Sigma y_t^2)^2}$$

$$= \frac{\Sigma y_t q_t}{\Sigma p_t y_t} = \begin{cases} \hat{\alpha}_2^{**} & \text{using indirect least squares} \\ \hat{\alpha}_2^{*} & \text{using instrumental variables} \end{cases}$$

Thus, identical parameter estimates will be obtained *if the equation is exactly identified* when 2SLS, indirect least-squares, and instrumental variables estimation techniques are used. In the overidentified case we have seen that the indirect least-squares procedure is no longer valid. However, it is still possible to show that 2SLS and instrumental variables are equivalent estimation procedures on the condition that the first stage of two-stage least squares involves all predetermined variables in the system, and on the condition that the instrument used in the instrumental variables procedure is the fitted value of the first-stage regression, i.e., the regression of the variable correlated with the error term on all predetermined variables in the system.

What happens to 2SLS when the supply equation is not identified, e.g., when the variables y and w appear in the equation? The answer is that 2SLS is impossible when the equation is unidentified. This is quite easy to visualize if one recalls that the fitted-value variable used in the second-stage regression is a weighted average (or linear combination) of the predetermined variables in the system. If the supply equation is unidentified, no excluded variables exist in that equation. In our example this means that the supply equation includes the variables y and w. When one attempts to regress q_t on $\hat{p}_t, y_t$, and w_t in the second stage, the perfect collinearity between the three regressors will make estimation impossible.

7.7 SERIAL CORRELATION IN THE PRESENCE OF LAGGED DEPENDENT VARIABLES

We have noted in the introduction to this chapter and in Section 7.3 that simultaneous-equation estimation becomes substantially more difficult when predetermined variables include lagged dependent variables and at the same time the error term is serially correlated. In fact, when serial correlation is present, the notion that lagged endogenous variables are predetermined loses its validity. To see this, consider the simplest possible example of a one-equation model with serially correlated errors. The model is

$$y_t = \beta y_{t-1} + \varepsilon_t \qquad \text{with } \varepsilon_t = \rho \varepsilon_{t-1} + v_t \qquad (7.27)$$

In general, were ordinary least squares used to estimate the slope parameter, inconsistent and biased results would be obtained. Recall that

$$\hat{\beta} = \frac{\Sigma y_t y_{t-1}}{\Sigma y_{t-1}^2} = \beta + \frac{\Sigma y_{t-1}\varepsilon_t}{\Sigma y_{t-1}^2} = \beta + \frac{\text{Cov }(y_{t-1},\, \varepsilon_t)}{\text{Var }(y_{t-1})}$$

But the covariance of y_{t-1} and ε_t is nonzero, since

$$\text{Cov }(y_{t-1},\, \varepsilon_t) = E(y_{t-1}\varepsilon_t) = E(\beta y_{t-2} + \varepsilon_{t-1})(\rho\varepsilon_{t-1} + v_t)$$

$$= \beta\rho E(\varepsilon_{t-1}y_{t-2}) + \rho E(\varepsilon_{t-1}^2) + \beta E(v_t y_{t-2}) + E(\varepsilon_{t-1}v_t)$$

$$= \beta\rho E(\varepsilon_{t-1}y_{t-2}) + \rho E(\varepsilon_{t-1}^2)$$

But
$$E(\varepsilon_{t-1}^2) = E(\varepsilon_t^2) \qquad \text{and} \qquad E(\varepsilon_{t-1}y_{t-2}) = E(\varepsilon_t y_{t-1})$$

Therefore,
$$E(y_{t-1}\varepsilon_t) = \beta\rho E(y_{t-1}\varepsilon_t) + \rho E(\varepsilon_t^2)$$

or
$$\text{Cov }(y_{t-1},\, \varepsilon_t) = \frac{\rho \text{ Var }(\varepsilon_t)}{1 - \rho\beta} \qquad (7.28)$$

This covariance will be 0 only when ρ is 0, that is, when there is no serial correlation in the model. Thus, the presence of serial correlation and lagged dependent variables is sufficient to render the ordinary least-squares estimation process biased and inconsistent. Intuitively speaking, the presence of serial correlation and a lagged dependent variable poses a parameter identification problem for the econometrician. If ordinary least squares is used to estimate Eq. (7.27), it will be impossible to tell to what extent the parameter estimate reflects the presence of a nonzero slope and to what extent there is serial correlation in the model.

Correct procedures for the estimation of single-equation models with serially correlated errors and a lagged dependent variable do exist. In general they involve the use of modified instrumental variables or maximum-likelihood techniques.† In addition, procedures for simultaneous equation estimation must also be revised when serial correlation and lagged dependent variables exist. In particular, two-stage least-squares estimation must be modified somewhat if consistent parameter estimates are to be obtained.‡

While we will not go into further detail in estimation here, it is important to be able to test for serial correlation simply to know whether or not these sophisticated estimated techniques are needed.§ The DW statistic is no longer useful here because when one or more lagged endogenous variables are present, the DW statistic will often be close to 2 even when the errors are serially correlated. Of course, one could simply look at the DW statistic as providing an indicator of serial correlation when the DW statistic is low, but this approach is strongly biased against finding serial correlation. Fortunately, there is a relatively easy alternative test provided by Durbin which is strictly valid for large samples of data but can be used for small samples as well. To see how the test is applied assume that we have estimated Eq. (7.29) using ordinary least squares

$$Y_t = \alpha + \beta Y_{t-1} + \gamma X_t + \varepsilon_t \tag{7.29}$$

The test statistic to be used is the Durbin h statistic, defined as

$$h = \hat{\rho}\sqrt{\frac{T}{1 - T[\text{Var}(\hat{\beta})]}} \tag{7.30}$$

where $\text{Var}(\hat{\beta})$ is estimated as the square of the standard error of the coefficient of the lagged endogenous variable, T is the number of observations, and $\hat{\rho}$ is the estimated first-order serial-correlation coefficient. We have already seen in Chapter 6 that $\hat{\rho}$ can be estimated directly from the DW statistic, since $\text{DW} \approx 2(1 - \hat{\rho})$. Solving for $\hat{\rho}$ and substituting, we find that

$$h = \left(1 - \frac{\text{DW}}{2}\right)\sqrt{\frac{T}{1 - T[\text{Var}(\hat{\beta})]}} \tag{7.31}$$

Since Durbin has shown that the h statistic is approximately normally distributed with unit variance, the test for first-order serial correlation can be done directly by using the normal distribution table (Table 1). As an example assume

† The interested reader should see ibid., pp. 316–320.

‡ A useful procedure is described by R. C. Fair in "The Estimation of Simultaneous Equation Models with Lagged Endogenous Variables and First Order Serially Correlated Errors," *Econometrica*, May 1970.

§ For further details on this subject see M. Nerlove and K. F. Wallis, "Use of the Durbin-Watson Statistic in Inappropriate Situations," *Econometrica*, vol. 34, no. 1, pp. 235–238, January 1966. The basic results are derived in J. Durbin, "Testing for Serial Correlation in Least-Squares Regression When Some of the Regressors Are Lagged Dependent Variables," *Econometrica*, vol. 38, pp. 410–421, 1970. For some more general results, see G. S. Maddala, *Econometrics* (New York: McGraw-Hill, 1970).

that the estimated version of Eq. (7.29) is as follows (standard errors in parentheses):

$$\hat{Y}_t = \underset{(.5)}{1.0} + \underset{(.10)}{.6} \ Y_{t-1} + \underset{(1.3)}{3.0} \ X_t \qquad T = 50 \qquad DW = 1.8 \qquad (7.32)$$

Then, Var $(\hat{\beta}) = .01$, so that

$$h = \left(1 - \frac{1.8}{2}\right)\sqrt{\frac{50}{1 - 50(.01)}} = 1.0$$

At the 5 percent level, the critical value of the normal distribution is 1.645. Since 1.0 is less than 1.645, we *cannot reject* the null hypothesis of no serial correlation. As a result, ordinary least-squares estimation can be used. Notice that if the value of the DW statistic had been 1.6, the value of h would be 2.0. In this case we would reject the null hypothesis and conclude that there was serial correlation. However, had we used the DW statistic directly, we would have incorrectly concluded that serial correlation was absent.

Finally, it is important to note that the Durbin h test is not valid when $T \ \mathrm{Var} \ (\hat{\beta})$ is greater than 1. (We cannot take the square root of a negative number.) In this case, Durbin proposes an alternative test which is only slightly more complicated. We obtain the residual variable $\hat{\varepsilon}_t$ from the ordinary least-squares regression and also create the lagged residual variable $\hat{\varepsilon}_{t-1}$. To simplify matters, the first observation should be dropped, so that all variables have $T - 1$ rather than T observations. We then estimate Eq. (7.33) as

$$\hat{\varepsilon}_t = \alpha + \rho^*\hat{\varepsilon}_{t-1} + \beta^* Y_{t-1} + \gamma^* X_t + u_t \qquad (7.33)$$

We then do a t test of the null hypothesis that ρ^* is not significantly different from 0. If we reject that null hypothesis, we conclude that first-order serial correlation is present. For example, if in the previous calculations we had obtained the same regression results with $T = 150$, we would find that the h statistic could not be calculated and Eq. (7.33) would have to be estimated.

Example 7.1 Demand for electricity The price elasticity of demand for electricity is an important policy parameter for those concerned with United States energy policy. A low elasticity (especially in the long run) means that substantial increases in price will be necessary to discourage consumer demand. A recent study of electricity demand provides such a price-elasticity estimate.† The model is specified as

$$\log Q = \alpha_1 + \alpha_2 \log P + \alpha_3 \log Y + \alpha_4 \log G + \alpha_5 \log D$$
$$+ \alpha_6 \log J + \alpha_7 \log R + \alpha_8 \log H + \varepsilon$$
$$\log P = \beta_1 + \beta_2 \log Q + \beta_3 \log L + \beta_4 \log K + \beta_5 \log F$$
$$+ \beta_6 \log R + \beta_7 \log I + \beta_8 \log T + U$$

---

† This example is taken from R. Halvorsen, "Residential Demand For Electric Energy," *Review of Economics and Statistics*, vol. 57, 1975, pp. 12–18. We have taken the liberty of simplifying the model and the discussion somewhat to clarify the exposition.

where Q = average annual residential electricity sales per customer

P = marginal price residential electricity (in real terms, i.e., deflated by Consumer Price Index)

Y = annual income per capita (real)

G = price for all types of residential gas

D = heating degree-days

J = average July temperature

R = percentage of population living in rural areas

H = average size of households

T = time

L = cost of labor

K = percentage of generation produced by publicly owned utilities

F = cost of fuel per kilowatt-hour of generation

I = ratio of total industrial sales to total residential sales

The first equation is a residential demand equation in which quantity demanded is a function of price and a host of demand-related variables. However, the second equation is not the usual supply relationship that one might expect; the supply of electricity is assumed to be fixed in the context of the model. The second equation arises because electric energy is sold at block rates, the price to a customer falling as the volume of sales increases. Thus, the price of electricity is itself a function of the sales. The other variables in the price equation are included to control for a host of variables which affect the price of the electricity sold.

Viewed as a system of equations, the model has two endogenous variables, P and Q, and is simultaneous, since Q appears on the right-hand side of the price equation and P appears on the right-hand side of the demand equation. The fact that both equations are identified can be seen without solving for the reduced form. The demand equation is identified because there are five exogenous variables in the price equation (L, K, F, I, T) which do not appear in the demand equation (in fact it is overidentified). The price equation is identified because there are five exogenous variables in the demand equation (Y, G, D, J, H) which do not appear in the price equation.

Both equations were estimated using 2SLS. In the first stage the endogenous variables were regressed against all the exogenous variables in the model. In the second stage, the structural equations were estimated using the predicted values of the first stage as instruments in place of the right-hand endogenous variables. The data are pooled time-series cross-section data for 48 states for the years 1961 to 1969. Note also that because the model is specified in logarithmic form, all coefficients including the price term are elasticities. The estimated results (with standard errors in parentheses) are:

$$\log \hat{Q} = -0.21 - \underset{(.03)}{1.15} \log P + \underset{(.06)}{.51} \log Y + \underset{(.01)}{.04} \log G - \underset{(.02)}{.02} \log D$$

$$+ \underset{(.12)}{.54} \log J + \underset{(.02)}{.21} \log R - \underset{(.12)}{.24} \log H \qquad R^2 = .91$$

$$\log \hat{P} = 0.57 - \underset{(.03)}{.60} \log Q + \underset{(.04)}{.24} \log L - \underset{(.01)}{.02} \log K + \underset{(.003)}{.01} \log F$$

$$+ \underset{(.01)}{.03} \log R - \underset{(.01)}{.12} \log I + \underset{(.003)}{.004} \log T \quad R^2 = .97$$

The results of the two-stage least-squares estimation of the demand equation show that the long-run direct elasticity of demand with respect to electricity price is somewhat greater than unity (1.15) in absolute value, a much higher elasticity than one would have expected in the short run. On the basis of detailed evidence on the trends in electricity pricing, the results suggest that the past growth of residential demand for electric energy has been due in good part to the decline in the real price of electricity.

We have not taken the time or space to discuss statistical tests or to analyze the equations in further detail. However, two issues ought to be raised. First, the usual t tests are not strictly appropriate when two-stage least squares is applied. Since parameter estimators are consistent but biased, only large-sample tests are appropriate. However, with the sample size of 432, there is little difference between the appropriate normal test and the usual t test. Second, assume that one wished to examine the effect of a tax on the use of electricity on long-run demand. The initial impact will be measured by the demand equation, but the price equation must also be taken into consideration since it measures the secondary effect of a change in quantity of purchases on price. Thus, to measure the *total* long-run elasticity of demand, and thus the long-run change in sales, the elasticity must be calculated from the reduced-form equation. When calculated from the reduced form, the total elasticity turns out to be -3.70, a much larger value than the direct effect given from the structural equation.

Example 7.2 Nondurable-goods consumption Assume that as a part of the task of building a large econometric model, one is interested in estimating a single equation in which the dependent variable is the aggregate quarterly expenditures of individuals on nondurable consumption items. A reasonable first choice for a single-equation regression model would be

$$CN_t = \beta_1 + \beta_2 YD_t + \beta_3 \left(\frac{PCN}{PC}\right)_t + \beta_4 CN_{t-1} + \varepsilon_t$$

where CN = personal consumption expenditures on nondurable goods, billions of 1958 dollars (data run quarterly from 1954-1 to 1971-4)

YD = disposable personal income, billions of 1958 dollars

PCN/PC = ratio of the Consumer Price Index for nondurable consumption items to the Consumer Price Index for all items (1957–1959 = 100)

We would expect the coefficients of the YD term and the CN term lagged one period both to be positive and the coefficient of the relative price term to be negative, the latter as a result of the shift into durable consumption likely to follow an increase in the relative price of nondurables. When ordinary least squares was used, the following regression results were obtained (with t statistics in parentheses):

$$\widehat{CN}_t = \underset{(3.9)}{85.49} + \underset{(4.8)}{.127}\,YD_t - \underset{(-3.5)}{66.7}\left(\frac{PCN}{PC}\right)_t + \underset{(6.6)}{.58}\,CN_{t-1}$$

$$R^2 = .998 \qquad s = 1.2 \qquad \text{Durbin } h = -.19$$

While the results appear quite reasonable, given prior expectations, the nature of the larger econometric model suggests that ordinary least-squares estimation is not appropriate. In particular, the fact that disposable income is determined (in a separate equation) in part by nondurable consumption (one component of disposable income) suggests that simultaneous-equation bias may exist. For this reason either 2SLS or instrumental-variables estimation ought to be used. Note also that the Durbin h was statistically insignificant, so that no serial-correlation correction was necessary. For pedagogical reasons we shall present the results associated with both estimation techniques.

In the first stage of the 2SLS estimation process, the explanatory variables were obtained by selection from among the right-hand variables appearing in the reduced form of the model system. When large econometric models are estimated, it is frequently impossible to use all reduced-form explanatory variables in the first-stage regression. For simplicity we have arbitrarily selected a few.† The first-stage regression contained YD_t on the left-hand side and YD_{t-1}, CN_{t-1}, and CD_{t-1}, durable goods consumption lagged, on the right-hand side. The results of the first-stage regression will not be printed here in order to save space. The first-stage results are important for our purposes only because they allow us to calculate fitted (or predicted) values for the variable YD. The results of the second-stage regression using those fitted values are as follows:

$$\widehat{CN}_t = \underset{(2.9)}{76.07} + \underset{(3.2)}{.110}\,\widehat{YD}_t - \underset{(-2.7)}{59.59}\left(\frac{PCN}{PC}\right)_t + \underset{(5.6)}{.637}\,CN_{t-1}$$

$$R^2 = .998 \qquad s = 1.3 \qquad \text{Durbin } h = .81$$

The results are identical in coefficient sign to the earlier least-squares results, although they differ slightly in terms of order of magnitude.

For purposes of comparison, the instrumental-variables estimation technique was used with two different choices of instruments. In the first case, the variable YD_{t-1}, disposable income lagged one quarter, was used as an

---

† For a more sophisticated method of variable selection see F. M. Fisher, "Dynamic Structure and Estimation in Economy-Wide Econometric Models," in Duesenberry, Fromm, Klein, and Kuh (eds.), *The Brookings Quarterly Econometric Model of the U.S.* (Chicago: Rand McNally, 1965), chap. 15.

instrument to replace YD_t. YD lagged should be a good instrument in terms of correlation with YD, but it may be less than desirable if serial correlation is present in the model. In any case, the instrumental-variables estimation results are

$$\widehat{CN}_t = 74.15 + .107\,YD_{t-1} - 58.15\left(\frac{PCN}{PC}\right)_t + .648\,CN_{t-1}$$
$$\quad\ \ (3.1) \qquad (3.4) \qquad\ \ (-2.8) \qquad\qquad (6.2)$$

$$R^2 = .998 \qquad s = 1.2 \qquad \text{Durbin } h = -1.37$$

The results are quite similar to those obtained by the 2SLS technique, an encouraging result since the choice between instrumental variables and 2SLS is often an arbitrary one.

In the second instrumental-variables case, the instrument chosen was the set of fitted values obtained from the first stage of the 2SLS results described earlier. The results are

$$\widehat{CN}_t = 76.07 + .110\,\widehat{YD}_t - 59.59\left(\frac{PCN}{PC}\right)_t + .637\,CN_{t-1}$$
$$\quad\ \ (3.26) \qquad (3.5) \qquad\ \ (-2.9) \qquad\qquad (6.1)$$

$$R^2 = .998 \qquad s = 1.2 \qquad \text{Durbin } h = -1.19$$

Notice that the instrumental-variables coefficient estimates are identical to the estimates obtained earlier. The two will be identical in the sample as long as all the right-hand exogenous variables in the original equation are among the variables chosen for inclusion in the process of instrument construction, i.e., the first-stage regression. The statistics associated with the parameter estimates are not identical, but this is due to the fact that the 2SLS program prints the outcome of the second-stage regression, while the instrumental-variables estimation output uses the parameter estimates and the *original variables* in the calculation of regression residual variance and R^2.

APPENDIX 7.1 INSTRUMENTAL-VARIABLES ESTIMATION IN MATRIX FORM

The technique of instrumental variables can be used to obtain consistent estimates of β when the right-hand variables are known to be correlated with the error term as a result of errors in variables or simultaneous-equation bias. If our original model is

$$Y = X\beta + \varepsilon \tag{A7.1}$$

the correlation of one or more X's and the error term ε is summarized as

$$\text{plim}\left(\frac{1}{N}X'\varepsilon\right) \neq 0 \tag{A7.2}$$

The expression "plim" refers to the probability limit as defined in Appendix 2.1. To see the difficulty which arises when (A7.2) holds, premultiply Eq. (A7.1) by the matrix $\mathbf{X}'$ to obtain

$$\mathbf{X}'\mathbf{Y} = \mathbf{X}'\mathbf{X}\boldsymbol{\beta} + \mathbf{X}'\boldsymbol{\varepsilon}$$

If plim $[(1/N)\mathbf{X}'\boldsymbol{\varepsilon}] = 0$, the last term goes to 0 in the probability limit and

$$\hat{\boldsymbol{\beta}} = (\mathbf{X}'\mathbf{X})^{-1}\mathbf{X}'\mathbf{Y} \tag{A7.3}$$

is a consistent estimate of $\boldsymbol{\beta}$. However, when the probability limit is nonzero, ordinary least-squares estimation becomes inconsistent.

Consistent estimates of $\boldsymbol{\beta}$ can be obtained through the use of an $N \times k$ matrix of instruments $\mathbf{Z} = (\mathbf{Z}_1, \mathbf{Z}_2, \ldots, \mathbf{Z}_k)$, where each instrument $\mathbf{Z}_i$ has N observations. $\mathbf{Z}$ satisfies the conditions necessary to be labeled a matrix of instruments if the following conditions hold:†

$$\text{plim} \left(\frac{1}{N} \mathbf{Z}'\boldsymbol{\varepsilon} \right) = \mathbf{0}. \tag{A7.4}$$

$$\text{plim} \left(\frac{1}{N} \mathbf{Z}'\mathbf{X} \right) = \boldsymbol{\Sigma} \text{ exists and is nonsingular (has an inverse).} \tag{A7.5}$$

$$\text{plim} \left(\frac{1}{N} \mathbf{Z}'\mathbf{Z} \right) = \boldsymbol{\Sigma}^* \text{ exists and is nonsingular.} \tag{A7.6}$$

The first condition guarantees that each instrument is uncorrelated with the error term, while the second guarantees a nonzero correlation between the Z's and the X's as well as the fact that all the Z's must be linearly independent. Thus, there is no reason that some of the original X's cannot be used as instruments in the instrumental-variables estimation process.

Given the appropriate instruments, we premultiply Eq. (A7.1) by $\mathbf{Z}'$ to get

$$\mathbf{Z}'\mathbf{Y} = \mathbf{Z}'\mathbf{X}\boldsymbol{\beta} + \mathbf{Z}'\boldsymbol{\varepsilon}$$

from which it follows that

$$\hat{\boldsymbol{\beta}}^* = (\mathbf{Z}'\mathbf{X})^{-1}\mathbf{Z}'\mathbf{Y} \tag{A7.7}$$

will be a consistent estimator of $\boldsymbol{\beta}$. $\hat{\boldsymbol{\beta}}^*$ will be consistent because

$$\hat{\boldsymbol{\beta}}^* = (\mathbf{Z}'\mathbf{X})^{-1}(\mathbf{Z}'\mathbf{X})\boldsymbol{\beta} + (\mathbf{Z}'\mathbf{X})^{-1}(\mathbf{Z}'\boldsymbol{\varepsilon}) = \boldsymbol{\beta} + (\mathbf{Z}'\mathbf{X})^{-1}(\mathbf{Z}'\boldsymbol{\varepsilon})$$

and $\quad \text{plim} \, \hat{\boldsymbol{\beta}}^* = \boldsymbol{\beta} + \text{plim} \left[(\mathbf{Z}'\mathbf{X})^{-1}(\mathbf{Z}'\boldsymbol{\varepsilon}) \right]$

$$= \boldsymbol{\beta} + \text{plim} \left[\left(\frac{1}{N} \mathbf{Z}'\mathbf{X} \right)^{-1} \left(\frac{1}{N} \mathbf{Z}'\boldsymbol{\varepsilon} \right) \right] \quad \text{from (A7.4) and (A7.5)}$$

$$= \boldsymbol{\beta} + \boldsymbol{\Sigma}^{-1}\mathbf{0} = \boldsymbol{\beta}$$

To find the appropriate distribution of $\hat{\boldsymbol{\beta}}^*$, we need to derive $\mathbf{V}$, the asymptotic

---

† With errors in variables Z must also be unrelated in the probability limit to the measurement error.

variance-covariance matrix for $\hat{\beta}^*$. To accomplish this, we use the fact that

$$\hat{\beta}^* - \beta = (Z'X)^{-1}(Z'\varepsilon)$$

and

$$(\hat{\beta}^* - \beta)(\hat{\beta}^* - \beta)' = (Z'X)^{-1}Z'\varepsilon\varepsilon'Z(X'Z)^{-1}$$

$$V = \left[\frac{1}{N}\text{plim}\left(\frac{1}{N}Z'X\right)^{-1}\right]\left[\text{plim}\left(\frac{1}{N}Z'\varepsilon\varepsilon'Z\right)\right]\left[\text{plim}\left(\frac{1}{N}X'Z\right)^{-1}\right]$$

from which it follows, using (A7.5) and (A7.6),† that

$$V = \frac{1}{N}\sigma^2\Sigma^{-1}\Sigma^*\Sigma^{-1} \tag{A7.8}$$

In practice, the true variance-covariance matrix can be consistently estimated by

$$s^2(Z'X)^{-1}(Z'Z)(X'Z)^{-1} \tag{A7.9}$$

where s^2 is a consistent estimate of σ^2:

$$s^2 = \frac{1}{N-k}(Y - X\hat{\beta}^*)'(Y - X\hat{\beta}^*)$$

Notice that s^2 is calculated from the residuals of the original equation, not the equation in which the instruments replace the original right-hand variables.

EXERCISES

7.1 Explain briefly why measurement error in the right-hand variables leads to inconsistent and biased parameter estimates while measurement error in the left-hand variables does not.

7.2 Show in the two-variable model that $\hat{\beta} = \Sigma y_i z_i / \Sigma z_i^2$ (where z is an instrument) will not yield a consistent estimate of the true slope parameter. Are there any conditions under which the instrumental-variables estimator described will yield a consistent estimate of β?

7.3 Consider the model

$$C_t = \alpha_1 + \alpha_2 Y_t + \varepsilon_t \qquad I_t = \beta_1 + \beta_2 Y_t + \beta_3 G_{t-1} + u_t \qquad Y_t = C_t + I_t + G_t$$

(a) Construct the reduced-form system of the model. From the reduced form determine the response of C in the first two periods to a one-unit change in G.

(b) Is the consumption-function equation identified? Is it overidentified?

(c) Is the investment equation identified? Overidentified?

(d) What would happen to your estimated marginal propensity to consume if it has been estimated by using ordinary least squares on an equation of the form $C_t = a + bY_t + \varepsilon_t$?

7.4 Consider the supply-demand model

$$Q_t^S = \alpha_1 + \alpha_2 P_t + \varepsilon_t$$

$$Q_t^D = \beta_1 + \beta_2 P_t + \beta_3 Y_t + \beta_4 P_{t-1} + u_t$$

$$Q_t^D = Q_t^S$$

where $E(\varepsilon_i \varepsilon_j) = 0$, $i \neq j$, and $E(u_i u_j) = 0$, $i \neq j$.

---

† See A. Goldberger, *Econometric Theory* (New York: Wiley, 1964), pp. 270–274.

(a) Is the supply equation identified? What would happen if the supply equation were estimated using ordinary least squares?

(b) Is the demand equation identified? What would happen if the demand equation were estimated using ordinary least squares?

(c) If you were told to estimate the supply equation using instrumental variables, what would you do? Be explicit.

(d) If you were told to estimate the supply equation using two-stage least squares, what would you do? How does this relate to part (c)?

(e) Could you use indirect least squares to estimate the demand equation? Why or why not?

(f) Would your results be different if you knew that ε was autocorrelated?

7.5 Consider the two-equation model system

$$Y_1 = a_1 Y_2 + a_2 Z_1 + u_1 \qquad Y_2 = b_1 Y_1 + b_2 Z_2 + u_2$$

(Assume $Z_1 \neq Z_2$.)

(a) Under what conditions will ordinary least-squares estimation of the first equation lead to consistent parameter estimates? *Hint:* There are two conditions, one relating to parameter values and the other to error variances and covariances.

(b) Under what assumptions is the first equation identified? *Hint:* Again there are two conditions, the first relating to parameter values and the second to error covariances.

7.6 Consider the two-equation model system

$$Y_1 = a_1 + a_2 Y_2 + u_1 \qquad Y_2 = b_1 + b_2 Y_1 + b_3 Z_1 + b_4 Z_2 + u_2$$

Assess the following approaches to the estimation of the first equation in terms of possible bias, inconsistency, and efficiency. Which of the estimators are instrumental-variables estimators? How does the last estimation process relate to the previous three?

(a) Ordinary least-squares estimation of the first equation

(b) Indirect least-squares estimation of the first equation

(c) Instrumental-variables estimation using Z_1 as an instrument in the first equation

(d) Two-stage least-squares estimation of the first equation

(e) Estimating the first equation as $\hat{Y}_1 = c_1 + c_2 Z_1 + c_3 Z_2$

FORECASTING WITH A SINGLE-EQUATION
REGRESSION MODEL

A principal purpose for constructing the single-equation regression models described in the last seven chapters is *forecasting*. A forecast is a quantitative estimate (or set of estimates) about the *likelihood* of future events based on past and current information. This past and current information is embodied in the form of a model—a single-equation structural model or, as we will discuss in Parts Two and Three of this book, a multi-equation model or a time-series model. By extrapolating our models out beyond the period over which they were estimated, we can use the information contained in them to make forecasts about future events. In this chapter we discuss in some detail how the single-equation regression model can be used as a forecasting tool.

The term *forecasting* is often thought to apply solely to time-series problems in which we predict the future given information about the past and the present. We shall remain consistent with this notion by orienting our notation and discussion toward time-series forecasting. We should stress, however, that our use of notation is for convenience only. Most of the analysis applies equally well to cross-section models and time-series models. In fact, our concern in this chapter is with *prediction*, the object of which is to obtain estimates or guesses as to the movement of certain variables, given additional information about the movement of other variables.

As we will see, two types of forecasts are found to be useful. *Point forecasts* predict a single number in each forecast period, while *interval forecasts* indicate in each forecast period an interval in which we hope the actual realized value will lie. We begin by discussing point forecasts, after which we consider how confidence intervals (interval forecasts) can be used to provide a margin of error around a point forecast.

The additional information provided by the forecasting process can be used in several different ways. Frequently forecasts are used as guides for public and private policy. A forecast of a high rate of inflation based on the assumption of a large budget deficit may lead policy makers to alter their budget plans, or a forecast of an increased world demand for crude oil may lead shipbuilders to invest in new supertankers. Forecasts are also useful as guidelines for model building. A forecast which is found to be way off target when actual data are available provides information which may lead to the revision of the model which provided the forecast.

It is useful to distinguish between two types of forecasting, *ex post* and *ex ante*. In terms of time-series models, both forecasts predict values of a dependent variable beyond the time period in which the model is estimated. However, in an *ex post* forecast the forecast period is such that observations on both endogenous variables and the exogenous explanatory variables are known with certainty. Thus, *ex post* forecasts can be checked against existing data and provide a means of evaluating a forecasting model. An *ex ante* forecast predicts values of the dependent variable beyond the estimation period, using explanatory variables which may or may not be known with certainty, depending on the nature of the data and the length of the lags associated with the explanatory variables. The distinction between *ex post* and *ex ante* forecasting can be seen in Fig. 8.1.

A distinction can also be made between *conditional* and *unconditional* forecasts. In an unconditional forecast, values for all the explanatory variables in the forecasting equation are known with certainty. Any *ex post* forecast is, of course, an unconditional forecast, but *ex ante* forecasts may also be unconditional. Suppose, for example, that for some industry, monthly sales $S(t)$ are linearly related to two variables X_1 and X_2 but with lags of 3 and 4 months, respectively:

$$S(t) = a_0 + a_1 X_1(t - 3) + a_2 X_2(t - 4) + \varepsilon(t) \tag{8.1}$$

If this equation were estimated, it could be used to produce unconditional forecasts of $S(t)$ 1, 2, and 3 months in the future. For example, to produce a 3-month forecast of $S(t)$, we would use the current value of X_1 and last month's value of X_2, both of which are known.

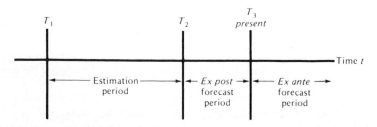

Figure 8.1 Types of forecasting.

In a conditional forecast, values for one or more explanatory variables are not known with certainty, so that guesses (or forecasts) for them must be used to produce the forecast of the dependent variable. If we wanted to use Eq. (8.1) to forecast $S(t)$ 4 months into the future, we would have to also forecast $X_1(t)$ 1 month into the future, making our forecast of $S(t)$ *conditional* upon our forecast of $X_1(t)$. Of course, if the right-hand side of the forecasting equation contained no lags, e.g., if it were of the form

$$S(t) - a_0 + a_1 X_1(t) + a_2 X_2(t) + e(t) \qquad (8.2)$$

every *ex ante* forecast generated by the equation would be a conditional forecast.†

Our primary concerns in this chapter are, first, the problem of obtaining good forecasts using a single-equation regression model, and, second, the problem of evaluating the nature of the resulting *forecasting error* using appropriate statistical tests. By a good forecast we really mean the *best* forecast possible, but the problem of selecting the best forecast is a difficult one as a general rule. For our purposes we define the best forecast as the one which yields a forecast error having the *minimum variance*. In the single-equation regression model, ordinary least-squares estimation yields the best forecast among all unbiased estimators which are based on linear equations. Other definitions of the best forecast are possible and indeed plausible. We shall extend our notion of the best forecast in later chapters when we consider minimum mean-square-error forecasts based on nonlinear equations and on estimation procedures which do not guarantee unbiased parameter estimates.

We shall see that the error associated with a forecasting procedure can come from a combination of four distinct sources. First, the random nature of the additive error process in a linear regression model guarantees that forecasts will deviate from true values even if the model is specified correctly and its parameter values are known with certainty. Second, the process of estimating the regression parameters introduces error because estimated parameter values are random variables which may deviate from the true parameter values. For any given sample, the estimated parameters are unlikely to equal the true values of the underlying parameters, even though they will (if they are unbiased) equal those parameters on the average. Third, in the case of a conditional forecast, errors are introduced when calculated guesses or forecasts are made for the values of the explanatory variables in the period in which the forecast is made. Finally, errors may be introduced because the model specification may not be an accurate representation of the "true" underlying model.

We proceed by discussing the best forecast and the properties of the resulting forecast error in three different cases. We deal first with unconditional forecasts generated by a linear regression model in which the error process obeys

---

† Even if the exogenous variables appeared with long lags in the equation, it may be the case that current values of the exogenous data are not known with certainty but contain errors and are subject to frequent and extreme revisions. The forecast would then be conditional on the exogenous data.

the classical assumptions of the linear model. Next, we treat the problem of unconditional forecasting when the error process is known to be serially correlated. Finally, we consider the added dimension of difficulty which arises when conditional forecasting is attempted.

8.1 UNCONDITIONAL FORECASTING

In order to produce an unconditional forecast from a regression model, it is necessary that the explanatory variables be known with certainty for the entire forecast period. As we saw before, one way this can occur is by having the explanatory variables appear with time lags. Even if explanatory variables do not appear with lags, we might be able to forecast them perfectly (or near perfectly)—and thus generate unconditional forecasts for the dependent variable—if they happen to be seasonal variables or demographic or economic variables which change slowly and predictably. For example, monthly forecasts over a 1-year horizon which use population and the month of the year as two explanatory variables will be unconditional, since population growth over this short period can be predicted rather precisely, and the month of the year is known with certainty.

In applied work it is desirable to construct models which can be used to generate unconditional forecasts, since this removes a large source of forecasting error. As a result, when constructing a forecasting equation, analysts will attempt to use explanatory variables that have long time lags or that can themselves be forecasted easily and precisely.

We begin our discussion of unconditional forecasting by considering the simple two-variable regression model:

$$Y_t = \alpha + \beta X_t + \varepsilon_t \qquad t = 1, 2, \ldots, T \tag{8.3}$$

$$\varepsilon_t \sim N(0, \sigma^2)$$

We pose the forecasting problem as follows: Given a *known* value X_{T+1}, what is the best single forecast that can be made for Y in period $T + 1$? In solving the problem, we begin by making the assumption that *the parameters α and β are known exactly*. If this is the case, the appropriate forecast for Y_{T+1} is given by

$$\hat{Y}_{T+1} = E(Y_{T+1}) = \alpha + \beta X_{T+1} \tag{8.4}$$

To see why this is so, consider the *forecast error*

$$\hat{e}_{T+1} = \hat{Y}_{T+1} - Y_{T+1} \tag{8.5}$$

The forecast error has two desirable properties:

1. $E(\hat{e}_{T+1}) = E(\hat{Y}_{T+1} - Y_{T+1}) = E(-\varepsilon_{T+1}) = 0$. Thus, our forecast of Y_{T+1} will be *unbiased*; i.e., it will be correct on the average.
2. The forecast error variance

$$\sigma_f^2 = E\left[(\hat{e}_{T+1})^2\right] = E\left[(\varepsilon_{T+1})^2\right] = \sigma^2$$

is the minimum variance possible among all possible forecasts based on linear equations.†

We should note that knowledge of the slope and intercept parameters α and β does not guarantee an accurate forecast every time. We are able to say only that the forecast error will have mean 0 and variance σ^2. The existence of forecast error is brought about because the value Y_{T+1} cannot be guaranteed to lie on the true regression line due to the presence of the disturbance term ε.

Since the error of forecast is normally distributed with mean 0 and variance σ^2, it is natural to consider the problem of statistical testing. We can perform significance tests on the forecasted value of Y by calculating the normalized error

$$\lambda = \frac{\hat{Y}_{T+1} - Y_{T+1}}{\sigma} \tag{8.6}$$

Since λ is normally distributed with mean 0 and standard deviation 1, we can determine a 95 percent (or any other) confidence interval by using the fact that

$$\text{Prob}\left(-\lambda_{.05} \leq \frac{\hat{Y}_{T+1} - Y_{T+1}}{\sigma} \leq \lambda_{.05}\right) = .95 \tag{8.7}$$

where $\lambda_{.05}$ is obtained from a table of the normal distribution. We write the 95 percent confidence interval as

$$\hat{Y}_{T+1} - \lambda_{.05}\sigma \leq Y_{T+1} \leq \hat{Y}_{T+1} + \lambda_{.05}\sigma \tag{8.8}$$

Notice that this interval is independent of values of the exogenous variable X. The 95 percent confidence interval for a typical two-variable regression model is shown in Fig. 8.2.

The confidence intervals determined above provide us with a simple means of testing the reliability of the regression model. When the actual value of Y_{T+1} is obtained, we can compare it with the previously forecasted value. If the actual observed value of Y_{T+1} lies within the 95 percent confidence interval, we can presume that the model is performing satisfactorily, but if the value lies outside the confidence interval, we may conclude that the model is not performing well. If this poor performance is known to be due to an extraordinary event not accounted for by the model, we are likely to wait for a second forecast before concluding that the model is unreliable, but as a general rule we would take the poor forecast as evidence of the need to revise the basic model structure. Of course economists do not often use a single forecast alone as a basis for accepting or rejecting a model; repeated observations and statistical tests are usually needed before a more definite conclusion can be drawn.

The reader should be aware that the use of forecasting as a means of evaluating model reliability is quite distinct from the classical t, F, and R^2 statistics described earlier in the book. A single-equation regression model can

---

† σ, the square root of the forecast error variance, is called the *standard error of the forecast*.

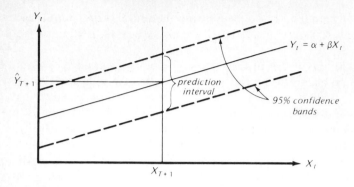

Figure 8.2 Forecast when equation parameters are known.

have significant t statistics and a high R^2 and still forecast very badly period after period. This may result from a structural change (in the economy) occurring during the forecast period and not explained by the model. Good forecasts, on the other hand, may come from regression models which have relatively low R^2's and one or more insignificant regression coefficients. This may happen because there is very little variation in the dependent variable, so that although it is not being explained well by the model, it is easy to forecast. We shall return to this model-building issue again in Parts Two and Three of the book.

Normally, of course, the parameters of our regression model are not known with certainty but instead are random variables that have been estimated. We also do not usually know the error variance σ^2, and this too is an estimated random variable. Let us therefore reconsider the problem of forecasting under the more realistic assumption that both the regression parameters and the error variance must be estimated. The best forecast for Y_{T+1} is then determined from a simple two-stage procedure:†

1. Estimate Eq. (8.3) using ordinary least squares.
2. Choose $\hat{Y}_{T+1} = \hat{\alpha} + \hat{\beta}X_{T+1}$.

The forecast error is then

$$\hat{e}_{T+1} = \hat{Y}_{T+1} - Y_{T+1} = (\hat{\alpha} - \alpha) + (\hat{\beta} - \beta)X_{T+1} - \varepsilon_{T+1} \qquad (8.9)$$

There are two sources of error involved in Eq. (8.9), the first due to the presence of the additive error term ε_{T+1} and the second due to the random nature of the estimated regression parameters. Recall that the estimated parameters are unbiased but are not *identical* to the true population parameters. While the former error source is due to the basic variance in the variable Y, the latter

† For a proof that this forecast is the best linear unbiased forecast, see J. Johnston, *Econometric Methods*, 2d ed. (New York: McGraw-Hill, 1972), pp. 38–40.

error source is sensitive to the estimation process and therefore to the number of degrees of freedom involved. We will see this as we examine the distribution of the error of forecast.

To begin with, the error of forecast is normally distributed, since it is a linear function of $\hat{\alpha}$, $\hat{\beta}$, and ε_{T+1}, all of which are normally distributed. Second, it has 0 mean, since

$$E(\hat{e}_{T+1}) = E(\hat{\alpha} - \alpha) + E(\hat{\beta} - \beta)X_{T+1} + E(-\varepsilon_{T+1}) = 0 \qquad (8.10)$$

(Remember that $\hat{\alpha}$ and $\hat{\beta}$ are unbiased estimators, and X_{T+1} is known.) Finally, we can determine the variance of $\hat{e}_{T+1}$:

$$\sigma_f^2 = E\big[(\hat{e}_{T+1})^2\big] = E\big[(\hat{\alpha} - \alpha)^2\big] + E\big[(\hat{\beta} - \beta)^2\big]X_{T+1}^2 + E\big[(\varepsilon_{T+1})^2\big]$$
$$+ E\big[(\hat{\alpha} - \alpha)(\hat{\beta} - \beta)\big]2X_{T+1} \qquad (8.11)$$

or $\qquad \sigma_f^2 = \text{Var}\,(\hat{\alpha}) + 2X_{T+1}\,\text{Cov}\,(\hat{\alpha}, \hat{\beta}) + X_{T+1}^2\,\text{Var}\,(\hat{\beta}) + \sigma^2 \qquad (8.12)$

Notice that all the cross-product terms involving estimated parameters and ε_{T+1} become 0 when expected values are taken, since $\hat{\alpha} - \alpha$ and $\hat{\beta} - \beta$ depend on $\varepsilon_1, \ldots, \varepsilon_T$, all of which are independent of ε_{T+1}. Recall that we have previously (Chapter 3) derived the variances of $\hat{\alpha}$ and $\hat{\beta}$ as well as their covariance:

$$\text{Var}\,(\hat{\alpha}) = \sigma^2 \frac{\Sigma X_t^2}{T\Sigma(X_t - \bar{X})^2} \qquad (8.13)$$

$$\text{Var}\,(\hat{\beta}) = \frac{\sigma^2}{\Sigma(X_t - \bar{X})^2} \qquad (8.14)$$

$$\text{Cov}\,(\hat{\alpha}, \hat{\beta}) = \frac{-\bar{X}\sigma^2}{\Sigma(X_t - \bar{X})^2} \qquad (8.15)$$

where the summation runs from 1 to T and $\bar{X}$ is the sample mean of X for the first T observations. Substituting Eqs. (8.13) to (8.15) into (8.12) and manipulating terms, we get

$$\sigma_f^2 = \sigma^2\left[\frac{\Sigma X_t^2}{T\Sigma(X_t - \bar{X})^2} - \frac{2\bar{X}X_{T+1}}{\Sigma(X_t - \bar{X})^2} + \frac{X_{T+1}^2}{\Sigma(X_t - \bar{X})^2} + 1 \right] \qquad (8.16)$$

But $\qquad \dfrac{\Sigma X_t^2}{T\Sigma(X_t - \bar{X})^2} = \dfrac{\Sigma(X_t - \bar{X})^2 + T\bar{X}^2}{T\Sigma(X_t - \bar{X})^2} = \dfrac{1}{T} + \dfrac{\bar{X}^2}{\Sigma(X_t - \bar{X})^2} \qquad (8.17)$

Therefore, $\qquad \sigma_f^2 = \sigma^2\left[1 + \dfrac{1}{T} + \dfrac{\bar{X}^2 - 2\bar{X}X_{T+1} + X_{T+1}^2}{\Sigma(X_t - \bar{X})^2} \right] \qquad (8.18)$

or
$$\sigma_f^2 = \sigma^2 \left[1 + \frac{1}{T} + \frac{\left(X_{T+1} - \bar{X} \right)^2}{\Sigma \left(X_t - \bar{X} \right)^2} \right] \qquad (8.19)$$

Equation (8.19) is of immediate interest because it tells us that the forecast error is sensitive to the size of the sample used in the estimation process, as well as to the variance in X and to the distance between X_{T+1} and $\bar{X}$.† Other things being equal then, the larger the sample size and the greater the variance in X the smaller the error of forecast will be. In addition, the error of forecast is smallest when X_{T+1} happens to be equal to the sample mean of X, since the last term in brackets in Eq. (8.19) then becomes 0. This suggests that the best forecasts about Y can be made for values of X around which the most sample information is available. This is not surprising; as the new value of X gets farther from the mean, it moves out of the range of experience used to estimate the model and generates less reliable forecasts. In general it is dangerous to extend a model much beyond its range of estimation. When time-series forecasts involve values of X_{T+1} substantially different from X, the resulting forecast error may be large.

If σ^2 were known, we could calculate σ_f^2 and then proceed to construct confidence intervals as before, relying on the knowledge that

$$\lambda = \frac{\hat{Y}_{T+1} - Y_{T+1}}{\sigma_f} \sim N(0, 1) \qquad (8.20)$$

However, σ^2 is usually not known, so that as a practical matter we must use an unbiased and consistent estimate of σ^2. Such an estimate would be

$$s^2 = \frac{1}{T - 2} \Sigma (Y_t - \hat{Y}_t)^2 \qquad (8.21)$$

As we saw in Chapter 3, this allows us to calculate confidence intervals using the t distribution. Writing the *estimated* forecast error variance

$$s_f^2 = s^2 \left[1 + \frac{1}{T} + \frac{\left(X_{T+1} - \bar{X} \right)^2}{\Sigma \left(X_t - \bar{X} \right)^2} \right] \qquad (8.22)$$

we know that the normalized error

$$\frac{\hat{Y}_{T+1} - Y_{T+1}}{s_f}$$

will be t-distributed with $T - 2$ degrees of freedom. The 95 percent confidence

---

† Equation (8.19) shows the error for a point forecast. If we forecast the expected value of the outcome, the equation is modified by omitting the 1 in the bracketed expression. That term adds to the expected value of the forecast the error variance associated with selecting a single forecast from the distribution of possible forecasts. Thus, a point forecast will have a higher variance than a forecast of the mean or expected outcome.

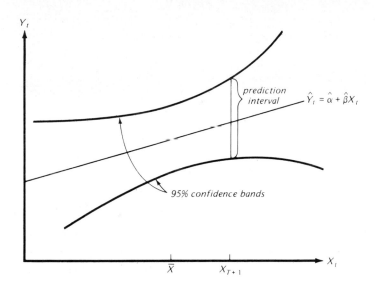

Figure 8.3 Forecast confidence intervals.

interval for $\hat{Y}_{T+1}$ is thus given by

$$\hat{Y}_{T+1} - t_{.05}s_f \leq Y_{T+1} \leq \hat{Y}_{T+1} + t_{.05}s_f \tag{8.23}$$

An example of the 95 percent confidence interval is shown in Fig. 8.3. It shows rather clearly the relationship between the forecast error and values of the explanatory variable X. At every value of X the distance between the regression line and one of the confidence bands is about twice the estimated standard error of the forecast.

These results (8.22) suggest that the farther into the future one forecasts the lower the reliability of the forecast is likely to be. Note that this diminished reliability occurs simply because the values of X associated with distant forecasts are outside the range of our normal experience and thus far from the mean value $\overline{X}$. The unreliability is not associated with an increased probability of specification error in the model, since we have presumed a correct specification at all times.

Our discussion so far has been in the context of the simple two-variable regression model, but the principles are the same and apply equally well to the multiple regression model. Confidence intervals for forecasts generated by a multiple regression model will have the same shape as those in Fig. 8.3. When two or more explanatory variables are present, however, the algebraic derivations of the forecast error distribution and forecast confidence interval become somewhat messy unless matrix notation is used. As a result, we will relegate the formal discussion of forecast error from a multiple regression model to Appendix 8.1. For now, let us examine some simple forecasting examples.

Example 8.1 Forecasting grade-point averages Reconsider the grade-point-average example discussed in Chapters 1 and 3. In that example we estimated a linear relationship between grade-point average and family income for a cross section of eight individuals. With the development of the forecasting techniques in this chapter, we are in a position to forecast the grade-point average of individuals not in the original sample, given only information about their family incomes. In terms of the notation used in Chapter 1, the relevant information about the grade-point sample is summarized as follows:

Estimated regression line $= \hat{Y}_i = 1.375 + .120X_i$ $i = 1, \ldots, N$

Estimated error variance $= s^2 = .111$ Number of observations $= N = 8$

Mean of $X = \bar{X} = 13.5$ Variation of $X = \Sigma(X_i - \bar{X})^2 = 162$

Assume for illustrative purposes that several individuals (not in the original sample) report their family income. We wish to predict grade-point average and to calculate a 95 percent confidence or prediction interval. The relevant calculations are summarized in Table 8.1, and 95 percent prediction intervals are shown graphically in Fig. 8.4.

Table 8.1 Grade-point-average forecast calculations

X_{N+1}	$\hat{Y}_{N+1}$	s_f^2	$\hat{Y}_{N+1} - 1.96s_f$	$\hat{Y}_{N+1} + 1.96s_f$
6.5	2.155	.158	1.375	2.935
10.0	2.575	.133	1.860	3.415
13.5	2.995	.125	2.303	3.687
17.0	3.315	.133	2.600	4.030
20.5	3.835	.158	3.055	4.615
24.0	4.155	.201	3.277	5.033
27.5	4.675	.259	3.677	5.673

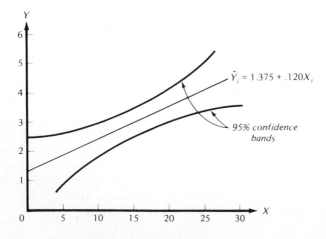

Figure 8.4 Confidence bands for estimated slope and intercept.

As can be seen in Table 8.1, the smallest error of forecast is associated with the family income of $13,500, the mean family income of the original sample. For that individual we can be reasonably confident that the final grade-point average will lie in the 2.3 to 3.7 range. The fact that the 95 percent prediction interval is so large, even at the point of minimum forecast error, suggests the limiting nature of the grade-point-average model. A more sophisticated model (with additional explanatory variables) and more sample observations would most likely lead to a smaller forecast interval. We should note, also, that the error of forecast grows nonlinearly when family income increases beyond its mean value. In fact, the forecast interval for the last individual (with family income of $27,500) is not only large but also unrealistic, since a grade-point average greater than 4.0 is not within the experience of the original sample. Forecasting in this particular cross-section example is clearly not worthwhile for family incomes outside the original range of experience.

Example 8.2   Forecasting interest rates In this example we reconsider the regression model that explains the short-term interest rate (the rate on 3-month Treasury bills).† The linear regression model is estimated using monthly time-series data over the period January 1958 to January 1970. The interest rate R is seen to depend on total disposable income YD, a moving sum of changes in the money supply M, and a moving sum of percent changes in the price level P (i.e., the inflation rate):

$$R_t = c_0 + c_1 YD_t + c_2(\Delta M_t + \Delta M_{t-1} + \Delta M_{t-2})$$
$$+ c_3\left(\frac{\Delta P_t}{P_t} + \frac{\Delta P_{t-1}}{P_{t-1}} + \frac{\Delta P_{t-2}}{P_{t-2}}\right) + \varepsilon_t$$

The results of the estimation are

$$R^2 = .853 \quad \text{Corrected } R^2 = .850$$
$$F(3/141) = 271.9 \quad \text{Standard error} = .552$$
$$\text{Sum of squared residuals} = 43.0 \quad \text{Durbin-Watson} = .24 \quad \overline{R} = 3.778$$

Coefficient	Estimated value	Standard error	t statistic	Mean of variable
c_0	−3.662	.388	−9.45	1.00
c_1	.053	.004	14.76	135.90
c_2	−.280	.046	−6.13	1.51
c_3	104.376	19.954	5.23	.006

† See Chapters 4 and 6.

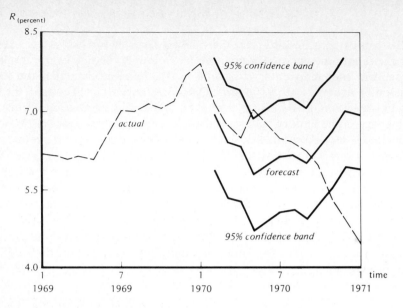

Figure 8.5 Interest-rate forecast.

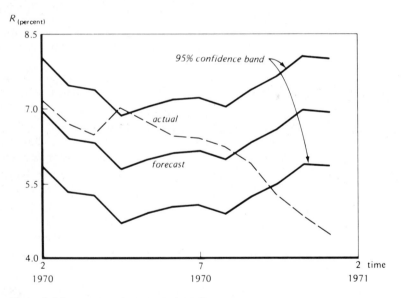

Figure 8.6 Interest-rate forecast (enlarged).

The estimated equation is then used to generate an *ex post* forecast over a 12-month period, from February 1970 to January 1971. The forecasted path for the interest rate, together with the 95 percent confidence interval and the path that the interest rate actually followed, is shown in Fig. 8.5 and again enlarged in Fig. 8.6. Note that the forecasted path is reasonably close to the actual path for the first 8 or 9 months of the forecast, but during the last 3 months the actual path is outside the boundaries of the 95 percent confidence interval. This would lead one to conclude that the model cannot be trusted for any intermediate or long-term forecasts. In fact, the main weakness of the model is revealed by the low Durbin-Watson statistic (.24), indicating that the error terms are serially correlated. We will deal with this problem of forecasting with serially correlated errors in the next section.

8.2 FORECASTING WITH SERIALLY CORRELATED ERRORS

Frequently we find that the error process is serially correlated in time-series models. When this is the case, the problem of determining the best forecast and its appropriate distribution becomes somewhat more difficult. Let us consider the two-variable model in which the errors are first-order serially correlated:

$$Y_t = \alpha + \beta X_t + \varepsilon_t \qquad \varepsilon_t = \rho \varepsilon_{t-1} + v_t$$

$$|\rho| < 1 \qquad v_t \sim N(0, \sigma_v^2) \tag{8.24}$$

The difficulty arises because we now have some additional information, namely that the error term is serially correlated, and we should take advantage of this information in producing our best forecast. In the previous section our best forecast for Y_{T+1} was determined by assigning ε_{T+1} the value 0 for the forecast period. This was reasonable, given that the error had 0 mean and that error terms were assumed independent over time. In the serially correlated case, however, the time-independence assumption no longer holds. It is now reasonable to expect that knowledge of the errors (or their estimates) in periods previous to the forecast period will allow us to modify our prediction of the error in period $T + 1$.

To pursue this matter further, let us assume (unrealistically) that all the regression parameters (α, β, and ρ) are known *a priori*. We proceed by choosing the forecasted value of Y_{T+1} as follows:

$$\hat{Y}_{T+1} = \alpha + \beta X_{T+1} + \hat{\varepsilon}_{T+1} \tag{8.25}$$

Rather than setting $\hat{\varepsilon}_{T+1} = 0$, as in the previous section, we calculate $\hat{\varepsilon}_{T+1}$ from the previous error term. Since $\varepsilon_{T+1} = \rho \varepsilon_T + v_T$, we choose $\hat{\varepsilon}_{T+1} = \rho \hat{\varepsilon}_T$ (since v_t has 0 mean and is uncorrelated over time).† Therefore,

$$\hat{Y}_{T+1} = \alpha + \beta X_{T+1} + \rho \varepsilon_T \tag{8.26}$$

---

† Since α and β are known, there is no estimation involved, so that $\hat{\varepsilon}_T = \varepsilon_T$.

If we wish to forecast farther into the future, the information provided by serial correlation becomes less and less useful, since

$$\hat{\varepsilon}_{T+2} = \rho \hat{\varepsilon}_{T+1} = \rho^2 \hat{\varepsilon}_T$$

$$\hat{\varepsilon}_{T+3} = \rho \hat{\varepsilon}_{T+2} = \rho^3 \hat{\varepsilon}_T$$

$$\cdots \cdots \cdots \cdots \cdots$$

$$\hat{\varepsilon}_{T+s} = \rho^s \hat{\varepsilon}_T$$

and ρ^s approaches zero as s gets arbitrarily large.

The reader should note that the identical prediction of Y_{T+1} would be obtained if we wrote the model in generalized difference form:

$$Y_t^* = \alpha(1 - \rho) + \beta X_t^* + v_t \tag{8.27}$$

where $\qquad Y_t^* = Y_t - \rho Y_{t-1} \qquad$ and $\qquad X_t^* = X_t - \rho X_{t-1}$

The appropriate forecast is then

$$\hat{Y}_{T+1}^* = \alpha(1 - \rho) + \beta X_{T+1}^* \tag{8.28}$$

where $\qquad \hat{Y}_{T+1}^* = \hat{Y}_{T+1} - \rho Y_T \qquad$ and $\qquad X_{T+1}^* = X_{T+1} - \rho X_T$

The equivalence of (8.28) and (8.26) becomes apparent by writing

$$\hat{Y}_{T+1} = \hat{Y}_{T+1}^* + \rho Y_T = \alpha(1 - \rho) + \beta X_{T+1}^* + \rho Y_T$$

$$= \alpha(1 - \rho) + \beta X_{T+1} + \rho Y_T - \beta \rho X_T$$

$$= \alpha(1 - \rho) + \beta X_{T+1} + \rho(Y_T - \beta X_T) \tag{8.29}$$

But $Y_T = \alpha + \beta X_T + \varepsilon_T$. Therefore,

$$\hat{Y}_{T+1} = \alpha(1 - \rho) + \beta X_{T+1} + \rho(\alpha + \varepsilon_T) = \alpha + \beta X_{T+1} + \rho \varepsilon_T \tag{8.30}$$

which is identical to Eq. (8.26).

If the parameters α, β, and ρ are all known, then the error of forecast is given simply by

$$\hat{e}_{T+1} = \hat{Y}_{T+1} - Y_{T+1} = (\alpha + \beta X_{T+1} + \rho \varepsilon_T) - (\alpha + \beta X_{T+1} + \varepsilon_{T+1})$$

$$= \rho \varepsilon_T - \varepsilon_{T+1} = -v_{T+1} \tag{8.31}$$

Thus the error of forecast is normally distributed with 0 mean and has a variance

$$\sigma_f^2 = E\left[(\rho \varepsilon_T - \varepsilon_{T+1})^2\right] = \rho^2 E(\varepsilon_T^2) + E(\varepsilon_{T+1}^2) - 2\rho E(\varepsilon_T \varepsilon_{T+1})$$

$$= \rho^2 E(\varepsilon_T^2) + E(\varepsilon_{T+1}^2) - 2\rho^2 E(\varepsilon_T^2)$$

$$= (1 - \rho^2)\sigma^2 = \sigma_v^2 \qquad \text{since } E(\varepsilon_{T+1}^2) = E(\varepsilon_T^2) = \sigma^2 \tag{8.32}$$

Note that this forecast error is *smaller*, by a factor of $1 - \rho^2$, than would be the case if we did not take serial correlation into account. Using the information about the serially correlated nature of the error terms makes it possible to reduce the forecast error.

Of course in practice all three parameters α, β, and ρ are usually not known, but they can be estimated using any one of the estimation techniques described in Chapter 6. To produce a best forecast, one simply uses the estimated equation in generalized difference form.† In other words, we calculate $\hat{Y}_{T+1}$ from

$$\hat{Y}_{T+1} = \hat{\rho}Y_T + \hat{\alpha}(1 - \hat{\rho}) + \hat{\beta}(X_{T+1} - \hat{\rho}X_T) \tag{8.33}$$

It can be proved (although we will not do so here) that the mean of the error of forecast will approach zero as the sample size gets large. It is somewhat difficult to determine an explicit expression for the variance of the error of forecast when all three parameters α, β, and ρ have been estimated, since the estimation process guarantees that the estimated slope and intercept parameters will be correlated with the residuals of the regression. In practice, to calculate the variance of the error of forecast (and thus calculate a confidence interval on the forecast itself), we assume that ρ has been estimated exactly, i.e., that $\hat{\rho} = \rho$. In this case the forecast variance of Eq. (8.19) applies to our estimated equation in *generalized difference form* (and thus with an error term v_t instead of ε_t). Once again the error of forecast for $\hat{Y}_{T+1}$ will have a smaller variance (and thus the 95 percent confidence bands will be narrower) than would be the case if serial correlation were not taken into account. We will examine this in more detail, and in the context of the multiple regression model, in Appendix 8.1. Let us now turn to an example of forecasting in the presence of serially correlated errors.

Example 8.3 Forecasting coal demand‡ In this example we construct and use a forecasting model to predict, on a monthly basis, the demand for bituminous coal. We begin by specifying a linear equation that relates coal demand (COAL) to the Federal Reserve Board index of iron and steel production (FIS), the Federal Reserve Board index of electrical utility production (FEU), the wholesale price index for coal (PCOAL), and the wholesale price index for natural gas (PGAS). We use monthly data over the period January 1965 to December 1972, and we use a seasonally adjusted series for coal demand. We begin by estimating the equation using ordinary least squares. The regression results are shown below, with t statistics in parentheses:

$$\widehat{COAL} = \underset{(3.51)}{12{,}262} + \underset{(6.46)}{92.34}\,FIS + \underset{(7.14)}{118.57}\,FEU - \underset{(-3.82)}{48.90}\,PCOAL$$

$$+ \underset{(3.18)}{118.91}\,PGAS \tag{8.34}$$

$R^2 = .692 \qquad \bar{R}^2 = .675 \qquad F(4/91) = 51.0 \qquad SER = 1{,}200 \qquad DW = .95$

The fit of this equation is quite good, as can be seen both from the statistics and from Figs. 8.7 and 8.8, which compare actual and fitted coal demand over 3- and 1-year periods, respectively. One problem with the

---

† For a proof that this is the best linear unbiased forecast, see A. S. Goldberger, "Best Linear Unbiased Prediction in the Linear Regression Model," *Journal of the American Statistical Association*, vol. 57, pp. 369–375, 1962.

‡ This example was first discussed in Chapter 6.

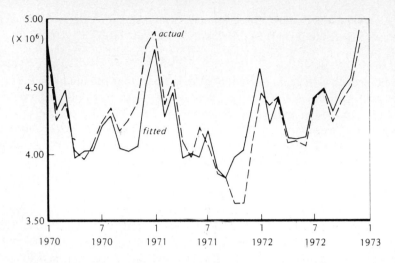

Figure 8.7 Coal demand, fitted versus actual.
Time bounds: January 1970 to December 1972.

model, however, is the low DW statistic, indicating a significant amount of serial correlation in the error terms.

We have seen that we can improve our forecasts by taking serial correlation into account. Therefore we will reestimate our equation using the Hildreth-Lu regression procedure, discussed in Chapter 6. Recall that in this procedure the equation is transformed using generalized differences:

$$(COAL - \rho COAL_{-1}) = c_0(1 - \rho) + c_1(FIS - \rho FIS_{-1}) + \cdots$$

$$(8.35)$$

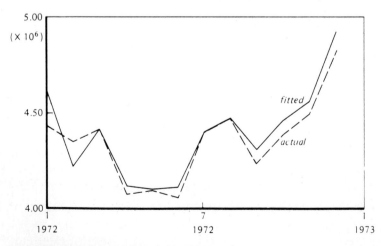

Figure 8.8 Coal demand, fitted versus actual.
Time bounds: January 1972 to December 1972.

Since ρ is not known, the Hildreth-Lu procedure performs OLS regressions on Eq. (8.35) using several different values of ρ. Each time a regression is performed, the sum of squared residuals (ESS) is calculated, and the value of ρ that gives the smallest ESS is used in the final result. The Hildreth-Lu regression results for our coal demand equation are

$$\widehat{\text{COAL}} = 16{,}245 + \underset{(3.29)}{75.29}\,\text{FIS} + \underset{(4.38)}{100.26}\,\text{FEU} - \underset{(-2.02)}{38.98}\,\text{PCOAL}$$

$$+ \underset{(1.96)}{105.99}\,\text{PGAS} \qquad\qquad (8.36)$$

$$R^2 = .774 \qquad \bar{R}^2 = .762 \qquad F(4/90) = 77.1 \qquad \text{SER} = 998 \qquad \text{DW} = 2.07$$

$$\hat{\rho} = .60$$

Note that the DW statistic is closer to 2.0, the central value in the range of the statistic, indicative of no serial correlation, and the standard error of the equation is smaller (998 versus 1,200 before). All the explanatory variables continue to be significant. The fit of the equation can be seen graphically in Figs. 8.9 and 8.10, which compare the actual and fitted series over 3- and 1-year periods, respectively. A comparison of Figs. 8.9 and 8.10 with Figs. 8.7 and 8.8 shows the better fit afforded by the Hildreth-Lu procedure.

We now generate *ex post* forecasts over the 12-month period January 1973 to December 1973 and compare these forecasts with actual coal demand over that period. First we use Eq. (8.34), which does not account for serial correlation. These forecast results, together with the 95 percent confidence band and the actual series for coal demand, are shown in Fig. 8.11. The results are quite good; the actual series always remains within the 95 percent confidence band and in fact is usually quite close to the predicted series.

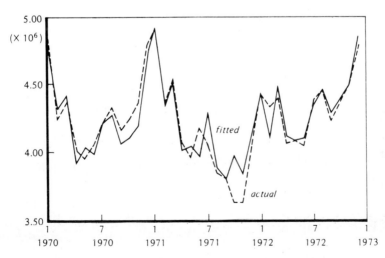

Figure 8.9 Coal demand, fitted versus actual with serial-correlation correction. Time bounds: January 1970 to December 1972.

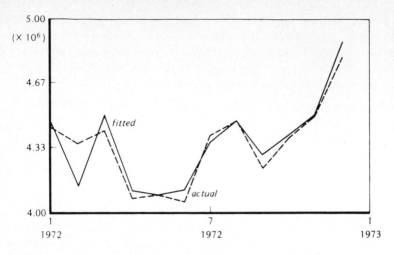

Figure 8.10 Coal demand, fitted versus actual with serial-correlation correction. Time bounds: January 1972 to December 1972.

We can generate better forecasts, however, by using Eq. (8.36) in its generalized difference form, i.e., by applying Eq. (8.28) or (8.33). These results, again together with the 95 percent confidence band and the actual series, are shown in Fig. 8.12. Compare Figs. 8.12 and 8.11 and notice that the 95 percent confidence band is *narrower* when the serial correlation has been taken into account. No matter whether our forecasts are *ex ante* or *ex post*, we will have greater confidence in them, i.e., expect smaller forecast errors, if we have correctly used the information provided by the serial correlation in the error terms. Finally, as we would expect, a comparison of

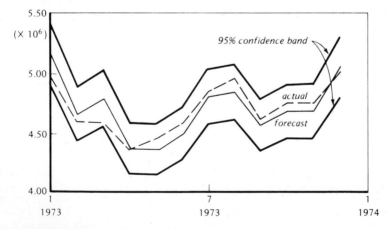

Figure 8.11 Forecast of coal demand using OLS regression. Time bounds: January 1973 to December 1973.

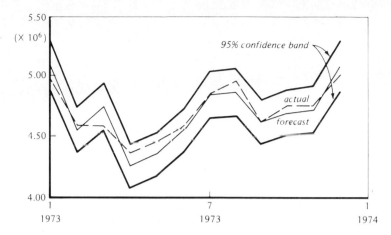

Figure 8.12 Forecast of coal demand using serial-correlation correction. Time bounds: January 1973 to December 1973.

the two figures shows that the forecasted series is closer to the actual series (i.e., the resulting forecast errors are indeed smaller) when serial correlation has been accounted for.†

8.3 CONDITIONAL FORECASTING

Our previous discussion about forecasting involved the assumption that all the explanatory variables are known without error, even in the forecast period. This may at times be an unrealistic assumption during *ex ante* forecasting, since some explanatory variables may have to be predicted into the future before the single-equation regression model can be used to forecast. One may intuitively expect that the stochastic nature of the predicted value of the X's will lead to forecasts of Y which are less reliable than in the fixed-X case. We shall see, in fact, that the 95 percent confidence intervals for the error of forecast are indeed increased in size when the X's must themselves be predicted. However, it is quite difficult to derive analytic results for the error of forecast in a general setting. We deal, therefore, with a special case, which, though somewhat restrictive, should be instructive.‡

Consider the following model:

$$Y_t = \alpha + \beta X_t + \varepsilon_t \qquad t = 1, 2, \ldots, T \tag{8.37}$$

† In Chapter 12 we present error measures that can be used to evaluate or compare forecasts. One measure that might be used is the sum of the squared errors over the forecast period. This measure is clearly smaller when the serial-correlation correction is used.

‡ This case is described in M. Feldstein, "The Error of Forecast in Econometric Models When the Forecast-Period Exogenous Variables Are Stochastic," *Econometrica*, vol. 39, pp. 55–60, January 1971.

where $\hat{X}_{T+1} = X_{T+1} + u_{T+1}$, $\varepsilon_t \sim N(0, \sigma^2)$, and $u_t \sim N(0, \sigma_u^2)$; ε_t and u_t are uncorrelated;

$$E\left[(\hat{X}_{T+1} - X_{T+1})(\hat{\beta} - \beta)\right] = E\left[(\hat{X}_{T+1} - X_{T+1})(\hat{\alpha} - \alpha)\right] = 0$$

and $\hat{\alpha}$ and $\hat{\beta}$ are the OLS estimates of α and β. The model presumes that X_{T+1} is forecasted in such a way that its error of forecast has 0 mean and constant variance. In addition, the error process associated with the forecast of X_{T+1} is assumed to be independent of the error process associated with each of the Y's in the model. Even though they are stochastic in nature, the X's are still presumed to be exogenous in the sense that they are uncorrelated with the equation error term. The restrictiveness of this model becomes clear when we consider the means by which forecasted values of X_{T+1} might be obtained. One frequently used procedure is to extrapolate from the sample values of X. While numerous extrapolation routines are available, the likelihood that the X variable is autocorrelated in a time-series model suggests that the error of forecast associated with the extrapolation procedure is itself likely to be serially correlated.

The forecasted value of Y in the time period $T + 1$ is defined by

$$\hat{Y}_{T+1} = \hat{\alpha} + \hat{\beta}\hat{X}_{T+1} \tag{8.38}$$

The error of forecast is then

$$\hat{e}_{T+1} = \hat{Y}_{T+1} - Y_{T+1} = (\hat{\alpha} - \alpha) + (\hat{\beta}\hat{X}_{T+1} - \beta X_{T+1}) - \varepsilon_{T+1} \tag{8.39}$$

It is easy to see that this error has 0 mean:

$$E(\hat{e}_{T+1}) = E(\hat{\alpha} - \alpha) + E(\hat{\beta}\hat{X}_{T+1}) - \beta X_{T+1} - E(\varepsilon_{T+1})$$
$$= E\left[\hat{\beta}(X_{T+1} + u_{T+1})\right] - \beta X_{T+1} = \beta X_{T+1} - \beta X_{T+1} = 0 \tag{8.40}$$

since $\hat{\beta}$ and u_{T+1} are uncorrelated.

The variance of the error of forecast is somewhat more difficult to derive:†

$$\sigma_f^2 = E\left[(\hat{e}_{T+1})^2\right] = E\left[(\hat{\alpha} - \alpha)^2\right] + E\left[(\hat{\beta}\hat{X}_{T+1} - \beta X_{T+1})^2\right] + E\left[(\varepsilon_{T+1})^2\right]$$
$$+ 2E\left[(\hat{\alpha} - \alpha)(\hat{\beta}\hat{X}_{T+1} - \beta X_{T+1})\right] \tag{8.41}$$

But
$$\hat{\beta}\hat{X}_{T+1} - \beta X_{T+1} = \hat{\beta}(\hat{X}_{T+1} - X_{T+1}) + X_{T+1}(\hat{\beta} - \beta) \tag{8.42}$$

Therefore,

$$E\left[(\hat{\beta}\hat{X}_{T+1} - \beta X_{T+1})^2\right] = E\left[\hat{\beta}(\hat{X}_{T+1} - X_{T+1}) + X_{T+1}(\hat{\beta} - \beta)\right]^2$$
$$= E\left[\hat{\beta}^2(\hat{X}_{T+1} - X_{T+1})^2\right] + X_{T+1}^2 E\left[(\hat{\beta} - \beta)^2\right]$$
$$= \left[\beta^2 + \text{Var}(\hat{\beta})\right]\sigma_u^2 + X_{T+1}^2 \text{Var}(\hat{\beta}) \tag{8.43}$$

---

† We have dropped out terms which are obviously equal to zero.

Note that in arriving at Eq. (8.43), we took advantage of the fact that $u_{T+1} = \hat{X}_{T+1} - X_{T+1}$, that u_{T+1} and $\hat{\beta}$ are uncorrelated, and, finally, that $\hat{\beta}^2 = \beta^2 + \mathrm{Var}\,(\hat{\beta})$. Next, we can use Eq. (8.42) to simplify the last term in Eq. (8.41):

$$E\big[(\hat{\alpha} - \alpha)(\hat{\beta}\hat{X}_{T+1} - \beta X_{T+1})\big]$$

$$= E\big[(\hat{\alpha} - \alpha)\hat{\beta}(\hat{X}_{T+1} - X_{T+1})\big] + X_{T+1}E\big[(\hat{\alpha} - \alpha)(\hat{\beta} - \beta)\big]$$

$$= X_{T+1}\,\mathrm{Cov}\,(\hat{\alpha}, \hat{\beta}) \tag{8.44}$$

(The first term on the right is zero by assumption.) Now, by combining terms, we find that

$$\sigma_f^2 = \mathrm{Var}\,(\hat{\alpha}) + \big[\beta^2 + \mathrm{Var}\,(\hat{\beta})\big]\sigma_u^2 + X_{T+1}^2\,\mathrm{Var}\,(\hat{\beta}) + 2X_{T+1}\,\mathrm{Cov}\,(\hat{\alpha}, \hat{\beta}) + \sigma^2$$

$$= \mathrm{Var}\,(\hat{\alpha}) + \mathrm{Var}\,(\hat{\beta})(X_{T+1}^2 + \sigma_u^2) + 2X_{T+1}\,\mathrm{Cov}\,(\hat{\alpha}, \hat{\beta}) + \sigma^2 + \beta^2\sigma_u^2 \tag{8.45}$$

When we put this in terms of our least-squares estimators, the formula for the variance of the error of forecast becomes

$$\sigma_f^2 = \sigma^2\left[1 + \frac{1}{T} + \frac{(X_{T+1} - \overline{X})^2 + \sigma_u^2}{\Sigma(X_t - \overline{X})^2}\right] + \beta^2\sigma_u^2 \tag{8.46}$$

A comparison of Eq. (8.46) with Eq. (8.19) from Section 8.1 makes it clear that the stochastic nature of the forecasted value of X increases the error of forecast. There are two additional nonnegative terms involved, both of which are minimized only when the forecast of X_{T+1} is made with 0 error variance. This result makes it quite clear that the 95 percent confidence intervals associated with the forecasted value of Y_{T+1} will be larger than the intervals described in the unconditional forecasting derivation. Unfortunately, it is quite difficult to describe the confidence intervals for the conditional error of forecast. The difficulty arises because the forecast variable $\hat{Y}_{T+1}$ is not normally distributed, since it involves the sum of *products* of normally distributed variables. While confidence intervals cannot be derived analytically, they can be approximated using computer simulation techniques. A rather crude estimate of the confidence interval might be obtained as follows:

1. Calculate the 95 percent confidence intervals associated with the forecast that would be obtained were we to select $\hat{X}_{T+1}$ to be two standard deviations higher or lower, i.e., the confidence intervals associated with $Y_{T+1}^* = \hat{\alpha} + \hat{\beta}(\hat{X}_{T+1} + 2\sigma_u)$ and $Y_{T+1}^{**} = \hat{\alpha} + \hat{\beta}(\hat{X}_{T+1} - 2\sigma_u)$.
2. The final interval prediction is taken to be the union of the two confidence intervals; i.e., it contains all the values of $\hat{Y}_{T+1}$ common to both confidence intervals.

This process is depicted in Fig. 8.13.

The results of this section help to accentuate some of the difficulties involved in the forecasting process. Even if the regression model has a good fit

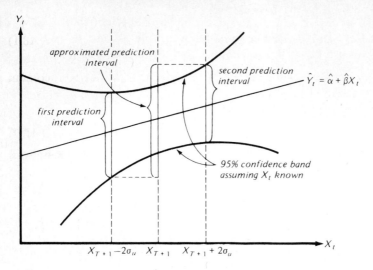

Figure 8.13 Approximating the prediction interval for a conditional forecast.

with statistically significant parameters, unconditional forecasts may not be very accurate. In addition, the process of forecasting or extrapolating the explanatory variables into the prediction period introduces additional forecast error which diminishes the reliability of the regression model. A good regression model in terms of unconditional forecasting may perform quite badly when conditional forecasting is attempted. One should not be too quick to reject a model with a high forecast error if the primary component of that error is due to a serious error in judgment or prediction involved with the determination of the value of the explanatory variables in the forecast period. In macroeconomic forecasting, the problem is even more difficult because an accurate initial conditional forecast may lead to a shift in policy and thus to an inaccurate forecast!

APPENDIX 8.1 FORECASTING WITH THE MULTIVARIATE REGRESSION MODEL

In this appendix we use matrix notation to generalize our discussion of the forecasting problem to the multivariate case. As we will see, the basic concepts that apply to the two-variable regression model also apply when additional independent variables are added to the right-hand side of the equation.

We begin by writing the general linear model in matrix form. The model contains a dependent variable and k independent variables (including the constant term) and is estimated over a total of T observations ($t =$

$1, 2, \ldots, T$):

$$\mathbf{Y} = \mathbf{X}\boldsymbol{\beta} + \boldsymbol{\varepsilon} \tag{A8.1}$$

Recall that $\mathbf{Y}$ is a $T \times 1$ column vector of dependent variable observations, $\mathbf{X}$ is a $T \times k$ matrix of independent variable observations, $\boldsymbol{\beta}$ is a $k \times 1$ column vector of unknown parameters, and $\boldsymbol{\varepsilon}$ is a $T \times 1$ column vector of error terms. Then the ordinary least-squares estimate of $\boldsymbol{\beta}$ will be given by

$$\hat{\boldsymbol{\beta}} = (\mathbf{X}'\mathbf{X})^{-1}\mathbf{X}'\mathbf{Y} \tag{A8.2}$$

Now let us examine the characteristics of a forecast made using this estimated equation. Suppose we have a new set of observations (or even forecasts or guesses) for the independent variables for period $T + 1$. Then the forecast for the dependent variable in period $T + 1$ will be given by

$$\hat{Y}_{T+1} = \mathbf{X}_{T+1}\hat{\boldsymbol{\beta}} \tag{A8.3}$$

Note that $\mathbf{X}_{T+1}$ is a $1 \times k$ row vector, so that $\hat{Y}_{T+1}$ is a *scalar*. Similarly, if we wanted a forecast for period $T + 2$, that would be given by

$$\hat{Y}_{T+2} = \mathbf{X}_{T+2}\hat{\boldsymbol{\beta}} \tag{A8.4}$$

Of course, if all the independent variables appeared with lags greater than or equal to two periods, then we could simply *observe* $\mathbf{X}_{T+2}$, but if some or all of the independent variables are not lagged, then $\mathbf{X}_{T+2}$ will itself have to be forecasted and the forecast of Y_{T+2} will be conditional on the forecast of $\mathbf{X}_{T+2}$.

Since Eqs. (A8.3) and (A8.4) apply for any time period, let us (in the interest of notational simplicity) drop the time subscript and rewrite our forecasting equation as†

$$\hat{Y} = \tilde{\mathbf{X}}\hat{\boldsymbol{\beta}} \tag{A8.5}$$

where $\hat{Y}$ is a forecast of Y_t for some period and $\tilde{\mathbf{X}}$ is a set of observations on the independent variables for that same period. Finally, let us denote the *actual* value of Y (which we must wait to observe) by $\tilde{Y}$. Then the *forecast error* is given by

$$\hat{e} = \hat{Y} - \tilde{Y} \tag{A8.6}$$

Since the actual value $\tilde{Y}$ of Y can be written as

$$\tilde{Y} = \tilde{\mathbf{X}}\boldsymbol{\beta} + \tilde{\varepsilon} \tag{A8.7}$$

where $\tilde{\varepsilon}$ is the actual value of the additive error term in the forecast period, we can write the forecast error as

$$\hat{e} = \tilde{\mathbf{X}}\hat{\boldsymbol{\beta}} - \tilde{\varepsilon} - \tilde{\mathbf{X}}\boldsymbol{\beta} = -\tilde{\varepsilon} - \tilde{\mathbf{X}}\boldsymbol{\beta} + \tilde{\mathbf{X}}(\mathbf{X}'\mathbf{X})^{-1}\mathbf{X}'\mathbf{Y} \tag{A8.8}$$

---

† For a proof that Eq. (A8.5) is the best predictor of Y, see H. Theil, *Principles of Econometrics* (New York: Wiley, 1971), p. 123.

Note that $\mathbf{Y}$ in Eq. (A8.8) is the $T \times 1$ vector of dependent-variable observations as given by Eq. (A8.1). Substituting (A8.1) into (A8.8), we have

$$\hat{e} = -\tilde{\varepsilon} - \tilde{\mathbf{X}}\boldsymbol{\beta} + \tilde{\mathbf{X}}(\mathbf{X}'\mathbf{X})^{-1}\mathbf{X}'(\mathbf{X}\boldsymbol{\beta} + \varepsilon) = -\tilde{\varepsilon} - \tilde{\mathbf{X}}\boldsymbol{\beta} + \tilde{\mathbf{X}}\boldsymbol{\beta} + \tilde{\mathbf{X}}(\mathbf{X}'\mathbf{X})^{-1}\mathbf{X}'\varepsilon$$

$$= -\tilde{\varepsilon} + \tilde{\mathbf{X}}(\mathbf{X}'\mathbf{X})^{-1}\mathbf{X}'\varepsilon \tag{A8.9}$$

We are interested in the variance of the forecast error, i.e., in

$$\sigma_f^2 = E[\hat{e}^2]$$

$$= E[\tilde{\varepsilon}^2] - 2\tilde{\mathbf{X}}(\mathbf{X}'\mathbf{X})^{-1}\mathbf{X}'E[\varepsilon\tilde{\varepsilon}] + \tilde{\mathbf{X}}(\mathbf{X}'\mathbf{X})^{-1}\mathbf{X}'E[\varepsilon\varepsilon']\mathbf{X}(\mathbf{X}'\mathbf{X})^{-1}\tilde{\mathbf{X}}'$$

$$\tag{A8.10}$$

We are assuming here that the additive error terms are not autocorrelated, and therefore $E[\varepsilon\tilde{\varepsilon}] = 0$. We are also assuming that the error terms are homoscedastic, so that

$$E[\varepsilon\varepsilon'] = \sigma^2\mathbf{I} \tag{A8.11}$$

We can thus write the variance of the forecast error as

$$\sigma_f^2 = \sigma^2 + \sigma^2\tilde{\mathbf{X}}(\mathbf{X}'\mathbf{X})^{-1}\mathbf{X}'\mathbf{I}\mathbf{X}(\mathbf{X}'\mathbf{X})^{-1}\tilde{\mathbf{X}}' = \sigma^2(1 + \tilde{\mathbf{X}}(\mathbf{X}'\mathbf{X})^{-1}\tilde{\mathbf{X}}') \tag{A8.12}$$

As was the case in the two-variable regression model, this variance (and therefore the 95 percent confidence interval implied by it) depends on what the particular values of the independent variables are in the forecast period; i.e., it depends on $\tilde{\mathbf{X}}$.

We might now ask what the *smallest possible* forecast error variance could be, i.e., what value of $\tilde{\mathbf{X}}$ would minimize σ_f^2. We can answer this question by solving a *constrained minimization* problem in which we make use of the method of Lagrange multipliers.† In order to minimize σ_f^2 we must minimize the matrix product on the right-hand side of Eq. (A8.12); that is, we want to solve

Minimize $\qquad \tilde{\mathbf{X}}(\mathbf{X}'\mathbf{X})^{-1}\tilde{\mathbf{X}}' \qquad$ subject to $\quad \tilde{X}_1 = 1$

The constraint that $\tilde{X}_1 = 1$ refers to the fact that the first element of $\tilde{\mathbf{X}}$ is the constant term, i.e., the intercept of the regression equation. Now we can write the *lagrangian* for this problem as

$$\mathcal{L} = \tilde{\mathbf{X}}(\mathbf{X}'\mathbf{X})^{-1}\tilde{\mathbf{X}}' - \lambda(\tilde{X}_1 - 1) \tag{A8.13}$$

where λ is the Lagrange multiplier. Now differentiating the lagrangian with

---

† Readers unfamiliar with the method of Lagrange multipliers can refer to M. Intriligator, *Mathematical Optimization and Economic Theory* (Englewood Cliffs, N.J.: Prentice-Hall, 1972), chap. 3; or K. Lancaster, *Mathematical Economics* (New York: Macmillan, 1968), chap. 4.

respect to $\tilde{\mathbf{X}}$ and setting the derivative equal to 0 gives

$$\frac{\partial \mathcal{L}}{\partial \tilde{\mathbf{X}}} = 2(\mathbf{X}'\mathbf{X})^{-1}\tilde{\mathbf{X}}' - \lambda \begin{bmatrix} 1 \\ 0 \\ \vdots \\ 0 \end{bmatrix} = 0 \tag{A8.14}$$

or

$$\tilde{\mathbf{X}}' = \frac{\lambda}{2}(\mathbf{X}'\mathbf{X})\begin{bmatrix} 1 \\ 0 \\ \vdots \\ 0 \end{bmatrix} \tag{A8.15}$$

Thus $\tilde{\mathbf{X}}'$ is proportional to the first column of $\mathbf{X}'\mathbf{X}$:

$$\tilde{\mathbf{X}}' = \frac{\lambda}{2}\begin{bmatrix} T \\ \Sigma X_2 \\ \Sigma X_3 \\ \vdots \\ \Sigma X_k \end{bmatrix} \tag{A8.16}$$

The summations in Eq. (A8.16) are over the T observations. From the first row of Eq. (A8.16) we have, since $\tilde{X}_1 = 1$,

$$\frac{\lambda}{2}T = 1 \qquad \text{or} \qquad \lambda = \frac{2}{T}$$

We can thus write Eq. (A8.16) as

$$\tilde{\mathbf{X}}' = \begin{bmatrix} 1 \\ \dfrac{\Sigma X_2}{T} \\ \dfrac{\Sigma X_3}{T} \\ \vdots \\ \dfrac{\Sigma X_k}{T} \end{bmatrix} \tag{A8.17}$$

But note that the right-hand side of (A8.17) is just the *point of means*. Thus, as was the case in the two-variable model, the forecast error variance is minimized when all the new observations on the independent variables are equal to their mean values. What is the value of this minimum forecast error variance? Writing (A8.17) as

$$\tilde{\mathbf{X}}' = \frac{1}{T}(\mathbf{X}'\mathbf{X})\begin{bmatrix} 1 \\ 0 \\ \vdots \\ 0 \end{bmatrix} \tag{A8.18}$$

and substituting this into (A8.12), we have

$$
\min \left(\sigma_f^2\right) = \sigma^2\left\{1 + \frac{1}{T}[1 \quad 0 \quad \cdots \quad 0](\mathbf{X'X})(\mathbf{X'X})^{-1}(\mathbf{X'X})\begin{bmatrix}1\\0\\\vdots\\0\end{bmatrix}\frac{1}{T}\right\}
$$

$$
= \sigma^2\left\{1 + \frac{1}{T^2}[1 \quad 0 \quad \cdots \quad 0](\mathbf{X'X})\begin{bmatrix}1\\0\\\vdots\\0\end{bmatrix}\right\}
$$

$$
= \sigma^2\left(1 + \frac{T}{T^2}\right) = \sigma^2\left(1 + \frac{1}{T}\right) \tag{A8.19}
$$

Note that as the number of observations T becomes infinitely large, this minimum forecast error variance approaches the variance of the additive error term σ^2. We would expect this be the case, since as T becomes infinitely large the estimated parameter values approach the true parameter values exactly, so that the only source of forecast error is the additive error term.

Now what will our 95 percent confidence regions look like? They will essentially be a multidimensional version of Fig. 8.3. In the case of two independent variables (in addition to the constant term), the 95 percent confidence region will be bounded by two hyperboloids. The confidence interval will be smallest at the mean values of X_1 and X_2.

EXERCISES

8.1 For the regression model $Y_t = \alpha + \beta X_t + \varepsilon_t$:

(a) Suppose α is *known*. What is the appropriate method for forecasting Y_{T+1}? Show that the error variance of the forecast is given by

$$
\sigma^2\left(\frac{1 + X_{T+1}^2}{\Sigma X_i^2}\right)
$$

(b) Suppose β is known. Find the appropriate method for forecasting Y_{T+1} and show that the error variance of the forecast will be

$$
\sigma^2\left(1 + \frac{1}{T}\right)
$$

Hint: (1) In the model $Y_t = \alpha + \varepsilon_t$, the least-squares estimator of α is given by $\hat{\alpha} = (1/T)\Sigma Y_i$ and the variance of $\hat{\alpha} = \sigma^2/T$, where $\sigma^2 = \text{Var}(\varepsilon_t)$. (2) In the model $Y_t = \beta X_t + \varepsilon_t$, the least-squares estimator of β is given by $\hat{\beta} = \Sigma X_i Y_i/\Sigma X_i^2$ and the variance of $\hat{\beta} = \sigma^2/\Sigma X_i^2$.

8.2 In Example 8.2, Fig. 8.5, the actual series for the interest rate diverges considerably from the forecasted series after November 1970. Suggest why the regression model failed to predict the downturn in interest rates that occurred at the end of 1970.

8.3 This problem uses the investment data set in Table 6.3. We know that $\text{IRC}_t = \beta_1 + \beta_2\text{YD}_t + \beta_3\text{DEL}_t + \beta_4\text{PIRC}_t + \varepsilon_t$, where ε_t follows a first-order autoregressive model, $\varepsilon_t = \rho\varepsilon_{t-1} + v_t$. Given observations on YD, DEL, PIRC for time period 1954-1 through 1979-1 and observations on IRC for the time period 1954-1 through 1977-1, we wish to forecast IRC for the time period 1977-2 through 1979-1.

(*a*) Using only data for time period 1954-1 to 1977-1, compute the OLS estimates of β_1, β_2, β_3, and β_4.

(*b*) Using the above OLS estimates, forecast IRC_t for the period 1977-2 to 1979-1 using the formula

$$\widehat{IRC}_t = \hat{\beta}_1 + \hat{\beta}_2 YD_t + \hat{\beta}_3 DEL_t + \hat{\beta}_4 PIRC_t$$

(*c*) Using only data for the time period 1954-1 to 1977-1 and a Cochrane-Orcutt type procedure, estimate β_1, β_2, β_3, β_4, and ρ.

(*d*) Forecast IRC_t for the time period 1977-2 to 1979-1 by the formula

$$\widehat{IRC}_t = \hat{\hat{\beta}}_1 + \hat{\hat{\beta}}_2 YD_t + \hat{\hat{\beta}}_3 DEL_t + \hat{\hat{\beta}}_4 PIRC_t$$

where $\hat{\hat{\beta}}_i$ is the estimate for β_i found in part (*c*) above.

(*e*) Take into full account the error structure and forecast IRC_t for the period 1977-2 to 1979-1 by the formula

$$\widehat{IRC}_t = \hat{\hat{\beta}}_1 + \hat{\hat{\beta}}_2 YD_t + \hat{\hat{\beta}}_3 DEL_t + \hat{\hat{\beta}}_4 PIRC_t + \hat{\hat{\rho}}^J \hat{C}_{1977-1}$$

where J = number of quarters of t after 1977-1 (e.g., $J = 5$ for $t = $ 1978-2)

$\hat{\hat{\rho}}$ = estimate for ρ found in part (*c*)

$$\hat{C}_{1977-1} = IRC_{1977-1} - (\hat{\hat{\beta}}_1 + \hat{\hat{\beta}}_2 YD_{1977-1} + \hat{\hat{\beta}}_3 DEL_{1977-1} + \hat{\hat{\beta}}_4 PIRC_{1977-1})$$

(*f*) Using the actual observations of IRC_t for the forecast periods compute both the sum of absolute error and the sum of squared errors of forecast for the three forecast methods.

SINGLE-EQUATION ESTIMATION:
ADVANCED TOPICS

In the last eight chapters we have completed the development of the core of econometrics, the general linear model. We began with a discussion of ordinary least-squares estimation and continued with an analysis of adjustments which must be made to ordinary least squares to guarantee unbiased, consistent, and efficient estimation. These adjustments included corrections for serial correlation, heteroscedasticity, and correlation between the regressors and the disturbance term. Finally, we showed how the linear model can be used for forecasting. In this chapter we continue our discussion of single-equation estimation by discussing problems associated with the econometric model.† The first topic in this chapter is a description of distributed lag models and their estimation. We focus on two of the most frequently used lag structures, the geometric lag and the polynomial distributed lag.

Second, we consider several means of resolving the dilemma which arises when there are missing observations. The loss of efficiency which results when observations are dropped from the sample is compared with the risks of replacing missing observations with suitable substitutes. Third, we provide a brief introduction to the estimation of regression models using cross-section and time-series data. Several alternative schemes for pooling data are contemplated, and whenever possible the corresponding estimation techniques are described.

† The four topics presented in this chapter can be read independently of each other and can be treated as optional for an introductory econometrics course.

Finally, the chapter concludes with an introduction to nonlinear estimation. We focus on some alternative techniques for estimating equations that are nonlinear in the parameters and see how these equations can be used for forecasting.

9.1 DISTRIBUTED LAGS

When constructing models, it is important to recognize that some amount of time usually lapses between the movement of the independent variables and the response of the dependent variable. In time-series models in particular, a substantial period of time may pass between the economic decision-making period and the final impact of a change in a given policy variable. If the decision-and-response period associated with a given model is sufficiently long, lagged explanatory variables should be included explicitly in the model specification. As an example, consider the specification of an aggregate consumption function which is to be estimated using quarterly macroeconomic data. One might specify aggregate consumption C_t to be a function of aggregate disposable income lagged one quarter Y_{t-1}. The one-period lag allows for the time involved in the consumption response to a change in disposable income. The specification of a model's lag structure is very much dependent on the time units of the data. If the same consumption function were specified using annual data, it might be reasonable to drop the lag in the income variable, since the period of measurement is substantially larger than the hypothesized reaction period.

This simple example assumes that the entire effect of the explanatory variable occurs in one time period $(t-1)$. More generally, one would account for the fact that economic changes take place gradually over time. For example, aggregate consumption may be a function of disposable income lagged one, two, three, or more periods. The fact that the impact of a variable can be distributed over a number of time periods is the basis of the *distributed lag model*, in which a series of lagged explanatory variables accounts for the time-adjustment process. In its most general form, the distributed lag model can be written

$$Y_t = \alpha + \beta_0 X_t + \beta_1 X_{t-1} + \beta_2 X_{t-2} + \cdots = \alpha + \sum_{s=0}^{\infty} \beta_s X_{t-s} + \varepsilon_t \quad (9.1)$$

Unless we state otherwise, we shall assume that the error term is normally distributed, independent of X, and neither serially correlated nor heteroscedastic. We allow the number of lags to be infinite in our specification, although many practical examples involve a finite lag structure. If the lag structure is infinite, however, the sequence of lag weights which describe the pattern of the lag response must have a finite sum. If this were not the case, the model would not have a finite solution.

If the number of terms in the distributed lag is very small, the equation can be estimated using ordinary least-squares regression. However, when there are many terms and little is known about the form of the lag, direct estimation becomes difficult for several reasons. First, the estimation of a lengthy lag structure uses up a large number of degrees of freedom, which are often in short supply in time-series models. Second, the estimation of an equation with a substantial number of lagged explanatory variables is likely to lead to imprecise parameter estimates because of the presence of multicollinearity. Multicollinearity arises when the X variable is highly autocorrelated; i.e., the variable observed at time t bears a close relationship to the variable measured at times $t - 1, t - 2$, etc. Both these difficulties can be resolved if one can specify *a priori* some conditions about the form of the distributed lag. We shall pursue this matter further by describing two of the most frequently posited lag structures. Our purpose is to introduce the reader to some of the problems involved in the specification of distributed lag models.†

9.1.1 Geometric Lag

The geometric lag assumes that the weights of the lagged explanatory variables are all positive and decline geometrically with time. The model is

$$Y_t = \alpha + \beta\left(X_t + wX_{t-1} + w^2X_{t-2} + \cdots\right) + \varepsilon_t$$

$$= \alpha + \beta \sum_{s=0}^{\infty} w^s X_{t-s} + \varepsilon_t \qquad 0 < w < 1 \tag{9.2}$$

The pattern of parameters associated with the model is depicted in Fig. 9.1 (for $w = \frac{1}{2}$). While the weights of the geometric lag model never become zero, they diminish so that beyond a reasonable time the effect of the explanatory variable becomes negligible.

It is often useful to describe the lag structure of a distributed lag model in terms of its mean or average lag and in terms of the long-run response of the dependent variable to a permanent change in one of the explanatory variables. The *long-run response m* in the geometric lag model is simply the parameter β times the sum of the lag weights Σw^s or $\beta/(1 - w)$.‡ m measures the change in Y associated with a one-unit increase in X which stays in effect for all time. The *mean lag*, on the other hand, is defined as a lag-weighted average of time, i.e.,

$$\text{Mean lag} = \frac{\displaystyle\sum_{s=0}^{\infty} s\beta_s}{\displaystyle\sum_{s=0}^{\infty} \beta_s} \qquad \text{where } \beta_s = \beta w^s$$

---

† For a more advanced discussion of distributed lag models, the reader is referred to P. Dhrymes, *Distributed Lags: Problem of Estimation and Formulation* (San Francisco: Holden-Day, 1971); Z. Griliches, "Distributed Lags: A Survey," *Econometrica*, vol. 35, pp. 16–49, 1967; L. M. Koyck, *Distributed Lags and Investment Analysis* (Amsterdam: North-Holland, 1954); and M. Nerlove, "Lags in Economic Behavior," *Econometrica*, vol. 40, pp. 221–251, 1972.

‡ Recall the sum of an infinite series such as $\Sigma w^s = 1/(1 - w)$. To prove this, let $\Sigma_{s=0}^{\infty} w^s = k$. Multiplying by w implies $\Sigma_{s=1}^{\infty} w^s = kw$. Subtracting, we get $1 = k(1 - w)$ or $k = 1/(1 - w)$.

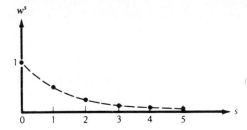

Figure 9.1 Geometric lag parameters.

In the geometric lag model, the mean lag is $w/(1 - w)$, since†

$$\frac{\sum\limits_{s=0}^{\infty} s\beta_s}{\sum\limits_{s=0}^{\infty} \beta_s} = \frac{\beta\sum sw^s}{\beta\sum w^s} = \frac{w/(1-w)^2}{1/(1-w)} = \frac{w}{(1-w)}$$

If $w = \frac{1}{2}$, for example, the mean lag of 1 suggests that half the impact of a change in Y will be felt during the first time period.

In its present form, the geometric lag model appears quite difficult to estimate, since it involves an infinite number of regressors. However, the parametric form of the lag weights allows for a substantial simplification of the model. To see this, we rewrite the original model [Eq. (9.2)] with all observations lagged one period:

$$Y_{t-1} = \alpha + \beta(X_{t-1} + wX_{t-2} + \cdots) + \varepsilon_{t-1} \tag{9.3}$$

Then we calculate the expression $Y_t - wY_{t-1}$ to obtain

$$Y_t - wY_{t-1} = \alpha(1 - w) + \beta X_t + u_t \tag{9.4}$$

where $u_t = \varepsilon_t - w\varepsilon_{t-1}$. Rewriting, we find that

$$Y_t = \alpha(1 - w) + wY_{t-1} + \beta X_t + u_t \tag{9.5}$$

Equation (9.5) makes it somewhat easier to measure the effect of a continuous one-unit change in X on the value of Y. In the first time period the effect is β. However, in the second period Y_{t-1} has increased by β, so that the effect is $\beta + \beta w = \beta(1 + w)$. After T periods the effect is $\beta\sum_{s=0}^{T-1}w^s = \beta(1 - w^T)/(1 - w)$,‡ while the long-run response is $\beta/(1 - w)$.

It is sometimes useful, although more difficult computationally, to calculate the *median lag*, i.e., the value of time T for which the fraction of adjustment

---

† The fact that $\sum sw^s = w/(1 - w)^2$ follows after some manipulation:

$$\sum sw^s = \sum_{s=1}^{\infty} w^s + \sum_{s=2}^{\infty} w^s + \sum_{s=3}^{\infty} w^s + \cdots = \frac{1}{1-w} \sum_{s=1}^{\infty} w^s = \frac{w}{(1-w)^2}$$

‡ Again, summing a geometric series.

completed is equal to $\frac{1}{2}$. To find the median lag we solve

$$\frac{T\text{-period response}}{\text{Long-run response}} = \frac{\beta(1 - w^T)/(1 - w)}{\beta/(1 - w)} = \frac{1}{2}$$

Solving for T, we find that

$$T = \frac{\log \frac{1}{2}}{\log w}$$

Equation (9.5) can be estimated more easily than (9.2), since only three parameters remain unknown. However, before considering the estimation of the equation, we shall pause to consider when such a model specification is appropriate. This is a relevant concern, because the autoregressive model [Eq. (9.5)], containing a single lagged endogenous variable, is frequently specified outside the distributed lag context.

Adaptive expectations model. The *adaptive expectations model* postulates that changes in Y are related to changes in the "expected" level of the explanatory variable X. We would write this model as

$$Y_t = \alpha^* + \beta^* X_t^* + \varepsilon_t^* \tag{9.6}$$

where X^* represents the desired or expected level of X. X^* might represent a notion of permanent income in the aggregate consumption example described previously, or it might represent an expected price in a microeconometric model. The expected level of X is defined by a second relationship, in which expectations are assumed to be altered every time period as an adjustment between the current observed value of X and the previous expected value of X. The relationship is

$$X_t^* - X_{t-1}^* = \theta(X_t - X_{t-1}^*) \qquad \text{where } 0 < \theta \le 1. \tag{9.7}$$

It is sometimes more useful to rewrite Eq. (9.7) as

$$X_t^* = \theta X_t + (1 - \theta)X_{t-1}^* \tag{9.8}$$

This suggests that the expected level of X (permanent income or expected price) is a weighted average of the present level of X and the previous expected level of X. Expected levels of X are adjusted period by period by taking into account present levels of X. To posit the adaptive expectations model in a form which allows econometric estimation, rewrite Eq. (9.8) by lagging the model period by period while at the same time multiplying by $(1 - \theta)^s$, where s is the number of periods involved in the lag process:

$$(1 - \theta)X_{t-1}^* = \theta(1 - \theta)X_{t-1} + (1 - \theta)^2 X_{t-2}^*$$

$$(1 - \theta)^2 X_{t-2}^* = \theta(1 - \theta)^2 X_{t-2} + (1 - \theta)^3 X_{t-3}^* \tag{9.9}$$

Now, substitute (9.9) into (9.8) and combine terms:

$$X_t^* = \theta\left[X_t + (1 - \theta)X_{t-1} + (1 - \theta)^2 X_{t-2} + \cdots\right] = \theta \sum_{s=0}^{\infty} (1 - \theta)^s X_{t-s} \tag{9.10}$$

Notice that the desired level of X is a weighted average of all present and previous values of X, since the weights sum to unity $[\theta\Sigma(1 - \theta)^s = 1]$. Substituting (9.10) into (9.6), we get

$$Y_t = \alpha^* + \beta^*\theta \sum_{s=0}^{\infty} (1 - \theta)^s X_{t-s} + \varepsilon_t^* \tag{9.11}$$

The equivalence of this model to the original geometric lag model [Eq. (9.2)] can be seen by letting

$$\alpha = \alpha^* \qquad \beta = \beta^*\theta \qquad w = (1 - \theta) \qquad \text{and} \qquad \varepsilon_t = \varepsilon_t^*$$

Thus, estimation of the economic specification associated with the adaptive expectations model is identical to the problem of estimating the Koyck geometric lag, with Eq. (9.5) now becoming

$$Y_t = \alpha^*\theta + \beta^*\theta X_t + (1 - \theta) Y_{t-1} + u_t^* \tag{9.12}$$

where $u_t^* = \varepsilon_t^* - (1 - \theta)\varepsilon_{t-1}^*$.

Stock adjustment model. The *stock adjustment model* assumes that the desired level of Y is dependent upon the current level of X, that is,

$$Y_t^* = \alpha' + \beta'X_t + \varepsilon_t' \tag{9.13}$$

In the consumption example Y_t^* might represent a desired or optimal expenditure level, while in the demand example it might represent the desired quantity to be supplied or the desired acreage to be farmed. In any given period, the actual value of Y may not adjust completely to obtain the desired level. Lack of knowledge, technical constraints, and other items might be responsible for this partial adjustment. We can represent the adjustment process as

$$Y_t - Y_{t-1} = \gamma(Y_t^* - Y_{t-1}) \qquad 0 < \gamma < 1 \tag{9.14}$$

The equation specifies that the change in Y will respond only partially to the difference between the desired stock of Y and the past value of Y, the rate of response being a function of the adjustment coefficient γ. Substituting for Y_t^* in Eq. (9.14) and solving for Y_t yields

$$Y_t = \alpha'\gamma + \gamma\beta'X_t + (1 - \gamma)Y_{t-1} + \gamma\varepsilon_t' \tag{9.15}$$

Once again the stock adjustment model bears a close relationship to the geometric lag model. The two are equivalent in form [see Eq. (9.5)] if we let

$$\alpha = \alpha' \qquad \beta = \gamma\beta' \qquad w = 1 - \gamma \qquad \text{and} \qquad u_t = \gamma\varepsilon_t'$$

However, the equivalence of the models is not complete, because they involve a different set of assumptions about the error structure. To see this, rewrite Eq. (9.15), lagging the model one period and then substituting for Y_{t-1}. Iterating this procedure and collecting terms, we obtain

$$Y_t = \alpha' + \beta'\gamma\left[X_t + (1 - \gamma)X_{t-1} + (1 - \gamma)^2 X_{t-2} + \cdots\right] + v_t \tag{9.16}$$

$$v_t = \gamma\varepsilon'_t + \gamma(1 - \gamma)\varepsilon'_{t-1} + \gamma(1 - \gamma)^2\varepsilon'_{t-2} + \cdots$$

or $\quad Y_t = \alpha' + \beta'\gamma \sum_{s=0}^{\infty} (1 - \gamma)^s X_{t-s} + \gamma \sum_{s=0}^{\infty} (1 - \gamma)^s \varepsilon'_{t-s}$ (9.17)

Unlike the original error specification, the error process associated with the stock adjustment model is a moving-average error process (moving-average error processes are discussed in another context in Chapter 17).

9.1.2 Geometric Lag Estimation

In this section we briefly outline some of the issues involved in the estimation of the geometric lag model.† Recall that such a model can be transformed into a single-equation autoregressive model with a single lagged dependent variable:

$$Y_t = \alpha(1 - w) + wY_{t-1} + \beta X_t + u_t \tag{9.18}$$

Depending on the model chosen, the error process may follow several alternative assumptions. Not surprisingly, the choice of estimation process depends heavily on the nature of the assumption that one is willing to make about the error process. Consider first the case in which the error term is normally distributed with constant variance and is not serially correlated. As a general rule, the Koyck specification will introduce serial correlation if the original error specified is not autocorrelated. However, the transformation procedure might conceivably eliminate any serial correlation that was originally present.‡ In such a case, the presence of a lagged dependent variable in the model causes ordinary least-squares parameter estimates to be biased, although they remain consistent.§ While it is possible to devise estimation procedures which remain consistent and are adjusted to remove bias, such procedures are not very popular, because the variance of the adjusted unbiased estimator tends to be large relative to the variance of the biased ordinary least-squares estimator.

Now consider the estimation problem when the error term follows the pattern suggested by the Koyck and adaptive expectations models, that is, $u_t = \varepsilon_t - w\varepsilon_{t-1}$. In this case we are less fortunate, because ordinary least-squares

† These estimation techniques also apply when we extend the two models just described by combining stock adjustment and adaptive expectations models, or by allowing more than one explanatory variable to involve a distributed lag.

‡ If $\varepsilon_t = w\varepsilon_{t-1} + u_t$, then the transformation process will yield the error process u_t, which is not autocorrelated.

§ For further details, see J. Johnston, *Econometric Methods*, 2d ed. (New York: McGraw-Hill, 1972), pp. 305–306.

estimates become inconsistent as well as biased. The difficulty arises because u_t and Y_{t-1} are correlated and the correlation does not disappear as the sample size gets larger (in the probability limit). A number of estimation procedures are available which involve the use of either an instrumental-variables technique or a maximum-likelihood technique, but they are too complex to present in detail here.† Perhaps the simplest procedure would be to use instrumental-variables estimation with X_{t-1} serving as an instrument for Y_{t-1}. This procedure will yield consistent estimates but is not likely to be very efficient in practice.

Finally, consider a third error specification involving first-order serial correlation, i.e.,

$$u_t = \rho u_{t-1} + \varepsilon_t$$

While this specification does not follow directly from any of the Koyck-related models, it should receive serious consideration, because autocorrelated disturbances often occur in models with lagged dependent variables. Once again, ordinary least-squares parameter estimates will be inconsistent and biased, with the direction of the large sample bias relating directly to the sign of ρ.‡ Both instrumental variables and maximum-likelihood estimation procedures are available to deal with the autoregressive model in the presence of serially correlated errors. The instrumental-variables estimation process yields consistent estimates but tends to be inefficient, given the known presence of serial correlation.§ The instrument to replace Y_{t-1} can be obtained by a first-stage regression in which Y_{t-1} is the dependent variable and a series of lagged values of X make up the explanatory variables. The efficiency of this estimator can be improved if the estimated intercept and slope parameters are used to obtain an estimate of the serial-correlation coefficient ρ.¶ We do this by calculating the residuals associated with the estimated intercept and slope parameters. A regression of u_t on u_{t-1} yields an estimate of the serial-correlation coefficient. Once ρ is estimated, the generalized differencing process can be used to reestimate the parameters of the original equation (see Chapter 6).

† For further details, see P. J. Dhrymes, "Efficient Estimation of Distributed Lags with Autocorrelated Error Terms," *International Economic Review*, vol. 10, pp. 47–67, February 1969; or A. Zellner and M. S. Geisel, "Analysis of Distributed Lag Models with Applications to Consumption Function Estimation," *Econometrica*, vol. 38, pp. 865–888, 1970. Two excellent discussions of distributed lag estimation appear in Johnston, op. cit., pp. 304–321, and J. Kmenta, *Elements of Econometrics* (New York: Macmillan, 1971), pp. 473–498.

‡ See Z. Griliches, "A Note on the Serial Correlation Bias in Estimates of Distributed Lags," *Econometrica*, vol. 29, pp. 65–73, 1971.

§ See N. Liviatan, "Consistent Estimation of Distributed Lags," *International Economic Review*, vol. 4, pp. 44–52, 1963.

¶ See K. F. Wallis, "Lagged Dependent Variables and Serially Correlated Errors: A Reappraisal of Three-Pass Least Squares," *Review of Economics and Statistics*, vol. 49, pp. 555–567, 1967.

9.1.3 Polynomial Distributed Lag

While the geometric lag formulation is quite useful, it is limited in its range of potential uses because it hypothesizes a declining set of lag weights.† A much more general formulation is the *polynomial distributed lag* model. The polynomial lag model assumes that the lag weights can be specified by a continuous function, which in turn can be approximated by evaluating a polynomial function at the appropriate discrete points in time. We might assume, for example, that $w_i = c_0 + c_1 i + c_2 i^2$ for $i = 0, 1, 2, 3, \ldots, 6$ and $w_i = 0$ for i less than 0 and greater than 6. This specifies lag weights that are to follow a second-degree polynomial for the first six lagged values and are 0 otherwise. The lag weights might appear as shown in Fig. 9.2.

We have considerable flexibility in specifying a polynomial distributed lag model. We should be careful, however, to be sure that the degree of the polynomial is less than the number of terms in the distributed lag minus one, or there will be no reduction in the number of lag parameters to be estimated.‡ The choice of endpoint restrictions is an optional one, however. If we do not wish to restrict the lag weights to be 0 outside the lag interval, one or both of the endpoint restrictions may be eliminated.

Usually a third- or fourth-degree polynomial will provide a sufficiently accurate approximation to the lag structure, although higher-degree polynomials are occasionally specified when sufficient data are available. The choice of length of lag depends more on the nature of the problem being specified, so that useful rules of thumb are not available. In practice it is common for researchers to vary the degree of the polynomial, the length of the lag, and the endpoint restrictions. Such a procedure is dangerous, however, because (see Chapters 8 and 12) an equation giving a good fit as measured by a high R^2 may turn out to be a poor-predicting equation.

To understand how the polynomial distributed lag model is estimated, consider the case of a third-degree polynomial with a five-period lag (no endpoint restrictions). The original lag specification is

$$Y_t = \alpha + \beta(w_0 X_t + w_1 X_{t-1} + \cdots + w_4 X_{t-4}) + \varepsilon_t \qquad (9.19)$$

Assume that

$$w_i = c_0 + c_1 i + c_2 i^2 + c_3 i^3 \qquad i = 0, 1, 2, 3, 4 \qquad (9.20)$$

---

† It is quite possible, of course, to allow the first several lag terms to be estimated freely and to impose the geometric lag assumption on lagged values of the explanatory variable beyond the first several terms. This allows for greater flexibility in the form of the distributed lag while maintaining the advantages associated with the simple geometric lag form.

‡ In addition, the number of observations available must be greater than or equal to the degree of the polynomial plus 2. The two extra observations are needed if the endpoints of the lag are fixed by assumption.

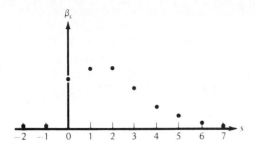

Figure 9.2 Polynomial distributed lag weights.

Substituting and rewriting the original specification, we get

$$Y_t = \alpha + \beta c_0 X_t + \beta(c_0 + c_1 + c_2 + c_3)X_{t-1}$$
$$+ \beta(c_0 + 2c_1 + 4c_2 + 8c_3)X_{t-2}$$
$$+ \beta(c_0 + 3c_1 + 9c_2 + 27c_3)X_{t-3}$$
$$+ \beta(c_0 + 4c_1 + 16c_2 + 64c_3)X_{t-4} + \varepsilon_t \qquad (9.21)$$

Combining terms, we have

$$Y_t = \alpha + \beta c_0(X_t + X_{t-1} + X_{t-2} + X_{t-3} + X_{t-4})$$
$$+ \beta c_1(X_{t-1} + 2X_{t-2} + 3X_{t-3} + 4X_{t-4})$$
$$+ \beta c_2(X_{t-1} + 4X_{t-2} + 9X_{t-3} + 16X_{t-4})$$
$$+ \beta c_3(X_{t-1} + 8X_{t-2} + 27X_{t-3} + 64X_{t-4}) + \varepsilon_t \qquad (9.22)$$

Equation (9.22) can be estimated using ordinary least squares. If the error term obeys the classical assumptions of econometrics, the estimated c's will be best linear unbiased estimates† (once the c's are known, it is a simple procedure to calculate the original lag weights, that is, the w's). Standard errors for each of the lag weights can be obtained from the variance-covariance matrix of the c's, but the calculations are too involved to display here.‡ In general, statistical tests that are performed must be done through the estimated equation (9.21) and not directly through the specified equation (9.22).

Example 9.1   Capital expenditures In her 1965 article,§ Almon used the polynomial distributed lag model to examine the relationship between

---

† As written, it is impossible to estimate β directly. One simply assumes that $\beta = 1$, allowing the estimated lag weights to incorporate the effect of the true parameter β. To estimate with endpoint restrictions we need to add constraints to (9.21) before doing the estimation in (9.22). For example, to set the tail = 0, we set $w_5 = 0$ in (9.20). Then, we substitute this constraint in (9.21) and obtain a new version of (9.22).

‡   See J. L. Murphy, *Introductory Econometrics* (Homewood, Ill.: Irwin, 1973), p. 277, for details.

§   See S. Almon, "The Distributed Lag between Capital Appropriations and Expenditures," *Econometrica*, vol. 33, pp. 178–196, 1965.

capital expenditures of manufacturing industries and capital appropriations. The model specified that capital expenditures E were determined by a series of seasonal dummy variables, S_1, S_2, and S_3, and by present and past values of appropriations A. The model was estimated using a seven-period lag structure and a third-degree polynomial, with both endpoints restricted to equal 0. The manufacturing industry results are

$$\hat{E}_t = -283 + 13S_{1t} - 50S_{2t} + 320S_{3t} + .048A_t + .099A_{t-1} + .141A_{t-2}$$
$$+ .165A_{t-3} + .167A_{t-4} + .146A_{t-5} + .105A_{t-6} + .053A_{t-7}$$
$$\bar{R}^2 = .92$$

A quick glance at the lag-weight coefficients shows that the lag structure follows an inverted U shape, lag weights first increasing and then decreasing. While not guaranteed by the specification of the model, this result is quite common when working with polynomial distributed lags.

Example 9.2 Consumption function In modeling the aggregate consumption function, it is plausible to assume that consumption in the present period C_t is a direct function of personal disposable income Y_t in the present and past periods and the interest rate r_t. We expect that a higher interest rate, other things being equal, will be associated with more savings and less consumption. If we were to regress C_t on Y_t and r, a low DW statistic would result, signaling the presence of positive first-order serial correlation. For this reason, a decision was made to estimate an elementary form of the aggregate consumption function, using first differences and a polynomial distributed lag formulation. The model is

$$\Delta C_t = \alpha + \beta_0 \Delta Y_t + \beta_t \Delta Y_{t-1} + \cdots + \beta_4 \Delta Y_{t-4} + \gamma r_t + \varepsilon_t$$

where C_t = quarterly personal consumption expenditures
    $\Delta C_t = C_t - C_{t-1}$
    Y_t = quarterly disposable personal income
    $\Delta Y_t = Y_t - Y_{t-1}$
    r_t = 3-month average of open market new issue rates of 3-month
        Treasury bills

A first attempt at model estimation using a five-period third-degree polynomial with no endpoint restrictions yielded the following regression results (t statistics in parentheses):

$$\hat{\Delta C}_t = \underset{(.43)}{.299} + \underset{(4.68)}{.445 \, \Delta Y_t} + \underset{(4.18)}{.219 \, \Delta Y_{t-1}} + \underset{(1.28)}{.086 \, \Delta Y_{t-2}} + \underset{(.82)}{.045 \, \Delta Y_{t-3}}$$
$$+ \underset{(.93)}{.098 \, \Delta Y_{t-4}} - \underset{(-.09)}{.037 \, r_t}$$

T (number of observations) = 68 (1953-1 to 1969-4)　　$R^2 = .62$

$$F = 25.6$$

DW = 2.56　　　Mean lag = 1.03　　　Sum of lag coefficients = .895

The coefficients of the lags can be interpreted as follows. An increase of $1 billion in the quarterly change in disposable income in the present time will result in an increase in the change in consumption of $445 million in the first quarter, $219 million in the second quarter, $86 million in the third quarter, etc. The interest rate is inversely related to changes in consumption, but the coefficient is not statistically significant. If one has reason to believe that the effect of changes in personal disposable income on changes in consumption will not be felt after four periods, it is reasonable to set the tail of the lag distribution equal to 0 in period $t - 5$. For illustrative purposes, we have reestimated the model using the zero tail restriction. The results exhibited in the following regression output show that the zero tail restriction forces neighboring lag weights to become close to zero. This is a natural consequence of the fact that polynomial functions are continuous.

$$\widehat{\Delta C_t} = \underset{(.37)}{.258} + \underset{(4.99)}{.394} \Delta Y_t + \underset{(5.09)}{.241} \Delta Y_{t-1} + \underset{(2.33)}{.125} \Delta Y_{t-2} + \underset{(.82)}{.005} \Delta Y_{t-3}$$

$$+ \underset{(.11)}{.046} \Delta Y_{t-4} + \underset{(.30)}{.004} r_t$$

$$T = 68 \qquad R^2 = .61 \qquad F = 33.8 \qquad DW = 2.57$$

$$\text{Mean lag} = .80 \qquad \text{Sum of lag coefficients} = .81$$

Finally, consider the regression output in which both the tail and the head of the lag distribution are assumed equal to 0:

$$\widehat{\Delta C_t} = \underset{(.25)}{.186} + \underset{(4.27)}{.166} \Delta Y_t + \underset{(4.24)}{.241} \Delta Y_{t-1} + \underset{(4.11)}{.224} \Delta Y_{t-2} + \underset{(2.09)}{.115} \Delta Y_{t-3}$$

$$- \underset{(-.91)}{.086} \Delta Y_{t-4} + \underset{(.96)}{.416} r_t$$

$$T = 68 \qquad R^2 = .56 \qquad F = 26.9 \qquad DW = 2.31$$

$$\text{Mean lag} = 1.05 \qquad \text{Sum of lag coefficients} = .66$$

The zero restriction on the head of the distribution substantially alters the pattern of the lag weights. The weights now approximate an inverted U structure. Once again the zero restriction and the continuity of the polynomial are crucial determinants of the lag pattern. The lag structures resulting from each of the three regressions are graphed in Fig. 9.3.

Example 9.3 Inventory investment In this example we construct a single-equation regression model which contains polynomial distributed lags and then use that equation for forecasting.† The example estimates the monthly change in manufacturers' inventories in the durable goods industries IND (end-of-period book value) as a function of shipments SHD, unfilled orders UNOD, and the wholesale price index WHMD. (All the independent

---

† This example came from a study done by Dynamics Associates, Inc., Cambridge, Mass. The reader may wish to refer to Chapter 8, in which the use of the single-equation model for forecasting is discussed.

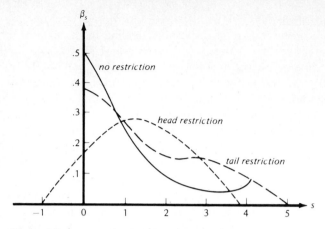

Figure 9.3 Consumption function lag structures.

variables relate to the category manufacturers' durable goods industries.) Monthly data from January 1965 to December 1972 have been used, and a polynomial distributed lag regression has been performed. The estimation results are shown below, with t statistics in parentheses, and a plot of estimated and actual values of the change in manufacturing durable inventories is presented in Fig. 9.4:

$$\widehat{\Delta IND}_t = -\underset{(-3.15)}{876.5} + \sum_{i=0}^{19} a_i \, SHD_{t-i} - \underset{(-3.50)}{.0809} \, IND_{t-1}$$

$$+ \underset{(2.44)}{45.82} \frac{WHMD_t - WHMD_{t-3}}{3} + \underset{(2.50)}{.177} \frac{UNOD_{t-3} - UNOD_{t-9}}{6}$$

$$R^2 = .573 \qquad \bar{R}^2 = .539 \qquad F(7/100) = 19.2$$

$$SER = 168.14 \qquad DW = 1.81$$

Third-degree polynomial lag coefficients:

$$a_0 = -\underset{(-2.91)}{.0394} \qquad a_1 = -\underset{(-2.69)}{.0196} \qquad a_2 = -\underset{(-.94)}{.0038} \qquad a_3 = \underset{(1.97)}{.0086}$$

$$a_4 = \underset{(3.17)}{.0177} \qquad a_5 = \underset{(3.88)}{.0241} \qquad a_6 = \underset{(4.60)}{.0279} \qquad a_7 = \underset{(5.53)}{.0295}$$

$$a_8 = \underset{(6.77)}{.0294} \qquad a_9 = \underset{(7.77)}{.0278} \qquad a_{10} = \underset{(6.89)}{.0251} \qquad a_{11} = \underset{(4.79)}{.0217}$$

$$a_{12} = \underset{(3.15)}{.0178} \qquad a_{13} = \underset{(2.11)}{.0139} \qquad a_{14} = \underset{(1.46)}{.0103} \qquad a_{15} = \underset{(1.03)}{.0073}$$

$$a_{16} = \underset{(.75)}{.0053} \qquad a_{17} = \underset{(.58)}{.0046} \qquad a_{18} = \underset{(.51)}{.0056} \qquad a_{19} = \underset{(.51)}{.0086}$$

$$\sum a_i = \underset{(3.64)}{.222}$$

Note that the final form of the equation expresses the relationship of inventories to shipments as a third-degree polynomial—the polynomial then

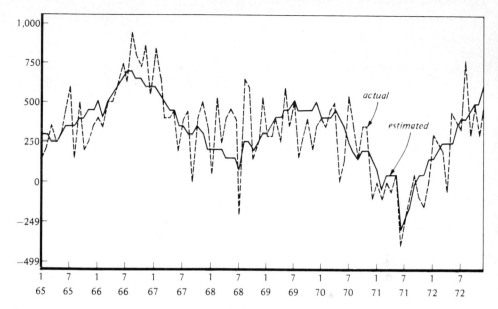

Figure 9.4 Change in manufacturer inventories in durable goods industries (in millions of dollars).

defining 20 coefficients of current and lagged shipments. The lagged level of inventories is included; the wholesale price index is introduced as the monthly change (averaged over 3 months); and unfilled orders are added using the monthly change (averaged over 6 months), lagged one quarter.

The regression equation can now be used to generate a set of *ex post* monthly forecasts (thus allowing us to compare the results with actual data) for the period January 1973 to December 1973. The resulting forecasted series, together with 95 percent confidence interval and the actual series, is shown in Fig. 9.5.

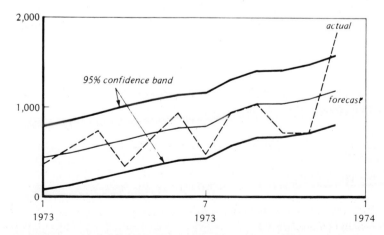

Figure 9.5 *Ex post* forecast of the changes in manufacturers' durable goods inventories.

One can observe that the forecasted series turned out to be a "smoothed" version of the actual series. Although the forecast did not successfully predict the short month-to-month "turning points" in the actual series, it did predict the overall trend. In fact the forecasted series is quite close to the actual series, at least for the first 9 or 10 months. Only in the last month of the forecast period is the actual value of the dependent variable outside the 95 percent confidence interval, and this may be due to an occurrence not properly modeled by the regression equation. On the whole we would probably be satisfied with the predictive performance of the regression equation.

9.1.4 Distributed Lags and Tests for Causality

In time-series analysis a frequent concern is the causal specification of a model. To be specific, assume that we wish to relate GNP to the money supply M in the United States macroeconomy. The usual procedure is to specify the model either with GNP as the dependent variable, and M the dependent variable or possibly both dependent within a simultaneous-equations model. Empirical testing usually follows the theoretical specification. However, when one believes that variables affect each other with lags, there are some empirical tests for causality which are possible.† In its simplest form the idea is easy to apply and thus potentially useful for a wide variety of research problems. To test for causality between GNP and M in the current example, we might estimate the model

$$\text{GNP}_t = \sum_{i=1}^{n} \beta_i M_{t-i} + \sum_{i=1}^{m} \alpha_i M_{t+i} + \varepsilon_t \tag{9.23}$$

The first expression on the right-hand side represents the usual distributed lag, in this case a finite n-period lag with the form of lag weights unspecified. The second expression on the right represents a distributed lag of future values of the money supply. If M affects GNP but the causality is not reversed, we would expect the coefficients on the α's to be statistically insignificant individually, or at least as a group. The test of significance of the set of α's is given by the usual F test described in Chapter 5. If, however, the F test on the coefficients of the first distributed lag is insignificant while the second is significant, we can expect that the causality is reversed. If both are significant, the causality runs both ways and a simultaneously determined model is called for.

---

† This discussion is based directly on the material in C. Sims, "Money, Income and Causality," *American Economic Review*, vol. 62, pp. 540–552, 1972. See also C. W. J. Granger, "Investigating Causal Relationships by Econometric Models and Cross-Spectral Methods," *Econometrica*, vol. 37, pp. 424–438, 1969; and, for an example of its relationship to the rational expectations literature, see Thomas J. Sargent, "A Classical Macroeconometric Model for the United States," *Journal of Political Economy*, vol. 86, pp. 207–238, 1976. For a more critical examination of these tests, see R. L. Jacobi, E. E. Leamer, and M. P. Ward, "The Difficulties with Testing for Causation," *Economic Inquiry*, vol. 17, pp. 401–413, 1979.

To see how such a test might be applied in our example, we report the result of an example used by Sims. Sims used variables in their logarithmic form, so that GNP represents the logarithm of United States GNP, while M denotes the logarithm of the money supply (here used as currency plus demand deposits).[†] First, GNP was regressed on M with eight past lags and four future lags. The F test of the hypothesis that the future lag coefficients were jointly equal to zero was .36, which clearly cannot reject the null hypothesis. On the other hand, when M was regressed on eight past lags of GNP and four future lags, the F test on the four future lags of GNP yielded a value of 4.29, significant at the 5 percent level. Since money affects future GNP but not vice versa, Sims concluded that GNP cannot be treated as an exogenous variable in explaining M but saw no evidence to contradict the usual procedure of regressing GNP on M, with the implicit assumption that M is exogenous.[‡]

9.2 MISSING OBSERVATIONS

Our empirical work is often complicated by the fact that observations for one or more variables may be missing. Since there is no best approach for dealing with the problem of missing observations, we proceed by discussing some of the relevant issues and suggesting some possible solutions. The choice of method for dealing with missing observations depends upon the nature of each particular regression model and the related data. For this reason, it is very difficult to state rules of thumb for dealing with missing observations. There is no substitute for careful thought on the part of the analyst.

Assume that the regression model is given by

$$Y_i = \beta_1 + \beta_2 X_i + \varepsilon_i \tag{9.24}$$

[†] The data were also prefiltered to remove serial correlation, an important initial step. See Sims, op. cit., for details.

[‡] More complex lag formulations can be made with the use of *rational distributed lags*. In general, rational lags are useful because they allow for lags of any length on either Y or X, and as such will be used frequently in Part Three. For a more serious discussion of the subject, see E. Kuh and R. Schmalensee, *An Introduction to Applied Macroeconomics* (Amsterdam: North-Holland, 1973), chap. 2, and D. W. Jorgenson, "Rational Distributed Lag Functions," *Econometrica*, pp. 135–139, January 1966. The rational lag may also be viewed as a generalization of the polynomial distributed lag. See A. Pagan, "Rational and Polynomial Lags," *Journal of Econometrics*, vol. 8, pp. 242–254, 1978. A number of other lag distributions are summarized in G. S. Maddala, *Econometrics* (New York: McGraw-Hill, 1977), chap. 16. See also R. J. Shiller, "A Distributed Lag Estimator Derived from Smoothness Priors," *Econometrica*, vol. 41, pp. 775–788, 1973. Distributed lag models have received a good deal of attention recently in the context of the *rational expectations* literature in economics. Rational expectations models suggest a number of possible lag specifications, all having the property that the parameters of the lag distribution are endogenous and may change over time. For details and some examples, see T. Sargent, "Observations on Improper Methods of Simulating and Teaching Friedman's Time Series Consumption Model," *International Economic Review*, vol. 18, pp. 445–462, 1977; R. J. Barro, "Unanticipated Money Growth and Unemployment in the United States," *American Economic Review*, vol. 67, pp. 101–115, 1977; Sargent, "A Classical Macroeconometric Model for the United States," op. cit.

We shall deal solely with the situation in which the right-hand variable (or variables when we generalize) has some missing observations.† If N observations on both X and Y are available, the least-squares estimator of the slope is

$$\hat{\beta}_2 = \frac{\sum_{i=1}^{N} (X_i - \bar{X}_N)(Y_i - \bar{Y}_N)}{\sum_{i=1}^{N} (X_i - \bar{X}_N)^2} \qquad (9.25)$$

where $\bar{X}_N$ and $\bar{Y}_N$ represent the sample means calculated for the first N observations. Assume that M additional observations are available for the dependent variable, but that there are M missing observations for the independent variable (there are a total of $M + N$ observations). A straightforward solution to the missing-observations problem is simply to drop the last M observations of Y from consideration. The resulting slope estimate is $\hat{\beta}_2$. If we are dealing with a cross-section problem and the missing observations appear to be missing at random (e.g., not available because of data reporting problems), then eliminating the observations is a reasonable procedure. Because the observations dropped are random, the least-squares slope estimator $\hat{\beta}_2$ will be an unbiased and consistent estimator of β_2 and the only effect of dropping the observations is a loss of efficiency. The loss of efficiency can be seen by comparing the variance of the slope estimator ($\hat{\beta}_2$) when missing observations are dropped to the variance of the slope estimator ($\hat{\beta}_2^*$) if all observations are available:

$$\text{Var}(\hat{\beta}_2) = \frac{\sigma^2}{\sum_{i=1}^{N} (X_i - \bar{X}_N)^2} \qquad (9.26)$$

$$\text{Var}(\hat{\beta}_2^*) = \frac{\sigma^2}{\sum_{i=1}^{N+M} (X_i - \bar{X}_{N+M})^2} \qquad (9.27)$$

where $\bar{X}_{N+M}$ is the overall mean of X. Then

$$\frac{\text{Var}(\hat{\beta}_2)}{\text{Var}(\hat{\beta}_2^*)} = \frac{\sum_{i=1}^{N+M} (X_i - \bar{X}_{N+M})^2}{\sum_{i=1}^{N} (X_i - \bar{X}_N)^2}$$

---

† In most cross-section studies the unavailability of observations on the dependent variable makes any information about the explanatory variables useless. For example, if we are predicting individual auto purchases on the basis of annual income, data on income for which there are no corresponding automobile expenditures data are likely to be of no value. The income observations (without expenditures) are best dropped from the model. In time-series analysis, however, missing-dependent-variable observations present a serious problem and necessitate a solution procedure.

But

$$\sum_{i=1}^{N+M} \left(X_i - \overline{X}_{N+M} \right)^2 = \sum_{i=1}^{N} \left[\left(X_i - \overline{X}_N \right) + \left(\overline{X}_N - \overline{X}_{N+M} \right) \right]^2$$

$$+ \sum_{i=N+1}^{N+M} \left(X_i - \overline{X}_{N+M} \right)^2$$

$$= \sum_{i=1}^{N} \left(X_i - \overline{X}_N \right)^2 + N \left(\overline{X}_N - \overline{X}_{N+M} \right)^2$$

$$+ \sum_{i=N+1}^{N+M} \left(X_i - \overline{X}_{N+M} \right)^2$$

Therefore,

$$\frac{\text{Var}\left(\hat{\beta}_2 \right)}{\text{Var}\left(\hat{\beta}_2^* \right)} = 1 + \frac{N \left(\overline{X}_N - \overline{X}_{N+M} \right)^2 + \sum\limits_{i=N+1}^{N+M} \left(X_i - \overline{X}_{N+M} \right)^2}{\sum\limits_{i=1}^{N} \left(X_i - \overline{X}_N \right)^2} \qquad (9.28)$$

It should be apparent from Eq. (9.28) that dropping the observations with only partial information available will increase the variance of the estimated slope parameter (note that all terms are nonnegative). Only when all missing observations are identical in value to the sample mean of the available X's will there be no loss of efficiency. In general, the closer the missing X's to the sample mean and the smaller the sample variance of the missing X's, the lower the efficiency loss caused by dropping the observations.

If many observations are missing, the potential loss of efficiency necessitates an alternative to simply dropping incomplete observations. If some *a priori* knowledge is available, the best alternative may very well be to assign values for the missing observations.† If the missing observations are random, with no *a priori* information available, another solution must be found. The most natural solution is to replace the missing observations by the sample mean of the available X observations. This so-called zero-order correction is equivalent to regressing X on a constant and assigning to each missing observation the estimated coefficient. To see the effect of this substitution, compare the least-squares estimator $\hat{\beta}_2$ with the least-squares estimator $\tilde{\beta}_2$ computed with the sample mean of X substituted for all missing observations:

$$\tilde{\beta}_2 = \frac{\sum\limits_{i=1}^{N} \left(X_i - \overline{X}_{N+M} \right)\left(Y_i - \overline{Y}_{N+M} \right) + \sum\limits_{i=N+1}^{N+M} \left(\overline{X}_N - \overline{X}_{N+M} \right)\left(Y_i - \overline{Y}_{N+M} \right)}{\sum\limits_{i=1}^{N} \left(X_i - \overline{X}_{N+M} \right)^2 + \sum\limits_{i=N+1}^{N+M} \left(\overline{X}_N - \overline{X}_{N+M} \right)^2}$$

† One must keep in mind, however, that the degrees of freedom in the model may be different from the degrees of freedom printed by the computer, so that statistical tests may be misleading.

By construction, $\bar{X}_N = \bar{X}_{N+M}$. Therefore,

$$\tilde{\beta}_2 = \frac{\sum_{i=1}^{N} (X_i - \bar{X}_N)(Y_i - \bar{Y}_{N+M})}{\sum_{i=1}^{N} (X_i - \bar{X}_N)^2} \tag{9.29}$$

But $\tilde{\beta}_2$ is identically equal to the least-squares estimator $\hat{\beta}_2$. To show this, we need simply to prove that the numerators of both estimators are equal [from (9.25) and (9.29)]. This result holds since

$$\sum_{i=1}^{N} (X_i - \bar{X}_N)(Y_i - \bar{Y}_N)$$

$$= \sum_{i=1}^{N} (X_i - \bar{X}_N)Y_i - \bar{Y}_N \sum_{i=1}^{N} (X_i - \bar{X}_N) = \sum_{i=1}^{N} (X_i - \bar{X}_N)Y_i$$

and

$$\sum_{i=1}^{N} (X_i - \bar{X}_N)(Y_i - \bar{Y}_{N+M}) = \sum_{i=1}^{N} (X_i - \bar{X}_N)Y_i - \bar{Y}_{N+M} \sum_{i=1}^{N} (X_i - \bar{X}_N)$$

$$= \sum_{i=1}^{N} (X_i - \bar{X}_N)Y_i$$

In addition, the variance of the estimator with the observations replaced will be identical to the estimator with observations dropped; that is,

$$\text{Var}(\tilde{\beta}_2) = \frac{\sigma^2}{\sum_{i=1}^{N} (X_i - \bar{X}_{N+M})^2 + \sum_{i=N+1}^{N+M} (\bar{X}_N - \bar{X}_{N+M})^2}$$

$$= \frac{\sigma^2}{\sum_{i=1}^{N} (X_i - \bar{X}_N)^2} = \text{Var}(\hat{\beta}_2) \tag{9.30}$$

Thus, the substitution of variable means for missing observations does not change the least-squares slope estimator or its variance. This result is discouraging but should not be taken out of context. If we were to generalize the model to one containing several independent variables, only one of which had missing observations, the substitution procedure described here *might* well yield different slope estimators and an improvement in efficiency. The proof of this is too complex to describe here,† but some examples in which the substitution of variable means is helpful appear later in the chapter.

In practice, the assumption that missing observations are random is unlikely to be realistic. More often than not, the pattern of missing observations is systematic. For example, in a study relating automobile expenditures to income, there may systematically be missing observations for low-income individuals, who tend to spend little on automobiles. Dropping observations or using the sample mean of X to replace missing observations is not the correct procedure, because no account is taken of the known correlation between income and expenditures. Equivalently, in doing time-series analysis, we can improve our analysis by accounting for the fact that most time-series variables tend to undergo relatively predictable rates of growth. To do so, we search for proxy variables which are highly correlated with the variables whose observations are missing and which involve little measurement error.

An elementary solution to the time-series problem would involve replacing missing observations with proxy observations obtained by regressing the known values of the independent variable X on time and by replacing the missing observations by the fitted values of the regression. In other words, the regression $X_t = \alpha_1 + \alpha_2 t + u_t$ would be run for all available X observations and $\hat{X}_t = \hat{\alpha}_1 + \hat{\alpha}_2 t$ would be calculated, where values of t are chosen to correspond to the time period of the missing observations. This procedure is only one of several ways in which missing observations can be replaced through the interpolation of the X variable.‡ It yields consistent parameter estimates *if the time variable t is uncorrelated with the error term in the original equation*. The procedure is perhaps most useful because it suggests a more general approach to the systematic missing-observations problem which also yields consistent parameter estimates.

Let us presume that a set of "instruments," $Z_2, \ldots, Z_k$, is available with respect to the variable with the missing observations. The nature of the instruments would vary, depending upon the particular problem and whether the data are cross-sectional or time-series. The instruments are presumed to be highly correlated with the variable X and uncorrelated with error term ε; that is, Cov $(Z_i, \varepsilon) = 0$, $i = 2, 3, \ldots, k$. It is necessary, of course, that all the observations be available for the instruments, which might be chosen (see Chapter 11) because they appear as predetermined variables in a simultaneous equation system. We can increase the efficiency of the original parameter estimates while maintaining the consistency of the parameter estimates by proceeding in a

---

† See Y. Haitovsky, "Estimation of Regression Equations When a Block of Observations Is Missing," *Proceedings of the American Statistical Association*, Business and Economics Statistics Section, 1968; A. A. Afifi and R. M. Elashoff, "Missing Observations in Multivariate Statistics II. Point Estimates in Simple Linear Regression," *Journal of the American Statistical Association*, vol. 62, pp. 10–29, 1967; and M. G. Dagenais, "The Use of Incomplete Observations in Multiple Regression Analysis," *Journal of Econometrics*, vol. 1, pp. 317–328, 1973.

‡ There are numerous methods of linear and geometric interpolation from which to choose.

manner which resembles the two-stage least-squares procedure described in Chapter 7.†

To do this first-order correction, regress X on the set of instruments for all observations with complete information:

$$X_i = \alpha_1 + \alpha_2 Z_{2i} + \cdots + \alpha_k Z_{ki} + u_i \qquad i = 1, 2, \ldots, N \qquad (9.31)$$

Then calculate fitted values for the missing observations:‡

$$\hat{X}_i = \hat{\alpha}_1 + \hat{\alpha}_2 Z_{2i} + \cdots + \hat{\alpha}_k Z_{ki} \qquad i = N + 1, \ldots, N + M \qquad (9.32)$$

We can then reestimate the original equation as follows:

$$Y_i = \beta_1 + \beta_2 \hat{X}_i + v_i \qquad (9.33)$$

where

$$\hat{X}_i = X_i \qquad \text{for } i = 1, 2, \ldots, N$$

$$v_i = \begin{cases} \varepsilon_i & \text{for } i = 1, 2, \ldots, N \\ \varepsilon_i - \beta_2 u_i & \text{for } i = N + 1, \ldots, N + M \end{cases} \qquad (9.34)$$

As long as the instruments are correctly chosen, the estimation of Eq. (9.33) will yield a consistent slope estimate.§

There are several problems associated with the instrumental variables approach just described. First, the error variances associated with missing observations will be larger than the remaining error variances [from Eq. (9.34)]:

$$\text{Var}(v_i) = \begin{cases} \sigma^2 & \text{for } i = 1, 2, \ldots, N \\ \sigma^2 + \beta_2^2 \text{ Var}(u_i) & \text{for } i = N + 1, \ldots, N + M \end{cases}$$

A more refined technique would use weighted least squares to adjust for the efficiency loss associated with heteroscedasticity. Such an approach is likely to be important only when many observations are missing. Second, it is possible that observations will be missing for more than one right-hand variable. Then, a series of instrumental variable regressions must be run to fill in the missing observations. Unfortunately, the order in which these procedures occur can affect the estimated parameters. Finally, the choice of proper instruments is often difficult. If one or more instruments are correlated with the error term, measurement error (a form of errors in variables) will be introduced when the missing observations are replaced by observations from the constructed proxy variable. For further details the reader should review Chapter 7, in which errors in variables and instrumental variables are discussed.¶

---

† If X is an endogenous variable, 2SLS can be used without any difficulty (as far as that particular equation is concerned) and the missing observations problem disappears!

‡ In time-series analysis, it is unlikely that the last set of observations will be missing. The analysis is quite general, however, because we need simply rearrange the numbering of the observations appropriately and all results will follow.

§ The proof is too difficult to describe here but is similar in nature to the proof that two-stage least-squares parameter estimates are consistent.

¶ For a distinctive and useful procedure for dealing with missing observations, see M. Glasser, "Linear Regression Analysis with Missing Observations among the Independent Variables," *Journal of the American Statistical Association*, vol. 59, pp. 834–844, 1964.

Example 9.4   Aid to states In order to understand how federal aid to states affects their spending decisions, public finance economists often estimate regression models in which state (and/or local) expenditures are determined by a number of important financial and demographic characteristics of that state. One rather simple specification of that model is

$$EXP = \beta_1 + \beta_2 POP + \beta_3 AID + \beta_4 INC + \varepsilon$$

where EXP = aggregate state expenditures in 1972
   POP = state population in 1972
   AID = total federal grants to each state in 1972
   INC = aggregate personal income in the state in 1970
We estimated the expenditure determinants model using data for all 50 states in the United States, obtaining the following result (t statistics in parentheses):†

$$\widehat{EXP} = -46,816 - \underset{(-.56)}{.60}\ POP + \underset{(13.6)}{.0032}\,AID + \underset{(8.1)}{.00019}\,INC$$

Then, as an illustration of how to treat the missing-observations problem, we assumed that the last five observations on INC were not available. We then tried three procedures for dealing with the missing observations problem. First, we simply dropped the last five observations from the model. Second, we replaced the missing observations with the mean of INC within the known sample of 45 observations. Third, we used the suggested first-order process for replacing missing observations by regressing INC on POP and AID within the sample of 45 observations. (The regression was $\widehat{INC}$ = $-1.7 \times 10^9 + 4.63AID + 4162POP$.) We then forecasted INC for the remaining five observations and replaced the missing observations with the forecasted values. The regression results in each of the three correction procedures are included along with the original results in the following table.

	Constant	POP	AID	INC
Original	− 46,816 (−.6)	− .60 (−5.7)	.0032 (13.6)	.00019 (8.1)
Drop missing observations	− 97,340 (−1.1)	− .62 (−5.9)	.0034 (14.1)	.00019 (8.3)
Zero-order correction	− 434,550 (−3.9)	.10 (1.6)	.0043 (14.1)	.00002 (2.6)
First-order correction	− 305,26 (−.4)	− .62 (−5.9)	.0033 (14.2)	.00019 (8.3)

In this particular case (our results will not necessarily hold generally), we find that the first procedure (omitting the observations) has relatively little effect on the regression results. However, replacing the missing observations by the mean of INC has a substantial impact, causing the

† The data upon which this example is based were given in Table 6.2.

estimated results to differ from the original. Finally, the first-order correction procedure yields very good results, the coefficient on AID becoming very close to the coefficient associated with the full sample. Why did the second procedure work so badly in this case? A partial answer can be obtained by comparing the values used to replace the missing observations with the original data (all values are in billions of dollars).

Observation	INC	Zero-order	First-order
46	15.7	17.9	15.4
47	9.5	17.9	9.4
48	103.8	17.9	102.1
49	1.7	17.9	0.5
50	4.2	17.9	2.4

Clearly, in this particular case (with INC varying so widely from state to state), the predicted or forecasted values of INC are much closer to the original than the mean of INC, and the first-order procedure works better. We stress, however, that this example does not generalize. Which of these elementary techniques is most appropriate depends upon one's implicit model explaining why the missing observations occurred in the first place. In addition, all correction procedures use up sample information and, implicitly, degrees of freedom. Thus, procedures 2 and 3 overstate the statistical significance of the results because they do not account directly for the fact that preliminary regressions were run to obtain the missing data.

9.3 POOLING OF CROSS-SECTION AND TIME-SERIES DATA

A practical problem of some importance occurs when observations are available for several individual units (households, firms, cities, etc.) over a period of time (usually years). Occasionally sufficient observations will not be available to estimate either a time-series or a cross-section equation, suggesting that some method of combining the data be used. As an example, assume that we are modeling the determination of profits of firms in an industry. A single-year cross-section model might include such cross-section explanatory variables as attributes of the firms' management, type of physical capital, and financial leverage.† If data were available for each firm over a series of years, we might question whether cross-section parameters remain constant over time. If they do, we can consider the possibility of combining the data to obtain more efficient parameter estimates. The process of combining cross-section and time-series

† This example was used by E. Kuh to discuss the stability of cross-section models and the specification of variables in *Capital Stock Growth: A Micro-Econometric Approach* (Amsterdam: North-Holland, 1963), pp. 116–117. Cross-section explanatory variables differ over individuals but remain constant over time. Time-series variables remain constant over individuals but vary over time. Some variables can both differ over individuals and vary over time.

data is called *pooling*. Cross-section parameters may shift over time, in which case pooling is not the appropriate procedure. On the other hand, there may be time-series-related explanatory variables such as expectations, prices, and interest rates which could be included in a pooled model. Pooling data in a model with both time-series and cross-section explanatory variables then becomes an acceptable procedure. However, the necessity of combining time-series and cross-section variables in the model adds a new dimension of difficulty to the problem of model specification. The model-specification problem in turn suggests that the structure of the disturbance term may be a complex one, since the disturbance term is assumed to result in part from the effects of omitted explanatory variables. The difficulty arises because the disturbance term is likely to consist of time-series-related disturbances, cross-section disturbances, and a combination of both.

We proceed by considering a simple regression model for which time-series and cross-section data are available. We discuss several alternative schemes by which the data might be pooled. The first technique is to combine all cross-section and time-series data and perform ordinary least-squares regression on the entire data set. A second procedure involves the recognition that omitted variables may lead to changing cross-section and time-series intercepts. *Covariance analysis* involves the addition of dummy variables to the model to allow for these changing intercepts. A third pooling technique improves the efficiency of the first least-squares estimation process by accounting for the existence of cross-section and time-series disturbances. The *error components* pooling procedure is a variation of the generalized least-squares estimation process described in the appendix to Chapter 6. Finally, we consider a set of techniques which accounts for the fact that the error term may be correlated over time and over cross-section units. Once again a variation of generalized least-squares estimation provides a useful solution to the problem.

Consider the two-variable model·†

$$Y_{it} = \alpha + \beta X_{it} + \varepsilon_{it} \qquad \text{for } \begin{array}{l} i = 1, 2, \ldots, N \\ t = 1, 2, \ldots, T \end{array} \qquad (9.35)$$

where N is the number of cross-section units (individuals) and T is the number of time periods. If all the classical error-term assumptions hold (no correlation with X, no autocorrelation, no heteroscedasticity, etc.), in principle, we could estimate separate cross-section regressions, each regression involving N observations. For time period $t = 1$, the cross-section regression would be

$$Y_{i1} = \alpha + \beta X_{i1} + \varepsilon_{i1} \qquad i = 1, 2, \ldots, N$$

There would be a total of T such equations. Similarly, we could estimate N time-series regressions with T observations in each. However, if both α and β are constant over time and over cross-section units, more efficient parameter estimates can be obtained if all the data are combined so that one large pooled regression is run with NT observations. In this most elementary pooling technique, there will be $NT - 2$ degrees of freedom (since estimation of the two parameters uses up two degrees of freedom).

† The use of a single explanatory variable does not limit the results of this section.

9.3.1 Covariance Model

The difficulty with the least-squares procedure just described is that the assumption of constant intercept and slope may be unreasonable in a pooled model. The obvious generalization of the ordinary least-squares model is to introduce dummy variables which allow for the intercept term to vary over time and to vary over cross-section units. If the slopes were to vary as well, each separate cross-section regression would involve a distinct model and pooling would be inappropriate.† We can introduce the dummy variables by writing the *covariance model* as follows:

$$Y_{it} = \alpha + \beta X_{it} + \gamma_2 W_{2t} + \gamma_3 W_{3t} + \cdots + \gamma_N W_{Nt}$$

$$+ \delta_2 Z_{i2} + \delta_3 Z_{i3} + \cdots + \delta_T Z_{iT} + \varepsilon_{it} \qquad (9.36)$$

where $\qquad W_{it} = \begin{cases} 1 & \text{for } i\text{th individual } i = 2, \ldots, N \\ 0 & \text{otherwise} \end{cases}$

$\qquad Z_{it} = \begin{cases} 1 & \text{for } t\text{th time period, } t = 2, \ldots, T \\ 0 & \text{otherwise} \end{cases}$

We have added $(N - 1) + (T - 1)$ dummy variables to the model and have omitted the remaining two, since their addition would result in perfect collinearity among the explanatory variables. If this model were estimated using ordinary least squares, unbiased and consistent estimates of all parameters (including the slope β) would be obtained. A total of $NT - 2 - (N - 1) - (T - 1)$, or $NT - N - T$, degrees of freedom would be involved. The dummy-variable coefficients would measure the change in the cross-section and time-series intercepts (with respect to the first individual in the first period of time). To see this, we can eliminate the dummy variables and rewrite the model associated with each of the NT observations:

$$\begin{aligned}
Y_{11} &= \alpha + \beta X_{11} + \varepsilon_{11} \\
Y_{12} &= (\alpha + \delta_2) + \beta X_{12} + \varepsilon_{12} \\
&\cdots\cdots\cdots\cdots\cdots\cdots\cdots \\
Y_{1T} &= (\alpha + \delta_T) + \beta X_{1T} + \varepsilon_{1T} \\
Y_{21} &= (\alpha + \gamma_2) + \beta X_{21} + \varepsilon_{21} \\
Y_{22} &= (\alpha + \gamma_2 + \delta_2) + \beta X_{22} + \varepsilon_{22} \\
&\cdots\cdots\cdots\cdots\cdots\cdots\cdots \qquad (9.37) \\
Y_{2T} &= (\alpha + \gamma_2 + \delta_T) + \beta X_{2T} + \varepsilon_{2T} \\
&\cdots\cdots\cdots\cdots\cdots\cdots\cdots \\
Y_{N1} &= (\alpha + \gamma_N) + \beta X_{N1} + \varepsilon_{N1} \\
Y_{N2} &= (\alpha + \gamma_N + \delta_2) + \beta X_{N2} + \varepsilon_{N2} \\
&\cdots\cdots\cdots\cdots\cdots\cdots\cdots \\
Y_{NT} &= (\alpha + \gamma_N + \delta_T) + \beta X_{NT} + \varepsilon_{NT}
\end{aligned}$$

The effect of the missing δ_1 and γ_1 coefficients is accounted for in the parameter

---

† Allowance for random variation in slope parameters is made in the random coefficients model literature. See, for example, H. Theil, *Principles of Econometrics* (New York: Wiley, 1971), pp. 622–627; and P. A. V. B. Swamy, "Efficient Inference in a Random Coefficient Regression Model," *Econometrica*, vol. 38, pp. 311–323, 1970.

α, the intercept of the first equation. Each of the δ's is then measured in terms of deviations from δ_1 (and the γ's in terms of deviations from γ_1) and thus from the "true" intercept α.

The choice of whether to pool data using ordinary least squares or to sacrifice degrees of freedom by using ordinary least squares with dummy variables is one which can be made on the basis of statistical testing. The test involves a comparison of the residual sum of squares associated with the two estimation techniques. Since the ordinary least-squares model includes more parameter restrictions than the covariance model (the intercepts are restricted to be equal over time and over individuals), we would expect the residual sum of squares to be higher for the ordinary least-squares model. If the increase in the residual sum of squares is not significant when the restrictions are added, we conclude that the restrictions are proper and ordinary least squares can be applied. If the residual sum of squares changes substantially, we opt for the covariance model. In our model the appropriate test statistic would be†

$$F_{N+T-2,\,NT-N-T} = \frac{(\mathrm{ESS}_1 - \mathrm{ESS}_2)/(N+T-2)}{(\mathrm{ESS}_2)/(NT-N-T)} \tag{9.38}$$

where ESS_1 and ESS_2 are the residual sum of squares using ordinary least squares and the covariance model, respectively. The numerator represents the increase in the residual sum of squares divided by the number of additional degrees of freedom when moving from the covariance model to the ordinary least-squares model, while the denominator represents the residual sum of squares for the covariance model divided by the number of degrees of freedom in the covariance model. On the null hypothesis that the equal-intercept restrictions are correct, the statistic F follows the F distribution with $N + T - 2$ and $NT - N - T$ degrees of freedom.

There are several important problems associated with the use of the covariance model for purposes of pooling. First, the use of dummies does not directly identify the variables which might cause the regression line to shift over time and over individuals. The use of dummy variables is an attempt to adjust for important missing information in the model. In doing so, a substantial portion of the error variation can be "explained" without the analyst's obtaining any useful knowledge about the model. Because of this fact, dummy-variable coefficients are difficult to interpret. Second, the dummy-variable technique uses up a substantial number of degrees of freedom ($N + T - 2$ in our model). The loss of degrees of freedom may substantially decrease the statistical power of the model. For example, the use of dummy variables for a study of 15 firms over a 4-year period would involve a reduction of degrees of freedom from 58 to 41, not an inconsequential number.‡

---

† For details concerning testing of the covariance model see Section 5.3.

‡ Despite the loss of degrees of freedom associated with the use of dummy variables, it is incorrect to drop those dummy variables whose coefficients are insignificant. This would bias the statistical tests when the new regression is run.

9.3.2 Error-Components Model

Since the inclusion of dummy variables represents a lack of knowledge about the model, it is natural to describe this lack of knowledge through the disturbance term of the equation. We might thus wish to choose a pooled cross-section and time-series model in which error terms may be correlated across time and correlated across individual units. Because of the limited number of available degrees of freedom, further restrictions on the error correlations must be made before a useful estimation procedure can be devised. The *error-components model* is a natural solution to this problem.†

The model is

$$Y_{it} = \alpha + \beta X_{it} + \varepsilon_{it} \tag{9.39}$$

$$\varepsilon_{it} = u_i + v_i + w_{it} \tag{9.40}$$

where $u_i \sim N(0, \sigma_u^2) =$ cross-section error component
$\quad v_t \sim N(0, \sigma_v^2) =$ time-series error component
$\quad w_{it} \sim N(0, \sigma_w^2) =$ combined error component

We assume also that individual error components are uncorrelated with each other and are not autocorrelated (across both cross-section and time-series units), that is,

$$\text{Cov}\,(u_i, v_t) = \text{Cov}\,(u_i, w_{it}) = \text{Cov}\,(v_t, w_{it}) = 0$$

$$\text{Cov}\,(u_i, u_j) = 0 \quad i \neq j$$

$$\text{Cov}\,(v_t, v_{t'}) = 0 \quad t \neq t'$$

$$\text{Cov}\,(w_{it}, w_{jt}) = 0 \quad i \neq j$$

$$\text{Cov}\,(w_{it}, w_{it'}) = 0 \quad t \neq t'$$

$$\text{Cov}\,(w_{it}, w_{jt'}) = 0 \quad \begin{matrix} i \neq j \\ t \neq t' \end{matrix}$$

The relationship between the error-components model and the covariance model can be seen by treating the intercept terms in the covariance model not as a set of distinct parameters but as two random variables, one a time-series variable and the other a cross-section variable. If both random variables are assumed to be normally distributed, degrees of freedom are saved because we need to be concerned only with the mean and variance of each of the error components.

† The model is discussed in P. Balestra and M. Nerlove, "Pooling Cross-Section and Time Series Data in the Estimation of a Dynamic Model: The Demand for Natural Gas," *Econometrica*, vol. 34, no. 4, pp. 585–612, 1966; T. D. Wallace and A. Hussain, "The Use of Error Components Models in Combining Cross Section with Time Series Data," *Econometrica*, vol. 37, no. 1, pp. 55–72, 1969; G. S. Maddala, "The Use of Variance Components Models in Pooling Cross Section and Time Series Data," *Econometrica*, vol. 39, no. 2, pp. 341–358, 1971; and M. Nerlove, "Further Evidence on the Estimation of Dynamic Economic Relations from a Time Series of Cross Sections," *Econometrica*, vol. 39, no. 2, pp. 359–381, 1971.

The error-components formulation is obtained from the covariance model by assuming that the mean effect of the random time-series and cross-section variables is included in the intercept term and the random deviations about the mean are equated to the error components, u_t and v_i, respectively.† To see this more clearly, consider the case in which no time-series error component exists. The use of dummy variables would force no restrictions on the pattern of shifting regression intercepts, while the error-components model would presume that the pattern follows a normal distribution. Specifically, we would assume that the cross-section intercepts have mean α_u and variance σ_u^2. The combined error component (which is analogous to the error term in the least-squares regression equation) is assumed to have mean 0 and variance σ_w^2. These two assumptions are equivalent to the assumption that the error component has variance $\sigma_u^2 + \sigma_w^2$, since

$$\text{Var}\,(\varepsilon_{it}) = \text{Var}\,(u_i) + \text{Var}\,(w_{it}) = \sigma_u^2 + \sigma_w^2 \tag{9.41}$$

The effect of the mean of the normally distributed intercepts (α_u) will be accounted for by the inclusion of a constant term in the pooled regression equation. If time-series intercepts had also been random, normally distributed with mean α_v and variance σ_v^2, we could allow the mean effect of the random intercepts (α_v) to be picked up by the constant term. At the same time the error term would consist of three components and would have variance

$$\text{Var}\,(\varepsilon_{it}) = \sigma_u^2 + \sigma_v^2 + \sigma_w^2 \tag{9.42}$$

The relationship between the error-components model and the pooled model using ordinary least squares can be seen directly from Eq. (9.42). If both σ_u^2 and σ_v^2 are identically equal to 0, the error term consists of a single combined disturbance and the correct procedure is to apply ordinary least-squares regression to the pooled data. In this case, we are assuming that intercept terms do not vary, either systematically, as in the covariance model, or randomly, as in the error-components model.

Since all the estimation techniques described will give unbiased and consistent parameter estimates, the central issue associated with pooling is one of efficiency. Error-components models are useful in this respect because they are estimated using a form of generalized least-squares regression (see Appendix 6.1) and can be shown under reasonable conditions to be more efficient than the covariance model estimation process.‡ The estimation of the error-components model is a generalization of the weighted least-squares technique because it weights observations in inverse relationship to their variances. To accomplish the weighting, a two-stage estimation process must be used, since error-component variances are generally not known. In the first stage, ordinary least squares is run on the entire pooled sample. The ordinary least-squares regression

---

† The relationship between the covariance model and the error components model is described in greater detail in Maddala, "The use of Variance Components Models in Pooling Cross Section and Time Series Data," loc. cit.

‡ See Wallace and Hussain, op. cit.

residuals are then used to calculate sample estimates of the variance components. The estimated variances are used in the second stage, in which the generalized least-squares parameter estimates are obtained.†

9.3.3 Time-Series Autocorrelation Model

There are several difficulties associated with the error-components model. First, its estimation can be computationally quite expensive, since the application of the generalized least-squares estimation procedure involves the inversion of an $NT \times NT$ matrix. Second, the technique is not directly applicable if there are lagged dependent variables in the equation or if the equation is part of a simultaneous-equations model.‡ Finally, the error-components specification is not the only error specification possible. It has the property that the correlation of disturbances over time is independent of the time gap between the disturbance terms.§ An alternative specification would predict a decline in the error correlation over time. This suggests that one ought to consider pooling cross-section and time-series data under error assumptions involving time-series (or cross-section) autocorrelation as well as cross-section (or time-series) heteroscedasticity. As one example of how this might be accomplished consider the model

$$Y_{it} = \alpha + \beta X_{it} + \varepsilon_{it} \qquad \varepsilon_{it} = \rho_i \varepsilon_{i, t-1} + u_{it} \qquad (9.43)$$

where
$$E(\varepsilon_{it}^2) = \sigma^2$$

$$E(\varepsilon_{it}\varepsilon_{jt}) = 0 \quad \text{and} \quad E(\varepsilon_{i, t-1} u_{jt}) = 0 \qquad i \neq j$$

$$u_{it} \sim N(0, \sigma_u^2)$$

The assumptions imply that cross-section disturbances are uncorrelated and have constant variance but time-series disturbances are autocorrelated. We allow ρ to vary from individual unit to individual unit but fix each error structure to involve first-order serial correlation. Efficient parameter estimates can be obtained by using a variant of generalized least squares, analogous to that described in Chapter 6. We estimate each ρ_i and then use the estimated $\hat{\rho}_i$ as a basis for the generalized least-squares regression. To estimate ρ_i, $i = 1, 2, \ldots, N$, we estimate the entire pooled sample using ordinary least squares. Since the parameter estimates are consistent (as well as unbiased), we can use them to calculate the regression residuals $\hat{\varepsilon}_{it}$. We then estimate each ρ_i con-

---

† More of the details are available in Wallace and Hussain, op. cit., and Kmenta, op. cit., pp. 515–516.

‡ For a discussion of some of these issues, see Maddala, loc. cit.

§ Recall that the time-series error components are assumed to be *independent*, identically distributed random variables.

sistently as follows:

$$\hat{\rho}_i = \frac{\sum\limits_{t=2}^{T} \hat{\varepsilon}_{it}\hat{\varepsilon}_{i,\,t-1}}{\sum\limits_{t=2}^{T} \hat{\varepsilon}_{i,\,t-1}^2} \qquad \text{for } i = 1, 2, \ldots, N \qquad (9.44)$$

We proceed by forming the generalized difference form of the original model:

$$Y_{it}^* = \alpha(1 - \hat{\rho}_i) + \beta X_{it}^* + u_{it}^* \qquad (9.45)$$

where $\quad Y_{it}^* = Y_{it} - \hat{\rho}_i Y_{i,\,t-1} \qquad X_{it}^* = X_{it} - \hat{\rho}_i X_{i,\,t-1} \qquad u_{it}^* = \varepsilon_{it} - \hat{\rho}_i \varepsilon_{i,\,t-1}$

The generalized difference form can now be estimated by applying ordinary least squares to the pooled model. $NT - N$ observations are used in the estimation, since one observation from each individual unit is dropped in the generalized differencing process. Corrections for heteroscedasticity or cross-section correlation between individual units would proceed in a fashion similar to that just described. If heteroscedasticity had been present in the model of Eq. (9.43), for example, we would use the residuals of the generalized difference model (pooled) to estimate the individual error variances and then apply weighted least squares in the third stage of the estimation process.

Example 9.5† Foreign aid An important empirical question facing development economists concerns the effect of foreign aid on the investment expenditures of less developed countries (LDCs). Some economists have argued that inflows of foreign capital to LDCs do not lead to increased investment but to increased public and private consumption. In order to deal with this issue, an economic model was developed which accounts for the interrelationship between taxing, spending, and borrowing decisions. The model makes a clear distinction between alternative types of foreign aid, such as grants and loans. The model used in the study of the fiscal behavior of LDC's presumes that local officials seek to maximize an objective function which is influenced by allocative choices between private consumption, public "civil" consumption, public "socioeconomic" consumption, public investment for development purposes, and public borrowing from domestic sources. Maximization of this objective function subject to a budget constraint yields a series of five simultaneous equations which must hold if maximization is to be achieved. In order to simplify matters we

---

† This example is adapted from Peter S. Heller, "An Econometric Analysis of the Fiscal Behavior of the Public Sector in Developing Countries: Aid, Investment and Taxation," *University of Michigan Center for Research on Economic Development, Discussion Paper 30,* Oct. 1973. An updated version appears as "A Model of Public Fiscal Behavior in Developing Countries: Aid, Investment, and Taxation," *American Economic Review,* pp. 368–379, June 1975.

shall examine two of these five equations:

$$T_t = \alpha_1 + \alpha_2 A_{1t} + \alpha_3 A_{2t} + \alpha_4 Y_t + \alpha_5 M_{t-1} + \alpha_6 I_t + \alpha_7 G_{s,t}$$
$$+ \alpha_8 G_{c,t-1} + \varepsilon_{1t}$$

$$I_t = \beta_1 + \beta_2 T_t + \beta_3 A_{1t} + \beta_4 A_{2t} + \beta_5 Y_{t-1} + \varepsilon_{2t}$$

where T_t = level of tax and nontax revenues at time t

$\qquad I_t$ = public investment for development purposes at time t

$\qquad G_{c,t}$ = public "civil" consumption (government administration, debt service, police, military) at time t

$\qquad G_{s,t}$ = public "socioeconomic" consumption (schools, hospitals, roads, agricultural projects) at time t

$\qquad A_{1t}$ = grants to the public sector at time t

$\qquad A_{2t}$ = loans to the public sector at time t

$\qquad Y_t$ = gross domestic product at time t

$\qquad M_t$ = imports at time t

The sample of LDCs included 11 African countries: Nigeria, Ghana, Zambia, Kenya, Uganda, Tanzania, Malawi, Liberia, Ethiopia, Tunisia, and Morocco. Time-series data on all variables were available for periods of approximately 6 years. The limited quantity of individual time-series and cross-section data necessitated that the data be pooled to obtain parameter estimates in each of the structural equations. Because the system of equations is simultaneous, the two-stage least-squares technique was chosen to estimate each equation. In addition, a decision was made to use an error-components model with two error components, a cross-section error term, and a combined error term, that is, $\varepsilon_{it} = u_i + w_{it}$. It was implicitly assumed that time-series intercepts remained constant during the period of study. However, the cross-section error component does account for the random nature of the cross-section intercepts. The error-components technique is likely to be more efficient than the direct inclusion of cross-section dummy variables in the model.

The estimation process proceeded in two steps. First, the reduced-form equations were estimated using ordinary least squares. The fitted values of the right-hand endogenous variables were calculated and substituted in the structural equations. The second stage of this 2SLS procedure was then estimated using a variant of the two-step generalized least-squares procedure described in the text. For each equation, the ratio of cross section to combined variance θ was calculated: $\theta = \sigma_u^2 / \sigma_w^2$. The estimated equations (with t statistics in parentheses and constant terms dropped) are

$$\hat{T}_t = - \underset{(-.58)}{.32} A_{1t} - \underset{(-1.98)}{.84} A_{2t} + \underset{(4.54)}{.23} Y_t - \underset{(-3.40)}{.39} M_{t-1} + \underset{(3.37)}{1.03} \hat{I}_t$$
$$- \underset{(-2.24)}{.71} G_{s,t} + \underset{(6.25)}{1.51} G_{c,t-1}$$

$$\theta = .45 \qquad N = \text{number of observations} = 57 \qquad R^2 = .89$$

and
$$\hat{I}_t = \underset{(3.21)}{.70} A_{1t} + \underset{(1.64)}{.24} A_{2t} + \underset{(11.10)}{.49} \hat{T}_t - \underset{(-1.23)}{.02} Y_{t-1}$$

$$\theta = .65 \qquad N = 61 \qquad R^2 = .89$$

The first equation verifies the expected result that higher grants and loans lead to lower domestically raised revenues (although the grants term is insignificant). Government investment and government civil consumption have a strong positive effect on tax revenues, but this is offset to some extent by the negative coefficient on the public socioeconomic consumption term. The results of the second equation indicate that foreign aid does have a positive effect on investment, but the value being less than 1 indicates that some of the foreign aid leaks into other expenditure areas. We can conclude that the estimated equations do verify the fiscal interdependence associated with current and capital budgets. Foreign loans can and do affect public consumption as well as investment.

9.4 NONLINEAR ESTIMATION

All the single-equation regression models we have studied to this point have been linear in their coefficients, and thus ordinary least squares or variations on ordinary least squares could be used to estimate them. In this section we examine the problem of estimating equations that are nonlinear in their coefficients. Although procedures for *nonlinear estimation* can be computationally expensive, they greatly increase the scope of model structures that can be fitted to data.

Recall that there is no problem in applying ordinary least squares to an equation that is nonlinear in the *independent variables*. Equations like

$$Y = \alpha_0 + \alpha_1 X_1^2 + \alpha_2 \log X_2 + \varepsilon \tag{9.46}$$

or
$$Y = \alpha_0 + \alpha_1 X_1^2 + \alpha_2 X_1 X_2 + \varepsilon \tag{9.47}$$

can be estimated using the methods discussed earlier in the book. In addition, some equations that are nonlinear in the coefficients can be transformed into linear equations. For example, the equation

$$Y = \alpha_0 X_1^{\alpha_1} X_2^{\alpha_2} \varepsilon \tag{9.48}$$

can be written equivalently as

$$\log Y = \log \alpha_0 + \alpha_1 \log X_1 + \alpha_2 \log X_2 + \log \varepsilon \tag{9.49}$$

and estimated by ordinary least squares. Our concern will be directed toward equations that are *inherently* nonlinear. For example, the equations

$$Y = \alpha_0 + \alpha_1 X_1^{\beta_1} + \alpha_2 X_2^{\beta_2} + \varepsilon \tag{9.50}$$

$$Y = \alpha_1 e^{\beta_1 X_1} + \alpha_2 e^{\beta_2 X_2} + \varepsilon \tag{9.51}$$

cannot be transformed into linear equations and thus do not lend themselves to linear regression.

Specifically, we consider equations of the form

$$Y = f(X_1, X_2, \ldots, X_k, \beta_1, \beta_2, \ldots, \beta_p) + \varepsilon \qquad (9.52)$$

where f is a nonlinear function of the k independent variables $X_1, \ldots, X_k$ and the p coefficients $\beta_1, \ldots, \beta_p$. The criterion used for determining the estimated values for the coefficients is the same as that used in a linear regression i.e., minimization of the *sum of squared errors*. If we have T observations on $Y, X_1, \ldots, X_k$, we can write the sum of squared errors as

$$S = \sum_{t=1}^{T} \left[Y_t - f(X_{1t}, \ldots, X_{kt}, \beta_1, \ldots, \beta_p) \right]^2 \qquad (9.53)$$

We call $\hat{\beta}_1, \ldots, \hat{\beta}_p$ the nonlinear least-squares estimates of $\beta_1, \ldots, \beta_p$, that is, the values of $\beta_1, \ldots, \beta_p$ that minimize the sum of squared errors S. If the error term ε is normally distributed, these estimates are equivalent to the maximum-likelihood estimates of $\beta_1, \ldots, \beta_p$.†

In the case of a linear regression, obtaining least-squares estimates is computationally straightforward. For a nonlinear equation, however, there are alternative computational approaches to finding coefficient estimates that minimize the sum of squared errors in Eq. (9.53).

9.4.1 Computational Methods for Nonlinear Estimation

There are three general approaches to the solution of the nonlinear estimation problem. Most numerical estimation methods involve one of the approaches or a combination of two of them. As we will see, the choice of approach will depend on the type of equation being estimated.

First, a *direct search* may be used; in this case the sum-of-squared-errors function is evaluated for alternative sets of coefficient values. Those values which result in a minimum are chosen as the estimates. This method may be effective if only one or two coefficients must be estimated. However, if more than two coefficients are involved (which is usually the case), an extremely large number of calculations must be made, so that the method becomes computationally very expensive. For example, if four coefficients must be estimated, and 20 alternative values for each coefficient are to be considered, the sum of squared errors must be calculated $(20)^4 = 160,000$ times! As a result, this method is almost never used, and we will not discuss it any further.

---

† The technique of maximum-likelihood estimation is discussed in Appendix 3.2. Since the likelihood function is

$$L = (2\pi\sigma_e^2)^{-T/2} e^{-S/2\sigma_e^2},$$

maximizing L with respect to $\beta_1, \ldots, \beta_p$ is equivalent to minimizing S with respect to $\beta_1, \ldots, \beta_p$.

A second approach involves *direct optimization*. Parameter estimates are obtained by differentiating the sum-of-squared-errors function with respect to each coefficient, setting the derivatives equal to zero (thus defining a minimum), and solving the resulting set of nonlinear equations (which are called the *normal equations*). Taking the derivatives of Eq. (9.53) with respect to $\beta_1, \ldots, \beta_p$ and setting them equal to zero, we find that the normal equations are

$$\sum_{t=1}^{T} 2 \big[Y_t - f(X_{1t}, \ldots, X_{kt}, \beta_1, \ldots, \beta_p) \big] \frac{\partial f}{\partial \beta_i} = 0 \qquad \text{for } i = 1, \ldots, p$$

(9.54)

These nonlinear equations must be solved simultaneously for $\beta_1, \ldots, \beta_p$, since each equation may contain all p coefficients. As one might expect, this approach can present computational difficulties, and is therefore seldomly applied directly. One variation of this approach that is computationally feasible is the *steepest-descent method*, which involves an iterative process to find the minimum of S. The method works by moving from one trial set of coefficient values for $\beta_1, \ldots, \beta_p$ to a new set in such a way that the derivatives $-\partial S/\partial \beta_1, \ldots, -\partial S/\partial \beta_p$ are as large as possible, resulting in rapid progress to those values of $\beta_1, \ldots, \beta_p$ that minimize S (and for which the derivatives are zero).†

The third approach is an iterative linearization method in which the nonlinear equation is linearized (using a Taylor series expansion) around some initial set of coefficient values. Then ordinary least squares is performed on this linear equation, generating a new set of coefficient values. The nonlinear equation is relinearized around these new coefficient values, ordinary least squares is again performed to generate new coefficient values, and the equation is relinearized around these values. This iterative process is repeated until *convergence* is attained, i.e., until the coefficient values do not change substantially after each new ordinary least-squares regression.

This approach has certain advantages, the first of which is computational efficiency. If the equation to be estimated is closely approximated by a linear equation, very few iterations may be necessary. A second advantage of the approach is that it provides a clear guideline for applying statistical tests that are usually applied only to linear regression. Since a linear regression is performed at each iteration, one can use standard statistics (R^2, t statistics, etc.) to evaluate the fit of the linearized equation. Because this approach has found application to computer systems for econometric modeling, we examine it in more detail.‡

---

† This technique is described in more detail in N. Draper and H. Smith, *Applied Regression Analysis* (New York: Wiley, 1966), pp. 270–272; and in H. A. Spang, "A Review of Minimization Techniques for Nonlinear Functions," *SIAM Review*, vol. 4, pp. 343–365, 1962.

‡ The approach and its application to an econometric software system are described in detail in M. Eisner and R. S. Pindyck, "A Generalized Approach to Estimation is Implemented in the TROLL/1 System," *Annals of Economic and Social Measurement*, vol. 2, no. 1, pp. 29–51, 1973.

We use the fact that any nonlinear function can be expressed as a *Taylor series expansion*. Specifically, we can write Eq. (9.52) in an expansion around a set of initial values $\beta_{1,0}, \ldots, \beta_{p,0}$ for the coefficients $\beta_1, \ldots, \beta_p$. (How these initial values were obtained is not important at this point; let us assume that they represent guesses of the true values.) The expanded equation would be

$$Y = f(X_1, \ldots, X_k, \beta_{1,0}, \ldots, \beta_{p,0}) + \sum_{i=1}^{p} \left(\frac{\partial f}{\partial \beta_i}\right)_0 (\beta_i - \beta_{i,0})$$

$$+ \frac{1}{2} \sum_{i=1}^{p} \sum_{j=1}^{p} \left(\frac{\partial^2 f}{\partial \beta_i \, \partial \beta_j}\right)_0 (\beta_i - \beta_{i,0})(\beta_j - \beta_{j,0}) + \cdots + \varepsilon \quad (9.55)$$

Here the subscript 0 on the partial derivatives denotes that these derivatives are evaluated at $\beta_1 = \beta_{1,0}, \ldots, \beta_p = \beta_{p,0}$.

A linear approximation to our nonlinear function is provided by the first two terms in the Taylor series expansion. Dropping the second- and higher-order terms and rewriting the equation, we get

$$Y - f(X_1, \ldots, X_k, \beta_{1,0}, \ldots, \beta_{p,0}) + \sum_{i=1}^{p} \beta_{i,0} \left(\frac{\partial f}{\partial \beta_i}\right)_0 = \sum_{i=1}^{p} \beta_i \left(\frac{\partial f}{\partial \beta_i}\right)_0 + \varepsilon$$

$$(9.56)$$

Observe that Eq. (9.56) has the form of a linear regression equation. The left-hand side is a constructed dependent variable. The right-hand side consists (in addition to the additive error term) of a set of unknown coefficients $(\beta_1, \ldots, \beta_p)$ multiplying a set of constructed independent variables. Thus, the coefficients can be estimated by performing an ordinary least-squares regression on Eq. (9.56).

The estimated coefficient values for $\beta_1, \ldots, \beta_p$ from Eq. (9.56), which are labeled $\beta_{1,1}, \ldots, \beta_{p,1}$, are used as a new set of initial estimates, and the nonlinear equation is *relinearized* around these values. The result is a new linear regression equation

$$Y - f(X_1, \ldots, X_k, \beta_{1,1}, \ldots, \beta_{p,1}) + \sum_{i=1}^{p} \beta_{i,1} \left(\frac{\partial f}{\partial \beta_i}\right)_1 = \sum_{i=1}^{p} \beta_i \left(\frac{\partial f}{\partial \beta_i}\right)_1 + \varepsilon$$

$$(9.57)$$

Ordinary least squares is applied to this equation, and a new set of coefficient estimates $\beta_{1,2}, \ldots, \beta_{p,2}$ is obtained. The process of relinearization is repeated until convergence occurs, i.e., until

$$\left| \frac{\beta_{i,j+1} - \beta_{i,j}}{\beta_{i,j}} \right| < \delta \quad i = 1, 2, \ldots, p \quad (9.58)$$

where δ is a small number whose choice depends in part on how much computational expense one is willing to entail in making repeated iterations.

There is no guarantee that this iterative process will converge to the maximum-likelihood estimate of the coefficients. The process may, for example, converge to a local, as opposed to global, minimum of the sum-of-squared-errors function. One way to check if this has occurred is to repeat the estimation starting with a different set of initial guesses for the coefficients. Usually the initial guesses $\beta_{1,0}, \ldots, \beta_{p,0}$ are based on values that would seem reasonable from a theoretical point of view. However, the set of guesses chosen for the second estimation should differ substantially from the first set of guesses.

Of crucial importance is the fact that the iterative process may not converge *at all*. Succeeding estimates of the coefficients may differ, and the left-hand side of Eq. (9.58) may grow larger with each new iteration (i.e., the process may *diverge*). Should divergence occur, one might begin the process over again using a new set of initial guesses for the coefficients. (Occasionally convergence is dependent on the particular initial guesses chosen.) If the process still does not converge, it becomes necessary to try a different estimation method, e.g., the direct optimization approach, through the solution of a set of normal equations, mentioned earlier.

An alternative method involves a variation on the iterative linearization method. Instead of using the successive estimates resulting from each linearization, estimates are computed from

$$\beta_{i,j+1} = \beta_{i,j} + \alpha\left(\hat{\beta}_{i,j+1} - \beta_{i,j}\right) \tag{9.59}$$

where $\hat{\beta}_{i,j+1}$ is the least-squares estimate from the $(j+1)$st iteration and α is a damping factor ($0 < \alpha < 1$). The damping factor α can be chosen to keep from overshooting the minimum of the sum-of-squared-errors function.†

Other methods for nonlinear estimation are available and may provide convergent estimates when the methods described above fail.‡ There is really no best method, since one method might converge more easily while another might involve less computational expense. Often alternative methods will be used as a way of checking that the global minimum of the sum-of-squared-errors function has been reached.

9.4.2 Evaluation of Nonlinear Regression Equations

The statistical tests used to evaluate the fit of a linear regression equation are not directly applicable to a nonlinear regression. An F statistic, for example, cannot be used to perform a significance test on the overall fit of a nonlinear

---

† The damping factor can also be used to change the step $\beta_{i,j+1} - \beta_{i,j}$ so that it is somewhere between that which would be indicated by the linearization method and that which would be indicated by the steepest-descent method. This is the basis for Marquardt's method. See D. W. Marquardt, "An Algorithm for Least Squares Estimation of Nonlinear Parameters," *Journal of the Society of Industrial and Applied Mathematics*, vol. 2, p. 431, 1963.

‡ For other methods that seem computationally quite efficient, see S. M. Goldfeld, R. E. Quandt, and H. F. Trotter, "Maximization by Quadratic Hill-Climbing," *Econometrica*, vol. 34, pp. 541–551, 1966. For a discussion of several alternative estimation methods and their statistical properties, see S. M. Goldfeld and R. E. Quandt, *Nonlinear Methods in Econometrics* (Amsterdam: North-Holland, 1972).

regression, nor can t statistics be used in the usual manner. One reason for this is that we cannot obtain an unbiased estimate of σ^2, the true variance of the error term ε, from the regression residuals. Even if ε is normally distributed with 0 mean, the residuals $\hat{\varepsilon}_t$ given by

$$\hat{\varepsilon}_t = Y_t - f(X_{1t}, \ldots, X_{kt}, \hat{\beta}_1, \ldots, \hat{\beta}_p) \tag{9.60}$$

will not be normally distributed (nor will they have 0 mean). Thus the sum of squared residuals will not follow a chi-square distribution, the estimated coefficients themselves will not be normally distributed, and standard t tests and F tests cannot be applied.

What we can do, however, is perform t tests and F tests on the *linear* regression that applies to the *final linearization of the iterative process* (if indeed we have estimated the equation using a linearization approach). These tests will provide some information about the fit of the regression for this last linearization. We would hope that this linearization provides a reasonable approximation to the nonlinear equation and that it fits the data. If this is not the case (as indicated by the statistics), doubt would be cast on the fit of the nonlinear equation as a whole. As a result, computer programs that perform nonlinear estimation via the linearization approach usually calculate t statistics (and associated standard errors) for the last linearization.†

The R^2, however, can be applied in its conventional sense to a nonlinear regression. Recall that the R^2 is calculated from

$$R^2 = 1 - \frac{\Sigma \hat{\varepsilon}_t^2}{\Sigma y_t^2} \tag{9.61}$$

(where y_t is measured in deviation form) and represents the fraction of the variation in y_t that is "explained" by the regression. The R^2 will retain this meaning if the equation is nonlinear and the residuals are calculated from Eq. (9.60). Recall, though, that the R^2 is solely a descriptive statistic that can be associated with overall fit. It cannot be used for significance or hypothesis testing.‡

9.4.3 Forecasting with a Nonlinear Regression Equation

Once a nonlinear regression equation has been estimated, it can be used to obtain forecasts. A forecasts of Y_t is given by

$$\hat{Y}_{T+1} = f(X_{1, T+1}, \ldots, X_{k, T+1}, \hat{\beta}_1, \ldots, \hat{\beta}_p) \tag{9.62}$$

We saw in Chapter 8 that for a linear regression this forecast is unbiased and has the minimum mean square error. This claim cannot be made, however, for a forecast generated from a nonlinear regression as in Eq. (9.62). The reason is

---

† See Eisner and Pindyck, op. cit.

‡ When the linearization approach is used for estimation, a second R^2 is usually calculated for the linear regression at the last iteration.

that the forecast errors will not be normally distributed with 0 mean as was the case for a linear equation. In such a case we cannot determine whether the forecast error is smaller than the error generated by a different set of coefficient estimates.

Furthermore, the formulas for the standard error of forecast (i.e., the standard deviation of the forecast error) and corresponding confidence intervals that were derived in Chapter 8 for the linear case do not apply to Eq. (9.62). There is, in fact, no analytical formula that can be used to compute directly forecast confidence intervals for the general nonlinear equation. One solution might involve the generation of confidence intervals through the use of Monte Carlo forecasting, as described in Chapter 13. This, however, requires that the coefficients be normally distributed (which is not the case) and that estimates be available for the coefficient standard errors and the standard error of the equation itself (which is also not the case). Thus, Monte Carlo techniques are not directly applicable here.

We suggest the following compromise approach. A Monte Carlo forecast is performed using normally distributed errors for the coefficients and the additive error term, and using the linear regression results from the last iteration to provide estimates for the standard errors. As an illustration, consider the nonlinear regression equation

$$Y_t = \beta_0 + \beta_1 X_t^{\beta_2} + \varepsilon_t \tag{9.63}$$

After the equation has been estimated and a forecast $\hat{Y}_{T+1}$ has been computed, the standard error of forecast would be computed as follows:

1. Rewrite the equation as

$$Y_t = (\beta_0 + \eta_0) + (\beta_1 + \eta_1) X_t^{\beta_2 + \eta_2} + \varepsilon_t \tag{9.64}$$

   where η_0, η_1, η_2, and ε_t are assumed to be normally distributed random variables with 0 mean and standard deviations equal to the *computed standard errors from the linear regression corresponding to the last iteration* of the estimation process.
2. Generate random numbers (from the appropriate normal distributions) for η_0, η_1, η_2, and ε_{T+1} to use for the forecast $\hat{Y}_{T+1}$. Compute this forecast accordingly.
3. Repeat step 2 approximately 50 times. Use the sample standard deviation of the resulting distribution of values for $\hat{Y}_{T+1}$ as the standard error of forecast. This approximate standard error of forecast can then be used to calculate confidence intervals.

There is no guarantee that this method provides even a close approximation to the true standard error of forecast. It does, however, at least provide some measure of forecast confidence.

Example 9.6 Consumption function In this example we estimate a *consumption function* that is nonlinear in the coefficients. The objective is to relate aggregate real (constant-dollar) consumption C to aggregate real disposable income YD in the United States, using quarterly time-series data. We would also like to test the hypothesis that the *marginal propensity to consume* MPC, defined as

$$\text{MPC} = \frac{dC}{d\text{YD}} \qquad (9.65)$$

declines as disposable income increases. This hypothesis is easy to support using cross-section data (regressing consumption against income for groups at different income levels), but not using time-series data.

Typically, the following consumption function, which is linear in the coefficients, is estimated:

$$C = \alpha_0 + \alpha_1\text{YD} + \alpha_2\text{YD}^2 + \varepsilon \qquad (9.66)$$

One would expect α_1 to be positive and α_2 to be negative, so that MPC decreases as YD increases. If Eq. (9.66) is estimated using cross-section data, a significant and negative value of α_2 will usually result, while if time-series data are used, the estimate of α_2 will invariably be insignificant, implying constant MPC (α_1 is always significant and positive).†

As an alternative to Eq. (9.66), we estimate the following nonlinear consumption function:

$$C = \alpha_0 + \alpha_1\text{YD}^{\alpha_2} + \varepsilon \qquad (9.67)$$

The quarterly time-series data used cover the period 1946-1 to 1974-3. The estimation is performed using the iterative linearization process. We use the value 1.0 as an initial guess for all three coefficients (we would expect α_1 and α_2 to be close to this value, but we have no expectation regarding the value of α_0).

The estimation results for each iteration are:

Iteration	α_0	α_1	α_2
Initial guess	1.0000	1.0000	1.0000
1	− 9.4974	1.1856	.9589
2	− 10.3366	1.2400	.9539
3	− 10.3517	1.2409	.9539
4	− 10.3507	1.2409	.9539

Convergence occurs quickly, requiring only four iterations. Standard errors are also calculated for the linear regression at the last iteration. The standard error for the equation as a whole is 4.732, and the standard errors

---

† See, for example, R. D. Husby, "A Nonlinear Consumption Function Estimated from Time-Series and Cross-Section Data," *Review of Economics and Statistics*, vol. 53, February 1971. Husby's consumption functions are nonlinear only in the independent variables, and not in the coefficients.

for α_0, α_1, and α_2 are 4.192, .0876, and .0098, respectively. Thus, the regression estimates at the last iteration are all significant. Finally, the R^2 for the fitted nonlinear equation is .9994. The estimated nonlinear equation is

$$\hat{C} = -10.3507 + 1.2409\text{YD}^{.9539} \tag{9.68}$$

For comparison, the following linear regression equation was also estimated (coefficient standard errors are in parentheses):

$$\hat{C} = 7.9852 + .8905\,\text{YD} \qquad R^2 = .9993 \qquad \text{SER} = 5.154 \tag{9.69}$$
$$\phantom{\hat{C} = }{}_{(1.0349)}\quad{}_{(.0022)}$$

Note that the MPC for this linear equation is a constant, .8905. For our nonlinear equation, the MPC is

$$\text{MPC} = \frac{dC}{d\text{YD}} = \alpha_1\alpha_2\text{YD}^{\alpha_2 - 1} \tag{9.70}$$

The mean value of YD (in billions of 1958 dollars) is 417, and at this value MPC is .876. Note that MPC indeed declines as YD increases; for YD equal to 600, MPC is .860.

It is important to stress that our estimation results are dependent upon the particular nonlinear estimation method used. As an illustration of this, Eq. (9.67) was reestimated using a steepest-descent method of direct optimization. Convergence occurred after 17 iterations, and the resulting equation is

$$\hat{C} = .005 + 1.0424\text{YD}^{.9779} \tag{9.71}$$

The result is a lower marginal propensity to consume. For YD equal to 417, the MPC is .850, and for YD equal to 600, the MPC is .841. While the results in Eqs. (9.68) and (9.71) differ, it is impossible to determine which is more "correct" on statistical grounds, since we lack statistical tests for nonlinear regression estimates. Therefore, the evaluation of the two equations would require comparing their performance in a series of *ex post* forecasts.

APPENDIX 9.1 ESTIMATING CONFIDENCE INTERVALS FOR LONG-RUN ELASTICITIES

Assume that we have estimated a distributed lag model with a geometric lag, specified as

$$\log Q_t = \beta_1 + \beta_2 \log P_t + \beta_3 \log Y_t + \beta_4 \log Q_{t-1} + \varepsilon_t \tag{A9.1}$$

where Q is quantity, P is own price, and Y is income. For this equation the short-run price and income elasticities are β_2 and β_3, respectively, but the *long-run* elasticities are†

$$\eta_{LR}^P = \frac{\beta_2}{1 - \beta_4} \qquad \text{and} \qquad \eta_{LR}^Y = \frac{\beta_3}{1 - \beta_4}$$

The problem is to estimate *standard errors* (and hence *confidence intervals*) for these elasticity estimates. It turns out that such confidence intervals can easily be obtained if one has estimates of the covariances of the *estimated regression coefficients*. Such covariances are usually calculated in most regression packages.

The procedure is as follows. Suppose we want to obtain a 90 percent confidence interval for the elasticity estimate given by the ratio $\hat{\beta}_2/(1 - \hat{\beta}_4)$, where $\hat{\beta}_2$ and $\hat{\beta}_4$ are the estimated values of β_2 and β_4. Then form the linear combination

$$\phi = \hat{\beta}_2 - z(1 - \hat{\beta}_4) = \hat{\beta}_2 + z\hat{\beta}_4 - z \tag{A9.2}$$

where z is yet to be determined. Now note that the variance of this linear combination is

$$\text{Var}\,(\phi) = \text{Var}\,(\hat{\beta}_2) + z^2\,\text{Var}\,(\hat{\beta}_4) + 2z\,\text{Cov}\,(\hat{\beta}_2, \hat{\beta}_4) \tag{A9.3}$$

If z is the true ratio $\beta_2/(1 - \beta_4)$, then ϕ would have a mean of zero. If the number of degrees of freedom is very large, e.g., more than 40, the distribution of ϕ is approximately normal, so that the probability is 90 percent that the sample value of ϕ is within plus or minus 1.645 times its standard deviation, where 1.645 is obtained from the normal table.‡ Thus,

$$\left(\hat{\beta}_2 - \hat{\beta}_4 z - z\right)^2 \le (1.645)^2\left[\text{Var}\,(\hat{\beta}) + \text{Var}\,(\hat{\beta}_4)z^2 + 2z\,\text{Cov}\,(\hat{\beta}_2, \hat{\beta}_4)\right] \tag{A9.4}$$

with probability 0.90. Now, to obtain the confidence interval, just treat Eq. (A9.4) above as an equality, i.e., as a *quadratic equation in z*. In other words, substitute in the estimates $\hat{\beta}_2$, $\hat{\beta}_4$, Var $(\hat{\beta}_2)$, Var $(\hat{\beta}_4)$, and Cov $(\hat{\beta}_2, \hat{\beta}_4)$ and solve the resulting quadratic equation for z. The result will be of the form

$$\hat{z} = \bar{\eta} \pm u$$

where $\bar{\eta}$ is the expected value of the elasticity [and *not* necessarily equal to $\hat{\beta}_2/(1 - \hat{\beta}_4)$], and $\pm u$ is the 90 percent confidence interval.

---

† If Eq. (A9.1) were in *linear* rather than logarithmic form, the elasticities would just be given by

$$\eta_{LR}^P = \frac{\beta_2}{1 - \beta_4}\frac{\bar{P}}{\bar{Q}} \qquad \text{and} \qquad \eta_{LR}^Y = \frac{\beta_3}{1 - \beta_4}\frac{\bar{Y}}{\bar{Q}}$$

where a bar indicates the mean value.

‡ See R. A. Fisher, *Statistical Methods for Research Workers*, 11th ed., 1950, for details.

EXERCISES

9.1 Suppose the equation to be estimated is

$$Y = \beta_1 + \beta_2 X_2 + \beta_3 X_3 + \beta_4 X_4 + \varepsilon$$

The researcher is missing the last five observations for X_4 but has available a variable Z which is known to be highly correlated with X_4. What should the researcher do, and what assumptions must hold for this to be a good procedure?

9.2 Consider the models $Y_t = \alpha + \beta X_t + \varepsilon_t$ and $Z_t = \gamma + \delta Y_t + u_t$.

(a) Suppose you are trying to estimate α and β but the last (Tth) observation on X_t is missing. What should you do?

(b) Suppose now that you are interested in forecasting Z_t and that you know γ, δ, and X_t for $t \le T$ and Y_t for $t \le T - 1$. What should you do?

9.3 Prove that replacing the missing X observation in the model described in part (a) of Exercise 9.2 by using time t as an instrument will yield a consistent slope estimate. What will happen if the error term is serially correlated?

9.4 Consider the model

$$Y_{it} = \alpha + \beta X_{it} + \varepsilon_{it} \qquad i = 1, 2, \ldots, N$$
$$t = 1, 2, \ldots, T$$

Assume that it is known that the time-series intercepts are constant. How would you test to see whether the covariance model ought to be used to account for varying cross-section intercepts?

9.5 How would you estimate a pooled time-series cross-section model when the cross-section error component is known to be heteroscedastic? Would a similar method work when it is the time-series component that is known to be heteroscedastic?

9.6 Assume that you are estimating a model with two explanatory variables, each of which has a Koyck geometric lag. Derive an equation to be estimated when both lags have identical weights.

9.7 Consider the following model:

$$Y_t = \alpha + \beta(w_0 X_t + w_1 X_{t-1} + w_2 X_{t-2} + w_3 X_{t-3}) + \varepsilon_t$$

Show how to estimate the model using the polynomial distributed lag model and a second-degree polynomial if:

(a) There are no endpoint restrictions.

(b) The tail and head of the distribution are assumed equal to 0 ($w_{-1} = w_4 = 0$).

9.8 Expand the consumption function

$$C = a_1 + a_2 YD^{a_3}$$

in a Taylor series expansion around some initial guess for a_1, a_2, and a_3. Set up the linear regression equation. Explain how the equation would be relinearized around the OLS estimates from the first regression.

9.9 Write the sum-of-squared-errors function S for the nonlinear consumption function

$$C = a_0 + a_1 YD^{a_2}$$

Take the derivatives of S with respect to a_0, a_1, and a_2 to obtain the *normal equations*. Describe how these normal equations could be solved to yield estimates of a_0, a_1, and a_2.

9.10 We wish to examine several alternatives for estimating an equation in the presence of missing data. The model we wish to estimate is

$$\text{EXP} = \beta_1 + \beta_2 \text{POP} + \beta_3 \text{AID} + \beta_4 \text{INC} + \varepsilon$$

where it is known (see Chapter 6) that $\text{VAR}(\varepsilon) = C(\text{POP}^2)$

(a) Transform each variable, dividing by POP. Define

$$\text{PCEXP} = \frac{\text{EXP}}{\text{POP}} \qquad \text{POP1} = \frac{1}{\text{POP}} \qquad \text{PCAID} = \frac{\text{AID}}{\text{POP}} \qquad \text{PCINC} = \frac{\text{INC}}{\text{POP}}$$

Using all the data, find efficient estimates of β_1, β_2, β_3, and β_4 by regressing PCEXP on POP1, PCAID, and PCINC (with a constant term included). These estimates are our reference set for the remainder of the problem. Denote them by β_1^A, β_2^A, β_3^A, β_4^A.

For the remainder of this problem we assume that the last five observations on INC are missing.

(b) Using only the first 45 observations and the transformed data, estimate the model. Label the estimates β_1^B, β_2^B, β_3^B, and β_4^B.

(c) Using observations 1 to 45, find the average of INC; call it $\widehat{\text{INC}}$. Define PCINCC by

$$\text{PCINCC}_t = \begin{cases} \text{PCINC}_t & \text{if } t \le 45 \\ \widehat{\text{INC}}/\text{POP}_t & \text{if } t \ge 46 \end{cases}$$

Regress PCEXP on POP1, AID, and PCINCC. Label the estimates β_1^C, β_2^C, β_3^C, and β_4^C.

(d) Regress INC on POP and AID using observations 1 to 45. Using the above, predict INC_t for $t = 46$ to 50. Label the predicted values $\widehat{\text{INC}}_t$. Define

$$\text{PCINCD}_t = \begin{cases} \text{PCINC}_t & t \le 45 \\ \dfrac{\widehat{\text{INC}}_t}{\text{POP}_t} & t \ge 46 \end{cases}$$

and regress PCEXP on POP1, PCAID, and PCINCD. Label the estimated coefficients β_1^D, β_2^D, β_3^D, β_4^D.

(e) Using the first 45 observations, find the average of PCINC. Denote this by $\widehat{\text{PCINC}}$. Define

$$\text{PCINCE}_t = \begin{cases} \text{PCINC}_t & t \le 45 \\ \widehat{\text{PCINC}} & t \ge 46 \end{cases}$$

Regress PCEXP on POP1, PCAID, and PCINCE. Label the estimates β_1^E, β_2^E, β_3^E, β_4^E, β_5^E.

(f) Using observations 1 to 45, regress PCINC on POP1 and PCAID. Using the above, predict PCINC_t for $t \ge 46$. Call the predicted values $\widehat{\text{PCINC}}_t$. Define

$$\text{PCINCF}_t = \begin{cases} \text{PCINC}_t & t \le 45 \\ \widehat{\text{PCINC}}_t & t \ge 46 \end{cases}$$

Regress PCEXP on POP1, PCAID, and PCINCF and label the estimated coefficients β_1^F, β_2^F, β_3^F, and β_4^F.

(g) Compare and contrast the results from procedures (a) to (f). Which seem to be the most reasonable methods for dealing with missing observations? Why?

MODELS OF QUALITATIVE CHOICE

Our objective in this chapter is to extend the tools of linear regression to construct models in which the dependent variable is not continuous. Specifically, we concern ourselves with models in which the dependent variable is associated with two or more qualitative choices. Such models are finding wider application to economics (and business) in part because of the recent emphasis on the analysis of survey data. In most surveys the behavioral responses are qualitative; one either votes yes or votes no in an election; one uses either the subway, the bus, or the automobile; one is either in the labor force or out of the labor force; etc.

Our approach will be to focus primarily on the analysis of models in which binary choices are made. In particular, we will discuss the specification and estimation of three models, the linear probability model, the probit model, and the logit model. The linear probability model provides a suitable starting point because it can be viewed as a direct extension of our earlier discussion (Chapter 5) of the use of dummy variables. Some of the difficulties associated with the interpretation of the probabilistic nature of this model suggest the usefulness of the probit and logit models. Throughout the chapter we attempt only to introduce the important modeling concepts involved and to outline some of the estimation problems which arise. To extend their understanding of this subject, some readers may wish to read some of the relevant source materials cited within the chapter. These studies include details about the estimation processes described in the chapter as well as proofs of some of the results.

10.1 BINARY-CHOICE MODELS

When one or more of the *explanatory* variables in a regression model are dichotomous in nature, we can represent them as dummy variables and proceed as in Chapter 5. However the application of the linear regression model when the *dependent variable* is dichotomous is more complex. *Binary-choice models* assume that individuals† are faced with a choice between two alternatives and that the choice they make depends on the characteristics of the individuals. Assuming that we have information about the attributes of each of the individuals and the choices they make, it is natural to ask whether we can estimate an equation which will predict the choices of individuals not in the original sample.‡ Suppose, for example, that we wish to build a model which will allow us to make predictions about how individuals will vote on a local bond issue. We might expect that individual income is a primary determinant of voting choice, and that (other things being equal) high-income individuals are more likely to vote yes on a bond issue than low-income individuals. Although it is reasonable to expect a direct relationship between income and voting behavior, our information is not sufficient to predict how each and every individual will vote with perfect accuracy. A more plausible objective is to predict the *likelihood* that an individual with a given income will vote yes.

As in the regression model, one purpose of qualitative choice models is to determine the probability that an individual with a given set of attributes will make one choice· rather than the alternative. A suitable model is one which (when properly estimated) will allow us to make statements of the following type: "The probability than an individual with an income of $15,000 will vote yes on the upcoming bond issue is .6." More generally, we wish to find a relationship between a set of attributes describing an individual and the probability that the individual will make a given choice. The choice model, like most models that we have studied, must be written in a form which is both useful for predictive purposes and easily estimated.

We will describe several possible model specifications and some of the trade-offs involved in selecting the appropriate one. In order to simplify our discussion, we will always assume that the probability of an individual making a given choice is a *linear* function of the individual attributes. Alternative model specifications arise because it is possible to make several assumptions about the probabilistic nature of the decision process. We will have more to say about the importance of the assumptions relating to probability after we study the most elementary specification of a binary-choice model, the linear probability model.

---

† We use the expression "individual" to refer to any choice-making entity. Thus, households, cities, and firms are all considered to be individuals in the discussion which follows.

‡ The problem of model estimation and its relationship to the theory of choice is described thoroughly in D. McFadden, "Conditional Logit Analysis of Qualitative Choice Behavior," in P. Zarembka (ed.), *Frontiers in Econometrics* (New York: Academic Press, 1973), and T. Domencich and D. McFadden, *Urban Travel Demand: A Behavioral Analysis* (Amsterdam: North-Holland, 1975). We shall implicitly restrict our analysis to cases in which prediction is to occur over the same set of choices available during the period of model estimation.

10.1.1 Linear Probability Model

We begin by examining the *linear probability model*. The regression form of the model is†

$$Y_i = \alpha + \beta X_i + \varepsilon_i \tag{10.1}$$

where X_i = value of attribute, e.g., income, for ith individual

$$Y_i = \begin{cases} 1 & \text{if first option is chosen (buy a car, vote yes)} \\ 0 & \text{if second option is chosen (not buy, vote no)} \end{cases}$$

ε_i = independently distributed random variable with 0 mean‡

The interpretation of Eq. (10.1) as a linear probability model comes about when we take the expected value of each dependent variable observation Y_i

$$E(Y_i) = \alpha + \beta X_i \tag{10.2}$$

Since Y_i can take on only two values, 1 and 0, we can describe the probability distribution of Y by letting $P_i = \text{Prob}\,(Y_i = 1)$ and $1 - P_i = \text{Prob}\,(Y_i = 0)$. Then,

$$E(Y_i) = 1(P_i) + 0(1 - P_i) = P_i$$

Thus, the regression equation can be interpreted as describing the probability that an individual will vote yes, given information about the person's income. The slope of the regression line measures the effect on the probability of voting yes of a unit change in the individual's income. Formally, the linear probability model is often written in the following form, which allows the dependent variable to be interpreted as a probability:

$$P_i = \begin{cases} \alpha + \beta X_i & \text{when} \quad 0 < \alpha + \beta X_i < 1 \\ 1 & \text{when} \quad \alpha + \beta X_i \geq 1 \\ 0 & \text{when} \quad \alpha + \beta X_i \leq 0 \end{cases}$$

We have not yet described the probability distribution of the error term in the model. The actual distribution is determined by substituting the values of Y_i (1 and 0) in Eq. (10.1), and is exhibited in Table 10.1.§ When X_i is fixed, the probability distribution of ε_i must be equivalent to the probability distribution of Y_i. (When X_i is stochastic, the probability distribution will be more complicated.) We can determine the relationship between the probability P_i and X_i by using our assumption that the error has 0 mean. It follows that

$$E(\varepsilon_i) = (1 - \alpha - \beta X_i)P_i + (-\alpha - \beta X_i)(1 - P_i) = 0$$

---

† We shall work with a single explanatory variable purely for purposes of simplicity.
‡ As in the classical linear regression model, we are assuming that X_i is fixed (or, if random, is independent of ε_i).
§ P_i measures the probability that $\varepsilon_i = 1 - \alpha - \beta X_i$, etc.

Table 10.1 Probability distribution of ε_i

Y_i	ε_i	Probability
1	$1 - \alpha - \beta X_i$	P_i
0	$-\alpha - \beta X_i$	$1 - P_i$

Solving for P_i, we find that

$$P_i = \alpha + \beta X_i$$
$$1 - P_i = 1 - \alpha - \beta X_i$$

The variance of the error term can now be calculated:

$$E(\varepsilon_i^2) = (1 - \alpha - \beta X_i)^2 P_i + (-\alpha - \beta X_i)^2 (1 - P_i)$$
$$= (1 - \alpha - \beta X_i)^2 (\alpha + \beta X_i) + (\alpha + \beta X_i)^2 (1 - \alpha - \beta X_i)$$
$$= (1 - \alpha - \beta X_i)(\alpha + \beta X_i) = P_i(1 - P_i)$$

or
$$\sigma_i^2 = E(\varepsilon_i^2) = E(Y_i)\big[1 - E(Y_i)\big]$$

This suggests quite properly that the error term is heteroscedastic; i.e., the variance of the error term is not constant for all observations. Observations for which P_i is close to 0 or close to 1 will have relatively low variances, while observations with P_i closer to $\frac{1}{2}$ will have higher variances. The presence of heteroscedasticity results in a loss of efficiency but does not in itself result in either biased or inconsistent parameter estimates.

An obvious means of correcting for heteroscedasticity is to estimate the variances of *each* of the Y_i and then to apply weighted least-squares estimation. To do this, we perform ordinary least squares on the original (0, 1) dichotomous dependent-variable model and estimate each of the error variances as follows:†

$$\hat{\sigma}_i^2 = \hat{Y}_i(1 - \hat{Y}_i) \qquad \text{where} \quad \hat{Y}_i = \hat{\alpha} + \hat{\beta} X_i \qquad (10.3)$$

The difficulty with weighted least squares is that there is no guarantee that the predicted value $\hat{Y}_i$ will lie in the (0, 1) interval.‡ If some values of $\hat{Y}_i$ do lie outside the (0, 1) range, the observations must either be dropped from the model or arbitrarily be set equal to numbers such as .01 and .99. In either case, the weighted least-squares procedure may not be efficient. It can be shown that as the sample size becomes arbitrarily large, weighted least squares is efficient, but it is not efficient for small samples. Since the weighted least-squares procedure is also quite sensitive to errors of specification, we advise against the indiscriminate use of the technique. Ordinary least-squares estimation is most likely a better alternative. An additional problem arises from the fact that the error

---

† $\hat{\sigma}_i^2$ will be a consistent estimate of σ_i^2.

‡ This, of course, presents a serious problem when the linear probability model is used for purposes of forecasting. See the discussion which follows.

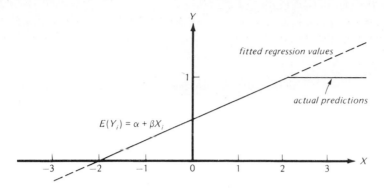

Figure 10.1 Prediction with the linear probability model.

distribution is not normal. We cannot apply the classical statistical tests to the estimated parameters, since the tests depend on the normality of the errors. (It is possible to develop statistical tests which are appropriate when the sample size gets large. However, the issues involved are too complex to be discussed here.†)

When we attempt to use the linear probability model for prediction, a serious weakness of the model becomes apparent. Since the linear probability model involves the interpretation of predicted values of Y as probabilities, we are faced with a problem when the predicted value lies outside the (0, 1) range. This possibility is depicted in Fig. 10.1. Even if the true linear probability model is correct, it is certainly possible that a given sample value of X will lie outside the $(-2, 2)$ interval. The fitted value of Y associated with this observation on X will be greater than 1 or less than 0 as the occasion arises. The obvious correction for this problem is to set extreme predictions equal to 1 or 0, thereby constraining predicted probabilities to be within the (0, 1) interval. This solution is not very satisfying, because it suggests that we might predict an occurrence with a probability of 1 when it is entirely possible that it may not occur or we might predict an occurrence with probability 0 when it may actually occur. While the estimation procedure might yield unbiased estimates, the predictions obtained from the estimation process are clearly biased.

An alternative approach is to reestimate the parameters α and β subject to the constraint that $0 \le \hat{Y}_i \le 1$. The determination of least-squares parameter estimates subject to inequality constraints is a nonlinear estimation problem, which in this particular case can be solved using a mathematical programming routine. The available evidence suggests that the addition of the inequality constraint leads to parameter estimates with lower variances, as expected, but

† For a discussion of some of the relevant issues, see S. Warner, "Asymptotic Variances for Dummy Variable Regression under Normality Assumptions," *Journal of the American Statistical Association*, vol. 62, pp. 1305–1314, 1967; and S. Warner, "Multivariate Regression of Dummy Variates under Normality Assumptions," *Journal of the American Statistical Association*, vol. 58, pp. 1054–1063, 1963.

there is no guarantee that the estimates will be unbiased.† Given this fact, and given the sensitivity of the constrained estimation procedure, it seems more appropriate to use the ordinary least-squares version of the linear probability model.

The problem of predicting outside the unit interval with the linear probability model suggests an additional problem associated with the model specification. The problem arises because observations in a given sample may be drawn excessively from attributes whose values are associated with extreme values of choice probabilities (0 and 1). Suppose, for example, that the independent attribute values are drawn randomly from a known population and that several observations lie outside the $(-2, 2)$ interval shown in Fig. 10.1. This possibility is depicted graphically in Fig. 10.2. In this case, the true regression model associates a probability of 1 with values of X greater than 2 and a probability of 0 with values of X less than -2. The sample contains several X values greater than 2 for which the first option was chosen and several values of X less than -2 for which the second was chosen. The resulting ordinary least-squares slope estimate will be biased, since it will underestimate the true regression slope. This bias is in reality a form of specification bias and cannot be eliminated by the use of nonlinear estimation procedures which account for loss of efficiency. It suggests the particular sensitivity to specification error which is associated with the linear probability model. We should note that the underestimated slope as shown in Fig. 10.2 is not a general result. If the attribute data are bunched somewhat differently, the slope might be overestimated. An example of this case is shown in Fig. 10.3.‡

Example 10.1 Predicting bond defaults A useful means of predicting bond failures is to analyze the factors that correlate highly with actual bond defaults.§ If we view the decision to default and the decision not to default as two options for local governments, we can estimate the probability of default using the linear probability model. A sample of 35 Massachusetts communities, several of which actually defaulted, was used in a cross-section study using 1930 data.¶ The goal of the estimation was to find a subset of characteristics of communities which best allows one to predict the probability of default. The model is

$$P_i = \beta_i + \beta_2 \text{TAX}_i + \beta_3 \text{INT}_i + \beta_4 \text{AV}_i + \beta_5 \text{DAV}_i + \beta_6 \text{WELF}_i + \varepsilon_i$$

---

† See Domencich and McFadden, op. cit., chap. 5.

‡ This bunching example is described in M. Nerlove and S. J. Press, "Univariate and Multivariate Log-Linear and Logistic Models," *Rand Corporation, R-1306-EDA/NIH,* Santa Monica, Calif., December 1973.

§ A bond default occurs when there is a delayed payment of either principal or interest on a bond. Some bondholders are repaid for partial or total loss of interest and payment, but only after some length of time.

¶ See D. Rubinfeld, "An Econometric Analysis of the Market for General Obligation Municipal Bonds," unpublished doctoral dissertation, M.I.T., June 1972.

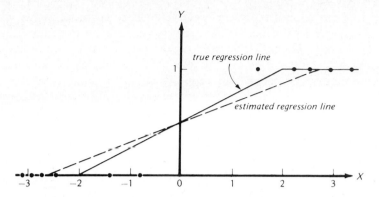

Figure 10.2 Underestimated slope.

where $P = 0$ if the municipality defaulted and 1 otherwise
   TAX = average of 1929, 1930, and 1931 tax rates
   INT = percentage of current budget allocated to interest payments in 1930
   AV = percentage growth in assessed property valuation from 1925 to 1930
   DAV = ratio of total direct net debt to total assessed valuation in 1930
   WELF = percentage of 1930 budget allocated to charities, pensions, and soldiers' benefits

The regression results were as follows (standard errors are in parentheses):

$$\hat{P} = 1.96 - \underset{(.009)}{.029}\,\text{TAX} - \underset{(2.13)}{4.86}\,\text{INT} + \underset{(.028)}{.063}\,\text{AV} + \underset{(.003)}{.007}\,\text{DAV} - \underset{(.88)}{.48}\,\text{WELF}$$
$$\underset{(.29)}{}$$

$$R^2 = .36$$

As we point out in Section 10.1.4, R^2 has limited validity as a measure of goodness of fit. However, the R^2 of .36 suggests that a good deal of variance in the model is still unexplained. Nonetheless one can still use the results of

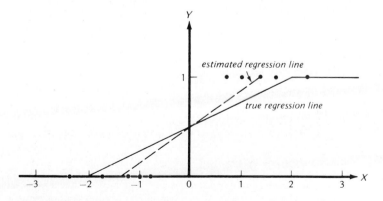

Figure 10.3 Overestimated slope.

the model to study several economic factors which do correlate highly with defaults. The coefficient of the tax rate variable is negative and significant, implying that, *ceteris paribus*, an increase in the tax rate of $1 per thousand will raise the probability of default by .029. The percentage of the budget allocated to interest payments also appears to be a good predictor of defaults, with higher-interest budget shares being positively correlated with the probability of default. This result is to be expected, given the near guarantee of the claim of interest payments on the current budget. The percentage of current budget allocated to welfare bears the same relationship to probability of default as the interest budget share, but is not significant. The rate of growth of actual assessed valuation is significant and inversely related to default probability. A growing tax base implies a low probability of default, at least in the short run. Finally, the debt-to-assessed-valuation ratio is also inversely related to default probability.

10.1.2 Probit Model

All the difficulties associated with the linear probability model point to the need for alternative model specifications. Since the most serious set of difficulties arises from the fact that predictions may lie outside the (0, 1) interval, it is natural to search for alternative distributional assumptions for which all predictions must lie within the appropriate interval. The obvious solution to the problem is to transform the original model in such a way that predictions will lie in the (0, 1) interval for all X. The constrained form of the linear probability model achieves this goal, but at some cost. Since our primary concern is to interpret the "dependent" variable in our model as the probability of making a choice (given information about the individual's attributes), it is reasonable to utilize some notion of probability as the basis of the transformation. The requirement of such a process is that it translate the values of the attribute X, which may range in value over the entire real line, to a probability which ranges in value from 0 to 1. We would also like the transformation to maintain the property that increases in X are associated with increases (or decreases) in the dependent variable for all values of X.† These requirements suggest that use of the *cumulative probability function* will provide a suitable transformation.‡ The resulting probability distribution might be represented as

$$P_i = F(\alpha + \beta X_i) = F(Z_i) \qquad (10.4)$$

where F is a cumulative probability function, and X is stochastic.

Under the assumption that we transform the model using a cumulative *uniform* probability function, we get the constrained version of the linear

---

† Such a transformation is called a *monotonic* transformation.

‡ The reader should recall that a *cumulative probability function* is defined as having as its value the probability that an observed value of a variable X (for every X) will be less than or equal to a particular X. The range of the cumulative probability function is the (0, 1) interval, since all probabilities lie between 0 and 1.

probability model $P_i = \alpha + \beta X_i$ (see Exercise 10.3). While numerous alternative cumulative probability functions are possible, we shall consider only two, the *normal* and the *logistic*.

The *probit probability model* is associated with the cumulative normal probability function.† To understand this model, assume that there exists a theoretical (but not actually measured) index Z_i which is determined by an explanatory variable X_i, as in the linear probability model. The index Z_i is assumed to be a continuous variable which is random and normally distributed for the usual econometric reasons. Thus, we can write

$$Z_i = \alpha + \beta X_i \tag{10.5}$$

What makes this problem different from the standard problem in econometrics is that we assume that observations on Z_i are not available. Instead we have data which distinguish only whether individual observations are in one category (high values of the index Z_i) or a second category (low values of Z_i). The problem which probit analysis solves is the problem of how to obtain estimates for the parameters α and β while at the same time obtaining information about the underlying unmeasured scale index Z.

To focus on this problem more specifically consider the analysis of voter behavior in an election. The individual is assumed to vote yes or no when faced with the choice of one of two candidates for an office. In this case, the index Z_i would represent the strength of feeling of individual i for the first candidate for the office. The index will, of course, vary by individual, but more importantly it is an index that is not observable from available survey data. All we are assumed to know is whether that individual voted for the candidate or not. Now, suppose that we also know that the index of strength of feeling is a linear function of income X. Then the probit model provides a suitable means of estimating the slope and intercept parameters of the relationship between the scale and income.

How does the underlying index Z relate to the actual voting information available? The answer is quite straightforward. Let Y represent a dummy variable which equals 1 when the first candidate is selected and 0 when the second candidate is chosen. Then assume that for each individual voter Z_i^* represents the critical cutoff value which translates the underlying index into a voting decision. Specifically, the

$$\text{Individual votes for} \begin{cases} \text{first candidate} & \text{if } Z_i > Z_i^* \\ \text{second candidate} & \text{if } Z_i \le Z_i^* \end{cases} \tag{10.6}$$

The probit model assumes that Z_i^* is a normally distributed random variable,‡ so that the probability that Z_i^* is less than (or equal to) Z_i can be computed from the cumulative normal probability function. (The cumulative

† For further details see D. J. Finney, *Probit Analysis*, 2d ed. (Cambridge: Cambridge University Press, 1964), and J. Tobin, "The Application of Multivariate Probit Analysis to Economic Survey Data," *Cowles Foundation Discussion Paper* 1, 1955.

‡ Z_i^* is usually normalized to have unit variance. A different normalization would have no substantive impact on the probit results.

normal function assigns to a number Z the probability that any arbitrary Z^* will be less than or equal to Z.) The standardized cumulative normal function is written

$$P_i = F(Z_i) = \frac{1}{\sqrt{2\pi}} \int_{-\infty}^{Z_i} e^{-s^2/2} \, ds \tag{10.7}$$

where s is a random variable which is normally distributed with mean zero and unit variance. By construction, the variable P_i will lie in the (0, 1) interval. P_i represents the probability of an event's occuring, in this case the probability of the individual's voting for the first candidate. Since this probability is measured by the area under the standard normal curve from $-\infty$ to Z_i, the event will be more likely to occur the larger the value of the index Z_i.

The reader unfamiliar with the cumulative normal function may find it helpful to examine Table 10.2, in which the relationship in Eq (10.7) is described for particular values of Z. (The normal distribution has mean 0 and variance 1.) The cumulative normal function is shown graphically in Fig. 10.4, which compares the probit and linear probability models.

To obtain an estimate of the index Z_i we apply the inverse of the cumulative normal function to Eq. (10.7):†

$$Z_i = F^{-1}(P_i) = \alpha + \beta X_i \tag{10.8}$$

We can interpret the probability P_i resulting from the probit model as an estimate of the conditional probability that an individual will vote yes (or an individual will go to college), given that the individual's income is X_i. This is equivalent to the probability that a standard normal variable will be less than or equal to $\alpha + \beta X_i$.

Note that the slope of the probit function as shown in Fig. 10.4 is larger than that of the linear probability function in the middle range but smaller at the extremes of the interval $(-2, 2)$. Outside the $(-2, 2)$ interval the linear probability model has a slope of 0. The graph is suggestive of some of the difficulties which might be associated with a misspecified linear probability

Table 10.2

Z	F(Z)	Z	F(Z)
−3.0	.001	.5	.691
−2.5	.006	1.0	.841
−2.0	.023	1.5	.933
−1.5	.067	2.0	.977
−1.0	.159	2.5	.994
−.5	.309	3.0	.999
0	.500	3.5	.999

† The variable Z_i can take on any real value.

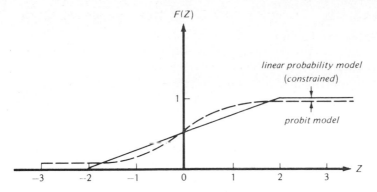

Figure 10.4 Probit model.

model. Assume, for example, that the probit specification is correct. Then estimation of the incorrect linear probability model will lead to the false inference that the slope of the function is constant when in fact the change in probability associated with a change in X is dependent upon the particular value of X selected.

While the probit model is more appealing than the linear probability model, it generally involves nonlinear estimation and thus added computational costs.[†] In addition, the theoretical justification for employing the probit model is often rather limited. Following several examples, we shall consider a somewhat more appealing model specification, *the logit model*.

Example 10.2 Voting behavior In a recent study of voting in the 1972 presidential election, a probit model was used to explain the probability of a citizen's voting for George McGovern.[‡] The authors assume that there is an underlying index Z_i, "propensity" to vote for McGovern, which is assumed to be a linear function of the positions that voters have taken on a number of policy issues. The underlying variable is not observed, the only voting information being whether the individual voted for McGovern or not.[§] The problem is to transform the linear relation between the index Z_i and the information about positions taken to obtain predicted probabilities of voting for McGovern. The probit results were obtained using a series of data drawn from the 1972 survey of the Center for Political Studies at the

---

† Because the cumulative normal transformation is nonlinear, ordinary least squares cannot generally be applied to estimate the probit model. However, we can obtain values for α and β using maximum-likelihood estimation. The use of maximum-likelihood estimation ensures that the parameter estimates will be consistent and the appropriate statistical tests can be performed. For further details, see Domencich and McFadden, op. cit.

‡ J. Aldrich and C. F. Cnudde, "Probing the Bounds of Conventional Wisdom: A Comparison of Regression, Probit, and Discriminant Analysis," *American Journal of Political Science*, vol. 19, pp. 571–608, Aug. 3, 1975.

§ Those who did not may have voted for Nixon, for a minor candidate, or abstained.

University of Michigan. The results of both the probit estimation and the comparable linear probability model regression are shown in Table 10.3. Each of the explanatory variables is actually a scale representing the individual's own view about how he or she feels about a given issue.

First, let us examine the regression coefficients. The results as given tell us the linear relationship between the estimated index Z_i and the position variables. The ratio of the estimated coefficient to the estimated standard error will approximate the normal distribution for large samples, so that the usual normal or t tests can be applied here.† An exact interpretation of the results would necessitate a more careful examination of the scaling survey techniques used in the study. However, the results do suggest that positions on federal jobs, taxation, and Vietnam, as well as one's liberal or conservative designation, serve best to explain why one may have chosen not to vote for McGovern. These results are not very different from the linear probability model results, except for the importance of the busing issue. However, the models can and do yield very different results when we interpret the exact numerical implications of the estimated coefficients. The easiest way to see this is to examine Fig. 10.3, which graphs the predicted *probability* of voting yes obtained from the probit model against the predicted probability obtained from the linear probability model. The linear probability model not only has the unfortunate property of predicting probabilities outside the 0 to 1 range, but it can give substantially different results from the probit model even within the 0 to 1 range. When we look at individual coefficients, we must be very careful in making any direct comparisons. The reason is

Table 10.3 Comparison of linear probability and probit predictions: probability of voting for McGovern, 1972

7-point issue	Probit model Z_i		Linear probability model	
	Coefficient	SE	Coefficient	SE
Federal jobs	− .375	.082	− .087	.018
Taxation	− .257	.066	− .050	.014
Vietnam	− .593	.092	− .145	.020
Marijuana	− .075	.058	− .019	.014
Busing	− .205	.083	− .067	.019
Women's rights	− .038	.046	− .010	.011
Rights of accused	− .046	.068	− .011	.015
Aid to minorities	− .136	.072	− .030	.017
Liberal or conservative	− .639	.113	− .168	.025
Constant	− .713		.303	
$N = 1130$		$R^2 = .530$		$R^2 = .347$

† The estimation procedure was a maximum-likelihood procedure; the t and normal distributions are essentially identical for $N = 1,130$.

that the normalization made in doing the probit estimation will generally lead to coefficients of an arbitrary scale. What matters for us is the relative magnitude of the coefficients, not their absolute size. For example, when the linear probability model was estimated, the liberal-conservative coefficient was 3.4 times the size of the taxation coefficient, while the ratio was only 2.5 when probit estimation was used.

How do we decide which model is appropriate? We have already seen that there are a number of undesirable properties associated with the linear probability model. But in this example we can go further by comparing measures of goodness of fit associated with the two models. Since the calculation of these measures is discussed later in the chapter we do not go into great detail here. However, when we calculate a measure of R^2 comparable to the R^2 associated with the linear probability model, the probit model clearly dominates. On net the probit model or one which is closely similar seems clearly preferable to the linear probability model. Its only deficiency is that of the added cost associated with finding and using a nonlinear estimation probit computer package.

Example 10.3 Voter turnout Another recent empirical study of voting used the 1972 Current Population Survey of the Bureau of the Census along with the 1972 survey of the Center for Political Studies at Michigan to analyze voter turnout in the 1972 general election.[†] Using a subsample of individual responses to the Michigan survey, the authors used a probit model to estimate the impact of voter registration laws on voter turnout. The estimated parameters of the probit model are exhibited in Table 10.4. The equation underlying the table describes the linear relationship between certain voting attributes and an underlying index of turnout (Z_i in our notation). To translate these results into measurements of the effect of voting attributes on the probability of turnout, the authors solved for P_i using the analog of Eq. (10.8). Since the resulting equation is nonlinear, the effect of each variable on the probability of turnout will vary depending upon the levels of each of the attribute variables. These results are described in Table 10.5.

A brief examination of Table 10.4 shows that both education and age of voters are significant determinants of turnout. In both cases, the authors added terms in the square of the variables to allow for nonlinearities in the relationship. When these variables were included, race had no independent effect on voter turnout. The second group of explanatory variables are all registration variables, and all were statistically significant at the 5 percent level. The final set of two variables were election rather than registration variables, but they also were somewhat helpful in explaining voter turnout.

---

† S. J. Rosenstone and R. E. Wolfinger, "The Effect of Registration Laws on Voter Turnout," *American Political Science Review*, vol. 72, no. 1, pp. 22–45, March 1978.

Table 10.4 Estimates of the effect of demographic variables and registration laws on turnout in 1972

Variable	Coefficient	SE
(Constant)	−2.7001	.2410
Education	.1847	.0120
Education squared	.0120	.0050
Age	.0707	.0045
Age squared	−.0006	.0001
Region	−.1371	.0413
Closing date	−.0073	.0015
Irregular office hours	−.1005	.0438
Open evening and/or Saturday	.1253	.0345
No absentee registration	−.0909	.0403
Hours polls open	.0336	.0159
Gubernatorial election	.0634	.0338
$N = 7,936$ Cases correctly predicted = 71.4%		

Note that as one measure of goodness of fit the authors used the probit model to classify individuals solely on the basis of the explanatory variable information as either having voted or not having voted. The procedure is a relatively straightforward one. The linear regression is used to predict the index of turnout Z_i for each individual. At the same time a cutoff point is determined to optimally classify voters with low Z_i's as not voting and those with high Z_i's as voting.† In this case, the probit model was able to classify 71.4 percent of the individuals correctly.

Table 10.5 The effect of registration requirements on the likelihood of an individual's voting

Probability of an individual's voting, %	30-day closing date	Irregular office hours	No Saturday or evening registration	No absentee registration
20	−6.7	−2.9	−3.8	−2.6
30	−8.1	−3.6	−4.7	−3.2
40	−8.7	−3.9	−5.1	−3.5
50	−8.7	−4.0	−5.5	−3.6
60	−8.2	−3.8	−4.9	−3.4
70	−8.1	−3.4	−3.4	−3.1
80	−5.6	−2.9	−3.4	−2.4
90	−3.3	−1.7	−2.1	−1.5

† The authors do not state how such a cutoff point was chosen.

To examine the effect of the registration provisions on the probability of voting, let us turn to Table 10.5. If we use Eq. (10.8) to solve for P_i, we find that $P_i = F(\alpha + \beta X_i)$. Table 10.5 exhibits the change in probability P_i with respect to a change in each attribute X_i.† Clearly the probability depends upon the value of the underlying index Z_i and thus implicitly on the probability of voting itself. For example, depending upon one's probability of voting otherwise, a 30-day closing date for registration (a value of 1 of the closing-date dummy variable) can decrease the probability of voting by as much as 8.7 percent or by substantially less. For each of the explanatory variables the probit results show a similar pattern. The impact of each of the voter registration variables on the probability of voting is greatest for those voters otherwise likely to vote with probability .5. This pattern is implicit in the form of the cumulative normal distribution function used in probit analysis.

10.1.3 Logit Model

The *logit model* is based on the cumulative logistic probability function and is specified as

$$P_i = F(Z_i) = F(\alpha + \beta X_i) = \frac{1}{1 + e^{-Z_i}} = \frac{1}{1 + e^{-(\alpha + \beta X_i)}} \qquad (10.9)$$

In this notation, e represents the base of natural logarithms, which is approximately equal to 2.718. P_i is the probability that an individual will make a certain choice, given knowledge of X_i. In our voting example, P_i would represent the probability that an individual will vote yes, given an income equal to X_i. To get a feeling for the cumulative logistic function, it might be useful to examine Table 10.6 and Fig. 10.5. Table 10.6 lists values of both the cumulative normal and cumulative logistic functions for various values of Z. As both the table and graph show, the logistic and probit formulations are quite similar; the only difference is that the logistic has slightly fatter tails.‡ Because it is quite similar in form to the cumulative normal function but easier to use from a computational point of view, the logit model is often used as a substitute for the probit model.

---

† We can calculate the entries in the table by differentiating P_i with respect to X_i for each attribute variable in the linear equation. In this case,

$$\frac{\partial P_i}{\partial X_i} = \frac{\partial F}{\partial Z} \frac{\partial Z}{\partial X_i} \qquad \text{or} \qquad \frac{\partial P_i}{\partial X_i} = f(Z_i)\beta$$

Here, $f(Z)$ represents the value of the standard normal density function associated with each possible value of the underlying index Z_i.

‡ E. A. Hanushek and J. E. Jackson, *Statistical Methods for Social Scientists* (New York: Academic, 1977) p. 189, point out that the logistic distribution closely resembles the t distribution with seven degrees of freedom. We have already seen in Chap. 2 that the t distribution approximates the normal as the number of degrees of freedom gets large.

Table 10.6 Values of cumulative probability functions†

Z	Cumulative normal $P_1(Z) = \dfrac{1}{\sqrt{2\pi}} \displaystyle\int_{-\infty}^{Z} e^{-s^2/2}\, ds$	Cumulative logistic $P_2(Z) = \dfrac{1}{1 + e^{-Z}}$
− 3.0	.0013	.0474
− 2.0	.0228	.1192
− 1.5	.0668	.1824
− 1.0	.1587	.2689
− .5	.3085	.3775
0	.5000	.5000
.5	.6915	.6225
1.0	.8413	.7311
1.5	.9332	.8176
2.0	.9772	.8808
3.0	.9987	.9526

† Each distribution is assumed to have zero mean and unit variance.

To show how the model specified in Eq. (10.9) can be estimated we first multiply both sides of the equation by $1 + e^{-Z_i}$ to get

$$(1 + e^{-Z_i})P_i = 1$$

Dividing by P_i, and then subtracting 1 leads to

$$e^{-Z_i} = \frac{1}{P_i} - 1 = \frac{1 - P_i}{P_i}$$

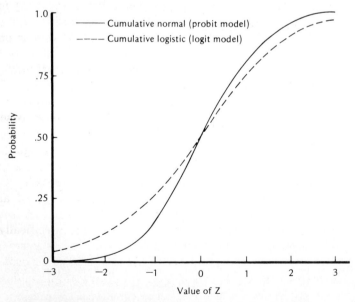

Figure 10.5 Comparison of logit and probit cumulative distributions.

By definition, however, $e^{-Z_i} = 1/e^{Z_i}$, so that

$$e^{Z_i} = \frac{P_i}{1 - P_i}$$

Now, by taking the natural logarithm of both sides,

$$Z_i = \log \frac{P_i}{1 - P_i}$$

or [from (10.9)]

$$\log \frac{P_i}{1 - P_i} = Z_i = \alpha + \beta X_i \qquad (10.10)$$

The dependent variable in this regression equation is simply the logarithm of the odds that a particular choice will be made. One important appeal of the logit model is that it transforms the problem of predicting probabilities within a (0, 1) interval to the problem of predicting the odds of an event's occurring within the range of the entire real line. The slope of the cumulative logistic distribution is greatest at $P = \frac{1}{2}$. In terms of the regression model, this implies that changes in independent variables will have their greatest impact on the probability of choosing a given option at the midpoint of the distribution. The rather low slopes near the endpoints of the distribution imply that large changes in X are necessary to bring about a small change in probability.† In our voting example, the logit model presumes that an increase in income will increase the probability of a yes vote only slightly for very low income individuals, who are unlikely to alter their vote under any conditions, and for high-income individuals, who are very likely to have voted yes before the increase in income. Only in the middle-income ranges, where individuals are more or less indifferent to voting yes or no, is the change in income likely to have a substantial impact on the probability of a yes vote.

If we were to attempt to estimate Eq. (10.10) directly, a serious difficulty would arise. If P_i happens to equal either 0 or 1, the odds, $P_i/(1 - P_i)$, will equal 0 or infinity and the logarithm of the odds will be undefined. Thus, the application of ordinary least-squares estimation to Eq. (10.10), where P_i is set equal to 1 if a given choice is made and 0 otherwise, is clearly inappropriate. The correct estimation of the logit model can best be understood by distinguishing between studies in which individual observations are the basic units of analysis and studies in which the analysis involves the use of grouped data.

Consider first the case in which information about the frequency of an event's occurring in a given subgroup of the population is available but there is no knowledge of the behavior of every individual in that subgroup. Specifically, assume that a single independent explanatory variable such as income is represented by G different values in the sample (for example, $5,000, $10,000), with n_1 individuals having income X_1, n_2 individuals having income X_2, and so

---

† The properties described hold in the probit model as well.

forth.† Also, let r_1 represent the number of times the first alternative is chosen by individuals with income X_1 (voting yes), r_2 the number of times the first alternative is chosen by individuals with income X_2, etc. Then it seems reasonable to estimate the logit model by using an estimate of the probability of a given choice *for each group* by identical individuals. Specifically, we approximate P_i as‡

$$\hat{P}_i = \frac{r_i}{n_i}$$

We can then estimate the logit probability model by using $\hat{P}_i$ to approximate P_i so that

$$\log \frac{P_i}{1 - P_i} \approx \log \frac{\hat{P}_i}{1 - \hat{P}_i}$$

and

$$\log \frac{\hat{P}_i}{1 - \hat{P}_i} = \log \frac{r_i/n_i}{1 - r_i/n_i} = \log \frac{r_i}{n_i - r_i} = \alpha^* + \beta^* X_i + \varepsilon_i \quad (10.11)$$

Equation (10.11) is linear in the parameters and can be estimated using ordinary least squares. For small samples the estimated parameters may be biased, but as the number of observations associated with each of the levels of X increases in magnitude, the results do improve. In fact, the estimated parameters are consistent when the sample *in each group* gets arbitrarily large. This requirement for consistency is more stringent than the usual requirement that the total sample size be large but is necessary to assure that the distribution of observations associated with each group X_i approaches normality.

We should note that this grouping procedure can also be used when individual observations are available. Since ordinary least squares is substantially cheaper than the more general logit estimation procedure to be described, one may opt to divide the independent variable (or variables) arbitrarily into groups and to calculate frequencies within each group. Once again, it is important to have a reasonable number of observations within each group so that the estimated frequency provides a good estimate of the true probability. To see how this procedure might apply, assume that we are analyzing voting behavior based on information about income (low, middle, high) and about size of family (small, large).§ For each voting district, we obtain data on the number of

---

† For details see J. Berkson, "Applications of the Logistic Function to Bio-Assay," *Journal of the American Statistical Association*, vol. 39, pp. 357–365, 1944; and D. R. Cox, *Analysis of Binary Data* (London: Methuen, 1970).

‡ This approximation is sensible if we take into account the fact that r_i obeys the binomial probability distribution, for which the mean frequency of occurrence is r_i/n_i.

§ This procedure is equivalent to the logit analysis of contingency tables and is described in H. Theil, "On the Estimation of Relationships Involving Qualitative Variables," *American Journal of Sociology*, vol. 76, pp. 103–154, July 1970; L. Goodman, "The Multivariate Analysis of Qualitative Data: Interactions among Multiple Classifications," *Journal of the American Statistical Association*, vol. 65, no. 329, pp. 226–256, 1970; and Hanushek and Jackson, op. cit.

registered voters voting for a given candidate associated with each of the six possible combinations of voters (small family, low income; small family, middle income; etc.). The data might be listed as follows:

$\hat{P}_1$ = fraction of low-income, small-family voters voting for candidate

$\hat{P}_2$ = fraction of low-income, large-family voters voting for candidate

$\hat{P}_3$ = fraction of middle-income, small-family voters voting for candidate

$\hat{P}_4$ = fraction of middle-income, large-family voters voting for candidate

$\hat{P}_5$ = fraction of high-income, small-family voters voting for candidate

$\hat{P}_6$ = fraction of high-income, large-family voters voting for candidate

Since there are six categories or groups defined by the six possible combinations of income and size of family, the least-squares regression will have six observations. The dependent-variable observations will be

$$\hat{Z}_1 = \log \frac{\hat{P}_1}{1 - \hat{P}_1}, \hat{Z}_2 = \log \frac{\hat{P}_2}{1 - \hat{P}_2}, \hat{Z}_3 = \log \frac{\hat{P}_3}{1 - \hat{P}_3}, \ldots$$

The independent variables in the linear regression will be a series of dummy variables defining the category to which each observation belongs. Thus, if we let

$$X_2 = \begin{cases} 1 & \text{for middle income voters,} \\ 0 & \text{otherwise} \end{cases}$$

$$X_3 = \begin{cases} 1 & \text{for high income voters} \\ 0 & \text{otherwise} \end{cases}$$

$$X_4 = \begin{cases} 1 & \text{for large family voters} \\ 0 & \text{otherwise} \end{cases}$$

the logit model will be *estimated* as

$$\log \frac{\hat{P}_i}{1 - \hat{P}_i} = \beta_1 + \beta_2 X_2 + \beta_3 X_3 + \beta_4 X_4 + \varepsilon_i \tag{10.12}$$

where $\hat{P}_i$ is the fraction of voters in each combination of income class (low, middle, high) and family size (small, large) in the sample.

Note that we have included a constant term but have omitted one dummy for each category to assure that perfect collinearity does not exist between the variables. Unlike the usual regression model, the error term arises, of course, because $\hat{P}_i$ is only an estimate of the true probability P_i.

Assuming for a moment that each $\hat{P}_i$ accurately measures the true frequency in the population, the interpretation of the logit model with grouped data is relatively straightforward. In this case,

$\hat{Z}_1 \approx Z_1 = \beta_1 =$ predicted odds of favorable voting by low-income,

small-family voters

$\hat{Z}_2 \approx Z_2 = \beta_1 + \beta_4 =$ predicted odds of favorable voting by low-income,

large-family voters

$\hat{Z}_3 \approx Z_3 = \beta_1 + \beta_2 =$ predicted odds of favorable voting by middle-income,

small-family voters

$\hat{Z}_4 \approx Z_4 = \beta_1 + \beta_2 + \beta_4 =$ predicted odds of favorable voting by middle-

income, large-family voters

$\hat{Z}_5 \approx Z_5 = \beta_1 + \beta_3 =$ predicted odds of favorable voting by high-income,

small-family voters

$\hat{Z}_6 \approx Z_6 = \beta_1 + \beta_3 + \beta_4 =$ predicted odds of favorable voting by high-income,

large-family voters

Thus, if we want to examine the impact on voting of having a large, rather than a small family, independent of income, the effect is measured by the coefficient β_4. Likewise, β_2 measures the difference in the logarithm of the odds of voting between middle- and low-income small families. The difference between middle and high income is measured by $\beta_3 - \beta_2$.

Because $\hat{P}_i$ does not equal P_i identically, there are some problems with the use of ordinary least-squares estimation in this grouped-data case. If we assume that each of the individual observations in a group is independent (and follows a binomial probability distribution), the estimated dependent variable,† $\log [r_i/(n_i - r_i)]$ will be (for large samples) approximately normally distributed with mean 0 and variance

$$V_i = \frac{n_i}{r_i(n_i - r_i)} \tag{10.13}$$

The result is that the error term implicit in the linear specification of Eq. (10.12) is heteroscedastic. The variance in each of the subgroups (six in our example) will be inversely related to the number of observations in each cell n_i and will also vary with the number of favorable votes r_i. The obvious correction for heteroscedasticity is to use weighted least squares, where each observation is multiplied by the weight $1/\sqrt{V_i}$. However, a number of other corrections have

---

† See Theil, op. cit., for details.

been proposed, mainly to help with the small-sample properties of the estimation process.†

If we wish to measure the goodness of fit associated with the grouped regression model, we can , of course, use the calculated R^2 statistic. However, a preferable statistic looks at the differences between the actual frequencies in each subgroup and the estimated frequencies obtained from the regression model. Specifically, let P_i^* be the estimated probability calculated for each observation from (10.9). Then the statistic‡

$$ s = \sum_{i=1}^{G} \frac{n_i (\hat{P}_i - P_i^*)^2}{P_i^*(1 - P_i^*)} $$

is distributed (for large samples) according to the chi-square distribution where the number of degrees of freedom is the number of subcategories G minus the number of estimated parameters.

The approximation leading to the specification of Eq. (10.12) is reasonable only when sufficient repetitions occur. In fact, when only one choice is associated with each set of explanatory variables, the left-hand side of Eq. (10.12) is undefined, so that the approximation to Eq. (10.10) is of no use. A useful rule of thumb for the application of the least-squares approximation is that for each value of X, n_i be at least equal to 5, but a more accurate rule would account for the fact that the least-squares approximation is poorest for levels of X in which the frequency of a given choice is close to 0 or 1. This can be seen in Eq. (10.13). When r_i/n_i approaches either 0 or 1, the expression for V_i gets arbitrarily large. The large variance in the frequency estimates guarantees inaccurate parameter estimates, making additional observations desirable. We should note that the approximation implicit in Eq. (10.12) is not strictly appropriate when the explanatory variable is continuous, since the continuous variable must be partitioned before the technique applied. Unfortunately, this partitioning process can introduce bias because partitioning introduces measurement error into the problem.

---

† One adjustment suggested by Cox, op. cit., and by Domencich and McFadden, op. cit., helps to improve the approximation involved in the specification given by Eq. (10.12). They suggest that the following equation be run in its place:

$$ \log \frac{r_i + \frac{1}{2}}{n_i - r_i + \frac{1}{2}} = \alpha + \beta X_i $$

An additional adjustment for heteroscedasticity is obtained if we use as weights the following estimates of the error variance:

$$ V_i^* = \frac{(n_i + 1)(n_i + 2)}{n_i(r_i + 1)(n_i - r_i + 1)} $$

Both corrections help with the small-sample properties of the estimation process but have no effect on the large-sample properties.

‡ See Theil, op. cit., and McFadden, op. cit., for details.

All these qualifications are rather discouraging, since most economic data are likely to be continuous, necessitating the use of a partitioning process. In addition, economic models are likely to contain several independent variables. With limited sample sizes, it is unlikely that sufficient repetitions will be available for groups of individuals defined over all possible combinations of attribute values, even if the attributes are qualitative rather than quantitative variables. To see this, assume that income and number of children are the two attributes which are used to predict voting behavior. If there are four income categories ($0 to $10,000; $10,000 to $20,000; $20,000 to $30,000; and $30,000 and over) and three categories representing the number of children (0, 1 or 2, 3 and over), there will be *twelve* groups of individuals (individuals with less than $10,000 in income and no children; $10,000 to $20,000 and no children, etc.).

The existence of continuous variables in models with several attributes as explanatory variables suggests that in the context of economic and business models it may be necessary to estimate a logit model in which only *one* choice is associated with each set of independent variables. Fortunately a maximum-likelihood estimation procedure which can be applied to the model in Eq. (10.12) does exist. The maximum-likelihood procedure does not necessitate that the data be grouped and thus allows for each individual observation within the sample to have a distinct probability associated with it. As in the case of the probit model, we refer the interested reader to Appendix 10.1 for a brief outline of the procedure and the statistical tests associated with it. Because it is possible to prove that a unique maximum always exists for the logit model, maximum-likelihood estimation is particularly appealing. Almost any nonlinear estimation routine will find the estimated parameters; the only question is one of computing costs. It is possible to prove that the maximum-likelihood estimation technique yields consistent parameter estimates, and the calculation of the appropriate large-sample statistics is not difficult. Thus, the only disadvantage of nonlinear logit estimation is its cost. Small-sample studies suggest that the signs (and frequently the relative magnitudes) of the estimated parameters obtained from the linear probability models and the maximum-likelihood logit estimators are usually the same. This provides an additional rationalization for the use of the linear probability model.†

---

† Essentially the same techniques described in this chapter can be applied to the study of models with a dependent variable having the property that many observations take on a single value (as in 0 dollars spent for a purchase). The remaining observations follow the usual characteristics of a continuous variable (dollars spent). Thus, the dependent is part qualitative (buy or not buy) and part quantitative (amount bought). The analysis of such a limited dependent variable is called *Tobit analysis*. It has received wide application to such problems as the study of automobile purchases, disequilibrium models of markets, and models of labor supply. For some theoretical discussion see J. Tobin, "Estimation of Relationships for Limited Dependent Variables," *Econometrica*, vol. 26, pp. 24–36, 1958; T. Amemiya, "Regression Analysis When the Dependent Variable Is Truncated Normal," *Econometrica*, vol. 41, pp. 997–1016, 1973; and J. Heckman, "The Common Structure of Statistical Models of Truncation, Sample Selection and Limited Dependent Variables and a Simple Estimator for Such Models," *Annals of Economic and Social Measurements*, vol. 5, pp. 475–492, 1976.

Example 10.4 Voting for a school budget The logit model was used to study the voting decisions of 425 individuals in a local school millage referendum in Troy, Michigan, in 1973.† The responses to the survey provide a list of attributes of voters, as well as estimates of household income and the price of education, measured as the cost to the individual of supporting an additional dollar per pupil of school spending in the community. The model takes the form

$$\log \frac{\text{Prob (yes)}}{1 - \text{Prob (yes)}} = \beta_1 + \beta_2 Z_2 + \cdots + \beta_k Z_k$$

where the Z's represent the voting attributes listed in Table 10.7 and Prob (yes) represents the probability of a voter supporting the millage referendum.‡ The estimated equation appears below, with asymptotic (large sample) standard errors in parentheses (* = significant at the 5 percent level). Note that since the observations are of individuals and not grouped, the logit model was estimated using a nonlinear maximum-likelihood estimation procedure.

$$- \underset{(3.84)}{23.15^*} + \underset{(.24)}{.24\,\text{SEX}} + \underset{(1.13)}{1.13\,\text{MAR}} + \underset{(1.47)}{1.09\,\text{OTHER}} + \underset{(.30)}{.08\,\text{A35-49}}$$

$$+ \underset{(.41)}{.61\,\text{A50-64}} + \underset{(.79)}{1.04\,\text{A65}} + \underset{(.34)}{1.44^*\text{PUB1}} + \underset{(.35)}{1.39^*\text{PUB2}}$$

$$+ \underset{(.42)}{1.30^*\text{PUB3}} + \underset{(.58)}{2.00^*\text{PUB4}} + \underset{(.79)}{2.16^*\text{PUB5}} - \underset{(.42)}{.56\,\text{PRIV}}$$

$$- \underset{(.01)}{.02^*\text{YEARS}} + \underset{(.84)}{3.07^*\text{SCHOOL}} + \underset{(.37)}{2.14^*(\log \text{INC})}$$

$$- \underset{(.44)}{1.21^*(\log \text{PRICE})}$$

The sex dummy was included to allow for the possibility that women and men might perceive the benefits and costs of educational expenditures differently. The expectation was that because women tend to bear a large share of the responsibility for child care, they would value the potential benefits associated with the educational system more highly than men. Whether women or men are more cognizant of the tax costs associated with

---

For some applications, see J. Heckman, "Shadow Prices, Market Wages and Labor Supply," *Econometrica*, vol. 42, pp. 679–694, 1974, R. C. Fair and D. M. Jaffee, "Methods of Estimation for Markets in Disequilibrium," *Econometrica*, vol. 40, pp. 597–614, 1972; and J. G. Cragg, "Some Statistical Models for Limited Dependent Variables with Application to the Demand for Durable Goods," *Econometrica*, vol. 39, pp. 829–844, 1971.

For a discussion of estimation in the context of simultaneous models with qualitative endogenous variables, see, T. Amemiya, "Multivariate Regression and Simultaneous Equation Models When the Dependent Variables Are Truncated Normal," *Econometrica*, vol. 42, pp. 999–1012, 1974.

† D. L. Rubinfeld, "Voting in a Local School Election: A Micro Analysis," *Review of Economics and Statistics*, vol. 59, no. 1, pp. 30–42, February 1977.

‡ The model shown here applies to those who actually voted in the election.

Table 10.7 Definition of variables

	1	0
SEX	If female	If male
MAR	If married with spouse present	Otherwise
OTHER	If separated, divorced, or widowed	Otherwise
A35–49	If aged 35–49	Otherwise
A50–64	If aged 50–64	Otherwise
A65 +	If aged 65 or over	Otherwise
PUB1	If 1 child is in public school	Otherwise
PUB2	If 2 children are in public school	Otherwise
PUB3	If 3 children are in public school	Otherwise
PUB4	If 4 children are in public school	Otherwise
PUB5	If 5 or more children are in public school	Otherwise
PRIV	If the family has 1 or more children in private school	Otherwise
SCHOOL	If individual is employed as a teacher (public or private)	Otherwise

YEARS = number of years living in Troy community
Log INC = natural logarithm of annual household income, dollars
Log PRICE = natural logarithm of price of public schooling, dollars

a favorable referendum outcome seemed less clear. The sex dummy coefficient was insignificant here but was significant as expected in a later election.

The effect of the age dummies is difficult to predict when income, number of children in school, and years in the community are held constant. Since we did not control for the total number of children in the household, our expectation was that as age increases in the eighteen to forty-nine range, the probability that an individual will have school-age children in the future declines and therefore the probability of voting yes should also decline. However, the results show that the age dummy coefficients were insignificant, generally with a positive sign.

The number of children in public school is perhaps the best measure for the direct benefits that households perceive from public schooling. When children are of school age, households are most likely to be aware of the costs and benefits associated with a vote for higher school taxes. The presence of at least one child in public school was expected to have a substantial positive impact on the probability of a yes vote. The presence of additional school-age children should also increase the probability of a yes vote, although we expected that, beyond a certain point, the marginal gain of reallocating the household budget toward private expenditures would outweigh the gain from public expenditures and the probability of a yes vote would decline. The presence of children in private school should have a strong negative effect, however. Families sending their children to private school are likely to perceive little benefit from the public school system while facing a substantial tax bill associated with it.

Each of the dummy-variable coefficients representing public school children was highly significant. The results suggest that the presence of the first public school child substantially raises the probability that the individual will vote yes in the election. After the first child, the probability of a yes vote remained roughly constant until the fourth and fifth school children were present, at which point it again increased substantially. The election results also suggest that in Troy the demand for educational expenditures per child actually levels off when the number of children grows to four or more, not an unreasonable result, given the large demands for private goods which arise with increased family size.

The private school dummy coefficient was negative but insignificant in the May election. This suggests that the presence of children in private school does increase the probability of a no vote, but the magnitude of this effect is small relative to the effect associated with the presence of at least one child in public school.

The number of years in residence was also included as an explanatory variable in the logit model. The results suggest that, to the extent that the other things (such as life-cycle stage) are constant, as the time of residence increases, voters tend to vote no, either in criticism of the educational system or possibly in opposition to the growing burden of local taxes.

The highly significant school dummy was included to account for the fact that the sample of respondents was overrepresented by school teachers and their spouses. As expected, school teachers are more likely to vote yes in the election relative to individuals with similar non-occupational attributes.

The income variable serves as a measure of the capacity of households to consume both private and public goods. On the assumption that local school education is a normal good, we expected, other things being equal, that income and the demand for public schools would be positively correlated. In the context of our voting model, this suggests a positive relationship between income and the probability of a yes vote. In the estimated equations the income variable was positive and significant, consistent with a positive income elasticity of demand for education.

As the price of schooling rises, other things being equal, we expected that the quantity of educational expenditures per pupil demanded would fall, as would the probability of voting yes in the election. Despite the fact that property tax payments are positively correlated with income, we found that the coefficient of the price of schooling variable was negative and significant. This result is consistent with a negative price elasticity of the demand for education.

Example 10.5 Predicting college-going behavior In a recent study of college choice,[†] a model was constructed to predict whether students attending college would choose to live on campus or to commute. This is a binary-choice problem for which the logit probability model was used. The goal was to predict the odds of a student attending college living on campus, conditional upon information about *individual* attributes and attributes of the particular college. The model is

$$\log \frac{P_i}{1 - P_i} = \beta_1 I_1 + \beta_2 I_2 + \beta_3 I_3 + \beta_4 I_4 + \beta_5 D + \beta_6 S + \beta_7 R$$

where P_i = probability that student will choose to live on campus
Y = logarithm (base 10) of family income
X = distance from home to campus
$I_1 = (100 - X)(5 - Y)/500$
$I_2 = X(5 - Y)/500$
$I_3 = (100 - X)Y/500$
$I_4 = XY/500$
D = percentage of students at college who live on campus
S = dummy variable representing sex of student; $S = 1$ if female and 0 otherwise
R = dummy variable representing residency preference; $R = 1$ if students said they preferred to live on campus and 0 otherwise

The logit model was estimated using the maximum-likelihood nonlinear estimation routine and a sample of students who actually attended college.[‡] The sample was part of the 1966 SCOPE survey, and consisted of a total of 10,600 college respondents. The estimation results (with standard errors in parentheses) are[§]

$$\log \frac{P_i}{1 - P_i} = -\underset{(1.73)}{16.59} I_1 - \underset{(.90)}{8.680} I_2 - \underset{(.40)}{.6277} I_3 + \underset{(.70)}{10.81} I_4 + \underset{(.0023)}{.01929} D$$

$$-\underset{(.11)}{.04789} S + \underset{(.16)}{1.470} R$$

The distance-income interaction variables are somewhat difficult to interpret on their own, but their import can be seen in the graph of Fig. 10.6, which shows that the probability of living on campus increases with distance from campus and is higher at all distances for the students with higher family incomes. The probability of campus residency increases with the percentage of students living on campus in the absence of monetary con-

---

[†] M. G. Kohn, C. F. Manski, and D. S. Mundel, "An Empirical Investigation of Factors Which Influence College Going Behavior," *Rand Corporation Report, R1470-NSF*, September 1974.

[‡] The ordinary least-squares approximation was not used here most likely because of the difficulty of grouping or categorizing individuals according to the set of attributes given. Despite the large sample size, the seven explanatory variables would have necessitated a substantial number of groups and would have involved arbitrary partitioning of the indices I_i and the D variable.

[§] We omit the 'hat' over the predicted value to simplify the presentation and will continue to do so in Parts II and III.

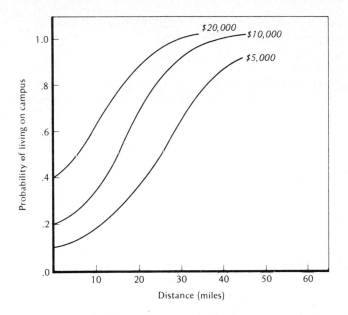

Figure 10.6 Probability of living on campus (for males attending a college with 50 percent dormitory capacity who prefer to live on campus).

straints. Finally, there is a slightly higher, but insignificant, probability of living on campus for males than females.

The interpretation of the individual estimated parameters must be done with care, since the left-hand side of the equation is the logarithm of the odds of choice, not the actual probability. For example, a 1 percent increase in the percentage of students living on campus at a given college will lead to an increase of .019 in the logarithm of the odds that the individual will choose to reside on that campus. To interpret the effect of a change in D on the probability of campus residence, we need to solve for the change in probability ΔP as follows:

$$\Delta \log \frac{P_i}{1 - P_i} = .019 \, \Delta D$$

To simplify, we utilize the fact that for any continuous variable x,† $\Delta \log x \approx \Delta x / x$, and the fact that $\log (x/y) = \log x - \log y$. Then

$$\Delta \log \frac{P_i}{1 - P_i} \approx \left(\frac{1}{P_i} + \frac{1}{1 - P_i} \right) \Delta P_i = \frac{1}{P_i(1 - P_i)} \, \Delta P_i$$

Since we have chosen $\Delta D = 1$, it follows that

$$\Delta P_i \approx .019 \left[P_i(1 - P_i) \right]$$

We find that the change in probability is a function of the probability itself. If P_i were equal to .5 , for example, ΔP_i would equal .076. Perhaps the most

---

† When x is a dummy variable, this approximation is no longer appropriate.

useful single value of P_i to choose for this interpretation is the mean, but examination of the responses in campus choice for numerous points of the probability distribution can be illuminating.

The campus choice model can easily be used to make predictions. Assume for example that we wish to predict the probability that a male student whose family income is $6,000 and who has stated a preference for living on campus rather than at home will indeed live on campus. We will assume that he attends a university located very near his home at which 50 percent of the students live on campus. To predict the odds of living on campus, we simply evaluate the right-hand side of the estimated equation:

$$I_1 = .2(5 - \log_{10} 6000) = .2444 \qquad D = 50$$

$$I_3 = .2(\log_{10} 6000) = .7556 \qquad S = 0$$

$$I_2 = I_4 = 0 \qquad R = 1$$

The calculated logarithm (base e) of the odds is -2.10. Taking antilogarithms and solving, we find that $P_i = .108$. Thus we predict that the student will live on campus with a probability of .108. We might wish to see how the probability of the student's living on campus would change as the distance between the university and home increased. Calculating P_i for different values of distance X, we would obtain:

Distance	0	10	20	30	40	50	60	70
Probability of living on campus	.108	.258	.500	.742	.892	.960	.986	.995

Notice that once the student's home is more than 50 miles from the campus, he will almost certainly choose to live on campus.

10.1.4 Forecasting

Forecasting with models that have a dichotomous dependent variable is somewhat more difficult than the continuous dependent variable case. As a general rule, the models developed in this chapter can be applied directly toward forecasting the probability (or the odds) that a given choice will be made. In the voting case, for example, assume that whatever the choice of specification, the predicted probability associated with one new individual observation is .8. We can interpret .8 as measuring our best forecast of the probability that an individual with a given income will vote yes in an election.† Of course, if we are

† Assume, for example, that our objective is to forecast so as to minimize the variance of the error of forecast. As before, let P equal the probability that an event occurs ($Y = 1$) and $1 - P$ equal the probability that the event does not occur ($Y = 0$). Let $\hat{P}$ be the forecast value of the probability that a given choice will be made. (Assume, for the moment, that our model is known so that the estimated probability is the true probability of the event occurring.) Then the error of

forecasting the *explicit* behavior of a single individual, a forecast of .8 can never be strictly correct.† If we wish to forecast individual choices, we are likely to predict an outcome of 1 (vote yes) if the predicted probability is greater than .5 and 0 if the predicted probability is less than .5.

This discussion suggests a problem with the use of R^2 as a measure of the goodness of fit of a linear equation. In the classical regression model R^2 can range in value between 0 and 1, with a value of close to 1 indicating a good fit. We have seen, however, that the dichotomous dependent variable model is not likely to yield an R^2 close to 1. Only in the extreme case that all predicted probabilities are either 0 or 1 can such a result possibly occur. Thus, if we are to use R^2 as a measure of goodness of fit, we must realize‡ that its upper limit is likely to be substantially less than 1. If we were to assume, for example, that the true probabilities of an event occurring were uniformly distributed across a given interval,§ it is possible to show¶ an upper bound for R^2 of $\frac{1}{3}$. Thus, it is not surprising that one who estimates a linear probability model is likely to obtain‖ a low R^2.

10.2 MULTIPLE-CHOICE MODELS

We now consider generalizing the results of the previous section to cases in which individuals make choices from three or more alternatives. (For example, an individual might choose to vote yes, vote no, or abstain.) In each case, we

---

forecast will be $1 - \hat{P}$ if the event occurs, and $0 - \hat{P}$ otherwise. The variance of the error of forecast is

$$\sigma_e^2 = P(1 - \hat{P})^2 + (1 - P)(-\hat{P})^2$$

Minimizing σ_e^2 with respect to $\hat{P}$ yields $\hat{P} = P$. Thus, to minimize the error of forecast, or equivalently to maximize the correlation between Y and the predicted probabilities, we choose our forecast to be the true probability of occurrence each time, rather than alternating between values of 0 and 1. The same general result would hold when we expand our deviation to include the effect of errors associated with the estimation and prediction processes.

  † It will be accurate only in the sense that it reflects the individual's uncertainty about a choice to be made.

  ‡ This issue is discussed in D. G. Morrison, "Upper Bounds for Correlations between Binary Outcomes and Probabilistic Predictions," *Journal of the American Statistical Association*, vol. 67, 1972; and J. Neter and E. S. Maynes, "Correlation Coefficient with a 0, 1 Dependent Variable," *Journal of the American Statistical Association*, vol. 65, pp. 501–509, 1970.

  § In the example given in the text the distribution of probabilities would result from an underlying distribution of the independent explanatory variable X.

  ¶ These results are described in Morrison, op. cit.

  ‖ There are, of course, alternative measures of goodness of fit for such models, but they are too involved to discuss at this point. One useful measure is the average conditional entropy as described by H. Theil in *Economics and Informational Theory* (Chicago: Rand McNally, 1967, and Amsterdam: North-Holland, 1967).

assume that all choices are mutually exclusive. There are several ways in which to analyze this problem, each dependent upon the statistical assumptions made and upon whether or not a natural ranking can be associated with each of the possible choices. We focus here on the case in which alternatives are unranked.†

First, consider the extension of the linear probability model to the multiple-choice case. If there are three choices $j = 1, 2, 3$, we would write

$$P_{1i} = \alpha_1 + \beta_1 X_i \qquad P_{2i} = \alpha_2 + \beta_2 X_i \qquad P_{3i} = \alpha_3 + \beta_3 X_i \qquad (10.14)$$

P_{ij} is the probability that individual i will choose the jth option, while X_i is the value of X for the ith individual. It appears reasonable to estimate each of the three equations in the model by ordinary least squares. In each case the dependent variable utilized will equal 1 if the choices is actually made and 0 otherwise. In practice it is not necessary to run all three of the linear probability regressions. Since the estimated probabilities are constrained to sum to 1, the estimated intercepts sum to 1 and the slope parameters sum to 0. To prove this, we use the fact that every observation is assigned to one and only one group. Then,

$$P_{1i} + P_{2i} + P_{3i} = 1 \qquad \text{for each } i$$

After averaging over all observations in the group, it follows that

$$\bar{P}_1 + \bar{P}_2 + \bar{P}_3 = 1$$

where $\bar{P}_j$ is the mean probability of choice j.. First examine the sum of the least-squares slope estimates:

$$\hat{\beta}_1 + \hat{\beta}_2 + \hat{\beta}_3 = \frac{\Sigma(P_{1i} - \bar{P}_1)(X_i - \bar{X})}{\Sigma(X_i - \bar{X})^2} + \frac{\Sigma(P_{2i} - \bar{P}_2)(X_i - \bar{X})}{\Sigma(X_i - \bar{X})^2}$$

$$+ \frac{\Sigma(P_{3i} - \bar{P}_3)(X_i - \bar{X})}{\Sigma(X_i - \bar{X})^2}$$

$$= \frac{\Sigma(P_{1i} + P_{2i} + P_{3i})(X_i - \bar{X}) - (\bar{P}_1 + \bar{P}_2 + \bar{P}_3)\Sigma(X_i - \bar{X})}{\Sigma(X_i - \bar{X})^2}$$

$$= \frac{\Sigma(X_i - \bar{X}) - \Sigma(X_i - \bar{X})}{\Sigma(X_i - \bar{X})^2} = 0$$

On the other hand, the intercepts sum to 1, since

$$\hat{\alpha}_1 + \hat{\alpha}_2 + \hat{\alpha}_3 = (\bar{P}_1 - \hat{\beta}_1\bar{X}) + (\bar{P}_2 - \hat{\beta}_2\bar{X}) + (\bar{P}_3 - \hat{\beta}_3\bar{X})$$

$$= (\bar{P}_1 + \bar{P}_2 + \bar{P}_3) - \bar{X}(\hat{\beta}_1 + \hat{\beta}_2 + \hat{\beta}_3) = 1$$

---

† In the case of ranked alternatives, it is possible to estimate a scale or set of scores associated with the available choices.

Therefore,

$$\hat{P}_{1i} + \hat{P}_{2i} + \hat{P}_{3i} = \left(\hat{\alpha}_1 + \hat{\beta}_1 X_i\right) + \left(\hat{\alpha}_2 + \hat{\beta}_2 X_i\right) + \left(\hat{\alpha}_3 + \hat{\beta}_3 X_i\right)$$

$$= \left(\hat{\alpha}_1 + \hat{\alpha}_2 + \hat{\alpha}_3\right) + \left(\hat{\beta}_1 + \hat{\beta}_2 + \hat{\beta}_3\right) X_i = 1$$

Thus, we need to run only two of the three least-squares regressions. A solution for the parameters of the third equations follows immediately.

If the X variables in each equation are not identical, the analysis becomes more difficult. The estimation process will not guarantee that the probabilities sum to 1, and ordinary least squares is no longer the most appropriate technique. A useful approach to this problem is provided by Zellner and Lee, who propose that a generalized least-squares estimation procedure be used to account for the correlation between the error terms associated with each equation in the multiple-choice model.†

The extension of the logit model in a manner analogous to that of the linear probability model is quite promising.‡ To extend the binary-choice logit model to the three-choice case, for example, we write

$$\log \frac{P_2}{P_1} = \alpha_{21} + \beta_{21} X \qquad \log \frac{P_3}{P_1} = \alpha_{31} + \beta_{31} X \qquad \log \frac{P_3}{P_2} = \alpha_{32} + \beta_{32} X$$

$$(10.15)$$

The subscript i, designating individual observations, has been dropped for notational simplicity. In this case, P_j, $j = 1, 2, 3$ indicates the probability that the jth choice will be made. Each equation presumes that the logarithm of the odds of one choice relative to a second choice is a linear function of the attribute X. These odds are dependent on the odds associated with the remaining two equations only in the sense that the system must be constrained so that the sum of the individual probabilities equals 1. As in the linear probability model, it is unnecessary to estimate each of the three equations separately. We can simplify matters by accounting for the fact that the choice of logit form forces constraints on the model which reduces the number of parameters to be estimated from six to four. To see why this is true, notice that

$$\log \frac{P_3}{P_2} = \log \frac{P_3}{P_1} + \log \frac{P_1}{P_2} = \log \frac{P_3}{P_1} - \log \frac{P_2}{P_1}$$

$$= (\alpha_{31} + \beta_{31} X) - (\alpha_{21} + \beta_{21} X) = (\alpha_{31} - \alpha_{21}) + (\beta_{31} - \beta_{21}) X$$

---

† See A. Zellner and T. H. Lee, "Joint Estimation of Relationships Involving Discrete Random Variables," *Econometrica*, vol. 33, pp. 382–394, April 1965.

‡ See McFadden, op. cit.; H. Theil, "A Multinomial Extension of the Linear Logit Model," *International Economic Review*, vol. 10, pp. 251–259, 1969; H. Theil, "On the Extension of Relationships Involving Qualitative Variables," *American Journal of Sociology*, vol. 76, pp. 103–154, 1970; and Nerlove and Press, op. cit. The probit extension is also possible. See, for example, J. Aitchison and S. Silvey, "The Generalization of Probit Analysis to the Case of Multiple Responses," *Biometrika*, vol. 44, pp. 131–140, 1957.

This creates two additional parameter constraints:

$$\alpha_{32} = \alpha_{31} - \alpha_{21} \qquad \beta_{32} = \beta_{31} - \beta_{21}$$

It is somewhat easier to view the logit model's form if we redefine all the unknown parameters as

$$\alpha_{21} = \alpha_2 - \alpha_1 \qquad \alpha_{31} = \alpha_3 - \alpha_1 \qquad \alpha_{32} = \alpha_3 - \alpha_2$$
$$\beta_{21} = \beta_2 - \beta_1 \qquad \beta_{31} = \beta_3 - \beta_1 \qquad \beta_{32} = \beta_3 - \beta_2 \qquad (10.16)$$

Then the model system of Eq. (10.15) can be rewritten

$$\log \frac{P_2}{P_1} = (\alpha_2 - \alpha_1) + (\beta_2 - \beta_1)X$$

$$\log \frac{P_3}{P_1} = (\alpha_3 - \alpha_1) + (\beta_3 - \beta_1)X \qquad (10.17)$$

$$\log \frac{P_3}{P_2} = (\alpha_3 - \alpha_2) + (\beta_3 - \beta_2)X$$

Since the parameters of the third equation can be calculated once we know the parameters of the first two equations, the third equation need not be estimated. Assume first that sufficient repetitions are available so that we can use the ordinary least-squares approximation to the correct estimation procedure. Then we proceed by using ordinary least squares to estimate the following two equations (i refers to each one of the k levels of X for which repetitions are available, not to the individual observations):

$$\log \frac{r_{2i}/n_i}{r_{1i}/n_i} = \log \frac{r_{2i}}{r_{1i}} = (\alpha_2 - \alpha_1) + (\beta_2 - \beta_1)X_i$$

$$\log \frac{r_{3i}/n_i}{r_{1i}/n_i} = \log \frac{r_{3i}}{r_{1i}} = (\alpha_3 - \alpha_1) + (\beta_3 - \beta_1)X_i \qquad (10.18)$$

The estimated parameters will determine the effect of changes in X on the logarithm of the ratios of the probabilities, which is sufficient for some uses of the model. If actual magnitudes are needed, one must take into account the constraint that the estimated probabilities must sum to 1. This can be done by renormalizing the estimated parameter values after the initial least-squares regression has been run. There are two difficulties associated with such a procedure. First, the errors are likely to be heteroscedastic, just as in the binary-choice model. A correction analogous to the one described previously can be applied to deal with this problem. Second, the cross-equation error correlation ought to be accounted for directly in the estimation process. As described before, this can be accomplished by the application of a form of generalized least-squares regression.†

---

† See Zellner and Lee, op. cit., and Theil, op. cit.

If sufficient repetitions are not available, a generalized version of the nonlinear maximum-likelihood procedure must be used. Once again the derivation of the estimator is not difficult, nor is the process of finding the maximum, but there is a large computing cost associated with the procedure. If computational costs are not a problem, the maximum-likelihood procedure should be considered desirable because it guarantees consistent parameter estimates and correct large-sample statistics.

Example 10.6 Occupational attainment In a recent study a multiple logit model was constructed to analyze occupational attainment of individuals.[†] The object was to predict the relative probability that an individual is in each of five occupational categories, professional, white collar, craft, blue collar, or menial, on the basis of individual's race, sex, education, and labor-market experience; 1,000 observations were used from years 1960 and 1970, each pertaining to a full-time working member of the labor force. The following model was estimated:

$$\log \frac{P_2}{P_1} = \alpha_{21} + \beta_{21}E_i + \gamma_{21}X_i + \delta_{21}R_i + \theta_{21}S_i$$

$$\log \frac{P_3}{P_1} = \alpha_{31} + \beta_{31}E_i + \gamma_{31}X_i + \delta_{31}R_i + \theta_{31}S_i$$

$$\log \frac{P_4}{P_1} = \alpha_{41} + \beta_{41}E_i + \gamma_{41}X_i + \delta_{41}R_i + \theta_{41}S_i$$

$$\log \frac{P_5}{P_1} = \alpha_{51} + \beta_{51}E_i + \gamma_{51}X_i + \delta_{51}R_i + \theta_{51}S_i$$

where subscript 1 = menial occupation
     subscript 2 = blue-collar occupation
     subscript 3 = craft occupation
     subscript 4 = white-collar occupation
     subscript 5 = professional occupation
     E_i = years of schooling of individual i
     X_i = years of work experience of individual i (age $- E - 5$)
     R_i = race of individual i (1 if white, 0 if black)
     S_i = sex of individual i (1 if male, 0 if female)
Statements for $\log (P_3/P_2)$, etc., can be derived from the above equations; for example,

$$\alpha_{32} = \alpha_{31} - \alpha_{21} \qquad \beta_{32} = \beta_{31} - \beta_{21}$$

The estimated coefficients are given in Table 10.8.

The estimation results demonstrate that more education makes it more likely for one to be in a higher-numbered occupation. Presumably, this is

† P. Schmidt and R. P. Strauss, "The Prediction of Occupation Using Multiple Logit Models," *International Economic Review*, vol. 16, no. 2, pp. 471–486, 1975.

Table 10.8 Estimated coefficients and t ratios†

Dependent variable	Constant		Education		Experience		Race		Sex	
	Coefficient	t ratio	Coefficient	t ratio	Coefficient	t ratio	Coefficient	t ratio	Coefficient	t ratio
1960‡										
$\log (P_2/P_1)$	1.293	2.18	−.1238	−2.71	−.02432	−2.74	1.244	4.46	.7988	3.23
$\log (P_3/P_1)$	−4.086	−4.56	.0490	.92	−.00957	−.94	2.747	5.02	2.138	5.34
$\log (P_4/P_1)$	−3.358	−4.05	.2163	4.17	−.01682	−1.70	2.8517	5.11	−.8087	−3.14
$\log (P_5/P_1)$	−6.025	−7.11	.4128	7.59	−.00126	−.12	1.879	3.83	.2263	.80
$\log (P_3/P_2)$	−5.379	−6.78	.1728	4.11	.01475	1.85	1.5030	2.85	1.3395	3.61
$\log (P_4/P_2)$	−4.651	−6.26	.3401	7.94	.00750	.95	1.6074	2.93	−1.6075	−7.62
$\log (P_5/P_2)$	−7.318	−9.09	.5366	11.66	.02306	2.72	.6347	1.32	−.5725	−2.33
$\log (P_4/P_3)$	.7280	.76	.1673	3.58	−.00725	−.80	.1044	.14	−2.947	−8.00
$\log (P_5/P_3)$	−1.939	−2.05	.3638	7.58	.00831	.89	−.8683	−1.31	−1.912	−4.93
$\log (P_5/P_4)$	−2.667	−3.11	.1965	4.69	.01556	1.86	−.9727	−1.45	1.035	4.66
1970‡										
$\log (P_2/P_1)$	1.056	1.56	−.1239	−2.53	−.01491	−1.75	.7000	2.32	1.2519	5.15
$\log (P_3/P_1)$	−3.769	−4.18	−.0014	−.03	.00776	.80	1.4575	3.35	3.1117	6.56
$\log (P_4/P_1)$	−3.305	−4.22	.2254	4.27	.00300	.35	1.7624	4.27	−.5233	−2.22
$\log (P_5/P_1)$	−5.959	−7.51	.4292	7.96	.00779	.88	.9758	2.62	.6557	2.65
$\log (P_3/P_2)$	−4.825	−6.14	.1225	2.86	.02268	2.85	.7575	1.90	1.8598	4.02
$\log (P_4/P_2)$	−4.361	−6.25	.3493	7.69	.01792	2.43	1.0624	2.60	−1.775	−8.35
$\log (P_5/P_2)$	−7.015	−10.03	.5531	11.89	.02270	3.02	.2758	.77	−.5962	−2.62
$\log (P_4/P_3)$	.4640	.52	.2268	4.57	−.00476	−.56	.3049	.59	−3.635	−7.97
$\log (P_5/P_3)$	−2.190	−2.49	.4306	8.71	.00002	.00	−.4817	−1.03	−2.456	−5.30
$\log (P_5/P_4)$	−2.654	−3.77	.2038	4.95	.00478	.67	−.7866	−1.77	1.179	5.96

†Ratio of the coefficient to the asymptotic error.

‡Group 5 = professional, 4 = white collar, 3 = craft, 2 = blue collar, 1 = menial.

what one expects; education enables one to move up the job scale. The only exception is that more education makes it less likely for one to be in a blue-collar position than a menial position. The effects of labor-market experience are much less strong across occupations and indicate that blue-collar workers tend to have little experience while professionals tend to have much more experience.

The results for sex are fairly apparent. If we order the occupations as follows:

White collar
Menial
Professional
Blue collar
Craft

then, other things being held constant, being *female* (male) makes one more likely to be in any occupational group relative to any other occupational group *lower* (higher) on the list.

Finally, if we order the occupations as follows:

Menial
Blue collar
Craft, professional
White collar

then being *black* (white) makes it more likely to be in any group relative to any other group *lower* (higher) on the list. Essentially what these results show is that being black makes it more likely to be in one of the less desirable groups—menial and blue collar. Furthermore, the worst discrimination is encountered in white-collar positions, not, as some might have expected, in the craft positions.

A final point worth noting is the intertemporal change of the race and sex variables. Movements toward zero represent decreases in discrimination. With this in mind, it is interesting to note that the race coefficient decreased in 9 out of 10 equations, while the sex coefficient increased in 9 out of 10 equations. While this suggests a decrease in occupational differences due to race and an increase in occupational differences due to sex, the reader is warned that none of the changes is significant at the 5 percent level.

There are a number of possible extensions of the probit model, but the one which is somewhat distinctive applies to models in which there is a known ordering to the categories associated with the dependent variable.† The model is

---

† This technique is discussed in R. D. McKelvey and W. Zavoina, "A Statistical Model for the Analysis of Ordinal Level Dependent Variables," *Journal of Mathematical Sociology*, vol. 4, pp. 103–120, 1975; and E. A. Hanushek and J. E. Jackson, *Statistical Methods for Social Scientists* (New York: Academic, 1977).

a straightforward generalization of the probit model discussed earlier. Assume, for example, that we are studying the voting process in which three parties offer candidates for office. The first candidate is conservative, the second is liberal, and the third is a socialist. In order to study the voting behavior of individuals, we might assume that there is an underlying index Z for each individual which measures (from their viewpoint) the extent to which each candidate feels that one ought to rely on the competitive market system. Assume that the actual observed dependent variable is measured as $Y_i = 3$ if conservative, 2 liberal, and 1 if socialist. Then the extended probit model assumes that there are cutoff points Z^* and Z^{**} which define the relationship between the observed and unobserved dependent variables. Specifically, in the case of a single explanatory variable, $Z_i = \alpha + \beta X_i$ (as before), and

$$
Y_i = \begin{cases} 3 & \text{if } Z_i \geq Z^{**} \\ 2 & \text{if } Z^* < Z_i < Z^{**} \\ 1 & \text{if } Z_i \leq Z^* \end{cases}
$$

As in the two-category probit model, the parameters will generally be estimated using a maximum-likelihood nonlinear estimation routine. While little is known about the small-sample properties of this estimation procedure, it is relatively straightforward to calculate the large-sample or asymptotic standard errors associated with each estimated coefficient. Since the technique is maximum likelihood and normality is assumed, it follows that the ratio of the estimated coefficient to the standard error follows the normal distribution, so that standard normal (as opposed to t) tests can be applied to test the significance of individual coefficients. There is also a test of the overall significance of the probit model analogous to an F test (actually the test uses the chi-square distribution) but we shall not go into the details here.

Example 10.7 Congressional vote on Medicare McKelvey and Zavoina used the multinomial model to analyze congressional voting on the 1965 Medicare bill.[†] The bill, which was reported by the Ways and Means Committee of the House of Representatives provided for a form of compulsory health insurance. However, before the bill was reported out by the committee a motion to recommit and thus weaken the bill was rejected. The authors analyzed votes on these two separate occasions to determine an indicator or index of each congressman's position on Medicare. There were three voting combinations which were the focus of the study. First, the greatest support position was from those congressman who voted against recommital and for passage of the bill. The second intermediate position was taken by those who voted for recommital and for passage, while the weakest position was by those who voted for recommital and against

---

† McKelvey and Zavoina, op. cit.

passage. The explanatory variables used were as follows:

$$\text{Party} = \begin{cases} 1 & \text{if Republican} \\ 0 & \text{if Democrat} \end{cases} \qquad \text{Region} = \begin{cases} 1 & \text{if South} \\ 0 & \text{otherwise} \end{cases}$$

Employment = % unemployed in the congressional district

Old = % over 65

Population = population density, thousands per square mile

Table 10.9 shows the results of estimating the model using probit analysis. As a means of comparison the data were also used to estimate a linear regression model in which the dependent variable was VOTE = 2 if strongly for Medicare, 1 if weakly for, and 0 if against. Because of the nature of the probit model, the regression and probit coefficients cannot be compared directly. The regression coefficients measure the change in the measured dependent variable associated with a change in the independent variable. These coefficients would, of course, change, if we were to rescale the dependent variable (2, 4, 6, for example). The coefficients of the probit model, on the other hand, measure the change in the *underlying* scale of Medicare preference, and thus the change in the probability of voting for Medicare, associated with a change in the independent variable. The outcome is that the magnitude of the resulting coefficients are not directly comparable. However, it is instructive to compare the relative magnitudes, the levels of significance, and the overall fit of each of the models.

While there are a number of ways to compare the resulting coefficients, the authors chose one which is very suitable. They reestimated each model after normalizing each variable to have zero mean and unit variance. The resulting standardized coefficients (the beta coefficients described in Chapter 4) are comparable. What is especially interesting to note is that the relative importance and significance of the variable does vary when the probit model is used as opposed to the regression model. In the regression analysis, party and region are by far the most important predictors of stance on Medicare, while in the probit analysis employment and especially population become much more important.

Table 10.9 Comparison of regression and probit analysis

| | Regression analysis | | | | Probit analysis | | | |
| | Coefficient | Standardized coefficient | Ratio† | R^2 | Coefficient | Standardized coefficient | Ratio† | R^2 |
Variables								
Party	−1.142	−.640	17.67	.52	−2.397	−.382	12.3	.88
Region	−.747	−.409	11.15		−1.730	−.269	8.9	
Old	.013	.003	.11		−.001	−.000	.0	
Employment	.055	.131	3.75		.204	.136	4.6	
Population	.004	.055	1.52		.192	.703	3.3	

†This represents the ratio of the coefficient to the asymptotic standard error.

In fact, population was insignificant at the 5 percent level in the regression analysis.

Which analytical technique is preferable? Since the linear regression model here has essentially the same defects as the linear probability model discussed earlier, probit is preferable. Indeed, if we were to compare the models on the basis of goodness of fit (R^2), probit would clearly dominate. The R^2 statistic calculated for the probit model measures the portion of the variation in the underlying scale explained by the model and is thus roughly comparable to its linear regression counterpart.

APPENDIX 10.1 MAXIMUM-LIKELIHOOD ESTIMATION OF THE LOGIT AND PROBIT MODELS

When using either the probit or the logit model with individual observations the most suitable estimation technique is that of maximum likelihood. To keep our discussion specific, assume that we wish to estimate the parameters of the logit model†

$$P_i = \frac{1}{1 + e^{-(\alpha + \beta X_i)}} \tag{A10.1}$$

Recall that the individual P_i are not observed; instead we have information for each observation on whether the first choice, e.g., candidate, was selected or whether the second was selected. Thus, the measured dependent variable is $Y_i = 1$ if the first choice is made and 0 if the second choice is made. Our objective is to find parameter estimators for α and β which make it most likely that the pattern of choices in the sample would have occurred. If we assume that the first candidate is chosen n_1 times and the second n_2 times ($n_1 + n_2 = N$), and if we order the data so that the first n_1 observations are associated with voting for the first candidate, then the likelihood function that we wish to maximize has the form

$$L = \text{Prob}\,(Y_1, \ldots, Y_N) = \text{Prob}\,(Y_1) \cdots \text{Prob}\,(Y_N) \tag{A10.2}$$

Note that we are assuming that each of the individual observations is independent of each other observation. Now, by taking into account the fact that the probability of the second candidate's being chosen is equal to 1 minus the probability that the first candidate is chosen, and using Π to represent the

---

† Maximum-likelihood estimation of the probit model is essentially similar to that of the logit model, except, of course, that the P_i represent the probabilities associated with the cumulative normal rather than the cumulative logistic probability function.

product of a number of factors, the likelihood function reduces to

$$L = P_1 \cdots P_{n_1}(1 - P_{n_1+1}) \cdots (1 - P_N) = \prod_{i=1}^{n_1} P_i \prod_{i=n_1+1}^{N} (1 - P_i)$$

$$= \prod_{i=1}^{N} P_i^{Y_i}(1 - P_i)^{(1-Y_i)}$$

The last expression follows because $Y_i = 1$ for the first n_1 observations, and 0 for the last n_2 observations.

As in Appendix 2.1, we choose to maximize the logarithm of L, rather than L itself, and do so by substituting for the logistic probability function from Eq. (A10.1). Note first that

$$1 - P_i = 1 - \frac{1}{1 + e^{-(\alpha + \beta X_i)}} = \frac{1 + e^{-(\alpha + \beta X_i)} - 1}{1 + e^{-(\alpha + \beta X_i)}}$$

$$= \frac{+e^{-\alpha + \beta X_i}}{1 + e^{-(\alpha + \beta X_i)}} = \frac{1}{1 + (1/e^{-(\alpha + \beta X_i)})} = \frac{1}{1 + e^{\alpha + \beta X_i}} \quad (A10.3)$$

Then
$$\log L = \sum_{i=1}^{n_1} \log P_i + \sum_{i=n_1+1}^{N} \log (1 - P_i)$$

To obtain the slope estimators $\hat{\alpha}$ and $\hat{\beta}$ we differentiate $\log L$ with respect to α and β, set the result equal to zero, and solve:

$$\frac{\partial(\log L)}{\partial \alpha} = \sum_{i=1}^{n} \frac{\partial P_i / \partial \alpha}{P_i} - \sum_{i=n_1+1}^{N} \frac{\partial P_i / \partial \alpha}{1 - P_i} = 0$$

$$\frac{\partial(\log L)}{\partial \beta} = \sum_{i=1}^{n} \frac{\partial P_i / \partial \beta}{P_i} - \sum_{i=n_1+1}^{N} \frac{\partial P_i / \partial \beta}{1 - P_i} = 0$$

In general, these two equations can be solved to obtain estimators of α and β. Since the equations are nonlinear, however, they must be solved using one of the techniques described in Chapter 9.

The maximum-likelihood estimation procedure has a number of desirable statistical properties. All parameter estimators are consistent and also efficient asymptotically, i.e., for large samples. In addition, all parameter estimators are known to be (asymptotically) normal, so that the analog of the regression t test can be applied. In this case the ratio of the estimated coefficient to its estimated standard error follows a normal distribution. If we wish to test the significance of all or a subset of the coefficients in the logit or probit model when maximum likelihood is used, a test using the chi-square distribution replaces the usual F test. For example, suppose that we wish to test the significance of the entire logit model. To do so, we first evaluate the likelihood function L when all parameters (other than the constant) are set equal to zero. We call this initial value L_0. We then evaluate the likelihood function at its maximum; call it L_{max}. Now, define the likelihood ratio, as

$$\lambda = \frac{L_0}{L_{max}}$$

The appropriate test follows directly from the fact that

$$-2 \log \lambda = -2(\log L_0 - \log L_{max})$$

follows a chi-square distribution with k degrees of freedom, where k is the number of parameters in the equation (other than the constant).

To use the maximum-likelihood results to obtain a measure of goodness of fit analogous to R^2 several options are possible. One simple option is to calculate $1 - L_0/L_{max}$. This statistic will equal 0 when the unconstrained likelihood function is no greater than the likelihood function in which all parameters are constrained equal to 0 and will increase towards 1 as L_{max} increases. A second option is to calculate residuals as follows:

$$\hat{\varepsilon}_i = Y_i - \hat{P}_i$$

These residuals will all be positive for those voting for the candidate and negative otherwise and will be smaller in absolute value the better the logit or probit model helps to explain the voting or other choices being made. From these residuals it is easy to calculate an analog to R^2. We proceed as follows. Let

$$\text{ESS} = \sum_{i=1}^{N} \hat{\varepsilon}_i^2 \qquad \text{TSS} = \sum_{i=1}^{N} (Y_i - \bar{Y})^2 \qquad \text{and} \qquad \hat{R}^2 = 1 - \frac{\text{ESS}}{\text{TSS}}$$

EXERCISES

10.1 In correcting the linear probability model for heteroscedasticity, why can't the least-squares residuals be used directly to calculate an estimate of the error variance σ_i^2 rather than using the formula in Eq. (10.3)?

10.2 What would happen to the coefficients of the linear probability model if the binary dependent variable were presented by a (0, 2) variable rather than by a (0, 1) variable? What does this suggest to you about the interpretation of the estimated least-squares parameters?

10.3 Prove that the transformation of the probability model described in Eq. (10.4) using a cumulative uniform probability function yields the constrained version of the linear probability model.

10.4 Consider the municipal-bond-default example (Example 10.1). Explain how you might reinterpret the bond default issue in terms of the probit model. What are some of the advantages and disadvantages of using the probit specification rather than the linear probability specification?

10.5 The logit model of Eq. (10.9) is linear in the parameters and yet must (usually) be estimated using a nonlinear estimation package. Explain this seeming inconsistency.

10.6 Using the following six data points, estimate a linear probability model using ordinary least squares:

X	-1	-2	0	1	1	1
Y	0	0	0	1	1	1

Calculate R^2 for the model. Then use the estimated model to classify individuals into the two categories. Calculate the number of correct classifications using the following classification rule:

$$\text{Classify} = \begin{cases} \text{first group } (Y = 1) & \text{if } \hat{Y} > \tfrac{1}{2} \\ \text{second group } (Y = 0) & \text{if } \hat{Y} \le \tfrac{1}{2} \end{cases}$$

Discuss the advantages and disadvantages of using R^2 and the percentage of correct classifications as measures of goodness of fit in the linear probability model.

10.7 Refer to the data set in Table 10.10.

(a) Using OLS, probit, and logit procedures, estimate the parameters in the model

$$\text{Prob (YESVM = 1)} = F \quad (\text{PUB1\&2, PUB3\&4, PUB5, PRIV,} \\ \text{YEARS, SCHOOL, INC, PTCON})$$

How do the results compare?

(b) Using the OLS estimates, predict for each case YESVM. How many cases actually result in predictions outside the 0 to 1 range. Discuss.

Table 10.10 Voting data set

Variables as in Table 10.7 with addition of PTCON = natural logarithm of property taxes paid per year, dollars; YESVM = dummy variable equal to 1 if individual voted yes in the election; 0 if individual voted no

Case	PUB1&2	PUB3&4	PUB5	PRIV	YEARS	SCHOOL	log INC	PTCON	YESVM
1	0	1	0	0	10	1	9.7700	7.0475	1
2	0	1	0	0	8	0	10.021	7.0475	0
3	1	0	0	0	4	0	10.021	7.0475	0
4	0	1	0	0	13	0	9.4335	6.3969	0
5	0	1	0	0	3	1	10.021	7.2792	1
6	1	0	0	0	5	0	10.463	7.0475	0
7	0	0	0	0	4	0	10.021	7.0475	0
8	0	1	0	0	5	0	10.021	7.2793	1
9	1	0	0	0	10	0	10.222	7.0475	0
10	0	1	0	0	5	0	9.4335	7.0475	1
11	1	0	0	0	3	0	10.021	7.0475	1
12	1	0	0	0	30	0	9.7700	6.3969	0
13	1	0	0	0	1	0	9.7700	6.7452	1
14	0	1	0	0	3	0	10.021	7.0475	1
15	0	1	0	0	3	0	10.820	6.7452	1
16	0	1	0	0	42	0	9.7700	6.7452	1
17	0	1	0	0	5	1	10.222	7.0475	1
18	1	0	0	0	10	0	10.021	7.0475	0
19	1	0	0	0	4	0	10.222	7.0475	1
20	1	0	0	1	4	0	10.222	6.7452	1
21	0	1	0	0	11	1	10.463	7.0475	1
22	0	0	0	0	5	0	10.222	7.0475	1

Table 10.10 Voting data set (Continued)

Case	PUB1&2	PUB3&4	PUB5	PRIV	YEARS	SCHOOL	log INC	PTCON	YESVM
23	0	1	0	0	35	0	9.7700	6.7452	1
24	0	1	0	0	3	0	10.463	7.2793	1
25	1	0	0	0	16	0	10.021	6.7452	1
26	0	0	0	1	7	0	10.463	7.0475	0
27	1	0	0	0	5	1	9.7700	6.7452	1
28	1	0	0	0	11	0	9.7700	7.0475	0
29	1	0	0	0	3	0	9.7700	6.7452	0
30	1	0	0	1	2	0	10.222	7.0475	1
31	0	1	0	0	2	0	10.021	6.7452	1
32	1	0	0	0	2	0	9.4335	6.7452	0
33	0	1	0	0	2	1	8.2940	7.0475	0
34	0	0	0	1	4	0	10.463	7.0475	1
35	1	0	0	0	2	0	10.021	7.0475	1
36	0	1	0	0	3	0	10.222	7.2793	0
37	1	0	0	0	3	0	10.222	7.0475	1
38	1	0	0	0	2	0	10.222	7.4955	1
39	0	1	0	0	10	0	10.021	7.0475	0
40	1	0	0	0	2	0	10.222	7.0475	1
41	1	0	0	0	2	0	10.021	7.0475	0
42	1	0	0	0	3	0	10.820	7.4955	0
43	1	0	0	0	3	0	10.021	7.0475	1
44	0	1	0	0	3	0	10.021	7.0475	1
45	1	0	0	0	6	0	10.021	6.7452	1
46	0	1	0	0	2	0	10.021	7.0475	1
47	1	0	0	0	26	0	9.7700	6.7452	0
48	0	0	0	1	18	0	10.222	7.4955	0
49	0	0	0	0	4	0	9.7700	6.7452	0
50	0	0	0	0	6	0	10.021	7.0475	0
51	0	0	0	0	12	0	10.021	6.7452	1
52	1	0	0	0	49	0	9.4335	6.7452	1
53	1	0	0	0	6	0	10.463	7.2793	1
54	0	0	0	1	18	0	9.7700	7.0475	0
55	1	0	0	0	5	0	10.021	7.0475	1
56	1	0	0	0	6	0	9.7700	5.9915	1
57	1	0	0	0	20	0	9.4335	7.0475	0
58	1	0	0	0	1	1	9.7700	6.3969	1
59	1	0	0	0	3	0	10.021	6.7452	1
60	1	0	0	0	5	0	10.463	7.0475	0
61	1	0	0	0	2	0	10.021	7.0475	1
62	0	0	1	1	5	0	10.820	7.2793	0
63	1	0	0	0	18	0	9.4335	6.7452	0
64	1	0	0	0	20	1	9.7700	5.9915	1
65	0	0	0	0	14	0	8.9227	6.3969	0
66	0	0	1	0	3	0	9.4335	7.4955	0
67	1	0	0	0	17	0	9.4335	6.7452	0
68	1	0	0	0	20	0	10.021	7.0475	0
69	0	1	0	1	3	0	10.021	7.0475	1
70	0	1	0	0	2	0	10.021	7.0475	1
71	0	0	0	0	5	0	10.222	7.0475	1

Case	PUB1&2	PUB3&4	PUB5	PRIV	YEARS	SCHOOL	log INC	PTCON	YESVM
72	1	0	0	0	35	0	9.7700	7.0475	1
73	0	1	0	0	10	0	10.021	7.2793	0
74	0	1	0	0	8	0	9.7700	7.0475	1
75	1	0	0	0	12	0	9.7700	7.0475	0
76	0	1	0	0	7	0	10.222	6.7452	1
77	1	0	0	0	3	0	10.463	6.7452	1
78	0	1	0	0	25	0	10.222	6.7452	0
79	1	0	0	0	5	1	9.7700	6.7452	1
80	0	1	0	0	4	0	10.222	7.0475	1
81	1	0	0	0	2	0	10.021	7.2793	1
82	0	1	0	0	5	0	10.463	6.7452	1
83	1	0	0	0	3	0	9.7700	7.0475	0
84	1	0	0	0	2	0	10.820	7.4955	1
85	0	0	0	1	6	0	8.9227	5.9915	0
86	1	0	0	1	3	0	9.7700	7.0475	1
87	0	0	1	0	12	0	9.4335	6.3969	1
88	0	0	0	0	3	0	9.7700	6.7452	1
89	0	1	0	0	3	0	10.021	7.0475	1
90	0	0	0	0	3	0	10.021	6.7452	1
91	1	0	0	0	3	0	10.222	7.2793	1
92	0	1	0	0	3	1	10.021	7.0475	1
93	0	0	1	0	5	0	10.021	7.0475	1
94	0	0	0	0	35	1	8.9227	5.9915	1
95	0	1	0	0	3	0	10.463	7.4955	0

MULTI-EQUATION
SIMULATION MODELS

In the next four chapters we concern ourselves with models that consist of more than one equation. In a single-equation regression model a dependent variable is related to a set of explanatory variables; e.g., an interest rate might be related to GNP, the rate of inflation, and the money supply. However, the single-equation model does not explain the interdependencies that may exist between the explanatory variables themselves or how these explanatory variables are related to other variables. In addition, the single-equation model explains causality in one direction; i.e., explanatory variables determine a dependent variable, but there is no feedback relationship between the dependent variable and the explanatory variables.

Multi-equation simulation models allow us to account simultaneously for all the interrelationships between a set of variables. Often these models consist of a set of regression equations which, after having been estimated, are solved simultaneously on a computer. However, simulation models can also consist of equations which are not estimated, such as accounting identities, or behavioral rules of thumb.

In Chapter 11 we describe some of the estimation problems involved in multi-equation models as well as the problem of model identification that was introduced in Chapter 7. We also examine some estimation techniques developed especially for multi-equation models, including two- and three-stage least squares.

In Chapters 12 and 13 we discuss some general issues involved in the construction, evaluation, and use of simulation models. In Chapter 12 we describe how the simulation of a model is actually carried out, how a simulation model can be evaluated, and how the particular estimation method used for the model affects its simulation performance. In Chapter 13 we examine the dynamic behavior of simulation models, methods of adjusting simulation models, and the use of stochastic simulation to determine confidence intervals for model forecasts.

Finally, in Chapter 14 we present three examples of simulation models. These include a model of the United States macroeconomy, a model of a particular industry, and a financial planning model for a corporation.

SIMULTANEOUS-EQUATION
ESTIMATION

In the first part of this book we concerned ourselves primarily with single-equation models. We found that in many cases, ordinary least-squares estimation was the most appropriate estimation procedure. We showed in Chapter 7, however, that the presence of simultaneity in a two-equation model causes ordinary least-squares parameter estimators to be inconsistent, so that an alternative method must be used to estimate each equation. In this chapter we change our emphasis by dealing explicitly with models consisting of several equations, in which the behavior of the variables is jointly determined.

Perhaps the simplest example of a simultaneous equation model is a two-equation model of market demand and supply, where price and quantity are both endogenous variables. More complex examples include industry, regional, and national economic models. All these examples are similar in that each model includes several endogenous variables which are simultaneously determined by an interrelated series of equations. The presence of two or more endogenous variables necessitates some additional model-building and estimation tools. We shall develop these tools by working with examples of two- or three-equation models. Our objective is to develop the important modeling and estimation techniques in as comprehensible a fashion as possible. The examples and derivations in the text have been chosen with an eye toward clarity and intuition, at the risk of loss of generality. However, Appendixes 11.1 through 11.4 do contain a more complete mathematical development of many of the techniques described in the text.

This chapter begins with a description of several types of *equation systems*. The discussion focuses on the distinction between alternative model systems, with emphasis given to the question of whether or not ordinary least squares is an appropriate estimation method. In the second section we return to the *identification problem* first discussed in Chapter 7. Model identification is analyzed in detail, with emphasis placed on rules of thumb which might be of use in the model-building process. The remaining sections of the chapter deal briefly with some of the estimation techniques available for multi-equation models. Section 11.3 completes the discussion of single-equation estimation techniques which can be applied to multi-equation models. In Section 11.4 we first introduce estimation techniques in which all the equations in the model are estimated simultaneously, thus providing greater estimation efficiency.

11.1 TYPES OF EQUATION SYSTEMS

We assume that in our econometric model there are as many equations as there are endogenous variables. If this were not the case, it would be impossible to solve the model to determine values for these endogenous variables (associated with values for the predetermined variables). A model with more equations than endogenous variables could have an infinite number of solutions, while one with fewer equations than endogenous variables would have no solution.

For purposes of model estimation it is important to distinguish between models which are truly simultaneous in nature and models which are not. We are referring, of course, to the structural form of the model which must be specified on the basis of known information. We shall proceed by describing several types of model systems, limiting ourselves on behalf of clarity to a three-equation system with two predetermined (exogenous and lagged endogenous) variables. We shall not concern ourselves with the identification of the structural parameters in the model until the following section.

11.1.1 Simultaneous-Equation Systems

The most general form of a three-equation simultaneous system is

$$Y_1 = \alpha_0 \qquad\qquad + \alpha_2 Y_2 + \alpha_3 Y_3 + \alpha_4 Z_1 + \alpha_5 Z_2 + u_1 \qquad (11.1)$$

$$Y_2 = \beta_0 + \beta_1 Y_1 \qquad\quad + \beta_3 Y_3 + \beta_4 Z_1 + \beta_5 Z_2 + u_2 \qquad (11.2)$$

$$Y_3 = \gamma_0 + \gamma_1 Y_1 + \gamma_2 Y_2 + \qquad\quad + \gamma_4 Z_1 + \gamma_5 Z_2 + u_3 \qquad (11.3)$$

Here each of the three endogenous variables, Y_1, Y_2, and Y_3, appears on the left-hand side of one and only one equation. The two predetermined variables, Z_1 and Z_2, appear on the right-hand side of the equations, along with the error terms, u_1, u_2, and u_3. We assume for now that the error term in each equation obeys the classical assumptions of least squares, that is, $u_i \sim N(0, \sigma_{u_i}^2)$ for $i = 1, 2, 3$. We also assume that there is no direct relationship between the three error processes, i.e., that $E(u_{it}u_{jt}) = 0$ for all t and for all $i \neq j$. (We shall drop this assumption in Section 11.4.)

If none of the coefficients in Eqs. (11.1) to (11.3) is 0, the model is a completely interdependent system, since it is impossible to solve for any single endogenous variable, say Y_1, without simultaneously solving all three equations. As a rule, ordinary least-squares estimation of this model will yield biased and inconsistent parameter estimates; we have seen why this is true in the two-equation model described in Chapter 7, and the logic extends to a model of three (or more) equations. Assume, for example, that we are trying to estimate Eq. (11.1). Ordinary least-squares estimates will be consistent only if both Y_2 and Y_3 are uncorrelated with the disturbance term u_1. Notice, however, what happens if there is a small movement in u_1. The movement in u_1 will cause an equivalent movement in Y_1 as depicted in Eq. (11.1). But Y_2 [in Eq. (11.2)] and Y_3 [in Eq. (11.3)] are both determined in part by Y_1, so that the movement in Y_1 will lead to a movement in Y_2 and Y_3. The result is that both Y_2 and Y_3 will be correlated with u_1, making ordinary least squares an inappropriate method of estimating Eq. (11.1).

Example 11.1 Consider the following three-equation macroeconomic model:

$$C_t = \alpha_0 + \alpha_2 I_t + \alpha_3 Y_t + \alpha_4 C_{t-1} + \alpha_5 R_t + u_{1t}$$

$$I_t = \beta_0 \qquad\qquad + \beta_3 Y_t \qquad\qquad + \beta_5 R_t + u_{2t}$$

$$Y_t = C_t + I_t + G_t$$

where C = aggregate consumption
$\quad I$ = gross investment
$\quad Y$ = gross national product
$\quad G$ = government spending
$\quad M$ = money supply
$\quad R$ = short-term interest rate

The three endogenous variables are C, I, and Y, while the predetermined variables are C_{t-1}, G_t, and R_t. The model is simultaneous, despite the fact that aggregate consumption is not a direct determinant of gross investment. Simultaneity occurs because the estimation of C and I in the first two equations cannot be accomplished unless values for Y are available, but Y is a function of C and I (as well as of G) in the third equation. Only when all three equations are solved simultaneously can a solution be found. (The fact that the third equation is an identity should not be a cause of concern. The identity differs from the previous behavioral equations only in that all its coefficients are known to be equal to 1.)

11.1.2 Recursive Equation Systems

A system of equations is *recursive* (rather than simultaneous) if each of the endogenous variables can be determined sequentially. Consider the model

$$Y_1 = \alpha_0 \qquad\qquad\qquad + \alpha_4 Z_1 + \alpha_5 Z_2 + u_1 \qquad\qquad (11.4)$$

$$Y_2 = \beta_0 + \beta_1 Y_1 \qquad\qquad + \beta_4 Z_1 + \beta_5 Z_2 + u_2 \qquad\qquad (11.5)$$

$$Y_3 = \gamma_0 + \gamma_1 Y_1 + \gamma_2 Y_2 + \gamma_4 Z_1 + \gamma_4 Z_2 + u_3 \qquad\qquad (11.6)$$

$$\text{Cov}\,(u_1, u_2) = \text{Cov}\,(u_1, u_3) = \text{Cov}\,(u_2, u_3) = 0$$

Although this system of equations seems simultaneous, it is actually recursive. To see this, assume that the true structural parameters are known. Given values for Z_1 and Z_2, we can solve directly for Y_1 in Eq. (11.4). Then, knowing Y_1 allows us to solve for Y_2 in Eq. (11.5). Finally, values for Y_1, Y_2, Z_1, and Z_2 allow us to solve for Y_3 in Eq. (11.6).

In a more general recursive model we see that (if the model is written appropriately) the solution for the nth endogenous variable involves only the first n equations of the model; thus the right-hand endogenous variables need not be correlated with the error terms. This property of recursive models makes ordinary least squares (OLS) an appropriate estimation procedure. OLS is obviously appropriate for the first equation, since Z_1 and Z_2 are predetermined and therefore uncorrelated with u_1. OLS is also appropriate for the second equation because the endogenous variable Y_1 is uncorrelated with u_2 (since the only error term affecting Y_1 is u_1 in the first equation). Finally, OLS can be applied to the third equation because (by similar reasoning) Y_1 and Y_2 are uncorrelated with u_3.

Remember that we have assumed that the errors across equations are themselves not correlated. We should note that the application of ordinary least squares would be inappropriate if this were not the case. We shall return to this problem in Section 11.4.

Example 11.2 Consider the following three-equation model:

$$P = \alpha_0 \qquad\qquad\qquad + \alpha_3 W + \qquad\quad + u_1$$

$$P' = \beta_0 + \beta_1 P \qquad\qquad\qquad + \beta_4 T + u_2$$

$$Q = \gamma_0 + \gamma_1 P + \gamma_2 P' + \gamma_3 W + \qquad\quad + u_3$$

where P = price of cotton
$\quad\quad P'$ = price of cotton goods
$\quad\quad Q$ = quantity of cotton goods sold
$\quad\quad W$ = index of weather conditions
$\quad\quad T$ = effective tax rate on cotton goods
The model specification is based on the presumption that the price of cotton is determined solely by weather conditions (there is no simultaneous interaction of demand and supply). The price of cotton goods is determined by the

price of cotton and by the tax rate on cotton goods. Finally, the quantity of cotton goods sold is determined by the two previously determined prices and by weather conditions. The model is clearly a recursive model and can be estimated using ordinary least squares.

11.1.3 Block-Recursive Equation Systems

A block-recursive equation system is a group of equations which can be broken up into groups or blocks of equations in such a way that equations *within* each block are simultaneous but groups of equations *across* blocks are recursive; i.e., knowledge of the endogenous variables in the first block permits the determination of the endogenous variables in the second block, etc. Consider the model

$$Y_1 = \alpha_0 \qquad\qquad + \alpha_2 Y_2 + \alpha_4 Z_1 + \alpha_5 Z_2 + u_1 \qquad (11.7)$$

$$Y_2 = \beta_0 + \beta_1 Y_1 + \qquad\quad + \beta_4 Z_1 + \beta_5 Z_2 + u_2 \qquad (11.8)$$

$$Y_3 = \gamma_0 + \gamma_1 Y_1 + \gamma_2 Y_2 + \gamma_4 Z_1 + \gamma_5 Z_2 + u_3 \qquad (11.9)$$

Equations (11.7) and (11.8) make up a block, i.e., a system of two equations which must be solved simultaneously to obtain values for Y_1 and Y_2. Once solutions are obtained, values for Y_1 and Y_2 can be substituted into Eq. (11.9) to obtain a value for Y_3. This particular model consists of two blocks, the first containing two equations and the second containing only one. To estimate this block-recursive system, we proceed by estimating the block of equations in which Y_1 and Y_2 are simultaneously determined. If identified, these equations can be estimated using either the instrumental variables or the two-stage least-squares technique. The third equation, however, can be estimated using ordinary least squares, since the recursive nature of the model guarantees that Y_1 and Y_2 will both be uncorrelated with u_3.

11.1.4 Systems of Seemingly Unrelated Equations

The seemingly unrelated model is a specific type of recursive model which occurs occasionally in business and economic modeling. It consists of a series of endogenous variables which are considered as a group because they bear a close conceptual relationship to each other. An example of such a model is

$$Y_1 = \alpha_0 + \alpha_4 Z_1 + \alpha_5 Z_2 + u_1 \qquad (11.10)$$

$$Y_2 = \beta_0 + \beta_4 Z_3 + \beta_5 Z_4 + u_2 \qquad (11.11)$$

$$Y_3 = \gamma_0 + \gamma_4 Z_5 + \gamma_5 Z_6 + u_3 \qquad (11.12)$$

A set of demand equations for related products might be specified in this form. If, in fact, the *disturbances* of each equation are unrelated (uncorrelated), then there is indeed no relationship between the equations. (Notice that no predetermined variable appears in more than one equation.) In such a case, ordinary least-squares estimation is quite proper. If the error terms are correlated between equations, efficient estimates can be obtained using a more sophisticated estimation technique.† Further details and examples appear in Section 11.4.

11.1.5 Modeling of Equation Systems

After having categorized equation systems, we might ask whether it is preferable to build models of one category (e.g., recursive) or another (e.g., simultaneous). The answer depends upon how one views the economic (and related) processes in the real world. One might argue that the world is best represented by a recursive model because very few markets are actually perfectly competitive; usually either price or quantity (or both) is influenced by a firm or firms with market power. Under monopoly, for example, one firm is a price setter, so that the notion of the simultaneous determination of price and quantity is irrelevant. In addition, the existence of lags in the reactions of buyers and sellers leads one to believe that with a proper time frame all variables to be explained could be seen as a function of predetermined variables (consisting, of many lagged endogenous variables, of course). On the other hand, the nature of the data available for econometric analysis makes analysis of reaction time very difficult, if not impossible, in most cases. The fact that quarterly macroeconomic data are available but weekly and daily are often not means that we may not be able to model weekly and daily lag adjustments. As a result, the majority of econometric models are appropriately simultaneous equation models. However, the choice of the type of equation system to be used depends in the end upon the judgment of the model builder.

11.2 THE IDENTIFICATION PROBLEM

We have seen in Chapter 7 that the study of a model's structure for purposes of identification is a prior step to model estimation. Within the context of a two-equation model, we discussed the relationship between structural forms, reduced forms, and the problem of identification. We found in certain cases that, given the reduced-form representation of the model, it was impossible to find the values of the parameters of the structural model. This corresponds, of course, to the case in which an equation is *unidentified* (or *underidentified*). When structural equation parameters can be uniquely determined, the equation in question is said to be *exactly identified*, and when more than one set of parameter estimates is available for one or more parameters, the equation is *overidentified*. Over- and underidentification are not symmetric concepts. Underidentification implies that structural model estimation is impossible. Overidentification implies only that a surfeit of information is available, forcing us to choose carefully from a set of possible estimation processes. Unless we specify

---

† Ordinary least-squares estimation will remain consistent and may be appropriate when the added computational costs are weighed against the gain in efficiency.

otherwise, we shall apply the concept of identification to individual equations in a model system. It is quite possible, of course, for one equation to be identified while another is unidentified.

In order to delve further into the nature of the identification problem, we consider a rather simple three-equation model:

$$y_1 = \alpha_3 y_3 + \alpha_4 z_1 + \alpha_5 z_2 + u_1 \tag{11.13}$$

$$y_2 = \beta_1 y_1 + u_2 \tag{11.14}$$

$$y_3 = \gamma_2 y_2 + u_3 \tag{11.15}$$

We have written the model using data in deviations form to eliminate unnecessary use of algebra. No loss of generality is involved in this simplification. If we were to solve the structural model for its reduced form, we would obtain

$$y_1 = \pi_{11} z_1 + \pi_{12} z_2 + v_1 \tag{11.16}$$

$$y_2 = \pi_{21} z_1 + \pi_{22} z_2 + v_2 \tag{11.17}$$

$$y_3 = \pi_{31} z_1 + \pi_{32} z_2 + v_3 \tag{11.18}$$

where
$$\pi_{11} = \frac{\alpha_4}{\delta} \qquad\qquad \pi_{12} = \frac{\alpha_5}{\delta} \tag{11.19}$$

$$\pi_{21} = \frac{\beta_1 \alpha_4}{\delta} \qquad\qquad \pi_{22} = \frac{\alpha_5 \beta_1}{\delta} \tag{11.20}$$

$$\pi_{31} = \frac{\beta_1 \gamma_2 \alpha_4}{\delta} \qquad\qquad \pi_{32} = \frac{\beta_1 \gamma_2 \alpha_5}{\delta} \tag{11.21}$$

$$\delta = 1 - \alpha_3 \beta_1 \gamma_2 \qquad v_1 = (u_1 + \alpha_3 \gamma_2 u_2 + \alpha_3 u_3)/\delta$$

$$v_2 = (\beta_1 u_1 + u_2 + \beta_1 \alpha_3 u_3)/\delta$$

$$v_3 = (\beta_1 \gamma_2 u_1 + \gamma_2 u_2 + u_3)/\delta$$

Since the right-hand variables are all predetermined, it is quite simple to estimate the reduced-form parameters using ordinary least squares. The identification problem poses the issue of whether structural-form parameter estimates can be deduced from the reduced-form estimates. From the reduced-form system we can see that the parameters β_1 and γ_2 can be obtained in two ways:

$$\hat{\beta}_1 = \frac{\hat{\pi}_{21}}{\hat{\pi}_{11}} \quad \text{or} \quad \hat{\beta}_1' = \frac{\hat{\pi}_{22}}{\hat{\pi}_{12}}$$

and
$$\hat{\gamma}_2 = \frac{\hat{\pi}_{31}}{\hat{\pi}_{21}} \quad \text{or} \quad \hat{\gamma}_2' = \frac{\hat{\pi}_{32}}{\hat{\pi}_{22}}$$

We conclude that Eqs. (11.14) and (11.15) are both identified (in fact, over-identified), since each of the parameters in the equation can be determined directly from the reduced-form parameter estimates in two different ways. A more careful examination of the reduced form should convince the reader that the first equation, (11.13), is unidentified, since there is no way to obtain estimates of the structural parameters α_3, α_4, and α_5.

As long as our concern lies solely with Eqs. (11.14) and (11.15), we can proceed with model estimation and use the resulting parameter estimates for prediction or other purposes. However, our analysis tells us that estimation of the first structural equation is not viable. While we could make calculated guesses of the parameter estimates, we would not be able to place much reliance, if any, on those guesses, since correct statistical estimation procedures are not applicable.

Although we will always check for identification before estimating a model, there may be cases in which prediction is our primary objective. In such cases models with unidentified equations may be valuable. If parameter estimates can be made for the unidentified equation, satisfactory predictions can be obtained. The gain in knowledge about the interaction of variables in the model may outweigh the costs associated with the potential unreliability of parameter estimates in unidentified equations. In fact, prediction can be accomplished directly with the use of the reduced-form parameters, so that knowledge of the structural-form parameters is not necessary for forecasting.

We have seen in Chapter 7 that identification necessitates *prior* information which allows us to distinguish the parameters of each equation from those of any other equation of the same form. While many kinds of prior information can help to resolve the identification problem, we limit ourselves to dealing with restrictions in the form of 0 coefficients on the endogenous and predetermined variables in the model.† Such a 0 coefficient occurs every time a variable which is present in at least one equation in the model is excluded from another equation. In our cotton example (Example 11.2), the first equation contains three zero restrictions, since only weather is expected to have a direct effect on the price of cotton. The second equation has two zero restrictions, given that neither weather nor the quantity of cotton goods affects the price of cotton goods directly. Finally, the third equation contains the single zero restriction that the tax rate will not directly affect the quantity of cotton goods sold.

Given that the test of whether an equation is identified involves a test of whether one can solve for the structural form from the reduced form, the most general conditions for identification in the case of zero restrictions involve some matrix-related conditions associated with the solution of a system of equations. These general conditions are described in Appendix 11.1. For our purposes it is useful only to describe in somewhat greater detail than in Chapter 7 what is necessary for identification to be possible.

The most useful rule for the purposes of identification is called the *order condition*. The order condition states that if an equation is to be identified, *the number of predetermined variables excluded from the equation must be greater than*

---

† Much of what we say about zero restrictions can be extended to all linear restrictions on the parameters. For details of this and related matters, see F. M. Fisher, *The Identification Problem in Econometrics* (New York: McGraw-Hill, 1966).

or equal to the number of included endogenous variables minus 1. The list of included endogenous variables should contain variables on the left-hand side and the right-hand side of the equation. For some purposes, it is useful to express the order condition in a somewhat different, but equivalent, form. A necessary condition for an equation to be identified is that the number of all variables excluded from the equation be greater than or equal to the number of endogenous variables in the model system minus 1.

Perhaps the best way to gain some intuition into why the order condition is necessary for identification is to consider the problem of estimating Eq. (11.13). Since the model is simultaneous, the variable y_3 will be correlated with the error term u_1. Consistent parameter estimates can be obtained if two-stage least squares or instrumental variables estimation is used. If we were to proceed thoughtlessly to use 2SLS, we would estimate y_3 in the reduced form as a weighted average of the two predetermined variables z_1 and z_2. We would then replace y_3 by $\hat{y}_3$ in the original equation and attempt to use an ordinary least-squares estimation procedure. Such a procedure would fail, however, because of the perfect collinearity between $\hat{y}_3$ and the variables z_1 and z_2 guaranteed by the first stage of the estimation process. In order for 2SLS to be used, at least one of the predetermined variables in the model must be excluded from the first equation. If y_2 were included in Eq. (11.13), the number of excluded predetermined variables would need to be at least 2 to guarantee identification. The presence of two right-hand endogenous variables necessitates the use of two potential instruments, both not already present in the equation.

The difficulty with the order condition is that it is not a sufficient condition; i.e., it is possible for the condition to be satisfied and for the equation to be unidentified. While the order condition is likely to be a satisfactory rule of thumb for identification, there is a possibility that it will fail on occasion. The extension of the order condition to include sufficient as well as necessary conditions for identification is somewhat difficult. Since it involves an understanding of the rank of a matrix, we leave that discussion to Appendix 11.1.†

Example 11.3 Reconsider the three-equation macroeconomic model described in Example 11.1. The first equation is clearly unidentified, since there are three endogenous variables and only one excluded predetermined variable (G_t). Estimation of the first equation using 2SLS is impossible, and prediction using any parameter estimates must be suspect. A more realistic consumption equation, not containing I_t (gross investment) as an explanatory variable, would be identified. The second equation is overidentified according to the order condition, since there are two excluded predetermined variables and only two included endogenous variables. Finally, the third equation is identified, without regard to the order condition, since it is an identity with all parameters known by definition. In this particular

---

† The sufficient condition for identifiability is called the *rank condition*.

example the order condition is sufficient to guarantee identification of the investment equation, since the rank condition also holds.

Example 11.4 Let us return to one of the rather simple supply-demand models examined in Chapter 7. The model is

Supply: $\qquad\qquad Q_t = \alpha_1 + \alpha_2 P_t + \qquad\quad + u_{1t}$

Demand: $\qquad\qquad Q_t = \beta_1 + \beta_2 P_t + \beta_3 Y_t + u_{2t}$

where P is price, Q is quantity, and Y is income. The demand equation is not identified by the order condition, since no predetermined variables are excluded. The necessary condition for the supply curve to be identified is satisfied, since there are two endogenous variables and one excluded predetermined variable. The sufficient condition will also hold when $\beta_3 \neq 0$. This makes intuitive sense, since $\beta_3 = 0$ implies that the original zero-exclusion restriction has no force in the model. With $\beta_3 = 0$ there is no way to distinguish between the supply and demand equations.

This simple example is useful because it suggests that the problem of identification should not be approached in a rigid manner. Assume, for example, that there is very little variability in the income variable Y, and that the associated coefficient is close to 0. While the strict rules for identification will be satisfied, it will still be difficult to distinguish the supply equation from the demand equation. This suggests that attempts to guarantee identifiability in each model equation by adding and deleting variables randomly will most likely lead to problems. While the strict order and rank conditions might be satisfied by such a process, the model is unlikely to have much predictive power, since some or all of the added variables may have little effect on the corresponding endogenous variables.

11.3 SINGLE-EQUATION ESTIMATION

Before discussing methods by which systems of equations can be estimated, let us once again consider the subject of single-equation estimation. We concern ourselves with the estimation of an overidentified equation, since the choice of estimation technique becomes uninteresting if the equation is exactly identified.† Our objective is to put the estimation techniques of instrumental variables and two-stage least squares in proper perspective by pointing out some practical difficulties. Each of the single-equation estimation techniques discussed here is a limited-information estimator in the sense that it does not use all the information available in the model. In particular, no account is taken of information associated with overidentifying restrictions in equations not being estimated.

---

† All the estimation techniques described here yield equivalent sample estimators if the equation is exactly identified.

Consider the simple two-equation model†

$$y_1 = \alpha_2 y_2 + u_1 \tag{11.22}$$

$$y_2 = \beta_1 y_1 + \beta_3 z_1 + \beta_4 z_2 + u_2 \tag{11.23}$$

The first equation is overidentified (as long as $\beta_3 \neq 0$ and $\beta_4 \neq 0$), while the second is unidentified. The reader should recall that the order condition is satisfied for Eq. (11.22) because there are two excluded predetermined variables and only two included endogenous variables. In Eq. (11.23), on the other hand, there are no excluded predetermined variables, so that the order condition is not satisfied.

For our purposes it will be sufficient to consider the problem of estimating the first equation. Ordinary least squares is clearly an inappropriate estimation procedure, since the simultaneous nature of the model guarantees that y_2 and u_1 will be correlated, regardless of sample size. One plausible estimation process is instrumental variables, since the proper choice of instruments guarantees that consistent parameter estimators will be utilized. If we were to choose the instrumental-variables technique as an estimation procedure, we would have a choice between at least two estimators of the parameter α_2, each choice associated with the use of a different predetermined variable as instrument ($\hat{\alpha}_2 = \Sigma z_1 y_1 / \Sigma z_1 y_2$ and $\hat{\hat{\alpha}}_2 = \Sigma z_2 y_1 / \Sigma z_2 y_2$). The two estimators will not coincide in the sample, so that we are faced with the necessity of finding a decision rule which allows us to choose between the two. Since both parameter estimators are consistent (i.e., in a large enough sample they will converge to the same estimate), some criterion must be used to choose between the two. One useful criterion‡ is to choose as an instrument the predetermined variable which is most highly correlated with y_2. This criterion guarantees that the *single* instrument chosen will lead to parameter estimators with the smallest variance among the set of parameter estimators associated with each predetermined variable taken individually. It makes sense intuitively,§ because an instrument which is very highly correlated with y_2 would be expected to lead to more accurate results than an instrument having a substantially lower correlation with y_2.

The choice of instruments just made is rather limiting, however, since we have restricted ourselves to choosing as our instrument one element from a set of predetermined variables. A more reasonable (and more efficient) procedure would be one which chooses as an instrument a weighted average of the two

---

† Portions of this section rely upon an excellent discussion in E. Malinvaud, *Principles of Econometrics* (Paris: North-Holland, 1966), pp. 534–540.

‡ This method of choosing instruments suggests one potential pitfall. If lagged endogenous variables are added to a model artificially to make each of the equations identified, the lagged variables may not be suitable choices as instruments. A variable such as y_{2t-1} is likely to be highly correlated with y_{2t}, but the high correlation makes it likely that it will also be correlated with u_{1t}, the error term. If such is the case, inconsistent parameter estimates will be obtained.

§ This result is quite difficult to prove. For details see Malinvaud, op. cit., p. 536.

available predetermined variables, the weights being selected so as to maximize the correlation between the single instrument and y_2. To get such an instrument, we simply regress y_2 on both z_1 and z_2 and calculate the fitted values $\hat{y}_2$. This procedure should be familiar to the reader, since it is the first stage of two-stage least squares. The 2SLS estimator is $\alpha_2^* = \Sigma \hat{y}_2 y_1 / \Sigma \hat{y}_2 y_2$. Thus, the 2SLS estimator is an instrumental variables estimator, where the instrument is chosen to maximize its correlation with y_2 and indirectly to minimize the variance of the estimated parameter.†

The 2SLS technique is frequently used in the estimation of business and economic models. As long as the number of predetermined variables in the reduced form of the model is relatively small (less than 20), 2SLS presents no computational problems. However, when the number of predetermined variables is quite large, the computational cost of 2SLS necessitates an alternative means of determining instruments. One solution is to reduce the number of predetermined variables through the technique of *principal components*. Principal components is a computational process in which a group of variables is reduced in number to a more fundamental set of variables. The reduced set of variables is used (sometimes in a modified form) as the reduced form for the first-stage estimation.‡ A second procedure selects a subset of predetermined variables from the original set according to a well-defined selection rule.§ Both techniques are used frequently in the estimation (and later simulation) of large econometric models.

Another complication with the use of 2SLS occurs when the error process in one or more equations of a model is autoregressive, i.e., when errors in a given equation are correlated over time. If the equations with autocorrelated errors do not contain lagged endogenous variables, and if the errors are first-order serially correlated, then the estimation problem is not very difficult.¶ Consider the simple example

$$y_{1t} = \alpha_2 y_{2t} + u_{1t} \tag{11.24}$$

$$y_{2t} = \beta_1 y_{1t} + \beta_3 z_t + u_{2t} \tag{11.25}$$

$$u_{1t} = \rho u_{1t-1} + \varepsilon_{1t} \tag{11.26}$$

where ε_{1t} and u_{2t} are not autocorrelated. We proceed first by applying the

---

† Ibid.

‡ For details see T. Kloek and L. B. Mennes, "Simultaneous Equation Estimation Based on Principal Components of Predetermined Variables," *Econometrica*, vol. 28, pp. 45–61, 1960; and L. R. Klein, "Estimation of Interdependent Systems in Macroeconometrics," *Econometrica*, vol. 37, pp. 171–192, 1969.

§ See F. M. Fisher, "Dynamic Structure and Estimation in Economy-Wide Econometric Models," chap. XV in J. Duesenberry,. G. Fromm, L. Klein, and E. Kuh (eds.), *The Brookings Quarterly Econometric Model of the United States*, 1965.

¶ The correct estimation technique when lagged endogenous variables appear in the equations is described by R. Fair in "The Estimation of Simultaneous Equation Models with Lagged Endogenous Variables and First Order Serially Correlated Errors," *Econometrica*, vol. 38, pp. 507–516, May 1970.

generalized differencing process to the first equation and then solving for the reduced form. This yields

$$y_{1t} = \frac{1}{1 - \alpha_2 \beta_1} (\rho y_{1t-1} - \alpha_2 \rho y_{2t-1} + \alpha_2 \beta_3 z_t + v_{1t}) \qquad (11.27)$$

$$y_{2t} = \frac{1}{1 - \alpha_2 \beta_1} (\beta_1 \rho y_{1t-1} - \beta_1 \alpha_2 \rho y_{2t-1} + \beta_3 z_t + v_{2t}) \qquad (11.28)$$

In order to estimate the first equation (11.24) we obtain fitted values for y_{2t} by applying ordinary least squares to the second reduced-form equation (11.28). Then, rewriting the first equation in generalized difference form and substituting the fitted values for y_{2t}, we obtain

$$y_{1t} - \rho y_{1t-1} = \alpha_2 (\hat{y}_{2t} - \rho \hat{y}_{2t-1}) + \hat{\varepsilon}_{1t}$$

The modified two-stage least-squares procedure is completed by estimating this equation using any one of the autoregressive estimation procedures described in Chapter 6.

11.4 ESTIMATION OF EQUATION SYSTEMS

All the single-equation estimation procedures just described yield consistent parameter estimates. As a general rule, however, each estimation technique yields inefficient parameter estimates (for large samples) because all the information available in the description of the system of equations is not used in the estimation procedure. We have argued that one way to view this loss of information is through the overidentifying restrictions in the system of equations that are not taken into account when single-equation estimation is done. An alternative source of inefficiency arises because single-equation estimation does not account for the fact that error terms across equations (for corresponding observations) are likely to be correlated. In either case, the problem of loss of efficiency can be resolved by using any of several methods of estimating systems of equations in which parameters for all equations are determined in a single procedure.

We describe in this section how techniques to estimate equation systems might be applied first to the seemingly unrelated-equation model and then to the simultaneous-equation model. Because of the complexity of the techniques, much of the mathematical detail is presented in the appendixes to the chapter. Our purpose is simply to provide an introduction to each of the important estimation procedures.

11.4.1 Seemingly Unrelated-Equation Model

The seemingly unrelated-equation model consists of a series of equations linked because the error terms across equations are correlated. As an example, assume that we are attempting to predict the percentage shares of a local government budget to be allocated to fire and police FP, to schools S, and to all other purposes O. The explanatory variables might include population density D, number of school-age children C, and median family income Y. Formally, the model is as follows (T = total budget):

$$\frac{FP_i}{T_i} = \alpha_0 + \alpha_1 D_i + \alpha_2 Y_i \qquad\qquad + u_{1i} \tag{11.29}$$

$$\frac{S_i}{T_i} = \beta_0 \qquad\qquad + \beta_2 Y_i + \beta_3 C_i + u_{2i} \tag{11.30}$$

$$\frac{O_i}{T_i} = \gamma_0 + \gamma_1 D_i + \gamma_2 Y_i + \gamma_3 C_i + u_{3i} \tag{11.31}$$

where the subscript i refers to individual cities. When none of the dependent budget-share variables appears on the right-hand side of any equation, the seemingly unrelated-equation model is appropriate. Each equation could be estimated independently using ordinary least-squares, and consistent and unbiased parameter estimates would be obtained. However, the efficiency of the parameter estimates could be improved if explicit account were taken of the correlation between error terms across equations. The correlation arises because of the restriction (by definition) that the sum of the individual budget shares is 100 percent, or 1. If in a given year a higher-than-average prediction is made for percentage expenditures on fire and police and on schools, the arithmetic of the model guarantees that a lower-than-average prediction should be made for the residual budget item. This correlation can be seen more formally by summing each of the three equations for each individual observation (city):

$$1 = (\alpha_0 + \beta_0 + \gamma_0) + (\alpha_1 + \gamma_1)D_i + (\alpha_2 + \beta_2 + \gamma_2)Y_i + (\beta_3 + \gamma_3)C_i$$
$$+ (u_{1i} + u_{2i} + u_{3i}) \tag{11.32}$$

Since Eq. (11.32) must hold identically for each observation, we conclude that $u_{1i} + u_{2i} + u_{3i} = 0$ for every observation.†

For efficient estimation one must take into account the correlation between equations by using a systems method of estimation. This can be done using a method devised by Zellner (called *Zellner estimation*).‡ Zellner suggests that efficiency in estimation can be gained if one views the system of seemingly unrelated equations as a single large equation to be estimated. Estimation of this

---

† There are additional parameter restrictions, of course, but they are not of immediate concern to us. The parameter restrictions are relevant, however, when the actual estimation process is undertaken. The restrictions that the sum of the intercept coefficients be 1 and that the sum of all slope coefficients be 0 necessitates the estimation of only two of the three equations listed. The coefficients of the third can be solved directly from the estimated coefficients of the first two equations.

‡ See A. Zellner, "An Efficient Method of Estimating Seemingly Unrelated Regressions and Tests for Aggregation Bias," *Journal of the American Statistical Association*, vol. 57, pp. 348–368, 1962.

single (system) equation is accomplished efficiently through the use of generalized least-squares estimation (see Appendix 6.2). Zellner estimation achieves an improvement in efficiency by taking into explicit account the fact that cross-equation error correlations may not be zero.

It will be instructive to examine a simple application of seemingly unrelated-equations estimation. Consider the two-equation model†

$$y_1 = \alpha x + u_1 \tag{11.33}$$

$$y_2 = \beta z + u_2 \tag{11.34}$$

We assume that the model is a cross-section model and that N observations are available for each of the variables in the model. Were the error terms in the two equations to be uncorrelated, then we would obtain efficient estimates of α and β by performing ordinary least-squares estimation on each separate equation, using N observations for each regression. However, under the assumption that u_1 and u_2 are correlated for identical cross-section units, we can improve upon the efficiency of ordinary least squares by writing the equation system as one combined equation, estimating that equation using generalized least-squares estimation.

In order to write the system as one large equation rather than two smaller equations, it is necessary to distinguish between observations associated with the first equation, (11.33), and observations associated with the second equation, (11.34). To do so, we shall relabel the observations, arbitrarily assigning observations 1 to N to the first-equation variables and observations $N + 1$ to $2N$ to the second-equation variables. We now define four new variables:

$$y^* = \begin{cases} y_{1i} & \text{if } i = 1, \ldots, N \\ y_{2i} & \text{if } i = N + 1, \ldots, 2N \end{cases} \qquad x^* = \begin{cases} x_i & \text{if } i = 1, \ldots, N \\ 0 & \text{otherwise} \end{cases}$$

$$z^* = \begin{cases} 0 & \text{if } i = 1, \ldots, N \\ z_i & \text{if } i = N + 1, \ldots, 2N \end{cases} \qquad u^* = \begin{cases} u_{1i} & \text{if } i = 1, \ldots, N \\ u_{2i} & \text{if } i = N + 1, \ldots, 2N \end{cases}$$

Also, $\qquad \sigma_1^2 = \text{Var}\,(u_1) \qquad \sigma_2^2 = \text{Var}\,(u_2) \qquad \sigma_{12} = \text{Cov}\,(u_1, u_2)$

With this new notation the combined equation can be written

$$y^* = \alpha x^* + \beta z^* + u^* \tag{11.35}$$

Applying the generalized least-squares procedure to Eq. (11.35) allows us to obtain parameter estimates for α and β. Since the algebra involved is substantial (despite the fact that we are working with data in deviations form), we shall simply present the results here:

$$\hat{\alpha} = \frac{1}{C}\left(A\sigma_1^2 \Sigma z^2 + B\sigma_{12}\Sigma xz\right) \tag{11.36}$$

$$\hat{\beta} = \frac{1}{C}\left(A\sigma_{12}\Sigma xz + B\sigma_2^2 \Sigma x^2\right) \tag{11.37}$$

---

† The observational subscripts have been dropped to simplify the exposition.

where
$$A = \sigma_2^2 \Sigma xy_1 - \sigma_{12} \Sigma xy_2$$
$$B = \sigma_1^2 \Sigma zy_2 - \sigma_{12} \Sigma zy_1$$
$$C = \sigma_1^2 \sigma_2^2 \Sigma x^2 \Sigma z^2 - \sigma_{12}^2 (\Sigma xz)^2$$

This example is instructive because it allows us to illustrate the two important cases in which Zellner estimation and ordinary least-squares estimation are identical. The first, and most obvious, situation occurs when the cross-equation covariance is identically 0 ($\sigma_{12} = 0$). The second, less obvious, situation occurs when the two explanatory variables (x and z) are identical. The details of these derivations are left to the reader (Exercise 11.6).

The application of generalized least squares necessitates obtaining estimates of the error covariances between equations. These estimates are obtained by first estimating each single equation using ordinary least squares. The variances and covariances of the estimated residuals then provide consistent estimators of the error variances and covariances. In our two-equation example, we would estimate σ_1^2, σ_2^2, and σ_{12} as follows:

$$\hat{\sigma}_1^2 = \frac{1}{N-2} \sum_{i=1}^{N} \hat{u}_{1i}^2 \qquad \hat{\sigma}_2^2 = \frac{1}{N-2} \sum_{i=N+1}^{2N} \hat{u}_{2i}^2 \qquad \hat{\sigma}_{12} = \frac{1}{N-2} \sum_{i=1}^{N} \hat{u}_{1i} \hat{u}_{1+N}$$

(11.38)

As a practical matter, Zellner estimation is a two-stage estimation procedure. It can be shown to be consistent as well as (asymptotically) efficient, but its small-sample properties are not well known.[†]

11.4.2 Simultaneous-Equation Model

The notion that the efficiency of parameter estimates can be improved using system estimation methods can be extended to simultaneous-equation models. The natural extension of Zellner estimation is the technique of three-stage least squares (3SLS).[‡] 3SLS involves the application of generalized least-squares estimation to the system of equations, each of which has first been estimated using 2SLS. In the first stage of the process, the reduced form of the model system is estimated. The fitted values of the endogenous variables are then used to get 2SLS estimates of all the equations in the system. Once the 2SLS parameters have been calculated, the residuals of each equation are used to estimate the cross-equation variances and covariances, just as in the Zellner estimation process described previously. In the third and final stage of the

---

[†] For some information about the properties of Zellner estimation, see A. Zellner, "Estimators of Seemingly Unrelated Regressions: Some Exact Finite Sample Results," *Journal of the American Statistical Association*, vol. 58, pp. 977–992, 1963; and J. Kmenta and R. F. Gilbert, "Small Sample Properties of Alternative Estimators of Seemingly Unrelated Regressions," *Journal of the American Statistical Association*, vol. 63, pp. 1180–1200, 1968.

[‡] See A. Zellner and H. Theil, "Three-Stage Least Squares: Simultaneous Estimation of Simultaneous Relations," *Econometrica*, vol. 30, pp. 54–78, 1962.

estimation process, generalized least-squares parameter estimates are obtained. The 3SLS procedure can be shown to yield more efficient parameter estimates than 2SLS because it takes into account cross-equation correlation.†

If one considers applying 3SLS, several items of information will prove valuable. First, all identities must be removed from the equation system before the estimation process is used.‡ Second, the application of the third stage of the procedure will not alter the 2SLS estimates in the special case in which all the cross-equation covariances are 0. Finally, any equation which is unidentified must be dropped from the equation system before 3SLS is applied. (Recall that 2SLS parameter estimates cannot be obtained for unidentified equations.)

Example 11.5 Public assistance The growth of public relief payments has long been a concern of professional economists. In an attempt to increase knowledge of the public relief problem, Brehm and Saving used statewide data to study the demand for public assistance.§ Data were collected on the number of general assistance recipients on an average per month basis, annually by state for the period 1951–1959. The model developed by the authors focuses on the effects of interstate migration on levels of participation in the general assistance program. This suggests the use of a cross-section estimation with individual observations associated with states of the United States. However, because time-series data were available for a period of 9 years, the authors decided that pooling their data might allow them to obtain more efficient parameter estimates. One equation which was estimated is of the form

$$N_{ij} = \beta_0 + \beta_1 \frac{P_{ij}}{W_{ij}} + \beta_2 U_{ij} + \beta_3 A_{ij} + \varepsilon_{ij}$$

where $i = 1, 2, \ldots, 48$ refers to observations across states

$\quad\quad\quad j = 1, 2, \ldots, 9$ refers to observations over time

$\quad\quad N_{ij}$ = percentage of ith state's population receiving general assistance payments (GAP) in jth year

$\quad\quad P_{ij}$ = average monthly GAP in ith state for jth year

$\quad\quad W_{ij}$ = average monthly manufacturing wage in ith state for jth year

$\quad\quad U_{ij}$ = unemployment rate in ith state for jth year

$\quad\quad A_{ij}$ = nonagricultural employment as percentage of population in ith state for jth year

On the basis of an extensive theoretical development the authors were able to predict that the percentage of the population receiving assistance will be

---

† See A. Madansky, "On the Efficiency of Three-Stage Least Squares Estimation," *Econometrica*, vol. 32, p. 55, 1964.

‡ This can be seen by substituting variables to eliminate the identities from the model, but such a procedure is unnecessary.

§ C. T. Brehm and T. R. Saving, "The Demand for General Assistance Payments," *American Economic Review*, vol. LIX, pp. 1002–1018, 1964.

directly related to average monthly assistance payments and inversely related to the ongoing wage rate. The latter result is expected because higher wages imply a higher opportunity cost of choosing to receive public assistance rather than to work. The unemployment rate appears in the model because it measures the number of individuals whose alternative to general assistance is a zero (or very low) wage. We would expect unemployment rates and public assistance recipient rates to be positively related. Finally, the nonagricultural employment rate that is included is used as a proxy variable for the ease of getting on general assistance rolls. The coefficient is expected to be positive since previous studies have shown a direct relationship between the degree of urbanization in a state and the assistance recipient rate.

In attempting to pool the data, the authors were concerned with the potential links that might exist between the nine individual cross-section relationships, one for each year in which data are available. The primary link is caused by the fact that the effect of migration of individuals from low to high general-assistance-level states takes place over a period of years. Since no lags are included explicitly in the model, it is reasonable to expect that disturbance terms for one state in a given year will be positively related to disturbance terms for that state in preceding as well as future years. The authors decided to improve the efficiency of the estimation process by using Zellner's seemingly unrelated regression technique rather than ordinary least squares. Zellner's generalized least-squares estimation process improves on efficiency by taking explicit account of the expected correlation between disturbance terms associated with separate cross-section equations. The results of their estimations are listed in Table 11.1.

The P/W term is generally the most significant of all the variables (significantly different from 0 at the 5 percent level in all cases but one). In all cases, the coefficient has the expected sign. The unemployment variable coefficient is significant in only three of the nine years, although it had an

Table 11.1 Results of seemingly unrelated estimation

Year	Constant		P/W		U		A	
	Est.	SE	Est.	SE	Est.	SE	Est.	SE
1951	− .7300	.4817	.0684	.0245	.1418	.0671	.0649	.0167
1952	− .8122	.4237	.0317	.0198	.1952	.0516	.0666	.0147
1953	.0673	.5558	.0808	.0257	.0938	.0760	.0177	.0198
1954	− .1399	.4992	.1006	.0189	.0443	.0388	.0251	.0174
1955	− .2245	.5043	.0967	.0185	− .0422	.0510	.0435	.0161
1956	.2102	.4985	.0729	.0175	.0402	.0469	.0254	.0148
1957	.2868	.5371	.0732	.0177	.0583	.0391	.0198	.0169
1958	− .8801	.8324	.0825	.0250	.1799	.0550	.0544	.0298
1959	− 1.0300	.9018	.0952	.0274	.2180	.0898	.0515	.0339
Mean	− .3614		.0780		.1033		.0400	

unexpected sign only once. Finally, the proxy variable for the ease of becoming a general assistance recipient has the expected sign in every case and is significantly different from 0 in four of the nine cases. The results of the study give additional support to the view that income-related variables such as the ratio of assistance payments to the wage rate are important determinants of recipient levels. The remaining variables have a somewhat lesser effect. The authors conclude that general assistance recipients are not unlike most consumers in that they react in expected ways to the economic incentives which exist.

Example 11.6 Macroeconomic model In their original article dealing with three-stage least-squares estimation, Zellner and Theil provide an insightful illustrative example.[†] In the example, 2SLS and 3SLS estimates of a simple macroeconomic model are compared. The model, known as *Klein's Model I*, includes three behavioral equations and three identities.[‡] The behavioral equations are

Consumption: $C = \alpha_0 + \alpha_1 \Pi + \alpha_2(W_1 + W_2) + \alpha_3 \Pi_{-1} + u_1$

Investment: $I = \beta_0 + \beta_1 \Pi + \beta_2 \Pi_{-1} + \beta_3 K_{-1} + u_2$

Demand for labor:

$$W_1 = \gamma_0 + \gamma_1(Y + T - W_2) + \gamma_2(Y + T - W_2)_{-1} + \gamma_3 t + u_3$$

where C=consumption
  Π=profits
  W_1=private wage bill
  W_2=government wage bill
  I=investment
  K=capital stock
  Y=national income
  T=indirect taxes
  t=time, years

The three behavioral equations are linked by three identities:

$$Y + T = C + I + G \qquad Y = W_1 + W_2 + \Pi \qquad K = K_{-1} + I$$

In total, the model includes six endogenous variables and eight predetermined variables. All three behavioral equations are overidentified. The results of the 2SLS and 3SLS estimations are provided in Table 11.2. The reader should pay particular attention to the variances of the coefficient estimators associated with both estimation processes. In all cases (as guaranteed by the estimation process), 3SLS parameter estimates have smaller variances than their 2SLS counterparts. The gain in efficiency associated with 3SLS is usually in the neighborhood of 5 percent. The

† Zellner and Theil, op. cit.
‡ From L. R. Klein, *Economic Fluctuations in the U.S., 1921–1941* (New York: Wiley, 1950).

Table 11.2 Three-stage and two-stage least-squares estimates of parameters

Equation	Coefficient of	3SLS Coefficient estimate	3SLS Variance of coefficient estimator	2SLS Coefficient estimate	2SLS Variance of coefficient estimator
Consumption	Π	.0479	.013119	.0173	.013936
	$W_1 + W_2$	.8170	.001490	.8102	.001620
	Π_{-1}	.1897	.010946	.2162	.011506
	1	16.1923	1.690	16.5548	1.745
Investment	Π	.2111	.028505	.1502	.030084
	Π_{-1}	.5667	.025220	.6159	.026499
	K_{-1}	− .1472	.001202	− .1578	.001305
	1	17.9210	52.516	20.2782	56.892
Demand for labor	$Y + T - W_2$	.4282	.001203	.4389	.001270
	$(Y + T - W_2)_{-1}$	.1543	.001422	.1467	.001508
	t	.1356	.000821	.1304	.000849
	1	1.6935	1.302	1.5003	1.317

example illustrates the benefits of using 3SLS but does not prove its necessity, since computational costs may be high enough to outweigh the efficiency gain.

11.5 COMPARISON OF ALTERNATIVE ESTIMATORS

We have now completed a survey of several single-equation and system estimation procedures. It is useful to pause for a moment and ask how one selects between alternative estimation techniques. The answer is a difficult one, for two reasons. First the choice of estimation procedure may depend in part upon the purpose for which the estimated system of equations is to be used. We shall see in the next chapter, for example, that the choice of estimation technique can have substantial effects on the dynamic properties of the estimated model. Second, most of our knowledge about the properties of estimators relates to large samples; i.e., we know that these estimators will be consistent and (sometimes) asymptotically efficient. We know little, however, about the small-sample properties of these estimators. Some small-sample studies examine the sensitivity of estimated parameters to different estimation techniques using real world data and previously developed models, while others apply *Monte Carlo* experimentation techniques to known artificial model structures.† While the

---

† See, for example, R. Summers, "A Capital Intensive Approach to the Small Sample Properties of Various Simultaneous Equation Estimators," *Econometrica*, vol. 33, pp. 1–41, 1965; J. Johnston, *Econometric Methods*, 2d ed. (New York: McGraw-Hill, 1972), pp. 408–420; G. Chow, "A Comparison of Alternative Estimators for Simultaneous Equations," *Econometrica*, vol. 32, pp. 532–553, October 1964.

results of the studies are varied and difficult to summarize, it would be worthwhile to mention a few of the important issues which arise from them.

Given a truly simultaneous system of equations, we know that ordinary least-squares estimation is inconsistent as well as biased. Two-stage least squares and instrumental variables provide consistent single-equation parameter estimates, but they are biased as well. On the other hand, studies suggest that 2SLS estimates have larger variance than OLS. Thus, if one's criterion is to minimize mean square error (which combines bias and variance), it is conceivable that OLS estimation will be more suitable than 2SLS and other consistent single-equation techniques. On the other hand, studies suggest that systems methods of estimation yield lower variance estimates than do single-equation methods. Since most modern computer packages allow for the use of generalized least-squares estimation, it is not unusual for one to bear the added expense of performing Zellner and 3SLS estimation. The difficulty with all systems estimation techniques, however, is that individual parameter estimates (by construction) are sensitive to the specification of the entire model system. A serious specification error in one equation can affect the parameter estimates in all equations of the model. Thus, the decision to use systems estimation involves a trade-off between the gain in efficiency and the potential costs of specification error.

APPENDIX 11.1 THE IDENTIFICATION PROBLEM IN MATRIX FORM

Representation of the Simultaneous-Equation Model

In order to consider the identification problem in its most general form, we need to develop some additional notation which will allow us to distinguish between endogenous and exogenous variables as well as structural and reduced forms. We assume that the model under investigation consists of G equations. Each equation contains G endogenous variables (some may have coefficients which are known to be equal to 0), K predetermined variables, and a randomly distributed error term. Written equation by equation, the structural form of the model is as follows:†

$$\beta_{11} y_{1i} + \beta_{12} y_{2i} + \cdots + \beta_{1G} y_{Gi} + \gamma_{11} x_{1i} + \gamma_{12} x_{2i} + \cdots + \gamma_{1K} x_{Ki} = u_{1i}$$
$$\beta_{21} y_{1i} + \beta_{22} y_{2i} + \cdots + \beta_{2G} y_{Gi} + \gamma_{21} x_{1i} + \gamma_{22} x_{2i} + \cdots + \gamma_{2K} x_{Ki} = u_{2i}$$
$$\cdots\cdots\cdots\cdots\cdots\cdots\cdots\cdots\cdots\cdots\cdots\cdots\cdots\cdots\cdots$$
$$\beta_{G1} y_{1i} + \beta_{G2} y_{2i} + \cdots + \beta_{GG} y_{Gi} + \gamma_{G1} x_{1i} + \gamma_{G2} x_{2i} + \cdots + \gamma_{GK} x_{Ki} = u_{Gi}$$

for $i = 1, 2, \ldots, N$. As in the text, the y's are the endogenous variables and the x's the predetermined variables. In each equation some of the coefficients are

---

† We have chosen a notation which is most nearly consistent with the notation used in other econometrics textbooks. In this notation, lowercase letters do not imply that variables are measured as deviations about their means.

equal to 0, and one of the endogenous variables is chosen to have a coefficient of 1. The variable with the coefficient 1 is viewed as the dependent variable (equations in the text are written in this form). The set of equations given previously can be written in matrix form as

$$\mathbf{B}\mathbf{y}_i + \mathbf{\Gamma}\mathbf{x}_i = \mathbf{u}_i \tag{A11.1}$$

where

$$\mathbf{y}_i = \begin{bmatrix} y_{1i} \\ y_{2i} \\ \vdots \\ y_{Gi} \end{bmatrix} \qquad \mathbf{x}_i = \begin{bmatrix} x_{1i} \\ x_{2i} \\ \vdots \\ x_{Ki} \end{bmatrix} \qquad \mathbf{u}_i = \begin{bmatrix} u_{1i} \\ u_{2i} \\ \vdots \\ u_{Gi} \end{bmatrix}$$

$$\mathbf{B} = \begin{bmatrix} \beta_{11} & \beta_{12} & \cdots & \beta_{1G} \\ \beta_{21} & \beta_{22} & \cdots & \beta_{2G} \\ \vdots & & & \vdots \\ \beta_{G1} & \beta_{G2} & \cdots & \beta_{GG} \end{bmatrix} \qquad \mathbf{\Gamma} = \begin{bmatrix} \gamma_{11} & \gamma_{12} & \cdots & \gamma_{1K} \\ \gamma_{21} & \gamma_{22} & \cdots & \gamma_{2K} \\ \vdots & & & \vdots \\ \gamma_{G1} & \gamma_{G2} & \cdots & \gamma_{GK} \end{bmatrix}$$

where $\mathbf{y}_i = G \times 1$ vector of endogenous variables
$\mathbf{x}_i = K \times 1$ vector of predetermined variables
$\mathbf{u}_i = G \times 1$ vector of disturbance terms
$\mathbf{B} = G \times G$ matrix of endogenous variable coefficients
$\mathbf{\Gamma} = G \times K$ matrix of predetermined variable coefficients

If we wish to include all N observations available for each y and each x and use the matrix notation, we can rewrite the model as

$$\mathbf{B}\mathbf{Y} + \mathbf{\Gamma}\mathbf{X} = \mathbf{U} \tag{A11.2}$$

where $\mathbf{Y} = G \times N$ matrix
$\mathbf{X} = K \times N$ matrix
$\mathbf{U} = G \times N$ matrix

$$\mathbf{Y} = \begin{bmatrix} y_{11} & y_{12} & \cdots & y_{1N} \\ y_{21} & y_{22} & \cdots & y_{2N} \\ \vdots & & & \vdots \\ y_{G1} & y_{G2} & \cdots & y_{GN} \end{bmatrix} \qquad \mathbf{X} = \begin{bmatrix} x_{11} & x_{12} & \cdots & x_{1N} \\ x_{21} & x_{22} & \cdots & x_{2N} \\ \vdots & & & \vdots \\ x_{K1} & x_{K1} & \cdots & x_{KN} \end{bmatrix}$$

$$\mathbf{U} = \begin{bmatrix} u_{11} & u_{12} & \cdots & u_{1N} \\ u_{21} & u_{22} & \cdots & u_{2N} \\ \vdots & & & \vdots \\ u_{G1} & u_{G2} & \cdots & u_{GN} \end{bmatrix}$$

The structural equation contains G equations and G unknowns. If all β's and γ's are known, we can in principle solve for the values of each of the y's, given values of the predetermined x's. To do so, we assume that $\mathbf{B}$ is nonsingular and solve to get the reduced-form representation of the model. Premultiplying both sides of Eq. (A11.1) by the matrix $\mathbf{B}^{-1}$, we get

$$\mathbf{y}_i + \mathbf{B}^{-1}\mathbf{\Gamma}\mathbf{x}_i = \mathbf{B}^{-1}\mathbf{u}_i$$

or

$$\mathbf{y}_i = \boldsymbol{\pi}\mathbf{x}_i + \mathbf{v}_i$$

where $\boldsymbol{\pi} = -\mathbf{B}^{-1}\mathbf{\Gamma}$ is a $G \times K$ matrix of reduced-form coefficients

$$\boldsymbol{\pi} = \begin{bmatrix} \pi_{11} & \pi_{12} & \cdots & \pi_{1K} \\ \pi_{21} & \pi_{22} & \cdots & \pi_{2K} \\ \vdots & & & \vdots \\ \pi_{G1} & \pi_{G2} & \cdots & \pi_{GK} \end{bmatrix}$$

and $\mathbf{v}_i = \mathbf{B}^{-1}\mathbf{u}_i$ is a $G \times 1$ vector of reduced-form disturbances. The reduced form of the model is

$$
\begin{aligned}
y_{1i} &= \pi_{11}x_{1i} + \pi_{12}x_{2i} + \cdots + \pi_{1K}x_{Ki} + v_{1i} \\
y_{2i} &= \pi_{21}x_{1i} + \pi_{22}x_{2i} + \cdots + \pi_{2K}x_{Ki} + v_{2i} \\
&\cdots \\
y_{Gi} &= \pi_{G1}x_{1i} + \pi_{G2}x_{2i} + \cdots + \pi_{GK}x_{Ki} + v_{Gi}
\end{aligned}
$$

In terms of all N equations, we would rewrite the system of equations as

$$
\mathbf{Y} = \pi\mathbf{X} + \mathbf{V} \tag{A11.3}
$$

where $\mathbf{Y} = G \times N$ matrix
  $\pi = G \times K$ matrix
  $\mathbf{X} = K \times N$ matrix
  $\mathbf{V} = G \times N$ matrix

In order to complete our description of the simultaneous-equation model, we need to specify the assumptions involving the error term $\mathbf{u}_i$. We shall assume that

$$
E(\mathbf{u}_i) = \mathbf{0} \tag{A11.4}
$$

and

$$
E(\mathbf{u}_i\mathbf{u}_i') = \Sigma \tag{A11.5}
$$

where Σ is a $G \times G$ matrix of variances and covariances between error terms of identical observations across equations. Σ need not be a multiple of the identity matrix, since covariances of identical observations across different equations may be nonzero. We also assume that

$$
E(\mathbf{u}_i\mathbf{u}_j') = \mathbf{0} \qquad i, j = 1, 2, \ldots, N \\
i \neq j \tag{A11.6}
$$

This assumption eliminates all correlations between errors associated with different observations, both within equations and across different equations.

It is also useful to relate the reduced-form error term to the structural error term. Reduced-form errors have 0 mean since

$$
E(\mathbf{v}_i) = E(\mathbf{B}^{-1}\mathbf{u}_i) = \mathbf{B}^{-1}E(\mathbf{u}_i) = \mathbf{0} \qquad i = 1, 2, \ldots, N \tag{A11.7}
$$

The variance-covariance matrix of the reduced-form errors Ω is

$$
\Omega = E(\mathbf{v}_i\mathbf{v}_i') = E\left[\mathbf{B}^{-1}\mathbf{u}_i\mathbf{u}_i'(\mathbf{B}')^{-1}\right] = \mathbf{B}^{-1}E(\mathbf{u}_i\mathbf{u}_i')(\mathbf{B}')^{-1} = \mathbf{B}^{-1}\Sigma(\mathbf{B}')^{-1} \tag{A11.8}
$$

Conditions for Identification

The presence of right-hand endogenous variables in the simultaneous-equation model guarantees that ordinary least-squares estimates of the structural form of the model will be inconsistent. However, ordinary least-squares estimates of the reduced form will be consistent, since only predetermined variables appear on the right-hand side of the reduced-form equations. Thus, it is natural to ask whether it is possible to obtain information about structural parameters, given that consistent estimates of reduced-form parameters can be obtained. The problem of expressing the β's and γ's in terms of the reduced-form coefficients (the π's) is the *identification problem*. We shall say that a structural parameter is identified if and only if it can be uniquely determined from the set of reduced-form parameters. In our notation, the link between the structural and reduced forms is provided by two equations:

$$\pi = -\mathbf{B}^{-1}\mathbf{\Gamma} \tag{A11.9}$$

$$\Omega = \mathbf{B}^{-1}\mathbf{\Sigma}(\mathbf{B}')^{-1} \tag{A11.10}$$

Knowledge of the reduced form is provided by the $G \times K$ elements of π. Unfortunately, our goal is to determine the $G \times G$ elements of $\mathbf{B}$ and the $G \times K$ elements of $\mathbf{\Gamma}$. Unless further information is known *a priori*, the goal will be impossible to obtain. What is required is information about restrictions on the structural-form parameters. As we have suggested in the text, *a priori* restrictions can be of several types. Restrictions may involve linear relationships between structural parameters as well as restrictions on elements of the variance-covariance matrix of the structural disturbances. We shall focus our attention on the most prevalent form of identifying restriction—the zero restriction on structural-form parameters.

We concentrate, without loss of generality, on the identification of the first equation. In addition, we presume that the variables with 0 coefficient restrictions are grouped after the variables with nonzero coefficients. We assume that of the G endogenous variables in the first equation, the first G_* have nonzero coefficients, while the remaining G_{**} are assumed to have 0 coefficients ($G = G_* + G_{**}$). In addition, K_0 of the predetermined variables have nonzero coefficients, while K_{00} are equal to 0 ($K = K_0 + K_{00}$). In other words, the first equation has G_{**} excluded endogenous variables and K_{00} excluded predetermined variables. The first equation can then be written

$$\begin{bmatrix} \beta_{11} & \beta_{12} & \cdots & \beta_{1G_*} & 0 & 0 & \cdots & 0 \end{bmatrix} \begin{bmatrix} y_{1i} \\ y_{2i} \\ \vdots \\ y_{Gi} \end{bmatrix}$$

$$+ \begin{bmatrix} \gamma_{11} & \gamma_{12} & \cdots & \gamma_{1K_0} & 0 & 0 & \cdots & 0 \end{bmatrix} \begin{bmatrix} x_{1i} \\ x_{2i} \\ \vdots \\ x_{Ki} \end{bmatrix} = \begin{bmatrix} u_{1i} \\ u_{2i} \\ \vdots \\ u_{Gi} \end{bmatrix}$$

We shall find it valuable to represent the equation as

$$\begin{bmatrix} \beta_* & \beta_{**} \end{bmatrix} \begin{bmatrix} y_* \\ y_{**} \end{bmatrix} + \begin{bmatrix} \gamma_0 & \gamma_{00} \end{bmatrix} \begin{bmatrix} x_0 \\ x_{00} \end{bmatrix} = \mathbf{u}_i \tag{A11.11}$$

where $y_* = G_* \times 1$ vector of observations on included endogenous variables

$y_{**} = G_{**} \times 1$ vector of observations on excluded endogenous variables

$\beta_* = 1 \times G_*$ vector of nonzero coefficients

$\beta_{**} = 1 \times G_{**}$ vector of 0's

$\gamma_0 = 1 \times K_0$ vector of nonzero coefficients

$\gamma_{00} = 1 \times K_{00}$ vector of 0's

$x_0 = K_0 \times 1$ vector of observations on included predetermined variables

$x_{00} = K_{00} \times 1$ vector of observations on excluded predetermined variables

We have dropped the i subscript in order to simplify the notation. We can rewrite the first equation as

$$\beta_* y_* + \gamma_0 x_0 = u \tag{A11.12}$$

by eliminating the terms with 0 coefficients. Using a similar notation, we can rewrite the reduced-form equation as

$$\begin{bmatrix} y_* & y_{**} \end{bmatrix} = \begin{bmatrix} \pi_{*,0} & \pi_{*,00} \\ \pi_{**,0} & \pi_{**,00} \end{bmatrix} \begin{bmatrix} x_0 & x_{00} \end{bmatrix} + \begin{bmatrix} v_* & v_{**} \end{bmatrix}$$

In the partitioned matrix of reduced-form coefficients the first subscript refers to the endogenous variables and the second to the predetermined variables:

$\pi_{*,0} = G_* \times K_0$ matrix

$\pi_{*,00} = G_* \times K_{00}$ matrix

$\pi_{**,0} = G_{**} \times K_0$ matrix

$\pi_{**,00} = G_{**} \times K_{00}$ matrix

$v_* = G_* \times 1$ vector of the first G_* reduced-form disturbances

$v_{**} = G_{**} \times 1$ vector of the remaining reduced-form disturbances

Now we are in a position to examine the conditions which are necessary and sufficient to identify the structural parameters. To do so, we rewrite Eq. (A11.9) as

$$B\pi = -\Gamma \tag{A11.13}$$

and then rewrite (A11.13) only in terms of the first equation of the simultaneous-equation system:

$$\begin{bmatrix} \beta_* & 0 \end{bmatrix} \begin{bmatrix} \pi_{*,0} & \pi_{*,00} \\ \pi_{**,0} & \pi_{**,00} \end{bmatrix} = -\begin{bmatrix} \gamma_0 & 0 \end{bmatrix}$$

It is useful to divide the previous matrix equation into two separate subequations:

$$\beta_* \pi_{*,0} = -\gamma_0 \tag{A11.14}$$

$$\beta_* \pi_{*,00} = 0 \tag{A11.15}$$

We have previously normalized one of the β's in the first equation to be equal to 1. Then Eq. (A11.14) has $G_* - 1$ unknown β's and K_0 unknown γ's. Equation (A11.15) involves only the $G_* - 1$ unknown β's. We shall focus for the moment on the second equation, which consists of K_{00} individual equations. We know that a necessary condition for the existence of a solution to (A11.15) is that there are at least $G_* - 1$ equations. This leads directly to the *order condition* for identification:

$$K_{00} \geq G_* - 1 \tag{A11.16}$$

where K_{00} is the number of excluded predetermined variables and G_* is the number of included endogenous variables. The order condition is not a sufficient condition for identification, because not all the K_{00} equations need be independent of each other. This suggests that a necessary and sufficient condition for identification will be one which guarantees that $G_* - 1$ of the K_{00} equations are in fact independent. This condition, often called the *rank condition*, can be stated as follows:†

$$\text{rank} \left[\pi_{*, 00} \right] = G_* - 1 \tag{A11.17}$$

Once the $G_* - 1$ unknown β's are determined from Eq. (A11.15), there is no difficulty in solving Eq. (A11.14) for the coefficients of the predetermined variables.

APPENDIX 11.2   TWO-STAGE LEAST SQUARES IN MATRIX FORM

Recall from Appendix 11.1 that the determination of the unknown structural coefficients depends upon a solution to the equation

$$\beta_* \pi_{*, 00} = 0 \tag{A11.18}$$

Given that one β has been set equal to 1, we seek (directly) to obtain values for the remaining $G_* - 1$ unknown β's. Such a solution will exist if $\text{rank}[\pi_{*, 00}] = G_* - 1$. If the rank condition is satisfied and $K_{00} = G_* - 1$, then the first equation is exactly identified. If $K_{00} > G_* - 1$, however, the equation is overidentified. Overidentification occurs because there are more than $G_* - 1$ equations in (A11.18) from which we wish to find estimates of the $G_* - 1$ unknown β's. There are several ways to combine the set of equations to obtain the value of β_*. In the overidentified case, two-stage least squares becomes an appropriate estimation procedure. Two-stage least squares uses all the information available in the equation system (A11.18) to obtain unique structural parameter estimates.

We shall describe the application of 2SLS to the estimation of the first structural equation, which we presume to be overidentified. To do so, it is useful to alter the notation of Appendix 11.1, expressing the first equation as

$$\mathbf{y}_1 = \mathbf{Y}_1 \boldsymbol{\beta}_1 + \mathbf{X}_1 \boldsymbol{\gamma}_1 + \mathbf{u}_1 \tag{A11.19}$$

---

† Since a detailed explanation of the rank condition necessitates a lengthy discussion of certain aspects of matrix algebra, we shall not pursue the matter further here.

where $y_1 = N \times 1$ vector of observations on endogenous variable with coefficient of 1 in first equation

$Y_1 = N \times (G_* - 1)$ matrix of observations on endogenous variables included in first equation (on right-hand side)

$\beta_1 = (G_* - 1) \times 1$ vector of coefficients for included endogenous variables

$X_1 = N \times K_0$ matrix of observations on included predetermined variables

$\gamma_1 = K_0 \times 1$ vector of predetermined variable coefficients

$u_1 = N \times 1$ vector of disturbances associated with first equation

As described in the text, the application of ordinary least squares to Eq. (A11.19) will yield inconsistent parameter estimates due to the fact that Y_1 and u_1 are (asymptotically) correlated. 2SLS yields consistent estimates by purging Y_1 of the component which is correlated with u_1 and then rerunning the new regression using OLS.

In the first stage, each of the right-hand endogenous variables is regressed on the *entire* set of predetermined variables in the model. This is equivalent to estimating the reduced-form equations associated with the $G_* - 1$ right-hand endogenous variables. We might represent this as

$$Y_1 = X_1\pi_1 + X_2\pi_2 + V \tag{A11.20}$$

or

$$Y_1 = X\pi + V \tag{A11.21}$$

where $X_2 = N \times K_{00}$ matrix of observations on predetermined variables excluded from first equation

$\pi_1 = K_0 \times (G_* - 1)$ matrix of reduced-form coefficients

$\pi_2 = K_{00} \times (G_* - 1)$ matrix of reduced-form coefficients

$V = N \times (G_* - 1)$ matrix of reduced-form disturbances

The resulting first-stage estimator is

$$\hat{\pi} = (X'X)^{-1}X'Y_1 \tag{A11.22}$$

from which we calculate the fitted values for Y_1:

$$\hat{Y}_1 = X\hat{\pi} \tag{A11.23}$$

In the second stage we perform an ordinary least-squares procedure of y_1 on $\hat{Y}_1$ and X_1. The estimated coefficients are the 2SLS parameter estimates of β_1 and γ_1. In terms of our matrix formulation, the second-stage estimators are

$$\begin{bmatrix} \hat{\beta}_1 \\ \hat{\gamma}_1 \end{bmatrix} = \{[\hat{Y}_1 \quad X_1]'[\hat{Y}_1 \quad X_1]\}^{-1}[\hat{Y}_1 \quad X_1]'y_1 \tag{A11.24}$$

or

$$\begin{bmatrix} \hat{\beta}_1 \\ \hat{\gamma}_1 \end{bmatrix} = \begin{bmatrix} \hat{Y}_1'\hat{Y}_1 & \hat{Y}_1'X_1 \\ X_1'\hat{Y}_1 & X_1'X_1 \end{bmatrix}^{-1} \begin{bmatrix} \hat{Y}_1'y_1 \\ X_1'y_1 \end{bmatrix} \tag{A11.25}$$

We can rewrite the 2SLS estimators in a more useful form by taking into account the fact that the residuals of the first-stage regression are uncorrelated with all the predetermined variables, that is,

$$\hat{V}'X = 0 = X'\hat{V} \tag{A11.26}$$

Also,
$$\hat{\mathbf{Y}}_1'\hat{\mathbf{V}} = \mathbf{0} \tag{A11.27}$$

since $\hat{\mathbf{Y}}_1$ is a linear combination of predetermined variables. Thus,
$$\mathbf{Y}_1'\mathbf{Y}_1 = (\hat{\mathbf{Y}}_1 + \hat{\mathbf{V}})'(\hat{\mathbf{Y}}_1 + \hat{\mathbf{V}}) = \hat{\mathbf{Y}}_1'\hat{\mathbf{Y}}_1 + \hat{\mathbf{V}}'\hat{\mathbf{V}}$$

Also
$$\mathbf{X}_1'\hat{\mathbf{Y}}_1 = \mathbf{X}_1'(\mathbf{Y}_1 - \hat{\mathbf{V}}) = \mathbf{X}_1'\mathbf{Y}_1$$

Therefore, we can rewrite Eq. (A11.25) as

$$\begin{bmatrix} \hat{\boldsymbol{\beta}}_1 \\ \hat{\boldsymbol{\gamma}}_1 \end{bmatrix} = \begin{bmatrix} \mathbf{Y}_1'\mathbf{Y}_1 - \hat{\mathbf{V}}'\hat{\mathbf{V}} & \mathbf{Y}_1'\mathbf{X}_1 \\ \mathbf{X}_1'\mathbf{Y}_1 & \mathbf{X}_1'\mathbf{X}_1 \end{bmatrix}^{-1} \begin{bmatrix} (\mathbf{Y}_1 - \hat{\mathbf{V}})'\mathbf{y}_1 \\ \mathbf{X}_1'\mathbf{y}_1 \end{bmatrix} \tag{A11.28}$$

As a comparison to the 2SLS estimator, the reader might find it useful to examine the inconsistent estimators which would be obtained if ordinary least squares were applied to the structural equation directly. The estimators are

$$\begin{bmatrix} \hat{\boldsymbol{\beta}}_1^0 \\ \hat{\boldsymbol{\gamma}}_1^0 \end{bmatrix} = \begin{bmatrix} \mathbf{Y}_1'\mathbf{Y}_1 & \mathbf{Y}_1'\mathbf{X}_1 \\ \mathbf{X}_1'\mathbf{Y}_1 & \mathbf{X}_1'\mathbf{X}_1 \end{bmatrix}^{-1} \begin{bmatrix} \mathbf{Y}_1'\mathbf{y}_1 \\ \mathbf{X}_1'\mathbf{y}_1 \end{bmatrix} \tag{A11.29}$$

Incidentally, it is not difficult to show that 2SLS is an instrumental variables estimator, where the fitted values of the first stage and the included predetermined variables of the first stage are the appropriate instruments. To see this, we write the instrumental variables estimator as follows:

$$\begin{bmatrix} \hat{\boldsymbol{\beta}}_1^* \\ \hat{\boldsymbol{\gamma}}_1^* \end{bmatrix} = \left\{ \begin{bmatrix} \hat{\mathbf{Y}}_1 & \mathbf{X}_1 \end{bmatrix}' \begin{bmatrix} \mathbf{Y}_1 & \mathbf{X}_1 \end{bmatrix} \right\}^{-1} \begin{bmatrix} \hat{\mathbf{Y}}_1 & \mathbf{X}_1 \end{bmatrix}' \mathbf{y}_1$$

Expanding terms and simplifying, we find that

$$\begin{bmatrix} \hat{\boldsymbol{\beta}}_1^* \\ \hat{\boldsymbol{\gamma}}_1^* \end{bmatrix} = \begin{bmatrix} \hat{\mathbf{Y}}_1'\mathbf{Y}_1 & \hat{\mathbf{Y}}_1'\mathbf{X}_1 \\ \mathbf{X}_1'\mathbf{Y}_1 & \mathbf{X}_1'\mathbf{X}_1 \end{bmatrix}^{-1} \begin{bmatrix} \hat{\mathbf{Y}}_1'\mathbf{y}_1 \\ \mathbf{X}_1'\mathbf{y}_1 \end{bmatrix}$$

$$= \begin{bmatrix} \mathbf{Y}_1'\mathbf{Y}_1 - \hat{\mathbf{V}}'\hat{\mathbf{V}} & \mathbf{Y}_1'\mathbf{X}_1 \\ \mathbf{X}_1'\mathbf{Y}_1 & \mathbf{X}_1'\mathbf{X}_1 \end{bmatrix}^{-1} \begin{bmatrix} \hat{\mathbf{Y}}_1'\mathbf{y}_1 \\ \mathbf{X}_1'\mathbf{y}_1 \end{bmatrix} = \begin{bmatrix} \hat{\boldsymbol{\beta}}_1 \\ \hat{\boldsymbol{\gamma}}_1 \end{bmatrix}$$

The consistency of 2SLS is too difficult to prove here, but it is important for statistical purposes to outline a derivation of the asymptotic variance-covariance matrix of the estimated parameters. To do so, we can use the formula for the asymptotic variance-covariance matrix of the instrumental variables estimator as described in the appendix to Chapter 7. In our notation the variance-covariance matrix is

$$\text{Var} \begin{bmatrix} \hat{\boldsymbol{\beta}}_1 \\ \hat{\boldsymbol{\gamma}}_1 \end{bmatrix} = \sigma^2 \left\{ \begin{bmatrix} \hat{\mathbf{Y}}_1 & \mathbf{X}_1 \end{bmatrix}' \begin{bmatrix} \mathbf{Y}_1 & \mathbf{X}_1 \end{bmatrix} \right\}^{-1}$$

$$\times \left\{ \begin{bmatrix} \hat{\mathbf{Y}}_1 & \mathbf{X}_1 \end{bmatrix}' \begin{bmatrix} \hat{\mathbf{Y}}_1 & \mathbf{X}_1 \end{bmatrix} \right\} \left\{ \begin{bmatrix} \mathbf{Y}_1 & \mathbf{X}_1 \end{bmatrix}' \begin{bmatrix} \hat{\mathbf{Y}}_1 & \mathbf{X}_1 \end{bmatrix} \right\}^{-1}$$

But
$$\mathbf{Y}_1'\mathbf{X}_1 = (\hat{\mathbf{Y}}_1 + \hat{\mathbf{V}})'\mathbf{X}_1 = \hat{\mathbf{Y}}_1'\mathbf{X}_1$$

Expanding the expression for Var $\begin{bmatrix} \hat{\beta}_1 \\ \hat{\gamma}_1 \end{bmatrix}$ using the previous result, we get

$$\text{Var}\begin{bmatrix} \hat{\beta}_1 \\ \hat{\gamma}_1 \end{bmatrix} = \sigma^2 \{ [\, \hat{Y}_1 \quad X_1 \,]'[\, Y_1 \quad X_1 \,] \}^{-1} = \sigma^2 \begin{bmatrix} Y_1'Y_1 - \hat{V}'\hat{V} & Y_1'X_1 \\ X_1'Y_1 & X_1'X_1 \end{bmatrix}^{-1}$$

(A11.30)

In practice, σ^2 is estimated by

$$s^2 = \frac{\hat{u}_1'\hat{u}_1}{N - [(G_* - 1) + K_0]} \qquad \text{where } \hat{u}_1 = y_1 - Y_1\hat{\beta}_1 - X_1\hat{\gamma}_1$$

Notice that the residuals utilized to calculate s^2 do not come from the second-stage regression alone, but are calculated from the *original* structural equation with the estimated parameters replacing the true parameters. The variance-covariance matrix, on the other hand, does account for the second-stage use of fitted values for Y_1, as seen by the fact that $Y_1'Y_1 - \hat{V}'\hat{V}$ $(= \hat{Y}_1'\hat{Y}_1)$ appears in the matrix to be inverted (rather than $Y_1'Y_1$ alone).

APPENDIX 11.3 ZELLNER ESTIMATION IN MATRIX FORM

As described in the text, Zellner estimation is simply the application of generalized least-squares estimation to a group of seemingly unrelated equations. The equations are related through the nonzero covariances associated with error terms across different equations at a given point in time. We can generalize the seemingly unrelated model by writing the system of G equations as follows:

$$Y_i = X_i\beta_i + u_i \qquad i = 1, 2, \ldots, G \qquad (A11.31)$$

where $Y_i = N \times 1$ vector
$\quad X_i = N \times K_i$ matrix
$\quad \beta_i = K_i \times 1$ vector
$\quad u_i = N \times 1$ vector

It will be useful to write the model in shorthand form as $Y = X\beta + u$, or

$$\begin{bmatrix} Y_1 \\ Y_2 \\ \vdots \\ Y_G \end{bmatrix} = \begin{bmatrix} X_1 & 0 & \cdots & 0 \\ 0 & X_2 & \cdots & 0 \\ \vdots & & & \vdots \\ 0 & 0 & \cdots & X_G \end{bmatrix} \begin{bmatrix} \beta_1 \\ \beta_2 \\ \vdots \\ \beta_G \end{bmatrix} + \begin{bmatrix} u_1 \\ u_2 \\ \vdots \\ u_G \end{bmatrix} \qquad (A11.32)$$

where $Y = GN \times 1$ matrix
$\quad X = GN \times \left(\sum\limits_{i=1}^{G} K_i \right)$ matrix
$\quad \beta = \left(\sum\limits_{i=1}^{G} K_i \right) \times 1$ matrix
$\quad u = GN \times 1$ matrix

According to the assumptions of the seemingly unrelated model, there is no autocorrelation within equations, but cross-equation correlation does exist; i.e.,

$$
E(\mathbf{u}_i\mathbf{u}_j') = \begin{bmatrix} \sigma_{ij} & 0 & \cdots & 0 \\ 0 & \sigma_{ij} & \cdots & 0 \\ \cdot & \cdot & \cdots & \cdot \\ 0 & 0 & \cdots & \sigma_{ij} \end{bmatrix} = \sigma_{ij}\mathbf{I} \tag{A11.33}
$$

where $\mathbf{I}$ is a $G \times G$ identity matrix. This relationship applies to the covariances between two arbitrary equations in the system of G equations. To generalize this result in matrix form, we write

$$
\Omega = E(\mathbf{u}\mathbf{u}') = \begin{bmatrix} E(\mathbf{u}_1\mathbf{u}_1') & E(\mathbf{u}_1\mathbf{u}_2') & \cdots & E(\mathbf{u}_1\mathbf{u}_G') \\ E(\mathbf{u}_2\mathbf{u}_1') & E(\mathbf{u}_2\mathbf{u}_2') & \cdots & E(\mathbf{u}_2\mathbf{u}_G') \\ \cdot & \cdot & \cdots & \cdot \\ E(\mathbf{u}_G\mathbf{u}_1') & E(\mathbf{u}_G\mathbf{u}_2') & \cdots & E(\mathbf{u}_G\mathbf{u}_G') \end{bmatrix}
$$

Substituting from (A11.33), we get

$$
\Omega = \begin{bmatrix} \sigma_{11}\mathbf{I} & \sigma_{12}\mathbf{I} & \cdots & \sigma_{1G}\mathbf{I} \\ \sigma_{21}\mathbf{I} & \sigma_{22}\mathbf{I} & \cdots & \sigma_{2G}\mathbf{I} \\ \cdot & \cdot & \cdots & \cdot \\ \sigma_{G1}\mathbf{I} & \sigma_{G2}\mathbf{I} & \cdots & \sigma_{GG}\mathbf{I} \end{bmatrix}
$$

All information about error covariances is contained in the matrix Ω. The most efficient estimation of Eq. (A11.32) is obtained by applying generalized least-squares estimation to get

$$
\hat{\beta} = (\mathbf{X}'\Omega^{-1}\mathbf{X})^{-1}(\mathbf{X}'\Omega^{-1}\mathbf{Y}) \tag{A11.34}
$$

with

$$
E\left[(\hat{\beta} - \beta)(\hat{\beta} - \beta)'\right] = (\mathbf{X}'\Omega^{-1}\mathbf{X})^{-1} \tag{A11.35}
$$

In practice the elements of Ω must be estimated. This is accomplished by using the residuals obtained when ordinary least-squares estimation is applied to each of the G equations:

$$
\hat{\sigma}_{ii} = \frac{\hat{\mathbf{u}}_i\hat{\mathbf{u}}_i'}{N - K_i}
$$

$$
\hat{\sigma}_{ij} = \frac{\hat{\mathbf{u}}_i\hat{\mathbf{u}}_j'}{\sqrt{(N - K_i)(N - K_j)}}
$$

$$
\hat{\mathbf{u}}_i = \mathbf{Y}_i - \mathbf{X}_i\hat{\beta}_i
$$

There are two important cases in which Zellner estimation is equivalent to the equation-by-equation application of ordinary least squares. The first case occurs when $\sigma_{ij} = 0$ for every i and j, $i \neq j$. Then Ω simplifies to

$$
\Omega = \begin{bmatrix} \sigma_{11}\mathbf{I} & 0 & \cdots & 0 \\ 0 & \sigma_{22}\mathbf{I} & \cdots & 0 \\ \cdot & \cdot & \cdots & \cdot \\ 0 & 0 & \cdots & \sigma_{GG}\mathbf{I} \end{bmatrix} \tag{A11.36}
$$

The use of simple matrix algebra [substituting (A11.36) into (A11.35)] is sufficient to prove the stated result. A second, less obvious case occurs when $\mathbf{X}_i = \mathbf{X}$ for every $i = 1, 2, \ldots, G$ ($K_i = K$ is implicit). This occurs when the identical set of independent variables appears in each equation. Once again the proof involves a straightforward application of the techniques of matrix algebra.

APPENDIX 11.4 MAXIMUM-LIKELIHOOD ESTIMATION OF EQUATION SYSTEMS

Limited-Information Maximum-Likelihood Estimation

The material on errors in variables discussed in Chapter 7 mentioned a disturbing property of the 2SLS estimation process. Before describing problems of simultaneity, we found that it was important to distinguish between errors in the dependent variable (no problem) and errors in the right-hand variables (a serious problem). In fact, the choice of left- and right-hand variables was related to our basic assumptions about both variable and equation error. Now reconsider Eqs. (11.22) and (11.23). Despite the fact that the endogenous variables are correlated with u_1, they are treated in the same way as predetermined variables when the 2SLS procedure is used. Both variables are replaced using the first-stage process, of course, but the residual sum of squares to be minimized in the second stage is based on deviations from the left-hand variable. The arbitrariness of this procedure is brought about because of the implicit normalization associated with the choice of dependent variable (with a coefficient of 1) for each equation. To see the arbitrariness of this normalization, rewrite each of the two equations, by solving the first for y_2 and the second for y_1. The revised equations are

$$y_2 = \frac{1}{\alpha_2} y_1 - \frac{u_1}{\alpha_2} \tag{A11.37}$$

$$y_1 = \frac{1}{\beta_1} y_2 - \frac{\beta_3}{\beta_1} z_1 - \frac{\beta_4}{\beta_1} z_2 - \frac{u_2}{\beta_1} \tag{A11.38}$$

Once again the first equation (A11.37) is overidentified, so that we might attempt to estimate α_2 by using 2SLS. In the first stage we would regress y_1 on the predetermined reduced-form variables z_1 and z_2 and obtain fitted values $\hat{y}_1$. A regression of y_2 on $\hat{y}_1$ would allow us to estimate the unknown parameter α_2:

$$\tilde{\alpha}_2 = \frac{1}{\sum \hat{y}_1 y_2 / \sum \hat{y}_1 \hat{y}_1} \tag{A11.39}$$

A careful check shows that $\tilde{\alpha}_2$ and α_2^* (Section 11.3) will not yield the same parameter estimate. The difficulty is equivalent to that discussed in Chapter 1 when minimization using vertical deviations was seen to be different from minimization using horizontal deviations.

As a solution to this troubling problem it is natural to look for an estimation process which is invariant to the type of normalization made, i.e., to the choice of left-hand variables in each equation. While the derivation of this new limited-information estimator† is beyond the scope of this book, we shall attempt to motivate it to some extent by using our original example. Our desire to find a "neutral" estimation process involves the search for a technique which yields parameter estimates somewhere between the two versions of 2SLS just described.

To motivate best the derivation of the new limited-information estimator, consider the following two-equation model:

$$y_1 = \alpha_2 y_2 + \alpha_4 z_1 + u_1 \tag{A11.40}$$

$$y_2 = \beta_1 y_1 + \beta_5 z_2 + \beta_6 z_3 + u_2 \tag{A11.41}$$

Assume that we wish to estimate the first equation without making the normalization that the coefficient of y_1 is equal to 1. To do so, we rewrite the first (overidentified) equation, replacing y_1 as the endogenous variable with a weighted average of the two endogenous variables y_1 and y_2. The artificially constructed variable is

$$y^* = \gamma_1 y_1 + \gamma_2 y_2 \tag{A11.42}$$

and the first equation can now be written

$$y^* = \gamma_4 z_1 + u_1 \tag{A11.43}$$

If our estimation procedure is properly chosen, y^* should be constructed so that Eq. (A11.43) fits the data as closely as possible. This objective is achieved by selecting γ_1 and γ_2 so that the coefficient γ_4 is significantly different from 0 while at the same time the deleted variables z_2 and z_3 add little or no explanatory power to the model. The only additional explanatory power which might exist will arise because the zero restrictions are only approximately satisfied in the particular sample being used.

If substantial explanatory power were added by the addition of z_2 and z_3 to Eq. (A11.43), then the restriction that allowed for the equation to be identified would be incorrect. This suggests that we ought to choose γ_1 and γ_2 jointly to minimize the following ratio:‡

$$\lambda = \frac{\text{residual variance after regressing } y^* \text{ on } z_1}{\text{residual variance after regressing } y^* \text{ on } z_1, z_2, \text{ and } z_3} \tag{A11.44}$$

---

† For an extensive discussion of this estimator see T. C. Koopmans and W. C. Hood, "The Estimation of Simultaneous Linear Economic Relationships," in Hood and Koopmans, *Studies in Econometric Method* (New York: Wiley, 1953), pp. 166–177. The authors prove that this estimation process is a limited-information maximum-likelihood estimator. It involves the use of a likelihood function relating to the observations on all endogenous variables included in the equation to be estimated.

‡ Because the solution to this problem involves the use of eigenvalues and matrix algebra, we do not include it here. For a brief summary of this material see J. Johnston, *Econometric Methods*, 2d ed. (New York: McGraw-Hill, 1972), pp. 384–387.

This ratio can never be less than unity, since the addition of any variable to a regression equation cannot increase the unexplained variance. If our model was correctly specified, we would expect λ to be close to 1 (but always greater than 1). This least-variance ratio technique (LVR) can be extended to apply to single-equation estimation in larger equation systems. The numerator becomes the residual variance associated with regressing the weighted endogenous variable y^* on all predetermined variables appearing in the equation, while the denominator becomes the residual variance associated with the regression of the weighted endogenous variable on all predetermined variables in the equation system. The solution values for the parameters will be good only up to scalar multiples,† so that a final normalization must be made. We usually achieve this by arbitrarily setting one of the parameters equal to 1. Note, however, that the normalization comes after the estimation procedure, not before, and is, therefore, quite distinct from the 2SLS normalization. Unlike 2SLS, least-variance ratio estimation has the property that parameter estimates are insensitive or invariant (up to scalar multiples) with respect to the choice of endogenous variable whose coefficient is to be set equal to 1.

The least-variance ratio estimator can be shown to be a maximum-likelihood estimator. As such, it is frequently referred to as the *limited-information maximum-likelihood* estimation process.‡ Least-variance ratio estimation can be applied to each identified equation in a model. It requires knowledge of the parametric form of the individual equation and knowledge of the list of all predetermined variables in the model system. It is a limited-information estimator, however, because it does not take into account any restrictions on the model which arise because equations other than the one to be estimated might be overidentified. As a practical matter, least-variance ratio estimation (or limited-information maximum-likelihood estimation) is not often used. The major reason is that LVR estimation is computationally much more difficult than 2SLS or IV estimation. In addition, researchers have found (using small-sample studies of limited-information estimators) that LVR is more sensitive to problems of multicollinearity than 2SLS.

While the least-variance ratio estimator appears to be quite distinct from the least-squares estimators described previously, there is, in reality, a close relationship. Recall that in our earlier discussion of instrumental variables estimation, we found that 2SLS is an instrumental variables estimator with $\hat{y}_2$ the appropriately chosen instrument. (Ordinary least squares, on the other hand, involves the use of y_2 as an instrument.) It seems reasonable, therefore, to ask what would happen if we took a weighted average of the 2SLS and OLS instruments. This is achieved by defining a new variable y_2^* as follows:

$$y_2^* = (1 - k)y_2 + k\hat{y}_2$$

As a general rule, all instruments of this type will not yield consistent parameter

---

† If a given set of parameter values is a solution to the estimation problem, multiplying each parameter by an identical constant will yield another solution.

‡ See Koopmans and Hood, op. cit., for a proof of this equivalence.

estimators (recall that OLS is inconsistent). However, if k is chosen appropriately, consistent estimation is possible.† What is surprising about this new class of instruments is that the least-variance ratio estimator is a *k-class estimator*, for k chosen equal to λ.‡ When the equation to be estimated is exactly identified, $\lambda = 1$ and LVR and 2SLS become equivalent. However, if the equation is overidentified, λ can be substantially greater than 1. Unfortunately, the larger the value of λ, the more unstable the parameter estimates are likely to be.

Full-Information Maximum-Likelihood Estimation

One of the difficulties with 3SLS arises because of the arbitrary nature of the normalization involved when 2SLS is used. This difficulty can be eliminated by an estimation procedure which is a generalization of the least-variance ratio, limited-information maximum-likelihood estimator described in the previous section. The new estimation process is alternately called a *full-information maximum-likelihood* (FIML) or a *least generalized residual variance* (LGRV) estimator. The former name applies because the estimation procedure arises as the solution to the application of the maximum-likelihood concept to the entire simultaneous equation system. The latter arises because the estimators can also be obtained by minimizing the determinant of the covariance matrix associated with the residuals of the reduced form of the equation system.§ Because it is not often used and is quite complex both theoretically and computationally, we shall not pursue the full-information maximum-likelihood estimator further.¶

EXERCISES

11.1 Explain intuitively (using a three-equation model) why the omission of one variable from each equation of a system of equations is insufficient to guarantee that each equation in the system is identified.

11.2 Prove that the two forms of the order condition for identifiability which are described in the text are equivalent.

11.3 Consider the three-equation model system

$$Y_1 = \alpha_1 + \alpha_2 Y_2 \qquad + \alpha_4 X_1 + \alpha_5 X_2 + u_1$$

$$Y_2 = \beta_1 \qquad + \beta_3 Y_3 \qquad + \beta_5 X_2 + u_2$$

$$Y_3 = \gamma_1 + \gamma_2 Y_2 \qquad + u_3$$

Which of the above equations (if any) are unidentified? Exactly identified? Overidentified?

---

† k must approach 1 in the probability limit.

‡ For a more thorough discussion of k-class estimators see A. Goldberger, *Econometric Theory* (New York: Wiley, 1964), pp. 341–344; or J. Kmenta, *Elements of Econometrics* (New York: Macmillan, 1972), pp. 565–571.

§ See Goldberger, op. cit., pp. 353–356, and Kmenta, op. cit., pp. 578–581, for details.

¶ For further details see ibid.

11.4 Consider the following simple macroeconomic model of an economy:

$$C_t = \alpha_1 + \alpha_2 Y_t + \alpha_3 r_t + u_{1t} \qquad I_t = \beta_1 + \beta_2 r_t + \beta_3(Y_t - Y_{t-1}) + u_{2t}$$

$$r_t = \gamma_1 + \gamma_2 I_t + \gamma_3 M_t + u_{3t} \qquad Y_t = C_t + I_t + G_t$$

Which of the equations are identified? Unidentified? How might you estimate the identified equations?

11.5 Consider the following two-equation recursive model:

$$Y_1 = \alpha_1 \qquad\quad + \alpha_3 X + u_1$$

$$Y_2 = \beta_1 + \beta_2 Y_1 \qquad\quad + u_2$$

(a) Explain why ordinary least squares is the appropriate estimation technique (assuming u_1 and u_2 are uncorrelated).

(b) Suppose that a naive researcher, seeing Y_1 on the right-hand side of the second equation, attempts to estimate it using two-stage least squares, i.e., regressing Y_2 on the fitted values of Y_1 determined by using ordinary least squares on the first equation. What will be the outcome of such an attempt? How might one obtain a value for β_2 if such a procedure is used?

(c) How would the answers to (b) differ if the second equation contained X explicitly as an independent variable?

11.6 Using the example in the text [Eqs. (11.33) and (11.34)], prove that Zellner estimation reduces to ordinary least-squares estimation when the cross-equation error covariance is 0 and when the independent variables in each equation are identical.

11.7 Consider the following two-equation supply-demand model:

Demand: $$P_t = \alpha_1 + \alpha_2 Q_t + u_{1t}$$

Supply: $$Q_t = \beta_1 + \beta_2 P_{t-1} + \beta_3 W_t + u_{2t}$$

(a) Discuss the identifiability of each equation.

(b) Under what condition is the model recursive?

(c) If the model is recursive, how would you estimate the demand equation?

(d) If the model is not recursive, how would you estimate the demand equation?

11.8 Explain why the simple process of lagging all right-hand variables in a simultaneous equation system does not necessarily make the model recursive.

11.9 Consider the model

$$y_1 = \alpha_2 y_2 + \alpha_3 x + u_1$$

$$y_2 = \beta_1 y_1 + \beta_4 z + \beta_5 w + u_2$$

Assume that you have estimated the reduced form of this model, first using ordinary least squares, and then using two-stage least-squares estimates of the structural parameters to solve for the reduced form. Explain why these estimates will differ.

INTRODUCTION TO SIMULATION MODELS

In this and the next two chapters we discuss the construction, evaluation, and analysis of simultaneous-equation simulation models and their use in policy analysis and forecasting. Simulation models, particularly large and complicated ones, are finding increasing use in the design of public policy.† It is therefore critical that those who construct or use such models be able to evaluate them properly and understand their behavior. Our coverage is somewhat limited, as most of our examples will be *econometric* simulation models. These models have an econometric orientation and are made up of equations which (except for accounting identities) are estimated using the standard econometric techniques described in Part One of this book. It is important to point out now, however, that the model-building techniques discussed in these chapters can also be applied to other types of models, including models of corporations‡ and models of social or political behavior.§ Economists do not have a monopoly on

---

† For a discussion of policy applications, see M. Greenberger, M. A. Crenson, and B. L. Crissey, *Models in the Policy Process* (New York: Russell Sage Foundation, 1976).

‡ See, for example, J. W. Elliott, *Econometric Analysis for Management Decisions* (Homewood, Ill.: Irwin, 1973), chap. 13; B. E. Davis, G. J. Cacappolo, and M. A. Chaudry, "An Econometric Planning Model for American Telephone and Telegraph Company," *Bell Journal of Economics and Management Science*, vol. 4, no. 1, 1973, or T. H. Naylor, *Corporate Planning Models* (Reading, Mass.: Addison-Wesley, 1979), chaps. 4 and 9. In Chapter 14 of this book we present an example of a corporate financial planning model.

§ See, for example, N. Choucri, M. Laird, and D. L. Meadows, "Resource Scarcity and Foreign Policy: A Simulation Model of International Conflict," *M.I.T. Center for International Studies Tech. Report* C/72-9. March 1972; and R. D. Brunner and G. D. Brewer, *Organized Complexity* (New York: Free Press, 1971).

simulation models; corporate planners, sociologists, political scientists, and others have been making increasing use of models as a framework for analysis and prediction.

One of our goals is to give the reader some idea of how a simulation model is constructed, since unfortunately much more is involved than simply putting together several individually estimated single equations. We will see that when individual regression equations, which may fit the historical data very well, are combined to form a simultaneous-equation model, simulation results may bear little resemblance to reality. The difficulty arises because the construction of a simulation model often involves understanding the dynamic structure of the system that results when individual equations are combined and thus may not be a straightforward process.

In order to construct and use simulation models, one must be able to evaluate them and to compare alternative models of the same physical process. Thus, we will be concerned at an early stage with the question of evaluating and validating simultaneous-equation simulation models. Model validation presents a less serious problem in the case of the single-equation regression, since one can look at a set of statistics such as the R^2 and t statistics to make a judgment about the goodness of fit of the equation. In a multiple-equation model each individual equation may have a very good statistical fit, but the model as a whole may do a very bad job in reproducing the historical data. The converse may also be true; the individual equations of a simulation model may have a very poor statistical fit, but the model when taken as a whole may reproduce the historical time series very closely. An important problem, then, is how to evaluate a simulation model properly.

Another objective is to compare the benefits of a simultaneous-equation model with the costs of building one. If our goal, for example, is to forecast a short-term interest rate, we know that it will be easier to produce a forecast using a single-equation regression model than using a multiple-equation simulation model of the money market. The question is whether the added benefit (measured in terms of an improved forecast) of the simultaneous-equation model outweighs the added cost involved in building it.

In this chapter we begin with a very elementary introduction to the simulation process. We then introduce the problem of evaluating simulation models and discuss a number of useful evaluation criteria. This discussion will be important for later developments, where we use these criteria routinely to evaluate alternative methods (and examples) of model construction. In the following section we discuss the problem of estimating a simultaneous-equation model (a problem which was discussed in great detail in the last chapter) and we relate the estimation method used to the simulation performance of the resulting model. Finally, we close the chapter with a brief discussion of alternative (noneconometric) approaches to the construction of simulation models. For example, we discuss the problem of building models of processes for which little or no data are available. In such a case, hypothetical relationships which cannot be statistically fitted or tested must be used.

12.1 THE SIMULATION PROCESS

Simulation, as we use the word, is simply the mathematical solution of a simultaneous set of difference equations.† A *simulation model* refers to that set of equations. As an example, consider the extremely simple macroeconomic model represented by

$$C_t = a_1 + a_2 Y_{t-1} \tag{12.1}$$

$$I_t = b_1 + b_2(Y_{t-1} - Y_{t-2}) \tag{12.2}$$

$$Y_t = C_t + I_t + G_t \tag{12.3}$$

where C = consumption
I = investment
Y = gross national product
G = government spending

and the error terms are suppressed. C, I, and Y are the *endogenous* variables, while G is an *exogenous* variable, i.e., determined from outside the model. This is the standard multiplier-accelerator model introduced in most elementary macroeconomics textbooks. Consumption is proportional to GNP (the multiplier), but investment is proportional to changes in GNP (the accelerator).

If values are given for the parameters a_1, a_2, b_1, and b_2, initial values are specified for the variables C and I, and a time path is given for the exogenous variable G, then the simultaneous solution of these three equations will give us time paths for each of the endogeneous variables C, I, and Y. This is what is meant by the simulation process. Given a model whose parameters have been estimated (or numerical values have been otherwise supplied), given initial values for the endogenous variables (i.e., base-year values), and given time series for the exogenous variables (these may be historical series, or they may represent hypotheses about the future behavior of the series), the model is solved over some range of time to yield solutions for each of the endogenous variables.

The model above is rather simple, and can be solved analytically by substituting Eqs. (12.1) and (12.2) into Eq. (12.3) and rearranging:

$$Y_t - (a_2 + b_2)Y_{t-1} + b_2 Y_{t-2} = (a_1 + b_1) + G_t \tag{12.4}$$

The result is a second-order difference equation whose solution will depend on two initial conditions, as well as all future values of the exogenous variable G_t.‡ We will see in the next chapter that the solution may not be stable; i.e., it may become increasingly large, or it may oscillate. In the case of a simple model, it is easy to determine the conditions that must hold for the parameters of the model

---

† A difference equation relates the current value of one variable to current and past values of other variables. Good examples of difference equations are given by the distributed lag models discussed in Chapter 9.

‡ For an introduction to difference equations and their solution, see W. J. Baumol, *Economic Dynamics* (New York: Macmillan, 1970), or A. C. Chiang, *Fundamental Methods of Mathematical Economics* (New York: McGraw-Hill, 1967), chaps. 16 and 17.

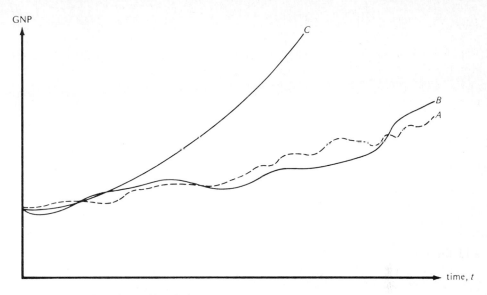

Figure 12.1 Stable and unstable solutions.

for it to be stable, while in the case of a more complex model (which may be nonlinear), the conditions for stability may be difficult to ascertain.

Model stability is important because we believe the real world (or at least most of it) to be stable. If, for example, the GNP moved over the past 20 years according to dotted line A in Fig. 12.1, we would expect a model which explained GNP to yield a solution which moved in the same characteristic way, perhaps as represented by solid line B. Solid line C would represent an unstable solution, since it diverges more and more rapidly from the range of actual values of GNP.† Other nonrepresentative modes of behavior are possible, such as the damped oscillations of solid line D in Fig. 12.2, and the explosive oscillations of line E in the same figure. Of course in some cases nonexplosive oscillations might be a desirable solution—if, for example, the model in question was being used to explain (or predict) business cycles for some commodity and the frequency of the oscillations closely matched the frequency of the actual cycles.

Solution characteristics like these are important and will be discussed in some detail in the next chapter. For now, however, we will limit ourselves to the problem of obtaining a solution i.e., performing a simulation. If the parameters are known for the small model of Eqs. (12.1) to (12.3), the solution is simple and can be obtained analytically. For a larger and perhaps nonlinear model, the simultaneous equations must be solved numerically (i.e., simulated) on a computer. Several computer programs exist that make the simulation of even a very large model quite easy, so that it is usually not necessary for an analyst to write

---

† A more precise definition of stability will be given in the next chapter.

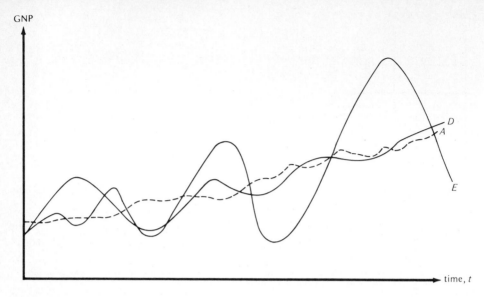

GNP

time, t

Figure 12.2 Oscillatory solutions.

a program of his or her own.† Most of these programs obtain solutions using an iterative procedure in which the nonlinear model is repeatedly linearized, perhaps renormalized, and then solved.‡

Simulations of a model might be performed for a variety of reasons, including model testing and evaluation, historical policy analysis, and forecasting. Usually the *time horizon* over which the simulation is performed will depend on the objective of the simulation. To see this, we examine some of the different types of simulations that might be performed over different time horizons.

In Fig. 12.3, T_1 and T_2 represent the time bounds over which the equations of a hypothetical model are estimated (the estimation period). T_3 represents the time today. The first mode of simulation is called an *ex post* or *historical simulation*. The simulation begins in year T_1 and runs forward until year T_2. Historical values in year T_1 are supplied as initial conditions for the endogenous

---

† Examples of more sophisticated simulation systems include the TROLL system, developed initially at MIT and then at the National Bureau of Economic Research, and now used in many universities; see *TROLL: A User's Manual* (Cambridge, Mass.: NBER Computer Research Center). Designed more for a commercial or applied environment is the XSIM system, developed by Dynamics Associates, Inc., Cambridge, Mass. (see "*XSIM Manual*," Dynamics Associates, Inc.). A small and convenient simulation package that can be used on almost any computer system is MODSIM, which is distributed by CONDUIT at the University of Iowa (see "MODSIM User's Manual," by C. Van Duyne, Williams College).

‡ We will not attempt to describe or explain these numerical solution methods; rather, it is assumed that readers who want to construct and simulate their own models will have access to the appropriate computer programs. Those readers interested in mathematical solution techniques and algorithms are referred to T. H. Naylor (ed.), *The Design of Computer Simulation Experiments* (Durham, N.C.: Duke University Press, 1969).

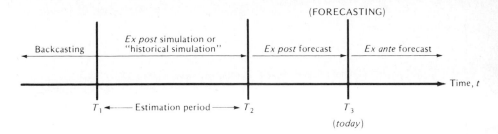

Figure 12.3 Simulation time horizons.

variables, and historical series beginning in T_1 and ending in T_2 are used for the exogenous variables. There is no reinitialization of the endogenous variables; after year T_1 values for the endogenous variables are determined by the simulation solution. By simulating the model during the period for which historical data for all variables are available, a comparison of the original data series with the simulated series for each endogenous variable can provide a useful test of the validity of the model. *Ex post* simulations can also be useful in policy analysis. By changing parameter values or letting exogenous policy variables follow different time paths one can examine and compare what might have taken place as a result of alternative policies. One can use a macroeconometric model to examine, for example, the economic consequences that would have resulted from changes in the level of government spending, tax rates, or the money supply.† Similarly, industry-wide models can be used to study the effects of alternative government regulatory policies, or the impact of macroeconomic growth and fluctuations on the industry.‡

Forecasting involves a simulation of the model forward in time beyond the estimation period. Of course, before a forecast can be made, one must have time series covering the entire forecast period for all the exogenous variables. In the simple macroeconomic model of Eqs. (12.1) to (12.3), for example, one must first predict (or at least make some assumption about) future values of government spending G_t. Typically, an analyst will generate a set of alternative forecasts, each of which is conditional on one particular set of assumptions about the exogenous variables.§

---

† We will examine how a macroeconometric model can be used for policy analysis in Chapter 14. The reader is also referred to G. Fromm and P. Taubman, *Policy Simulation with an Econometric Model* (Washington: Brookings, 1968).

‡ We will provide an example of an industry-wide model in Chapter 14. Other examples can be found in T. Naylor, *Computer Simulation Experiments with Economic Systems* (New York: Wiley, 1971). For a detailed example of an application of an industry-wide econometric model to the analysis of government price regulatory policy, see P. W. MacAvoy and R. S. Pindyck, "Alternative Regulatory Policies for Dealing with the Natural Gas Shortage," *Bell Journal of Economics and Management Science*, Autumn 1973; and P. W. MacAvoy and R. S. Pindyck, *The Economics of the Natural Gas Shortage* (Amsterdam, North-Holland, 1975).

§ This is more useful to the user of the model (or the model's forecasts), since the future values of the exogenous variables are not known and the sensitivity to those values may be particularly important.

As we saw in Chapter 8, we can distinguish between two types of forecasts. If the estimation period did not extend to the current year (that is, T_2 is less than T_3), one might want to begin the forecast at the end of the estimation period and extend it to the present, perhaps comparing the results with available data. This type of simulation is called an *ex post* forecast, and is often performed to test the forecasting accuracy of a model. On the other hand, a forecast made by beginning the simulation in the current year and extending it into the future is called an *ex ante* forecast.

It should be clear that forecasting is useful not only for predictive purposes but also for sensitivity analysis and policy analysis. Forecasts can be used to study the effects of changes in exogenous variables or particular parameters. They can also be used to compare the effects of alternative policies, where policies are stated as movements in exogenous variables that are controllable (such as G_t in our examples) or as changes in the values of policy parameters (such as tax rates). We will examine in more detail in Chapter 14 how policy analyses of this sort can be performed.

One last type of simulation, the "backcast" simulation, should also be mentioned. It is occasionally of interest to simulate a model *backward* in time beginning at the start of the estimation period. One reason for doing this would be to test a model's dynamic stability as it evolved backward in time instead of forward. Another reason might be to analyze hypotheses about events that took place just before the estimation period. Note that in a backcast one begins with initial conditions for all variables in period T_1 (see Fig. 12.3 again) and then, using specified values for the exogenous variables before period T_1, solves the model backward one period at a time. Since time runs forward in the real world, there is little reason to expect the model to reproduce the real world when it is simulated backward: for this reason backcasting is usually done only over a short time period. The word *backcasting* is often misused and confused with *ex post*, or historical, simulation. Occasionally books or articles describing simulation models will refer to an historical simulation as a backcast. However, for purposes of clarity we will use the definition of backcasting given above.

12.2 EVALUATING SIMULATION MODELS

In constructing a simulation model, we are faced with the same difficulty that exists in constructing a single-equation regression model (or, as we will see in Part Three of this book, that exists in constructing a time-series model). The problem is how to evaluate or test the goodness of the model. We have seen that in the case of the single-equation regression model there exists a set of statistical tests (R^2, F test, t tests, etc.) that can be used to judge the significance (in a statistical sense) of the model and its individual estimated coefficients. Other statistics exist (e.g., the DW statistic) to test the underlying assumptions of the model. Even with these tests, however, the choice of whether to accept or reject a single-equation model, particularly in comparison with other single-equation models, is not a straightforward task. One must decide whether the structural specification of the model is reasonable and whether the estimated coefficients make sense. The model's evaluation must also depend on the *purpose* for which the model was built. A model designed for forecasting purposes should have as small a standard error of forecast as possible, while t statistics are more important in a model designed to test a specific hypothesis or measure some elasticity.

The same considerations apply to a multi-equation simulation model, except that the evaluation criteria become more complicated. The fact that there are several equations means that high statistical significance for some equations may have to be balanced against low statistical significance for other equations. Even more important, however, is the fact that the model as a whole will have a dynamic structure which is much richer than that of any one of the individual equations of which it is composed. Thus even if all the individual equations fit the data well and are statistically significant, we have no guarantee that the model as a whole, when simulated, will reproduce those same data series closely. Finally, it is possible that in an *ex post* (or historical) simulation some of the endogenous variables will track the original data series closely while others will not. Just as in the case of a single-equation model, the evaluation of the multi-equation model must depend on the purpose for which the model was built. Some models are built primarily for forecasting, while others are built primarily for descriptive purposes and hypothesis testing. As in the single-equation case, different criteria will apply depending on the model's purpose.

We shall examine criteria that can be used to evaluate multi-equation models, beginning with the individual equations of the model. Do the equations, on a one-by-one basis, fit the data well; i.e., are they statistically significant? This question can be answered by using the same criteria (statistical and otherwise) that were used in the construction and evaluation of single-equation regression models. As we saw in Part One, judgments can be made regarding the theoretical reasonableness of each equation, as well as the statistical significance of the equation's coefficients and overall fit.

Even if a multi-equation estimation procedure was used to estimate all the model's coefficients, the statistical fit of each of the model's individual equations can be judged. Recall from Chapter 11 that Zellner and three-stage least-squares estimates increase the estimation efficiency by accounting for cross-equation error covariances. Each individual equation, however, will still have an associated set of standard errors and t statistics which can be used to evaluate statistical fit just as in the case of ordinary least-squares or other single-equation estimation methods.

In examining the equations of a model, one typically finds that some of the equations fit the data very well while others do not. Thus a judgment must be made regarding the overall statistical fit of the multi-equation model. The model builder makes this judgment as the model is constructed. One might find, for example, that some of the model's equations are easy to fit, in the sense that there is little difficulty in specifying equation forms which fit the data well. Construction of other parts of the model might prove more difficult. In fact the estimated forms of some equations may not fit the data well even when several alternative specifications are tried. In practice, it may be necessary to use specifications for some of the equations in the model that are less desirable from a statistical point of view but that improve the ability of the model to simulate well (according to criteria that we will discuss below). The model builder is thus forced to make some compromises, accepting some equations which do not have a particularly good statistical fit in order to build a complete structural model.

Another criterion that is used to evaluate a simulation model is the fit of the individual variables in a *simulation context*. One would expect the results of a historical simulation (i.e., a simulation through the estimation period) to match the behavior of the real world rather closely. One way to test the performance of the model is to perform an historical simulation and examine how closely each endogenous variable tracks its corresponding historical data series. It is therefore desirable to have some quantitative measure of how closely individual variables track their corresponding data series. The measure that is most often used is called the *rms* (root-mean-square) *simulation error*. The rms simulation error for the variable Y_t is defined as

$$\text{rms error} = \sqrt{\frac{1}{T} \sum_{t=1}^{T} (Y_t^s - Y_t^a)^2} \tag{12.5}$$

where Y_t^s = simulated value of Y_t
Y_t^a = actual value
T = number of periods in the simulation

The rms error is thus a measure of the deviation of the simulated variable from its actual time path. Of course, the magnitude of this error can be evaluated only by comparing it with the average size of the variable in question.

Other measures of simulation fit exist and are often used. Another simulation error statistic is the *rms percent error*, which is defined as

$$\text{rms percent error} = \sqrt{\frac{1}{T} \sum_{t=1}^{T} \left(\frac{Y_t^s - Y_t^a}{Y_t^a} \right)^2} \tag{12.6}$$

This is also a measure of the deviation of the simulated variable from its actual time path but in percentage terms. Other measures are the *mean simulation error*, defined as

$$\text{Mean error} = \frac{1}{T} \sum_{t=1}^{T} (Y_t^s - Y_t^a) \tag{12.7}$$

and the *mean percent error*, defined as

$$\text{Mean percent error} = \frac{1}{T} \sum_{t=1}^{T} \frac{Y_t^s - Y_t^a}{Y_t^a} \tag{12.8}$$

The problem with mean errors is that they may be close to 0 if large positive

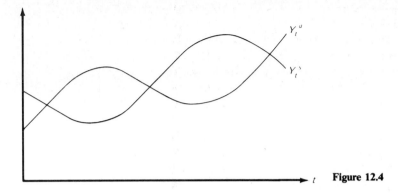

Y_t^a

Y_t^s

t **Figure 12.4**

errors cancel out large negative errors. In Fig. 12.4, for example, the mean simulation error would probably be close to 0, while the rms simulation error would be large. The rms simulation error would be a better measure of the simulation performance.†

Note that it is entirely possible for an equation that has a very good statistical fit to have a very poor simulation fit. In an industry market model, for example, an equation which explains the market price of the good being sold (i.e., price is the dependent variable) may have a very good statistical fit (large R^2, small standard errors, etc.). At the same time, however, when the model as a whole is simulated, that same price variable might have a very poor simulation fit; i.e., it might have a very large rms simulation error. It is for this reason that simulation-error statistics are important criteria for evaluating a multi-equation model while estimation statistics alone are insufficient.

It is also possible that the results of an historical simulation will show some endogenous variables to have a small rms simulation error while others will have large errors. In this case model evaluation will involve a consideration of which variables are most critical as well as the *reasons* that large errors have occurred. Usually one can trace through the structure of the model in order to find out why certain variables seem to diverge from their historical paths during the simulation. The simulation performance of the model can often be improved by substituting new equation forms, which may have poorer statistical fits but improve the dynamic structure of the model.

Low rms simulation errors are only one desirable measure of simulation fit. Another important criterion is how well the model simulates *turning points* in the historical data. Consider Fig. 12.5, where dotted line *A* represents the historical time series for some endogenous variable *X* and solid lines *B* and *C* represent the simulated values of that same variable using two different models. From that figure alone, one would probably pick the model that produced line *C* as the

† Mean *absolute* errors (and mean absolute percent errors) can also be calculated to avoid the problem of positive and negative errors canceling, but rms errors are used more often in practice, since they penalize large individual errors more heavily. See Exercise 12.1.

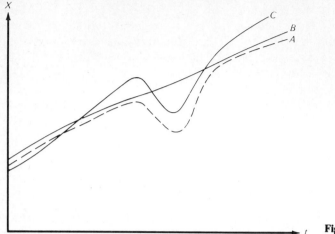

Figure 12.5

better model, since despite its larger rms simulation error it duplicates the marked change in variable X that occurred historically. The model that produced line B failed to predict the *turning point*, i.e., the sudden change in the historical data. It did track the historical data closely during the rest of the simulation period, but any simple trend model could have done this without really explaining the underlying physical processes. Thus the ability of a simulation model to duplicate turning points or rapid changes in the actual data is an important criterion for model evaluation.

If the model has been designed for forecasting purposes, then the *ex post rms forecast error* is another very important criterion for model performance. In an *ex post* forecast, the forecast results can be compared to recent data. The rms forecast error, i.e., the rms simulation error computed over the forecast range, provides a measure of the ability of the model to forecast well. Again it is possible in a multi-equation model for some endogenous variables to have large rms forecast errors while others have very small errors. Unless the forecasting objective is centered on only one or two variables, all the rms forecast errors must be evaluated together to judge the model as a whole.

A useful simulation statistic related to the rms simulation error and applied to the evaluation of historical simulations or *ex post* forecasts is Theil's *inequality coefficient*, defined as

$$U = \frac{\sqrt{\dfrac{1}{T} \sum_{t=1}^{T} (Y_t^s - Y_t^a)^2}}{\sqrt{\dfrac{1}{T} \sum_{t=1}^{T} (Y_t^s)^2} + \sqrt{\dfrac{1}{T} \sum_{t=1}^{T} (Y_t^a)^2}} \tag{12.9}$$

Note that the numerator of U is just the rms simulation error, but the scaling of the denominator is such that U will always fall between 0 and 1. If $U = 0$,

$Y_t^s = Y_t^a$ for all t and there is a perfect fit. If $U = 1$, on the other hand, the predictive performance of the model is as bad as it possibly could be. When $U = 1$, simulated values are always 0 when actual values are nonzero, or nonzero predictions have been made when actual values are zero and hence easy to predict, or simulated values are positive (negative) when actual values are negative (positive).†

The Theil inequality coefficient can be decomposed in an interesting way. It can be shown with a little algebra that

$$\frac{1}{T} \sum (Y_t^s - Y_t^a)^2 = (\bar{Y}^s - \bar{Y}^a)^2 + (\sigma_s - \sigma_a)^2 + 2(1 - \rho)\sigma_s \sigma_a \quad (12.10)$$

where $\bar{Y}^s$, $\bar{Y}^a$, σ_s, and σ_a are the means and standard deviations of the series Y_t^s and Y_t^a, respectively, and ρ is their correlation coefficient.‡ We can then define the *proportions of inequality* as

$$U^M = \frac{(\bar{Y}^s - \bar{Y}^a)^2}{(1/T)\Sigma(Y_t^s - Y_t^a)^2} \quad (12.11)$$

$$U^S = \frac{(\sigma_s - \sigma_a)^2}{(1/T)\Sigma(Y_t^s - Y_t^a)^2} \quad (12.12)$$

and

$$U^C = \frac{2(1 - \rho)\sigma_s \sigma_a}{(1/T)\Sigma(Y_t^s - Y_t^a)^2} \quad (12.13)$$

The proportions, U^M, U^S, and U^C are called the *bias*, the *variance*, and the *covariance proportions*, respectively, and they are useful as a means of breaking the simulation error down into its characteristic sources. [Note from Eq. (12.10) that $U^M + U^S + U^C = 1$.]

The bias proportion U^M is an indication of systematic error, since it measures the extent to which the *average* values of the simulated and actual series deviate from each other. Whatever the value of the inequality coefficient U, we would hope that U^M would be close to zero. A large value of U^M (above .1 or .2) would be quite troubling, since it would mean that a systematic bias is present, so that revision of the model is necessary.

The variance proportion U^S indicates the ability of the model to replicate the degree of variability in the variable of interest. If U^S is large, it means that the actual series has fluctuated considerably while the simulated series shows little fluctuation, or vice versa. This would also be troubling and might lead us to a revision of the model.

Finally, the covariance proportion measures what we might call unsystematic error; i.e., it represents the remaining error after deviations from average

---

† The inequality coefficient was introduced in H. Theil, *Economic Forecasts and Policy* (Amsterdam: North-Holland, 1961), pp. 30–37, and is also discussed in H. Theil, *Applied Economic Forecasting* (Amsterdam: North-Holland, 1966), pp. 26–35. Theil also shows that if U is not large (say, below .3), its variance can be approximated by Var $(U) \approx U^2/T$.

‡ That is, $\rho = (1/\sigma_s \sigma_a T)\Sigma(Y_t^s - \bar{Y}^s)(Y_t^a - \bar{Y}^a)$.

values and average variabilities have been accounted for. Since it is unreasonable to expect predictions that are perfectly correlated with actual outcomes, this component of error is less worrisome. Indeed, for any value of $U > 0$, the ideal distribution of inequality over the three sources is $U^M = U^S = 0$, and $U^C = 1$.

It would be useful to have a measure of performance associated with an *ex ante* forecast for a multi-equation model. We saw in Chapter 8, for example, that for a single-equation regression model a standard error of forecast and a corresponding confidence interval could be computed. Unfortunately there is no simple way to calculate analytically confidence intervals for the forecast from a multi-equation model. This is due to the fact that forecast errors can be compounded in a complex way by the feedback structure of the model. One can, however, *experimentally* compute confidence intervals for the *ex ante* forecast through the process of *stochastic*, or *Monte Carlo*, simulation, as will be discussed in Chapter 13. Often *ex post* rms forecast errors are used as criteria for forecast performance. However, one must remember that the *ex ante* errors are likely to be larger than the *ex post* errors.

Even if a model tracked well, i.e., had small rms simulation and forecast errors for most or all of the endogenous variables, one would also want to investigate whether or not it responds to stimuli (e.g., large changes in exogenous variables or policy parameters) in a manner consistent with economic theory and with empirical observation. In the case of a macroeconometric model, for example, the simulation of a $1 billion increase in government expenditures should result in increases in GNP (over time) that at least roughly match both our theoretical expectations and recent observations of the relationship of these two variables. Thus the *dynamic response* of the model (which will be discussed in some detail in the next chapter) is another evaluation criterion.†

An additional criterion of model performance is the overall *sensitivity* of the model to such factors as the initial period in which the simulation is begun, minor changes in estimated coefficients, and small changes in the time paths of exogenous variables. If, for example, a model was estimated using data from 1955 to 1970, then one would expect the historical simulation to fit well whether it was begun in 1955 or in 1960. If the model truly represents the real world, it should not matter very much in what year the simulation is begun. Thus alteration of the initial simulation period provides one test for model sensitivity. We would also expect that small changes in the model's coefficients (at least within one-half of the estimated standard error for the coefficient) should not affect the model's simulation performance very drastically. Another sensitivity test, then, is to simulate the model after making small changes in individual coefficients. A third sensitivity test is to alter the time paths for exogenous variables over the simulation period. Again, *small* changes in these time paths

---

† This and other evaluation criteria are discussed in H. T. Shapiro, "Is Verification Possible? The Evaluation of Large Econometric Models," *American Journal of Agricultural Economics*, vol. 55, May 1973; and in L. R. Klein, *An Essay on the Theory of Economic Prediction* (Chicago: Markham, 1971). Also, see R. Fair, "An Evaluation of a Short-Run Forecasting Model," *International Economic Review*, June 1974.

for exogenous variables should not affect the simulation performance drastically.

We have seen that there is a wide variety of criteria which can be (and are) used to evaluate the performance of a simulation model, but problems may arise in the use of these criteria.† What can one say if the rms simulation errors are all very small but the model is very sensitive to the initial starting date in the simulation? What if the *ex post* rms forecast errors are all small, but the model fails to reproduce turning points? What if the Theil inequality coefficient U is very small but the bias component U^M is large? Unfortunately, we can offer no formulas for what should be done in cases like these. Model building is very much an art, and part of that art is learning to trade off alternate criteria in different ways.

12.3 A SIMULATION EXAMPLE

As a simple example of a multi-equation simulation model we look at a small linear macroeconomic model, which is given by Eqs. (12.14) to (12.17). (The reader can check that all the equations are identified.)

$$C_t = 2.537 + .185\ Y_t + .714\ C_{t-1} \tag{12.14}$$
$$\underset{(1.90)}{} \quad \underset{(5.95)}{} \quad \underset{(13.8)}{}$$

$$R^2 = .999 \qquad \text{SER} = 2.40 \qquad \text{DW} = 2.08$$

$$\hat{I}_t = 5.020 + .392\ (Y_t - Y_{t-1}) + .1634\ Y_{t-1} - 3.856\ R_{t-4} \tag{12.15}$$
$$\underset{(2.69)}{} \quad \underset{(4.25)}{} \quad \underset{(23.80)}{} \quad \underset{(-5.23)}{}$$

$$R^2 = .980 \qquad \text{SER} = 4.22 \qquad \text{DW} = .62$$

$$R_t = -\ .072 + .0024\ Y_t + .011\ (Y_t - Y_{t-1}) - .189\ (M_t - M_{t-1})$$
$$\quad \underset{(-.25)}{} \quad \underset{(2.14)}{} \quad \underset{(.74)}{} \quad \underset{(-2.30)}{}$$

$$+ .347\ (R_{t-1} + R_{t-2}) \tag{12.16}$$
$$\underset{(6.24)}{}$$

$$R^2 = .867 \qquad \text{SER} = .59 \qquad \text{DW} = .92$$

$$Y_t = C_t + I_t + G_t \tag{12.17}$$

where C = aggregate personal consumption
I = gross domestic investment
Y = GNP (net of exports and imports)
G = government spending
M = money stock
R = short-term interest rate

† For examples of research in the development of other evaluation criteria for econometric models, see M. K. Evans, Y. Haitkovsky, and G. Treyz, "An Analysis of the Forecasting Properties of U.S. Econometric Models," and V. Zarnowitz, C. Boschan, and G. H. Moore, "Business Cycle Analysis of Econometric Model Simulations," both articles in B. Hickman (ed.), *Econometric Models of Cyclical Behavior* (New York: National Bureau of Economic Research, 1972). For a summary of the state of the art of model evaluation, see P. J. Dhrymes et al., "Criteria for Evaluation of Econometric Models," *Annals of Economic and Social Measurement*, vol. 1, pp. 291–324, 1972.

C, Y, I, and G are all measured in billions of 1958 dollars, while R is in percent per year. The equations are estimated using quarterly time-series data from 1955 through the end of 1971. The t statistics (in parentheses below each estimated coefficient), the R^2, the standard error, and the DW statistic are shown for each equation.† Except for (12.17), which is an identity, the equations were all estimated using ordinary least squares, a method which could be improved upon, as will be demonstrated in the next section.

Equation (12.14) for aggregate consumption consists of a multiplier with a Koyck lag distribution.‡ The investment equation contains both a multiplier and an accelerator, with investment also depending on the short-term interest rate R, with a long time delay. An equation is also estimated for this interest rate, which is positively related to the GNP and changes in the GNP, and negatively related to changes in the money stock. Finally, the model is completed with the addition of the GNP accounting identity in Eq. (12.17). The model thus consists of four endogenous variables and four equations, as well as two exogenous variables—the money stock and government expenditures.

Despite the simplicity of this model, its simulation performance is surprisingly good. To see this, we can examine an *ex post* (historical) simulation over the estimation period 1955-1 to 1971-4. In performing this simulation, the historical values are used for the two exogenous variables—government spending and the money supply. The results are shown graphically in Figs. 12.6 to 12.9, in which the actual and simulated series for each endogenous variable are plotted on the same set of axes.

Presumably one would use the results of this historical simulation to help in evaluating the model. Looking at Figs. 12.6 to 12.9, we observe that the simulated series do seem to reproduce the general long-run behavior of the actual series, although short-run fluctuations in the actual series are not reproduced well, and some turning points are missed altogether. We could also examine the rms and mean simulation errors and percent simulation errors for

---

† The reader should be aware of the fact that because Eqs. (12.14) and (12.16) contain lagged dependent variables, their DW statistics are biased toward 2 and thus provide no guarantee that there is no serial correlation. This point is discussed in Chapter 7.

‡ The use of the lagged dependent variable C_{t-1} in Eq. (12.14) is equivalent to a lag distribution of Y_t with geometrically declining weights. Consider the equation

$$C_t = a_0 + a_1 Y_t + a_1 \lambda Y_{t-1} + a_1 \lambda^2 Y_{t-2} + a_1 \lambda^3 Y_{t-3} + \cdots$$

where λ is a coefficient greater than 0 but less than 1. Now subtract from the left- and right-hand sides of this equation the equation

$$\lambda C_{t-1} = \lambda a_0 + a_1 \lambda Y_{t-1} + a_1 \lambda^2 Y_{t-2} + a_1 \lambda^3 Y_{t-3} + \cdots$$

The result is the equation

$$C_t = a_0(1 - \lambda) + a_1 Y_t + \lambda C_{t-1}$$

as in Eq. (12.14). This geometrically declining lag distribution, called a Koyck distribution, is described in some detail in Chapter 9.

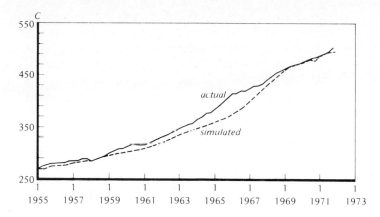

Figure 12.6 Historical simulation of consumption. Time bounds: 1955-1 to 1971-4.

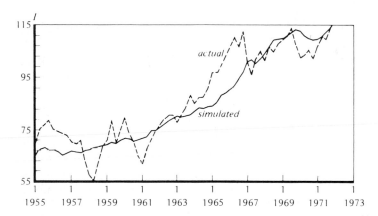

Figure 12.7 Historical simulation of investment. Time bounds: 1955-1 to 1971-4.

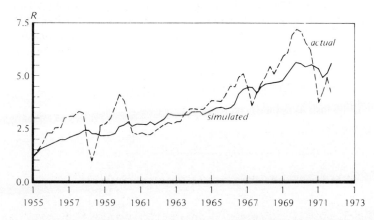

Figure 12.8 Historical simulation of interest rates. Time bounds: 1955-1 to 1971-4.

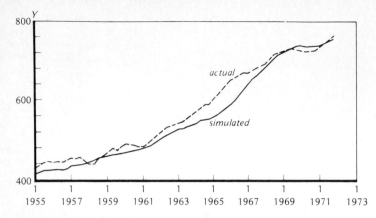

Figure 12.9 Historical simulation of GNP. Time bounds: 1955-1 to 1971-4.

each variable, which are shown in Table 12.1 along with the mean value of each variable.

The results are reasonable, given the simplistic nature of the model. Recall also that the model was estimated using ordinary least squares. We will see in the next section that the use of alternative estimation methods can result in an improved simulation performance. In the meanwhile, however, we will illustrate the use of this model for forecasting.

We begin with an *ex post* forecast, in which the model is simulated forward starting at the end of the estimation period (1971-4) and continuing as long as historical data are available (in this case 1973-2). The results of this simulation are shown in Figs. 12.10 to 12.13. The results are also shown numerically for each endogenous variable in Table 12.2.

Note that the rms errors and rms percent errors for the *ex post* forecast are for the most part larger than those for the historical simulation. This is not surprising, since in the *ex post* forecast the model is being extrapolated outside the period over which its coefficients were estimated. In Fig. 12.10, for example, the forecasted series for consumption fails to predict the upturn in consumer spending that actually occurred in 1972 and the first quarter of 1973. One reason

Table 12.1 Results of historical simulation

	C	I	R	Y
Mean	369.8	87.3	3.72	574.0
rms error	15.3	7.04	.776	24.0
rms percent error	3.97%	8.26%	26.2%	4.12%
Mean error	−11.3	−1.95	−.284	−16.9
Mean percent error	−3.10%	−1.92%	−3.90%	−3.04%

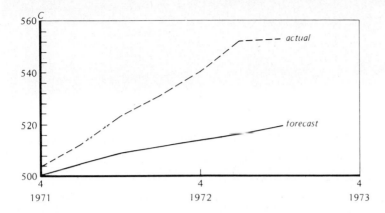

Figure 12.10 *Ex post* forecast of consumption. Time bounds: 1971-4 to 1973-2.

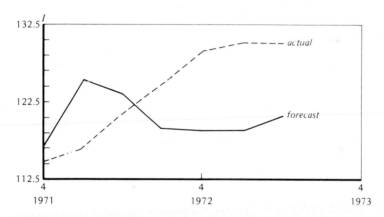

Figure 12.11 *Ex post* forecast of investment. Time bounds: 1971-4 to 1973-2.

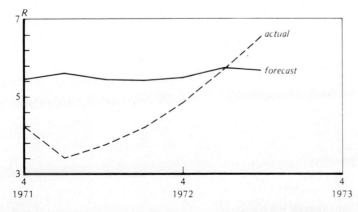

Figure 12.12 *Ex post* forecast of interest rate. Time bounds: 1971-4 to 1973-2.

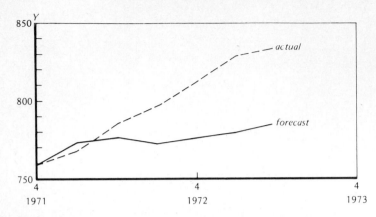

Figure 12.13 *Ex post* forecast of GNP. Time bounds: 1971-4 to 1973-2.

Table 12.2 Ex post forecast results

	Actual	Forecast	Error	Percent error
Consumption *C*				
1971-4	504.1	500.81	− 3.28	− .651
1972-1	512.5	505.28	− 7.21	− 1.408
1972-2	523.4	509.27	− 14.12	−2.697
1972-3	531.	511.71	− 19.28	−3.632
1972-4	540.5	514.21	− 26.28	−4.863
1973-1	552.7	516.66	− 36.03	−6.520
1973-2	553.3	519.40	− 33.89	−6.126
Mean	531.1	511.1	− 20.02	−3.7
rms	531.4†	511.1†	23.22	4.25
Investment *I*				
1971-4	114.8	116.54	1.74	1.516
1972-1	116.5	125.44	8.94	7.674
1972-2	121.	123.63	2.63	2.176
1972-3	124.8	119.24	− 5.55	−4.448
1972-4	129.1	118.97	− 10.12	−7.844
1973-1	130.2	118.92	− 11.27	−8.657
1973-2	130.2	120.72	− 9.47	−7.278
Mean	123.8	120.5	− 3.30	−2.41
rms	123.9	120.5	7.93	6.27

† These are the rms values of the actual and forecasted series, for example,

$$\text{rms (actual)} = \sqrt{\frac{1}{T}\sum_{t=1}^{T} C_t^2}$$

	Actual	Forecast	Error	Percent error
Interest rate R				
1971-4	4.23	5.44	1.21	28.66
1972-1	3.43	5.60	2.16	63.11
1972-2	3.77	5.45	1.68	44.62
1972-3	4.22	5.43	1.21	28.68
1972-4	4.86	5.49	.63	13.00
1973-1	5.7	5.75	.05	1.03
1973-2	6.60	5.67	− .92	− 14.04
Mean	4.69	5.55	.86	23.58
rms	4.80	5.55	1.29	33.78
GNP Y				
1971-4	759.	758.9	− .04	− .00
1972-1	768.	773.4	5.42	.70
1972-2	785.6	776.9	− 8.68	− 1.10
1972-3	796.7	772.7	− 23.94	− 3.00
1972-4	812.3	776.6	− 35.61	− 4.38
1973-1	829.3	779.9	− 49.30	− 5.94
1973-2	834.3	785.3	− 48.97	− 5.87
Mean	797.9	774.9	− 23.02	− 2.80
rms	798.3	774.9	31.11	3.78

for this might have been an increase in the actual propensity to consume, which the model, with its constant coefficients, could not have accounted for.†

We will take the example one step further and use the model to produce an *ex ante* forecast. We begin the simulation in the second quarter of 1973 (using the actual data as initial values for the endogenous variables) and continue the simulation through the fourth quarter of 1975. Before this simulation can be performed, however, some forecast or assumption must be made regarding the exogenous variables G_t and M_t. We assumed that G_t and M_t would grow at an annual rate of 4 percent from their actual values in the second quarter of 1973 (this is close to their average historical growth rates).

The results of this *ex ante* forecast are shown for consumption and investment in Figs. 12.14 and 12.15. Even though the *ex ante* forecast is not compared with actual data, some judgment can be made regarding reasonableness. The forecast for GNP predicts a growth rate after the second quarter of 1974 of about 10 percent, which is too high to be reasonable. Rapid forecasted investment growth during this period (in response to falling forecasted interest rates

---

† The forecasts for the interest rate and gross investment also contain sizable errors, with the interest rate failing to reproduce the sharp upturn that actually occurred in 1972 and early 1973, and forecasted investment decreasing while actual investment increased. The reader can investigate the reasons for this (see Exercise 12.4). One would not expect to be able to predict macroeconomic behavior in any detail with a four-equation model; we present it only as an example of how a simulation is performed and how the results can be analyzed.

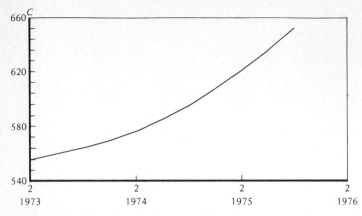

Figure 12.14 *Ex ante* forecast of consumption. Time bounds: 1973-2 to 1975-4.

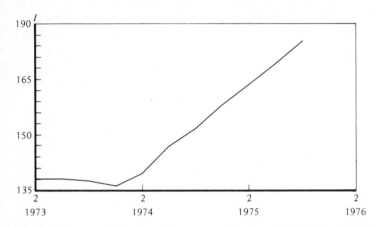

Figure 12.15 *Ex ante* forecast of investment. Time bounds: 1973-2 to 1975-4.

earlier) may be part of the reason for this, but in any case such forecasts would invite skepticism.

12.4 MODEL ESTIMATION

In this section we demonstrate how alternative estimation methods can affect the simulation performance of a model. The model given by Eqs. (12.14) to (12.17) was estimated using ordinary least squares, which can result in inconsistent and biased estimates of the coefficients. It is interesting to see how the choice of estimation method affects the performance of the model when simulated as a whole. To see this we estimate the model using two-stage least squares

(2SLS). The 2SLS estimates are

$$C_t = .940 + .125\ Y_t + .814\ C_{t-1} \qquad\qquad (12.18)$$
$${}_{(.54)}{}_{(2.86)}{}_{(11.15)}$$

$$R^2 = .999 \qquad SER = 2.82 \qquad DW = 2.23$$

$$I_t = 4.964 + .341\ (Y_t - Y_{t-1}) + .164\ Y_{t-1} - 3.948\ R_{t-4} \qquad (12.19)$$
$${}_{(2.44)}{}_{(3.86)}\phantom{(Y_t-Y_{t-1}) + }{}_{(22.13)}\phantom{Y_{t-1} - }{}_{(-4.83)}$$

$$R^2 = .976 \qquad SER = 4.62 \qquad DW = .94$$

$$R_t = -\ .057 + .016\ Y_t + .041\ (Y_t - Y_{t-1}) - .265\ (M_t - M_{t-1})$$
$${}_{(-.22)}{}_{(1.71)}{}_{(3.39)}\phantom{(Y_t - Y_{t-1}) - }{}_{(-3.34)}$$

$$+\ .384\ (R_{t-1} + R_{t-2}) \qquad\qquad (12.20)$$
$${}_{(4.48)}$$

$$R^2 = .886 \qquad SER = .55 \qquad DW = .93$$

Presumably the use of 2SLS will reduce the possibility of inconsistency introduced by the model's simultaneity. The equations look reasonable, except that two of them, (12.19) and (12.20), have rather low DW statistics, indicating likely serial correlation in the error terms. If these equations could be reestimated using an autoregressive transformation to correct for this serial correlation, more efficient estimates would be obtained. Using the Hildreth-Lu method[†] to reestimate the equations gives the results shown in Eqs. (12.21) to (12.23) below.[‡] The value of ρ used in the autoregressive correction is shown with each equation:

$$C_t = .940 + .125\ Y_t + .814\ C_{t-1} \qquad\qquad (12.21)$$
$${}_{(.54)}{}_{(2.86)}{}_{(11.15)}$$

$$R^2 = .999 \qquad SER = 2.82 \qquad DW = 2.23 \qquad \rho = 0$$

$$I_t = 5.239 + .207\ (Y_t - Y_{t-1}) + .161\ Y_{t-1} - 3.247\ R_{t-4} \qquad (12.22)$$
$${}_{(1.33)}{}_{(3.19)}\phantom{(Y_t-Y_{t-1}) + }{}_{(17.07)}\phantom{Y_{t-1} - }{}_{(-3.15)}$$

$$R^2 = .984 \qquad SER = 3.81 \qquad DW = 2.01 \qquad \rho = .6$$

$$R_t = .433 + .004\ Y_t + .020\ (Y_t - Y_{t-1}) - .194\ (M_t - M_{t-1})$$
$${}_{(.49)}{}_{(2.77)}{}_{(2.52)}\phantom{(Y_t - Y_{t-1}) - }{}_{(-2.96)}$$

$$+\ .144\ (R_{t-1} + R_{t-2}) \qquad\qquad (12.23)$$
$${}_{(2.06)}$$

$$R^2 = .926 \qquad SER = .43 \qquad DW = 1.50 \qquad \rho = .8$$

We now have three versions of this model, the first estimated by ordinary least squares, the second by two-stage least squares, and the third combining

† The Hildreth-Lu technique is described in Chapter 6.

‡ Combining 2SLS with an autoregressive correction as we have done actually may yield inconsistent estimates. A method for obtaining consistent estimates using these two methods together has been derived by Fair (R. Fair, "The Estimation of Simultaneous Equation Models with Lagged Endogenous Variables and First Order Serially Correlated Errors," *Econometrica*, May 1970), but was not computationally available. In any case, it was felt here that the benefit from more efficient estimates outweighed the probably small error introduced by combining the techniques. An alternative estimation method is used to construct a larger macroeconomic model in Chapter 14.

Table 12.3 Summary simulation statistics

	Version 1 OLS		Version 2 2SLS		Version 3 autoregressive	
	rms error	rms percent error	rms error	rms percent error	rms error	rms percent error
Gross national product Y	16.44	2.16	12.43	1.70	8.15	1.12
Consumption C	10.03	2.06	6.86	1.50	6.22	1.35
Investment I	7.22	6.49	6.62	6.00	2.29	1.96
Interest rate R	.86	17.67	.88	19.03	.27	5.43

two-stage least squares with an autoregressive correction. Each of these models was simulated from the first quarter of 1961 to the last quarter of 1971, and the rms simulation error and rms percent error were computed for each endogenous variable. The results are shown in Table 12.3.

Note that the simulation of the two-stage least-squares version of the model yields smaller rms simulation errors than the ordinary least-squares version for every variable except the interest rate. Version 3, which contains the autoregressive correction for serial correlation in the error terms, does even better, with the rms errors for investment and the interest rate less than one-third of what they were before.† The reason that the autoregressive corrections improve the performance of the model is that they add information to it. Even though we may not know why the additive error terms behave the way they do, we can observe that they are serially correlated, and include that information in the model.

In Part Three of this book we will discuss time-series models, i.e., models which describe and predict the behavior of random processes. The autoregressive correction that we employed to estimate the third version of our small model makes the implicit assumption that the additive error terms are of the form

$$\varepsilon_t = \rho\varepsilon_{t-1} + \varepsilon_t^* \tag{12.24}$$

where ε_t^* is the uncorrelated part of ε_t. Equation (12.24) is actually a simple time-series model for ε_t (a first-order autoregressive model, to be exact). By combining this model with the structural relationships of each equation, the predictive performance of the model as a whole can be improved. In fact a more complicated time-series model than that of Eq. (12.24) can be used to "explain" the behavior of the additive error term, and we will see in Chapter 20 that the result can be an even greater improvement in model performance.

The important point for the time being, however, is that the ability of a model to simulate the forecast well can depend on the particular method used to

---

† The reason that the rms error for consumption does not decrease as dramatically is that the estimated value for ρ in that equation was 0, so that in effect there was no autoregressive correction in the consumption equation.

estimate the model's coefficients. We have examined only two alternatives to ordinary least squares, but a variety of other estimation methods are available. R. Fair made a comparison of 10 alternative estimation methods.† Each method was used to estimate the seven behavioral equations of a macroeconomic forecasting model that had been previously developed.‡ Historical simulations were then performed for each of the 10 resulting versions of the model, and the rms simulation errors for each endogenous variable compared. Nine of the estimation methods used were§

1. Ordinary least squares (OLS)
2. Two-stage least squares (2SLS)
3. OLS plus first-order autoregressive correction (OLSAUTO1)
4. 2SLS plus first-order autoregressive correction (2SLSAUTO1)
5. OLS plus second-order autoregressive correction (OLSAUTO2)
6. 2SLS plus second-order autoregressive correction (2SLSAUTO2)
7. Full-information maximum likelihood (FIML)
8. FIML plus first-order autoregressive correction (FIMLAUTO1)
9. FIML plus second-order autoregressive correction (FIMLAUTO2)

The rms simulation errors are shown below for one variable, GNP, for the entire sample period (42 observations) and for a four-quarter forecast:

	Entire period	Four quarters
1 OLS	8.45	7.51
2 2SLS	8.07	7.21
3 OLSAUTO1	8.61	6.44
4 2SLSAUTO1	8.27	6.42
5 OLSAUTO2	8.40	6.14
6 2SLSAUTO2	7.78	5.90
7 FIML	7.38	5.34
8 FIMLAUTO1	6.55	4.79
9 FIMLAUTO2	6.99	4.95

Note that it is with the four-quarter forecast that the estimation method used is most critical, with the range of rms errors extending from 7.51 (OLS) to 4.79 (FIMLAUTO1). Since most forecasting is done over the short term, the results for the first four quarters are presented separately from those for the

† See R. Fair, "A Comparison of Alternative Estimators of Macroeconomic Models," *International Economic Review*, vol. 14, no. 2, pp. 261–277, June 1973.

‡ The model is described in detail in R. Fair, *A Short-Run Forecasting Model of the United States Economy* (Lexington, Mass: Heath, 1971).

§ The tenth method was an experimental procedure that accounts for the dynamic structure of the equations on a one-by-one basis. This method has rarely been used in practice, and so we will not describe it here.

entire sample period. In both cases, however, the use of FIMLAUTO1 seems to yield the best result. This method accounts for correlations between error terms across equations as well as first-order serial correlation in the individual error terms, and the gain that results in its use seems quite large. The results, however, do not prove one method to be better than any other: they simply demonstrate the use of the alternative methods on one particular model. In general, the model builder must experiment with alternative estimation methods on each and every model being developed.

12.5 OTHER KINDS OF
MULTI-EQUATION SIMULATION MODELS

Our discussion of multi-equation simulation models has focused largely on econometric models, i.e., models constructed from sets of equations that were estimated using standard econometric techniques. One of the criteria that we used to judge or evaluate a simulation model, for example, was the degree of statistical fit of the model's individual equations. We said that if the model contained several equations that did not fit the data well or were otherwise statistically insignificant, we might question the validity of the model as a whole. Thus, the reader may have been lead to believe that econometric estimation is essential to the construction of a simulation model. In fact there exist other approaches to modeling, and there are other applications of multi-equation simulation models besides micro- and macroeconomic forecasting and policy analysis.†

A simulation model need not contain equations that are estimated by fitting them to data. One of the newest and most important applications of multi-equation simulation is in corporate financial planning. A financial simulation model can be thought of as an econometric model in which the equations describe the financial accounting structure of a particular corporation, together with some decision risks that describe dividend payouts, bond issues, etc. Since all the equations are accounting relationships or decision rules (as opposed to behavioral relationships), the model consists of a set of identities, and there is no estimation involved in its construction. Financial simulation models can be extremely useful for forecasting and analyzing the impact of alternative financial strategies on a company's development. By simulating such a model into the future using different assumptions about capitalization, debt, future revenue streams, etc., one can generate *pro forma* balance sheets and income statements that can provide a useful input to corporate planning. We will present an example of a financial simulation model and demonstrate its use in Chapter 14.‡

There may be other situations in which a simulation model is constructed without the use of econometric estimation. Suppose that one wanted to construct

---

† For an overview of simulation techniques as they apply to economic problems, see T. Naylor, *Computer Simulation Experiments with Economic Systems* (New York: Wiley, 1971).

‡ For another example of a financial simulation model, see J. M. Warren and J. P. Shelton, "A Simultaneous Equation Approach to Financial Planning," *Journal of Finance*, December 1971.

a model to be simulated over a very long time horizon, perhaps 100 years. Such a model might be used to explain long-run economic growth, changes in population and fertility rates, or some other economic, social, or political process which evolves slowly over a long period of time. It is very possible that data would not exist for many of the variables in such a model. One reason for this might be that some of the variables are unobservable and thus unmeasurable; an example would be some attitudinal parameters in a sociological model. On the other hand, the variable may be observable, but perhaps data have never been collected for it. This is often the case in less developed countries and presents a problem to the economist constructing a planning model for economic development policy. Finally, even if data were available, they might span only a short time period, say 10 or 20 years. Even if the data were used to estimate the coefficients of the model, the resulting estimates might have limited meaning when the model was simulated over a 100-year period.

In this situation the model builder could begin by specifying a set of hypothetical relationships. In the case of an econometric model, those relationships would be estimated and tested by fitting them to available data. If data were not available (or the model builder chose not to use available data), it would be necessary to "specify" values for the coefficients based either on "intuition" or else on estimates produced by examining averages, sporadic data points, or perhaps just the opinion of "experts." As far as the testing of the individual relationships is concerned, all one can really do in this case is to simulate the model as a whole and assess its performance over some limited time period for which data are available.

One of the problems of this modeling technique is that it provides no safety check on the reasonableness of the individual relationships that make up the model, and this limits the ability to validate the model as a whole. Since the model builder is free to pick the coefficient values instead of fitting them to data, it becomes possible to adjust the coefficients until the model succeeds in reproducing the historical data. In such a case the model might appear to simulate well, even though the relationships that go into it are largely invalid, so that the model itself is invalid in terms of its forecasts or policy implications.

Anyone who has constructed an econometric model knows that many hypothetical relationships must be tested against data before one is found that is statistically acceptable. This provides an important check on model builders, forcing them to test statistically each of the relationships originally specified. This check is missing in the data-less approach to modeling, and it is thus important that that approach be used only with great caution.†

---

† One of the more prominent proponents of the data-less approach to modeling has been J. W. Forrester, who has constructed models of, among other things, the dynamics of urban growth and world resource use. See J. W. Forrester, *Urban Dynamics* (Cambridge, Mass.: M.I.T. Press, 1969); J. W. Forrester, *World Dynamics* (Cambridge, Mass.: Wright-Allen, 1971); and D. Meadows et al., *The Limits to Growth* (Cambridge, Mass.: Wright-Allen, 1972). Forrester's work has been criticized because many of the relationships used in his models have not been substantiated or validated; see, for example, W. D. Nordhaus, "World Dynamics: Measurement without Data," *Economic Journal*, December 1974.

Simulation models have over the past few years found acceptance and application in a wide variety of social science disciplines. Sociologists and political scientists, finding them a natural vehicle for the representation, analysis, and forecasting of complex social phenomena, have been applying them to a variety of problems. Sociological and political simulation models have been constructed by combining econometric estimation methods with the data-less techniques described above. In some cases these modeling efforts have resulted in methodological advances for dealing with situations when data are limited or unreliable. Although the perspective of this book is largely limited to econometric models of the economy, individual markets, and individual firms, the reader should be aware that the applicability of the techniques that we are presenting is quite broad.†

EXERCISES

12.1 The rms simulation error penalizes heavily for large individual errors. In what cases is it a more, or less, desirable performance criterion than the mean absolute error (MAE), defined as

$$\text{MAE} = \frac{1}{T} \sum_{t=1}^{T} \frac{|Y_t^s - Y_t^a|}{Y_t^a}$$

12.2 The mean error may be small even though the rms error is large, if positive and negative errors cancel. In what situation does the mean error provide useful information for evaluating a model not provided by the rms error?

12.3 Two sets of actual and predicted series are shown below. Note that the series in the second set are equal to the first increased by 100.

t	x_t^a	x_t^s	y_t^a	y_t^s
1	−3	−1	97	99
2	5	7	105	107
3	10	7	110	107
4	−4	−1	96	99

Calculate the rms simulation errors and Theil inequality coefficients for the two variables x_t and y_t. Decompose the inequality coefficients into the proportions U^M, U^S, and U^C, and interpret the results.

† For examples of some of the more interesting applications of multi-equation simulation models to sociology and political science, see Brunner and Brewer, op. cit.; G. D. Brewer, *Politicians, Bureaucrats, and the Consultant: a Critique of Urban Problem Solving* (New York: Basic Books, 1973); J. M. Dutton and W. H. Starbuck, *Computer Simulation of Human Behavior* (New York: Wiley, 1971); and J. P. Crecine, "A Computer Simulation Model of Municipal Budgeting," *Management Science*, vol. 13, pp. 786–815, July 1967. This last model, which describes the process by which mayors make their budgeting decisions, consists of a set of logical rules of thumb, and is not unlike the financial simulation models described above.

12.4 Reexamine the historical simulation of the four-equation macroeconometric model in Figs. 12.6 to 12.9. Based on this historical simulation (and the model itself) explain why the *ex post* forecast (Figs. 12.10 to 12.13) underpredicts GNP.

12.5† Specify, estimate, and simulate your own macroeconometric model. [Equations (12.14) to (12.17) could be used as a starting point.] Produce *ex post* and *ex ante* forecasts, and evaluate these forecasts. If possible, experiment with alternative estimation techniques. Attempt to improve upon the performance of the four-equation model in the text. (The experience gained in this kind of exercise is invaluable for learning the art of model building.)

† This exercise is for students who have access to an econometric computer facility.

THIRTEEN

DYNAMIC BEHAVIOR OF SIMULATION MODELS

We saw in the last chapter that a multi-equation simulation model can sometimes provide a representation of the real world that is considerably richer than that of a single-equation regression model. Because variables can interact with each other across equations and through time, a multi-equation model can describe and explain the dynamic behavior of the world in a much more complete way than a single-equation model can. Because the multi-equation model is constructed to represent the dynamic behavior of the real world, its own time-dynamic behavior is of central concern in both its construction and its use. It is the time-dynamic behavior of multi-equation simulation models that is the focus of this chapter.

Since a simulation model is a set of difference equations that can be solved simultaneously through time, we are interested in the properties of difference-equation solutions. We want to know, for example, what makes the solution to a difference equation (or set of difference equations) oscillate, since oscillatory behavior would be important in a model designed to explain (or forecast) cyclical market phenomena. We begin, then, by reviewing difference equations and their solutions.

Simulation models are often used to study and compare the short-run and the long-run responses of one variable (or set of variables) to another variable. The second section of this chapter deals with the notion of *dynamic multipliers* and dynamic response. We may know, for example, that a change in price may result in a change in demand for some good, but how long does it take for that change in demand to occur? We know that an increase in government spending results in an increase in GNP with a multiplier effect—but the size of that multiplier depends on how much time elapses after the level of government spending is increased. By discussing dynamic multipliers and dynamic elasticities, we will see how simulation models can be used as a tool for analyzing the dynamic response of one set of economic variables to changes in other variables.

In the third section of the chapter we describe how a simulation model can be modified or adjusted to improve its performance, i.e., to improve its forecasting ability or its ability to provide information regarding policy alternatives. As we will see, misspecification or biased estimation in one part of a model may cause the whole model to perform poorly in a simulation context. These problems can sometimes be reduced or eliminated by modifying the structure of the model slightly.

The chapter closes with an introductory discussion of *stochastic simulation* (or *Monte Carlo* simulation). Since the equations of an econometric model are estimated by fitting them to data, the resulting parameter estimates are themselves random variables. Furthermore, each equation has an implicit additive error term associated with it. Stochastic simulation allows us to recognize this random character of the model explicitly—as well as the simulation and forecast errors that it implies. When a model is used for policy analysis, the results are subject to some margin of error. Stochastic simulation allows one to get a better quantitative grasp of what this margin of error is and to estimate its magnitude. Stochastic simulation is similarly useful when a model is used for forecasting, as it allows one to obtain confidence intervals for the forecast.

13.1 MODEL BEHAVIOR: STABILITY AND OSCILLATIONS

The structural richness of a multi-equation simulation model makes it somewhat more difficult to build, analyze, evaluate, and use. Life is relatively simple in a single-equation world; a regression equation can easily be evaluated based on its statistical fit, and directly used to produce a forecast. As we saw in the last chapter, however, things may not be so simple in the case of a simulation model. Each of the regression equations that make up the model may have an excellent statistical fit, but when they are put together and simulated, the results may be meaningless. The reason for this may be that a *structural instability* was built into the model that is unrepresentative of the real world. Such an instability may not appear in any single equation but could result when the equations of the model are combined and solved simultaneously. Of course a single-equation model can be simulated by itself, and it too may (or may not) be structurally unstable. A single-equation model can in fact have a rather complicated dynamic structure (e.g., long and complicated distributed lags), but it is more crucial that one be concerned about questions of stability when dealing with multi-equation models.

In this section we present the conditions for determining stability (and oscillations) in simple linear models. In particular, we show how these conditions depend not only on the structure of the model (i.e., the particular causal relationships that have been specified), but also on the estimated values of the coefficients of the individual equations. We discuss nonlinear models only briefly, since there is little in the way of analytical tools available for analyzing their dynamic properties. Some discussion is necessary, however, since many econometric models are nonlinear.

13.1.1 Linear Models†

We say that a model is *linear* if all the difference equations that constitute it are linear. Sets of linear difference equations can be solved rather easily, and the determination of whether or not the system is stable is relatively straightforward. We will begin by demonstrating how one can analyze a linear model to determine whether or not it is stable and/or oscillatory. We will illustrate the method using as an example the simple three-equation multiplier-accelerator model presented at the beginning of the last chapter:

$$C_t = a_1 + a_2 Y_{t-1} \tag{13.1}$$

$$I_t = b_1 + b_2(Y_{t-1} - Y_{t-2}) \tag{13.2}$$

$$Y_t = C_t + I_t + G_t \tag{13.3}$$

where C = consumption
  I = investment
  G = government spending (exogenous)
  Y = GNP

The analysis of this linear model begins by combining the three equations into a *single* difference equation, which we call the *fundamental dynamic equation*. Substituting (13.1) and (13.2) into (13.3), we have as our fundamental dynamic equation the following second-order difference equation for Y_t:

$$Y_t - (a_2 + b_2) Y_{t-1} + b_2 Y_{t-2} = (a_1 + b_1) + G_t \tag{13.4}$$

We are interested in determining if and how the endogenous variable Y_t reaches a new equilibrium value in response to a change in the exogenous variable G_t. In other words, if at time $t = 0$, G_t increases by 1 and then *remains fixed at that higher level*, what will happen to Y_t over all future time? We are thus interested in the pattern by which Y_t reaches a new equilibrium value (if indeed it does reach a new equilibrium value). This pattern, called the *transient solution* for Y_t, is found by setting the right-hand side of the fundamental

† Readers who are not familiar with the solution of linear difference equations and the analysis of their properties may have some difficulty with this section. These readers may wish to read W. J. Baumol, *Economic Dynamics* (New York: Macmillan, 1951); R. G. D. Allen, *Mathematical Economics* (New York: Macmillan, 1956); or A. C. Chiang, *Fundamental Methods of Mathematical Economics* (New York: McGraw-Hill, 1967), for a detailed but introductory presentation of difference equations.

dynamic equation equal to 0:

$$Y_t - (a_2 + b_2)Y_{t-1} + b_2Y_{t-2} = 0 \tag{13.5}$$

and then *assuming* the solution of this equation to be of the form†

$$Y_t = A\lambda^t \tag{13.6}$$

If (13.6) above is a solution, then it should satisfy Eq. (13.5). Substituting (13.6) into (13.5) and dividing through the equation by $A\lambda^{t-2}$, we obtain the *characteristic equation* for our model:

$$\lambda^2 - (a_2 + b_2)\lambda + b_2 = 0 \tag{13.7}$$

The solutions to the characteristic equation, called the *characteristic roots* of the model, determine the solution properties of the model. In our example the characteristic equation is quadratic, and so the characteristic roots (i.e., the solutions to the equation) are easy to find:

$$\lambda_1, \lambda_2 = \frac{(a_2 + b_2) \pm \sqrt{(a_2 + b_2)^2 - 4b_2}}{2} \tag{13.8}$$

We now have two transient solutions to our model, $Y_t = A_1\lambda_1^t$ and $Y_t = A_2\lambda_2^t$, where A_1 and A_2 are constants that depend on the initial value that Y_t happens to take. We had assumed that the solutions were of the form $A\lambda^t$, but since λ_1 and λ_2 both satisfy the characteristic equation, we can verify that $A_1\lambda_1^t$ and $A_2\lambda_2^t$ are indeed solutions. If we substitute $A_1\lambda_1^t$ for Y_t in Eq. (13.5), we will obtain the characteristic equation in terms of λ_1, and since λ_1 is known to be a solution to the characteristic equation, we can be sure that $A_1\lambda_1^t$ is a transient solution. In fact, it is easy to see that if $A_1\lambda_1^t$ and $A_2\lambda_2^t$ are both solutions to (13.5), the *sum* $Y_t = A_1\lambda_1^t + A_2\lambda_2^t$ is also a solution. The reader can verify this by substituting $A_1\lambda_1^t + A_2\lambda_2^t$ for Y_t in (13.5).

Depending on the values of a_2 and b_2, the behavior of the solution can be characterized in four possible ways: (1) The solution may be stable, converging without oscillation. This requires that both λ_1 and λ_2 be less than 1 in magnitude and have no imaginary component. (2) The solution may be stable, converging with damped oscillations. This occurs if the solutions to the characteristic equation are both less than 1 in magnitude but have imaginary components. (3) The solution may be unstable and nonoscillatory. This results if either solution to the characteristic equation is greater than 1 in magnitude but there is no imaginary component. (4) The solution may be unstable and oscillatory (i.e., it exhibits ever-diverging oscillations). This occurs if one or both of the characteristic roots are greater than 1 in magnitude and there is an imaginary component.

It is easy to see how these conditions on the characteristic roots λ_1 and λ_2 determine the behavior of the model if one remembers that the transient solution to the fundamental dynamic equation is given by

$$Y_t = A_1\lambda_1^t + A_2\lambda_2^t$$

† Again we are assuming that the reader has some familiarity with difference-equation solutions. If our discussion seems somewhat confusing, the reader should turn to one of the references mentioned in the previous footnote.

Clearly if either λ_1 or λ_2 is greater than 1 in magnitude, the solution will grow explosively, and if λ_1 and λ_2 are complex (i.e., have imaginary components), the solution will be sinusoidal (i.e., will oscillate).†

The type of solution which results will depend on the values of the two parameters a_2 and b_2. For example, if a_2 and b_2 take on the values .6 and .1, respectively, the characteristic roots are given by

$$\lambda_1, \lambda_2 = \frac{.7 \pm \sqrt{.49 - .4}}{2} = .35 \pm .15$$

Since the largest root has a value of .5 and neither root has an imaginary component, the solution will be stable and nonoscillatory. If a_2 and b_2 have the values .6 and .8, respectively, the characteristic roots would be

$$\lambda_1, \lambda_2 = \frac{1.4 \pm \sqrt{1.96 - 3.2}}{2} \approx .7 \pm .56i$$

Now the characteristic roots are both less than 1 in magnitude, but they have an imaginary component, so that the solution will be stable but will oscillate. The reader can see that values of a_2 and b_2 equal to .6 and 1.5, respectively, would result in a solution that is unstable (explosive) and oscillatory, while values of .6 and 3.0 would result in a solution that is unstable and nonoscillatory. In fact (and the reader can verify this), as long as a_2 and b_2 are both less than 1, the solution will be stable, while if either is larger than 1 the solution will be unstable. We can also find an algebraic relationship between a_2 and b_2 that will determine whether the solution is oscillatory. The characteristic roots [see Eq. (13.8)] will have an imaginary component if

$$4b_2 > (a_2 + b_2)^2 \qquad (13.9)$$

or $$a_2 < 2\sqrt{b_2} - b_2 \qquad (13.10)$$

In Fig. 13.1 the plane is divided into regions that indicate the range of parameter values that would result in each of the four types of solutions. The region that indicates those values of a_2 and b_2 that would result in a stable and nonoscillatory solution has been shaded.

In Fig. 13.2 and Table 13.1 we show as an illustration four solutions for Y_t corresponding to the four pairs of values for a_2 and b_2 from above, that is, $(a_2, b_2) = (.6, .1), (.6, .8), (.6, 1.5)$, and $(.6, 3.0)$. These solutions begin with the initial conditions $C_t = 90$, $I_t = 0$, $G_t = 10$, and $Y_t = 100$. After three periods G_t is increased to 12, and a solution is obtained for the next 30 periods. In each case, the values 30 and 0 are used for the parameters a_1 and b_1, respectively.

In order to obtain the fundamental dynamic equation for our three-equation model (and thus the characteristic equation and characteristic roots), we could have begun by combining the equations of the model for any one endogenous variable. If, for example, we had substituted Eqs. (13.2) and (13.3) into Eq. (13.1)

---

† If the characteristic roots are complex, then they will occur as complex conjugates; i.e., they will be of the form $\lambda_1, \lambda_2 = \alpha \pm \beta i$. These complex roots, when substituted into $Y_t = A_1\lambda_1^t + A_2\lambda_2^t$, will result in a solution for Y_t that will be a sinusoidal function of time. For a proof and further discussion of this, see Baumol, op. cit., or Chiang, op. cit.

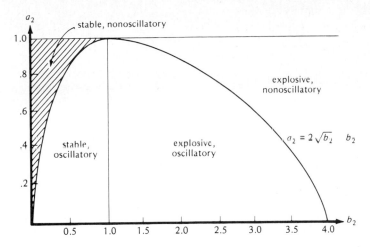

Figure 13.1 Solution behavior for simple multiplier-accelerator model.

for C_t, we would have the following fundamental dynamic equation in terms of C_t:

$$C_t = a_1 + a_2 C_{t-1} + a_2 b_1 + a_2 b_2 \left(\frac{C_{t-1}}{a_2} - \frac{a_1}{a_2} \right) - a_2 b_2 \left(\frac{C_{t-2}}{a_2} - \frac{a_1}{a_2} \right) + a_2 G_{t-1}$$

$$(13.11)$$

or $$C_t - (a_2 + b_2) C_{t-1} + b_2 C_{t-2} = (a_1 + a_2 b_1) + a_2 G_{t-1} \qquad (13.12)$$

It is easy to see that this yields the same characteristic equation as (13.7) and thus the same characteristic roots. The reader can verify that the same characteristic equation would also result if Eqs. (13.1) and (13.3) were substituted into Eq. (13.2) to yield a single fundamental dynamic equation in terms of investment I_t.

Suppose that we *estimate* the coefficients of our model and obtain values for a_2 and b_2 that result in an oscillatory (but stable) solution. How should the model then be interpreted? If the oscillations in GNP predicted by the model in a historic simulation bear no resemblance to the actual past behavior of GNP, we should doubt the validity of the model (even if the *individual* equations have good statistical fit). On the other hand, if the periodicity and magnitude of the oscillations predicted by the model bear a reasonable resemblance to the actual behavior of the economy, we might conclude that the dynamic structure of the model is representative of that of the actual economy. One might, for example, try to explain the presence of business cycles in the American economy using a multiplier-accelerator interaction. From Eq. (13.8) a range of values for a_2 and b_2 could be found that would result in oscillations with periodicity close to that observed in business cycles. Statistical tests could then be performed to determine whether data could support values of a_2 and b_2 in that range.†

---

† See, for example, P. A. Samuelson, "Interactions between the Multiplier Analysis and the Principle of Acceleration," *Review of Economics and Statistics*, May 1939; and G. C. Chow, "Multiplier, Accelerator, and Liquidity Preference in the Determination of National Income in the United States," *Review of Economics and Statistics*, February 1967.

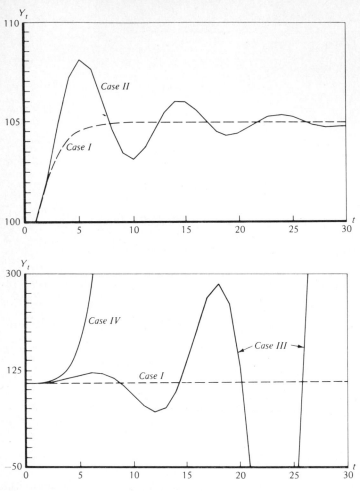

Figure 13.2 Simulations of multiplier-accelerator model: case I: $b_2 = .1$; case II: $b_2 = .8$; case III: $b_2 = 1.5$; case IV: $b_2 = 3.0$.

A simple multiplier-accelerator model would probably not suffice to explain the cycles and other fluctuations in the economy. However, the larger and more complicated models which have been constructed recently have to some extent been able to explain and predict economic fluctuations. The principle holds that the dynamic structure implicit in a set of simultaneous time-dependent equations can provide a model of real world structure. It is for this reason that a multiequation model can often describe more about the actual physical system being modeled than single-equation models can.

13.1.2 Analyzing Larger Models

As models become larger, an analysis of their dynamic behavior becomes more difficult and less straightforward. As long as the model remains linear, a

Table 13.1 Simulations of multiplier-accelerator model

t	Case I $(b_2 = .1)$	Case II $(b_2 = .8)$	Case III $(b_2 = 1.5)$	Case IV $(b_2 = 3.0)$
0	100	100	100	100
1	100	100	100	100
2	102	102	102	102
3	103.4	104.8	106.2	109.2
4	104.18	107.12	112.02	129.12
5	104.586	108.128	117.942	179.232
6	104.792	107.683	121.648	299.875
7	104.896	106.254	120.548	583.854
8	104.948	104.609	112.679	1,244.25
9	104.974	103.45	97.8034	2,769.74
10	104.987	103.142	78.3680	6,280.3
11	104.993	103.639	59.8696	14,341.9
12	104.997	104.581	50.1727	32,831.8
13	104.998	105.502	57.5584	75,210.9
14	104.999	106.038	87.6135	172,306
15	105	106.052	139.651	394,710
16	105	105.642	203.846	904,080
17	105	105.057	260.601	2.071×10^6
18	105	104.566	283.493	4.742×10^6
19	105	104.347	246.433	1.086×10^7
20	105	104.433	134.27	2.487×10^7
21	105	104.728	−45.6819	5.695×10^7
22	105	105.073	−255.337	1.304×10^8
23	105	105.32	−425.685	2.986×10^8
24	105	105.389	−468.933	6.838×10^8
25	105	105.289	−304.231	1.566×10^9
26	105	105.093	106.513	3.586×10^9
27	105	104.899	722.025	8.210×10^9
28	105	104.784	1,398.48	1.880×10^{10}
29	105	104.779	1,895.77	4.305×10^{10}
30	105	104.863	1,925.4	9.859×10^{10}

characteristic equation can be derived, although a solution to that equation may offer computational problems. Consider, for example, the four-equation macro-economic model constructed in the last chapter [Eqs. (12.14) to (12.17)].

This is a very simple model, but if the equations are combined into a single fundamental dynamic equation for Y, the difference equation will be of fifth order, i.e., of the form

$$Y_t + \alpha_1 Y_{t-1} + \alpha_2 Y_{t-2} + \alpha_3 Y_{t-3} + \alpha_4 Y_{t-4} + \alpha_5 Y_{t-5} = \alpha_6 Z_t \quad (13.13)$$

The characteristic equation will also be fifth order and will have five solutions (i.e., five characteristic roots). A fifth-order equation is harder to solve analytically than the simple characteristic equation of (13.7). Thus if the size of the econometric model is substantial, an analysis of the properties of the solution becomes difficult.

Computer programs exist that can be used to solve a characteristic equation of high order. In fact some of the computer packages that have been written to solve simulation models also provide a solution of the characteristic equation—either directly, if the model is linear, or for a linearization of the model around a particular simulation solution if it is nonlinear. If an appropriate program is available, one can examine the characteristic roots of a model (there might be 100 or 200 such characteristic roots if the model is large). Those characteristic roots which are greater than 1 in magnitude will yield instabilities in the model, and those characteristic roots which are complex (i.e., have imaginary components) will contribute to the oscillatory behavior of the model.

When actually simulating a linear econometric model, it might be useful to look at the values of the characteristic roots. It is possible that the model may exhibit oscillatory or unstable behavior, but that the period of the oscillation may be much larger than the simulation period being used, or that the rate of divergence might be very slow. For example, if an econometric model is built to be simulated over 40 time periods, the period of oscillation might be more than 100 or 200 time periods and will not become apparent in a 40-period simulation. By examining the values of the characteristic roots, the model builder can immediately determine whether or not the model will have long-term oscillatory characteristics.

It is quite possible that a large model will have some characteristic roots that are greater than 1 (and some that are complex) but that the model will be quite useful as a forecasting tool. If a few roots exist that are only slightly larger than 1, their destabilizing effects may be minimal, becoming evident only if the model is simulated over a long time horizon. The importance of stability for a model's forecasting performance thus depends very much on the length of the forecast. In particular, a technical instability may be of little consequence for a short-term forecasting model.

In the simple model of Eqs. (13.1) to (13.3), it was easy to determine whether or not the solution was stable and to determine whether or not a small change in one of the coefficients (that is, a_2 or b_2) would change the solution characteristic from stable to unstable. Suppose, for example, that the estimated values of a_2 and b_2 yield a stable and nonoscillatory solution, and we would like to know if a small change in a_2 would result in unstable behavior. It is very easy to determine analytically whether or not this would be the case, since one need look only at how the solution to the characteristic equation changes as a result of the change in a_2. Such an analysis is difficult or impossible, however, if the model is large. Even if we can determine the characteristic roots for the model, we would probably not be able to determine how those characteristic roots are related to all the individual coefficients in the model. Thus, it becomes difficult to determine analytically how sensitive the solution is to small changes in any of the coefficients. We usually cannot say (without actually performing a simulation) whether or not a small change in one of the coefficients will move the solution from stable to unstable or from nonoscillatory to oscillatory.

If the model is nonlinear, the situation becomes even more difficult, because we cannot use the solution to a characteristic equation to tell us about the stability or instability of the model solution. Most computer solution algorithms for nonlinear models involve iterative solutions in which a linearization is made in each iteration. Thus, as far as characteristic roots are concerned, the best one can do is derive a set of characteristic roots based on a linearization about some nominal solution path. (The model might, for example, be simulated and then linearized around the resulting solution.) If these characteristic roots are all less than 1 in magnitude, the *linearization* of the nonlinear model (i.e., about the particular nominal path) is stable. We still have no guarantee, however, that the full nonlinear model will exhibit stability. Unfortunately, the current state of the art of mathematical stability theory is of limited use when it comes to nonlinear models. Methods do exist for determining the stability of nonlinear models, but these methods are largely analytical and do not readily yield computational algorithms that can be applied to models of any reasonable size. As a result we have no simple and direct way of determining the stability of a nonlinear model.†

Is there any way to determine the solution properties for a medium to large simultaneous equation model that contains nonlinearities (as many models do)? Usually one must resort to performing a series of simulations, over different periods of time, and using different time paths for the exogenous variables in the model. If the model is nonlinear and complex, the best that one can do to determine whether or not it is stable in the long term is to simulate it over a long period of time. Similarly, in analyzing the sensitivity of the model to parameter changes, often the simplest thing to do (and the most revealing) is to make trial-and-error experiments with parameter values. After experimenting with models over a period of time, one usually obtains a sense of a model's characteristics and how they are determined. Experimentation with parameter changes, etc., then becomes more intuitive and less a matter of trial and error. Clearly, this aspect of model building is more of an art than a science.

13.2 MODEL BEHAVIOR: MULTIPLIERS AND DYNAMIC RESPONSE

We often build models to predict how a change in one variable is likely to affect other variables over time. We might construct a macroeconometric model, for

---

† Most of the analytical methods that do exist have come out of the field of control theory. An approach that has recently received some attention by economists and econometricians (called *Lyapunov's direct method*) provides a sufficient condition for stability in the form of an existence theorem. If a certain function (called a *Lyapunov function*) can be shown to exist for a given model, then the model is guaranteed to be stable. Unfortunately there is no simple computational algorithm for determining whether or not such a function exists for a particular model. For an introduction to the applications of Lyapunov's method to economic models the reader is referred to K. Fox, J. Sengupta, and E. Thorbecke, *The Theory of Quantitative Economic Policy* (Amsterdam: North-Holland, 1966). For a detailed treatment of the dynamic analysis of both linear and nonlinear models, see G. C. Chow, *Analysis and Control of Dynamic Economic Systems* (New York: Wiley, 1975).

example, to determine how changes in government expenditures, the money supply, or some other exogenous policy variable will affect future values of the GNP and its components, prices, employment, etc. We might construct a microeconometric model of some industry to forecast the future impact on market equilibrium of changes in personal income (or other demand-determining exogenous variables), changes in export demand, or (if the industry is a regulated one) changes in the government's regulatory policy. In any case, we will want to use our models to make statements about the *dynamic response*, i.e., the response over time, of the macroeconomy, an industry, or a firm to changes in particular variables. One way to quantify these statements is to calculate and examine the *multipliers* associated with the model's exogenous variables.

In the case of our simple three-equation multiplier-accelerator model, Eqs. (13.1) to (13.3), we can determine what change in Y_t would result from a \$1 increase in G_t (or we could determine the corresponding change in C_t or I_t). Assuming that the model's parameters are such that the simulation solution is stable, we would expect that the initial increase in G_t would result in ever-diminishing increases in Y_t. These changes in Y_t are called *dynamic multipliers*. The initial (first-period) change in Y_t is called the *impact multiplier*, while the *total long-run multiplier* is just the sum of all the dynamic multipliers over time. Thus, the long-run multiplier indicates the total long-run change in Y_t that results from a unit change in G_t. In this section we examine dynamic multipliers in some detail, and see how they can be used to provide information about a model's behavior.†

13.2.1 Dynamic Multipliers

Let us return to our simple model of Eqs. (13.1) to (13.3) with parameter values $a_1 = 30$, $a_2 = .6$, $b_1 = 0$, and $b_2 = .1$. We can obtain the dynamic multipliers directly from our simulation of the model in which we increased G_t by 2. Taking the *changes* in Y_t and dividing these by 2 (to correspond to an increase in G_t of 1), we obtain the dynamic multipliers, tabulated in Table 13.2. We also show in Table 13.2 the dynamic multipliers that result for $a_2 = .6$ and $b_2 = .8$, which, as expected, are oscillatory. The impact multiplier is the initial first-period change in Y_t (1.0), and the total long-run multiplier is the sum of all the dynamic multipliers. Note that in both cases the total long-run multiplier is 2.50. The two transient solutions are quite different, but they both bring Y_t to the same equilibrium value.

The impact multiplier can also be determined algebraically. First, rewrite Eq. (13.4) as

$$Y_t = (a_2 + b_2)Y_{t-1} - b_2Y_{t-2} + (a_1 + b_1) + G_t \qquad (13.14)$$

---

† For a detailed discussion of dynamic multipliers and their application to the analysis of a larger econometric model, see A. S. Goldberger, *Impact Multipliers and the Dynamic Properties of the Klein-Goldberger Model* (Amsterdam: North-Holland, 1959).

Table 13.2 Dynamic multipliers for multiplier-accelerator model

t	Case I $(b_2 = .1)$	Case II $(b_2 = .8)$	t	Case I $(b_2 = .1)$	Case II $(b_2 = .8)$
2	1.0	1.0	18	.000023	− .2453
3	.699997	1.39999	19	.000015	− .109543
4	.389999	1.16	20	.000007	.042877
5	.202995	.503998	21	.000004	.147667
6	.103096	− .222397	22	0	.172432
7	.051872	− .714554	23	0	.123268
8	.025993	− .822464	24	0	.03463
9	.013008	− .579803	25	0	− .050133
10	.006508	− .153755	26	0	− .097885
11	.003258	.248581	27	0	− .096931
12	.001625	.471016	28	0	− .057396
13	.000816	.460564	29	0	− .002815
14	.000404	.267975	30	0	.041977
15	.000206	.006714	$\vdots$		
16	.000099	− .204979	Sum	2.5000	2.5000
17	.000053	− .292343			

Now taking first differences across this equation,

$$\Delta Y_t = (a_2 + b_2) \, \Delta Y_{t-1} - b_2 \, \Delta Y_{t-2} + \Delta G_t \tag{13.15}$$

we see that for $\Delta G_t = 1$ the first-period change in Y_t will also be 1. In general, one can obtain the impact multipliers directly from the reduced-form version of a model (the reduced-form coefficient of each unlagged exogenous variable is that variable's impact multiplier). The remaining dynamic multipliers, however, cannot be determined from inspection of the model. Instead, one must perform a simulation in which each exogenous variable is increased appropriately and the resulting changes in the endogenous variables are obtained by examining the simulation solution.

It is also important to keep in mind the fact that if a model is *nonlinear*, the dynamic multipliers will depend on the *size* of the variation of the particular exogenous variable as well as the starting values of all the endogenous variables. The simple model of Eqs. (13.1) to (13.3) is linear, so that the same multipliers would be obtained by increasing G_t by 4 as by increasing it by 2 (we would simply divide the changes in Y_t by 4 instead of 2). Furthermore, the multipliers would be the same whatever the initial values of Y_t and its components. This would *not* be the case, however, if the model were nonlinear. With a nonlinear model large increases in G_t could yield different multipliers than a small increase in G_t, and those multipliers would also differ for different starting values of Y_t. For this reason dynamic multipliers for nonlinear models should be presented together with information about how they were calculated.

Example 13.1   St. Louis model An application of dynamic multipliers is provided by the St. Louis model of Andersen and Carlson of the St. Louis Federal Reserve Bank.[†] They set out to test the monetarist position regarding macroeconomic policy. This viewpoint holds that only the money supply (and therefore monetary policy) has any long-run impact on the GNP and that government expenditures, while perhaps having some immediate impact on GNP, have almost no long-run impact. The model constructed by Andersen and Carlson included as exogenous variables both government expenditures and the money supply. Simulations of the model were used to determine the dynamic and total long-run multipliers corresponding to each of these exogenous variables. The result was that the total long-run multiplier for government expenditures was close to zero, while that for the money supply was large.

We will not describe the St. Louis model in detail, since that would require a lengthy discussion. The results described above, however, are largely the outcome of only one of the model's eight equations, one which relates changes in total spending (in current dollars) ΔY to changes in the money supply ΔM and changes in government expenditures ΔG. The estimated form of that equation uses polynomial distributed lags (see Chapter 9) and constrains each of the independent variables to lie on a fourth-degree polynomial with the head and tail set at 0. The estimated equation is shown below, with t statistics in parentheses:[‡]

$$\frac{\widehat{\Delta Y_t}}{Y_t} = \underset{(3.23)}{2.65} + \sum_{i=0}^{4} m_i \frac{\Delta M_{t-i}}{M_{t-i}} + \sum_{i=0}^{4} g_i \frac{\Delta G_{t-i}}{G_{t-i}} \qquad (13.16)$$

$$m_0 = .394\ (2.89) \qquad\qquad g_0 = .071\ (1.97)$$

$$m_1 = .443\ (5.69) \qquad\qquad g_1 = .057\ (2.27)$$

$$m_2 = .289\ (2.38) \qquad\qquad g_2 = .002\ (0.07)$$

$$m_3 = .071\ (0.91) \qquad\qquad g_3 = -.053\ (-2.11)$$

$$m_4 = -.071\ (-0.51) \qquad\quad g_4 = -.067\ (-1.91)$$

$$\Sigma m_i = 1.127\ (6.40) \qquad\qquad \Sigma g_i = .010\ (0.14)$$

[†] L. C. Andersen and K. M. Carlson, "A Monetarist Model for Economic Stabilization," *Federal Reserve Bank of St. Louis, Monthly Review*, April 1970. For a general reference on the monetarist view, see K. Brunner, "The Role of Money and Monetary Policy," *Federal Reserve Bank of St. Louis, Monthly Review*, July 1968. For a textbook discussion, see R. Dornbusch and S. Fischer, *Macroeconomics* (New York: McGraw-Hill, 1978). The complete St. Louis model is available with the MODSIM computer program (distributed by Conduit at the University of Iowa), and its equations are described in the MODSIM User's Manual.

[‡] This equation is from the April 1979 version of the model, as estimated by the Federal Reserve Bank of St. Louis using data over the period 1953-1 through 1978-4. The form of the equation differs only slightly from that in the original model (the three variables are now in percentage change rather than first difference form). For a discussion of changes in the specification, see K. M. Carlson, "Does the St. Louis Model Now Believe in Fiscal Policy?," *Federal Reserve Bank of St. Louis Review*, February 1978.

As can be seen from this equation, an increase in G will initially have a small positive impact on Y, but after two or three quarters it will have a negative impact, with a total (long-run) impact that is close to zero. The money supply, on the other hand, has a significant long-run impact ($\Sigma m_i = 1.127$).†

13.2.2 Dynamic Elasticities

When constructing a microeconometric model, we are usually interested in describing (and predicting) the dynamic response of a particular industry or market. Corresponding to the dynamic multipliers described above, we would calculate dynamic *elasticities*. A dynamic elasticity would tell how the demand for a good would change *over time* in response to a change in price or in consumers' incomes. We often make statements about the price or income elasticity of some good without explicitly recognizing that the value of the elasticity depends on how much time is allowed to elapse after price or income has changed.‡ In fact it is much more meaningful to look at a dynamic elasticity, such as

$$E_p(\tau) = -\frac{P_t}{Q_t}\frac{Q_{t+\tau} - Q_t}{\Delta P_t} \tag{13.17}$$

Here ΔP_t is a change in price (occurring at time t), and $Q_{t+\tau} - Q_t$ is the change in quantity demanded after a time interval τ has elapsed. Other dynamic elasticities (e.g., income, cross-price, etc.) would be defined in the same way.

By simulating the model (with a change in price), we can calculate and plot the elasticity as a function of the time interval τ. We would normally expect the elasticity to grow monotonically with increasing τ and approach some asymptotic value, as in Fig. 13.3. It is quite possible, however, that as a result of the model's structure (which we hope reflects the true market structure) the elasticity would oscillate (still approaching some asymptotic long-run value as long as the model is stable), as in Fig. 13.4.

The behavior of dynamic elasticities is clearly important if a model is being used to forecast or analyze the impact of a price increase, or a change in the price of some competing good, on an industry's (or a company's) sales. That impact must be described in dynamic terms. It is possible that a price increase would result in a drop in demand, but only after a long period of time has elapsed. On the other hand, it might result in an initially large drop in demand but later (after consumers' perceptions of relative prices have changed) an

---

† One criticism of the model has been that this equation is not easily justified. It is not our purpose to enter into this debate but to use it as an example of how impact multipliers alone (describing a static or short-run response) are not sufficient as a mode of analysis. It is the dynamic response of the St. Louis model that makes it interesting.

‡ By definition price elasticity of demand = $E_p = -\dfrac{P}{Q}\dfrac{\Delta Q}{\Delta P}$. Income elasticity = $E_t = \dfrac{I}{Q}\dfrac{\Delta Q}{\Delta I}$.

The problem, of course, is that given some ΔP (or ΔI), how much time should be allowed to elapse before we measure ΔQ?

$E(\tau)$

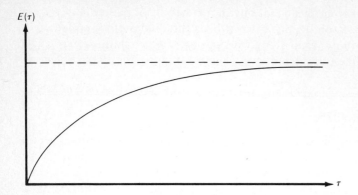

Figure 13.3 Dynamic elasticity.

$E(\tau)$

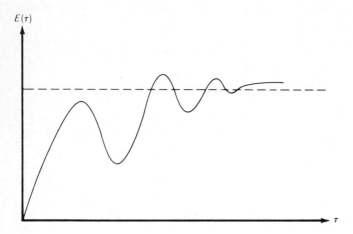

Figure 13.4 Oscillating dynamic elasticity.

increase in demand, so that the net decrease is small. The time required for these changes to occur is likely to vary considerably from industry to industry. Because of this, a company, trying to plan its production and marketing in anticipation of a planned change in prices, must have some idea of how much time will pass before it experiences a resulting change in sales.

Example 13.2   Automobile demand The dynamic characteristics of elasticities are very important when analyzing the demand for automobiles. To see why, let us examine a quarterly model of automobile demand constructed by Hymans.†

---

† S. H. Hymans, "Consumer Durable Spending: Explanation and Prediction," *Brookings Papers on Economic Activity*, no. 2, pp. 173–199, 1970.

The demand for cars (a flow variable) will depend on the *stock in circulation* at that time and provides the means of adjusting the stock to some desired or equilibrium level. We therefore begin by writing an equation for the *desired stock* of cars KA*:

$$KA_t^* = a + b(DI_{t-1}) + c(UM_{t-1}) + d(PA_t) + \varepsilon_t \qquad (13.18)$$

where DI = disposable personal income, net of transfers, 1958 dollars
UM = unemployment rate for males twenty years of age and over, percent
PA = a real (constant-dollar) price index of cars (1958 = 1.0)
Given this desired stock, gross real expenditures on cars (CARK) can be described by

$$CARK_t = w(KA_t^* - KA_{t-1}) + v(KA_{t-1}) \qquad (13.19)$$

where KA = actual car stock
w = quarterly rate of adjustment between desired and actual stocks
v = quarterly rate of depreciation of actual stock
Equation (13.18) can then be substituted for KA* in (13.19) to yield an equation for CARK that can be estimated. Hymans added a dummy variable to account for strikes against General Motors in 1964 and Ford in 1967 and obtained the following estimated equation using quarterly data over 1954-1 through 1968-4 and using a Hildreth-Lu correction for serial correlation:†

$$CARK_t = \underset{(2.93)}{19.009} + \underset{(9.14)}{0.206\,DI_{t-1}} - \underset{(-3.73)}{0.753\,UM_{t-1}} - \underset{(-4.40)}{25.861\,PA_t}$$

$$- \underset{(-6.33)}{0.157\,KA_{t-1}} + \underset{(3.94)}{1.626\,STRIKE} \qquad (13.20)$$

To simulate the model and forecast the effects of price or income changes, Eq. (13.20) is combined with the following identity for the stock of cars:

$$KA_t = (1 - v)KA_{t-1} + CARK_t \qquad (13.21)$$

Hymans uses a calculated value of 0.078 for the quarterly depreciation rate v. Equations (13.20) and (13.21) thus comprise a two-equation simulation model for expenditures on cars.

What is interesting about this model is that it implies that long-run price and income elasticities are *smaller* in magnitude than the short-run elasticities. In particular, the short-run (impact) *price* elasticity is −1.07, while the long-run elasticity is −0.36. The short-run *income* elasticity is 3.08, while the

---

† STRIKE = − 2 in 1964-4, 1 in 1965-1 and 1965-2, −1 in 1967-4, and $\frac{1}{2}$ in 1968-1 and 1968-2.

long-run elasticity is 1.02. The reason, of course, is the *stock adjustment effect*. When price goes up (or income goes down) consumers may initially cut down drastically on purchases of new cars. After a few years go by, however, old cars will have depreciated so that purchases of new cars will pick up, reaching a new equilibrium level that is below, but not that much below, what it was before the price increase.

Example 13.3 Another macroeconometric model The St. Louis model discussed above represents just one example of an attempt to study fiscal and monetary policy. As a second example, let us look at a quarterly model constructed by Kmenta and Smith.† Their model is also rather simple, and should help make clear the notion of dynamic multipliers and their application.

The equations of the model, which were estimated with quarterly data over the period 1954 to 1963, using three-stage least squares, are shown below with standard errors in parentheses below each coefficient:

$$C_t = -1.7951 + .1731 Y_t + .0421\left(L_t - .7275 L_{t-1}\right) + .7275 C_{t-1}$$
$$(.7803) \quad (.0131) \quad (.0277) \quad\quad (.0665) \quad\quad (.0665)$$

$$R^2 = .9968 \tag{13.22}$$

$$I_t^d = 2.5624 - .4411 r_t + .1381\left(S_{t-1} - S_{t-2}\right) + .0237 t + .8917 I_{t-1}^d$$
$$(1.0759) \quad (.1891) \quad (.0501) \quad\quad (.0110) \quad (.0700)$$

$$R^2 = .8961 \tag{13.23}$$

$$I_t^r = 3.6083 - .5127 r_t + .1267\left(S_{t-1} - S_{t-2}\right) + .0218 t + .6483 I_{t-1}^r$$
$$(.5779) \quad (.1133) \quad (.0335) \quad\quad (.0059) \quad (.0668)$$

$$R^2 = .8394 \tag{13.24}$$

$$I_t^i = 3.0782 - .8934 r_t + .3713\left(S_{t-1} - S_{t-2}\right) + .0450 + .3178 I_{t-1}^i$$
$$(1.3610) \quad (.4089) \quad (.1303) \quad\quad (.0208) \quad (.1181)$$

$$R^2 = .5341 \tag{13.25}$$

$$r_t = 13.8928 + .0261 Y_t - .1501 M_t + .0588 M_{t-1} \tag{13.26}$$
$$(1.8706) \quad (.0042) \quad (.0335) \quad (.0338)$$

$$R^2 = .8538$$

$$Y_t = C_t + I_t^d + I_t^r + I_t^i + G_t \tag{13.27}$$

$$S_t = Y_t - I_t^i \tag{13.28}$$

$$L_t = M_t + TD_t \tag{13.29}$$

† J. Kmenta and P. E. Smith, "Autonomous Expenditures versus Money Supply: An Application of Dynamic Multipliers," *Review of Economics and Statistics*, vol. LV, pp. 299–307, August 1973.

where $Y=$ gross national product

$C=$ consumption expenditures

$I^d=$ producer's outlays on durable plant and equipment

$I^r=$ residential construction

$I^i=$ increase in inventories

$G=$ government purchases of goods and services plus net foreign investment

$S=$ final sales of goods and services

$t=$ time in quarters (first quarter of $1954=0$)

$r=$ yield on all corporate bonds, percent per annum

$M=$ money supply, i.e., demand deposits plus currency outside banks

$TD=$ time deposits in commercial banks

$L=$ money supply plus time deposits in commercial banks (representing liquid wealth)

All the variables except for t and r are measured in billions of 1958 dollars, and the variables G, M, TD, and t are taken to be exogenous (there are thus eight equations and eight endogenous variables). No prices or wages are included in the model, since during the time period it describes prices were relatively stable.

To examine the dynamic characteristics of this model, we can begin by writing the reduced-form equation for GNP. This is found by expressing the current endogenous variables in Eq. (13.27) in terms of the exogenous and lagged endogenous variables. Making those substitutions gives the reduced form equation

$$Y_t = -20.8070 + \underset{(.1024)}{.3168} M_t - \underset{(.0755)}{.1242} M_{t-1} + \underset{(.0308)}{.0481} L_t - \underset{(.0224)}{.0350} L_{t-1}$$

$$+ \underset{(.0286)}{1.1427} G_t + \underset{(.0489)}{.1035} t + \underset{(.0356)}{.8313} C_{t-1} + \underset{(.1796)}{.7270} (S_{t-1} - S_{t-2})$$

$$+ \underset{(.0853)}{1.0190} I^d_{t-1} + \underset{(.0802)}{.7409} I^r_{t-1} + \underset{(.1350)}{.3631} I^i_{t-1} \tag{13.30}$$

According to this equation, the impact effect of a \$1 billion increase in government expenditures G_t is to increase GNP by \$1.1427 billion, while the impact effect of a \$1 billion increase in money supply M_t is to increase GNP by \$.3649 billion (.3168 plus .0481, since M_t is a component of L_t).

Before examining the dynamic multipliers, let us determine what type of solution the model will have by finding the characteristic roots. First, by substituting for C_{t-1}, S_{t-1}, S_{t-2}, I^d_{t-1}, I^r_{t-1}, and I^i_{t-1} in Eq. (13.30) we obtain the fundamental dynamic equation, which expresses current GNP in terms of its own lagged values and in terms of current and lagged values of the exogenous variables:

$$Y_t = 3.0716\,Y_{t-1} - 3.6561\,Y_{t-2} + 2.0850\,Y_{t-3} - .5585\,Y_{t-4} + .0535\,Y_{t-5}$$
$$+ 1.1427\,G_t - 2.5300\,G_{t-1} + 1.3779\,G_{t-2} + .5853\,G_{t-3} - .7463\,G_{t-4}$$
$$+ .1784\,G_{t-5} + .3168\,M_t - .7499\,M_{t-1} + .6253\,M_{t-2} - .2000\,M_{t-3}$$
$$+ .0082\,M_{t-4} + .0046\,M_{t-5} + .0481\,L_t - .1065\,L_{t-1} + .0580\,L_{t-2}$$
$$+ .0246\,L_{t-3} - .0314\,L_{t-4} + .0075\,L_{t-5} + .1034t - .2050(t-1)$$
$$+ .1267(t-2) - .0192(t-3) - .0032(t-4) - .5113 \qquad (13.31)$$

From Eq. (13.31) we can determine the characteristic equation of the model:

$$\lambda^5 - 3.0716\lambda^4 + 3.6561\lambda^3 - 2.0850\lambda^2 + .5585\lambda - .0535 = 0 \qquad (13.32)$$

The characteristic roots (i.e., the solutions to this equation) are

$$\lambda_1 = .2081 \qquad \lambda_{2,3} = .8475 \pm .0809i \qquad \lambda_{4,5} = .5843 \pm .1156i$$

Since all the roots are less than 1 in magnitude (λ_2 and λ_3 have a magnitude of .8513), and four of them are complex, the solution will be stable, and we will observe damped oscillations. The dynamic multipliers, then, should also exhibit damped oscillations and should converge toward 0 as the length of the time lag increases. This is indeed the case, as can be seen in Table 13.3.

Table 13.3 Dynamic GNP multipliers

Lag k	Multipliers of			
	G_{t-k}	M_{t-k}	L_{t-k}	$t-k$
0	1.14271	.31683	.04811	.10341
1	.98001	.22330	.04126	.11262
2	.21029	.15287	.00885	.09459
3	.03086	.11372	.00130	.07525
4	− .01519	.08722	− .00064	.05920
5	− .02878	.06775	− .00121	.04660
6	− .03352	.05291	− .00141	.03679
7	− .03539	.04135	− .00149	.02908
8	− .03604	.03210	− .11052	.02298
9	− .03592	.02487	− .00151	.01808
10	− .03520	.08196	− .00148	.01412
11	− .00396	.01410	− .00143	.01091
12	− .03227	.01036	− .00136	.00820
13	− .03024	.00729	− .00127	.00619
14	− .02795	.00486	− .00188	.00448
15	− .02552	.00295	− .00107	.00312
16	− .02303	.00148	− .00097	.00204
17	− .02056	.00037	− .00086	.00120
18	− .01816	− .00044	− .00076	.00055
19	− .01589	− .00102	− .00067	.00006
. . .	. . .	. . .	. . .	. . .

By summing the multipliers listed in the table, we see that the total long-run multiplier for government expenditures is 1.8406, that for the money supply (the combined effect of M_t and L_t) is 1.2270, and that for the time trend is .6363. These results are quite different from those of the St. Louis model, and support the view that both government expenditures and the money supply are effective as policy instruments.†

13.3 TUNING AND ADJUSTING SIMULATION MODELS

By making changes or adjustments in a simulation model, its forecasting performance can often be improved. The structure of a model might be such that its dynamic behavior verges on being unstable, and minor changes in the structure might be sufficient to stabilize the behavior. On the other hand, a bias in an individual estimated coefficient might result in consistent under or over prediction by the model as a whole which could be corrected by an adjustment in the coefficient value. In this section we discuss how one can tune or make changes in, a simulation model so as to improve its forecasting performance. We begin with a brief review of how we might change a regression equation to improve its fit and explanatory power.

Suppose we estimated a regression equation to forecast an interest rate into the future. The result might have been Eq. (12.16). Presumably, this equation has been compared with other regression equations that used different explanatory variables, different lag structures, and even different functional forms. The reason for having selected this particular equation might have been based solely on statistical grounds; i.e., it might have a higher R^2, better t statistics, etc. Suppose we take the equation and use it to produce a predicted series for the interest rate over the historical time period, by using historical values for the independent variables. It may turn out to be the case that the predicted series is very close to the actual series for the interest rate during those periods when the interest rate does not change very much, i.e., during periods of relative interest rate stability. On the other hand, during periods when the interest rate is changing rapidly, the predicted series may miss the turns in the actual series. Thus, although the overall fit of the equation is good, the equation may fail to pick up turns in the variable that is being explained. If this is the case, we might want to change the equation, perhaps by introducing additional explanatory variables or by changing the functional form or the lag structure. The result might have an overall statistical fit that is not as good but might be more useful for purposes of prediction or analysis. The point is that in selecting an individual regression equation one must usually experiment with different equations and keep in mind the ultimate purpose of building the single-equation model.

---

† The reader might wish to examine this model, the St. Louis model, and the macroeconometric model developed in the next chapter in more detail and make a personal evaluation of their rather different implications for fiscal and monetary policy.

Once a single-equation regression model has been built, one would probably not want to manipulate the coefficient values that have been estimated (although alternative estimation techniques might be used). This may not be the case with a simulation model. Let us consider as an example the four-equation model from Chapter 12, the equations of which (ordinary least-squares version) are shown again below:

$$C_t = \underset{(1.90)}{2.537} + \underset{(5.95)}{.185} \, Y_t + \underset{(13.8)}{.714} \, C_{t-1} \tag{12.14}$$

$$R^2 = .999 \qquad \text{SER} = 2.40 \qquad \text{DW} = 2.08$$

$$I_t = \underset{(2.69)}{5.020} + \underset{(4.25)}{.392} \, (Y_t - Y_{t-1}) + \underset{(23.80)}{.1634} \, Y_{t-1} - \underset{(-5.23)}{3.856} \, R_{t-4} \tag{12.15}$$

$$R^2 = .980 \qquad \text{SER} = 4.22 \qquad \text{DW} = .62$$

$$R_t = \underset{(-.25)}{-.072} + \underset{(2.14)}{.0024} \, Y_t + \underset{(.74)}{.011} \, (Y_t - Y_{t-1}) - \underset{(-2.30)}{.189} \, (M_t - M_{t-1})$$

$$+ \underset{(6.24)}{.347} \, (R_{t-1} + R_{t-2}) \tag{12.16}$$

$$R^2 = .867 \qquad \text{SER} = .59 \qquad \text{DW} = .92$$

$$Y_t = C_t + I_t + G_t \tag{12.17}$$

Suppose we wanted to use this model to forecast the interest rate. We might be satisfied with each of the above equations taken by itself, but we might not be happy with the simulation performance of the model as a whole. The model might be overly sensitive to changes in an exogenous variable, or it simply may be unstable or oscillate. One approach to improve its performance (as discussed in Chapter 12) is to use alternative methods for estimating the model's coefficients. Aside from the use of two-stage least squares to ensure consistency (discussed in some detail in Chapter 11), we saw in Section 12.4 that the use of simple single-equation estimation techniques such as an autoregressive correction (for serially correlated error terms) can greatly improve a model's forecasting performance, and the use of full-information techniques can result in still further improvement. Let us assume, then, that the model builder has used the estimation "tool kit" as extensively as possible to obtain coefficient estimates, and see what else can be done to improve the performance of the model.†

Other techniques are available for making major or minor changes in the model, and are often used interdependently. The first of these is to analyze all the feedback and feedforward loops in the model. To do this, one begins with a *block diagram* of the model. A block diagram, an example of which is shown for our simple four-equation model in Fig. 13.5, illustrates all the causal flows between variables and blocks of variables. Feedback loops are essentially

---

† It should be noted that some estimation methods, such as three-stage least squares and full-information maximum likelihood, can require a large amount of numerical computation, and thus may not be feasible for a model builder whose computational facilities are limited. The estimation tool kit, then, should be used as extensively as possible, given such constraints.

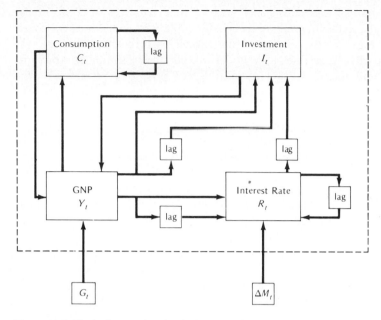

Figure 13.5 Block diagram for simple four-equation model.

circular causal flows; an example in Fig. 13.5 is the loop between consumption and GNP; consumption is at least in part determined by GNP, but it is also a component of (and therefore helps determine) GNP.

The model builder can use a block diagram to identify mechanisms in the model that could result in an unstable performance. In our four-equation model, for example, consumption and investment both depend on total GNP, while at the same time contribute to total GNP. Thus, if the multiplier coefficients in these equations are too large, a feedback loop could result that would continually magnify small changes in consumption or investment demand into very large changes in the GNP. If this is the case, one might want to restructure one of the demand equations, e.g., the consumption equation, so as to reduce the dependence on total GNP. One could, for example, introduce another explanatory variable that would eliminate some of the dependence of consumption on GNP. Thus a restructuring of the model can be used to eliminate feedback loops or at least reduce their impact. Note that the restructuring of individual equations will be done for very different reasons than would be the case in a single-equation model. In a single-equation model, one is usually concerned only with the statistical fit, either overall or at particular turning points. In a simulation model, however, one is also concerned with the dynamic interaction of the equations which compose the model. Thus, we might want to restructure an equation even though it has a very satisfactory statistical fit.

There is a second method that is often used to make minor adjustments in large econometric models, particularly those used for forecasting purposes. This method is called *tuning*, and consists of making small changes in some of the model's coefficients, as well as introducing adjustable parameters at key points in the model to improve the ability of the model to forecast.† Suppose, for example, that one of the variables in a model is consistently simulated above its actual values. There might be several reasons for this; one or more of the coefficients in the consumption equation might be biased, some of the coefficients in other equations that feed into the consumption equation might be biased, or the structure of the model may simply build an upward trend into that particular variable. One way of dealing with this problem is to adjust some of the coefficients in the equation for the variable that is simulating badly.

Some equations may have autoregressive terms; i.e., lagged dependent variables. An adjustment of the coefficient of the autoregressive term provides a simple means of changing the overall dynamic response of the particular dependent variable, and is thus another means by which trend effects and built-in dynamic adjustments can be modified.

Tuning a model can be a somewhat tricky business. By adjusting some of the coefficients, the analyst might make the model track the historical data very well, even though it is really a very poor representation of the real world, with little predictive value. Coefficients should be adjusted only with great caution and to a very limited extent, and only if they are not statistically significant. A statistically significant coefficient indicates that the data have information to convey, and this information should be accounted for when making a forecast.

There are other techniques for the construction and adjustment of simulation models. One technique that has proved quite effective in many cases involves constructing a separate model for the random error term of each equation. In effect, the use of an autoregressive correction is an example of this technique, since one is constructing (and estimating) a simple serial correlation model of the error term. In the case of first-order serial correlation, one constructs the model

$$\varepsilon_t = \rho \varepsilon_{t-1} + v_t \tag{13.33}$$

Note that Eq. (13.33) does not *explain* the behavior of the error term; it simply replicates (to some extent) its past behavior and conveys some information about its future behavior. If Eq. (13.33) is a correct representation of the error term, its inclusion in the model will improve the model's forecasting performance.‡

---

† These parameters are often called *add factors* and *mul factors*, depending on whether they are introduced additively or multiplicatively in the equation. Add and mul factors have come to be used in large macroeconometric forecasting models, particularly those constructed for commercial or business application (often they are adjusted to keep the forecast in line with intuitive forecasts—thus to some extent negating the predictions of the model). Needless to say, they can easily be misused (and often are).

‡ For a study of the effectiveness of this and a number of other forecast adjustment techniques, see Y. Haitovsky and G. Treyz, "Forecasts with Quarterly Macroeconometric Models, Equation Adjustments, and Benchmark Predictions: The U.S. Experience," *Review of Economics and Statistics*, August 1972.

Much more complicated and sophisticated models can be constructed for the random error term than that of Eq. (13.33). These models, called *time-series models*, are the subject of Part Three. After discussing how to build time-series models in Chapters 16 to 19 we will see in Chapter 20 how they can be used to improve the forecasting performance of a structural econometric model (and how they can be used for other forecasting purposes).

Related to the problem of adjusting a model to improve its forecasting performance is the question of how literally a model's forecasts should be taken. Usually forecasters and policy makers allow for a considerable amount of interaction between their models and their judgment. In this way a model becomes more than just a mathematical forecasting tool and also serves as a means of processing and making consistent available information that was not originally contained in the model.

13.4 STOCHASTIC SIMULATION

In Chapter 8 we saw how the forecasts produced by a single-equation regression model are subject to four sources of error:

1. The regression equation contains an implicit additive error term.
2. The estimated values of the coefficients of the equation are themselves random variables and will therefore differ from the true values.
3. The exogenous variables may have to be forecasted themselves, and these forecasts may contain errors.
4. The equation itself may be misspecified; i.e., the functional form may not be representative of the real world.

We showed in Chapter 8 how we could calculate a confidence interval on a forecast that would account for the first three sources of error. (We cannot account for the fourth source of error, so that all our confidence intervals are calculated under the assumption that the model is correctly specified.)

In the case of a multi-equation simulation model, the four sources of error listed above still apply, although now misspecification can occur not only for individual equations but also for the dynamic structure contained in the model as a whole. Furthermore, even if the model is totally specified correctly, errors in each equation of the first three types may become multiplied across equations and thus magnified.

As an example, consider the four-equation model of Eqs. (12.14) to (12.17), repeated above, along with the corresponding block diagram in Fig. 13.5. When the model is simulated, the consumption equation will generate a prediction of consumption which will be in error as a result of both the implicit additive error term in that equation and the fact that the equation's coefficients are not known with certainty. Since consumption is a component of GNP, the error in consumption will contribute to an error in GNP, and this error in GNP will contribute to the error term in the prediction of investment (together with the additive error term and coefficient errors in the investment equation). Investment is also a component of GNP, so that the error in investment will also contribute to an error in GNP. Likewise, consumption is a function of GNP, so that the error in consumption will become still larger as a result of the accumulated error in GNP.

If the model is linear, the final forecasting error variances associated with each endogenous variable can be calculated exactly, although to do so is not computationally trivial.† Generally a more fruitful approach (particularly for nonlinear models) is to perform a *stochastic simulation* (also called *Monte Carlo simulation*). This is done by specifying, for each equation of the model, a probability distribution for the additive error term and for each estimated coefficient. Next, a large number (say 50 or 100) of simulations are performed, and in each simulation values for the additive error terms and estimated coefficients are chosen at random from the corresponding probability distributions. For any particular endogenous variable, the results of the simulation (i.e., the resulting set of forecasts) yield points that trace out a probability distribution of that variable's forecasted value. Thus the dispersion of the forecasts about their mean value can be used to define a forecast confidence interval.

If unbiased and consistent estimates have been obtained for all the model's coefficients, the determination of the appropriate probability distributions for the additive error terms and the estimated coefficients is straightforward. For each equation, the additive error can be assumed to be normally distributed with 0 mean and standard deviation equal to the standard error of the regression. The coefficients of each equation can be assumed to follow a *joint* normal distribution, where the mean of each coefficient is given by its estimated value, the standard deviation of each coefficient is given by its estimated standard error, and the covariances between coefficients are given by the estimated covariance matrix.

In order to illustrate the technique, let us take the four-equation model as an example. To perform a stochastic simulation, the equations of the model would be written

$$C_t = (2.537 + v_{11}) + (.185 + v_{12})Y_t + (.714 + v_{13})C_{t-1} + \varepsilon_{1t} \qquad (13.34)$$

$$I_t = (5.020 + v_{21}) + (.392 + v_{22})(Y_t - Y_{t-1}) + (.1634 + v_{23})Y_{t-1}$$
$$- (3.856 + v_{24})R_{t-4} + \varepsilon_{2t} \qquad (13.35)$$

$$R_t = -(.072 + v_{31}) + (.0024 + v_{32})Y_t + (.011 + v_{33})(Y_t - Y_{t-1})$$
$$- (1.89 + v_{34})(M_t - M_{t-1}) + (.347 + v_{35})(R_{t-1} + R_{t-2}) + \varepsilon_{3t}$$
$$(13.36)$$

$$Y_t = C_t + I_t + G_t \qquad (13.37)$$

---

† The techniques for doing this are the result of recent advances in modern control and system theory, and are beyond the scope of this book. The interested reader is referred to K. Anstrom, *Introduction to Stochastic Control Theory* (New York: Academic, 1970).

In the first equation the "error terms" v_{11}, v_{12}, and v_{13} should be assumed to follow a joint normal distribution. In some situations it may be computationally difficult to generate random numbers from joint distributions, and if the covariances are small, it would be reasonable to perform the stochastic simulation under the approximating assumption that the covariances between coefficients are zero. It is important to remember, however, that ignoring the covariances between coefficients will usually tend to *overestimate* the size of the model's forecast errors. The majority of the estimated covariances are usually negative and cancel part of the variance in each coefficient. Ignoring the covariances thus tends to overemphasize the degree of fluctuation in the coefficients, and forecast confidence intervals obtained in this way will thus be somewhat conservative.

Ignoring covariances for purposes of this example, the error term v_{11} is assumed to be normally distributed random variable with 0 mean and a standard deviation of 1.33 (which is the estimated standard error of the coefficient 2.537 in the consumption equation). Similarly, v_{12} is normally distributed with 0 mean and a standard deviation of .031, and v_{13} is normally distributed with 0 mean and a standard deviation of .051. The additive error term ε_{1t} is, *for each period t*, a normally distributed random variable with 0 mean and a standard deviation of 2.40 (the standard error of the equation). The remaining error terms in Eqs. (13.35) and (13.36) are similarly defined.

Now suppose that we would like to obtain a stochastic one-period-ahead forecast of the interest rate R_t (under the assumption that the exogenous variables M_t and G_t are known with certainty). We do this by performing 50 or 100 simulations of the model one period ahead.† In each simulation we select a value for v_{11} at random from a normal distribution with mean 0 and standard deviation 1.33, we select a value for v_{12} at random from a normal distribution with mean 0 and standard deviation .031, etc. The result of these 50 or 100 simulations will be a range of forecasted values of R_t. This range will have some sample mean, and the 50 or 100 simulated values themselves will determine a probability distribution about this mean (if the model is nonlinear, this probability distribution will not be normal). Next, we can calculate the standard deviation of this sample distribution, which will give us an estimated value for the standard error of the forecast. We can then use this standard error of forecast just as we did in Chapter 8 to determine forecast confidence intervals.

It should be pointed out that if the model is linear, then as the number of simulations included in the sample becomes large, the sample mean will approach the deterministic forecast (i.e., the forecast corresponding to all the random parameters set at 0). If the model is nonlinear, however, there is no guarantee that the sample mean will approach the deterministic forecast as the sample size increases, and in fact it usually will not. In addition, it may be

---

† The choice of how many simulations to peform may depend somewhat on one's research budget. Obviously, performing a large number of simulations can entail a considerable computational expense.

necessary for an unacceptably large number of simulations to be performed before the sample means for each variable converge at all. We therefore center our confidence intervals on the *deterministic forecast* rather than on the sample mean of the stochastic simulations.

The process would be exactly the same if we wanted to forecast over a time horizon longer than one period. For each simulation we simply select a *different* random value for ε_{1t}, ε_{2t}, and ε_{3t} for *each period*, but we use the *same* random value for v_{11}, v_{12}, etc., during the entire simulation (since the equations of the model were specified and estimated under the assumption that the coefficients are constant over time). Furthermore, if the future values of the exogenous variables G_t and M_t were not known with certainty but had to be forecasted themselves, standard errors could be associated with their forecasts. The exogenous variables could then be treated as normally distributed random variables (with means equal to their forecasted values and standard deviations equal to their standard errors of forecast) in our stochastic simulation. For example, Eq. (13.37) could be rewritten to include an error term associated with G_t (which now must itself be forecasted):

$$Y_t = C_t + I_t + (\hat{G}_t + \eta_t) \tag{13.38}$$

Here $\hat{G}_t$ is a forecast of G_t, and η_t is a normally distributed random variable (defined for each period t) with mean 0 and standard deviation equal to the standard error of the forecast $\hat{G}_t$. Note that our forecast is now a *conditional* forecast; i.e., it is conditional on $\hat{G}_t$.

Example 13.4 Stochastic simulation Let us examine the results of an actual stochastic simulation based on Eqs. (13.34) to (13.37). We forecast the model over four periods, beginning with the first quarter of 1972 and ending with the last quarter of that year. Actual values for G_t are used, so that the forecast is unconditional.

The results of a sample of 25 simulations are shown in Figs. 13.6 to 13.9 for each of the four endogenous variables. Each figure shows the 25 different forecast paths for a particular variable that resulted from different random errors. Note that there is a good deal of dispersion in the forecasts.

A sample standard deviation can be calculated for each variable for each of the four periods in the forecast. These sample deviations can be interpreted as estimated standard errors of forecast and thus can be used to determine confidence intervals for the forecast. In Figs. 13.10 to 13.13 we show forecasts for each variable from a simulation in which no random errors are introduced, and these forecasts can be compared with the actual values of the variables. Also shown in each figure are 95 percent confidence intervals for the forecasts. These are based on the sample standard deviations calculated from the stochastic simulation (the 95 percent confidence interval is approximately 2 standard deviations above and below the forecast). These confidence intervals are rather large, and would have been

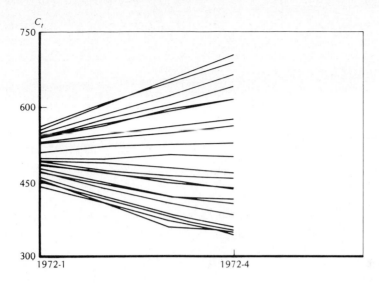

Figure 13.6 Stochastic simulation: consumption.

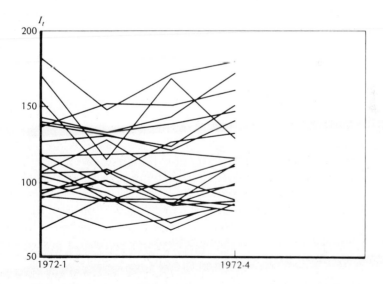

Figure 13.7 Stochastic simulation: investment.

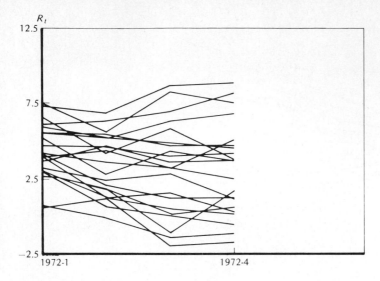

Figure 13.8 Stochastic simulation: interest rate.

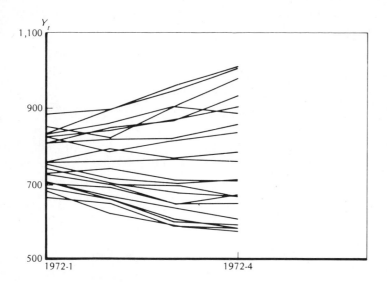

Figure 13.9 Stochastic simulation: GNP.

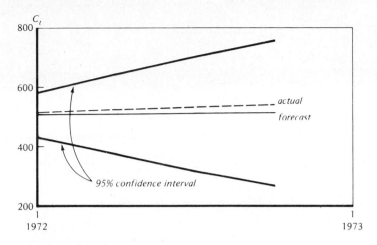

Figure 13.10 Forecast of consumption.

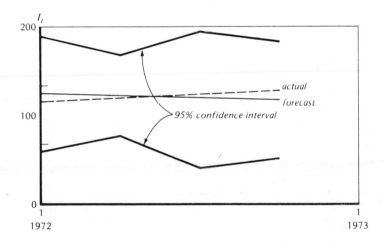

Figure 13.11 Forecast of investment.

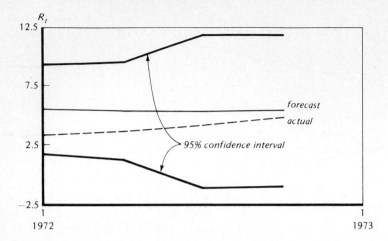

Figure 13.12 Forecast of interest rate.

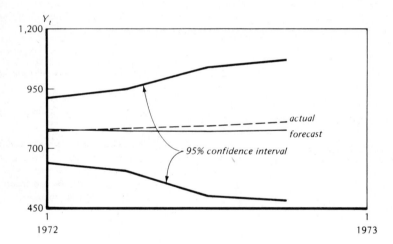

Figure 13.13 Forecast of GNP.

considerably smaller had we accounted for the covariances between the coefficients of each equation. However they provide a conservative measure of the model's forecasting accuracy.

EXERCISES

13.1 Show that if $A_1\lambda_1^t$ and $A_2\lambda_2^t$ are both transient solutions to a model, i.e., both satisfy an equation such as (13.5), then the sum $A_1\lambda_1^t + A_2\lambda_2^t$ must also be a solution.

13.2 Consider the following simple multiplier-accelerator macroeconomic model:

$$C_t = a_1 + a_2 Y_{t-1} \qquad I_t = b_1 + b_2(C_t - C_{t-1}) \qquad Y_t = C_t + I_t + G_t$$

Note that investment is now a function of changes in consumption, rather than changes in total GNP.

(a) Determine the characteristic equation for this model, and find the associated characteristic roots.

(b) Find the relationships between values of a_2 and b_2 that determine what kind of solution the model will have. Draw a diagram that corresponds to that of Fig. 13.1.

(c) What is the impact multiplier corresponding to a change in G_t? What is the *total* long-run multiplier corresponding to a change in G_t?

13.3 The following equations describe a simple "cobweb" model of a competitive market:

Demand: $\qquad\qquad\qquad\qquad Q_t^D = a_1 + a_2 P_t \qquad a_2 < 0$

Supply: $\qquad\qquad\qquad\qquad Q_t^S = b_1 + b_2 P_{t-1} \qquad b_2 > 0$

When the market is in equilibrium, $Q_t^D = Q_t^S$. Now suppose that the market is temporarily out of equilibrium, i.e., that $Q_t^D \neq Q_t^S$ temporarily.

(a) Show that the price will converge stably to an equilibrium value if $b_2/a_2 < 1$.

(b) Show that the path to equilibrium will be oscillatory if $b_2 > 0$ and will not be oscillatory if $b_2 < 0$.

13.4 Examine the 95 percent confidence intervals in Figs. 13.10 to 13.13 from the stochastic simulation of Example 13.4. What can you say about the forecasting accuracy of the four-equation model used in the simulation? Examine the model again [Eqs. (12.14) to (12.17)] and the corresponding block diagram in Fig. 13.5, and indicate potential sources of forecasting error. Which coefficients of the model seem to be most critical in terms of introducing forecast error? How might you restructure and/or reestimate the model to improve its forecasting performance?

EXAMPLES OF SIMULATION MODELS

This chapter provides three examples of the construction and application of multi-equation simulation models. All the models are quite different in terms of the level of aggregation and scope of the economic activity they describe and in terms of the ways they are constructed.

We begin with a small model of the United States economy. This model is designed to demonstrate how one might construct a macroeconometric model and use it to forecast over a 2-year period. Because the model is illustrative, it is therefore simple and highly aggregated, representing the economy in a way that is consistent with most introductory Keynesian macroeconomics textbooks. As a result, it does not represent the state of the art of macroeconometric modeling and forecasting; other models exist (most of them much larger) that are likely to be more reliable as tools for forecasting and policy analysis.† It is, however, a good starting point for students who are interested in macroeconomic modeling.

---

† One of the well-known large models is the Wharton econometric model, described in M. D. McCarthy, *The Wharton Quarterly Econometric Forecasting Model, Mark III*, Wharton School of Finance and Commerce, University of Pennsylvania, and in V. G. Duggal, L. R. Klein, and M. D. McCarthy, "The Wharton Model Mark III: A Modern IS-LM Construct," *International Economic Review*, October 1974. Two other good examples of large econometric models are the "MPS Model," developed jointly at M.I.T., the University of Pennsylvania, and the Federal Reserve, and described in A. Ando and F. Modigliani, *The MPS Econometric Model: Its Theoretical Foundation and Empirical Findings* (unpublished), and the University of Michigan Model, described in S. H. Hymans and H. T. Shapiro, "The Structure and Properties of the Michigan Quarterly Econometric Model of the U.S. Economy," *International Economic Review*, October 1974. For examples of smaller quarterly models see R. Fair, *A Short-Run Forecasting Model of the United States Economy* (Lexington, Mass.: Heath, 1971); R. Fair, *A Model of Macroeconomic Activity*, vols. *I and II*, (Cambridge, Mass.: Ballinger Press, 1975); and E. Kuh and R. Schmalensee, *An Introduction to Applied Macroeconomics* (Amsterdam: North-Holland, 1973). Finally, for an example of a *monthly* macroeconometric model, see T. C. Liu and E. C. Hwa, "Structure and Applications of a Monthly Econometric Model of the U.S.," *International Economic Review*, June 1974.

The next example is a model that describes a particular industry. It is small and relatively simple, but it serves to show how *microeconometric* models can be constructed and used for industry forecasting and analysis. As we shall see, an industry-wide econometric model can provide a consistent framework which accounts for the interactions of producers and consumers that determine the behavior of price, demand, and other market variables.

Finally, our last example shows how a noneconometric simulation model can be used to describe and analyze a corporations's financial structure. Since all the equations in such a model represent financial accounting identities or decision rules, no statistical estimation is required for the model's construction. The example shows, however, how a set of simultaneous time-dependent equations can provide a useful tool for corporate analysis and planning.

14.1 A SMALL MACROECONOMETRIC MODEL

Our first example is designed to take the reader through the steps involved in the construction of a small, quarterly model of the United States economy and to demonstrate how that model can be used to perform some simple policy experiments. As we discussed in Chapter 12, the design or construction of any model as well as the criteria used to validate the model depend very much on the purpose for which the model is built. Since the major objective of our model is short-term macroeconomic forecasting, to be useful the model must contain several basic macroeconomic variables—consumption, investment, GNP, an interest rate, a price level, wages, and unemployment. Because we are also concerned with the means by which the government might control the economy, we will include in the model some basic policy variables—the money supply, government spending, and a crude tax mechanism. Since the model is intended to be illustrative, it is convenient to design its structure to be consistent with conventional macroeconomic theory. Therefore, validation of the model will involve a check to see whether the estimated coefficients are statistically significant with the proper sign, as well as whether the simulated time series correlate well with the historical time series.

We begin by specifying the overall structure of the model, including the rough functional form for each equation. Since our purpose in this book is not to teach macroeconomic theory, the theoretical motivation for each equation is presented in a compressed summary form.† We then discuss the estimation of the model's equations and the evaluation of the model's simulation performance. Finally, we use the model to perform some simple forecasting and policy experiments.

---

† The reader interested in the application of macroeconomic theory to macroeconometric modeling is referred to E. Kuh and R. Schmalensee, op. cit., or M. K. Evans, *Macroeconomic Activity* (New York: Harper & Row, 1969).

14.1.1 Structure of the Model

The model consists of 13 equations, of which 10 are behavioral and three are identities. The specification of the model involves a considerable degree of interrelationship between the endogenous variables. This interrelationship is easiest to see from a block diagram, and one is presented in Fig. 14.1. The endogenous and exogenous variables of the model (with equation references) are listed in Table 14.1. The reader may find it useful to refer to Fig. 14.1 and Table 14.1 during the discussion of the model's structure.

The model assumes that exports and imports are always equal and therefore can be dropped from the GNP accounting relationship. GNP and its components, consumption C, total investment I, and government expenditures G, are all in real (constant-dollar) terms. Total investment is disaggregated, and separate equations are estimated to explain nonresidential investment (fixed plant

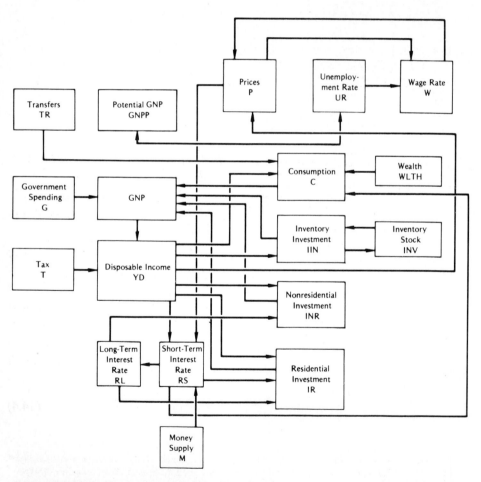

Figure 14.1 Block diagram of macroeconomic model.

Table 14.1 Variables in the model

Variables		Equation number
Endogenous:		
C	Consumption	(14.6)
GNP	Gross national product	(14.1) (identity)
IIN	Inventory investment	(14.16)
INR	Nonresidential investment	(14.11)
INV	Stock of inventories	(14.13) (identity)
IR	Residential investment	(14.12)
P	Price level	(14.19)
RL	Long-term interest rate	(14.18)
RS	Short-term interest rate	(14.17)
T	Taxes	(14.2)
UR	Unemployment rate	(14.21)
W	Nominal wage rate	(14.20)
YD	Disposable income	(14.3) (identity)
Exogenous:		
G	Government spending	
GNPP	Potential GNP	
M	Money supply	
T_0	Surtax	
TR	Transfer payments	
WLTH	Wealth	

and equipment) INR, residential investment IR, and investment in inventories IIN. The GNP identity, then, can be written as

$$GNP = C + INR + IR + IIN + G \qquad (14.1)$$

The tax mechanism in the model is extremely simple. The total tax flow T (net of transfer payments) is given by

$$T = t(GNP) + T_0 \qquad (14.2)$$

where t is an average tax rate and T_0 is a surtax.† Thus, disposable income YD is given by the identity

$$YD = (1 - t)GNP - T_0 \qquad (14.3)$$

Let us now turn to the specification of the consumption function. As one might expect, consumption can be largely explained by disposable income. A consumption function of the form

$$C_t = \sum_{i=0}^{n} \beta_i YD_{t-i} + \varepsilon_{0t} \qquad (14.4)$$

---

† Thus personal income taxes, corporate profits taxes, and indirect business taxes are averaged together. If GNP is roughly constant at some nominal level $(GNP)_0$, we could think of T_0 in terms of a tax surcharge of S percent, where $S = T_0/t(GNP)_0$.

or, using a geometric lag distribution,

$$C_t = a_0 + a_1 YD_t + a_2 C_{t-1} + \varepsilon_{0t} \tag{14.5}$$

should provide a reasonable fit to the data.† However, we have chosen to restructure the consumption function to include a measure of wealth, which would have an impact on consumption independent of that of income.‡ Wealth can be defined in a variety of ways and is difficult to measure, but we use an index of real wealth developed as part of the MIT–Federal Reserve–Penn econometric model.

In addition, we divide disposable income into two components, transfer payments TR and all other disposable income. The reason for this is that over a cross section of the population, the average and marginal propensities to consume fall as income increases. Since lower-income families generally consume out of transfer payments, the propensity to consume out of transfers should be higher than for other income.

Finally, consumption should also depend on the cost and availability of consumer credit. (This is particularly true for major durable goods such as automobiles and large appliances.) We can use an interest rate in the consumption function as a measure of the cost of credit. Our consumption function, then, is of the form

$$C = f_1[(YD - TR), TR, WLTH, RS, C_{-1}] + \varepsilon_1 \tag{14.6}$$

Nonresidential investment is also taken to depend on disposable income.§ Because there is usually a significant lead time between an investment decision and an investment expenditure, income should enter the investment function as a distributed lag. Nonresidential investment should also depend on long-term interest rates RL (probably with a long lag) and on the capital stock K.¶ Our equation is of the form

$$INR = f_2(YD, RL, K) + \varepsilon_2 \tag{14.7}$$

However, since there are no published capital stock data, we treat the investment equation in *differenced* form. To do this, we use the identity that the level

---

† The reader may wish to review the discussion of distributed lags in Chapter 9.

‡ The problem with Eqs. (14.4) and (14.5) is that the heavy dependence of consumption on income (together with the fact that consumption is itself a large proportion of income) is likely to result in a structural instability in this simultaneous-equation model. If the coefficients in (14.4) or (14.5) were large enough, some of the characteristic roots of the model would be greater than 1 in magnitude (see Chapter 13). Then, an overprediction of C_t would result in an overprediction of YD_t, which would result in *still larger* an overprediction of C_t, etc. This instability is inconsistent with our expectations concerning the behavior of the entire system of equations, rather than the consumption equation alone.

§ It could be argued that GNP should be used instead, but this would eliminate the influence of direct and indirect business taxes. Thus in order to keep the tax mechanism simple and consistent, we use YD instead of GNP both here and throughout the rest of the model.

¶ If the capital stock is large relative to the *desired* capital stock (which in turn would be roughly proportional to planned output), the level of investment will be lower. Thus investment should depend *negatively* on the capital stock.

of investment in plant and equipment is equal to the change in the stock of plant and equipment ΔK plus the rate of depreciation D:

$$INR = \Delta K + D \tag{14.8}$$

Now by assuming that the capital-stock variable is separable from the disposable-income and interest-rate variables, we can write the investment function as

$$INR = f_2(YD, RL) + \beta_1 K + \varepsilon_2 \qquad \beta_1 < 0 \tag{14.9}$$

and by first differencing we get

$$\Delta INR = \Delta f_2(YD, RL) + \beta_1 \Delta K + u_2 \tag{14.10}$$

or $\qquad \Delta INR = f_2^*(\Delta YD, \Delta RL, INR, D) + u_2 \tag{14.11}$

In our model D is assumed to be relatively constant, so that its effect is measured by the intercept term in the estimated nonresidential investment equation.

Residential (housing) investment is difficult to explain accurately in a small macroeconomic model. It depends on mortgage interest rates, mortgage availabilities, and construction costs, none of which are included in our model. We explain residential investment by relating it to income, the short-term interest rate RS, and the difference between the long-term and short-term interest rates:

$$IR = f_3(YD, RS, RL - RS) + \varepsilon_3 \tag{14.12}$$

The interest rates are used both as a proxy for mortgage rates and as a crude measure of credit availability (credit becomes tighter as the short-term rate approaches the long-term rate). The dependence on interest rates is expected to be greater than with nonresidential investment, in terms of both magnitude and speed of response.

Inventory investment IIN is related to the stock of inventories INV by the identity

$$INV_t = INV_{t-1} + IIN_t \tag{14.13}$$

To describe inventory investment, we assume that the present stock of inventories is a linear function of present GNP, present consumption, and the stock of inventories last quarter:

$$INV_t = d_1 GNP_t + d_2 C_t + d_3 INV_{t-1} + \varepsilon_4 \tag{14.14}$$

The coefficient d_1 should be positive, and the coefficient d_2 should be negative, since consumption spending is expected to deplete the stock of inventories. First-differencing this equation, recognizing from (14.13) that IIN $= \Delta$INV, and replacing GNP with our income variable YD, we have

$$IIN_t = d_1 \Delta YD_t + d_2 \Delta C_t + d_3 IIN_{t-1} + \varepsilon_4 \tag{14.15}$$

We would also expect inventory investment to depend negatively on the *stock* of inventories, since if the stock is large (relative to the desired stock), downward adjustments are made by decreasing inventory investment. This means that we must add to our model the identity in Eq. (14.13). Thus inventory investment can be specified as

$$\text{IIN} = f_4(\Delta\text{YD}, \Delta\text{C}, \text{INV}, \text{IIN}_{-1}) + u_4 \qquad (14.16)$$

Our model contains both a short-term and a long-term interest rate, with the long-term rate assumed to adjust with lags to the expected value of the short-term rate. The short-term interest rate RS is a function of the level of income YD, the rate of change in the real money supply $\Delta M/M$, and current and past values of the rate of inflation $\Delta P/P$. The interest rate does not depend explicitly on the level of the money supply, but there is an indirect dependency through the income variable YD.† Our equation, then, has the form

$$\text{RS} = f_5\!\left(\text{YD}, \frac{\Delta M}{M}, \frac{\Delta P}{P}\right) + \varepsilon_5 \qquad (14.17)$$

The long-term interest rate RL responds (with a geometric lag) to the level of the short-term rate as well as changes in the short-term rate. Hence monetary policy, i.e., changes in the money supply, can affect RL only indirectly (through RS). The equation for the long-term interest rate, then, is of the form

$$\text{RL} = f_6(\text{RS}, \Delta\text{RS}, \text{RL}_{-1}) + \varepsilon_6 \qquad (14.18)$$

An important variable in the model is the price level P, which we would expect to depend on the nominal wage rate W and the level of income. Our equation explains the rate of change in the price level, i.e., the inflation rate, which is linked to the rate of change in the wage rate and changes in real income. Changes in real income also serve as a measure of excess demand for goods and services in the economy; when excess demand is large, we would expect increased inflation. Finally, today's rate of inflation should also depend on rates of inflation that existed in the recent past. When the rate of inflation is high for a year or more, people develop inflationary expectations, which in turn have an inflationary impact on current and future prices. Thus we include a moving average of past inflation rates in our price equation. That equation is thus of the form

$$\frac{\Delta P}{P} = f_7\!\left(\frac{\Delta W}{W}, \Delta\text{YD}, \frac{\Delta P_{-1}}{P_{-1}}\right) + \varepsilon_7 \qquad (14.19)$$

What remains now is to explain the wage rate W and the unemployment rate UR. As in the price equation, our wage equation explains the rate of change in the wage level. The rate of change in the nominal wage level is related to the

---

† We are viewing the demand for money as being proportional to YD, so that if YD increases, the demand for money increases, and if M is held fixed, the interest rate must rise. We could have included the level of the money supply in the interest-rate equation, but collinearity with YD would make a good estimate of its coefficient impossible.

rate of change in prices, as well as the unemployment rate:†

$$\frac{\Delta W}{W} = f_8\left(\frac{\Delta P}{P}, \text{UR}\right) + \varepsilon_8 \tag{14.20}$$

Finally, the unemployment rate depends on past and current changes in income (the unemployment rate is lowest when GNP is growing rapidly), as well as the extent of slack capacity in the economy. To measure slack capacity, we introduce an exogenous variable into the model, potential GNP (GNPP). Excess capacity is thus measured by the difference GNPP − GNP.‡ Our unemployment-rate equation is then of the form

$$\text{UR} = f_9(\Delta \text{YD}, \text{GNPP} - \text{GNP}, \text{UR}_{-1}) + \varepsilon_9 \tag{14.21}$$

14.1.2 Estimation of the Model

All the equations of the model were estimated using quarterly data over the period 1956-1 to 1976-4.§ The average tax rate t was found by regressing T (taxes net of transfer payments) on GNP and forcing the regression line through the origin. The estimated value of t was .11925. The tax surcharge variable T_0 was set at zero when estimating all the behavioral equations.

All the other behavioral equations were estimated using two-stage least squares, but for those equations which do not contain a lagged dependent variable a correction for first-order serial correlation was also used. In order to obtain consistent estimates of both the equation coefficients and the serial-correlation coefficient, a procedure was devised to combine these estimation techniques. This procedure involves an iterative process in which a first estimate of the serial-correlation coefficient ρ is obtained, two-stage least squares is performed on the equation in its generalized difference form, a new estimate of ρ is obtained, two-stage least squares is again performed, etc. This procedure is described in more detail in Appendix 14.1.

This estimation technique cannot be applied to all the equations of the model, even if serial correlation is present. The estimate of ρ would be inconsistent for those equations which contain a lagged dependent variable; these

---

† The derivation of the wage and unemployment rate equations is too lengthy to be presented here. For a more detailed explanation of why these equations are specified as they are, see R. S. Pindyck, *Optimal Planning for Economic Stabilization* (Amsterdam: North-Holland, 1973), chap. 4.

‡ Potential GNP is that GNP which would result if the economy were operating at full capacity. It is measured in real terms, and it is essentially a 4 percent trend line. For a discussion of the concept of potential GNP, see A. M. Okun, "Potential GNP: Its Measurement and Significance," *Papers and Proceedings of the Business and Economic Statistics Section of the American Statistical Association*, pp. 98–104, 1962.

§ The data used to estimate the model were obtained from the National Bureau of Economic Research Data Bank and are presented in Appendix 14.1. Note that all real variables are measured in *1958 dollars*. Students are encouraged to use the data to modify and reestimate parts or all of the model.

equations are therefore estimated using two-stage least squares without a serial-correlation correction.† In presenting the behavioral equations, we simply show the final estimates obtained in the last step of the procedure. Equations are presented in their original form, even if they have been estimated in generalized difference form, but the estimated value for ρ is included.

We begin with the consumption equation. As explained earlier, we try to identify the dependence of consumption on two components of disposable income, transfer payments TR and all other disposable income. Changes in the level of income should affect consumption only slowly, so the dependence occurs through a geometric lag (i.e., lagged consumption appears in the equation). The lagged dependent variable also imposes a geometric lag on wealth. Because of this and because we expect increases (and decreases) in wealth to affect consumption, we use the change in the wealth index rather than the level of the index in the equation. Finally, consumption depends on interest rates; here we use a four-quarter moving average of the short-term rate. The final estimated consumption function, then (t statistics are in parentheses),‡ is

$$
\begin{aligned}
C = \ & \underset{(0.58)}{1.77276} + \underset{(2.98)}{0.14020}\,(\mathrm{YD} - \mathrm{TR}) + \underset{(2.62)}{0.47305}\,\mathrm{TR} + \underset{(4.00)}{44.10080}\ \Delta\mathrm{WLTH} \\
& - \underset{(-1.74)}{0.18347}\,(\mathrm{RS} + \mathrm{RS}_{-1} + \mathrm{RS}_{-2} + \mathrm{RS}_{-3}) + \underset{(9.50)}{0.78927}\,C_{-1} \qquad (14.22)
\end{aligned}
$$

$$
R^2 = 0.999 \qquad \mathrm{SER} = 2.3861 \qquad F(5/75) = 2.17 \times 10^4 \qquad \mathrm{DW} = 2.13
$$

Note that the propensity to consume out of transfer payments is indeed considerably larger than out of the remainder of disposable income.

As we explained earlier, our equation for nonresidential investment is estimated in differenced form so that we may capture the capital stock effect. A

---

† If the error terms are serially correlated, the estimate of the coefficient of the lagged dependent variable will also be inconsistent. It could be argued that for this reason it is not desirable to include lagged dependent variables in equations. The lagged dependent variable, however, sometimes provides the best means of imposing a lagged distribution on the equation, and this benefit may outweigh the associated statistical problems.

‡ In the earlier version of this model (which appeared in the first edition of this book) disposable income as it appeared in the consumption function was not divided into transfer payments and all other disposable income. In addition, a liquidity measure (LIQ) equal to the sum of demand deposits plus time deposits was used instead of wealth, and no interest rate was introduced. We reestimated that equation using the more recent data, and obtained

$$
C = - \underset{(-0.65)}{1.2290} + \underset{(1.49)}{0.0462}\,\mathrm{YD} + \underset{(2.58)}{0.3160}\,\Delta\mathrm{LIQ} + \underset{(23.35)}{0.9465}\ C_{-1}
$$

$$
R^2 = .9987 \qquad \mathrm{SER} = 3.259 \qquad F(3/77) = 1.94 \times 10^4 \qquad \mathrm{DW} = 1.52
$$

However, because of the heavy dependence on disposable income, this equation results in an instability when combined with the other equations of the model. We also estimated other versions of Eq. (14.22) in which disposable income is not divided into its two components, but again marginal propensities to consume turned out to be close to 1, and the model as a whole became unstable.

five-quarter distributed lag is used for the income term, and the long-term interest rate appears in the equation with a four-quarter lag. Finally, a two quarter moving sum of the level of nonresidential investment is used as the capital stock proxy. The estimated equation is

$$\Delta INR = - \underset{(-3.61)}{0.00531} (INR_{-1} + INR_{-2}) + \underset{(3.92)}{0.08036} \Delta YD + \underset{(6.06)}{0.06307} \Delta YD_{-1}$$

$$+ \underset{(4.16)}{0.05266} \Delta YD_{-2} + \underset{(4.82)}{0.04912} \Delta YD_{-3} + \underset{(2.88)}{0.05246} \Delta YD_{-4}$$

$$- \underset{(-2.17)}{1.35401} \Delta RL_{-4} \qquad (14.23)$$

$$R^2 = 0.617 \qquad SER = 0.9602 \qquad F(4/76) = 30.605 \qquad DW = 1.94$$

$$\hat{\rho} = 0.224$$

Residential investment is related to income, the difference between the long- and short-term interest rates, and the short-term interest rate (with lags). These variables are not sufficient to explain the cyclical behavior of housing starts (and thus of residential investment), including the steep drop that occurred between the second quarter of 1966 and the end of 1967. Since we are restricted to the use of a simple macroeconomic model, we provide part of the explanation of this cyclical behavior through a second-order autoregressive relationship for residential investment. (Autoregressive models are discussed in detail in Part Three.) This means introducing the dependent variable lagged one and two periods, and this in turn imposes a distributed lag on income and the interest rates. The estimated equation is†

$$IR = - \underset{(-0.53)}{0.33033} + \underset{(4.50)}{0.01149} YD + \underset{(1.98)}{0.47200} (RL_{-2} - RS_{-2}) - \underset{(-2.19)}{0.38887} RS_{-1}$$

$$+ \underset{(12.97)}{1.29240} IR_{-1} - \underset{(-4.88)}{0.45175} IR_{-2} \qquad (14.24)$$

$$R^2 = 0.977 \qquad SER = 0.9436 \qquad F(5/75) = 637.18 \qquad DW = 1.93$$

Inventory investment is regressed against lagged income YD, two-quarter differences in income and consumption, the lagged stock of inventories INV,

---

† We also estimated this equation leaving out the dependent variable lagged two periods:

$$IR = - \underset{(-1.90)}{1.2713} + \underset{(5.31)}{0.0149} YD + \underset{(3.50)}{0.8868} (RL_{-2} - RS_{-2}) - \underset{(-2.81)}{0.5572} RS_{-1} + \underset{(25.24)}{0.8271} IR_{-1}$$

$$R^2 = .9698 \qquad SER = 1.075 \qquad F(4/76) = 609.2 \qquad DW = 1.11$$

However, this equation is much less able to replicate the behavior of residential investment, particularly during the latter years. Ideally, residential investment should be explained through a detailed model of the housing market, but that of course is beyond the scope of this simple macroeconomic model.

and the dependent variable lagged two quarters:†

$$IIN = -4.10794 + 0.13038\,YD_{-1} + 0.37372\,\Delta_2 YD - 0.56866\,\Delta_2 C$$
$$\quad\quad (-3.31) \quad\quad (4.18) \quad\quad\quad (4.51) \quad\quad\quad\quad (-4.44)$$

$$\quad\quad -0.40114\,INV_{-1} + 0.36996\,IIN_{-2} \quad\quad (14.25)$$
$$\quad\quad (-3.90) \quad\quad\quad\quad (4.00)$$

$$R^2 = 0.818 \quad SER = 2.1537 \quad F(5/75) = 67.33 \quad DW = 1.85$$

Note that all the explanatory variables are statistically significant and have the correct sign.

The short-term interest rate is related to income, changes in income, the rate of growth of the money supply RGM, and a three-period moving sum of past inflation rates:‡

$$RS = -0.21727 + 0.00630\,YD + 0.01380\,\Delta YD_{-1} - 24.50340\,RGM$$
$$\quad\quad (-0.21) \quad\quad (3.14) \quad\quad\quad (1.48) \quad\quad\quad\quad (-2.58)$$

$$\quad\quad + 37.85490\left(\frac{\Delta P_{-1}}{P_{-1}} + \frac{\Delta P_{-2}}{P_{-2}} + \frac{\Delta P_{-3}}{P_{-3}}\right) \quad\quad (14.26)$$
$$\quad\quad\quad (3.19)$$

$$R^2 = 0.348 \quad SER = 0.5215 \quad F(4/76) = 10.15 \quad DW = 1.60$$
$$\hat{\rho} = 0.818$$

The long-term interest rate responds, with a geometric lag, to the short-term rate and to changes in the short-term rate:

$$RL = 0.12535 + 0.04534\,RS + 0.13063\,\Delta RS + 0.94306\,RL_{-1} \quad\quad (14.27)$$
$$\quad\quad (1.52) \quad\quad (1.91) \quad\quad\quad (3.04) \quad\quad\quad (28.86)$$

$$R^2 = 0.985 \quad SER = 0.1564 \quad F(3/77) = 1646.1 \quad DW = 2.10$$

Note that the coefficient of the lagged dependent variable is large (.943), which indicates that the adjustment of long-term rates occurs only slowly.

The price and wage equations are estimated in terms of rates of change. The explanatory variables in the price equation include the rate of change of the wage rate, a two-quarter change in income, and a two-quarter moving sum of past inflation rates (which is used to represent the expected rate of inflation). In addition, a dummy variable (DUM) is included to account for the exogenously induced inflation that occurred in 1974 as a result of steep increases in the world price of oil as well as increases in the prices of grains and other food commodities. (The dummy variable takes on the value 1 during the period 1973-4 to

---

† Single-quarter differences in income and consumption could have been used instead of two-quarter differences and would result in a good fit. The resulting equation, however, would be somewhat unstable in a simulation framework. This would be an example of statistical fit that is somewhat artificial; we are in effect regressing a noisy variable against its own noise. For this reason, two-quarter differences are used. (Note that $\Delta_2 YD = YD - YD_{-2}$.)

‡ Note that if the inflation term were moved to the left-hand side of the equation, what would remain would be very close to the *real* interest rate, i.e., the nominal interest rate minus the average rate of inflation.

1974-4 and is zero otherwise.) The estimated equation is

$$\frac{\Delta P}{P} = \underset{(-0.86)}{-0.00156} + \underset{(1.76)}{0.2188} \frac{\Delta W}{W} + \underset{(2.65)}{0.00011934} \Delta_2 YD + \underset{(3.45)}{0.00763} DUM$$

$$+ \underset{(7.23)}{0.32983} \left(\frac{\Delta P_{-1}}{P_{-1}} + \frac{\Delta P_{-2}}{P_{-2}} \right) \qquad (14.28)$$

$$R^2 = 0.745 \qquad SER = 3.30 \times 10^{-3} \qquad F(4/76) = 55.65 \qquad DW = 1.98$$

The wage equation explains the rate of change of the average money wage rate expressed in dollars per hour. Explanatory variables include the rate of change of prices and the lagged unemployment rate. The estimated equation is

$$\frac{\Delta W}{W} = \underset{(5.32)}{0.01677} + \underset{(4.65)}{0.48601} \frac{\Delta P}{P} - \underset{(-2.12)}{0.00116} UR_{-3} \qquad (14.29)$$

$$R^2 = 0.289 \qquad SER = 5.55 \times 10^{-3} \qquad F(2/78) = 15.86 \qquad DW = 2.19$$

Finally, the unemployment rate (measured in percent) is related to changes in income (and thus output), the difference between actual and potential GNP, and its own lagged value. The equation is

$$UR = \underset{(3.00)}{0.50222} - \underset{(-7.36)}{0.04062} \Delta YD_{-1} - \underset{(-1.90)}{0.00128} (GNP_{-1} - GNPP_{-1})$$

$$+ \underset{(27.22)}{0.9325} UR_{-1} \qquad (14.30)$$

$$R^2 = 0.940 \qquad SER = 0.3184 \qquad F(3/77) = 401.15 \qquad DW = 1.73$$

Note that most of the explanation in the equation comes from income. If GNP and income are rising rapidly, the equation will predict a low unemployment rate.

14.1.3 Simulation of the Model

The model can now be simulated as a complete system. Two historical simulations and an *ex post* forecast were performed in order to evaluate the model's ability to replicate the actual data.† The first simulation was begun at the beginning of the estimation period (1956-1) and ended in 1977-4 (four quarters beyond the end of the estimation period), the second runs from the first quarter of 1972 to the fourth quarter of 1977, and the *ex post* forecast covers the 2-year period 1976-1 through 1977-4. The results of these simulations are summarized in Table 14.2. For each simulation, rms errors and rms percent errors are shown for 11 endogenous variables in the model. In addition, actual and simulated values for the endogenous variables are plotted in Figs. 14.2 to 14.11 for the historical simulation that begins in 1972 and in Figs. 14.12 to 14.14 for the *ex post* forecast.

---

† All simulations are *dynamic*, in the sense that *simulated* (rather than actual) values for the endogenous variables in a given period are used as inputs when the model is solved in future periods. See Chapter 12 for details of the simulation process.

Table 14.2 Results of historical simulations

Variable	1956-1 to 1977-4		1972-1 to 1977-4		1976-1 to 1977-4 (*ex post* forecast)	
	rms error	rms % error	rms error	rms % error	rms error	rms % error
C	9.6Q	2.02	9.27	1.73	2.83	0.48
INR	5.34	7.56	4.92	5.79	4.83	5.43
IR	3.82	13.87	4.93	17.17	2.13	6.32
IIN	3.98	308.68	5.68	421.62	5.90	1016.97
INV	4.01	2.15	4.13	1.93	3.68	1.67
RS	1.00	29.34	1.47	25.85	1.34	27.62
RL	0.41	8.73	0.43	6.16	0.43	6.38
P	7.44	5.68	7.08	3.66	2.37	1.13
W	0.16	3.72	0.19	2.80	0.17	2.46
UR	0.75	12.75	0.82	12.57	0.45	6.12
GNP	17.91	2.50	20.48	2.60	12.42	1.42

Note that the model reproduces the general trends for most variables but does not capture the sharp recession that occurred in 1975. Because nonresidential and residential investment failed to pick up the sharp downturn that occurred in 1974 and continued through the beginning of 1975, GNP (and its major component consumption) are over predicted during 1975. As a result, the steep increase in the unemployment rate that occurred during 1975 is also not reproduced. It appears that the main source of error here lies in the nonresidential and residential investment equations. Investment spending is volatile and is

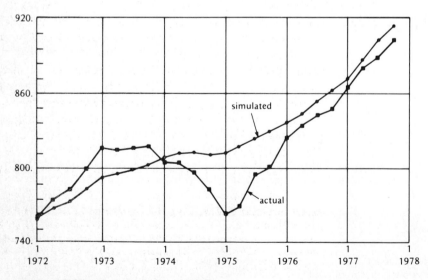

Figure 14.2 Historical simulation of GNP.

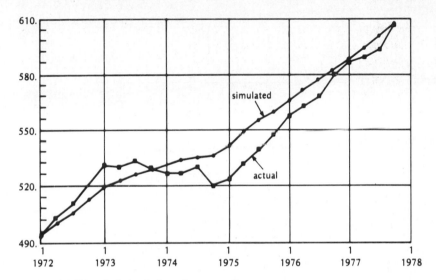

Figure 14.3 Historical simulation of consumption.

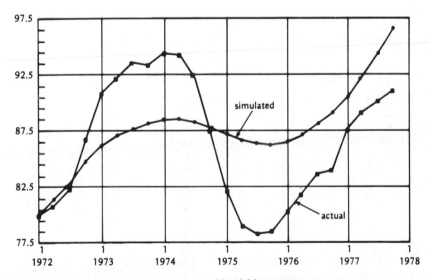

Figure 14.4 Historical simulation of nonresidential investment.

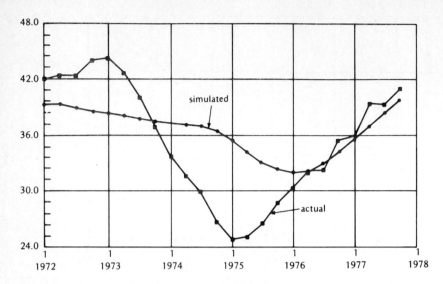

Figure 14.5 Historical simulation of residential investment.

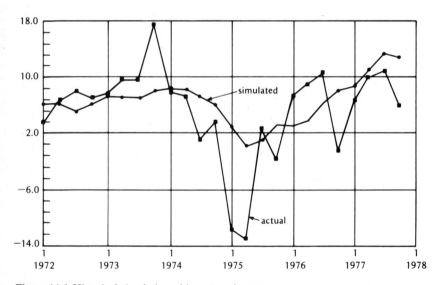

Figure 14.6 Historical simulation of inventory investment.

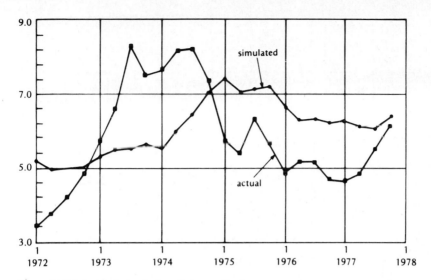

Figure 14.7 Historical simulation of short-term interest rate.

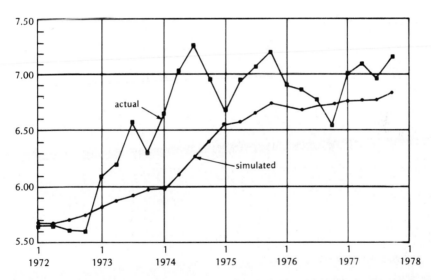

Figure 14.8 Historical simulation of long-term interest rate.

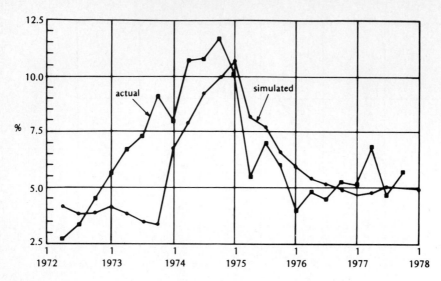

Figure 14.9 Historical simulation of annual rate of growth of price level.

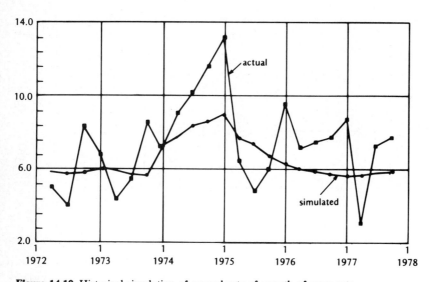

Figure 14.10 Historical simulation of annual rate of growth of wage rate.

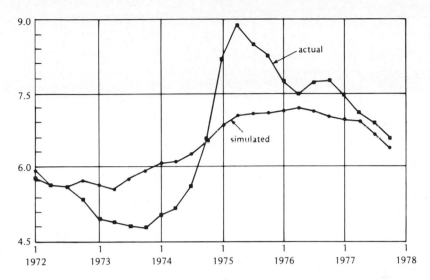

Figure 14.11 Historical simulation of unemployment rate.

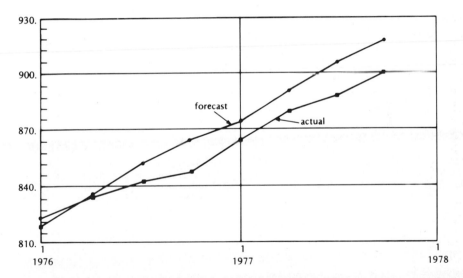

Figure 14.12 *Ex post* forecast of GNP.

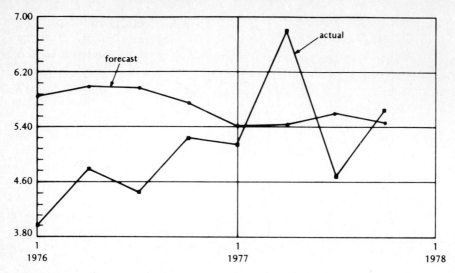

Figure 14.13 *Ex post* forecast of annual rate of growth of price level.

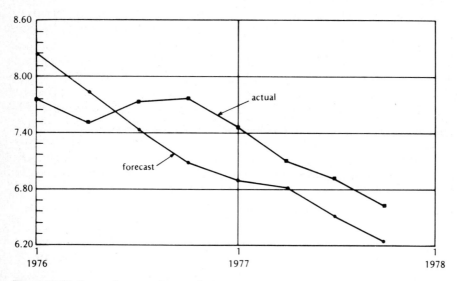

Figure 14.14 *Ex post* forecast of unemployment rate.

a major determinant of short-term macroeconomic fluctuations. Explaining investment spending is one of the most challenging tasks involved in the construction of any macroeconometric model that is to be used for serious forecasting work.

Also observe that the rms errors for GNP and its components, prices, wages, and unemployment are considerably lower in the *ex post* forecast than in either of the two historical simulations. However, this is in large part due to the more stable behavior of the economy during 1976 and 1977. As can be seen in Figs. 14.12 to 14.14, GNP grew fairly steadily and the unemployment rate, after remaining about level for a year, slowly dropped. The model replicated this behavior fairly closely, but rms errors for such variables as interest rates and nonresidential investment were still large.

We probably would not want to rely on this model as a serious tool for macroeconomic forecasting. Nonetheless, the model still provides a good example for macroeconometric policy analysis, as we will see below.

Dynamic multipliers Before using the model to perform some simple policy experiments, it would be interesting to calculate the dynamic GNP multipliers that correspond to changes in government spending and the money supply. These total multipliers, representing the net change in GNP after the specified number of periods has elapsed, are shown in Table 14.3. The government spending multipliers were obtained by increasing that variable by $1 billion above its historical path beginning in the first quarter of 1972. The simulated series for GNP corresponding to the historical series for government spending was then subtracted from the simulated series for GNP resulting from this higher value of government spending. Next, the money supply was increased by $1 billion in the first quarter of 1972 and all quarters thereafter, and corresponding changes in GNP were similarly calculated. Note that the government spending multiplier grows steadily for about 18 to 20 quarters. The impact multiplier is 1.86, and the long-run multiplier is about 4.5. (These multipliers are larger than those predicted by most of the current large-scale macroeconometric

Table 14.3 Government spending and money-supply multipliers

	ΔGNP			ΔGNP	
Period	From ΔG	From ΔM	Period	From ΔG	From ΔM
0	1.86	.026	18	4.20	.124
2	2.38	.447	20	4.30	.094
4	2.81	.664	22	4.39	.067
6	2.99	.487	24	4.45	.050
8	3.24	.349	26	4.49	.033
10	3.48	.236	28	4.52	.012
12	3.71	.188	30	4.54	− .005
14	3.91	.172	32	4.54	− .022
16	4.07	.154			

models.) The money-supply multiplier oscillates slowly and approaches zero after several periods. This is expected, since it is only *changes* in the money supply that enter the interest-rate equation. Thus, a change in the money supply has an impact on the GNP only in the first several quarters. Monetary policy experiments in this model must therefore involve changes in the *percentage growth rates* in the money supply and not changes in the level of the money supply.

14.1.4 Use of the Model for Forecasting and Policy Analysis

We now use the model to perform some simple forecasting and policy experiments. In each experiment we simulate the model 3 years into the future, beginning in the fourth quarter of 1977. Our objective is to forecast the effects of alternative economic policies by formulating those policies in terms of trajectories for the exogenous policy variables. In particular, we perform the following four simulation experiments.

1. **Base forecast** In this first experiment, we generate a forecast out to the end of 1980 under the assumption that all the exogenous variables, including the policy variables, grow at their historical rates of growth. This means that wealth (in real terms) grows at a rate of 2 percent per year, the money supply (in real terms) grows at 2 percent per year, and government spending (also in real terms) grows at 4 percent per year. In addition, the tax surcharge variable T_0 is set at zero.
2. **Tax surcharge experiment** In this experiment, wealth, the money supply, and government spending grow at the same rates as in the base forecast, but a 5 percent tax surcharge is imposed over the period 1978-1 to 1980-4. The objective is to determine how large an impact this tax surcharge will have on GNP, interest rates, unemployment, and the rate of inflation.
3. **Money growth experiment** Now the money supply grows at the annual rate of 6 percent per year; government spending again grows at 4 percent per year; and the tax surcharge is set at zero. This more rapid expansion of the money supply should result in a more rapid growth of GNP (through lower interest rates and more investment) but may also result in more inflation.
4. **Expansion of government spending** In this last experiment, the rate of growth of government spending is set at 6 percent. The other exogenous variables follow the same paths as in experiment 1. The objective is to examine how an increase in government spending will affect GNP, prices, and other variables.

The results of all these experiments are presented graphically in Figs. 14.15 to 14.24. The results are not at all surprising. The 5 percent tax surcharge (experiment 2) results in lower levels of GNP, consumption, and nonresidential investment through the multiplier effect. Note that residential investment, however, is only slightly below its level for the base case. This is because the drop in

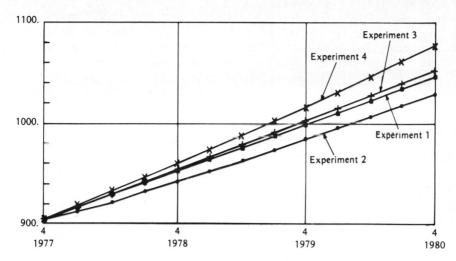

Figure 14.15 Forecasts of GNP.

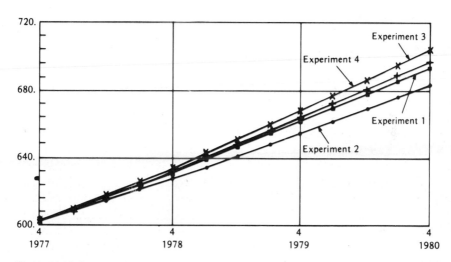

Figure 14.16 Consumption.

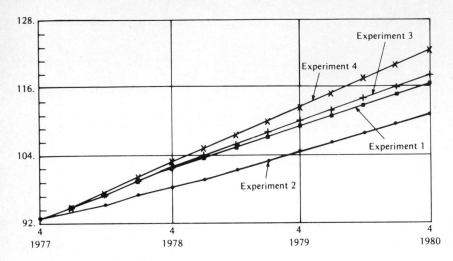

Figure 14.17 Nonresidential investment.

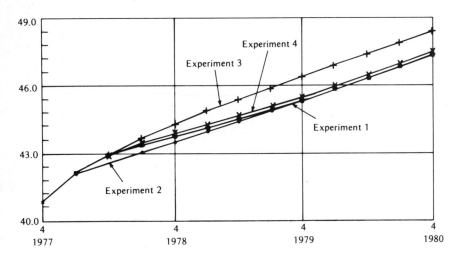

Figure 14.18 Residential investment.

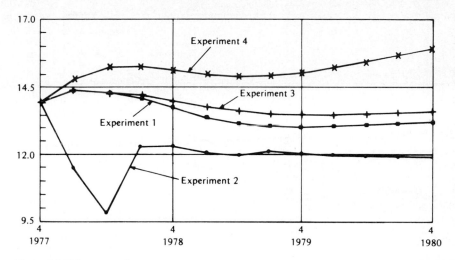

Figure 14.19 Inventory investment.

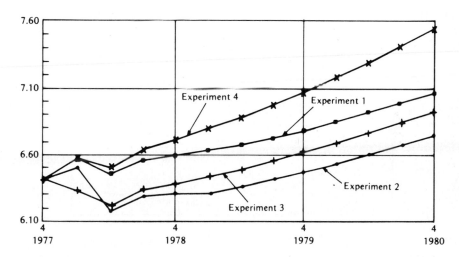

Figure 14.20 Short-term interest rate.

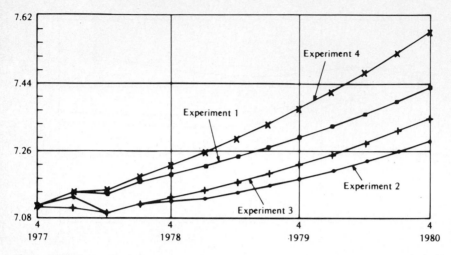

Figure 14.21 Long-term interest rate.

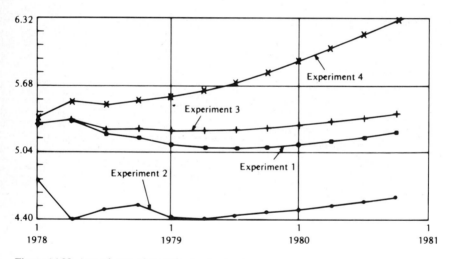

Figure 14.22 Annual rate of growth of price level.

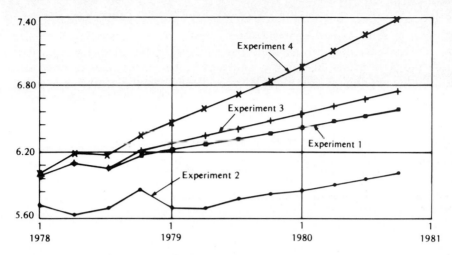

Figure 14.23 Annual rate of growth of wage rate.

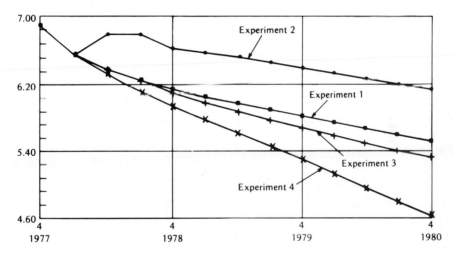

Figure 14.24 Unemployment rate.

GNP results in lower interest rates, which in turn stimulate residential investment (and, to some extent, nonresidential investment). The tax surcharge also results in less inventory investment, particularly in the first few quarters. Because the GNP grows less rapidly with the surcharge, the rates of price and wage inflation are about a half point lower and the unemployment rate is a half point higher.

The more rapid growth of the money supply (experiment 3) results in only a small increase in GNP and its components. The impact on GNP occurs through interest rates, which are between a quarter and a half point lower. This in turn stimulates residential and nonresidential investment, but the impact is small in magnitude.

The more rapid growth of government spending has a sizable impact on GNP, inflation, and unemployment. We leave the interpretation of these results to the reader (see Exercise 14.1).

The model could, of course, be used to perform other forecasting experiments. For example, the effects of a change in the propensity to consume could be measured by changing the coefficient multiplying disposable income net of transfer payments in the consumption equation and then simulating the model into the future. Readers who have access to the appropriate computer simulation package may wish to use this model and perform their own simulation experiments (see Exercise 14.2).

14.2 AN INDUSTRY-WIDE ECONOMETRIC MODEL

As our microeconometric example we examine a model of the United States tobacco industry constructed by Vernon, Rives, and Naylor.[†] The model attempts to explain the behavior of the tobacco industry over the 18-year period 1949 to 1966, and was constructed using annual data for that time period. The model determines the annual production (supply) of flue-cured tobacco leaf, the annual production of cigarettes (and thus the demand for tobacco leaf), and by equating demand and supply, the price of tobacco leaf. All these variables are at least partly dependent on certain government controls. An important use of the model, then, would be as a tool to forecast tobacco prices and measure the impact on prices of government controls.

---

† J. M. Vernon, N. W. Rives, Jr., and T. H. Naylor, "An Econometric Model of the Tobacco Industry," *Review of Economics and Statistics*, May 1969. For other examples of microeconometric simulation models, see W. H. Wallace, T. H. Naylor, and W. E. Sasser, "An Econometric Model of the Textile Industry in the United States," *Review of Economics and Statistics*, February 1968; F. M. Fisher, P. H. Cootner, and M. N. Baily, "An Econometric Model of the World Cooper Industry," *Bell Journal of Economics and Management Science*, vol. 3, no. 2, 1972; J. M. Griffin, "The Effects of Higher Prices on Electricity Consumption," *Bell Journal of Economics and Management Science*, vol. 5, no. 2, 1974; and P. W. MacAvoy and R. S. Pindyck, *The Economics of the Natural Gas Shortage* (Amsterdam: North-Holland, 1975).

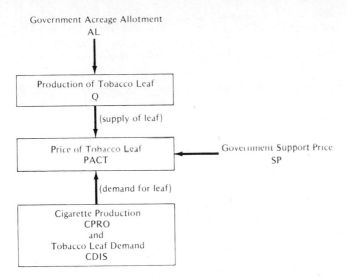

Figure 14.25 Simplified block diagram of tobacco leaf model.

The model is completely recursive; i.e., endogenous variables affect other endogenous variables only with a time lag, so that there is no simultaneity, and ordinary least squares (rather than two-stage least squares) is used to estimate the model's behavioral equations. The model, which contains a total of seven behavioral equations and eleven identities, can best be understood by breaking it up into three blocks, as shown in Fig. 14.25. The first block contains six equations, which explain the production of tobacco leaf and the effect of government restrictions on leaf output. The second block describes the determination of leaf price and the effects of government support prices. Finally, the third block describes cigarette manufacturing, which in turn determines the demand for tobacco leaf. The leaf price is determined in the second block of equations by equilibrating leaf supply (from the first block) with this demand for tobacco leaf.

Since 1933, the United States government has placed certain controls on the operation of the tobacco leaf market which are accounted for in the model. In particular, output restrictions have been placed on leaf production, and support prices for tobacco leaf were maintained by the government.† These controls are embodied in the model via two policy variables, acreage allotment AL and the support price SP.

Let us now turn to the econometric model, and examine it on a block-by-block basis.

---

† The maintenance of high leaf prices by the government was justified on the grounds that leaf producers formed a competitive industry whereas the buyers of tobacco leaf, namely the cigarette manufacturing companies, were highly concentrated and thus represented an oligopsony. Government policies were intended to offset the oligopsony power of the cigarette manufacturers.

14.2.1 Production of Tobacco Leaf

In this model, leaf production is treated separately from the determination of leaf price. This is based on the assumption that price and production are not determined simultaneously. It is assumed instead that production depends on the lagged price, while price depends on current production. Thus production and price are determined recursively.†

Leaf production Q is determined in the model as being proportional to the amount of acreage planted A. This first equation, then, can be written as

$$Q = A \times \overline{\text{YPA}} \tag{14.31}$$

$\overline{\text{YPA}}$ is the yield per acre, which should depend on such factors as weather and technical change. This variable is made exogenous to the model, however, so that once the amount of producing acreage is determined, production is also determined.‡ The remaining equations serve to determine A, the amount of acreage planted.

The dollar value of producing acreage AVAL is determined by the identity

$$\text{AVAL} = \frac{\overline{\text{YPA}} \times \text{PACT}}{\overline{\text{WPX}}} \tag{14.32}$$

where PACT is the tobacco leaf price and $\overline{\text{WPX}}$ is the wholesale price index. Thus, acre value is just the yield per acre times the price per unit of that yield deflated by the wholesale price index so that the value is in real terms.

Under free-market conditions, one would expect a supply relationship to exist between producing acreage and the value of acreage, that is, $A = f(\text{AVAL}_{-1})$. Because of government intervention, however, it is impossible to estimate such a supply relationship. Instead of explaining acreage directly, an equation is estimated to explain the difference between the acreage allotment of the government $\overline{\text{AL}}$ and the acreage planted A. This difference is called the *underage* (UND $= \overline{\text{AL}} - A$) and is the number of acres not planted even though permitted by the government allotment. We would expect that UND will be the lower the greater the economic incentive to growers.

The authors of the model take the approach of estimating an acreage equation using 1910–1930 data, and then extrapolating this equation forward to create a hypothetical free-market acreage (AFR) over the 1949–1966 period. The estimated equation for free-market acreage is shown below, with standard errors in parentheses:

$$\text{AFR} = \underset{(89.07)}{197.60} + \underset{(.0738)}{.9089} A_{-1} + \underset{(.8684)}{3.1058} \text{AVAL}_{-1} \tag{14.33}$$

$$\overline{R}^2 = .9025 \qquad \text{DW} = 2.14 \qquad \text{SER} = 84.54$$

---

† This assumption is reasonable, since tobacco growers decide on leaf production in the spring of each year, based upon the price received for the crop in the preceding fall. The tobacco is then harvested during the summer and taken to market.

‡ Exogenous variables have a bar over them.

Using the estimate of free-market acreage obtained from Eq. (14.33), free-market acreage less the government allotment (AFRMAL) is determined by the identity

$$\text{AFRMAL} = \widehat{\text{AFR}} - \overline{\text{AL}} \tag{14.34}$$

Underage can now be estimated econometrically by relating it to the free-market acreage less allotment. The underage equation contains two dummy variables in addition to AFRMAL. The first (SBDMY) is equal to 1 during the years 1957 and 1958 and is 0 otherwise and accounts for the effects of the government soil bank program at that time. The second dummy variable (LBDMY) represents the year 1965 and accounts for a change in allotments that occurred after planting was over in that year.†

The estimated equation for underage is

$$\text{UND} = \underset{(6.672)}{26.964} - \underset{(.0085)}{.0160}\,\text{AFRMAL} + \underset{(5.227)}{46.397}\,\text{SBDMY} + \underset{(7.537)}{33.642}\,\text{LBDMY}$$

$$\tag{14.35}$$

$$\overline{R}^2 = .8296 \qquad \text{DW} = 1.56 \qquad \text{SER} = 6.90$$

Finally, actual acreage is determined as the difference between the acreage allotment and estimated underage

$$\hat{A} = \overline{\text{AL}} - \widehat{\text{UND}} \tag{14.36}$$

14.2.2 The Price of Tobacco Leaf

This part of the model determines the actual leaf price (PACT) by explaining the mutual dependence between that variable and the amount of leaf pledged by growers T at the support price $\overline{\text{SP}}$. Since T depends upon the support price, the model thus explains the impact of the support price on the actual price.

One would expect that T, the amount of leaf pledged at the support price, would depend upon the difference between $\overline{\text{SP}}$ and a hypothetical free-market price PFR, which represents what the price would have been if the government control program were not in effect. As we shall see, this hypothetical free-market price can be estimated from an equation for the actual price by setting the amount of leaf pledged under the support program to 0.

The actual leaf price is a function of two variables, disposable income and the ratio of the net leaf supply to domestic leaf consumption (or disappearance). This second variable (SQNET) is given by the identity

$$\text{SQNET} = \frac{\text{STK}_{-1} + Q - T - \overline{X}}{\text{DDISP}} \tag{14.37}$$

---

† The original allotment was set at 515,425 acres in December 1964 but was increased in May 1965 to 607,335 acres as a result of a new government control program.

where STK_{-1} = stock of tobacco leaf remaining from previous year

$\quad\quad X$ = exports of tobacco leaf

$\quad\quad Q$ = leaf production

$\quad\quad DDISP$ = leaf disappearance, determined from cigarette consumption in third block of model

Q was determined in the first block of equations, and the determination of T will be discussed shortly. The leaf stock is also given by an identity:

$$STK = STK_{-1} + Q - DDISP - \bar{X} \quad\quad (14.38)$$

The variable SQNET thus represents a ratio of inventory stock to sales. Since cigarette manufacturers attempt to maintain a constant ratio of leaf supply to leaf use, this variable should have a negative effect on the leaf price.

The other explanatory variable in the leaf price equation is per capita disposable income ($\overline{PCAPY}$). This variable accounts for shifts in demand and thus should have a positive impact on the price. The estimated equation for the leaf price is

$$\log PACT = -\underset{(.1108)}{.2833} \log SQNET + \underset{(.0189)}{.5858} \log \overline{PCAPY} \quad\quad (14.39)$$

$$\bar{R}^2 = .7873 \quad\quad DW = 1.66 \quad\quad SER = .043$$

It is still necessary to determine the amount of leaf pledged, which is related to the support price less the free-market price. The hypothetical free-market price (PFR) is determined from the actual leaf price equation under the assumption that $T = 0$, that is, from

$$\log PFR = -.2833 \log SQ + .5858 \log \overline{PCAPY} \quad\quad (14.40)$$

where

$$SQ = \frac{STK_{-1} + Q - \bar{X}}{DDISP} \quad\quad (14.41)$$

The support price less the free-market price (SPMFP) is thus determined by the identity

$$SPMFP = \overline{SP} - PFR \quad\quad (14.42)$$

Finally, the amount of leaf pledged (T) under the support program is given by the estimated equation

$$\log T = \underset{(.1609)}{5.4038} + \underset{(.0352)}{.1472} SPMFP \quad\quad (14.43)$$

$$\bar{R}^2 = .4922 \quad\quad DW = 1.27 \quad\quad SER = .439$$

14.2.3 Cigarette Production and the Demand for Tobacco Leaf

One of the variables that determines leaf price is DDISP, the domestic disappearance of tobacco leaf, and this of course is related to cigarette production. Domestic leaf disappearance is given by

$$DDISP = CDIS + \overline{OTHDIS} \quad\quad (14.44)$$

where CDIS is leaf disappearance into cigarette production and $\overline{\text{OTHDIS}}$ is disappearance into other tobacco products. The variable CDIS is in turn determined by the identity

$$CDIS = 1000(LFPCIG \times CPRO) \qquad (14.45)$$

where LFPCIG is quantity of leaf per cigarette and CPRO is cigarette production.

The quantity of leaf per cigarette has been declining slightly over time and is predicted using the exponential trend equation

$$\log LFPCIG = \underset{(.0156)}{.6161} - \underset{(.0017)}{.0289} \overline{\text{TIME}} \qquad (14.46)$$

$$\bar{R}^2 = .9531 \qquad DW = 1.38 \qquad SER = .028$$

Cigarette production is equal to domestic cigarette consumption (CCON, measured in packs) plus tax-free withdrawals and exports of cigarettes ($\overline{\text{TXFWD}}$):

$$CPRO = 20(CCON) + \overline{\text{TXFWD}} \qquad (14.47)$$

One remaining equation is needed to explain domestic cigarette consumption. A log-log demand function is estimated that relates cigarette consumption to the real retail price of cigarettes ($\overline{\text{RPCIG}}$) and real disposable income ($\overline{\text{RDISY}}$):

$$\log CCON = -\underset{(.1349)}{.4250} \log \overline{\text{RPCIG}} + \underset{(.0765)}{.7721} \log \overline{\text{RDISY}} \qquad (14.48)$$

$$\bar{R}^2 = .9094 \qquad DW = .5900 \qquad SER = 0.467$$

The estimated price elasticity of $-.425$ and income elasticity of $.772$ are comparable to estimates obtained from other studies.

14.2.4 Simulation of the Model

The authors of this model performed an historical simulation to test the model's validity. The simulated and actual values for the more important endogenous variables in the model are shown graphically in Figs. 14.26 to 14.29.

Note that flue-cured underage tracks the historical series quite closely, while the stock of flue-cured tobacco leaf veers away from the actual series after several years. Since the stock of tobacco leaf in the current year depends in part on the stock of the previous year, there is a tendency for errors in the estimation of this variable to accumulate over time.

The actual price of tobacco leaf tracks only the broad trend of the historical series, missing the sharp upturn that occurs around 1960, and the usefulness of the model as a tool for forecasting tobacco leaf prices is thus rather limited. One reason for this is that the equations that determine cigarette production, and thus leaf demand, fail to pick up the turning points in these variables. Note, for example, that the simulated values for domestic cigarette consumption also track only the broad trend in the actual series.

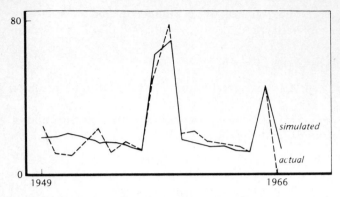

Figure 14.26 Flue-cured underage (1,000 acres).

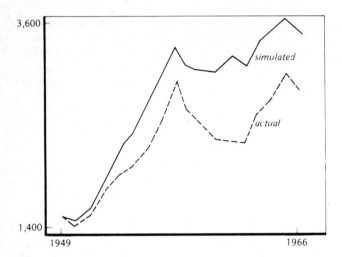

Figure 14.27 Stocks of flue-cured tobacco leaf (1,000 pounds).

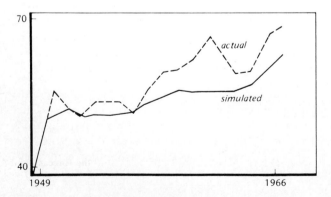

Figure 14.28 Actual price of flue-cured tobacco leaf (cents).

446

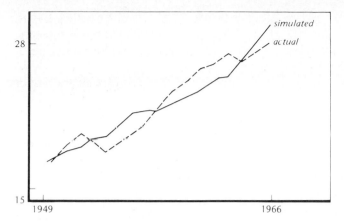

Figure 14.29 Domestic cigarette consumption, United States (billions of cigarettes).

These results indicate that the model, while providing an overall description of the tobacco industry, would be of only limited use for forecasting. This is not surprising. The model is rather simple, so that one would not expect it to provide a full representation for what is a rather complex industry.† The model does, however, provide a good starting point for what could be a more detailed econometric analysis of the tobacco industry.

14.3 SIMULATION MODELS FOR CORPORATE FINANCIAL PLANNING

As we explained in Chapter 12, a simulation model need not consist only of equations that are statistically estimated. A *financial simulation model*, containing equations all of which are accounting identities that describe the financial structure of a particular corporation, is an example of a noneconometric model. Although the equations of a financial simulation model are not behavioral, many of them will be *time-dependent*, enabling the model to describe the dynamic characteristics of the firm's financial structure. By simulating the model into the future, one can forecast and analyze the effects of economic conditions, changing revenue streams, or alternative financial strategies on the firm's financial position. Typically, these models are used to generate *pro forma* balance sheets and *pro forma* income statements, i.e., balance sheets and income statements that would apply in the future under specific assumptions about capitalization, debt, future costs and revenues, etc.

Financial simulation models have become an important addition to the quantitative tool kit of corporate planners and business analysts. They are

† In addition, the difficulty of obtaining information about some of the exogenous variables (such as acreage allotment and tobacco leaf exports) may substantially complicate the forecasting process.

particularly valuable for planning because they provide a consistent framework that simultaneously accounts for all the interrelationships in a firm's financial structure. Thus, although they are still new, their usefulness has become increasingly accepted.

In this section we provide a brief introduction to the construction and use of financial simulation models. As we will see, building such a model basically boils down to specifying all of the firm's accounting relationships as well as its financial decision rules. We also present a detailed example of a financial simulation model, which will help illustrate how such a model is constructed and applied to corporate financial planning.

To begin with, let us see how an extremely simple set of accounting relationships can serve as the basis of a model of a firm's income statement and balance sheets. The relationships of interest are as follows:

1. The cost of goods sold (CGS) is equal to 85 percent of sales but can never drop by more than 10 percent from one year to the next (because of fixed costs, contracts, inertia, etc.). Thus, CGS is equal to 85 percent of sales *or* 90 percent of last year's CGS, *whichever is larger*.
2. Gross profit (GROSSPR) equals sales minus cost of goods sold.
3. Interest expense (INT) equals 9 percent of debt.
4. Pretax profit (PRETXPR) equals gross profit minus interest.
5. Taxes equal 48 percent of pretax profit.
6. Net profit (NETPR) equals pretax profit less taxes.
7. Retained earnings (RETEARN) equals the previous year's retained earnings plus net profit.
8. The cash level is equal to that in the previous year plus net profit plus the change in debt from the previous year.
9. Total assets (TOTASST) is equal to cash plus fixed assets (FIXASST), with the latter assumed to be constant at $500,000 per year.
10. Total liabilities (TOTLIAB) is equal to debt plus retained earnings.

Note that the first six relationships described the firm's income statement, while the last four describe the balance sheet. We can now summarize these relationships in the form of a simple simulation model:

$$CGS = \max(.85SALES, .9CGS_{-1}) \tag{14.49}$$

$$GROSSPR = SALES - CGS \tag{14.50}$$

$$INT = .09DEBT \tag{14.51}$$

$$PRETXPR = GROSSPR - INT \tag{14.52}$$

$$TAXES = .48PRETXPR \tag{14.53}$$

$$NETPR = PRETXPR - TAXES \tag{14.54}$$

$$RETEARN = RETEARN_{-1} + NETPR \tag{14.55}$$

$$CASH = CASH_{-1} + NETPR + \Delta DEBT \tag{14.56}$$

$$TOTASST = CASH + FIXASST \tag{14.57}$$

$$TOTLIAB = DEBT + RETEARN \tag{14.58}$$

This model contains 10 equations, 10 endogenous variables, and 3 exogenous variables (SALES, DEBT, and FIXASST). The model is simulated into the future using hypothetical data for 1980, assuming that debt is fixed at $200,000 each year and that sales fall from $1,000,000 in 1980 to $700,000 in 1981 and then rise to $1,100,000 in 1982 and $1,400,000 in 1983. The resulting *pro forma* income statement and balance sheet are shown in Table 14.4.

Observe that the model projects that the firm's cash level will fall to $56,840 in 1981. Suppose that the firm needs a minimum cash level of $100,000 to operate and management is interested in finding a debt policy that will satisfy this constraint. We can easily use the model to solve this debt management problem by making DEBT an endogenous variable and adding the following equation to the model:

$$DEBT = \max (DEBT_{-1} + 100,000 - CASH_{-1} - NETPR, 0) \quad (14.59)$$

This equation simply says that this year's debt is equal to last year's plus the $100,000 target cash level less cash already on hand less (plus) any net profits (losses), provided that debt is not to fall below zero.

By resimulating the model with Eq. (14.59) added we can find the debt policy needed to satisfy the firm's cash needs. Doing this, we find that debt must increase by $45,279 in 1981, but total debt can be reduced to $167,309 in 1982 and $60,962 in 1983.

Table 14.4 Simulation of simplest model

	1980	1981	1982	1983
		Income statement		
Sales	$1,000,000	$700,000	$1,100,000	$1,400,000
Cost of goods sold	850,000	765,000	935,000	1,190,000
Gross profit	$ 150,000	$(65,000)	$ 165,000	$ 210,000
Interest	18,000	18,000	18,000	18,000
Pretax profit	$ 132,000	$(83,000)	$ 147,000	$ 192,000
Taxes	63,360	(39,840)	70,560	92,160
Net profit	$ 68,640	$(43,160)	$ (76,440)	$ 99,840
		Balance sheet		
Cash	$ 100,000	$ 56,840	$ 133,280	$ 233,120
Fixed assets	500,000	500,000	500,000	500,000
Total assets	$ 600,000	$556,840	$ 633,280	$ 733,120
Debts	200,000	200,000	200,000	200,000
Retained earnings	400,000	356,840	433,280	533,120
Total liabilities and net worth	600,000	556,840	633,280	733,120

This model is, of course, extremely simple, and hardly realistic. Let us therefore turn to a more detailed example of a financial simulation model.† The firm described in this example is also imaginary, and its financial structure is still a simple one. However, the example embodies many of the principles of financial decision making encountered in actual situations.

The objective of this model is to generate *pro forma* financial statements that describe the financial condition of the firm for any assumed pattern of sales in the future. Particular attention is paid to the determination of retained earnings, dividends paid, and securing additional funds through the flotation of long-term debt or the sale of common and preferred stock. A given sales pattern implies a set of asset requirements; these, in turn, are combined with a number of decision rules supplied by management to calculate the distribution of retained earnings and the levels and types of new financing.

The equations of the model include both descriptive relationships between financial variables such as those discussed earlier and basic decision rules specified in a very general form. The descriptive relationships are accounting relationships and definitions. The decision rules, on the other hand, are not written in the form of conventional algebraic equations. They are described algebraically using *conditional operators*, consisting of statements of the type: "IF . . . THEN . . . ELSE." A decision rule describes what to do given a binary choice (or series of binary choices). For example, suppose we wanted to express the following decision rule algebraically: "If X is greater than 0, then Y is set equal to X divided by 2. Otherwise, Y is set equal to 0." Using the symbol "GT" to represent "greater than," we use the conditional operator "IF . . . THEN . . . ELSE" to write the decision rule algebraically as:

$$Y = \text{IF } X \text{ GT } 0 \text{ THEN } X/2 \text{ ELSE } 0 \qquad (14.60)$$

Suppose that we wanted the decision rule instead to read: "If X is greater than 0, then Y is set equal to X divided by 2. Otherwise, Y depends on Z. If Z is less than 3 times X, then Y is set equal to 0, but otherwise Y is set equal to Z." The equation for this rule would be

$$Y = \text{IF } X \text{ GT } 0 \text{ THEN } X/2 \text{ ELSE IF } Z \text{ LT } 3X \text{ THEN } 0 \text{ ELSE } Z \qquad (14.61)$$

Equations (14.60) and (14.61) are highly nonlinear relationships, but models that include relationships of this kind can be solved using appropriate computer simulation packages.

Data for our corporate model include a set of financial variables calculated by the equations of the model and various types of parameters which are supplied by management. Examples of input data are historical values such as stock outstanding in a previous period, "environmental" data such as the expected interest rate on new debt or tax rates, observed or assumed characteris-

---

† The example was constructed by Robert B. Anthonyson and J. Phillip Cooper for Dynamics Associates, Inc., Cambridge, Mass., and is used here by permission. Our introductory discussion was based on a publication by Dynamics Associates entitled "Financial Modeling in XSIM."

tics of the business operation such as the ratio between accounts receivable and sales, and financial decision variables such as the maximum desired debt-equity ratio. In the present example, the focus is on the pattern of sales, and the financing decision problem is solved for alternative sales scenarios. The technique is perfectly general, however, since any one or any combination of the input variables or parameters could be chosen for a sensitivity analysis.

Table 14.5 presents a list of the variables used in the model; there are 37 unknown variables that are solved for by the model and 22 parameters to be supplied by management. There are a total of 37 equations in the model, and they are listed in Table 14.6, broken down into three functional blocks.† The basic logic of the model is described below.

In each time period, the assumed level of sales is used to generate the earnings of the firm in the first block of equations. Input parameters (supplied by management) relate the cost of goods sold to sales, operating costs to both sales and fixed assets, and so on, leading to values for earnings before and after taxes. Earnings per share are converted to an implied stock price using a supplied price-earnings ratio.

The asset side of the balance sheet is also highly aggregated. Assets required to support the sales level are generated as simple functions of sales in the second block of equations. (The net book value is assumed to be an appropriate measure of assets for this purpose.) The asset equations determine expected values for accounts receivable and "required" values for inventories, cash, and fixed assets.

The liability side of the balance sheet includes relationships similar to those used above; for example, accounts payable is related proportionally to inventories, and other current liabilities is a simple function of last year's long-term debt. There are, in addition, more complicated equations which embody the decision rules used by the hypothetical financial officer. Some examples of these decision rules follow:

1. A minimum desired dollar addition to retained earnings (FRETMIN) and a normal retention rate for earnings (B) are specified as parameters by management. The targeted addition to retained earnings (RETMIN) is chosen (in the fourth equation of block III) according to the relationship between the two constraints imposed by management and the simulated (i.e., calculated) value for earnings available for common stock less a minimum dividend payout.
2. The determination of actual dividends paid (CMDIV) takes into account the targeted addition to retained earnings and also a maximum dividend payout ratio (DPSMAX).
3. After calculating the funds needed (NF) to meet asset changes, dividends, and maturing debt, the amount of long-term debt to be floated (NL) is

---

† The equations are written in the format of the XSIM simulation language. The model itself was simulated using XSIM, a system that is particularly applicable to the construction and solution of financial simulation models.

Table 14.5 Unknowns and parameters supplied by management

Unknowns

1. A	Total assets		20. LIAB	Total liabilities and equity
2. AP	Accounts payable		21. NF	Needed funds
3. AR	Accounts receivable		22. NFA	New fixed assets
4. CA	Current assets		23. NL	New long-term debt
5. CASH	Cash		24. NPFDSK	New preferred stock
6. CGS	Cost of goods sold		25. NS	New common stock
7. CL	Current liabilities		26. NUMCS	Number of common shares
8. CMDIV	Common dividends			outstanding
9. DEP	Depreciation		27. OC	Operating costs
10. DPS	Dividends per share		28. OCL	Other current liabilities
11. EAFCD	Earnings available for		29. OI	Operating income
	common dividends		30. P	Price per common share
12. EAT	Earnings after taxes		31. PFDIV	Preferred dividends
13. EBT	Earnings before taxes		32. PRDSK	Preferred stock
14. EPS	Earnings per share		33. R	Retained earnings
15. EQTY	Total equity		34. RCASH	Minimum cash requirement
16. FA	Net plant and equipment		35. RETMIN	Desired addition to retained
17. INT	Interest			earnings
18. INV	Inventories		36. S	Common stock
19. L	Long-term debt		37. TAX	Income taxes

Parameters supplied by management

1. B		Retention rate as percentage of earnings
2. DPSMAX		Maximum desired common dividend per share
3. DPSMIN		Minimum desired common dividend per share
4. FINV		Fixed (buffer) inventory
5. FRETMIN		Minimum desired addition to retained earnings
6. I		Interest rate in percent
7. K		Maximum desired debt as fraction of debt + equity
8. M		Multiplier (P/E ratio)
9. NFAS		Minimum increment size for plant and equipment
10. PROD		Turnover rate for plant and equipment
11. RAP		Accounts payable as percentage of inventory
12. RAR		Accounts receivable as percentage of sales
13. RCGS		Cost of goods sold as percentage of sales
14. RDEP		Depreciation as percentage of fixed assets
15. RINV		Variable inventory as percentage of sales
16. RL		Current portion of long-term debt as percentage of long-term debt
17. ROCA		Operating costs dependent on fixed assets as percentage
18. ROCS		Operating costs dependent on sales as percentage
19. RPFDIV		Preferred stock dividend rate as percent
20. RRCASH		Minimum cash requirement as percentage of sales
21. SALES		Sales
22. T		Tax rate in percent

Table 14.6 Equations of the financial simulation model†

Block I: Generation of sales and earnings

CGS = RCGS/100*SALES
OC = ROCS/100*SALES + ROCA/100*(FA + FA(−1))/2
OI = SALES − CGS − OC
INT = I/100*(L + L(−1))/2
DEP = RDEP/100*(FA(−1) + NFA/2)
PFDIV = RPFDIV/100*PFDSK
EBT = OI − INT − DEP
TAX = EBT*T/100
EAT = EBT − TAX
EAFCD = EAT − PFDIV
EPS = EAFCD/NUMCS
P = EPS*M

Block II: Generation of required assets

AR = RAR/100*SALES
INV = RINV/100*SALES + FINV
RCASH = RRCASH/100*SALES
CA = CASH + AR + INV
NFA = IF SALES(−1)/PROD GT FA(−1) − DEP THEN(SALES(−1)/PROD − (FA(−1)
    −DEP))ELSE 0
FA = FA(−1) − DEP + NFA
A = CA + FA

Block III: Financing the required asset level

AP = RAP/100*INV
OCL = RL/100*L(−1)
CL = AP + OCL
RETMIN = IF B/100*EAFCD GT EAFCD − DPSMIN*NUMCS AND EAFCD
    −DPSMIN*NUMCS GT FRETMIN THEN EAFCD − DPSMIN*NUMCS ELSE IF
    B/100*EAFCD GT FRETMIN THEN B/100*EAFCD ELSE FRETMIN
CMDIV = IF EAFCD − RETMIN GT DPSMAX*NUMCS THEN DPSMAX*NUMCS
    ELSE IF EAFCD − RETMIN LT 0 THEN 0 ELSE EAFCD − RETMIN
R = R(−1) + EAFCD − CMDIV
EQTY = PFDSK + S + R
NF = NFA + DEL(AR) + DEL(INV) − DEL(AP) + OCL(−1) + CMDIV − EAFCD
    −DEP + RCASH − CASH(−1)
NL = IF NF GT 0 THEN IF NF LT K*(EQTY + L(−1) − OCL + NF) − L(−1)
    +OCL THEN NF ELSE K*(EQTY + L) − L(−1) + OCL ELSE IF − NF GT L(−1)
    −OCL THEN − L(−1) + OCL ELSE NF
L = L(−1) − OCL + NL
NS = IF NF − NL GT 0 THEN IF EAFCD − RETMIN GT NUMCS(−1)*DPSMIN
    THEN IF NF − NL GT P*(EAFCD − RETMIN − NUMCS(−1)*DPSMIN)/
    DPSMIN THEN P*(EAFCD − RETMIN − NUMCS(−1)*DPSMIN)/DPSMIN
    ELSE NF − NL ELSE 0 ELSE 0

† GT and LT refer to "greater than" and "less than," respectively. DEL refers to a first difference, for example, DEL(AR) = AR − AR(−1). An asterisk (*) refers to multiplication.

Table 14.6 Equations of the financial simulation model (*Continued*)

Block III: Financing the required asset level

NUMCS = NUMCS(−1) + NS/P
S = S(−1) + NS
NPFDSK = IF NF − NL − NS GT 0 THEN NF − NL − NS ELSE IF − (NF − NL − NS)
   GT PFDSK(−1)THEN − PFDSK(−1)ELSE NF − NL − NS
DPS = CMDIV/NUMCS
PFDSK = PFDSK(−1) + NPFDSK
CASH = RCASH − NF + NL + NS + NPFDSK
LIAB = CL + L + EQTY

chosen in light of a prespecified leverage ratio; if no new debt is needed, the amount of existing debt that should be retired is chosen.

4. The amount of common stock to be issued (NS) is chosen on the basis of funds needed which are not financed by new long-term debt, but is constrained by the responsibility to meet minimum dividend payments. Preferred stock (NPFDSK) is issued to make up any remaining deficiency. Excess funds can be used to retire preferred stock.

It would be difficult to diagram the decision tree reflecting the set of rules referred to above for two reasons. First, these rules have been stated succinctly using conditional statements (IF . . . THEN . . . ELSE). If the options involved were to be written in detail, a very large number of possibilities would have to be evaluated. Second, and far more important, these calculations could not progress in a straightforward manner from start to end. Because the branches of the decision tree are tied together in a number of places, there are many feedback loops in the model, so that the determination of additions to retained earnings, dividends paid, debt floated, and stock issued must be a simultaneous one.

The concept of simultaneity, as it enters our example, can be illustrated as follows. A sales figure was used to generate earnings and this in turn led to, among other items, the level of long-term debt required. Yet the level of debt affects the interest expense incurred within the current year and therefore earnings. Furthermore, as earnings are affected, so is the price at which new shares are issued, the number of shares to be sold, and thus earnings per share. Earnings per share then feeds back into the stock price calculation.

Let us now examine how this model can be used. The model was simulated into the future to generate a *pro forma* income statement and balance sheet. "Actual" data were used for 1980, and the simulation was run through 1983. The variables SALES was set at its "actual" value of $1 million in 1980, and was assumed to drop to $900,000 in 1981, and then increase to $1.1 million in 1982 and $1.4 million in 1983.† The results of this simulation are shown in Table 14.7.

---

† Note that an econometric forecasting model could have been used to generate these sales forecasts. Typically, a financial simulation model is linked in this way to an econometric model.

Table 14.7 Simulation results

	1980	1981	1982	1983
Pro forma income statement for 1980–1983				
Sales	$1,000,000	$ 900,000	$1,100,000	$1,400,000
Cost of goods sold	600,000	540,000	660,000	840,000
Operating costs	125,000	115,600	140,400	176,200
Operating income	$ 275,000	$ 244,400	$ 299,600	$ 383,800
Depreciation	25,000	26,200	31,200	37,100
Interest	2,000	1,400	4,300	12,900
Earnings before taxes	$ 247,200	$ 216,700	$ 264,100	$ 333,800
Income taxes	118,600	104,000	126,800	160,200
Earnings after taxes	$ 128,500	$ 112,700	$ 137,400	$ 173,600
Preferred dividends	0	0	0	0
Earnings available for common	$ 128,500	$ 112,700	$ 137,400	$ 173,600
Earnings per share	$1.29	$1.13	$1.37	$1.74
Common dividends	$ 75,000	$ 56,400	$ 75,000	$ 86,800
Dividends per share	$ .75	$ .56	$ .75	$ .87
Pro forma balance sheet for 1980–1983				
Assets				
Cash	$ 126,000	$ 90,200	$ 110,000	$ 140,000
Accounts receivable	70,000	63,000	77,000	98,000
Inventories	430,000	397,000	463,000	562,000
Current assets	$ 626,000	$ 550,200	$ 650,000	$ 800,000
Net plant and equipment	475,000	548,800	667,600	780,400
Total assets	$1,101,000	$1,098,900	$1,317,600	1,580,400
Liabilities				
Accounts payable	$ 107,500	$ 99,200	$ 115,700	$ 140,500
Other current liabilities	5,000	2,400	0	7,100
Current liabilities	$ 112,500	$ 101,600	$ 115,700	$ 147,600
Long-term debt	47,500	0	142,100	286,400
Equity				
Preferred stock	0	0	0	0
Common stock	500,000	500,000	500,000	500,000
Retained earnings	441,000	497,400	559,700	646,500
Total equity	$ 941,000	$ 997,400	$1,059,700	$1,146,500
Total liabilities and equity	$1,101,000	$1,099,000	$1,317,600	$1,580,500

Observe from the income statement that the decrease and then increase in sales result in a decrease and then increase in both earnings and dividends. We see in the balance sheet that no new stock (preferred or common) is issued, however, and long-term debt drops to zero in 1981 and then increases in the following 2 years. An additional sale of stock is unnecessary, because retained earnings increase steadily over the 4 years. The 1-year drop in sales, then, has no adverse long-term effect on the company's financial position. This may not be the case, however, if sales drop more dramatically and remain low over a longer period of time. The model can easily be simulated to determine the impact of alternative sales flows on the company's future income statements and balance sheets.

Note that in this simulation, we chose sales to be an external input variable and we solved the model for various financial measures contingent upon the given values for sales. We might also have asked the following question: What would the value of sales have to be for earnings to be zero; i.e., what is the *breakeven* point for sales? This question could be answered easily by resolving the model, making sales an internal unknown variable and earnings an external input parameter. (See Exercise 14.6.)

APPENDIX 14.1 ESTIMATION METHOD AND DATA SERIES FOR THE MACROECONOMETRIC MODEL

Estimation

Two of the behavioral equations in the macroeconomic model [Eqs. (14.23) and (14.26)] were estimated using a procedure that combines two-stage least squares with a first-order serial-correlation correction. To explain this procedure, let us go through the steps involved in estimating Eq. (14.26) for the short-term interest rate.

The short-term interest rate is taken to be related linearly to income, lagged changes in income, the rate of growth in the money supply, and a moving sum of recent inflation rates. This equation was first estimated using a simple Cochrane-Orcutt procedure for first-order serial-correlation correction. (For a review of this procedure, see Chapter 6.) The estimation results are shown below with t statistics in parentheses. The R^2, F statistic, standard error (SER), Durbin-Watson (DW) statistic, and the estimated value of ρ used in the serial-correlation correction are also shown.

$$\text{RS} = \underset{(-1.31)}{-1.75421} + \underset{(3.53)}{.00914\,\text{YD}} + \underset{(1.32)}{.01228\ \Delta\text{YD}_{-1}} - \underset{(-2.56)}{24.0402\,\text{RGM}}$$

$$+ \underset{(2.84)}{34.03730}\left(\frac{\Delta P_{-1}}{P_{-1}} + \frac{\Delta P_{-2}}{P_{-2}} + \frac{\Delta P_{-3}}{P_{-3}}\right) \qquad \text{(A14.1)}$$

$$R^2 = .3626 \qquad \text{SER} = .5170 \qquad F(4/76) = 10.808 \qquad \text{DW} = 1.58 \qquad \hat{\rho} = 0.8159$$

Note that this equation contains an unlagged endogenous variable YD. Two-stage least squares must therefore be applied, with YD being regressed against the set of exogenous variables in the model as well as lagged endogenous variables. This results in a fitted series for YD, which we call YDFIT. We now reestimate our equation using *ordinary least squares* but with YDFIT instead of YD:

$$\text{RS} = \underset{(-3.95)}{-2.17531} + \underset{(8.14)}{.01173}\,\text{YDFIT} - \underset{(-0.41)}{.00672}\,\Delta\text{YD}_{-1} - \underset{(-4.33)}{63.9380}\,\text{RGM}$$

$$+ \underset{(.43)}{4.57416}\left(\frac{\Delta P_{-1}}{P_{-1}} + \frac{\Delta P_{-2}}{P_{-2}} + \frac{\Delta P_{-3}}{P_{-3}}\right) \tag{A.14.2}$$

$$R^2 = .7980 \qquad \text{SER} = .7912 \qquad F(4/76) = 75.05 \qquad \text{DW} = 0.65$$

The residuals $\hat{\varepsilon}_{5t}$ from Eq. (A14.2) are then regressed against their own lagged values $\hat{\varepsilon}_{5,\,t-1}$ to obtain a new estimate for the coefficient of serial correlation:

$$\hat{\varepsilon}_{5t} = \underset{(7.83)}{.68568}\,\hat{\varepsilon}_{5,\,t-1} - \underset{(-0.16)}{.01029} \tag{A14.3}$$

Our original equation is now transformed autoregressively using .68568 as an estimated value for ρ. Note that this value for ρ is substantially lower than that obtained when the Cochrane-Orcutt procedure was applied to the original equation. Our equation is now of the form

$$\text{RS} - .68568\text{RS}_{-1} = \beta_0(1 - .68568\,Y) + \beta_1(\text{YD} - .68568\text{YD}_{-1})$$

$$+ \beta_2(\Delta\text{YD}_{-1} - .68568\,\Delta\text{YD}_{-2}) + \cdots \tag{A14.4}$$

This equation is now estimated using two-stage least squares. This is done by regressing the generalized difference $\text{YD} - .68568\text{YD}_{-1}$ against a set of exogenous and lagged endogenous variables that are in the same generalized difference form; i.e., we perform the regression

$$(\text{YD} - .68568\text{YD}_{-1}) = \alpha_0 + \alpha_1(Z_1 - .68568Z_{1,\,-1})$$

$$+ \alpha_2(Z_2 - .68568Z_{2,\,-1}) + \cdots \tag{A14.5}$$

where Z_1, Z_2, etc., are exogenous and lagged endogenous variables. A fitted series thus results for the generalized difference $\text{YD} - .68568\text{YD}_{-1}$, which we call YDDIF. This fitted series is now substituted for $\text{YD} - .68568\text{YD}_{-1}$ in Eq. (A14.4):

$$(\text{RS} - .68568\text{RS}_{-1}) = \beta_0(1 - .68568) + \beta_1\text{YDDIF}$$

$$+ \beta_2(\Delta\text{YD}_{-1} - .68568\,\Delta\text{YD}_{-2}) + \cdots$$

$$\tag{A14.6}$$

We now continue iteratively, by estimating Eq. (A14.6) using the Cochrane-Orcutt procedure and obtaining a new value for ρ, using this value to obtain a new generalized difference form for YD, etc. We continue until our estimate of ρ converges, i.e., until successive iterations result in almost no change in the estimated value for ρ.

Usually convergence will occur after three or four iterations; for the interest-rate equation above, three iterations were sufficient. We obtained a final estimate for ρ of .8184. We repeat the two-stage least-squares procedure described above using this last estimate for ρ to obtain the final coefficient estimates for our interest-rate equation:

$$RS - .8184RS_{-1} = -\underset{(-.21)}{.21727}(1 - .8184) + \underset{(3.14)}{.00630}\,YDDIF$$

$$+ \underset{(1.48)}{.01380}(\Delta YD_{-1} - .8184\,\Delta YD_{-2}) - \underset{(-2.58)}{24.50340}(RGM - .8184RGM_{-1})$$

$$+ \underset{(3.19)}{37.85490}\left[\left(\frac{\Delta P_{-1}}{P_{-1}} - .8184\frac{\Delta P_{-2}}{P_{-2}}\right) + \left(\frac{\Delta P_{-2}}{P_{-2}} - .8184\frac{\Delta P_{-3}}{P_{-3}}\right)\right.$$

$$\left. + \left(\frac{\Delta P_{-3}}{P_{-3}} - .8184\frac{\Delta P_{-4}}{P_{-4}}\right)\right] \tag{A14.7}$$

$$R^2 = .3483 \qquad SER = .5215 \qquad F(4/67) = 10.154 \qquad DW = 1.60$$

Data Series

Some readers may wish to repeat the estimation of the model themselves, or estimate alternative versions of one or more equations (see Exercise 14.2). All the data used in the construction of the model are therefore presented in Table 14.8.

Table 14.8

Quarter	1	2	3	4
	C = personal consumption expenditures, billions of 1958 dollars			
1956	279.1	279.6	280.5	283.3
1957	285.1	285.2	287.3	288.0
1958	284.7	287.1	291.6	294.4
1959	300.3	304.6	307.0	307.6
1960	310.3	314.4	313.2	313.8
1961	314.3	318.2	319.4	325.6
1962	328.4	332.2	334.6	339.2
1963	341.4	344.2	348.9	351.1
1964	357.3	363.5	369.7	370.4
1965	377.7	380.9	386.7	397.1
1966	401.7	402.5	407.1	408.2
1967	411.2	416.3	418.3	420.6
1968	428.7	433.6	442.5	444.8
1969	449.2	451.1	453.6	457.2
1970	459.8	461.9	465.3	461.3
1971	471.1	476.5	479.0	485.3
1972	493.0	503.1	509.4	520.0
1973	530.5	529.5	532.2	528.9
1974	526.2	526.3	529.4	520.0
1975	522.9	532.1	539.7	547.5
1976	557.7	563.1	568.2	580.2
1977	587.3	590.0	594.2	607.5

Quarter	1	2	3	4

	G = government purchases of goods and services, billions of 1958 dollars			
1956	84.6	85.8	85.2	86.4
1957	89.3	89.8	90.1	90.4
1958	92.2	94.2	95.5	98.2
1959	96.3	96.2	95.5	95.0
1960	95.0	96.8	97.8	98.5
1961	100.6	101.4	102.4	105.6
1962	107.2	107.6	109.1	109.3
1963	110.0	109.5	111.8	112.3
1964	113.2	114.2	113.6	114.1
1965	113.5	116.3	118.6	121.9
1966	123.9	125.9	131.1	133.9
1967	137.1	138.7	140.4	141.0
1968	143.6	145.9	146.5	146.0
1969	144.6	145.0	143.5	143.1
1970	141.5	139.8	139.9	140.4
1971	139.9	138.6	140.6	140.8
1972	142.6	142.1	141.4	142.1
1973	143.2	141.0	141.3	141.4
1974	143.8	144.6	145.0	145.0
1975	145.6	147.2	148.6	148.9
1976	148.1	148.4	148.5	148.5
1977	147.9	151.6	153.8	155.5

	GNP = gross national product, billions of 1958 dollars			
1956	437.3	437.7	437.9	441.5
1957	443.3	443.7	447.8	442.3
1958	434.2	437.0	448.4	461.4
1959	468.9	481.6	474.0	479.6
1960	489.2	486.4	482.1	478.3
1961	479.8	490.3	497.3	508.5
1962	517.3	523.1	527.1	529.1
1963	533.8	539.3	550.1	553.4
1964	561.1	570.0	575.9	578.1
1965	594.1	601.7	612.2	626.3
1966	638.4	643.8	650.6	654.4
1967	653.8	657.7	666.0	672.7
1968	680.4	692.0	700.6	704.6
1969	711.6	715.0	716.4	712.9
1970	709.3	709.8	714.5	707.8
1971	724.1	732.5	736.1	744.5
1972	760.7	775.1	783.5	799.7
1973	816.2	815.1	816.5	818.1
1974	806.3	804.3	797.6	783.1
1975	763.8	770.3	795.1	801.9
1976	823.6	834.6	843.0	847.8
1977	865.4	880.4	888.4	901.2

Table 14.8 (*Continued*)

Quarter	1	2	3	4
	GNPP = potential GNP, billions of 1958 dollars			
1956	413.4	415.1	419.6	421.6
1957	424.4	429.5	435.7	441.9
1958	450.1	455.3	460.4	467.4
1959	474.5	480.9	482.3	485.4
1960	487.4	490.4	494.1	495.5
1961	499.9	507.2	512.0	517.9
1962	524.9	526.8	532.3	539.1
1963	545.7	547.6	554.2	558.2
1964	560.8	568.5	574.2	580.9
1965	592.0	594.7	603.0	612.5
1966	619.9	629.6	641.2	648.2
1967	655.7	662.9	671.9	685.4
1968	698.1	704.3	714.6	728.5
1969	736.9	747.0	755.4	764.6
1970	774.6	784.4	793.9	806.9
1971	820.5	837.2	843.7	861.0
1972	884.7	892.7	898.6	912.0
1973	919.4	929.1	927.6	935.3
1974	946.0	957.0	957.0	966.6
1975	976.2	986.0	995.8	1005.7
1976	1015.8	1026.0	1036.3	1046.6
1977	1057.1	1067.9	1078.6	1089.4

	IIN = Inventory investment: change in business inventories, billions of 1958 dollars			
1956	6.39	4.54	4.28	4.45
1957	2.15	2.34	3.23	−2.22
1958	−5.43	−5.12	0.10	4.08
1959	3.94	10.18	0.00	6.32
1960	10.91	4.14	2.30	−2.78
1961	−2.88	1.53	4.85	4.74
1962	7.81	6.66	5.99	3.81
1963	5.37	4.90	6.64	5.13
1964	4.29	5.83	5.43	5.51
1965	9.95	8.02	9.21	6.70
1966	10.03	13.19	11.15	14.87
1967	10.39	5.13	8.58	9.64
1968	4.31	8.44	6.37	5.58
1969	6.76	8.21	8.99	4.63
1970	1.84	3.05	4.17	1.85
1971	5.25	6.62	3.28	2.37
1972	3.14	6.71	7.97	7.03
1973	7.57	9.72	9.54	17.56
1974	8.13	7.45	1.29	3.71
1975	−11.70	−13.16	2.52	−1.83
1976	7.28	9.08	10.55	−0.44
1977	6.60	10.20	10.96	6.18

Quarter	1	2	3	4

INV = level of business inventories,
billions of 1958 dollars

Year	1	2	3	4
1956	111.3	112.5	113.5	114.7
1957	115.2	115.8	116.6	116.0
1958	114.7	113.4	113.4	114.4
1959	115.4	117.8	117.8	119.6
1960	122.3	123.3	123.9	123.2
1961	122.5	122.9	124.1	125.3
1962	127.2	128.9	130.4	131.3
1963	132.7	133.9	135.6	136.8
1964	137.9	139.4	140.7	142.1
1965	144.6	146.6	148.9	150.6
1966	153.1	156.4	159.2	162.9
1967	165.5	166.8	168.9	171.3
1968	172.4	174.5	176.1	177.5
1969	179.2	181.2	183.5	184.6
1970	185.1	185.9	186.9	187.4
1971	188.8	190.3	191.2	191.7
1972	192.5	194.2	196.2	198.0
1973	199.9	202.3	204.7	209.1
1974	211.1	212.9	213.3	214.2
1975	211.3	208.0	208.6	208.2
1976	210.0	212.3	214.9	214.8
1977	216.6	219.0	221.7	223.2

INR = fixed nonresidential investment,
billions of 1958 dollars

Year	1	2	3	4
1956	45.27	46.03	46.58	46.32
1957	46.43	46.37	47.40	46.24
1958	43.27	41.32	40.44	41.59
1959	42.67	44.06	45.43	45.56
1960	47.10	47.33	46.09	46.02
1961	45.12	46.02	46.31	47.69
1962	48.70	50.26	50.95	50.35
1963	49.85	51.37	52.66	53.91
1964	54.73	56.38	57.97	59.60
1965	63.56	66.22	68.52	71.73
1966	73.96	74.84	75.55	75.13
1967	73.21	72.92	72.55	73.50
1968	75.47	74.81	76.21	78.58
1969	80.41	80.20	81.29	80.58
1970	78.80	78.85	78.21	74.84
1971	76.10	75.61	75.85	77.39
1972	80.01	80.87	82.27	86.71
1973	90.70	92.19	93.55	93.45
1974	94.55	94.45	92.15	87.65
1975	82.30	79.12	78.32	78.52
1976	80.20	81.87	83.63	83.98
1977	87.69	89.18	90.11	91.01

Table 14.8 (*Continued*)

Quarter	1	2	3	4

IR = fixed residential investment in nonfarm structures,
billions of 1958 dollars

	1	2	3	4
1956	21.95	21.81	21.35	21.01
1957	20.41	19.95	19.77	19.84
1958	19.43	19.41	20.78	23.08
1959	25.68	26.58	26.05	25.11
1960	25.97	23.74	22.68	22.74
1961	22.74	23.04	24.34	24.84
1962	25.23	26.32	26.46	26.36
1963	27.32	29.37	30.09	31.09
1964	31.55	30.14	29.18	28.57
1965	29.41	30.24	29.21	28.88
1966	28.84	27.38	25.70	22.36
1967	21.88	24.56	26.05	27.98
1968	28.38	29.25	29.04	29.64
1969	30.58	30.46	28.94	27.30
1970	27.33	26.14	26.94	29.44
1971	31.76	35.18	37.33	38.64
1972	41.90	42.33	42.38	43.95
1973	44.29	42.73	40.00	36.87
1974	33.57	31.54	29.74	26.70
1975	24.73	25.06	26.52	28.80
1976	30.30	32.15	32.16	35.51
1977	35.98	39.43	39.37	41.05

M = money supply: demand deposits and currency (M1),
billions of 1958 dollars

	1	2	3	4
1956	144.3	143.5	142.0	141.5
1957	140.1	139.6	138.4	137.5
1958	136.8	138.1	138.6	139.9
1959	140.6	140.8	141.0	139.6
1960	138.0	137.5	138.1	138.2
1961	138.9	139.4	139.6	140.7
1962	140.4	140.5	139.9	139.9
1963	140.6	141.9	142.8	143.3
1964	143.7	144.6	146.2	147.6
1965	147.4	147.8	148.5	150.3
1966	151.2	151.3	150.3	149.1
1967	149.6	151.2	153.2	153.7
1968	153.8	155.0	156.7	157.7
1969	158.6	158.2	156.7	155.6
1970	154.7	154.8	155.4	155.3
1971	155.6	157.3	158.5	158.2
1972	158.9	160.9	162.8	164.7
1973	165.4	165.1	164.3	162.7
1974	161.9	159.6	157.0	154.0
1975	150.3	150.8	150.8	149.5
1976	149.0	150.3	150.2	150.7
1977	150.3	150.9	152.6	153.0

Quarter	1	2	3	4

P = implicit price deflator for GNP (1958 = 100)

	1	2	3	4
1956	93.9	94.7	95.8	96.6
1957	97.7	98.1	99.0	99.1
1958	99.5	99.7	100.3	100.6
1959	101.4	102.1	102.5	102.9
1960	103.6	103.8	104.2	104.4
1961	104.3	104.8	105.2	105.4
1962	106.3	106.6	106.9	107.6
1963	108.0	108.1	108.4	109.1
1964	109.5	109.8	110.4	110.7
1965	111.6	112.2	112.9	113.5
1966	114.6	116.0	116.6	117.7
1967	118.4	118.8	120.0	121.4
1968	122.9	124.4	125.5	127.3
1969	128.6	130.3	132.4	134.0
1970	136.0	137.7	138.9	140.8
1971	143.0	145.0	146.2	147.5
1972	149.6	150.6	151.9	153.6
1973	155.8	158.5	161.4	165.1
1974	168.5	173.2	178.0	183.3
1975	188.1	190.7	194.1	197.1
1976	199.1	201.5	203.8	206.5
1977	209.2	212.8	215.3	218.4

RL = long-term interest rate: market yield on long-term
U.S. Government Bonds
(nominal rate, % per annum, not seasonally adjusted)

	1	2	3	4
1956	2.887	2.990	3.127	3.300
1957	3.273	3.433	3.630	3.533
1958	3.250	3.150	3.570	3.753
1959	3.913	4.060	4.157	4.167
1960	4.223	4.107	3.823	3.907
1961	3.827	3.803	3.973	4.007
1962	4.060	3.890	3.977	3.877
1963	3.910	3.980	4.013	4.103
1964	4.157	4.163	4.143	4.140
1965	4.150	4.143	4.197	4.347
1966	4.557	4.583	4.777	4.697
1967	4.440	4.710	4.933	5.327
1968	5.243	5.303	5.073	5.417
1969	5.883	5.917	6.137	6.530
1970	6.563	6.820	6.650	6.267
1971	5.820	5.883	5.750	5.507
1972	5.650	5.657	5.603	5.607
1973	6.093	6.217	6.587	6.307
1974	6.637	7.047	7.270	6.977
1975	6.673	6.960	7.080	7.223
1976	6.910	6.880	6.780	6.553
1977	7.010	7.100	6.970	7.150

Table 14.8 (*Continued*)

Quarter	1	2	3	4

RS = short-term interest rate: market yield on 3-month
Treasury bills
(nominal rate, % per annum, not seasonally adjusted)

1956	2.327	2.567	2.583	3.033
1957	3.100	3.137	3.353	3.303
1958	1.760	0.957	1.680	2.690
1959	2.773	3.000	3.540	4.230
1960	3.873	2.993	2.360	2.307
1961	2.350	2.303	2.303	2.460
1962	2.723	2.713	2.840	2.813
1963	2.907	2.937	3.293	3.497
1964	3.530	3.477	3.497	3.683
1965	3.890	3.873	3.867	4.167
1966	4.610	4.587	5.043	5.210
1967	4.513	3.660	4.300	4.753
1968	5.050	5.520	5.197	5.587
1969	6.093	6.197	7.023	7.353
1970	7.210	6.677	6.330	5.353
1971	3.840	4.250	5.010	4.230
1972	3.437	3.770	4.220	4.863
1973	5.700	6.603	8.323	7.500
1974	7.617	8.153	8.190	7.360
1975	5.750	5.393	6.330	5.627
1976	4.917	5.157	5.150	4.673
1977	4.630	4.840	5.497	6.100

TRANSFERS = federal government transfer payments,
billions of 1958 dollars

1956	16.11	16.33	16.57	16.69
1957	16.78	18.36	18.02	19.19
1958	20.12	21.71	22.05	21.59
1959	21.47	21.10	21.45	22.23
1960	21.67	22.41	22.87	23.79
1961	25.38	26.02	25.89	25.38
1962	25.48	25.07	25.44	25.88
1963	26.58	25.90	26.08	26.25
1964	26.65	26.26	26.14	26.32
1965	26.81	26.65	29.12	27.81
1966	28.77	27.66	28.79	30.86
1967	32.33	32.75	33.20	32.64
1968	33.35	35.28	36.00	36.05
1969	36.14	36.97	36.23	36.49
1970	36.67	42.05	41.52	42.72
1971	42.43	45.99	45.92	45.84
1972	45.93	45.38	45.34	50.04
1973	49.66	50.43	50.77	50.58
1974	53.57	55.79	57.07	58.18
1975	61.66	65.79	66.21	66.05
1976	67.10	65.27	67.05	66.76
1977	67.33	65.71	67.06	66.64

Quarter	1	2	3	4

	UR = unemployment rate, percentage terms, seasonally adjusted			
1956	4.033	4.200	4.133	4.133
1957	3.933	4.100	4.233	4.933
1958	6.300	7.367	7.333	6.637
1959	5.833	5.100	5.267	5.600
1960	5.133	5.233	5.533	6.267
1961	6.800	7.000	6.767	6.200
1962	5.633	5.533	5.567	5.533
1963	5.767	5.733	5.500	5.567
1964	5.467	5.200	5.000	4.967
1965	4.900	4.667	4.367	4.100
1966	3.867	3.833	3.767	3.700
1967	3.833	3.833	3.800	3.900
1968	3.733	3.567	3.533	3.400
1969	3.400	3.433	3.567	3.567
1970	4.167	4.733	5.167	5.867
1971	5.900	5.900	6.033	5.967
1972	5.767	5.633	5.600	5.333
1973	4.933	4.900	4.800	4.767
1974	5.033	5.167	5.600	6.567
1975	8.233	8.867	8.500	8.300
1976	7.733	7.500	7.733	7.767
1977	7.467	7.100	6.900	6.633

	W = nominal wage rate, dollars per hour			
1956	1.904	1.932	1.969	2.013
1957	2.043	2.067	2.083	2.118
1958	2.156	2.178	2.219	2.227
1959	2.254	2.258	2.283	2.317
1960	2.374	2.381	2.396	2.414
1961	2.434	2.496	2.527	2.551
1962	2.570	2.606	2.649	2.682
1963	2.704	2.726	2.764	2.800
1964	2.854	2.886	2.937	2.956
1965	2.976	2.988	3.068	3.117
1966	3.161	3.226	3.308	3.365
1967	3.414	3.489	3.545	3.593
1968	3.687	2.753	3.837	3.882
1969	3.934	2.993	4.085	4.157
1970	4.273	4.327	4.420	4.457
1971	4.562	4.610	4.717	4.725
1972	4.809	4.870	4.920	5.025
1973	5.114	5.172	5.245	5.360
1974	5.457	5.584	5.731	5.904
1975	6.105	6.207	6.283	6.381
1976	6.539	6.660	6.798	6.924
1977	7.077	7.133	6.277	7.413

Table 14.8 (*Continued*)

Quarter	1	2	3	4
	WLTH = index of real household wealth†			
1956	1.335	1.343	1.351	1.358
1957	1.349	1.363	1.374	1.373
1958	1.371	1.394	1.419	1.460
1959	1.498	1.530	1.556	1.576
1960	1.573	1.575	1.577	1.586
1961	1.619	1.657	1.680	1.712
1962	1.721	1.700	1.673	1.674
1963	1.711	1.758	1.785	1.803
1964	1.841	1.873	1.895	1.928
1965	1.948	1.973	1.988	3.018
1966	2.026	1.989	1.938	1.901
1967	1.936	2.008	2.048	2.056
1968	2.056	2.100	2.153	2.190
1969	2.192	2.178	2.153	2.139
1970	2.123	2.083	2.056	2.074
1971	2.129	2.180	2.185	2.172
1972	2.202	2.274	2.311	2.354
1973	2.401	2.406	2.400	2.387
1974	2.361	2.322	2.254	2.179
1975	2.182	2.251	2.283	2.287
1976	2.341	2.404	2.442	2.464
1977	2.495	2.526	2.557	2.589
	YD = disposable income, billions of 1958 dollars			
1956	385.2	385.5	385.7	388.8
1957	390.5	390.8	394.4	389.6
1958	382.4	384.9	394.9	406.4
1959	413.0	424.1	417.4	422.4
1960	430.9	428.4	424.6	421.3
1961	422.6	431.8	438.0	447.8
1962	455.6	460.7	464.3	466.0
1963	470.2	475.0	484.5	487.4
1964	494.2	502.0	507.3	509.2
1965	523.3	530.0	539.2	551.6
1966	562.3	567.0	573.0	576.4
1967	575.8	579.3	586.5	592.5
1968	599.3	609.5	617.1	620.6
1969	626.7	629.8	631.0	627.9
1970	624.7	625.1	629.3	623.4
1971	637.7	645.1	648.3	655.7
1972	670.0	682.6	690.0	704.4
1973	718.9	717.9	719.2	720.6
1974	710.2	708.4	702.5	689.7
1975	672.8	678.4	700.3	706.3
1976	725.3	735.1	742.5	746.7
1977	762.2	775.4	782.5	793.8

† Data series for Household Net Worth obtained from the MIT–Federal Reserve–Penn econometric model data bank and deflated by price level *P*.

466

EXERCISES

14.1 Note in Figs. 14.15 to 14.24 that the higher rate of growth of government spending has a significant impact on most of the endogenous variables in the model, and in particular results in significantly lower unemployment but greater inflation. Explain the results of experiment 4 by tracing through the effects of the increased government spending. Why is residential investment in experiment 4 almost the same as in the base case even though GNP is so much greater?

14.2 (Possible term project.) The data that were used in the estimation of the macroeconomic model are listed in Table 14.8 and should be used to reconstruct the model. Begin by reestimating all the equations as they are specified in the text. Next experiment with alternative equation specifications. For example, alternative lag structures might be used in the consumption or investment equations. After the new version of the model has been estimated, the student should test it by performing a historical simulation and calculating rms simulation errors. Finally, the student should use the model to conduct a set of forecasting experiments. For example, the model might be used to predict the effects of a change in the propensity to consume or a change in the average tax rate.

14.3 Construct a complete block diagram for the tobacco model discussed in Section 14.2. The diagram should show the interrelationships between all the variables in the model. Use arrows in your diagram to indicate directions of causality.

14.4 (*a*) Suppose the government increases the tobacco support price SP. Using the tobacco model, explain how this will affect the actual price of tobacco leaf PACT and the production of tobacco leaf Q. Indicate all the causal links and the time lags (if any) between a change in the support price and changes in leaf price and leaf production. You may refer to the block diagram from Exercise 14.3.

   (*b*) Repeat the above analysis for a change in the government acreage allotment AL. Again, indicate all causal links and time lags between a change in acreage allotment and changes in leaf price and leaf production.

14.5 In using the financial simulation model to generate *pro forma* income statements and balance sheets, it was hypothesized that sales would drop to $900,000 in 1981 and then increase to $1.1 million in 1982 and $1.4 million in 1983. Suppose instead that sales drop to $800,000 in 1982 and $700,000 in 1983. Trace through the equations of the model to explain (qualitatively) how this would affect the company's financial position in 1982 and 1983. Indicate where preferred or common stock might be issued, and how long-term debt would change. (Students with access to a computer simulation package should actually perform the simulation.)

14.6 Rewrite the equations of the financial simulation model (Table 14.6) so that the model can be used to determine the breakeven point for sales, i.e., the value of sales that produces zero earnings. Note that this can be done by making sales an endogenous variable and earnings an input parameter.

THREE

TIME-SERIES MODELS

In the first two parts of this book we saw how econometric models—both single-equation regression models and multi-equation models—can be constructed and used to explain and forecast the future movements of one or more variables. In Part Three of the book we are again interested in constructing models and using them for forecasting, but these models are quite different from those that we worked with earlier. We no longer predict future movements in a variable by relating it to a set of other variables in a causal framework; instead we base our prediction solely on the past behavior of the variable and that variable alone.

As an example, consider the time function $y(t)$ drawn in the figure below, which might represent the historical performance of some economic or business variable—a stock market index, an interest rate, a production index, or perhaps the daily sales volume for some commodity. We may or may not been able to explain (based on economic theory, intuitive reasoning, etc.) why $y(t)$ behaved the way it did. If $y(t)$ represents the sales volume of some good, for example, it may have moved up or down partly in response to changes in prices, personal income, and interest rates (or so we might believe). However, much of its movement may have been due to factors that we may have simply not been able to explain, such as the weather, changes in consumer taste, or simply seasonal (or aseasonal) cycles in consumer spending.

It may be difficult or impossible to explain the movement of $y(t)$ through the use of a structural model, i.e., by relating it explicitly to other economic variables. This might happen if, for example, data are not available for those explanatory variables which are believed to affect $y(t)$. Or if data were available,

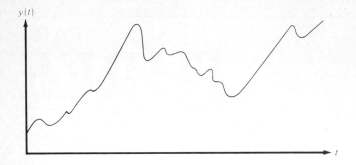

the estimation of a regression model for $y(t)$ might result in standard errors that are so large as to make most of the estimated coefficients insignificant and the standard error of forecast unacceptably large.

Even if we could estimate a statistically significant regression equation for $y(t)$, the result may not be useful for forecasting purposes. To obtain a forecast for $y(t)$ from a regression equation, those explanatory variables that are not lagged must themselves be forecasted, and this may be more difficult than forecasting $y(t)$ itself. The standard error of forecast for $y(t)$ with future values of the explanatory variables known may be small (if the regression equation fits well). However, when the future values of the explanatory variables are unknown, their forecast errors may be so large as to make the total forecast error for $y(t)$ too large to be acceptable.

Clearly, then, situations may exist where it is impossible or undesirable to "explain" $y(t)$ using a structural model, and we might ask whether there is an alternative means of obtaining a forecast of $y(t)$. Are there ways in which we can observe the time series in the figure and draw some conclusions about its *past* behavior that would allow us to infer something about its probable *future* behavior? For example, is there some kind of overall upward trend in $y(t)$ which, because it has dominated the past behavior of the series, might dominate its future behavior? Or does the series exhibit some kind of cyclical behavior which we could extrapolate into the future? If some kind of systematic behavior of this type is present, we can attempt to construct a *model* for the time series which does not offer a structural explanation for its behavior in terms of other variables but does replicate its past behavior in a way that might help us forecast its future behavior. On this basis the *time-series model* accounts for patterns in the past movements of a particular variable, and uses that information to predict future movements of the variable. In a sense a time-series model is just a sophisticated method of extrapolation. Yet, as we will see in this part of the book, it may often provide a very effective tool for forecasting.

In this book we have divided economic and business forecasting models into three general classes, each of which involves a different level of comprehension about the real world processes that one is trying to model. In Part One of the book we discussed single-equation regression models, where the variable of interest is explained by a single function (linear or nonlinear) of explanatory variables. Next, in Part Two of the book we examined multi-equation simulation models, where two or more endogenous variables are related to each other (and perhaps to one or more exogenous variables) through a set of equations, which can be solved simultaneously (i.e., simulated) to produce forecasts over time. In this third part of the book we concern ourselves with time-series models, in which we have no structural knowledge about the real world causal relationships that affect the variable we are trying to forecast.

Clearly a choice will often have to be made as to which type of model should be developed in order to best make a forecast. This choice may be difficult and will depend not only on how much we know about the workings of the real world process but also on how much time and energy we can afford to spend on the modeling process. The development of a single-equation regression model may not be too difficult, but the construction of a multi-equation simulation model might require large expenditures of time and effort. The gains that result from this effort might include a better understanding of the relationships and structure involved as well as the ability to make a better forecast. However, in some cases, these gains may be so small that they are outweighed by the heavy cost involved.

The choice of a time-series model will usually result in cases where little information is known about the determinants of the variable of primary concern and a sufficiently large amount of data is available to construct a time series of reasonable length. An example might be to forecast on a weekly or monthly basis a cyclical series for the production of a commodity (we will present as an example a time-series model to forecast monthly hog production). In some cases we will have information about the physical processes involved, and it will not be obvious as to whether a time-series model or a single-equation regression model is preferable as a means of forecasting. One choice would be to build a regression model; a second choice would be to build a time-series model; and, as will see in Chapter 20, a third choice is to *combine* time-series analysis with regression analysis. We will see that a powerful method of forecasting involves constructing a regression model in which, say, an interest rate is related to several economic variables, after which a time-series model is constructed to explain the behavior of the residual term from the regression.

The following chapters will present an introduction, on a rather elementary level, to the science and art of developing time-series models for purposes of forecasting. The models that we deal with are actually only a subset of a broader class of models and techniques for data analysis that falls under the general rubric of time-series analysis. We do not discuss, for example, recent developments in the theory of *spectral analysis* and its application to economic modeling and forecasting. Instead we concentrate on a class of linear time-series models introduced by Box and Jenkins that have recently found wide application to economic and business forecasting.†

Since time-series analysis builds on the development of the single-equation regression model, we treat time-series models in the last part of the book, even

---

† G. E. P. Box and G. M. Jenkins, *Time Series Analysis* (San Francisco: Holden-Day, 1970).

though they are the "simplest" class of models in terms of their explanation of the real world. To forecast a short-term interest rate, we might use a regression model to relate that variable to GNP, prices, and the money supply. A time series for interest rates would relate that variable to its past values, and to variables that describe the random nature of its past behavior. The model, like most regression models, is an equation containing a set of coefficients that must be estimated. Unlike regression models, however, the equation is nonlinear in the coefficients, so that a nonlinear version of ordinary least squares is necessary for estimation purposes.

Part Three begins with a brief survey of simple extrapolation methods (in effect deterministic models of time series), as well as methods for smoothing and seasonally adjusting time series. Extrapolation techniques have been used widely for many years and for some applications provide a simple and yet adequate means of forecasting. Smoothing and seasonal adjustment are also useful techniques, which in many instances can facilitate the forecasting or interpretation of a time series.

In Chapter 16 we present a brief introduction to the nature of stochastic (i.e., random) time series. We discuss how stochastic processes are generated, what they look like, and most important, how they are described. We also discuss some of the characteristics of stochastic processes and in particular develop the concept of stationarity. Then we describe autocorrelation functions and show how they can be used as a means of describing time series and as a tool for testing their properties. The concepts and tools developed in this chapter are essential to the discussion of time-series models in the chapters that follow.

Chapter 17 develops linear models for time series, including moving average models, autoregressive models, and mixed autoregressive–moving average models for stationary time series. We show how certain types of nonstationary time series can be differenced one or more times so as to produce a stationary series. This enables us to develop a general integrated autoregressive–moving average model (ARIMA model) for time series. Finally, we show how autocorrelation functions can be used to specify and characterize a time-series model for any particular time series.

Chapters 18 and 19 deal with use of time-series models to make forecasts. Chapter 18 explains how parameters of a time-series model are estimated and how a specification of the model can be verified. Chapter 19 discusses how the model can then be used to produce a forecast. We also show how time series are adaptive in nature, i.e., how they produce forecasts in a way that adapts to new information. The last part of Chapter 19 deals with forecast errors and shows how confidence intervals can be determined for forecasts.

The last chapter of Part Three develops some examples of applications of time-series models to economic and business forecasting. While Chapters 15 to 19 concentrate on the science of time-series model building, Chapter 20 is concerned largely with the art of time-series models. In that chapter we lead the reader step by step through the construction of several time-series models and their application to forecasting problems.

FIFTEEN

SMOOTHING AND EXTRAPOLATION
OF TIME SERIES

As explained in the introduction to Part Three, time-series models in effect provide a sophisticated method of extrapolating time series. There are situations, however, when less sophisticated methods of extrapolation can be used for forecasting purposes. Such situations might arise when projections for a large number of time series must be generated quickly, so that time and resources do not permit the use of formal time-series modeling techniques, or when there is good reason to believe that a particular time series follows a single trend, thus obviating the need for a more complicated model. We therefore begin by discussing some simple (and not so simple) methods of extrapolation. As we will see, these extrapolation techniques represent *deterministic models* of time series.

There are also situations when it is desirable to *smooth* a time series and thereby eliminate some of the more volatile short-term fluctuations. Smoothing might be done before making a forecast or simply to make the time series easier to analyze and interpret. Smoothing might also be done to remove seasonal fluctuations, i.e., to *deseasonalize* (or *seasonally adjust*) a time series. We will discuss smoothing and seasonal adjustment in the second section of this chapter.

15.1 SIMPLE EXTRAPOLATION MODELS

We begin by explaining how to construct simple models that can be used to forecast the future behavior of a time series on the basis of its past behavior. These models are *deterministic* in that no reference is made to the sources or nature of the underlying randomness in the series. Essentially the models involve extrapolation techniques that have been standard tools of the trade in economic and business forecasting for years. Although they usually do not provide as much forecasting accuracy as the modern stochastic time-series models that will be developed in later chapters, there are situations in which they provide a simple, inexpensive, and still quite acceptable means of forecasting. It is therefore important to understand these techniques.

Most of the time series that we encounter are not continuous in time; instead they consist of discrete observations made at regular intervals of time. A typical time series might be given by Fig. 15.1. We denote the values of that series by y_t, so that y_1 represents the first observation, y_2 the second, and y_T the *last* observation that we have for the series.† Our objective is to build a model describing the series y_t and to use that model to make a forecast of y_t beyond the last observation y_T. We denote the forecast one period ahead by $\hat{y}_{T+1}$, two periods ahead by $\hat{y}_{T+2}$, and l periods ahead by $\hat{y}_{T+l}$.

If the number of observations is not too large, the simplest and most complete representation of y_t would be given by polynomial whose degree is 1 less than the number of observations; i.e., we could describe y_t by a continuous function of time $f(t)$, where

$$f(t) = a_0 + a_1 t + a_2 t^2 + \cdots + a_n t^n \tag{15.1}$$

and $n = T - 1$. Such a polynomial (if the a's are chosen correctly) will pass through *every point* in the time series y_t. Thus, we can be sure that $f(t)$ will equal y_t at every time t from 1 to T. Can we, however, have any confidence that the *forecast* of y_t one or more periods ahead generated by $f(t)$ will be at all close to

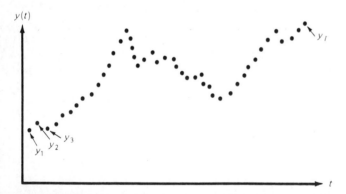

Figure 15.1 Discrete time series.

---

† In Part Three of the book we use small letters, for example, y_t, to denote time series. The reader should not confuse this with the notation in Part One of the book, where a small letter denotes deviations from the mean.

the actual future values taken on by y_t? Will, for example, the forecast

$$f(T + 1) = a_0 + a_1(T + 1) + a_2(T + 1)^2 + \cdots + a_{T-1}(T + 1)^{T-1} = \hat{y}_{T+1}$$

be close to the actual future value y_{T+1}? Unfortunately, we have no way of knowing the answer to this question unless additional prior information is available. The difficulty with the model given by Eq. (15.1) is that it does not describe y_t; it merely *reproduces* y_t. It does not capture any characteristics of y_t that might repeat themselves in the future. Thus, although $f(t)$ correlates perfectly with y_t, it is of little use for forecasting y_t.

15.1.1 Simple Extrapolation Models

One of the basic characteristics of y_t that can be described is its long-run growth pattern. Despite the short-run up-and-down movement, it is possible that y_t might exhibit a clear-cut upward trend. If we believe that this upward trend exists and will continue (and there may not be any reason why we should), we can construct a simple model that describes that trend and can be used to forecast, i.e., extrapolate, y_t.

The simplest extrapolation model is the *linear trend model*. If one believes that a series y_t will increase in constant absolute amounts each time period, one can predict y_t in the future by fitting the trend line

$$y_t = c_1 + c_2 t \tag{15.2}$$

where t is time and y_t is the value of y at time t. t is usually chosen to equal 0 in the base period (first observation) and to increase by 1 during each successive period. For example, if we determine by regression that

$$y_t = 27.5 + 3.2t \tag{15.3}$$

we can predict that the value of y in period $t + 1$ will be 3.2 units higher than the previous value.

It may be more realistic to assume that the series y_t grows with constant percentage increases, rather than constant absolute increases. This assumption is the basis for the second simple example of a trend model which is the *exponential growth curve*:

$$y_t = f(t) = Ae^{rt} \tag{15.4}$$

Here A and r would be chosen to maximize the correlation between $f(t)$ and y_t. A forecast one period ahead would then be given by

$$\hat{y}_{T+1} = Ae^{r(T+1)} \tag{15.5}$$

and l periods ahead by

$$\hat{y}_{T+l} = Ae^{r(T+l)} \tag{15.6}$$

This is illustrated in Fig. 15.2. The parameters A and r can be estimated by taking the logarithms of both sides of (15.4) and fitting the log-linear regression

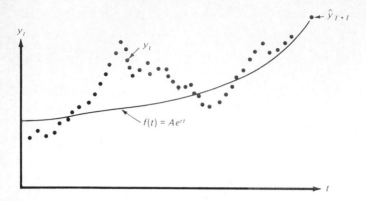

Figure 15.2 Exponential growth curve.

equation†

$$\log y_t = c_1 + c_2 t \tag{15.7}$$

where $c_1 = \log A$
$\qquad c_2 = r$

A third extrapolation method is based on the *autoregressive trend model*

$$y_t = c_1 + c_2 y_{t-1} \tag{15.8}$$

In using such an extrapolation procedure, one has the option of fixing $c_1 = 0$, in which case c_2 represents the rate of change of the series y. If, on the other hand, c_2 is set equal to 1, with c_1 not equal to 0, the extrapolated series will increase by the same absolute amount each time period. The autoregressive trend model is illustrated in Fig. 15.3 for three different values of c_2 (in all cases $c_1 = 1$).

A variation of the previous model is the *logarithmic autoregressive trend model*

$$\log y_t = c_1 + c_2 \log y_{t-1} \tag{15.9}$$

If c_1 is fixed to be 0, then the value of c_2 is the compounded rate of growth of the series y. Both linear and compound extrapolation based on the autoregressive model are commonly used as a simple means of forecasting.

Note that the four models described above basically involve regressing y_t (or $\log y_t$) against a function of time (linear or exponential) and/or itself lagged. Alternative models can be developed by making the function slightly more complicated. As examples, let us examine two other simple extrapolation models, the *quadratic trend model*, and the *logistic growth curve*.

The quadratic trend model is a simple extension of the linear trend model and just involves adding a term in t^2

$$y_t = c_1 + c_2 t + c_3 t^2 \tag{15.10}$$

---

† Note that in the exponential growth model the logarithm of y_t is assumed to grow at a constant rate. If $y_{t+1} = Ae^{rt}$, then $y_{t+1}/y_t = e^r$, and $\log y_{t+1} - \log y_t = r$.

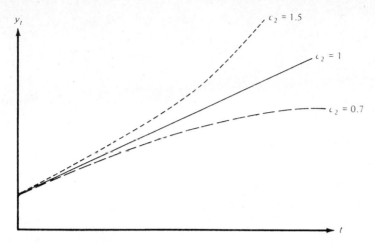

Figure 15.3 Autoregressive trend model.

If c_2 and c_3 are both positive, y_t will always be increasing but even more rapidly as time goes on. If c_2 is negative and c_3 positive, y_t will at first decrease but later increase. If both c_2 and c_3 are negative, y_t will always decrease. The various cases are illustrated in Fig. 15.4 ($c_1 > 0$ in each case). Note that even if the data show that y_t has generally been increasing over time, estimation of Eq. (15.10) might yield a positive value for c_3 but a negative value for c_2. This can occur (as shown in Fig. 15.4) because the data usually only span a portion of the trend curve.

A somewhat more complicated model, at least in terms of its estimation, is the *logistic curve*, given by

$$y_t = \frac{1}{k + ab^t} \qquad b > 0 \qquad\qquad (15.11)$$

This equation is nonlinear in the parameters (k, a, and b) and therefore must be estimated using a nonlinear estimation procedure (as described in Chapter 9). While this can add computational expense (and perhaps difficulty), there are some cases in which it is worth it. As shown in Figure 15.5, Eq. (15.11) represents an S-shaped curve which might be used to represent the sales of a product that will someday saturate the market (so that the total stock of the good in circulation will approach some plateau, or, equivalently, additional sales will approach zero).†

---

† If the estimation of (15.11) turns out to be problematical, the following *approximation* to the logistic curve can be estimated using ordinary least squares:

$$\frac{\Delta y_t}{y_{t-1}} = c_1 - c_2 y_{t-1}$$

The parameter c_2 should always be less than 1 and would typically be in the vicinity of 0.05 to 0.5. This equation is in fact a discrete-time approximation to the differential equation $dy/dt = c_2 y(c_1 - y)$, and the *solution* to this differential equation has the form of Eq. (15.11).

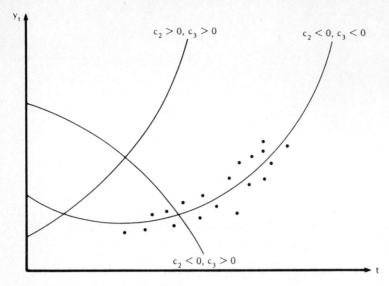

Figure 15.4 Quadratic trend model.

Other S-shaped curves can be used in addition to the logistic curve. One very simple function with an S shape that can be used to model sales saturation patterns is given by

$$y_t = e^{k_1 - (k_2/t)} \qquad (15.12)$$

Note that if we take the logarithms of both sides, we have an equation linear in the parameters α and β that can be estimated using ordinary least squares:

$$\log y_t = k_1 - \frac{k_2}{t} \qquad (15.13)$$

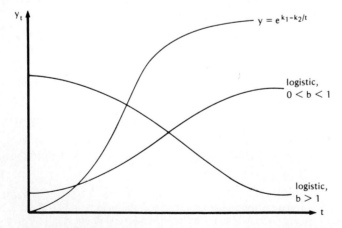

Figure 15.5 S-shaped curves.

This curve is also shown in Fig. 15.5. Note that it begins at the origin and rises more steeply than the logistic curve.

Example 15.1 Forecasting department store sales In this example simple extrapolation models are used to forecast monthly retail sales of department stores. The time series is listed below, where monthly observations are seasonally adjusted and cover the period from January 1968 to March 1974, the units of measurement are millions of dollars, and the source of the data is the U.S. Department of Commerce.

	1968	1969	1970	1971	1972	1973	1974
January	2,582	2,839	3,034	3,287	3,578	4,121	4,456
February	2,621	2,876	3,029	3,342	3,650	4,233	4,436
March	2,690	2,881	3,045	3,336	3,664	4,439	4,699
April	2,635	2,967	3,066	3,427	3,643	4,167	
May	2,676	2,944	3,077	3,413	3,838	4,326	
June	2,714	2,939	3,046	3,503	3,792	4,329	
July	2,834	3,014	3,094	3,472	3,899	4,423	
August	2,789	3,031	3,053	3,511	3,845	4,351	
September	2,768	2,995	3,071	3,618	4,007	4,406	
October	2,785	2,998	3,186	3,554	4,092	4,357	
November	2,886	3,012	3,167	3,641	3,937	4,485	
December	2,842	3,031	3,230	3,607	4,008	4,445	

One might wish to forecast monthly sales for April, May, and the months following in 1974. For instructional purposes, we extrapolate sales for April 1974. The results of four regressions associated with four of the trend models described above are listed below. Standard regression statistics are shown with t statistics in parentheses:

Linear trend model:

$$SALES_t = 2463.1 + 26.70\,t \qquad (15.14)$$
$$\;(84.9)\quad\;\;(39.5)$$

$$R^2 = .995 \qquad F(1/73) = 2{,}000 \qquad SER = 126.9 \qquad DW = .38$$

Logarithmic linear trend model (exponential growth):

$$\log SALES_t = 7.849 + .0077\,t \qquad (15.15)$$
$$\;(1{,}000)\quad\;\;(52.6)$$

$$R^2 = .974 \qquad F(1/73) = 3{,}000 \qquad SER = .027 \qquad DW = .56$$

Autoregressive trend model:

$$SALES_t = 4.918 + 1.007\,SALES_{t-1} \qquad (15.16)$$
$$\;(.09)\quad\;\;(65.05)$$

$$R^2 = .983 \qquad F(1/73) = 4{,}000 \qquad SER = 78.07 \qquad DW = 2.82$$

Logarithmic autoregressive trend model:

$$\log \text{SALES}_t = \underset{(.16)}{.0188} + \underset{(70.37)}{.9987} \log \text{SALES}_{t-1} \qquad (15.17)$$

$$R^2 = .985 \qquad F(1/73) = 5{,}000 \qquad \text{SER} = .021 \qquad \text{DW} = 2.80$$

In the first regression, a time variable running from 0 to 74 was constructed and then used as the independent variable. When $t = 75$ is placed in the right-hand side of the equation

$$\text{SALES} = 2{,}463.1 + 26.70t \qquad (15.18)$$

the resulting forecast is 4,465.8. The use of the second log-linear equation yields a forecast of 4,551.5. The third regression, based on an autoregressive process, yields an extrapolated value for April 1974 of 4,736.8:

$$4{,}736.8 \approx 4.92 + 1.007 \times 4{,}699$$

If the constant term were dropped from Eq. (15.17), the extrapolated value would be 4,738.24. The fourth regression result is based on the logarithmic

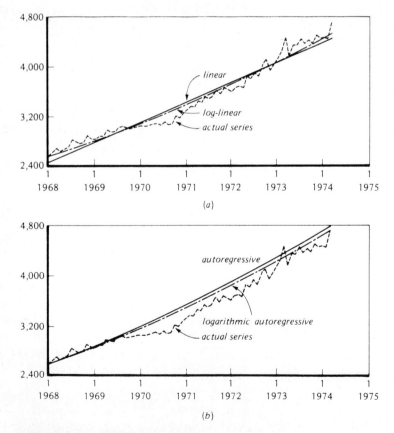

Figure 15.6 Simulated and actual sales.

autoregressive model. The extrapolated value in this case is 4,735.6. If one were to calculate a compounded growth rate for the series and to extrapolate on the basis that the growth rate remains unchanged, the extrapolated value would be 4,739.3.

The simulated and actual series are plotted for each of the four extrapolation models in Fig. 15.6a and b. One can see from the figure that the two autoregressive models are closer to the actual series at the end of the period. Of course, other trend models could be used to extrapolate the data. For example, the reader might try to calculate a forecast based on a quadratic trend model (see Exercise 15.1).

Simple extrapolation methods such as those used in the preceding example are frequently the basis for making casual long-range forecasts of variables ranging from GNP to population to pollution indices. Although they can be useful as a way of quickly formulating initial forecasts, they usually provide little forecasting accuracy. The analyst who estimates an extrapolation model is at least advised to calculate a standard error of forecast and forecast confidence interval following the methods presented in Chapter 8.† More important, the analyst should realize that there are alternative models that can be used to obtain forecasts with smaller standard errors.

15.1.2 Moving Average Models

Another class of deterministic models that are often used for forecasting consists of *moving average models*. As a simple example, assume that we are forecasting a monthly time series. We might use the model

$$f(t) = \tfrac{1}{12}(y_{t-1} + y_{t-2} + \cdots + y_{t-12}) \tag{15.19}$$

Then, a forecast one period ahead would be given by

$$\hat{y}_{T+1} = \tfrac{1}{12}(y_T + y_{T-1} + \cdots + y_{T-11}) \tag{15.20}$$

The moving average model is useful if we believe that a likely value for our series next month is a simple average of its values over the past 12 months. It may be unrealistic, however, to assume that a good forecast of y_t would be given by a simple average of its past values. It is often more reasonable to have more recent values of y_t play a greater role than earlier values. In such a case recent values should be weighted more heavily in the moving average. In other words, if y_{T+1} is to be an average of all the past values of y_t, we might, in taking the average, want to weight y_T most heavily, y_{T-1} somewhat less heavily, etc. A deterministic forecasting model that accomplishes this is the *exponentially*

---

† One should keep in mind that the autoregressive models of Eqs. (15.8) and (15.9) involve regression with a lagged dependent variable. If the additive error process is serially correlated, the coefficient estimates will be biased, as will the estimate of the standard error of forecast.

weighted moving average (EWMA) model:

$$\hat{y}_{T+1} = \alpha y_T + \alpha(1 - \alpha)y_{T-1} + \alpha(1 - \alpha)^2 y_{T-2} + \cdots$$

$$= \alpha \sum_{\tau=0}^{\infty} (1 - \alpha)^{\tau} y_{T-\tau} \tag{15.21}$$

Here α is a number between 0 and 1 that indicates how heavily we weight recent values relative to older ones.† With $\alpha = 1$, for example, our forecast becomes

$$\hat{y}_{T+1} = y_T \tag{15.22}$$

and we ignore any values of y that occurred before y_T. As α becomes smaller, we place greater emphasis on more distant values of y.‡ Note that Eq. (15.21) represents a true average, since

$$\alpha \sum_{\tau=0}^{\infty} (1 - \alpha)^{\tau} = \frac{\alpha}{1 - (1 - \alpha)} = 1 \tag{15.23}$$

so that the weights indeed sum to unity.

If we want to make a forecast $\hat{y}_{T+l}$ more than one period ahead using an exponentially weighted moving average model, we can modify Eq. (15.21) to include a weighted average of the more recent short-run forecasts $\hat{y}_{T+l-1}$, $\hat{y}_{T+l-2}, \ldots, \hat{y}_{T+1}$. This logical extension of the EWMA model is given by

$$\hat{y}_{T+l} = \alpha\hat{y}_{T+l-1} + \alpha(1 - \alpha)\hat{y}_{T+l-2} + \cdots + \alpha(1 - \alpha)^{l-2}\hat{y}_{T+1}$$

$$+ \alpha(1 - \alpha)^{l-1}y_T + \alpha(1 - \alpha)^l y_{T-1} + \alpha(1 - \alpha)^{l+1}y_{T-2}$$

$$+ \alpha(1 - \alpha)^{l+2}y_{T-3} + \cdots \tag{15.24}$$

As an example, consider a forecast two periods ahead ($l = 2$), which would be given by

$$\hat{y}_{T+2} = \alpha\hat{y}_{T+1} + \alpha(1 - \alpha)y_T + \alpha(1 - \alpha)^2 y_{T-1} + \cdots$$

$$= \alpha\left[\alpha y_T + \alpha(1 - \alpha)y_{T-1} + \cdots\right] + \alpha(1 - \alpha)y_T$$

$$+ \alpha(1 - \alpha)^2 y_{T-1} + \cdots$$

$$= \alpha^2 \sum_{\tau=0}^{\infty} (1 - \alpha)^{\tau} y_{T-\tau} + \alpha(1 - \alpha) \sum_{\tau=0}^{\infty} (1 - \alpha)^{\tau} y_{T-\tau}$$

$$= \alpha \sum_{\tau=0}^{\infty} (1 - \alpha)^{\tau} y_{T-\tau} \tag{15.25}$$

---

† The reader might note that this model is similar to the Koyck distributed lag model discussed in Chapter 9. In fact Eq. (15.21) says that y_t is related to a Koyck lag distribution of past values of y_t —rather than past values of some explanatory variable x_1, as in Chapter 9.

‡ The reader might suspect that if the series has an upward (downward) trend, the EWMA model will underpredict (overpredict) future values of y_t. This will indeed be the case, since the model averages past values of y_t to produce a forecast. If y_t has been growing steadily in the past, the EWMA forecast $\hat{y}_{T+1}$ will thus be *smaller* than the most recent value y_T, and if the series continues to grow steadily in the future, $\hat{y}_{T+1}$ will be an underprediction of the true value y_{T+1}. This suggests that one ought to remove any trend from the data before using the EWMA technique. Once an untrended initial forecast has been made, the trend term can be added in order to obtain a final forecast for the time series.

Note that the two-period forecast is the same as the one-period forecast. The weightings on $y_T, y_{T-1}, \dots,$ in the EWMA model are the same as they were before, but we are now extrapolating the average ahead an extra period. In fact, it is not difficult to show (see Exercise 15.4) that the l-period forecast $\hat{y}_{T+l}$ is also given by Eq. (15.25).

The moving average forecasts represented by Eqs. (15.20), (15.21), and (15.24) are all *adaptive forecasts*. By "adaptive" we mean that they automatically adjust themselves to the most recently available data. Consider, for example, a simple four-period moving average. Suppose y_{20} in Fig. 15.7 represents the most recent data point. Then our forecast will be given by

$$\hat{y}_{21} = \tfrac{1}{4}(y_{20} + y_{19} + y_{18} + y_{17}) \qquad (15.26)$$

and a forecast two periods ahead will be given by

$$\hat{y}_{22} = \tfrac{1}{4}(\hat{y}_{21} + y_{20} + y_{19} + y_{18}) = \tfrac{5}{16}y_{20} + \tfrac{5}{16}y_{19} + \tfrac{5}{16}y_{18} + \tfrac{1}{16}y_{17} \quad (15.27)$$

These forecasts are represented by crosses in Fig. 15.7. If y_{21} were known, we would forecast y_{22} one period ahead as

$$\hat{\hat{y}}_{22} = \tfrac{1}{4}(y_{21} + y_{20} + y_{19} + y_{18})$$

This forecast is represented by a circled cross in Fig. 15.7. Now suppose that the *actual* value of y_{21} turns out to be larger than the predicted value, i.e.,

$$y_{21} > \hat{y}_{21}$$

The actual value of y_{22} is, of course, not known, but we would expect that $\hat{\hat{y}}_{22}$ would provide a better forecast than $\hat{y}_{22}$ because of the extra information used in the adaptive process. The EWMA forecast would exhibit the same adaptive behavior. Note, however, that the simple exponential trend model of Eq. (15.4) is not adaptive, i.e., does not change in response to a new data point.

Although the moving average models described above are certainly useful, they do not provide us with information about *forecast confidence*. The reason is that no regression is used to estimate the model, so that we cannot calculate standard errors, nor can we describe or explain the stochastic (or unexplained) component of the time series. It is this stochastic component that creates the error in our forecast. Unless the stochastic component is explained through the

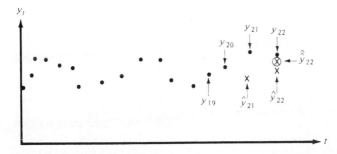

Figure 15.7 Adaptive forecasts.

modeling process, little can be said about the kinds of forecast errors that might be expected. This is one reason why stochastic time-series models often turn out to be more useful tools for forecasting.

15.2 SMOOTHING AND SEASONAL ADJUSTMENT

Smoothing techniques provide a means of removing or at least reducing volatile short-term fluctuations in a time series. This can be useful since it is often easier to discern trends and cyclical patterns and otherwise visually analyze a smoothed series. Seasonal adjustment is really a special form of smoothing; it removes seasonal (cyclical) oscillations from the series rather than irregular short-term fluctuations.

15.2.1 Smoothing Techniques

In the last section we discussed moving average models (simple and exponentially weighted) in the context of forecasting, but these models also provide a basis for smoothing time series. For example, one of the simplest ways to smooth a series is to take an *n-period moving average*. Denoting the original series by y_t and the smoothed series by $\tilde{y}_t$, we have

$$\tilde{y}_t = \frac{1}{n}(y_t + y_{t-1} + \cdots + y_{t-n+1}) \tag{15.28}$$

Of course, the larger the n the smoother the $\tilde{y}_t$ will be. One problem with this moving average is that it uses only *past* (and current) values of y_t to obtain each value of $\tilde{y}_t$. This problem is easily remedied by using a *centered moving average*. For example, a five-period centered moving average is given by

$$\tilde{y}_t = \tfrac{1}{5}(y_{t+2} + y_{t+1} + y_t + y_{t-1} + y_{t-2}) \tag{15.29}$$

Exponential smoothing simply involves the use of the exponentially weighted moving average model for smoothing. (Recall that this model assigns heavier weights to recent values of y_t.) The exponentially smoothed series $\tilde{y}_t$ is given by

$$\tilde{y}_t = \alpha y_t + \alpha(1 - \alpha)y_{t-1} + \alpha(1 - \alpha)^2 y_{-2} + \cdots \tag{15.30}$$

where the summation in Eq. (15.30) extends all the way back through the length of the series. In fact, $\tilde{y}_t$ can be calculated much more easily if we write

$$(1 - \alpha)\tilde{y}_{t-1} = \alpha(1 - \alpha)y_{t-1} + \alpha(1 - \alpha)^2 y_{t-2} + \cdots \tag{15.31}$$

Now subtracting (15.31) from (15.30) we obtain a recursive formula for the computation of $\tilde{y}_t$:

$$\tilde{y}_t = \alpha y_t + (1 - \alpha)\tilde{y}_{t-1} \tag{15.32}$$

Note that the closer α is to 1 the more heavily the current value of y_t is weighted in generating $\tilde{y}_t$. Thus smaller values of α imply a more heavily smoothed series.

There are instances in which one might wish to heavily smooth a series but not give very much weight to past data points. In such a case the use of Eq.

(15.32) with a small value of α (say 0.1) would not be acceptable. Instead one can apply *double exponential smoothing*. As the name implies, the singly smoothed series $\tilde{y}_t$ from Eq. (15.32) is just smoothed again:

$$\tilde{\tilde{y}}_t = \alpha\tilde{y}_t + (1 - \alpha)\tilde{\tilde{y}}_{t-1} \tag{15.33}$$

In this way a larger value of α can be used, and the resulting series $\tilde{\tilde{y}}_t$ will still be heavily smoothed.

The simple exponential smoothing formula of Eq. (15.32) can also be modified by incorporating average *changes* in the long-run trend (secular increase or decline) of the series. This is the basis for *Holt's two-parameter exponential smoothing* method (which is still best applied after basic long-run trend has been removed).[†] Now the smoothed series $\tilde{y}_t$ is found from two recursive equations and depends on two smoothing parameters, α and γ, both of which must lie between 0 and 1 (again, the smaller the α and γ the heavier the smoothing):

$$\tilde{y}_t = \alpha y_t + (1 - \alpha)(\tilde{y}_{t-1} + r_{t-1}) \tag{15.34}$$

$$r_t = \gamma(\tilde{y}_t - \tilde{y}_{t-1}) + (1 - \gamma)r_{t-1} \tag{15.35}$$

Here r_t is a smoothed series representing the trend, i.e., average rate of increase, in the smoothed series $\tilde{y}_t$. This trend is added in when computing the smoothed series $\tilde{y}_t$ in Eq. (15.34), thereby preventing $\tilde{y}_t$ from deviating considerably from recent values of the original series y_t. This is particularly useful if the smoothing method is going to be used as a basis for forecasting. An *l*-period forecast can be generated from Eqs. (15.34) and (15.35) using

$$\hat{y}_{T+l} = \tilde{y}_T + lr_T \tag{15.36}$$

Thus the *l*-period forecast takes the most recent smoothed value $\tilde{y}_T$ and adds in an expected increase lr_T based on the (smoothed) long-run trend. (If the data have been detrended, the trend should be added back to the forecast.)

As the reader may have gathered by this point, smoothing methods tend to be rather *ad hoc*, particularly when they are used to generate forecasts. One problem is that we have no way of determining the "correct" values of the smoothing parameters, so that their choice becomes somewhat arbitrary. If our objective is simply to smooth the series to make it easier to interpret or analyze, then this is not really a problem, since we can choose the smoothing parameters to give us the extent of smoothing desired. We must be careful, however, when using an equation like (15.36) for forecasting and recognize that the resulting forecast will be somewhat arbitrary.[‡]

[†] C. C. Holt, "Forecasting Seasonals and Trends by Exponentially Weighted Moving Averages," unpublished research report, Carnegie Institute of Technology, Pittsburgh, 1957.

[‡] A number of other smoothing techniques exist, several of which are often applied to forecasting problems. For a detailed treatment of some of these other techniques, see C. W. J. Granger and P. Newbold, *Forecasting Economic Time Series* (New York: Academic, 1977); and S. Makridakis and S. C. Wheelwright, *Forecasting Methods and Applications* (New York: Wiley, 1978).

Example 15.2 Monthly housing starts The time series for monthly housing starts in the United States provides a good example for the application of smoothing and seasonal adjustment methods.† The series fluctuates considerably and also exhibits strong seasonal variation. In this example we smooth the series using the moving average and exponential smoothing methods.

We begin by using three- and seven-period centered moving averages to smooth the series; i.e., we generate the smoothed series $\tilde{y}_t$ from the original series y_t using

$$\tilde{y}_t = \frac{1}{n} \sum_{i=0}^{n-1} y_{t+(1/2)(n-1)-i} \tag{15.37}$$

where $n = 3$ or 7. Note that since the moving average is centered, there is no need to detrend the series before smoothing it. The original series, together with the two smoothed series, are shown in Fig. 15.8. Observe that the use of the seven-period moving average heavily smoothes the series and even eliminates some of the seasonal variation.

We now use the exponential smoothing method, i.e., we apply Eq. (15.32). Since the original series is growing over time and the exponentially weighted moving average is not centered, the smoothed series will underestimate the original series unless we first detrend the series. To detrend the original series we assumed a linear trend (we could of course test alternative

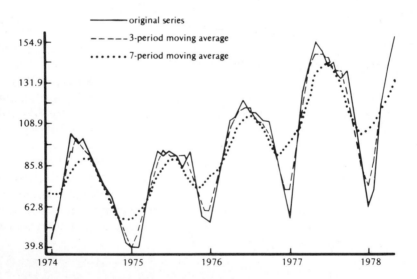

Figure 15.8 Smoothing using moving averages.

---

† The original data series is in thousands of units per month and is *not* seasonally adjusted. U.S. Bureau of the Census.

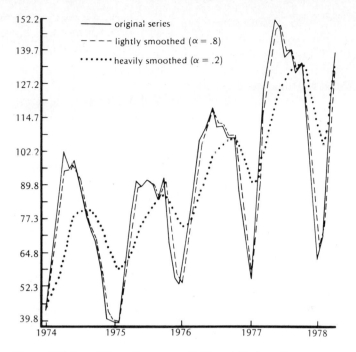

Figure 15.9 Smoothing using exponentially weighted moving averages.

time trends), and ran the regression

$$y_t = -156.81 + 1.2083\, t \qquad R^2 = .360 \qquad (15.38)$$
$$\quad\; (-3.36) \quad\;\; (5.37)$$

The *residuals* u_t from this regression, that is, $u_t = y_t + 156.81 - 1.2083t$, provide the detrended series.

We next apply exponential smoothing to this detrended series. We use two alternative values of the smoothing parameter, $\alpha = 0.8$ (light smoothing) and $\alpha = 0.2$ (heavy smoothing). Finally we take the smoothed detrended series $\tilde{u}_t$ and add the trend back in; i.e., we compute $\tilde{y}_t = \tilde{u}_t - 156.81 + 1.2083t$.

The original series and the smoothed series are shown in Fig. 15.9. Observe from the figure that the seasonal variations, while reduced, are pushed forward by heavy exponential smoothing. This occurs because the exponentially weighted moving average is not centered. Thus if a series shows strong seasonal variations, exponential smoothing should be used only after the series has been seasonally adjusted.

15.2.2 Seasonal Adjustment

Seasonal adjustment techniques are basically *ad hoc* methods of computing *seasonal indices* (that attempt to measure the seasonal variation in the series) and then using those indices to *deseasonalize* (i.e., seasonally adjust) the series by removing those seasonal variations. National economic data in the United States is usually seasonally adjusted by the *Census II method* (or one of its variants), which was developed by the Bureau of the Census of the U.S. Department of Commerce. The Census II method is a rather detailed and complicated procedure (and is amazingly *ad hoc*), and we therefore will not attempt to describe it here.† Instead, we discuss the basic idea that lies behind all seasonal adjustment methods (including Census II) and present a very simple method that in many cases is quite adequate.

Seasonal adjustment techniques are based on the idea that a time series y_t can be represented as the product of four components:

$$y_t = L \times S \times C \times I \tag{15.39}$$

where L = value of the long-term secular trend in series
S = value of seasonal component
C = (long-term) cyclical component
I = irregular component

The objective is to eliminate the seasonal component S.

To do this we first try to isolate the combined long-term trend and cyclical components $L \times C$. This cannot be done exactly; instead an *ad hoc* smoothing procedure is used to remove (as much as possible) the combined seasonal and irregular components $S \times I$ from the original series y_t. For example, suppose that y_t consists of monthly data. Then a *12-month moving average* $\tilde{y}_t$ is computed:

$$\tilde{y}_t = \tfrac{1}{12}(y_{t+6} + \cdots + y_t + y_{t-1} + \cdots + y_{t-5}) \tag{15.40}$$

Presumably $\tilde{y}_t$ is relatively free of seasonal and irregular fluctuations and is thus an *estimate* of $L \times C$.

We now divide the original data by this estimate of $L \times C$ to obtain an estimate of the combined seasonal and irregular components $S \times I$:

$$\frac{L \times S \times C \times I}{L \times C} = S \times I = \frac{y_t}{\tilde{y}_t} = z_t \tag{15.41}$$

The next step is to eliminate the irregular component I as best as possible in order to obtain the seasonal index. To do this, we *average the values of $S \times I$ corresponding to the same month*. In other words, suppose that y_1 (and hence z_1) corresponds to January, y_2 to February, etc., and there are 48 months of data. We thus compute

$$\begin{aligned}
\tilde{z}_1 &= \tfrac{1}{4}(z_1 + z_{13} + z_{25} + z_{37}) \\
\tilde{z}_2 &= \tfrac{1}{4}(z_2 + z_{14} + z_{26} + z_{38}) \\
&\quad\cdot\cdot\cdot\cdot\cdot\cdot\cdot\cdot\cdot\cdot\cdot\cdot\cdot \\
\tilde{z}_{12} &= \tfrac{1}{4}(z_{12} + z_{24} + z_{36} + z_{48})
\end{aligned} \tag{15.42}$$

---

† The Census II method is described in detail in Makridakis and Wheelwright, op. cit., and in L. Salzman, *Computerized Economic Analysis* (New York: McGraw-Hill 1968).

The rationale here is that when the seasonal-irregular percentages z_t are averaged for each month (each quarter if the data are quarterly), the irregular fluctuations will be largely smoothed out.

The 12 averages $\tilde{z}_1, \ldots, \tilde{z}_{12}$ will then be estimates of the seasonal indices. They should sum close to 12 but will not do so exactly if there is any long-run trend in the data. Final seasonal indices are computed by multiplying the indices in (15.42) by a factor that brings their sum to 12. (For example, if $\tilde{z}_1, \ldots, \tilde{z}_{12}$ add to 11.7, multiply each one by 12.0/11.7 so that the revised indices will add to 12.) We denote these final seasonal indices by $\bar{z}_1, \ldots, \bar{z}_{12}$.

The deseasonalization of the original series y_t is now straightforward; just divide each value in the series by its corresponding seasonal index, thereby removing the seasonal component while leaving the other three components. Thus the seasonally adjusted series y_t^a is obtained from $y_1^a = y_1/\bar{z}_1$, $y_2^a = y_2/\bar{z}_2, \ldots, y_{12}^a = y_{12}/\bar{z}_{12}, y_{13}^a = y_{13}/\bar{z}_1, y_{14}^a = y_{14}/\bar{z}_2$, etc.

Again, we must emphasize that this procedure, as well as its more sophisticated variants such as the Census II method, are *ad hoc*, and one has no guarantee that it will remove *all* the seasonality from the original series. What is more troubling is that procedures such as this might remove *more* than the seasonality from the original series. For this reason, seasonal adjustment should be done with care and only when it has a clear purpose.

Example 15.3 Monthly housing starts Let us now apply the seasonal adjustment technique to our series for monthly housing starts (see Example 15.2). To do this we first compute a 12-month average $\tilde{y}_t$ of the original series y_t using Eq. (15.40) and then divide y_t by $\tilde{y}_t$ that is, compute $z_t = y_t/\tilde{y}_t$. Note that z_t contains (roughly) the seasonal and irregular components of the original series. We remove the irregular component by averaging the values of z_t that correspond to the same month; i.e., we compute $\tilde{z}_1, \tilde{z}_2, \ldots, \tilde{z}_{12}$ using Eq. (15.42). We then compute the final *seasonal indices* $\bar{z}_1, \bar{z}_2, \ldots, \bar{z}_{12}$ by multiplying the $\tilde{z}_1, \ldots, \tilde{z}_{12}$ by a factor that brings their sum to 1. The final seasonal indices are as follows:

Month	Index	Month	Index
January	0.5552	July	1.1900
February	0.7229	August	1.1454
March	0.9996	September	1.0675
April	1.1951	October	1.0823
May	1.2562	November	0.8643
June	1.2609	December	0.6584

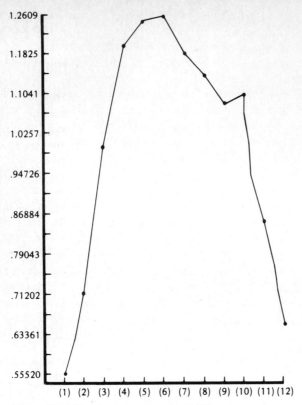

Figure 15.10 Housing starts: seasonal indices.

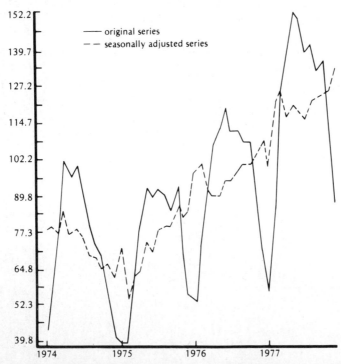

Figure 15.11 Seasonal adjustments of housing starts data.

These seasonal indices have also been plotted in Fig. 15.10.

To deseasonalize the original series y_t we just divide each value in the series by its corresponding seasonal index, thereby removing the seasonal component. The original series y_t together with the seasonally adjusted series y_t^a are shown in Fig. 15.11. Observe that the seasonal variation has been eliminated in the adjusted series, while the long-run trend and short-run irregular fluctuations remain.

EXERCISES

15.1 Go back to Example 15.1 and use the data for monthly department store sales to estimate a quadratic trend model. Use the estimated model to obtain an extrapolated value for sales for April 1974. Try to evaluate your model in comparison to the other four estimated in Example 15.1, and explain how and why your forecast for April differs from the other forecasts in the example.

15.2 Which (if any) of the simple extrapolation models presented in Section 15.1 do you think might be suitable for forecasting the GNP? The Consumer Price Index? A short-term interest rate? Annual production of wheat? Explain.

15.3 Show that the exponentially weighted moving average (EWMA) model will generate forecasts that are adaptive in nature.

15.4 Show that the EWMA forecast l periods ahead is the same as the forecast one period ahead, i.e.,

$$\hat{y}_{T+l} = \alpha \sum_{\tau=0}^{\infty} (1 - \alpha)^{\tau} y_{T-\tau}$$

15.5 Three years of monthly interest rate data are shown in Table 15.1.

Table 15.1 3-month Treasury bill rate

	1976		1977		1978
Jan.	4.961	Jan.	4.597	Jan.	6.448
Feb.	4.852	Feb.	4.662	Feb.	6.457
Mar.	5.047	Mar.	4.613	Mar.	6.319
Apr.	4.878	Apr.	4.540	Apr.	6.306
May	5.185	May	4.942	May	6.430
June	5.443	June	5.004	June	6.707
July	5.278	July	5.146	July	7.074
Aug.	5.153	Aug.	5.500	Aug.	7.036
Sept.	5.075	Sept.	5.770	Sept.	7.836
Oct.	4.930	Oct.	6.188	Oct.	8.132
Nov.	4.810	Nov.	6.160	Nov.	8.787
Dec.	4.355	Dec.	6.063	Dec.	9.122

SOURCE: Economic Report of the President, 1979.

(*a*) Exponentially smooth this data using a value of 0.9 for the smoothing parameter α. Repeat for a value of 0.2.

(b) Now smooth the data using Holt's two-parameter exponential smoothing method. Set $\alpha = 0.2$ and $\gamma = 0.2$. Explain how and why the results differ from those in (a) above. Now use Eq. (15.36) to forecast the series out 1, 2, and 3 months.

15.6 Again using the interest-rate data from Exercise 15.5, apply the seasonal adjustment procedure described in the text. Plot the 12 final seasonal indices as a function of time and try to explain the shape of the curve.

PROPERTIES OF STOCHASTIC TIME SERIES

In the last chapter we presented and discussed a number of simple extrapolation techniques. In this chapter we begin our treatment of the construction and use of time-series models. We will see that time-series models provide a much more sophisticated method of extrapolating time series and that extrapolation using time-series models differs in a fundamental way from simple extrapolations. The difference arises because time-series analysis presumes that the series to be forecasted has been generated by a *stochastic* (or *random*) *process*, with a structure that can be characterized and described. In other words, a time-series model provides a description of the random nature of the (stochastic) process that generated the sample of observations under study. The description is given not in terms of a cause-and-effect relationship (as would be the case in a regression model) but in terms of how that randomness is embodied in the process. Time-series analysis is, therefore, more sophisticated than simple extrapolation, since extrapolation does not account for the fact that the time series is stochastic. This point will become clearer as we proceed through this and the following chapters.

This chapter begins with an introduction to the nature of stochastic time-series models and shows how those models characterize the stochastic structure of the underlying process that generated the particular series. The chapter then turns to the properties of stochastic time series, focusing in particular on the concept of *stationarity*. This material will be important for the discussion of model construction in the following chapters.

16.1 INTRODUCTION TO STOCHASTIC TIME-SERIES MODELS

The time-series models developed in this and the following chapters are all based on an important assumption—that the time series to be forecasted has been generated by a *stochastic process*. In other words, we assume that each value $y_1, y_2, \ldots, y_T$ in the series is drawn randomly from a probability distribution. In modeling such a process, we attempt to describe the characteristics of its randomness. This should help us to infer something about the probabilities associated with alternative future values of the series.

To be completely general, we could assume that the observed series $y_1, \ldots, y_T$ is drawn from a set of *jointly distributed random variables*, i.e., that there exists some probability distribution function $p(y_1, \ldots, y_T)$ that assigns probabilities to all possible combinations of values of $y_1, \ldots, y_T$. If we could somehow numerically specify the probability distribution function for our series, then we could actually determine the probability of one or another future outcome.

Unfortunately, the complete specification of the probability distribution function for a time series is almost always impossible, particularly if the series contains more than about six data points. However, it usually is possible to construct a simplified model of the time series which explains its randomness in a manner that is useful for forecasting purposes. For example, we might believe that the values of $y_1, \ldots, y_T$ are normally distributed, and are correlated with each other according to a simple first-order Markov process (recall the serially correlated error process described in Chapter 6). The actual distribution of $y_1, \ldots, y_T$ may in fact be much more complicated, but this simple model may be a reasonable approximation. Of course, the usefulness of such a model depends on how closely it captures the true probability distribution and thus the true random behavior of the series. Note that it *need not* (and usually will not) match the actual past behavior of the series *since the series and the model are stochastic*. It should simply capture the characteristics of the series' randomness.

We take as our first (and simplest) example of a stochastic time series the *random walk* process.† Of course, there are few series that are actually random walk processes, but there are several for which a random walk model is not a bad approximation. In the simplest random walk process, each successive *change* in y_t is drawn *independently* from a probability distribution with 0 mean. Thus, y_t is determined by

$$y_t = y_{t-1} + \varepsilon_t \tag{16.1}$$

with $E(\varepsilon_t) = 0$ and $E(\varepsilon_t \varepsilon_s) = 0$ for $t \neq s$. Such a process could be generated by successive flips of a coin, where a head receives a value of $+1$ and a tail receives a value of -1.

---

† The random walk process has often been used as a model for the movement of stock market prices. See, for example, E. F. Fama, "Random Walks in Stock Market Prices," *Financial Analysts Journal*, September-October 1965; or P. H. Cootner (ed.), *The Random Character of Stock Market Prices* (Cambridge, Mass.: M.I.T. Press, 1964).

Suppose we wanted to make a forecast for such a random walk process; i.e., we knew the past history $y_1, y_2, \ldots, y_T$ and we wanted to obtain a forecast $\hat{y}_{T+1}$. The forecast is given by

$$\hat{y}_{T+1} = E(y_{T+1} | y_T, \ldots, y_1) \qquad (16.2)$$

But $y_{T+1} = y_T + \varepsilon_{T+1}$ is independent of $y_T, y_{T-1}, \ldots, y_1$. Thus, the forecast one period ahead is simply

$$\hat{y}_{T+1} = y_T + E(\varepsilon_{T+1}) = y_T \qquad (16.3)$$

The forecast two periods ahead is

$$\hat{y}_{T+2} = E(y_{T+2} | y_T, \ldots, y_1) = E(y_{T+1} + \varepsilon_{T+2})$$
$$= E(y_T + \varepsilon_{T+1} + \varepsilon_{T+2}) = y_T \qquad (16.4)$$

Similarly, the forecast l periods ahead is also y_T.

Although the forecast $\hat{y}_{T+l}$ will be the same no matter how large l is, the variance of the forecast error will grow as l becomes larger. For the one-period forecast, the forecast error is given by

$$e_1 = y_{T+1} - \hat{y}_{T+1} = y_T + \varepsilon_{T+1} - y_T = \varepsilon_{T+1} \qquad (16.5)$$

and its variance is just $E(\varepsilon_{T+1}^2) = \sigma_\varepsilon^2$. For the two-period forecast,

$$e_2 = y_{T+2} - \hat{y}_{T+2} = y_T + \varepsilon_{T+1} + \varepsilon_{T+2} - y_T = \varepsilon_{T+1} + \varepsilon_{T+2} \qquad (16.6)$$

and its variance is

$$E\left[(\varepsilon_{T+1} + \varepsilon_{T+2})^2 \right] = E(\varepsilon_{T+1}^2) + E(\varepsilon_{T+2}^2) + 2E(\varepsilon_{T+1}\varepsilon_{T+2}) \qquad (16.7)$$

Since ε_{T+1} and ε_{T+2} are independent, the third term in (16.7) is 0 and the error variance is $2\sigma_\varepsilon^2$. Similarly, for the l-period forecast, the error variance is $l\sigma_\varepsilon^2$. Thus, the *standard error of forecast* (i.e., the standard deviation of the forecast error) increases with the square root of l. We can thus obtain *confidence intervals* for our forecasts, and these intervals will become wider as the forecast horizon increases. This is illustrated in Fig. 16.1. Note that the forecasts $\hat{y}_{T+1}, \hat{y}_{T+2}$, etc., are all equal to the last observation y_T but the confidence intervals represented by 1 standard deviation in the forecast error increase as the square root of l.

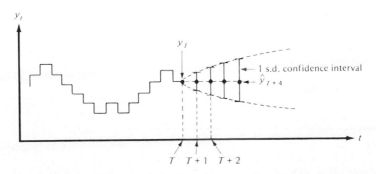

Figure 16.1 Forecasting a random walk.

The fact that we can generate confidence intervals of this sort is an important advantage of stochastic time-series models and makes them much more useful for forecasting than the simple extrapolation techniques discussed in the last chapter. A point forecast is usually of only limited value for policy making. As we explained in Chapter 8, policy makers usually need to know the margin of error that has to be associated with a particular forecast, and for this reason confidence intervals can be as important as the forecasts themselves.

A simple extension of the random walk process discussed above is the random walk with drift. This process accounts for a trend (upward or downward) in the series y_t and thereby allows us to embody that trend in our forecast. In this process, y_t is determined by

$$y_t = y_{t-1} + d + \varepsilon_t \qquad (16.8)$$

so that on the average the process will tend to move upward (for $d > 0$). Now the one-period forecast is

$$\hat{y}_{T+1} = E(y_{T+1}|y_T, \ldots, y_1) = y_T + d \qquad (16.9)$$

and the l-period forecast is

$$\hat{y}_{T+l} = y_T + ld \qquad (16.10)$$

The standard error of forecast will be the same as before. For one period,

$$e_1 = y_{T+1} - \hat{y}_{T+1} = y_T + d + \varepsilon_{T+1} - y_T - d = \varepsilon_{T+1} \qquad (16.11)$$

as before. The process, together with forecasts and forecast confidence intervals, is illustrated in Fig. 16.2. As can be seen in that figure, the forecasts increase linearly with l, and the standard error of forecast increases with the square root of l.

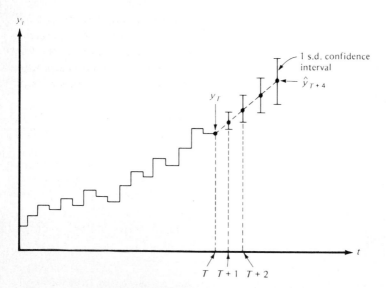

Figure 16.2 Forecasting a random walk with drift.

In the next chapter we examine a general class of stochastic time-series models. Later, we will see how that class of models can be used to make forecasts for a wide variety of time series. First, however, it is necessary to introduce some basic concepts about stochastic processes and their properties.

16.2 STATIONARY AND NONSTATIONARY TIME SERIES

As we begin to develop models for time series, we want to know whether or not the underlying stochastic process that generated the series can be assumed to be *invariant with respect to time*. If the characteristics of the stochastic process change over time, i.e., if the process is *nonstationary*, it will often be difficult to represent the time series over past and future intervals of time by a simple algebraic model.† On the other hand, if the stochastic process is fixed in time, i.e., if it is *stationary*, then, as we will see, it is possible to model the process via an equation with fixed coefficients that can be estimated from past data. This is analogous to the single-equation regression model in which one economic variable is related to other economic variables, with coefficients that are estimated under the assumption that the structural relationship described by the equation is invariant over time (i.e., is stationary). If the structural relationship changed over time (i.e., was nonstationary), then we could hardly expect to follow the techniques of Chapter 8 in using a regression model estimated from past data to forecast future data. Time-series models do not use economic relationships. However, our task of describing a stochastic process will be much easier if the characteristics of that process do not change over time. Thus, stationarity is an important characteristic of the stochastic processes we will model.

The stochastic time-series models developed in detail in the next chapter of the book are stationary models. Specifically, the stochastic processes are assumed to be in equilibrium over time about a constant mean level. The probability of a given fluctuation in the process from that mean level is assumed to be the same *at any point in time*. In other words, the stochastic properties of the stationary process are assumed to be *invariant with respect to time*.

One would suspect that many of the time series that one encounters in business and economics are not generated by stationary processes. The GNP, for example, has for the most part been growing steadily, and for this reason alone its stochastic properties in 1980 are different from those in 1933. Although it is quite difficult to build models of nonstationary processes, we will see that certain classes of nonstationary processes can easily be transformed into stationary or approximately stationary processes. Many time series that arise in economic and business applications belong to one of these classes of nonstationary processes.

---

† The random walk with drift is one example of a nonstationary process for which a simple forecasting model can be constructed.

16.2.1 Properties of Stationary Processes

We have said that any stochastic time series $y_1, \ldots, y_T$ can be thought of as having been generated by a set of jointly distributed random variables; i.e., the set of data points $y_1, \ldots, y_T$ represents a particular outcome of the joint probability distribution function $p(y_1, \ldots, y_T)$.† Similarly, a *future* observation y_{T+1} can be thought of as being generated by a *conditional probability distribution function* $p(y_{T+1}|y_1, \ldots, y_T)$, that is, a probability distribution for y_{T+1} given the past observations $y_1, \ldots, y_T$. We define a *stationary* process, then, as one whose joint distribution and conditional distribution both are *invariant with respect to displacement in time*. In other words, if the series y_t is stationary, then

$$p(y_t, \ldots, y_{t+k}) = p(y_{t+m}, \ldots, y_{t+k+m}) \tag{16.12}$$

and

$$p(y_t) = p(y_{t+m}) \tag{16.13}$$

for any t, k, and m.

Note that if the series y_t is stationary, the *mean* of the series, defined as

$$\mu_y = E(y_t) \tag{16.14}$$

must also be stationary, so that $E(y_t) = E(y_{t+m})$, for any t and m. Furthermore, the *variance* of the series,

$$\sigma_y^2 = E\left[(y_t - \mu_y)^2\right] \tag{16.15}$$

must be stationary, so that $E[(y_t - \mu_y)^2] = E[(y_{t+m} - \mu_y)^2]$, and finally, for any lag k, the *covariance* of the series,

$$\gamma_k = \text{Cov}(y_t, y_{t+k}) = E\left[(y_t - \mu_y)(y_{t+k} - \mu_y)\right] \tag{16.16}$$

must be stationary, so that $\text{Cov}(y_t, y_{t+k}) = \text{Cov}(y_{t+m}, y_{t+m+k})$.‡

If a stochastic process is stationary, the probability distribution $p(y_t)$ is the same for all time t and its shape (or at least some of its properties) can be inferred by looking at a histogram§ of the observations $y_1, \ldots, y_T$ that make up the observed series. Also, an estimate of the mean μ_y of the process can be obtained from the *sample mean* of the series

$$\bar{y} = \frac{1}{T} \sum_{t=1}^{T} y_t \tag{16.17}$$

and an estimate of the variance σ_y^2 can be obtained from the *sample variance*

$$\hat{\sigma}_y^2 = \frac{1}{T} \sum_{t=1}^{T} (y_t - \bar{y})^2 \tag{16.18}$$

---

† This outcome is called a *realization*. Thus $y_1, \ldots, y_T$ represent one particular realization of the stochastic process represented by the probability distribution $p(y_1, \ldots, y_T)$.

‡ It is possible for the mean, variance, and covariances of the series to be stationary but not the joint probability distribution. If the probability distributions are stationary, we term the series *strict-sense stationary*. If the mean, variance, and covariances are stationary, we term series *wide-sense stationary*. Note that strict-sense stationarity implies wide-sense stationarity but that the converse is not true.

§ A histogram is a plot of the frequency distribution of a set of observations.

16.2.2 The Autocorrelation Function

While it is usually impossible to obtain a complete description of a stochastic process (i.e., actually specify the underlying probability distributions), the autocorrelation function is extremely useful in helping us to obtain a partial description of the process for modeling purposes. The autocorrelation function provides us with a measure of how much correlation there is (and by implication how much interdependency there is) between neighboring data points in the series y_t. We define the *autocorrelation with lag k* as

$$\rho_k = \frac{E\left[(y_t - \mu_y)(y_{t+k} - \mu_y)\right]}{\sqrt{E\left[(y_t - \mu_y)^2\right]E\left[(y_{t+k} - \mu_y)^2\right]}} = \frac{\text{Cov}(y_t, y_{t+k})}{\sigma_{y_t}\sigma_{y_{t+k}}} \quad (16.19)$$

For a stationary process the variance at time t in the denominator of (16.19) is the same as the variance at time $t + k$; thus the denominator is just the variance of the stochastic process, and

$$\rho_k = \frac{E\left[(y_t - \mu_y)(y_{t+k} - \mu_y)\right]}{\sigma_y^2} \quad (16.20)$$

Note that the numerator of (16.20) is the covariance between y_t and y_{t+k}, γ_k, so that

$$\rho_k = \frac{\gamma_k}{\gamma_0} \quad (16.21)$$

and thus $\rho_0 = 1$ for *any* stochastic process.

Suppose that the stochastic process is simply

$$y_t = \varepsilon_t \quad (16.22)$$

where ε_t is an independently distributed random variable with zero mean. Then it is easy to see from Eq. (16.20) that the autocorrelation function for this process is given by $\rho_0 = 1$, $\rho_k = 0$ for $k > 0$. The process of Eq. (16.22) [identical to first-differencing the random walk process of (16.1)], is called *white noise*, and there is no model that can provide a forecast any better than $\hat{y}_{T+l} = 0$ for all l. Thus if the autocorrelation function is zero (or close to zero) for all $k > 0$, there is little or no value in using a model to forecast the series.

Of course the autocorrelation function in (16.20) is purely theoretical, in that it describes a stochastic process for which we have only a limited number of observations. In practice, then, we must calculate an *estimate* of the autocorrelation function, called the *sample autocorrelation function*:†

$$\hat{\rho}_k = \frac{\sum_{t=1}^{T-k}(y_t - \bar{y})(y_{t+k} - \bar{y})}{\sum_{t=1}^{T}(y_t - \bar{y})^2} \quad (16.23)$$

---

† Other estimates of the autocorrelation function have been suggested. For a discussion of their properties, see G. M. Jenkins and D. G. Watts, *Spectral Analysis and Its Applications* (San Francisco: Holden-Day, 1968). Equation (16.23), however, seems to provide the most robust estimate.

If the number of observations in the time series is large, then the estimated autocorrelation function will closely approximate the true population autocorrelation function.

It is easy to see from their definitions that both the theoretical and estimated autocorrelation functions are symmetrical, i.e., that the correlation for a positive displacement is the same as that for a negative displacement, so that

$$\rho_k = \rho_{-k} \tag{16.24}$$

Then, when plotting an autocorrelation function (i.e., plotting ρ_k for different values of k), one need consider only positive values of k.

It is often useful to determine whether a particular value of the sample autocorrelation function $\hat{\rho}_k$ is close enough to zero to permit assuming that the *true* value of the autocorrelation function ρ_k is indeed equal to zero. It is also useful to test whether *all* the values of the autocorrelation function for $k > 0$ are equal to zero. (If they are, we know that we are dealing with white noise.) Fortunately, simple statistical tests exist that can be used to test the hypothesis that $\rho_k = 0$ for a particular k or to test the hypothesis that $\rho_k = 0$ for all $k > 0$.

To test whether a particular value of the autocorrelation function ρ_k is equal to zero we use a result obtained by Bartlett. He showed that if a time series has been generated by a *white noise* process, i.e., consists of independently distributed random variables, the sample autocorrelation coefficients (for $k > 0$) are approximately distributed according to a normal distribution with mean 0 and standard deviation $1/\sqrt{T}$ (where T is number of observations in the series).† Thus, if a particular series consists of, say, 100 data points, we can attach a standard error of 0.1 to each autocorrelation coefficient. Therefore, if a particular coefficient was greater in magnitude than 0.2, we could be 95 percent sure that the true autocorrelation coefficient is not zero.

To test the *joint hypothesis* that *all* of the autocorrelation coefficients are zero we use the Q statistic introduced by Box and Pierce. We will discuss this statistic in some detail in Chapter 18 in the context of performing diagnostic checks on estimated time-series models, so here we only mention it in passing. Box and Pierce show that the statistic

$$Q = T \sum_{k=1}^{K} \hat{\rho}_k^2 \tag{16.25}$$

is (approximately) distributed as chi square with K degrees of freedom. Thus if the calculated value of Q is greater than, say, the critical 5 percent level, we can be 95 percent sure that the *true* autocorrelation coefficients $\rho_1, \ldots, \rho_k$ are not all zero.

In practice people tend to use the critical 10 percent level as a cutoff for this test. For example, if Q turned out to be 18.5 for a total of $K = 15$ lags, we would

---

† See M. S. Bartlett, "On the Theoretical Specification of Sampling Properties of Autocorrelated Time Series," *Journal of the Royal Statistical Society*, ser. B8, vol. 27, 1946. Also see G. E. P. Box and G. M. Jenkins, *Time Series Analysis* (San Francisco: Holden-Day, 1970).

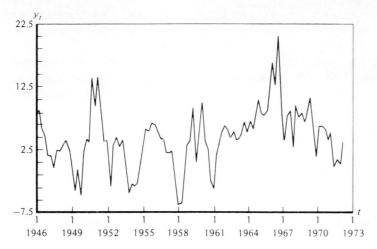

Figure 16.3 Nonfarm inventory investment.

observe that this is below the critical level of 22.31 and accept the hypothesis that the time series was generated by a white noise process.

Let us now turn to an example of an estimated autocorrelation function for a stationary economic time series. We have calculated $\hat{\rho}_k$ for quarterly data on nonfarm inventory investment. The time series itself (covering the years 1946 to 1972) is shown in Fig. 16.3, and the sample autocorrelation function is shown in Fig. 16.4. Note that the autocorrelation function falls off rather quickly as the lag k increases. This is typical of a stationary time series, such as inventory investment. In fact, as we will see, the autocorrelation function can be used to test whether or not a series is stationary. If $\hat{\rho}_k$ does not fall off quickly as k increases, this is an indication of nonstationarity.

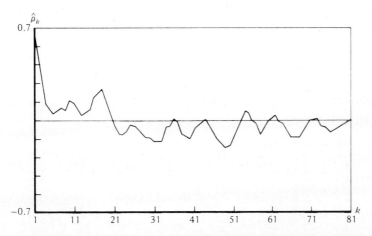

Figure 16.4 Nonfarm inventory investment, sample autocorrelation function.

If a time series is stationary, there exist certain analytical conditions which place bounds on the values that can be taken by the individual points of the autocorrelation function. However, the derivation of these conditions is somewhat complicated and will not be presented at this point. Furthermore, the conditions themselves are rather cumbersome and of limited usefulness in applied time-series modeling. Therefore, we have chosen to include the mathematical details in Appendix 16.1. We turn our attention now to the properties of those time series which are nonstationary, but which can be transformed into stationary series through a simple mathematical operation.

16.2.3 Homogeneous Nonstationary Processes

Probably very few of the time series one meets in practice are stationary. Fortunately, however, many of the nonstationary time series encountered (and this includes most of those that arise in economics and business) have the desirable property that if they are *differenced one or more times, the resulting series will be stationary*. Such a nonstationary series is termed *homogeneous*. The number of times that the original series must be differenced before a stationary series results is called the *order* of homogeneity. Thus, if y_t is first-order homogeneous nonstationary, the series

$$w_t = y_t - y_{t-1} = \Delta y_t \qquad (16.26)$$

is stationary. If y_t happened to be second-order homogeneous, the series

$$w_t = \Delta^2 y_t = \Delta y_t - \Delta y_{t-1} \qquad (16.27)$$

would be stationary.

As an example of a first-order homogeneous nonstationary process, consider the simple random walk process that we introduced earlier:

$$y_t = y_{t-1} + \varepsilon_t \qquad (16.28)$$

Let us examine the variance of this process:

$$\gamma_0 = E(y_t^2) = E\left[(y_{t-1} + \varepsilon_t)^2\right] = E(y_{t-1}^2) + \sigma_\varepsilon^2 = E(y_{t-2}^2) + 2\sigma_\varepsilon^2 \qquad (16.29)$$

or $\qquad \gamma_0 = E(y_{t-n}^2) + n\sigma_\varepsilon^2 \qquad (16.30)$

Observe that the variance grows over time. In fact the variance becomes infinite and is undefined. In addition, the covariances grow over time, since, for example

$$\gamma_1 = E(y_t y_{t-1}) = E\left[y_{t-1}(y_{t-1} + \varepsilon_t)\right] = E(y_{t-1}^2) \qquad (16.31)$$

Now let us look at the series that results from differencing the random walk process, i.e., the series

$$w_t = \Delta y_t = y_t - y_{t-1} = \varepsilon_t \qquad (16.32)$$

Since the ε_t are assumed independent over time, w_t clearly is a stationary process. Thus, we see that the random walk process is first-order homogeneous.

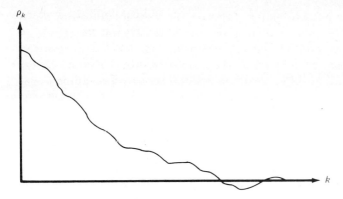

Figure 16.5 Stationary series.

In fact, w_t is just a white noise process, and it has the autocorrelation function $\rho_0 = 1$, but $\rho_k = 0$ for $k > 0$.

16.2.4 Stationarity and the Autocorrelation Function

The GNP or a series of sales figures for a firm are both likely to be non-stationary. Each has been growing (on average) over time, so that the mean of each series is time-dependent. It is quite likely, however, that if the GNP or company sales figures are first-differenced one or more times, the resulting series will be stationary. Thus, if we want to build a time-series model to forecast the GNP, we can difference the series one or two times, construct a model for this new series, make our forecasts, and then *integrate* (i.e., remove the effect of the differencing) the model and its forecasts to arrive back at the GNP.

How can we decide whether a series is stationary or determine the appropriate number of times a homogeneous nonstationary series should be differenced to arrive at a stationary series? Usually these questions can be answered by looking at a plot of the autocorrelation function (called a *correlogram*). Figures 16.5 and 16.6 show autocorrelation functions for stationary and

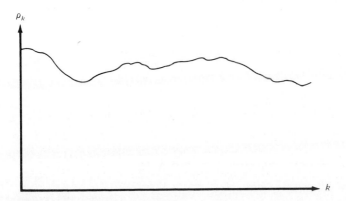

Figure 16.6 Nonstationary series.

nonstationary series. The autocorrelation function for a stationary series drops off as k, the number of lags, becomes large, but this is usually not the case for a nonstationary series. If we are differencing a nonstationary series, we can test each succeeding difference by looking at the autocorrelation function. If, for example, the second round of differencing results in a series whose autocorrelation function drops off rapidly, we can determine that the original series is second-order homogeneous. If the resulting series is still nonstationary, the autocorrelation function will remain large even for long lags.

Example 16.1   Interest rate Often in applied work it will not be clear how many times a nonstationary series should be differenced, and one must make a judgment based on experience and intuition. As an example, take the time series for the interest rate on 4- to 6-month commercial paper. This series (consisting of quarterly data from 1947 to 1973) is shown in Fig. 16.7, and its sample autocorrelation function is shown in Fig. 16.8. The autocorrelation function does seem to decline as the number of lags becomes large, so that one might at first suspect that the series is stationary. The series, however, exhibits an upward trend (so that the mean is not constant over time), and the autocorrelation function declines very slowly. We can therefore conclude that this series has been generated by a homogeneous non-stationary process. To check, we difference the series and recalculate the sample autocorrelation function.

The differenced series is shown in Fig. 16.9. Its sample autocorrelation function, shown in Fig. 16.10, appears more stationary (as does the series itself). The series is then differenced a second time (see Fig. 16.11), and the resulting autocorrelation function (Fig. 16.12) appears stationary. In fact, it declines more rapidly than the autocorrelation function associated with

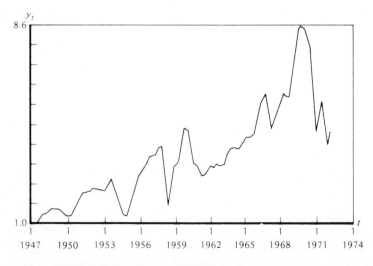

Figure 16.7 Interest rate on commercial paper.

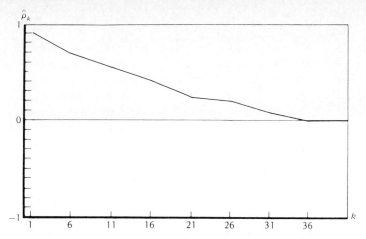

Figure 16.8 Interest rate on commercial paper, sample autocorrelation function.

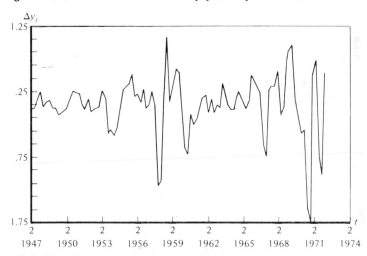

Figure 16.9 Interest rate on commercial paper, Δy_t.

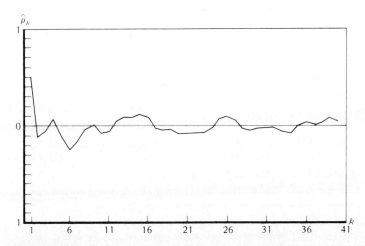

Figure 16.10 Interest rate on commercial paper: autocorrelation function of Δy_t.

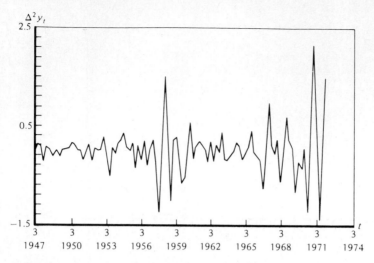

Figure 16.11 Interest rate on commercial paper: $\Delta^2 y_t$.

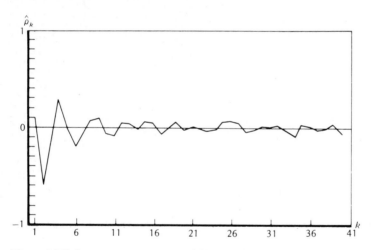

Figure 16.12 Interest rate on commercial paper: autocorrelation function of $\Delta^2 y_t$.

differencing only once.† To conclude our example, we can attempt to obtain a more stationary series by differencing a third time. The thrice-differenced series is shown in Fig. 16.13 and the corresponding sample autocorrelation function in Fig. 16.14. The results do not seem qualitatively different than the previous case. Our conclusion, then, would be that differencing once, or at most twice, should be sufficient to ensure stationarity.

---

† For our purposes what is important for stationarity is the sharp decline in $\hat{\rho}_k$ over the first eight or ten time periods. The remaining portion of the graph appears to be random with 0 mean.

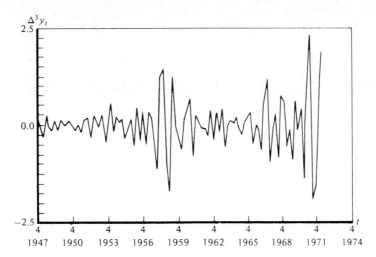

Figure 16.13 Interest rate on commercial paper: $\Delta^3 y_t$.

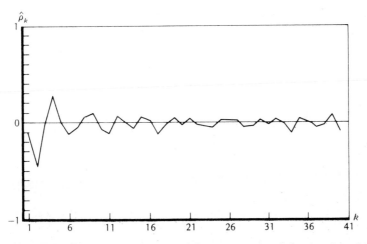

Figure 16.14 Interest rate on commercial paper: autocorrelation function of $\Delta^3 y_t$.

Example 16.2   Daily hog prices† As a second example, let us examine a time series for the daily market price of hogs. If a forecasting model could be developed for this series, one could conceivably make money by speculating on the futures market for hogs and using the model to outperform the market.

---

† This example is from a paper by R. Leuthold, A. MacCormick, A. Schmitz, and D. Watts, "Forecasting Daily Hog Prices and Quantities: A Study of Alternative Forecasting Techniques," *Journal of the American Statistical Association*, March 1970, Applications Section, pp. 90–107.

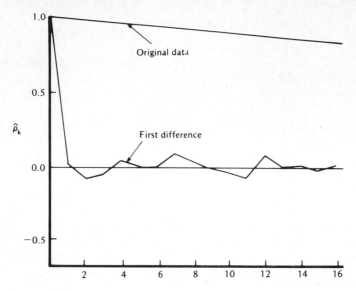

Figure 16.15 Sample autocorrelation functions of daily hog price data.

The series consists of 250 daily data points covering all the trading days in 1965. The price variable is the average price in dollars per hundredweight of all hogs sold in the eight regional markets in the United States on a particular day. The sample autocorrelation functions for the original price series and for the first difference of the series are shown in Fig. 16.15.

Observe that the original series is clearly nonstationary. The autocorrelation function barely declines, even after a 16-period lag. The series is, however, first-order homogeneous, since its first difference is clearly stationary.

In fact, not only is the first-differenced series stationary but it appears to resemble white noise, since the sample autocorrelation function $\hat{\rho}_k$ is close to zero for all $k > 0$. To determine whether the differenced series is indeed white noise, let us calculate the Q statistic for the first 15 lags. The value of this statistic is 14.62, which, with 15 degrees of freedom, is insignificant at the 10 percent level. We can therefore conclude that the differenced series is white noise and that the original price series can best be modeled as a *random walk*:

$$P_t = P_{t-1} + \varepsilon_t \tag{16.33}$$

As is the case of most stock market prices, our best forecast of P_t is its most recent value, and (sadly) there is no model that can help us outperform the market.

16.2.5 Seasonality and the Autocorrelation Function

We have just seen that the autocorrelation function can reveal information about the stationarity of a time series. In the remaining chapters of this book we will see that a good deal of other information about time series can also be obtained from its autocorrelation function. This information will be useful in helping us to construct stochastic models of time series. However, we continue here by examining the relationship between the autocorrelation function and the *seasonality* of a time series.

As discussed in the previous chapter, seasonality is just a cyclical behavior that occurs on a regular calendar basis, i.e., in cycles with periodicity that is annual, semiannual, quarterly, monthly, or any other unit of calendar time. An example of a highly seasonal time series would be toy sales, which exhibit a strong peak every Christmas. Sales of ice cream and iced-tea mix show seasonal peaks each summer in response to increased demand brought about by warmer weather; Peruvian anchovy production shows seasonal troughs once every 7 years in response to decreased supply brought about by cyclical changes in the oceans currents.

Often seasonal peaks and troughs are easy to spot simply by direct observation of the time series. On many occasions, however, if the time series fluctuates considerably, seasonal peaks and troughs will not be distinguishable from the other fluctuations. Recognition of seasonality is important, since it provides information about "regularity" in the series that can aid us in making a forecast. Fortunately, that recognition can be made easier with the help of the autocorrelation function.

If a monthly time series y_t exhibits annual seasonality, the data points in the series should show some degree of correlation with the corresponding data points which lead or lag by 12 months. In other words, we would expect to see some degree of correlation between y_t and y_{t-12}. Since y_t and y_{t-12} will be correlated, as will y_{t-12} and y_{t-24}, we should also see correlation between y_t and y_{t-24}. Similarly there will be correlation between y_t and y_{t-36}, y_t and y_{t-48}, etc. These correlations should manifest themselves in the sample autocorrelation function $\hat{\rho}_k$, which will exhibit peaks at $k = 12, 24, 36, 48$, etc. Thus we can identify seasonality by observing regular peaks in the autocorrelation function, even if seasonal peaks cannot be discerned in the time series itself.

Example 16.3 **Hog production** As an example, look at the time series for the monthly production of hogs in the United States, shown in Fig. 16.16. It would take a somewhat experienced eye to discern easily seasonality in that series. The seasonality of the series, however, is readily apparent in its sample autocorrelation function, which is shown in Fig. 16.17. Note the peaks that occur at $k = 12, 24$, and 36, indicating annual cycles in the series.

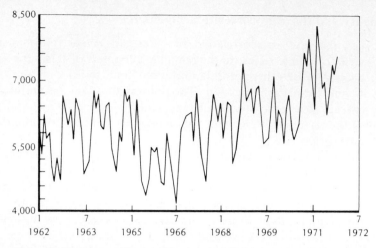

Figure 16.16 Hog production (in thousands of hogs per month). Time bounds: January 1962 to December 1971.

A crude method of removing the annual cycles ("deseasonalizing" the data) would be to take a 12-month difference, obtaining a new series $z_t = y_t - y_{t-12}$. As can be seen in Fig. 16.18, the sample autocorrelation function for this 12-month differenced series does not exhibit strong seasonality. We will see in later chapters that z_t represents an extremely simple time-series model for hog production, since it accounts only for the annual cycle. We can complete this example by observing that the autocorrelation function in Fig. 16.18 declines only slowly, so that there is some doubt as to whether z_t is a stationary series. We therefore first-differenced this series, to obtain $w_t = \Delta z_t = \Delta(y_t - y_{t-12})$. The sample autocorrelation function of

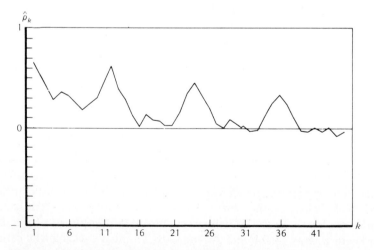

Figure 16.17 Sample autocorrelation function for hog production series.

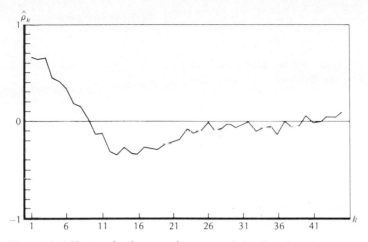

Figure 16.18 Hog production: sample autocorrelation function of $y_t - y_{t-12}$.

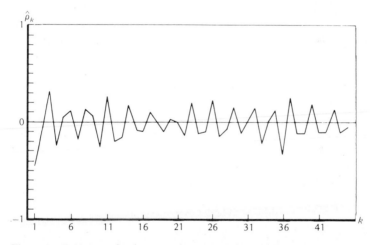

Figure 16.19 Hog production: sample autocorrelation function of $\Delta(y_t - y_{t-12})$.

this series, shown in Fig. 16.19, declines rapidly and remains small, so that we can be confident that w_t is a stationary, nonseasonal time series.

APPENDIX 16.1 THE AUTOCORRELATION FUNCTION FOR A STATIONARY PROCESS

In this appendix we derive a set of conditions that must hold for an autocorrelation function of a stationary process. Let y_t be a stationary process and let L_t be any linear function of y_t and lags in y_t, for example,

$$L_t = \alpha_1 y_t + \alpha_2 y_{t-1} + \cdots + \alpha_k y_{t-k+1} \qquad (A16.1)$$

Now since y_t is stationary, the covariances of y_t are stationary, and

$$\text{Cov}\,(y_{t+i}, y_{t+j}) = \gamma_{|i-j|} \tag{A16.2}$$

independent of t. Then, by squaring both sides of Eq. (A16.1), we see that the variance of L_t is given by

$$\text{Var}\,(L_t) = \sum_{i=1}^{k+1}\sum_{j=1}^{k+1} \alpha_i \alpha_j \gamma_{|i-j|} \tag{A16.3}$$

If the α's are not all 0, the variance of L_t must be greater than 0 and therefore we must have, for all i and j,

$$\gamma_{|i-j|} > 0 \qquad \text{for } i = j \tag{A16.4}$$

Now, for n observations, write the covariances of y_t as a matrix:

$$\Gamma_n = \begin{bmatrix} \gamma_0 & \gamma_1 & \gamma_2 & \cdots & \gamma_{n-1} \\ \gamma_1 & \gamma_0 & \gamma_1 & \cdots & \gamma_{n-2} \\ \cdots & \cdots & \cdots & \cdots & \cdots \\ \gamma_{n-1} & \gamma_{n-2} & \gamma_{n-3} & \cdots & \gamma_0 \end{bmatrix} \tag{A16.5}$$

This matrix must be positive definite because the variance of L_t is always greater than zero. Note that

$$\Gamma_n = \sigma_y^2 \begin{bmatrix} 1 & \rho_1 & \rho_2 & \cdots & \rho_{n-1} \\ \rho_1 & 1 & \rho_1 & \cdots & \rho_{n-2} \\ \cdots & \cdots & \cdots & \cdots & \cdots \\ \rho_{n-1} & \rho_{n-2} & \rho_{n-3} & \cdots & 1 \end{bmatrix} = \sigma_y^2 \mathbf{P}_n \tag{A16.6}$$

where $\mathbf{P}_n$ is the matrix of autocorrelations, and is itself positive definite. Thus the determinant of $\mathbf{P}_n$ and its principal minors must be greater than 0.

As an example, let us consider the case of $n = 2$. The condition on the determinant of $\mathbf{P}_n$ becomes

$$\det \begin{bmatrix} 1 & \rho_1 \\ \rho_1 & 1 \end{bmatrix} > 0$$

which implies that

$$1 - \rho_1^2 > 0$$

or

$$-1 < \rho_1 < 1 \tag{A16.7}$$

Similarly, for $n = 3$, it is easy to see that the following three conditions must all hold:

$$-1 < \rho_1 < 1 \tag{A16.8}$$

$$-1 < \rho_2 < 1 \tag{A16.9}$$

$$-1 < \frac{\rho_2 - \rho_1^2}{1 - \rho_1^2} < 1 \tag{A16.10}$$

Sets of conditions can also be derived for $n = 4$, $n = 5$, etc., but it should become clear that as the number of observations n becomes large, the number of conditions that must hold also becomes quite large. Although these conditions can provide an analytical check on the stationarity of a time series, in applied work, it is more typical to judge stationarity from a visual examination of both the series itself and the sample autocorrelation function. For our purposes it will be sufficient to remember that for $k > 0$, $-1 < \rho_k < 1$ for a stationary process.

EXERCISES

16.1 Show that the random walk process with drift is first-order homogeneous nonstationary.

16.2 Consider the time series 1, 2, 3, 4, 5, 6, ..., 20. Is this series stationary? Calculate the sample autocorrelation function $\hat{\rho}_k$ for $k = 1, 2, ..., 5$. Can you explain the shape of this function?

16.3 Go back to the monthly interest rate data presented in Exercise 15.5. Calculate the sample autocorrelation function $\hat{\rho}_k$ for $k = 1, ..., 10$. Does it exhibit stationarity and/or seasonality? Now difference the series and recalculate the sample autocorrelation function. Does the differenced series appear stationary?

SEVENTEEN

LINEAR TIME-SERIES MODELS

In the last chapter we introduced stochastic processes and discussed some of their properties. Now we turn to the main focus of the remainder of this book, the construction of models of stochastic processes and their use in forecasting. Our objective is to develop models that "explain" the movement of a time series y_t. Unlike the regression model, however, a set of explanatory variables will not be used. Instead we explain y_t by relating it to its own past values and to a weighted sum of current and lagged random disturbances.

While there are many functional forms that can be used to relate y_t to its past values and lagged random disturbances, we use here a linear specification. The assumption of linearity allows us to make quantitative statements about the stochastic properties of the models and the forecasts generated by the models (e.g., to calculate confidence intervals around our forecasts). In addition, our models apply to stationary processes and to homogeneous nonstationary processes (which can be differenced one or more times to yield stationary processes). Finally, the models are written as equations with fixed estimated coefficients, representing a stochastic structure that does not change over time. Although models with time-varying coefficients of nonstationary processes have been developed recently, they are well beyond the scope of this book.

In the first two sections of the chapter we examine simple moving average and autoregressive models for stationary processes. In a moving average model, the process y_t is described completely by a weighted sum of current and lagged random disturbances. In the autoregressive model, y_t depends on a weighted sum of its past values and a random disturbance term. In the third section we introduce mixed autoregressive–moving average models. In these models the process y_t is a function of both lagged random disturbances and its past values, as well as a current disturbance term. Even if the original process is nonstationary, it often can be differenced one or more times to produce a new series that is stationary and for which a mixed autoregressive–moving average model can be constructed. This model can be used to produce a forecast one or more periods into the future, after which the forecasted stationary series can be integrated one or more times to yield a forecast for the original time series. The integrated autoregressive–moving average model is the most complex model that we discuss in this chapter. It provides a general framework for the modeling of homogeneous nonstationary time series.

When building an integrated autoregressive–moving average model for a nonstationary time series, we must first specify how many times the series is to be differenced before a stationary series results. We must also specify the number of autoregressive terms and lagged disturbance terms to be included in the model of the stationary series. We have seen in Chapter 16 that the autocorrelation function can be used to tell us how many times we must difference a homogeneous nonstationary process in order to produce a stationary process. In this chapter, we see how the autocorrelation function can also be used to help determine the number of disturbance terms in the moving average portion and the number of lags in the autoregressive portion of our model.

17.1 MOVING AVERAGE MODELS

In the *moving average process of order q* each observation y_t is generated by a weighted average of random disturbances going back q periods. We denote this process as MA(q) and write its equation as

$$y_t = \mu + \varepsilon_t - \theta_1 \varepsilon_{t-1} - \theta_2 \varepsilon_{t-2} - \cdots - \theta_q \varepsilon_{t-q} \tag{17.1}$$

where the parameters $\theta_1, \ldots, \theta_q$ may be positive or negative.

In the moving average model (and also in the autoregressive model, which will follow) the random disturbances are assumed to be independently distributed across time, i.e., generated by a *white noise* process. In particular, each disturbance term ε_t is assumed to be a normal random variable with mean 0, variance σ_ε^2, and covariance $\gamma_k = 0$ for $k \neq 0$.† White noise processes may not occur very commonly in nature, but, as we will see, weighted sums of a white noise process provide a good representation of processes that are nonwhite.

The reader should observe that the *mean* of the moving average process is independent of time, since $E(y_t) = \mu$. Each ε_t is assumed to be generated by the same white noise process, so that $E(\varepsilon_t) = 0$, $E(\varepsilon_t^2) = \sigma_\varepsilon^2$, and $E(\varepsilon_t \varepsilon_{t-k}) = 0$ for $k \neq 0$. The process MA(q) is thus described by exactly $q + 2$ parameters, the mean μ, the disturbance variance σ_ε^2, and the parameters $\theta_1, \theta_2, \ldots, \theta_q$ that determine the weights in the moving average.

---

† As we saw in the last chapter, the autocorrelation function for a white noise process is simply

$$\rho_k = \begin{cases} 1 & \text{for } k = 0 \\ 0 & \text{for } k \neq 0 \end{cases}$$

Let us now look at the *variance*, denoted by γ_0, of the moving average process of order q:

$$\text{Var}(y_t) = \gamma_0 = E\left[(y_t - \mu)^2\right]$$

$$= E\left(\varepsilon_t^2 + \theta_1^2\varepsilon_{t-1}^2 + \cdots + \theta_q^2\varepsilon_{t-q}^2 - 2\theta_1\varepsilon_t\varepsilon_{t-1} - \cdots\right)$$

$$= \sigma_\varepsilon^2 + \theta_1^2\sigma_\varepsilon^2 + \cdots + \theta_q^2\sigma_\varepsilon^2$$

$$= \sigma_\varepsilon^2\left(1 + \theta_1^2 + \theta_2^2 + \cdots + \theta_q^2\right) \tag{17.2}$$

Note that the expected values of the cross terms are all 0, since we have assumed that the ε_t's are generated by a white noise process for which $\gamma_k = E(\varepsilon_t\varepsilon_{t-k}) = 0$ for $k \neq 0$.

Equation (17.2) imposes a restriction on the values that are permitted for $\theta_1, \ldots, \theta_q$. We would expect the variance of y_t to be finite, since otherwise a realization of the random process (i.e., a time series generated by it) would involve larger and larger deviations from a fixed reference point as time increased. This, in turn, would violate our assumption of stationarity, since stationarity requires that the probability of being some arbitrary distance from a reference point be invariant with respect to time. Thus, if y_t is the realization of a stationary random process, we must have

$$\sum_{i=1}^{q} \theta_i^2 < \infty \tag{17.3}$$

In a sense this result is trivial, since we have only a finite number of θ_i's, and thus their sum is finite. However, the assumption of a fixed number of θ_i's can be considered to be an approximation to a more general model. A complete model of most random processes would require an infinite number of lagged disturbance terms (and their corresponding weights). Then, as q, the order of the moving average process, becomes infinitely large, we must require that the sum $\sum_{i=0}^{\infty}\theta_i^2$ converge. Convergence will usually occur if the θ's become smaller as i becomes larger. Thus, if we are representing a process, believed to be stationary, by a moving average model of order q, we expect the θ_i's to become smaller as i becomes larger. We will see later that this implies that if the process is stationary, its correlation function ρ_k will become smaller as k becomes larger. This is consistent with our result of the last chapter that one indicator of stationarity is an autocorrelation function that approaches zero.

Now we examine some simple moving average processes, calculating the mean, variance, covariances, and autocorrelation function for each. These statistics are important, first because they provide information that helps characterize the process, and second because they will help us to identify the process when we actually construct models in the next chapter.

We begin with the simplest moving average process, the moving average process of order 1. The process is denoted by MA(1), and its equation is

$$y_t = \mu + \varepsilon_t - \theta_1\varepsilon_{t-1} \tag{17.4}$$

This process has mean μ and variance $\gamma_0 = \sigma_\varepsilon^2(1 + \theta_1^2)$. Now let us derive the *covariance* for a one-lag displacement, γ_1:

$$\gamma_1 = E\big[(y_t - \mu)(y_{t-1} - \mu)\big] = E\big[(\varepsilon_t - \theta_1\varepsilon_{t-1})(\varepsilon_{t-1} - \theta_1\varepsilon_{t-2})\big]$$
$$= -\theta_1\sigma_\varepsilon^2 \tag{17.5}$$

In general we can determine the covariance for a k-lag displacement to be

$$\gamma_k = E\big[(\varepsilon_t - \theta_1\varepsilon_{t-1})(\varepsilon_{t-k} - \theta_1\varepsilon_{t-k-1})\big] = 0 \qquad \text{for } k > 1 \tag{17.6}$$

Thus the MA(1) process has a covariance of 0 when the displacement is more than one period. We say, then, that the process has a *memory* of only one period; any value y_t is correlated with y_{t-1} and with y_{t+1}, but with no other time-series values. In effect, the process forgets what happened more than one period in the past; i.e., events occurring more than one period in the past (and that are independent of y_{t-1}) have no effect on where the process is now. In general the limited memory of a moving average process is important. It suggests (and we will see this to be the case in Chapter 19) that a moving average model provides forecasting information only a limited number of periods into the future [one period into the future for an MA(1) model].

We can now determine the autocorrelation function for the process MA(1):

$$\rho_k = \frac{\gamma_k}{\gamma_0} = \begin{cases} \dfrac{-\theta_1}{1 + \theta_1^2} & k = 1 \\[2mm] 0 & k > 1 \end{cases} \tag{17.7}$$

An example of a first-order moving average process might be given by

$$y_t = 2 + \varepsilon_t + .8\varepsilon_{t-1} \tag{17.8}$$

The autocorrelation function for y_t is shown in Fig. 17.1, and a typical realization is shown in Fig. 17.2.

Now let us proceed by examining the moving average process of order 2. The process is denoted by MA(2), and its equation is

$$y_t = \mu + \varepsilon_t - \theta_1\varepsilon_{t-1} - \theta_2\varepsilon_{t-2} \tag{17.9}$$

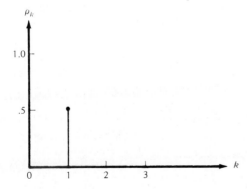

Figure 17.1 Autocorrelation function for $y_t = 2 + \varepsilon_t + .8\varepsilon_{t-1}$.

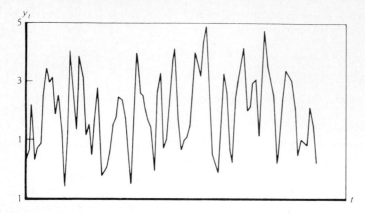

Figure 17.2 Typical realization of $y_t = 2 + \varepsilon_t + .8\varepsilon_{t-1}$.

This process has mean μ, variance $\sigma_\varepsilon^2(1 + \theta_1^2 + \theta_2^2)$, and covariances given by

$$\gamma_1 = E\big[(\varepsilon_t - \theta_1\varepsilon_{t-1} - \theta_2\varepsilon_{t-2})(\varepsilon_{t-1} - \theta_1\varepsilon_{t-2} - \theta_2\varepsilon_{t-3})\big]$$

$$= -\theta_1\sigma_\varepsilon^2 + \theta_2\theta_1\sigma_\varepsilon^2 = -\theta_1(1 - \theta_2)\sigma_\varepsilon^2 \tag{17.10}$$

$$\gamma_2 = E\big[(\varepsilon_t - \theta_1\varepsilon_{t-1} - \theta_2\varepsilon_{t-2})(\varepsilon_{t-2} - \theta_1\varepsilon_{t-3} - \theta_2\varepsilon_{t-4})\big] = -\theta_2\sigma_\varepsilon^2 \tag{17.11}$$

and $\quad \gamma_k = 0 \qquad$ for $k > 2$ $\tag{17.12}$

The autocorrelation function is given by

$$\rho_1 = \frac{-\theta_1(1 - \theta_2)}{1 + \theta_1^2 + \theta_2^2} \tag{17.13}$$

$$\rho_2 = \frac{-\theta_2}{1 + \theta_1^2 + \theta_2^2} \tag{17.14}$$

and $\qquad\qquad\qquad \rho_k = 0 \qquad$ for $k > 2$ $\tag{17.15}$

The process MA(2) has a memory of exactly two periods, so that the value of y_t is influenced only by events that took place in the current period, one period back, and two periods back.

An example of a second-order moving average process might be

$$y_t = 2 + \varepsilon_t + .6\varepsilon_{t-1} - .3\varepsilon_{t-2} \tag{17.16}$$

The autocorrelation function is shown in Fig. 17.3, and a typical realization is shown in Fig. 17.4.

We leave to the reader a proof that the moving average process of order q has a memory of exactly q periods, and that its autocorrelation function ρ_k is given by the following (see Exercise 17.3):

$$\rho_k = \begin{cases} \dfrac{-\theta_k + \theta_1\theta_{k+1} + \cdots + \theta_{q-k}\theta_q}{1 + \theta_1^2 + \theta_2^2 + \cdots + \theta_q^2} & k = 1, \ldots, q \\[2mm] 0 & k > q \end{cases} \tag{17.17}$$

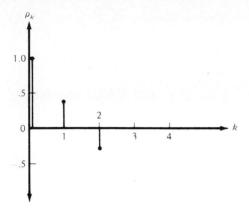

Figure 17.3 Autocorrelation function for $y_t = 2 + \varepsilon_1 + 6\varepsilon_{t-1} - .3\varepsilon_{t-2}$.

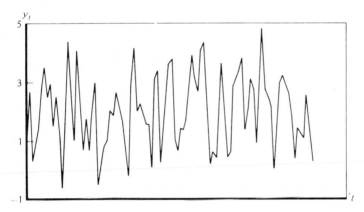

Figure 17.4 Typical realization of $y_t = 2 + \varepsilon_t + .6\varepsilon_{t-1} - .3\varepsilon_{t-2}$.

We can now see why the sample autocorrelation function can be useful in specifying the order of a moving average process (assuming that the time series of concern is generated by a moving average process). The autocorrelation function ρ_k for the MA(q) process has q nonzero values, and is then 0 for $k > q$. As we proceed through this and later chapters, we will attempt to give the reader an understanding of how the sample autocorrelation function can be used to identify the stochastic process that may have generated a particular time series.

17.2 AUTOREGRESSIVE MODELS

In the *autoregressive process of order p* the current observation y_t is generated by a weighted average of past observations going back p periods, together with a random disturbance in the current period. We denote this process as AR(p) and write its equation as

$$y_t = \phi_1 y_{t-1} + \phi_2 y_{t-2} + \cdots + \phi_p y_{t-p} + \delta + \varepsilon_t \qquad (17.18)$$

Here δ is a constant term which relates (as we will see) to the mean of the stochastic process.

17.2.1 Properties of Autoregressive Models

If the autoregressive process is stationary, then its mean, which we denote by μ, must be invariant with respect to time; that is, $E(y_t) = E(y_{t-1}) = E(y_{t-2}) = \cdots = \mu$. The mean μ is thus given by

$$\mu = \phi_1 \mu + \phi_2 \mu + \cdots + \phi_p \mu + \delta \tag{17.19}$$

or
$$\mu = \frac{\delta}{1 - \phi_1 - \phi_2 - \cdots - \phi_p} \tag{17.20}$$

This formula for the mean of the process also gives us a condition for stationarity. If the process is stationary, the mean μ in (17.20) must be finite. If this were not the case, the process would drift farther and farther away from any fixed reference point and could not be stationary. (Consider the example of the random walk with drift, that is, $y_t = y_{t-1} + \delta + \varepsilon_t$. Here $\phi_1 = 1$, and $\mu = \infty$, and if $\delta > 0$, the process continually drifts upward.) If μ is to be finite, it is necessary that

$$\phi_1 + \phi_2 + \cdots + \phi_p < 1 \tag{17.21}$$

This condition is not sufficient to ensure stationarity, since there are other necessary conditions that must hold if the AR(p) process is to be stationary. We discuss these additional conditions in more detail in Appendix 17.1.

Now let us examine the properties of some simple autoregressive processes. Again we will determine the mean, covariances, etc., for each. We begin with the first-order process AR(1):

$$y_t = \phi_1 y_{t-1} + \delta + \varepsilon_t \tag{17.22}$$

[The reader should notice the resemblance between AR(1) and the first-order autoregressive error process discussed in Chapter 6.] This process has mean

$$\mu = \frac{\delta}{1 - \phi_1} \tag{17.23}$$

and is stationary if $|\phi_1| < 1$. Again, recall that the random walk with drift is a first-order autoregressive process that is *not* stationary. In that process $\phi_1 = 1$, and, as we saw in Chapter 16, the variance of the process becomes larger and larger with time.

Let us now calculate γ_0, the variance of this process about its mean. Assuming stationarity, so that we know that the variance is constant (for $|\phi_1| < 1$), and setting $\delta = 0$ (to scale the process to one that is zero mean), we have†

$$\gamma_0 = E\left[(\phi_1 y_{t-1} + \varepsilon_t)^2\right] = E(\phi_1^2 y_{t-1}^2 + \varepsilon_t^2 + 2\phi_1 y_{t-1}\varepsilon_t) = \phi_1^2 \gamma_0 + \sigma_\varepsilon^2$$

so that

$$\gamma_0 = \frac{\sigma_\varepsilon^2}{1 - \phi_1^2} \tag{17.24}$$

We can also calculate the covariances of y_t about its mean:

$$\gamma_1 = E\left[y_{t-1}(\phi_1 y_{t-1} + \varepsilon_t)\right] = \phi_1 \gamma_0 = \frac{\phi_1 \sigma_\varepsilon^2}{1 - \phi_1^2} \tag{17.25}$$

$$\gamma_2 = E\left[y_{t-2}(\phi_1^2 y_{t-2} + \phi_1 \varepsilon_{t-1} + \varepsilon_t)\right] = \phi_1^2 \gamma_0 = \frac{\phi_1^2 \sigma_\varepsilon^2}{1 - \phi_1^2} \tag{17.26}$$

Similarly the covariance for a k-lag displacement is

$$\gamma_k = \phi_1^k \gamma_0 = \frac{\phi_1^k \sigma_\varepsilon^2}{1 - \phi_1^2} \tag{17.27}$$

The autocorrelation function for AR(1) is thus particularly simple—it begins at $\rho_0 = 1$ and then declines geometrically:

$$\rho_k = \frac{\gamma_k}{\gamma_0} = \phi_1^k \tag{17.28}$$

Note that this process has an *infinite memory*. The current value of the process depends on *all past values*, although the magnitude of this dependence declines with time.‡

An example of a first-order autoregressive process would be the process defined by

$$y_t = .9y_{t-1} + 2 + \varepsilon_t \tag{17.29}$$

The autocorrelation function for this process is shown in Fig. 17.5, and a typical realization is shown in Fig. 17.6. The realization differs from that of a first-order

---

† Setting $\delta = 0$ is equivalent to measuring y_t in terms of deviations about its mean, since if y_t follows Eq. (17.22), then the series $\tilde{y}_t = y_t - \mu$ follows the process $\tilde{y}_t = \phi_1 \tilde{y}_{t-1} + \varepsilon_t$. The reader can check to see that the result in Eq. (17.24) is also obtained (although with more algebraic manipulation) by calculating $E[(y_t - \mu)^2]$ directly.

‡ It can be shown that if the AR(1) process is stationary, it is equivalent to a moving average process of *infinite order* (and thus with infinite memory). In fact, for any stationary autoregressive process of any order there exists an equivalent moving average process of infinite order (so that the autoregressive process is *invertible* into a moving average process). Similarly, if certain *invertibility* conditions are met (and these will be discussed in Appendix 17.1) any finite-order moving average process has an equivalent autoregressive process of infinite order. For a more detailed discussion of invertibility, the reader is referred to G. E. P. Box and G. M. Jenkins, *Time Series Analysis* (San Francisco: Holden-Day, 1970); C. Nelson, *Applied Time Series Analysis* (San Francisco: Holden-Day, 1973), chap. 3; or C. W. J. Granger and P. Newbold, *Forecasting Economic Time Series* (New York: Academic, 1977).

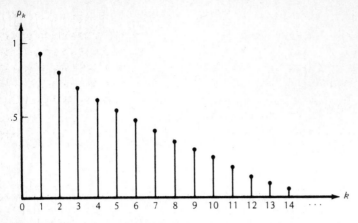

Figure 17.5 Autocorrelation function for $y_t = .9y_{t-1} + 2 + \varepsilon_t$.

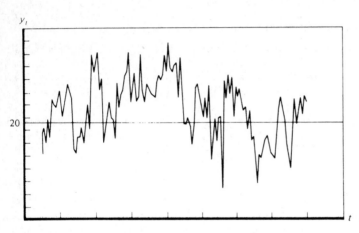

Figure 17.6 Typical realization of the process $y_t = .9y_{t-1} + 2 + \varepsilon_t$.

moving average process in that each observation is highly correlated with those surrounding it, resulting in discernible overall up-and-down patterns.

Let us now look at the second-order autoregressive process AR(2):

$$y_t = \phi_1 y_{t-1} + \phi_2 y_{t-2} + \delta + \varepsilon_t \qquad (17.30)$$

The process has mean

$$\mu = \frac{\delta}{1 - \phi_1 - \phi_2} \qquad (17.31)$$

and a necessary condition for stationarity is that $\phi_1 + \phi_2 < 1.$†

---

† This is not a sufficient condition for stationarity. Necessary and sufficient conditions are presented in Appendix 17.1.

Let us now calculate the variances and covariances of y_t (when y_t is measured in deviations form):

$$\gamma_0 = E[y_t(\phi_1 y_{t-1} + \phi_2 y_{t-2} + \varepsilon_t)] = \phi_1 \gamma_1 + \phi_2 \gamma_2 + \sigma_\varepsilon^2 \qquad (17.32)$$

$$\gamma_1 = E[y_{t-1}(\phi_1 y_{t-1} + \phi_2 y_{t-2} + \varepsilon_t)] = \phi_1 \gamma_0 + \phi_2 \gamma_1 \qquad (17.33)$$

$$\gamma_2 = E[y_{t-2}(\phi_1 y_{t-1} + \phi_2 y_{t-2} + \varepsilon_t)] = \phi_1 \gamma_1 + \phi_2 \gamma_0 \qquad (17.34)$$

and in general, for $k \geq 2$,

$$\gamma_k = E[y_{t-k}(\phi_1 y_{t-1} + \phi_2 y_{t-2} + \varepsilon_t)] = \phi_1 \gamma_{k-1} + \phi_2 \gamma_{k-2} \qquad (17.35)$$

We can solve (17.32), (17.33), and (17.34) simultaneously to get γ_0 in terms of ϕ_1, ϕ_2, and σ_ε^2. Equation (17.33) can be rewritten as

$$\gamma_1 = \frac{\phi_1 \gamma_0}{1 - \phi_2} \qquad (17.36)$$

Substituting (17.34) into (17.32) yields

$$\gamma_0 = \phi_1 \gamma_1 + \phi_2 \phi_1 \gamma_1 + \phi_2^2 \gamma_0 + \sigma_\varepsilon^2 \qquad (17.37)$$

Now using (17.36) to eliminate γ_1 gives us

$$\gamma_0 = \frac{\phi_1^2 \gamma_0}{1 - \phi_2} + \frac{\phi_2 \phi_1^2 \gamma_0}{1 - \phi_2} + \phi_2^2 \gamma_0 + \sigma_\varepsilon^2$$

which, after rearranging, yields

$$\gamma_0 = \frac{(1 - \phi_2)\sigma_\varepsilon^2}{(1 + \phi_2)[(1 - \phi_2)^2 - \phi_1^2]} \qquad (17.38)$$

These equations can also be used to derive the autocorrelation function ρ_k. From (17.34) and (17.36),

$$\rho_1 = \frac{\phi_1}{1 - \phi_2} \qquad (17.39)$$

$$\rho_2 = \phi_2 + \frac{\phi_1^2}{1 - \phi_2} \qquad (17.40)$$

From (17.35) one can see that for $k \geq 2$,

$$\rho_k = \phi_1 \rho_{k-1} + \phi_2 \rho_{k-2} \qquad (17.41)$$

and this can be used to calculate the autocorrelation function for $k > 2$.

A comment is in order regarding Eqs. (17.39) and (17.40), which are called the *Yule-Walker equations*. Suppose we have the sample autocorrelation function for a time series which we believe was generated by a second-order autoregressive process. We could then take a measurement of ρ_1 and ρ_2 and substitute these numbers into Eqs. (17.39) and (17.40). We would then have two algebraic equations which could be solved simultaneously for the two unknowns ϕ_1 and ϕ_2. Thus, we could use the Yule-Walker equations to obtain estimates of the autoregressive parameters ϕ_1 and ϕ_2. (We will discuss the methods by which

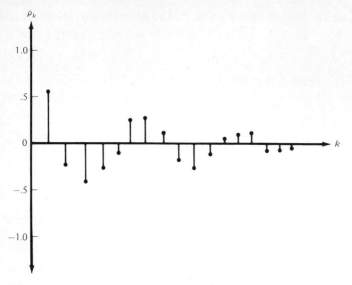

Figure 17.7 Autocorrelation function for $y_t = .9y_{t-1} - .7y_{t-2} + 2 + \varepsilon_t$.

we obtain estimates for the parameters of our time-series models in considerable detail in the next chapter.)

Let us look at an example of a second-order autoregressive process:

$$y_t = .9y_{t-1} - .7y_{t-2} + 2 + \varepsilon_t \qquad (17.42)$$

The autocorrelation function for this process is shown in Fig. 17.7. Note that it is a sinusoidal function that is geometrically damped. As we will see from further examples, autocorrelation functions for autoregressive processes (of order greater than 1) are typically geometrically damped, oscillating, sinusoidal functions.

· The reader should note that *realizations* of second- (and higher-) order autoregressive processes may or may not be cyclical, depending on the numerical values of the parameters ϕ_1, ϕ_2, etc. Equation (17.30), for example, is a second-order difference equation in y_t (with an additive error term). We saw in Chapter 13 that the values of ϕ_1 and ϕ_2 determine whether the solution to this difference equation is oscillatory.

17.2.2 The Partial Autocorrelation Function

One problem in constructing autoregressive models is identifying the *order* of the underlying process. For moving average models this is less of a problem, since if the process is of order q the sample autocorrelations should all be close to zero for lags greater than q. (As we saw in the last chapter, Bartlett's formula provides approximate standard errors for the autocorrelations, so that the order of a moving average process can be determined from significance tests on the sample autocorrelations.) Although some information about the order of an autoregressive process can be obtained from the oscillatory behavior of the sample autocorrelation function, much more information can be obtained from the *partial autocorrelation function*.

To understand what the partial autocorrelation function is and how it can be used, let us first consider the covariances and autocorrelation function for the autoregressive process of order p. First, notice that the covariance with displacement k is determined from

$$\gamma_k = E\left[y_{t-k}(\phi_1 y_{t-1} + \phi_2 y_{t-2} + \cdots + \phi_p y_{t-p} + \varepsilon_t) \right] \qquad (17.43)$$

Now letting $k = 0, 1, \ldots, p$, we obtain the following $p + 1$ difference equations that can be solved simultaneously for $\gamma_0, \gamma_1, \ldots, \gamma_p$:

$$
\begin{aligned}
\gamma_0 &= \phi_1 \gamma_1 + \phi_2 \gamma_2 + \cdots + \phi_p \gamma_p + \sigma_\varepsilon^2 \\
\gamma_1 &= \phi_1 \gamma_0 + \phi_2 \gamma_1 + \cdots + \phi_p \gamma_{p-1} \\
&\cdots\cdots\cdots\cdots\cdots\cdots\cdots\cdots\cdots \\
\gamma_p &= \phi_1 \gamma_{p-1} + \phi_2 \gamma_{p-2} + \cdots + \phi_p \gamma_0
\end{aligned}
\qquad (17.44)
$$

For displacements k greater than p the covariances are determined from

$$\gamma_k = \phi_1 \gamma_{k-1} + \phi_2 \gamma_{k-2} + \cdots + \phi_p \gamma_{k-p} \qquad (17.45)$$

Now by dividing the left-hand and right-hand sides of the equations in (17.44) by γ_0, we can derive a set of p equations that together determine the first p values of the autocorrelation function:

$$
\begin{aligned}
\rho_1 &= \phi_1 + \phi_2 \rho_1 + \cdots + \phi_p \rho_{p-1} \\
&\cdots\cdots\cdots\cdots\cdots\cdots\cdots\cdots\cdots \\
\rho_p &= \phi_1 \rho_{p-1} + \phi_2 \rho_{p-2} + \cdots + \phi_p
\end{aligned}
\qquad (17.46)
$$

For displacement k greater than p we have, from Eq. (17.45),

$$\rho_k = \phi_1 \rho_{k-1} + \phi_2 \rho_{k-2} + \cdots + \phi_p \rho_{k-p} \qquad (17.47)$$

The equations (17.46) are the Yule-Walker equations; if $\rho_1, \rho_2, \ldots, \rho_p$ are known (i.e., measured from a sample autocorrelation function), then the equations can be solved for $\phi_1, \phi_2, \ldots, \phi_p$. (As in the case of the second-order autoregressive process, the Yule-Walker equations provide one means of obtaining estimates of the parameters $\phi_1, \ldots, \phi_p$.)

Unfortunately, solution of the Yule-Walker equations, at least as they are presented in (17.46), requires knowledge of p, the order of the autoregressive process, and determining p is the problem in the first place. Therefore, suppose that we solve the Yule-Walker equations for *successive values of p*. In other words, suppose we begin by hypothesizing that $p = 1$. Then Eqs. (17.46) boil down to $\rho_1 = \phi_1$ or, using the sample autocorrelations, $\hat{\rho}_1 = \hat{\phi}_1$. Thus, if the calculated value $\hat{\phi}_1$ is significantly different from zero, we know that the autoregressive process is *at least* order 1. Let us denote this value $\hat{\phi}_1$ by a_1.

Now let us consider the hypothesis that $p = 2$. To do this we just solve the Yule-Walker equations (17.46) for $p = 2$. Doing this gives us a new set of estimates $\hat{\phi}_1$ and $\hat{\phi}_2$. If $\hat{\phi}_2$ is significantly different from zero we can conclude that the process is *at least* order 2, while if $\hat{\phi}_2$ is approximately zero, we can conclude that $p = 1$. Let us denote the value $\hat{\phi}_2$ by a_2.

We now repeat this process for successive values of p. For $p = 3$ we obtain an estimate of $\hat{\phi}_3$ which we denote by a_3, for $p = 4$ we obtain $\hat{\phi}_4$ which we denote by a_4, etc. We call this series $a_1, a_2, a_3, \ldots$ the *partial autocorrelation function* and note that we can infer the order of the autoregressive process from its behavior. In particular, if the true order of the process is p, we should observe that $a_j \approx 0$ for $j > p$.

17.3 MIXED AUTOREGRESSIVE–MOVING AVERAGE MODELS

Many stationary random processes cannot be modeled as purely moving average or as purely autoregressive, since they have the qualities of both types of processes. The logical extension of the models presented in the last two sections is the *mixed autoregressive–moving average process of order* (p, q). We denote this process as ARMA(p, q) and represent it by

$$y_t = \phi_1 y_{t-1} + \cdots + \phi_p y_{t-p} + \delta + \varepsilon_t - \theta_1 \varepsilon_{t-1} - \cdots - \theta_q \varepsilon_{t-q} \quad (17.48)$$

We assume that the process is stationary, so that its mean is constant over time and is given by

$$\mu = \phi_1 \mu + \cdots + \phi_p \mu + \delta$$

or

$$\mu = \frac{\delta}{1 - \phi_1 - \cdots - \phi_p} \quad (17.49)$$

This gives a necessary condition for the stationarity of the process, that is,†

$$\phi_1 + \phi_2 + \cdots + \phi_p < 1 \quad (17.50)$$

Now let us consider the simplest mixed autoregressive–moving average process, the process ARMA(1, 1):

$$y_t = \phi_1 y_{t-1} + \delta + \varepsilon_t - \theta_1 \varepsilon_{t-1} \quad (17.51)$$

The variances and covariances of this process are determined jointly as follows (setting $\delta = 0$):

$$\gamma_0 = E\left[y_t(\phi_1 y_{t-1} + \varepsilon_t - \theta_1 \varepsilon_{t-1}) \right] = E\left[(\phi_1 y_{t-1} + \varepsilon_t - \theta_1 \varepsilon_{t-1})^2 \right]$$

$$= \phi_1^2 \gamma_0 - 2\phi_1 \theta_1 E\left[y_{t-1} \varepsilon_{t-1} \right] + \sigma_\varepsilon^2 + \theta_1^2 \sigma_\varepsilon^2 \quad (17.52)$$

Since $E(y_{t-1} \varepsilon_{t-1}) = \sigma_\varepsilon^2$, we have

$$\gamma_0(1 - \phi_1^2) = \sigma_\varepsilon^2(1 + \theta_1^2 - 2\phi_1 \theta_1) \quad (17.53)$$

so that the variance is given by‡

$$\gamma_0 = \frac{1 + \theta_1^2 - 2\phi_1 \theta_1}{1 - \phi_1^2} \sigma_\varepsilon^2 \quad (17.54)$$

---

† Again, this is not a sufficient condition. See Appendix 17.1.
‡ For $|\phi_1| < 1$.

We can now determine the covariances $\gamma_1, \gamma_2, \ldots,$ recursively:

$$\gamma_1 = E\big[\, y_{t-1}(\phi_1 y_{t-1} + \varepsilon_t - \theta_1 \varepsilon_{t-1})\big] = \phi_1 \gamma_0 - \theta_1 \sigma_\varepsilon^2$$

$$= \frac{(1 - \phi_1\theta_1)(\phi_1 - \theta_1)}{1 - \phi_1^2}\, \sigma_\varepsilon^2 \tag{17.55}$$

$$\gamma_2 = E\big[\, y_{t-2}(\phi_1 y_{t-1} + \varepsilon_t - \theta_1 \varepsilon_{t-1})\big] = \phi_1 \gamma_1 \tag{17.56}$$

and similarly,

$$\gamma_k = \phi_1 \gamma_{k-1} \qquad k > 2 \tag{17.57}$$

The autocorrelation function, then, is given by

$$\rho_1 = \frac{\gamma_1}{\gamma_0} = \frac{(1 - \phi_1\theta_1)(\phi_1 - \theta_1)}{1 + \theta_1^2 - 2\phi_1\theta_1} \tag{17.58}$$

and for displacement k greater than 1,

$$\rho_k = \phi_1 \rho_{k-1} \qquad k \geq 2 \tag{17.59}$$

Thus, the autocorrelation function begins at its starting value ρ_1 (which is a function of both ϕ_1 and θ_1) and then decays geometrically from this starting value. This reflects the fact that the moving average part of the process has a memory of only one period.

Let us examine the autocorrelation functions of some typical ARMA(1, 1) processes. The autocorrelation function for the process

$$y_t = .8y_{t-1} + 2 + \varepsilon_t - .9\varepsilon_{t-1} \tag{17.60}$$

is shown in Fig. 17.8. The starting value ρ_1 is negative, and the function decays toward 0 from this value.

The autocorrelation function for the process

$$y_t = -.8y_{t-1} + 2 + \varepsilon_t + .9\varepsilon_{t-1} \tag{17.61}$$

will exhibit oscillatory behavior, as shown in Fig. 17.9. Note that it oscillates between positive and negative values, since ϕ_1 is negative.

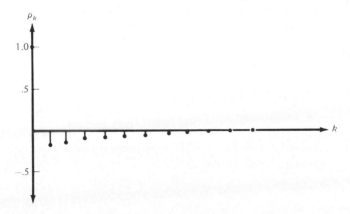

Figure 17.8 Autocorrelation function for $y_t = .8y_{t-1} + 2 + \varepsilon_t - .9\varepsilon_{t-1}$.

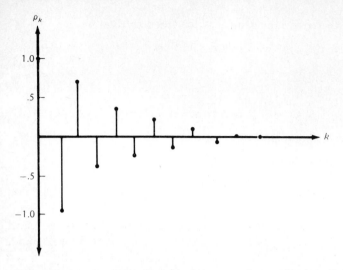

Figure 17.9 Autocorrelation function for $y_t = -.8y_{t-1} + 2 + \varepsilon_t + .9\varepsilon_{t-1}$.

For higher-order processes, i.e., the general ARMA(p, q) process, the variance, covariances, and autocorrelation function are solutions to difference equations that usually cannot be solved by inspection. It can be shown easily, however, that

$$\gamma_k = \phi_1\gamma_{k-1} + \phi_2\gamma_{k-2} + \cdots + \phi_p\gamma_{k-p} \qquad k \geq q+1 \qquad (17.62)$$

and thus
$$\rho_k = \phi_1\rho_{k-1} + \phi_2\rho_{k-2} + \cdots + \phi_p\rho_{k-p} \qquad k \geq q+1 \qquad (17.63)$$

Note that q is the memory of the moving average part of the process, so that for $k \geq q+1$ the autocorrelation function (and covariances) exhibit the properties of a purely autoregressive process.

This completes our discussion of models for stationary stochastic processes. Before we turn to models for homogeneous nonstationary processes, it will be useful to introduce a new notational device. Often it is convenient to write or describe time lags using the *backward shift operator* B. The operator B imposes a one-period time lag each time it is applied to a variable. Thus, $B\varepsilon_t = \varepsilon_{t-1}$, $B^2\varepsilon_t = \varepsilon_{t-2}, \ldots, B^n\varepsilon_t = \varepsilon_{t-n}$. Using this operator, we can now rewrite Eq. (17.1) for the MA(q) process as

$$y_t = \mu + \left(1 - \theta_1 B - \theta_2 B^2 - \cdots - \theta_q B^q\right)\varepsilon_t = \mu + \theta(B)\varepsilon_t \quad (17.64)$$

where $\theta(B)$ denotes a polynomial function of the operator B. Similarly Eq. (17.18) for the AR(p) process can be rewritten as

$$\left(1 - \phi_1 B - \phi_2 B^2 - \cdots - \phi_p B^p\right)y_t = \delta + \varepsilon_t \qquad (17.65)$$

or
$$\phi(B)y_t = \delta + \varepsilon_t \qquad (17.66)$$

Finally, Eq. (17.48) for the ARMA(p, q) process can be rewritten as

$$\left(1 - \phi_1 B - \phi_2 B^2 - \cdots - \phi_p B^p\right)y_t = \delta + \left(1 - \theta_1 B - \theta_2 B^2 - \cdots - \theta_q B^q\right)\varepsilon_t$$

(17.67)

or

$$\phi(B)y_t = \delta + \theta(B)\varepsilon_t$$

(17.68)

We will use the backward shift operator for notational ease throughout the remainder of Part Three of the book.

17.4 HOMOGENEOUS NONSTATIONARY PROCESSES: ARIMA MODELS

In practice, many of the time series we will work with are nonstationary, so that the characteristics of the underlying stochastic process change over time. In this section we construct models for those nonstationary series which can be transformed into stationary series by differencing one or more times. We say that y_t is *homogeneous nonstationary of order d* if

$$w_t = \Delta^d y_t$$

(17.69)

is a stationary series. Here Δ denotes differencing, i.e.,

$$\Delta y_t = y_t - y_{t-1} \qquad \Delta^2 y_t = \Delta y_t - \Delta y_{t-1}$$

and so forth. A discussion of the autoregressive characteristics of homogeneous nonstationary series is given in Appendix 17.1.

Observe that if we have a series w_t, we can get back to y_t by *summing* w_t a total of d times. We write this as

$$y_t = \Sigma^d w_t$$

(17.70)

where Σ is the summation operator:

$$\Sigma w_t = \sum_{i=-\infty}^{t} w_i$$

(17.71)

$$\Sigma^2 w_t = \sum_{j=-\infty}^{t} \sum_{i=-\infty}^{j} w_i$$

(17.72)

and so forth. Note that the summation operator Σ is just the *inverse* of the difference operator Δ. Since $\Delta y_t = y_t - y_{t-1}$, we can write that $\Delta = 1 - B$, and thus $\Sigma = \Delta^{-1} = (1 - B)^{-1}$.

When computing this sum for an actual time series, we begin with the first observation on the original undifferenced series (y_0), and then add successive values of the differenced series. Thus if $w_t = \Delta y_t$, we would compute y_t from

$$y_t = \Sigma w_t = \sum_{i=-\infty}^{t} w_i = \sum_{i=-\infty}^{0} w_i + \sum_{i=1}^{t} w_i = y_0 + w_1 + w_2 + \cdots + w_t$$

(17.73)

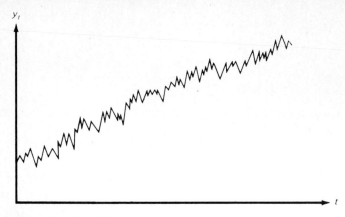

Figure 17.10 An ARIMA process with $d = 1$.

If y_t had been differenced twice, so that $w_t = \Delta^2 y_t$, we could compute y_t from w_t by summing w_t twice.†

After we have differenced the series y_t to produce the stationary series w_t, we can model w_t as an ARMA process. If $w_t = \Delta^d y_t$, and w_t is an ARMA(p, q) process, then we say that y_t is an integrated autoregressive–moving average process of order (p, d, q), or simply ARIMA(p, d, q). We can write the equation for the process ARIMA(p, d, q), using the backward shift operator, as

$$\phi(B)\Delta^d y_t = \delta + \theta(B)\varepsilon_t \tag{17.74}$$

with
$$\phi(B) = 1 - \phi_1 B - \phi_2 B^2 - \cdots - \phi_p B^p \tag{17.75}$$

and
$$\theta(B) = 1 - \theta_1 B - \theta_2 B^2 - \cdots - \theta_q B^q \tag{17.76}$$

We call $\phi(B)$ the *autoregressive operator* and $\theta(B)$ the *moving average operator*.

Note that the mean of $w_t = \Delta^d y_t$ is given by

$$\mu_w = \frac{\delta}{1 - \phi_1 - \phi_2 - \cdots - \phi_p} \tag{17.77}$$

Thus if δ is not equal to 0, the *integrated series* y_t will have a built-in *deterministic trend*. Suppose, for example, that $d = 1$ and $\delta > 0$. Then $y_t = \Sigma w_t$ will grow linearly over time. An example of such a series might be the one drawn in Fig. 17.10. The series has a linear time trend that is independent of the random disturbances, i.e., that is deterministic. The series drawn in Fig. 17.11, on the

---

† Summing w_t the first time gives us Δy_t:

$$\Delta y_t = \Sigma w_t = \sum_{i=-\infty}^{0} w_i + \sum_{i=1}^{t} w_i = \Delta y_0 + w_1 + w_2 + \cdots + w_t$$

Now summing Δy_t yields y_t:

$$y_t = \Sigma(\Delta y_t) = \Sigma(\Delta y_0 + w_1 + w_2 + \cdots + w_t) = y_0 + (\Delta y_0 + w_1) + (\Delta y_0 + w_1 + w_2) + \cdots$$
$$+ (\Delta y_0 + w_1 + w_2 + \cdots + w_t)$$

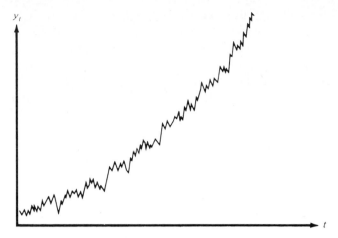

Figure 17.11 An ARIMA process with $d = 2$.

other hand, has an average slope that is increasing linearly in time. This series would most likely have been generated by a process that is ARIMA with $d = 2$ and $\delta > 0$. Thus $w_t = \Delta^2 y_t$ will have no time trend, $\Sigma w_t = \Delta y_t$ will have a linear time trend, and $\Sigma\Sigma w_t = y_t$ will have a time trend whose rate of increase is constant.

It is possible that the stationary series w_t will not be mixed, i.e., will be completely autoregressive or moving average. If w_t is just $AR(p)$, then we call y_t an integrated autoregressive process of order (p, d), and denote it as $ARI(p, d, 0)$. If w_t is just $MA(q)$, then we call y_t an integrated moving average process of order (d, q), and denote it as $IMA(0, d, q)$.

17.5 SPECIFICATION OF ARIMA MODELS

We have seen that any homogeneous nonstationary time series can be modeled as an ARIMA process of order (p, d, q). The practical problem is to choose the most appropriate values for p, d, and q, that is, to *specify* the ARIMA model. This problem is partly resolved by examining both the autocorrelation function and the partial autocorrelation function for the time series of concern.

Given a series y_t that one would like to model, the first problem is to determine the degree of homogeneity d, that is, the number of times that the series must be differenced to produce a stationary series. To determine the appropriate value of d, we make use of the fact that *the autocorrelation function ρ_k for a stationary series must approach 0 as the displacement k becomes large.* To see why this must be so, consider a stationary ARMA process of order (p, q). We know that the autocorrelation function for the *moving average part* of this process becomes 0 for $k > q$, as the process has a memory of only q periods.

Thus, if y_t is MA(q), then $\rho_k = 0$ for $k > q$. We also know that the autocorrelation function for the *autoregressive part* of a stationary ARMA process is geometrically damped (see the examples in Figs. 17.5 to 17.7). Finally, the autocorrelation function for the complete ARMA process has moving average characteristics for the first $q - p$ periods, but after that it is autoregressive in character; i.e., it has an envelope that declines geometrically.

The procedure for specifying the value of d is straightforward. Look at the autocorrelation function of the original series y_t and determine whether it is stationary. If it is not, difference the series and examine the autocorrelation function for Δy_t to determine stationarity. Repeat this process until a value for d is reached such that $\Delta^d y_t$ is stationary; i.e., the autocorrelation function goes to 0 as k becomes large.† One should also examine the time series itself to check for stationarity. If the series appears to have an overall trend, it is probably not stationary.

After d is determined, one can work with the stationary series $w_t = \Delta^d y_t$ and examine both its autocorrelation function and its partial autocorrelation function to determine the proper specification of p and q. For low-order processes this can be rather simple, since the autocorrelation functions for processes such as AR(1), AR(2), MA(1), MA(2), and ARMA(1, 1) are easy to recognize and distinguish from each other (see Figs. 17.1 to 17.9). Fortunately, many of the time series encountered in economic applications can, if they are seasonally adjusted, be modeled as low-order ARMA processes, i.e., as processes with $p \leq 2$ and $q \leq 2$. When this is not the case, the specification of p and q becomes more difficult, and requires closer inspection of the full and partial autocorrelation functions. For example, spikes in the autocorrelation function are indicative of moving average terms, and the partial autocorrelation function can be used for guidance in determining the order of the autoregressive portion of the process.

Unfortunately, if both the autoregressive and moving average parts of the process are of high order, one may at best only be able to make a tentative guess for p and q. As we will see later, however, it is possible to check that guess after the parameters in the ARMA(p, q) model have been estimated. As a first step in this process of *diagnostic checking* one can calculate the autocorrelation function for the estimated ARMA(p, q) model and compare it with the autocorrelation function of the original series to see how well the two match. If they do not match well, a new specification can be tried.

The process of diagnostic checking will be discussed in more detail in Chapter 18. However, it is important to realize that the specification of an ARMA model is an art, rather than a science. As one gains more experience in

---

† Remember that in practice we have no guarantee that the time series being modeled is homogeneous nonstationary. One might be unlucky and discover that one's time series is *nonhomogeneous* nonstationary. In this case, no matter how many times the series was differenced, the autocorrelation function would not damp down to 0. Models of nonhomogeneous nonstationary series are beyond the scope of this book; suffice it to say, they are difficult to construct and estimate.

constructing time-series models, it becomes easier to recognize autocorrelation functions and to link them to the appropriate specification of p and q. When sound judgment is used, diagnostic checking becomes simpler.

Example 17.1 Price of newsprint† As a first example of model specification, let us examine a quarterly series for the average price of newsprint in the United States over the period 1965-2 through 1977-3 (50 data points).

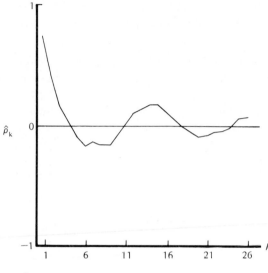

Figure 17.12 Newsprint price: autocorrelation function of Δy_t.

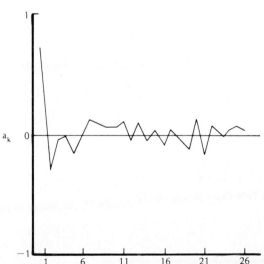

Figure 17.13 Newsprint price: partial autocorrelation function of Δy_t.

† This example was constructed by Dynamics Associates, Inc., Cambridge, Mass., and is used by permission.

The series itself (not shown here) rises steadily over time, indicating that it is nonstationary. However, the differenced series Δy_t does appear to be stationary, as can be seen from its sample autocorrelation function in Fig. 17.12. The autocorrelation function has the damped sinusoidal shape of a second-order autoregressive process and no spikes indicative of moving average terms. The partial autocorrelation function, shown in Fig. 17.13, has significant spikes at lags 1 and 2, confirming a second-order autoregressive interpretation of the differenced series. We might thus estimate an ARI(2, 1, 0) model.

Example 17.2 Interest rate As a second example of model specification, reconsider the time series for the interest rate on commercial paper we examined in Chapter 16. After repeatedly differencing the series and examining the sample autocorrelation functions, we established that it was probably second-order homogeneous nonstationary, so that d equals 2 in a specification of an ARIMA model. Now if we examine the autocorrelation function for $\Delta^2 y_t$ in Fig. 17.14 in more detail, we see that it exhibits moving average properties that are second order; i.e., it begins decaying after the point $k = 2$. The periodicity of the oscillations in the autocorrelation function would probably indicate that the autoregressive part of the model should be of order 4, although a second-order autoregressive specification might also be suggested by the periodic behavior. Thus two specifications might be appropriate, namely the ARIMA(2, 2, 2) and the ARIMA(4, 2, 2) models.

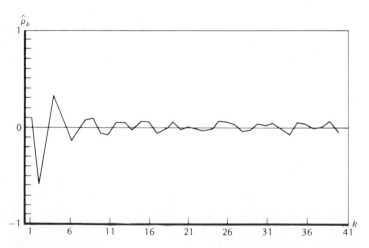

Figure 17.14 Interest rate on commercial paper: autocorrelation function of $\Delta^2 y_t$.

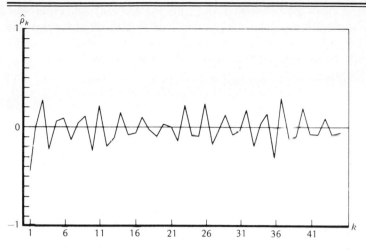

Figure 17.15 Monthly hog production: autocorrelation function of $(1 - B)(1 - B^{12})y_t$.

Example 17.3 Hog production A third example is the monthly series for hog production which was also examined in the last chapter. We took a 12-month difference of the series to eliminate seasonal cycles and then found that differencing once was sufficient to ensure stationarity. The autocorrelation function for $(1 - B)(1 - B^{12})y_t$ is shown again in Fig. 17.15.† Observe that the sample autocorrelation function begins declining immediately at $k = 1$, and has peaks roughly once every three periods. We might thus suspect that $(1 - B)(1 - B^{12})y_t$ is autoregressive of order 3, so that y_t could be specified by the model (using backward shift operator notation):

$$\left(1 - \phi_1 B - \phi_2 B^2 - \phi_3 B^3\right)(1 - B)(1 - B^{12})y_t = \varepsilon_t \qquad (17.78)$$

Readers should not be disturbed at this point if they find the art of model specification somewhat bewildering. We will go through several more examples of model specification in Chapter 20.

APPENDIX 17.1 STATIONARITY, INVERTIBILITY, AND HOMOGENEITY

We saw before that a necessary condition for an ARMA(p, q) process to be stationary is that

$$\phi_1 + \phi_2 + \cdots + \phi_p < 1 \qquad (A17.1)$$

† Recall the meaning of the backward shift operator B:

$$(1 - B)(1 - B^{12})y_t = \Delta(y_t - y_{t-12})$$

We now present a strict (i.e., necessary and sufficient) condition for stationarity, and use it to demonstrate a particular property of homogeneous nonstationary processes.

Note that the process ARMA(p, q) can be written in the form

$$(1 - \phi_1 B - \cdots - \phi_p B^p)\tilde{y}_t = (1 - \theta_1 B - \cdots - \theta_q B^q)\varepsilon_t \quad \text{(A17.2)}$$

or

$$\phi(B)\tilde{y}_t = \theta(B)\varepsilon_t \quad \text{(A17.3)}$$

where B is the backward shift operator and $\tilde{y}_t$ is the deviation of y_t from its mean, that is,

$$\tilde{y}_t = y_t - \mu \quad \text{(A17.4)}$$

Now let us rewrite Eq. (A17.3) as

$$\tilde{y}_t = \phi^{-1}(B)\theta(B)\varepsilon_t \quad \text{(A17.5)}$$

If y_t is a stationary process, then $\phi^{-1}(B)$ must converge. This requires that the roots of the *characteristic equation*

$$\phi(B) = 0 \quad \text{(A17.6)}$$

all be *outside* the unit circle.† Thus the solutions $B_1, \ldots, B_p$ to (A17.6) must all be greater than 1 in magnitude.

Now suppose that the process $\tilde{y}_t$ in (A17.3) is *nonstationary* but in such a way that exactly d of the roots of $\phi(B)$ are on the unit circle and the remainder are outside the unit circle. This process can then be rewritten in the form

$$\omega(B)(1 - B)^d\tilde{y}_t = \theta(B)\varepsilon_t \quad \text{(A17.7)}$$

where $\omega(B)$ is a stationary autoregressive operator of order $p - d$ and the operator $(1 - B)^d$ has d roots all equal to unity. But $1 - B$ is a *first-difference* operator, that is,

$$(1 - B)\tilde{y}_t = \Delta\tilde{y}_t = \tilde{y}_t - \tilde{y}_{t-1} \quad \text{(A17.8)}$$

Thus (A17.7) can be rewritten as

$$\omega(B)\Delta^d\tilde{y}_t = \theta(B)\varepsilon_t \quad \text{(A17.9)}$$

or

$$\omega(B)w_t = \theta(B)\varepsilon_t \quad \text{(A17.10)}$$

where $w_t = \Delta^d\tilde{y}_t$ is stationary, since it resulted from differencing $\tilde{y}_t$ d times. We call $\tilde{y}_t$ *homogeneous nonstationary with order d*, and we note the conclusion that such a process has an autoregressive operator $\phi(B)$ such that

$$\phi(B) = \omega(B)(1 - B)^d \quad \text{(A17.11)}$$

where the roots of $\omega(B)$ are all outside the unit circle.

Analogous to the stationarity condition for the autoregressive operator is the *invertibility condition* for the moving average operator. We say that y_t is invertible if we can write (A17.3) as

$$\theta^{-1}(B)\phi(B)\tilde{y}_t = \varepsilon_t \quad \text{(A17.12)}$$

---

† See Box and Jenkins, op. cit., for a proof of this.

i.e., if the ARMA process (or more specifically the moving average part of the ARMA process) can be inverted into a purely autoregressive process. Now, if y_t is invertible, $\theta^{-1}(B)$ must converge. This requires that the roots of the *characteristic equation*

$$\theta(B) = 1 - \theta_1 B - \theta_2 B^2 - \cdots - \theta_q B^q = 0 \qquad (\text{A}17.13)$$

must all lie outside the unit circle; i.e., the solutions $B_1, B_2, \ldots, B_q$ to Eq. (A17.13) must all be greater than 1 in absolute value.†

As an example, consider the first-order moving average process (that is, $q = 1$), whose characteristic equation is

$$1 - \theta_1 B = 0 \qquad (\text{A}17.14)$$

Then the invertibility condition becomes

$$|B| = \frac{1}{|\theta_1|} > 1 \qquad (\text{A}17.15)$$

or

$$|\theta_1| < 1$$

For the second-order moving average process ($q = 2$) the characteristic equation is

$$1 - \theta_1 B - \theta_2 B^2 = 0 \qquad (\text{A}17.16)$$

and

$$B = \frac{-\theta_1 \pm \sqrt{\theta_1^2 + 4\theta_2}}{2\theta_2} \qquad (\text{A}17.17)$$

Both these values of B must be outside the unit circle, which implies that

$$\theta_2 + \theta_1 < 1 \qquad (\text{A}17.18)$$
$$\theta_2 - \theta_1 < 1 \qquad (\text{A}17.19)$$

and

$$|\theta_2| < 1 \qquad (\text{A}17.20)$$

EXERCISES

17.1 Calculate the covariances γ_k for MA(3), the moving average process of order 3. Determine the autocorrelation function for this process. Plot the autocorrelation function for the MA(3) process

$$y_t = 1 + \varepsilon_t + .8\varepsilon_{t-1} - .5\varepsilon_{t-2} + .3\varepsilon_{t-3}$$

17.2 What are the characteristics that one would expect of a realization of the following MA(1) process?

$$y_t = 1 + \varepsilon_t + .8\varepsilon_{t-1}$$

---

† This invertibility condition is proved in detail in U. Grenander and M. Rosenblatt, *Statistical Analyses of Stationary Time Series* (New York: Wiley, 1957). A brief discussion is also presented in Box and Jenkins, op. cit.

How would these characteristics differ from those of a realization of the following MA(1) process?

$$y_t = 1 + \varepsilon_t - .8\varepsilon_{t-1}$$

17.3 Show that the covariances γ_k of MA(q), the moving average process of order q, are given by

$$\gamma_k = \begin{cases} (-\theta_k + \theta_1\theta_{k+1} + \cdots + \theta_{q-k}\theta_q)\sigma_\varepsilon^2 & k = 1, \ldots, q \\ 0 & k > q \end{cases}$$

and that the autocorrelation function for MA(q) is given by

$$\rho_k = \begin{cases} \dfrac{-\theta_k + \theta_1\theta_{k+1} + \cdots + \theta_{q-k}\theta_q}{1 + \theta_1^2 + \theta_2^2 + \cdots + \theta_q^2} & k = 1, \ldots, q \\ 0 & k > q \end{cases}$$

as in Eq. (17.17).

17.4 Derive the autocorrelation function for the ARMA(2, 1) process

$$y_t = \phi_1 y_{t-1} + \phi_2 y_{t-2} + \varepsilon_t - \theta_1\varepsilon_{t-1}$$

that is, determine ρ_1, ρ_2, etc., in terms of ϕ_1, ϕ_2, and θ_1. Draw this autocorrelation function for $\phi_1 = .6$, $\phi_2 = .3$, and $\theta_1 = .9$. Repeat for $\phi_1 = .6$, $\phi_2 = .3$, and $\theta_1 = -.9$. Repeat for $\phi_1 = .6$, $\phi_2 = -.3$, and $\theta_1 = -.9$.

17.5 Show that the autocorrelation function for the general ARMA(p, q) process is given by

$$\rho_k = \phi_1\rho_{k-1} + \phi_2\rho_{k-2} + \cdots + \phi_p\rho_{k-p} \qquad k \geq q + 1$$

as in Eq. (17.63).

17.6 Suppose that y_t is first-order homogeneous nonstationary, and that $w_t = \Delta y_t$ can be represented by the ARMA(1, 1) model

$$w_t = .9w_{t-1} + \varepsilon_t - .6\varepsilon_{t-1} + 1$$

If $y_t = 0$ for $t = 0$, what is $E(y_t)$ as a function of time?

17.7 Relate the summation operator to the backward-shift operator by showing that

$$\Sigma = (1 - B)^{-1} = 1 + B + B^2 + B^3 + \cdots +$$

17.8 Refer back to the time series for nonfarm inventory investment in Fig. 16.7 and its sample autocorrelation function in Fig. 16.8. Can you suggest one or more ARMA(p, q) processes that might have generated that time series? (In other words, how many autoregressive terms p and moving average terms q should the process have?)

ESTIMATION OF TIME-SERIES MODELS

In this chapter we discuss the procedure by which the parameters of an ARIMA model are estimated. As we shall see, if the model contains moving average terms, this involves the application of a nonlinear estimation method similar to that described in Chapter 9. Following this we describe *diagnostic checking*, a procedure used to test whether the model has been correctly specified (i.e., whether p, d, and q have been chosen correctly).

The material in this chapter is at a somewhat more advanced mathematical level than that in the previous three chapters. Readers unfamiliar with vector and matrix notation should skip over some of the mathematical details involved in the estimation procedure. A basic understanding of the estimation procedure and its application can be obtained by reading through the chapter and paying special attention to the examples.

We begin by summarizing the procedures involved in the estimation and diagnostic checking of a time-series model. Once a tentative specification of the time-series model has been made, i.e., once values of p, d, and q have been chosen for the ARIMA model,†

$$\phi(B)\Delta^d y_t = \phi(B)w_t = \theta(B)\varepsilon_t \tag{18.1}$$

with $\phi(B) = 1 - \phi_1 B - \phi_2 B^2 - \cdots - \phi_p B^p$ and $\theta(B) = 1 - \theta_1 B - \theta_2 B^2$

---

† We assume for simplicity here that $\delta = 0$, that is, that w_t, is measured as a deviation from its mean value.

$- \cdots - \theta_q B^q$, then estimates can be obtained for the p autoregressive parameters $\phi_1, \ldots, \phi_p$ and the q moving average parameters $\theta_1, \ldots, \theta_q$. As in the case of the regression model, we choose parameter values that will minimize the sum of squared differences between the actual time series $w_t = \Delta^d y_t$ and the fitted time series $\hat{w}_t$.

To put this another way, rewrite Eq. (18.1) in terms of the error term series ε_t†:

$$\varepsilon_t = \theta^{-1}(B)\phi(B)w_t \tag{18.2}$$

The objective in estimation is to find a vector of autoregressive parameters $\phi = (\phi_1, \ldots, \phi_p)$ and a vector of moving average parameters $\theta = (\theta_1, \ldots, \theta_q)$ that *minimize the sum of squared errors*

$$S(\phi, \theta) = \sum_t \varepsilon_t^2 \tag{18.3}$$

We denote the vectors of parameters that minimize (18.3) by $\hat{\phi} = (\hat{\phi}_1, \ldots, \hat{\phi}_p)$ and $\hat{\theta} = (\hat{\theta}_1, \ldots, \hat{\theta}_q)$, and the residuals associated with these parameter values by $\hat{\varepsilon}_t$, so that $\hat{\varepsilon}_t = \hat{\theta}^{-1}(B)\hat{\phi}(B)w_t$. Thus,

$$S(\hat{\phi}, \hat{\theta}) = \sum_t \hat{\varepsilon}_t^2$$

This estimation can be difficult if moving average terms are present, since then Eq. (18.2) is nonlinear in the parameters. For this reason an iterative method of nonlinear estimation must be used in the minimization of (18.3). In addition, the first error term in the series, ε_1, depends on the past and unobservable values $w_0, w_{-1}, \ldots, w_{-p+1}$ and $\varepsilon_0, \varepsilon_{-1}, \ldots, \varepsilon_{-q+1}$. Thus some method must be used to initialize the series (i.e., choose numbers for these unobservable values) before the nonlinear estimation process is applied.

After the parameters of the model have been estimated, a procedure of *diagnostic checking* is used to test whether the initial specification of the model was correct. We would expect the *residuals* $\hat{\varepsilon}_t$, $t = 1, \ldots, T$, to resemble closely the true errors ε_t, which, by assumption, are uncorrelated. A diagnostic check is used to test whether these residuals are indeed uncorrelated. If they are not, we would want to respecify the model (i.e., choose new values for p, d, and q), estimate this new model, and perform another diagnostic check to determine if it has been correctly specified.

Once the model has been checked to satisfaction, it can be used for forecasting future movements in the time series. We will see that the optimal (minimum mean square error) forecast $\hat{y}_T(l)$ of the series y_t made at time T for the value l periods in the future is the conditional expectation of y_{T+l} taken at time T. The properties of this forecast, as well as the method of determining confidence intervals, will be discussed in Chapter 19.

---

† It should be more clear now why we were concerned with the invertibility of $\theta(B)$ in Appendix 17.1.

18.1 THE ESTIMATION PROCEDURE

We assume that a total of $T + d$ observations are available for the homogeneous nonstationary time series of order d, y_t, and we denote these observations as $y_{-d+1}, \ldots, y_0, y_1, \ldots, y_T$. After differencing this series d times, we obtain a stationary series w_t with T observations $w_1, \ldots, w_T$. The problem is to estimate the parameter vectors ϕ and θ for the ARMA(p, q) model which has been specified for the series w_t. To do this, we utilize the fact that (by assumption) the error terms $\varepsilon_1, \ldots, \varepsilon_T$ are all *normally distributed* and independent, with mean 0 and variance σ_ε^2. Then the *conditional log likelihood function* associated with the parameter values ($\phi, \theta, \sigma_\varepsilon$) is given by

$$L(\phi, \theta, \sigma_\varepsilon) = -T \log \sigma_\varepsilon - \frac{S(\phi, \theta)}{2\sigma_\varepsilon^2} \qquad (18.4)$$

We say that $L(\phi, \theta, \sigma_\varepsilon)$ is the *conditional* logarithmic likelihood function because the sum of squared errors $S(\phi, \theta)$ depends on (i.e., is conditional on) the past and unobservable values $w_0, w_{-1}, \ldots, w_{-p+1}, \varepsilon_0, \varepsilon_{-1}, \ldots, \varepsilon_{-q+1}$. This can be seen by writing the equation for the first observable error term ε_1 in the expanded form of the ARMA model:

$$\varepsilon_1 = w_1 - \phi_1 w_0 - \phi_2 w_{-1} - \cdots - \phi_p w_{-p+1} + \theta_1 \varepsilon_0 + \cdots + \theta_q \varepsilon_{-q+1}$$
$$(18.5)$$

Setting aside for the moment the problem of determining the past values of w_t and ε_t, Eq. (18.4) makes it clear that the maximum-likelihood estimate of ϕ and θ is given by the *minimization* of the sum of squared residuals $S(\phi, \theta)$. Thus, under the assumption of normally distributed errors, the maximum-likelihood estimate is the same as the *least-squares* estimate.†

18.1.1 Initialization of the Series

Because the sum-of-squares function $S(\phi, \theta)$ and thus the likelihood function $L(\phi, \theta, \sigma_\varepsilon)$ are both conditional on the past unobservable values of w_t and ε_t ($w_0, \ldots, w_{-p+1}$ and $\varepsilon_0, \ldots, \varepsilon_{-q+1}$), the least-squares estimates that we obtain depend on the choice of values made for $w_0, w_{-1}, \ldots,$ etc. For this reason we must choose initial starting values for $w_0, w_{-1}, \ldots,$ to be used in the minimization of the conditional sum-of-squares function.

One solution is to set $w_0, \ldots, w_{-p+1}$ and $\varepsilon_0, \ldots, \varepsilon_{-q+1}$ equal to their *unconditional* *expected* *values*. The unconditional expected values of $\varepsilon_0, \ldots, \varepsilon_{-q+1}$ are all 0, and, if $\delta = 0$ (i.e., the process has no deterministic component), the unconditional expected values of $w_0, \ldots, w_{-p+1}$ are 0 as well. This solution will provide a reasonably good approximation to the correct procedure if the actual values of $\phi_1, \ldots, \phi_p$ are not very close to 1 and if the number of observations T is large relative to p and q.

---

† For a review of maximum-likelihood estimation, see Appendix 3.2.

In Appendix 18.1 we discuss an alternative method of initializing the series. The procedure determines *conditional expected values* for $w_0, \ldots, w_{-p+1}$, that is, values that are conditional on the observed values of $w_1, \ldots, w_T$ and the estimated values of $\varepsilon_1, \ldots, \varepsilon_T$. This procedure is technically difficult and computationally expensive, however, and its benefits (in terms of increased efficiency in the parameter estimates) may not be substantial. In fact, as the sample size becomes large, the influence of the initial values disappears. We therefore recommend using the unconditional expected values for $w_0, \ldots, w_{-p+1}$, that is, setting them equal to 0 (when $\delta = 0$).

18.1.2 Nonlinear Estimation of Model Parameters

Our estimation problem is to find values of ϕ and θ that minimize the sum of squared errors

$$S(\phi, \theta) = \sum_t \varepsilon_t^2 = \sum_t \left[\varepsilon_t | \phi, \theta, \mathbf{w} \right]^2 \tag{18.6}$$

where $\mathbf{w}$ is the vector of observations of w_t and the errors ε_t are conditional on ϕ, θ, and $\mathbf{w}$. Assuming that the initialization of the series is based, as we suggest, on the unconditional expected values (which are all 0) of $w_0, \ldots, w_{-p+1}$ and $\varepsilon_0, \ldots, \varepsilon_{-q+1}$, the time bounds in the summation of Eq. (18.6) would be $t = 1$ to T. Thus our problem is to minimize

$$S(\phi, \theta) = \sum_{t=1}^{T} \left[\varepsilon_t | \phi, \theta, \mathbf{w} \right]^2 \tag{18.7}$$

Now suppose that the model was purely autoregressive, i.e., was of the form

$$\phi(B) w_t = \varepsilon_t \tag{18.8}$$

or

$$w_t = \phi_1 w_{t-1} + \cdots + \phi_p w_{t-p} + \varepsilon_t \tag{18.9}$$

Observe that since Eq. (18.9) is of the general form

$$y_t = \beta_0 + \beta_1 x_{1t} + \beta_2 x_{2t} + \cdots + \varepsilon_t \tag{18.10}$$

it can be estimated simply as a linear regression.† Although for a purely autoregressive model the estimation process is essentially a linear regression, the problem is more difficult if the model contains a moving average component as well. In that case we can represent the model as

$$\theta^{-1}(B) \phi(B) w_t = \varepsilon_t \tag{18.11}$$

Clearly, this "regression equation" is nonlinear in the parameters, and cannot be

---

† Ignoring problems of initialization (i.e., selection of values for $w_0, w_{-1}, \ldots, w_{-p+1}$), our estimate for ϕ would be given by

$$\hat{\phi} = (\mathbf{X}'\mathbf{X})^{-1}\mathbf{X}'\mathbf{Y} \quad \text{where } \mathbf{X} = \begin{bmatrix} w_p & w_{p-1} & \cdots & w_1 \\ w_{p+1} & w_p & \cdots & w_2 \\ \cdots & \cdots & \cdots & \cdots \\ w_{T-1} & w_{T-2} & \cdots & w_{T-p} \end{bmatrix} \text{ and } \mathbf{Y} = \begin{bmatrix} w_{p+1} \\ w_{p+2} \\ \cdots \\ w_T \end{bmatrix}$$

that is, $\mathbf{X}$ is a $(T - p) \times p$ matrix and $\mathbf{Y}$ is a $(T - p) \times 1$ vector.

estimated by a simple application of ordinary least squares. However, it can be estimated by a general iterative nonlinear estimation routine. The process is nearly identical to that discussed in Section 9.4 and used in standard nonlinear regression programs.

The nonlinear estimation process uses the first two terms in a Taylor series expansion to linearize Eq. (18.11) around an initial guess for ϕ and θ. A linear regression is then performed on this linearized equation, least-squares estimates of θ and ϕ are obtained, and a new linearization of (18.11) is made around these estimates. Again a linear regression is performed, a second set of estimates of θ and ϕ is obtained, and a new linearization of (18.11) is made around this second set of estimates. This process is repeated iteratively until convergence occurs, i.e., until the estimates of θ and ϕ do not change after repeated iterations.

To look at this iterative estimation process in more detail, let the vector β represent the $p + q$ parameters (θ, ϕ) that we wish to estimate. We wish to choose numerical values for β which minimize

$$S(\beta) = \sum_{t=1}^{T} \left[\varepsilon_t | \mathbf{w}, \beta \right]^2 = \sum_{t=1}^{T} \left[\varepsilon_t \right]^2 \tag{18.12}$$

Remember that the notation $[\varepsilon_t]$ means that the errors are conditional on the values of $\mathbf{w}$ and β. Now let us expand $[\varepsilon_t]$ in a Taylor series around some initial guess β_0 for the parameter values:†

$$\left[\varepsilon_t \right] = \left[\varepsilon_t | \mathbf{w}, \beta_0 \right] + \sum_{i=1}^{p+q} (\beta_i - \beta_{i,0}) \frac{\partial \left[\varepsilon_t \right]}{\partial \beta_i} \bigg|_{\beta = \beta_0}$$

$$+ \frac{1}{2} \sum_{i=1}^{p+q} (\beta_i - \beta_{i,0})^2 \frac{\partial^2 \left[\varepsilon_t \right]}{\partial \beta_i^2} \bigg|_{\beta = \beta_0} + \cdots + \tag{18.13}$$

Here $\beta_{i,0}$ is the value of the first guess for the parameter β_i, and thus is the ith component of the vector β_0. We will approximate $[\varepsilon_t]$ by the first two terms of this Taylor series expansion. When we let

$$x_{i,t} = - \frac{\partial \left[\varepsilon_t \right]}{\partial \beta_i} \bigg|_{\beta = \beta_0} \tag{18.14}$$

† Recall that if $y = f(x_1, x_2)$ is a nonlinear function of two variables x_1 and x_2, it can be represented by a Taylor series around the numerical values $x_{1,0}$ and $x_{2,0}$ as follows:

$$y = f(x_{1,0}, x_{2,0}) + (x_1 - x_{1,0}) \frac{\partial f}{\partial x_1} \bigg|_{\substack{x_1 = x_{1,0} \\ x_2 = x_{2,0}}} + (x_2 - x_{2,0}) \frac{\partial f}{\partial x_2} \bigg|_{\substack{x_1 = x_{1,0} \\ x_2 = x_{2,0}}} + \frac{1}{2}(x_1 - x_{1,0})^2 \frac{\partial^2 f}{\partial x_1^2} \bigg|_{\substack{x_1 = x_{1,0} \\ x_2 = x_{2,0}}}$$

$$+ \frac{1}{2}(x_2 - x_{2,0})^2 \frac{\partial^2 f}{\partial x_2^2} \bigg|_{\substack{x_1 = x_{1,0} \\ x_2 = x_{2,0}}} + (x_1 - x_{1,0})(x_2 - x_{2,0}) \frac{\partial^2 f}{\partial x_1 \partial x_2} \bigg|_{\substack{x_1 = x_{1,0} \\ x_2 = x_{2,0}}} + \cdots +$$

(Note that the derivatives are evaluated at $x_{1,0}$ and $x_{2,0}$.) A linear approximation of $f(x_1, x_2)$ is thus given by the first three terms on the right-hand side of the above equation.

and
$$[\varepsilon_{t,0}] = [\varepsilon_t | \mathbf{w}, \boldsymbol{\beta}_0] \tag{18.15}$$

it follows that (approximately)

$$[\varepsilon_t] = [\varepsilon_{t,0}] - \sum_{i=1}^{p+q} (\beta_i - \beta_{i,0}) x_{i,t} \tag{18.16}$$

which can be rewritten as

$$[\varepsilon_{t,0}] + \sum_{i=1}^{p+q} \beta_{i,0} x_{i,t} = \sum_{i=1}^{p+q} \beta_i x_{i,t} + [\varepsilon_t] \tag{18.17}$$

The left-hand side of Eq. (18.17) can be thought of as a composite dependent variable, which will have different numerical values for $t = 1, 2, \ldots, T$. (Note that $[\varepsilon_{t,0}]$ is just the value of the error term at time t, given the first guess $\boldsymbol{\beta}_0$.) On the right-hand side of (18.17) are $p + q$ independent variables (multiplied by the $p + q$ unknown parameters β_i) as well as an additive error term. It should be clear, then, that the parameters β_i can be estimated from Eq. (18.17) via a linear regression.† This ordinary least-squares regression is performed to produce a new estimate of $\boldsymbol{\beta}$, which we call $\hat{\boldsymbol{\beta}}_1$.

Next, using a new Taylor series expansion of $[\varepsilon_t]$ around this $\hat{\boldsymbol{\beta}}_1$, we obtain a new version of (18.17) which can also be estimated by ordinary least squares to yield a new estimate $\hat{\boldsymbol{\beta}}_2$. This process is repeated over and over again until

$$\hat{\boldsymbol{\beta}}_k - \hat{\boldsymbol{\beta}}_{k-1} \approx 0 \tag{18.18}$$

We call k the *convergence number*, i.e., the number of iterations required until convergence occurs. $\hat{\boldsymbol{\beta}}_k$ will then be our final estimate of the parameters $\phi_1, \ldots, \phi_p$ and $\theta_1, \ldots, \theta_q$.

The standard errors and t statistics for our parameter estimates would be calculated from the *last* linearization, as is typically done in a nonlinear estimation procedure (see Chapter 9). Thus t statistics have limited meaning, indicating only the significance of the least-squares parameter estimates obtained for the final linearization of the nonlinear equation. An R^2 can be calculated in the same way, and has similar relevance. For this reason, we should not necessarily reject a time-series equation with a low R^2. Despite a low

---

† Let $\mathbf{Y}$ be the $T \times 1$ vector representing the left-hand side of (18.17) for different values of t, let $\mathbf{X}$ be the $T \times (p + q)$ matrix of independent variables, and let $\boldsymbol{\beta}$ be the $(p + q) \times 1$ vector of unknown parameters:

$$\mathbf{Y} = \begin{bmatrix} [\varepsilon_{1,0}] + \sum_{i=1}^{p+q} \beta_{i,0} x_{i,1} \\ \cdots\cdots\cdots\cdots \\ [\varepsilon_{T,0}] + \sum_{i=1}^{p+q} \beta_{i,0} x_{i,T} \end{bmatrix} \quad \mathbf{X} = \begin{bmatrix} x_{1,1} & x_{2,1} & \cdots & x_{p+q,1} \\ \cdots\cdots\cdots\cdots\cdots \\ x_{1,T} & x_{2,T} & \cdots & x_{p+q,T} \end{bmatrix} \quad \boldsymbol{\beta} = \begin{bmatrix} \beta_1 \\ \cdot \\ \beta_{p+q} \end{bmatrix}$$

Now letting $[\varepsilon]$ be the $T \times 1$ vector of (unobservable) error terms, we obtain the linear regression equation

$$\mathbf{Y} = \mathbf{X}\boldsymbol{\beta} + [\varepsilon]$$

R^2 for the last iteration, it is possible that the full nonlinear model will have considerable predictive power.

It is important to point out that there can be no guarantee that the estimation process described above will converge *at all* to a final estimate of the parameters. It is quite possible for the process to *diverge*, i.e., for the successive estimates $\hat{\beta}_1, \hat{\beta}, \ldots, \hat{\beta}_k$ to be farther and farther apart. Furthermore, it is also possible for *multiple solutions* to exist; in this case convergence occurs, but different initial guesses result in different final estimates for one or more of the parameters. Whether or not divergence or multiple solutions occur would depend both on the specification of the ARIMA model and on the data to which that specification is fitted.

Should divergence occur, the model can be reestimated one or more times using different initial guesses. A new initial guess may result in convergence, although one cannot be sure that this will be the case. If it turns out to be impossible to reach a convergent solution, a new model specification will have to be chosen.

Even if convergence occurs on the first try, it is wise to test for multiple solutions by reestimating the model with a different initial guess. If multiple solutions do occur, the final estimate should be that which gives the smallest value of the sum of squared errors. This estimate would correspond to the global minimum of the sum of squared errors function, as opposed to one or more local minima.

18.1.3 Obtaining an Initial Guess for the Parameter Values

Before a nonlinear estimation can be performed on Eq. (18.11), an initial guess $\beta_0 = (\phi_0, \theta_0)$ must be made for the parameter values. Convergence of the estimation process may be faster if the initial guess is a good one, i.e., if β_0 is close to the "true" parameter values. On the other hand, if the initial guess is very poor, it is possible that the iterative process may not converge at all.

The sample autocorrelation function can sometimes be used to help produce the initial guess. As one might expect, this may work for a simple (i.e., low-order) time-series model, but can be virtually useless if the model is at all complicated. For example, if the series w_t is modeled as first-order autoregressive, one need only look at the sample value of ρ_1. If that is, say, .9, a reasonable first guess for ϕ_1 is $\phi_{1,0} = .9$. If, however, our model for w_t is complex, this inspection method is unlikely to produce much useful information.

Even if we cannot determine the initial guess by simply inspecting a correlogram, we can still use the numerical values for the sample autocorrelation function to obtain the initial guess. As we demonstrated in the last chapter, the theoretical autocorrelation function can be related to the theoretical parameter values through a series of equations. If these equations are inverted, they can be used to solve for the parameter values *in terms of the autocorrelation function*. This is straightforward at least in the case of a purely autoregressive model. As an example, consider the autoregressive process of order p, and recall from Eq.

(17.47) that the difference equation for its autocorrelation function is given by

$$\rho_k = \phi_1 \rho_{k-1} + \phi_2 \rho_{k-2} + \cdots + \phi_p \rho_{k-p}$$

Using the fact that $\rho_k = \rho_{-k}$, we can rewrite this equation as a set of p simultaneous linear equations relating the parameters $\phi_1, \ldots, \phi_p$ to $\rho_1, \ldots, \rho_p$:

$$
\begin{aligned}
\rho_1 &= \phi_1 \quad\;\; + \phi_2 \rho_1 + \cdots + \phi_p \rho_{p-1} \\
\rho_2 &= \phi_1 \rho_1 + \phi_2 \quad\; + \cdots + \phi_p \rho_{p-2} \\
&\;\cdots\cdots\cdots\cdots\cdots\cdots\cdots\cdots\cdots \\
\rho_p &= \phi_1 \rho_{p-1} + \phi_2 \rho_{p-2} + \cdots + \phi_p
\end{aligned}
\tag{18.19}
$$

Recall from the last chapter that these are the *Yule-Walker equations*.† By using them to solve for the parameters $\phi_1, \ldots, \phi_p$ in terms of the *estimated* values of the autocorrelation function, we arrive at what are called the *Yule-Walker estimates* of the parameters. These estimates can be used to provide a reasonable first guess for the parameter values.‡ This first guess is, however, of limited value, since the purely autoregressive model can be estimated by ordinary least squares.

If the time-series model contains a moving average part, the Yule-Walker equations that relate the values of the autocorrelation function to the values of the parameters will not be linear. Recall, for example, that the process MA(1) has the autocorrelation function

$$
\rho_k = \begin{cases} \dfrac{-\theta_1}{1 + \theta_1^2} & k = 1 \\[2mm] 0 & k > 1 \end{cases}
$$

Suppose in this example that $\rho_1 = .4$ in the sample autocorrelation function. Then

$$
\theta_1 = \frac{-1 \pm \sqrt{1 - 4\rho_1^2}}{2\rho_1} = \frac{-1 \pm .6}{.8}
\tag{18.20}
$$

Thus the first estimate for θ_1 is -2 or $-.5$. Since invertibility necessitates that $|\theta_1| < 1$, we select the value $\theta_{1,0} = -.5$ for our first guess in the nonlinear

---

† G. U. Yule, "On a Method of Investigating Periodicities in Disturbed Series, with Special Reference to Wölfer's Sunspot Numbers," *Philosophical Transactions*, vol. A226, p. 267, 1927; and G. Walker, "On Periodicity in Series of Related Terms," *Proceedings of the Royal Society*, vol. A131, p. 518, 1931.

‡ Writing Eq. (18.19) in matrix notation

$$\rho = P\phi$$

where
$$
\rho = \begin{bmatrix} \rho_1 \\ \rho_2 \\ \vdots \\ \rho_p \end{bmatrix} \qquad
P = \begin{bmatrix} 1 & \rho_1 & \cdots & \rho_{p-1} \\ \rho_1 & 1 & \cdots & \rho_{p-2} \\ \cdots\cdots\cdots\cdots\cdots\cdots \\ \rho_{p-1} & \rho_{p-2} & \cdots & 1 \end{bmatrix} \qquad \text{and} \qquad
\phi = \begin{bmatrix} \phi_1 \\ \phi_2 \\ \vdots \\ \phi_p \end{bmatrix}
$$

we can solve for ϕ as simply $\phi = P^{-1}\rho$.

estimation process. Unfortunately, the solution for θ in terms of ρ becomes more difficult as the moving average order q becomes larger. In fact, to get initial estimates for the model MA(q), it is necessary to solve q simultaneous nonlinear equations.

One might ask why a first guess for the parameter values based on the Yule-Walker equations is not sufficient for practical purposes. This would eliminate the use of the iterative nonlinear estimation method. One reason is that the sample autocorrelation function is only an *estimate* of the actual autocorrelation function and thus is subject to error. In fact, for small samples (e.g., time series with less than 50 data points) the sample autocorrelation function will be biased (downward) from the true autocorrelation function. A second reason is that the sample autocorrelation function does not contain as much information as the actual time series. It contains only a part of the information that is very useful for model specification. In order to use as much information as possible in the estimation of the model's parameters, we calculate our final estimates based on the actual time series.

Example 18.1   Estimation of ARMA(1, 1) As an example of the iterative nonlinear estimation method described in Section 18.1.2, let us see how the estimation of ϕ_1 and θ_1 in an ARMA(1, 1) model for a stationary series w_t would be carried out. Writing the ARMA(1, 1) model in terms of Eq. (18.11), we have

$$\varepsilon_t = \frac{1 - \phi_1 B}{1 - \theta_1 B} w_t \tag{18.21}$$

This equation is nonlinear in θ_1, but it can be approximated by a Taylor series expansion. This involves calculating the first derivatives of ε_t with respect to ϕ_1 and θ_1, and evaluating them at the initial guess $\phi_{1, 0}$ and $\theta_{1, 0}$.[†]

$$x_{1, t} = -\left. \frac{\partial \varepsilon_t}{\partial \phi_1} \right|_{\phi_{1, 0}, \theta_{1, 0}} = \frac{B}{1 - \theta_{1, 0} B} w_t \tag{18.22}$$

$$x_{2, t} = -\left. \frac{\partial \varepsilon_t}{\partial \theta_1} \right|_{\phi_{1, 0}, \theta_{1, 0}} = -\frac{B - \phi_{1, 0} B^2}{(1 - \theta_{1, 0} B)^2} w_t \tag{18.23}$$

Numerical time series can be computed for $x_{1, t}$ and $x_{2, t}$ (they will be used to perform the linear regression) over the time period $t = 1$ to T by expanding Eqs. (18.22) and (18.23). Taking Eq. (18.22) for $x_{1, t}$, for example, we get

$$x_{1, t} = \theta_{1, 0} x_{1, t-1} + w_{t-1} \tag{18.24}$$

Setting $w_0 = x_{1, 0} = 0$, we can solve Eq. (18.24) repeatedly to generate a

---

† Recall that the initial guesses for $\phi_{1, 0}$ and $\theta_{1, 0}$ could be obtained from inspection of the autocorrelation function. If one is unable to make a reasoned initial guess (e.g., for a high-order model), then initial guesses of 0 could be used.

series for $x_{1,t}$. The first value $x_{1,1}$ would be equal to 0, the second value $x_{1,2}$ would equal w_1, the third value $x_{1,3}$ would equal $\theta_{1,0}w_1 + w_2$, etc. The same thing is done for $x_{2,t}$ by expanding Eq. (18.23):

$$x_{2,t} = 2\theta_{1,0}x_{2,t-1} - \theta_{1,0}^2 x_{2,t-2} - w_{t-1} + \phi_{1,0}w_{t-2} \qquad (18.25)$$

We would begin the computation of $x_{2,t}$ by setting

$$x_{2,1} = x_{2,0} = w_0 = w_{-1} = 0 \qquad (18.26)$$

Thus, the first value $x_{2,1}$ would just be equal to 0, while $x_{2,2}$ would be equal to $-w_1$, $x_{2,3}$ would be equal to $2\theta_{1,0}x_{2,2} - w_2 + \phi_{1,0}w_1$, etc.

Finally, a time series must also be computed for $\varepsilon_{t,0}$ for t ranging from 1 to T. This is done simply by writing

$$\varepsilon_{t,0} = \frac{1 - \phi_{1,0}B}{1 - \theta_{1,0}B} w_t \qquad (18.27)$$

and using the series for w_t to obtain the series for $\varepsilon_{t,0}$. Note that this is just a series of residuals based on the first-guess estimates $\phi_{1,0}$ and $\theta_{1,0}$.

We are now ready to perform a linear regression. Equation (18.17) becomes

$$\varepsilon_{t,0} + \phi_{1,0}x_{1,t} + \theta_{1,0}x_{2,t} = \phi_1 x_{1,t} + \theta_1 x_{2,t} + \varepsilon_t \qquad (18.28)$$

Equation (18.28) is a linear regression equation, and ordinary least squares can be used to estimate ϕ_1 and θ_1. If these estimates of ϕ_1 and θ_1 are significantly different from the first guesses $\phi_{1,0}$ and $\theta_{1,0}$, they are used as *new* first guesses, and the *entire process is repeated* all over again, to yield *new* estimates for ϕ_1 and θ_1. Again, if the change is significant, then the process is repeated. With luck, the estimates for ϕ_1 and θ_1 will converge after a few iterations, but we have no guarantee of this, nor, in fact, do we even have a guarantee that the process will converge *at all*. (If the estimation process fails to converge at all, it should be started again using a new and different initial guess for the parameters.)

18.2 DIAGNOSTIC CHECKING

After a time-series model has been specified and its parameters have been estimated, a check must be made to test whether or not the original specification was correct. This process of diagnostic checking usually involves two steps. First, the autocorrelation function for the simulated series (i.e., the time series generated by the model) can be compared with the sample autocorrelation function of the original series. If the two autocorrelation functions seem very different (and we offer no quantitative measure of just how different that is), some doubt may be cast on the validity of the model and a respecification may be in order. If the two autocorrelation functions are not markedly different (and this will most often be the case), a quantitative analysis can be made of the *residuals* generated by the model.

Remember that we have assumed that the random error terms ε_t in the actual process are normally distributed and *independent of each other*. Then if the model has been specified correctly, the *residuals* $\hat{\varepsilon}_t$ (which are *estimates* of the unobservable error terms) should have close to the same properties; i.e., they should resemble a white noise process. In particular, we would expect the residuals to be *nearly uncorrelated* with each other, so that a *sample autocorrelation function* of the residuals would be close to 0 for displacement $k \geq 1$.

Recall that the residuals of the model are simply

$$\hat{\varepsilon}_t = \hat{\theta}^{-1}(B)\hat{\phi}(B)w_t \tag{18.29}$$

These residuals should be nearly uncorrelated if the model has been correctly specified. Let us denote the sample autocorrelation function (for displacement k) of the residuals as $\hat{r}_k$. It is calculated by

$$\hat{r}_k = \frac{\sum_t \hat{\varepsilon}_t \hat{\varepsilon}_{t-k}}{\sum_t \hat{\varepsilon}_t^2} \tag{18.30}$$

As we mentioned in Chapter 16, a very convenient test, based on statistical results obtained by Box and Pierce, can be applied to this sample autocorrelation function.[†] *If the model is correctly specified*, then for large displacements k (for example, $k > 5$ for low-order models) *the residual autocorrelations $\hat{r}_k$ are themselves uncorrelated, normally distributed random variables with mean 0 and variance $1/T$*, where T is the number of observations in the time series. This fact makes it possible to devise a simple diagnostic test.

Consider the statistic Q composed of the first K residual autocorrelations $\hat{r}_1, \ldots, \hat{r}_K$:[‡]

$$Q = T \sum_{k=1}^{K} \hat{r}_k^2 \tag{18.31}$$

This statistic is a sum of squared independent normal random variables, each with mean 0 and variance $1/T$ and is therefore itself approximately distributed as *chi-square* (see Chapter 2). We say "approximately" because the first few autocorrelations r_1, r_2, etc., will have a variance slightly less than $1/T$, and may themselves be correlated. Box and Pierce demonstrate that the approximation is quite close, and that the statistic Q will be distributed as $\chi^2(K - p - q)$, i.e., chi square with $K - p - q$ degrees of freedom.[§] Therefore, a statistical hypothesis

---

† G. E. P. Box and D. A. Pierce, "Distribution of Residual Autocorrelations in Autoregressive-Integrated Moving Average Time Series Models," *Journal of the American Statistical Association*, vol. 65, December 1970.

‡ For low-order models, K equal to 15 or 20 is certainly sufficient.

§ In Chapter 16 we said that the Q statistic is chi square with K degrees of freedom. Note, however, that that was in reference to a test of the hypothesis that the *original data series* (as opposed to the residuals from our estimated ARMA model) is white noise. For the original data series, $p = q = 0$.

test of model accuracy can be performed by comparing the observed value of Q with the appropriate points from a chi-square table.

Suppose, for example, that we have specified an ARMA(1, 1) model for a series w_t, that the model has been estimated, and that the statistic Q is calculated to be 31.5 with $K = 20$. From a chi-square table we see that the 90 percent point for $K - p - q = 18$ degrees of freedom is 26.0, and the 95 percent point is 28.9. Thus the statistic Q is too large and we can reject the model, since the probability that the residuals are not white noise is at least 95 percent. Suppose that a new model, ARMA(2, 2), is specified and estimated, and the statistic Q is now 22.0, again with $K = 20$. From the chi-square table we see that the 90 percent point for 16 degrees of freedom is 23.5. Thus we need not accept the hypothesis that the residuals are nonwhite, and this second model would be acceptable.† To determine the "best" specification, we might want to specify and estimate some other ARMA models to see whether a lower chi-square statistic can be obtained.

If the calculated value of Q is between the 90 and 95 percent points of the chi-square tail, some doubt would be thrown on the model. At the very least a second test should be applied. This second test would involve observing the individual values of $\hat{r}_k$ for all k between, say, $K/4$ and K, for example, between $k = 5$ and $k = 20$. Since these $\hat{r}_k$ are normal with variance $1/T$, we can test to see if they are all within two or three standard deviations from their means of 0. If several of the $\hat{r}_k$ are larger than $2/\sqrt{T}$ (two standard deviations of the normal variable), evidence exists that the model is misspecified. In addition the evidence might suggest how the model should be respecified. For example, if for an ARMA(2, 1) model $\hat{r}_3$ is very much larger than $2/\sqrt{T}$, this would indicate that the model should be respecified with the inclusion of a third-order moving average term.

In constructing a time-series model one often estimates several alternative specifications. It may be the case that two or more specifications pass the diagnostic checks described above. In this case additional tests must be used to determine the "best" specification. One test is to compare the "simulated series" (i.e., the time series generated by the model) for each specification with the original series. The specification that yields the smallest rms simulation error would then be retained.‡ However, unless one specification has a markedly lower rms error, we suggest retaining all the specifications (that pass the diagnostic checks) and choosing among them based on their *forecasting* performance. The generation and evaluation of forecasts from a time-series model is discussed in the next chapter.

Example 18.2 Interest rate In the last two chapters we began analyzing a time series containing quarterly data for the interest rate on 4- to 6-month

---

† Note that this chi-square test is a "weak" hypothesis test. A value of Q below the 90 percent point on the chi-square distribution indicates that it is not necessary to accept the hypothesis that the residuals are nonwhite, since the probability that the hypothesis is true is less than 90 percent. It is thus only an *indirect* test of the hypothesis that the residuals are white.

‡ Calculation of the rms simulation error is discussed in Chapter 12.

commercial paper from the beginning of 1947 to the second quarter of 1972, and a time series consisting of monthly data for hog production in the United States from the beginning of 1960 to the end of 1967. Let us now estimate some alternative ARIMA models for these two time series.

Review the sample autocorrelation functions in Figs. 16.7, 16.9, and 16.11 for the interest rate series undifferenced, differenced once, and differenced twice. Recall that we suggested that these autocorrelation functions indicate that the series is second-order homogeneous nonstationary. In addition, in Chapter 17, we suggested that ARIMA(2, 2, 2) or ARIMA(4, 2, 2) might be appropriate specifications for a model of the series. Suppose, however, that one judged the autocorrelation function of the *undifferenced* series to be stationary, and indicative of a first-order autoregressive model. Since the sample autocorrelation function declines geometrically from a value of $\hat{\rho}_1 = .9$, some indication of an ARIMA(1, 0, 0) model with $\phi_1 \approx .9$ does exist. For this reason we estimated the ARIMA(1, 0, 0) model, with the following results:

ARIMA(1, 0, 0): $(1 - .9607B)y_t = .1783 + \varepsilon_t$ (18.32)

$$R^2 = .939 \qquad \chi^2(1, 20) = 37.38$$

Note that while the R^2 of Eq. (18.32) is high, one should not be misled into thinking that the equation is necessarily a good one. Remember that the R^2 measures fit in terms of the dependent variable of the regression, which in this case is a level variable. A more revealing statistic is the chi-square, which is equal to 37.38. With 19 degrees of freedom (20 lags minus one estimated parameter), this value is above the critical 95 percent level, so that we may conclude (with at least 95% certainty) that the residuals from the ARIMA(1, 0, 0) model are autocorrelated. Thus, we must turn to a homogeneous nonstationary model for our interest-rate series.

We next estimate the ARIMA(2, 2, 2) and ARIMA(4, 2, 2) models that we suggested earlier. The results are shown below:

ARIMA(2, 2, 2):

$$(1 - .2604B + .3019B^2) \Delta^2 y_t = -.0008 + (1 - .4563B - .5434B^2)\varepsilon_t$$

(18.33)

$$R^2 = .114 \qquad \chi^2(4, 20) = 15.12$$

ARIMA(4, 2, 2):

$$(1 - .1675B + .1867B^2 + .0915B^3 - .2100B^4) \Delta^2 y_t$$
$$= -.0008 + (1 - .3627B - .6372B^2)\varepsilon_t$$

(18.34)

$$R^2 = .101 \qquad \chi^2(6, 20) = 13.63$$

Note that both models have approximately the same statistical fit. The R^2's are low, but that is merely reflective of the fact that the dependent variable has been differenced twice. (If the R^2's were calculated in terms of the *undifferenced* variable y_t, their values would be approximately .95.) Both models have about the same chi-square statistic (they are both insignificant at the 95 percent level), so that in each case we may conclude that the residuals are not autocorrelated. In practice, sets of forecasts should be produced using both models, so that their performance can be compared. We will produce forecasts using the (4, 2, 2) model in the next chapter.

Example 18.3 Hog production Let us now turn to the series for monthly hog production. Recall from the last chapter that we suggested that an appropriate model for the series might be

$$(1 - \phi_1 B - \phi_2 B^2 - \phi_3 B^3)(1 - B)(1 - B^{12})y_t = \varepsilon_t$$

This model was estimated over the period January 1960 to December 1967, with the results

$$(1 + .6681 B + .2015 B^2 - .1298 B^3)(1 - B)(1 - B^{12})y_t = .0014 + \varepsilon_t$$

$$\tag{18.35}$$

$$R^2 = .365 \qquad \chi^2(3, 20) = 12.83$$

The model is acceptable, and will be used to forecast in the next chapter. The reader might wonder, however, whether another model specification might provide a better fit to the data. Perhaps, for example, the addition of moving average terms would improve the model. To test this, we estimated a model that includes first- and second-order moving average terms:

$$(1 + .6626 B + .3945 B^2 - .0179 B^3)(1 - B)(1 - B^{12})y_t$$

$$= .0015 + (1 + .0168 B - .2191 B^2)\varepsilon_t \tag{18.36}$$

$$R^2 = .349 \qquad \chi^2(5, 20) = 13.01$$

Inclusion of the moving average terms results in a slightly lower value for the R^2. Of greater importance, however, is the fact that the estimated values of ϕ_1, ϕ_2, and ϕ_3 add up to a number greater than 1. The result is a nonstationary model for a series that we believe to be stationary. We would thus reject this model, and retain the model of Eq. (18.35).

APPENDIX 18.1 INITIALIZATION OF THE TIME SERIES

We saw in Section 18.1.1 that the sum-of-squares function $S(\phi, \theta)$ and thus the likelihood function $L(\phi, \theta, \sigma_\varepsilon)$ are conditional on the past unobservable values of w_t and ε_t. For this reason the least-squares estimates will depend on the choice of values that we use for $w_0, w_{-1}, \ldots,$ etc. We suggested using unconditional expected values of $w_0, \ldots, w_{-p+1}$ and for $\varepsilon_0, \ldots, \varepsilon_{-q+1}$, i.e., setting them all equal to 0.

A procedure also exists for finding *conditional expected values* for $w_0, \ldots, w_{-p+1}$, that is, values that are conditional on the *observed* values of $w_1, \ldots, w_T$ and the *estimated* values of $\varepsilon_1, \ldots, \varepsilon_T$. Essentially one can *initially* set $w_0, \ldots, w_{-p+1}$ and $\varepsilon_0, \ldots, \varepsilon_{-q+1}$ to 0, estimate the ARMA model by minimizing $S(\phi, \theta)$ conditional on these 0 values, and then *backcast* the model to generate new values for $w_0, \ldots, w_{-p+1}$. Since the differenced series w_t is stationary, the ARMA process of Eq. (18.1) can be turned around in time; i.e., it is equivalent (statistically so in a large sample) to the process

$$\phi(F)w_t = \theta(F)\varepsilon_t \qquad (A18.1)$$

where F is the *forward lag operator:*

$$Fw_t = w_{t+1} \qquad F^2w_t = w_{t+2}$$

and so forth, and $\phi(\ )$ and $\theta(\ )$ are the same polynomials as in (18.1). Thus (A18.1) can be written as

$$w_t = \phi^{-1}(F)\theta(F)\varepsilon_t \qquad (A18.2)$$

and can be used to solve for $\hat{w}_0, \hat{w}_{-1}, \ldots, \hat{w}_{-p+1}$ in terms of the estimated values of $\varepsilon_1, \ldots, \varepsilon_T$. These estimated values are the residuals formed by subtracting the actual series for w_t from the predicted series generated by the initially estimated ARMA model. We can obtain *new* least-squares estimates for ϕ and θ by minimizing $S(\phi, \theta, \sigma_\varepsilon)$ *conditional* on $w_0 = \hat{w}_0$, $w_1 = \hat{w}_1$, etc. A new round of estimates for $\hat{w}_0, \hat{w}_1, \ldots, \hat{w}_{-p+1}$ can then be computed from (A18.2), and the process repeated until the estimates converge, i.e., until $\hat{\phi}$ and $\hat{\theta}$ stop changing in value. We have no guarantee, unfortunately, that this process will converge. If it does not, one may be forced to fix $\hat{w}_0, \hat{w}_1, \ldots, \hat{w}_{-p+1}$ at their initial estimates.

The determination of conditional expected values for the series $w_0, \ldots, w_{-p+1}$ is difficult, and usually involves a good deal of computation. Thus it is reasonable to ask whether or not our estimates of ϕ and θ will be very sensitive to this initialization of the series. The answer depends on the length of the observed time series that is to be modeled and, in particular, the length of the series relative to the values of p and q. If the time series is long relative to p and q, the conditional sum-of-squares function will be nearly equal to the unconditional sum-of-squares function, and our estimates of ϕ and θ will be very insensitive to the initialization process. In this case one can simply set all the initial values to 0. If the time series is short (relative to p and q), some gain in efficiency would probably result from the use of conditional expected values of $w_0, \ldots, w_{-p+1}$, but we cannot determine how large this gain in efficiency would be. Our knowledge of the statistical properties of the parameter estimates is based on asymptotical results, i.e., on large samples. Unfortunately the small-sample properties of the estimates are not known.

Usually one would not want to model a time series as an ARMA process anyway unless a reasonably large number of observations are available (e.g., more than 50). Otherwise it is unlikely that one could obtain a reasonable statistical fit for the model and the model will be of limited value for forecasting. Furthermore, many of the ARMA models that one would construct in economic or business applications are of low order; that is, p and q are not more than 2 or 3. In this case the initialization of the series will usually not be a problem, and one can simply set all the initial values equal to 0. We suggest this practice, and we apply it to all the numerical examples in this chapter and the next.

EXERCISES

18.1 Following the example in Section 18.1.4, show how the estimation of ϕ_1, ϕ_2, and θ_1 for an ARMA(2, 1) model would be carried out. Go through the steps of the Taylor series expansion, show how the data series are generated, and indicate how the linear regressions are performed.

18.2 Suppose that an ARMA(0, 2) model has been estimated for a time series that has been generated by an ARMA(1, 2) process.

(a) How would the diagnostic test indicate that the model has been misspecified?

(b) What will the residual autocorrelations $\hat{r}_k$ look like? What characteristics of these autocorrelations might indicate that ARMA(1, 2) is a more correct specification?

18.3 Repeat Exercise 18.2 for an ARMA(0, 2) model estimated for a time series that has been generated by an ARMA(2, 3) process.

18.4 Suppose that a particular homogeneous nonstationary time series y_t can be modeled as a stochastic process that is ARIMA(1, 1, 1).

(a) How would you calculate the sample autocorrelation functions for y_t and its differences and use them to verify that ARIMA(1, 1, 1) is indeed a proper specification for y_t?

(b) Suppose you did not have access to a computer package for nonlinear estimation. How would you use a *linear regression* to obtain *approximate* estimates of the parameters in the model? (Explain the steps involved clearly.)

CHAPTER NINETEEN

FORECASTING WITH
TIME-SERIES MODELS

Once a time-series model has been estimated and its original specification has been checked, it can be used for forecasting. In this chapter we explain how one can use the general ARIMA model

$$\phi(B)\, \Delta^d y_t = \theta(B)\varepsilon_t \tag{19.1}$$

to obtain a forecast of y_t for period $T + l$ (that is, l periods ahead, with $l \geq 1$). We denote this forecast by $\hat{y}_T(l)$, and call it the *origin-T forecast for lead time l*. We assume for now that the true parameters of the model are known and examine the properties both of the forecast and of the forecast error. Later we will see how imperfect knowledge of the true parameter values increases the forecast error.

We begin this chapter by discussing the basis for making forecasts, after which we go through the steps of actually computing a forecast. Then we discuss the nature of forecast errors, showing how forecast confidence intervals can be computed. In order to give the reader an understanding of the characteristics of time-series forecasts, we examine in detail the properties of the forecasts of some simple ARIMA models. Finally, we present two examples in which we generate forecasts for an interest rate and for hog production using the time-series models estimated at the end of the last chapter. In discussing these examples we attempt to give the reader some feeling for the strengths and weaknesses of time-series forecasts.

19.1 MINIMUM MEAN SQUARE ERROR FORECAST

Our objective in forecasting is to predict future values of a time series subject to as little error as possible. For this reason we consider the optimum forecast to be that forecast which has the *minimum mean square forecast error*. Since the forecast error is a random variable, we minimize the *expected value*. Thus we wish to choose our forecast $\hat{y}_T(l)$ so that $E[e_T^2(l)] = E\{[y_{T+l} - \hat{y}_T(l)]^2\}$ is minimized.† We show that this forecast is given by the *conditional expectation* of y_{T+l}, that is, by

$$\hat{y}_T(l) = E(y_{T+l}|y_T, y_{T-1}, \ldots, y_1) \tag{19.2}$$

To prove that the minimum mean square error forecast is given by Eq. (19.2), we begin by rewriting the ARIMA model in Eq. (19.1) above as

$$\phi(B)(1 - B)^d y_t = \theta(B)\varepsilon_t \tag{19.3}$$

since $\Delta = 1 - B$, as explained in Chapter 17. Therefore,

$$y_t = \phi^{-1}(B)(1 - B)^{-d}\theta(B)\varepsilon_t = \psi(B)\varepsilon_t = \sum_{j=0}^{\infty} \psi_j \varepsilon_{t-j} \tag{19.4}$$

Here we have expressed the ARIMA model as a purely moving average process of infinite order.‡ Then

$$y_{T+l} = \psi_0 \varepsilon_{T+l} + \psi_1 \varepsilon_{T+l-1} + \cdots + \psi_l \varepsilon_T + \psi_{l+1} \varepsilon_{T-1} + \cdots$$

$$= \psi_0 \varepsilon_{T+l} + \psi_1 \varepsilon_{T+l-1} + \cdots + \psi_{l-1} \varepsilon_{T+1} + \sum_{j=0}^{\infty} \psi_{l+j} \varepsilon_{T-j} \tag{19.5}$$

In Eq. (19.5) we have divided the infinite sum into two parts, the second part beginning with the term $\psi_l \varepsilon_T$, and thus describing information up to and including time period T.

Of course the forecast $\hat{y}_T(l)$ can be based only on information available up to time T. Our objective is to compare this forecast with the actual value y_{T+l} as expressed in Eq. (19.5). To do so, we write the forecast as a weighted sum of those error terms *which we can estimate*, namely, $\varepsilon_T, \varepsilon_{T-1}, \ldots$. Then, the desired forecast is

$$\hat{y}_T(l) = \sum_{j=0}^{\infty} \psi_{l+j}^* \varepsilon_{T-j} \tag{19.6}$$

where the weights ψ_{l+j}^* are to be chosen optimally so as *to minimize the mean square forecast error*. We can now write an expression for the forecast error,

---

† In this way, "mean square forecast error" refers to the *variance* of the forecast error.

‡ Any ARIMA process can be equivalently expressed as purely moving average or as purely autoregressive. We could have, for example, rewritten Eq. (19.3) as $\phi(B)(1 - B)^d \theta^{-1}(B)y_t = \varepsilon_t$, or $\xi(B)y_t = \varepsilon_t$. This is a purely autoregressive process of infinite order. The reason that we do not originally specify the ARIMA process as purely autoregressive or purely moving average (of infinite order) is that we would then have an infinite number of parameters to estimate.

$e_T(l)$, using Eqs. (19.5) and (19.6):

$$e_T(l) = y_{T+l} - \hat{y}_T(l) = \psi_0 \varepsilon_{T+l} + \psi_1 \varepsilon_{T+l-1} + \cdots + \psi_{l-1} \varepsilon_{T+1}$$

$$+ \sum_{j=0}^{\infty} (\psi_{l+j} - \psi_{l+j}^*) \varepsilon_{T-j} \qquad (19.7)$$

Since by assumption $E(\varepsilon_i \varepsilon_j) = 0$ for $i \neq j$, the mean square forecast error is

$$E[e_T^2(l)] = (\psi_0^2 + \psi_1^2 + \cdots + \psi_{l-1}^2)\sigma_\varepsilon^2 + \sum_{j=0}^{\infty} (\psi_{l+j} - \psi_{l+j}^*)^2 \sigma_\varepsilon^2 \qquad (19.8)$$

Clearly this expression is minimized by setting the "optimum" weights ψ_{l+j}^* equal to the true weights ψ_{l+j}, for $j = 0, 1, \ldots$. But then our optimum forecast $\hat{y}_T(l)$ is just the conditional expectation of y_{T+l}. This can be seen by taking the conditional expectation of y_{T+l} in Eq. (19.5). The expected values of $\varepsilon_{T+l}, \ldots, \varepsilon_{T+1}$ are all 0, while the expected values of $\varepsilon_T, \varepsilon_{T-1}, \ldots,$ are just the actual observed errors, i.e., the residuals from the estimated equation. Thus we have

$$\hat{y}_T(l) = \sum_{j=0}^{\infty} \psi_{l+j} \hat{\varepsilon}_{T-j} = E(y_{T+l} | y_T, \ldots, y_1) \qquad (19.9)$$

This provides the basic principle for calculating forecasts from our **ARIMA** models. Now we apply this principle to the actual computation of forecasts.

19.2 COMPUTING A FORECAST

The actual computation of the forecast $\hat{y}_T(l)$ can be done recursively using the estimated ARIMA model. This involves first computing a forecast one period ahead, using this forecast to compute a forecast two periods ahead, and continuing until the l-period forecast has been reached. Let us write the ARIMA(p, d, q) model as

$$w_t = \phi_1 w_{t-1} + \cdots + \phi_p w_{t-p} + \varepsilon_t - \theta_1 \varepsilon_{t-1} - \cdots - \theta_q \varepsilon_{t-q} + \delta \qquad (19.10)$$

with

$$y_t = \Sigma^d w_t \qquad (19.11)$$

To compute the forecast $\hat{y}_T(l)$, we begin by computing the *one-period* forecast of w_t, $\hat{w}_T(1)$. To do so, we write Eq. (19.10) with the time period modified:

$$w_{T+1} = \phi_1 w_T + \cdots + \phi_p w_{T-p+1} + \varepsilon_{T+1} - \theta_1 \varepsilon_T - \cdots - \theta_q \varepsilon_{T-q+1} + \delta \qquad (19.12)$$

We then calculate our forecast $\hat{w}_T(1)$ by taking the conditional expected value of w_{T+1} in Eq. (19.12):

$$\hat{w}_T(1) = E(w_{T+1} | w_T, \ldots) = \phi_1 w_T + \cdots + \phi_p w_{T-p+1}$$

$$- \theta_1 \hat{\varepsilon}_T - \cdots - \theta_q \hat{\varepsilon}_{T-q+1} + \delta \qquad (19.13)$$

where the $\hat{\varepsilon}_T$, $\hat{\varepsilon}_{T-1}$, etc., are observed residuals. Note that the expected value of

ε_{T+1} is 0. Now using the one-period forecast $\hat{w}_T(1)$, we can obtain the *two-period forecast* $\hat{w}_T(2)$:

$$\hat{w}_T(2) = E(w_{T+2}|w_T, \dots)$$

$$= \phi_1 \hat{w}_T(1) + \phi_2 w_T + \cdots + \phi_p w_{T-p+2} - \theta_2 \hat{\varepsilon}_T - \cdots - \theta_q \hat{\varepsilon}_{T-q+2} + \delta \quad (19.14)$$

The two-period forecast is then used to produce the three-period forecast, and so on, until the *l*-period forecast $\hat{w}_T(l)$ is reached:

$$\hat{w}_T(l) = \phi_1 \hat{w}_T(l-1) + \cdots + \phi_l w_T + \cdots + \phi_p w_{T-p+l}$$

$$- \theta_l \hat{\varepsilon}_T - \cdots - \theta_q \hat{\varepsilon}_{T-q+l} + \delta \quad (19.15)$$

Note that if $l > p$ and $l > q$, then this forecast will be

$$\hat{w}_T(l) = \phi_1 \hat{w}_T(l-1) + \cdots + \phi_p \hat{w}_T(l-p) \quad (19.16)$$

Once the differenced series w_t has been forecasted, a forecast can be obtained for the original series y_t simply by applying the summation operation to w_t, that is, by summing w_t d times. Suppose, for example, that $d = 1$. Then our *l*-period forecast of y_t would be given by

$$\hat{y}_T(l) = y_T + \hat{w}_T(1) + \hat{w}_T(2) + \cdots + \hat{w}_T(l) \quad (19.17)$$

On the other hand, if the model for y_t were ARIMA with $d = 2$, then the *l*-period forecast $\hat{y}_T(l)$ would be given by

$$\hat{y}_T(l) = y_T + \left[\Delta y_T + \hat{w}_T(1)\right] + \left[\Delta y_T + \hat{w}_T(1) + \hat{w}_T(2)\right] + \cdots$$

$$+ \left[\Delta y_T + \hat{w}_T(1) + \cdots + \hat{w}_T(l)\right]$$

$$= y_T + l\,\Delta y_T + l\hat{w}_T(1) + (l-1)\hat{w}_T(2) + \cdots + \hat{w}_T(l) \quad (19.18)$$

Here the summation operator has been applied twice.† The procedure is similar for larger values of d.

19.3 THE FORECAST ERROR

As we saw before, if we express the ARIMA model as a purely moving average process of infinite order, the forecast error l periods ahead is given by

$$e_T(l) = y_{T+l} - \hat{y}_T(l) = \psi_0 \varepsilon_{T+l} + \psi_1 \varepsilon_{T+l-1} + \cdots + \psi_{l-1} \varepsilon_{T+1} \quad (19.19)$$

Remember that the weights ψ_j are determined from

$$\psi(B) = \phi^{-1}(B)(1-B)^{-d}\theta(B) \quad (19.20)$$

We assume that the model parameters $\phi_1, \dots, \phi_p$ and $\theta_1, \dots, \theta_q$ are known exactly and therefore the weights $\psi_0, \psi_1, \dots,$ are also known exactly. In this case the *variance* of the forecast error is given by

$$E\left[e_T^2(l)\right] = \left(\psi_0^2 + \psi_1^2 + \cdots + \psi_{l-1}^2\right)\sigma_\varepsilon^2 \quad (19.21)$$

---

† The reader may wish to review the use of the summation operator as described in Chapter 17.

Therefore, the algebraic form for the forecast error variance depends on the particular ARIMA specification that has been adopted. In the next section we examine the forecast error in more detail for some simple ARIMA models. For now, however, there are two things that the reader should observe.

First, we know from the definition of $\psi(B)$ above that $\psi_0 = 1$.† Therefore, for *any* ARIMA specification, we know that the forecast error *one period* ahead is just

$$e_T(1) = \varepsilon_{T+1} \tag{19.22}$$

and this has variance σ_ε^2. Thus the forecast error variance one period ahead is always the variance of the error term.

Second, we must keep in mind the fact that our calculation of the forecast error was based on the assumption that we knew the parameter values $\phi_1, \ldots, \phi_p$ and $\theta_1, \ldots, \theta_q$ with certainty, i.e., that we had obtained perfect estimates of the parameter values. Needless to say, this is never the case. The parameters are estimated via a nonlinear least-squares regression, and, as in any least-squares regression, the estimates are random variables with means and variances. Therefore the *actual* forecast error variance will be *larger* than the variance calculated above. To determine exactly *how much larger*, we must know the variances (or standard errors) of the parameter estimates in the ARIMA model. Because the parameters are estimated nonlinearly, however, the variances of their estimates are difficult to determine. The best we could do, in fact, would be to calculate standard errors for the parameter estimates based on the *last iteration* of the nonlinear estimation procedure.‡ In other words, we could take the ordinary least-squares regression from the last iteration, calculate the residuals of that linearized equation, and obtain standard errors in the manner discussed in Chapter 8. The residuals from this linearization could also be used to calculate an estimate of the variance σ_ε^2.

The difficulty here is that the meaning of the standard errors for the linearization in the last (or any particular) iteration is somewhat limited—certainly they are not "true" estimates of the actual standard errors for the parameter values. As a practical matter, one has the choice of using these standard errors in the calculation of the forecast error variance or ignoring them and simply calculating the forecast error variance based on Eq. (19.21) above.

19.4 FORECAST CONFIDENCE INTERVALS

We base our forecast confidence intervals on the assumption that the parameter values are known. However, these confidence intervals will be overoptimistic if

---

† Remember that the ARIMA model (with 0 mean) is $w_t = \phi_1 w_{t-1} + \cdots + \phi_p w_{t-p} + \varepsilon_t - \theta_1 \varepsilon_{t-1} - \cdots - \theta_q \varepsilon_{t-q}$. The only unlagged term on the right-hand side is ε_t (which has a weight of 1). Thus ψ_0 must equal 1 in Eq. (19.4).

‡ Assuming that the procedure is based on repeated linearizations of the nonlinear model. As we mentioned in Section 9.4 there exist other approaches to nonlinear estimation.

the standard errors for the parameter estimates based on the last iteration are large (e.g., if the corresponding t statistics are less than 5). When generating forecasts from a linear single-equation regression model (in Chapter 8), we calculated confidence intervals which accounted for errors due to imperfect knowledge of the model's parameter values. As we explained above, however, this is difficult to do in the case of a time-series model, because the model is nonlinear in the parameters.

Before we can calculate a confidence interval for our forecast, we need an estimate $\hat{\sigma}_\varepsilon^2$ for the variance of the disturbance term. This estimate would logically be based on the sum of squared residuals $S(\hat{\phi}, \hat{\theta})$ obtained after final estimates of the parameters have been obtained:

$$\hat{\sigma}_\varepsilon^2 = \frac{S(\hat{\phi}, \hat{\theta})}{T - p - q} = \frac{\sum\limits_{t=1}^{T} \hat{\varepsilon}_t^2}{T - p - q} \tag{19.23}$$

Here $T - p - q$ is the number of degrees of freedom in the linear regression. We see from Eq. (19.21) and the fact that $\psi_0 = 1$ that a *confidence interval of n standard deviations* around a forecast l periods ahead would be given by

$$C_n = \hat{y}_T(l) \pm n\left(1 + \sum_{j=1}^{l-1} \psi_j^2\right)^{1/2} \hat{\sigma}_\varepsilon \tag{19.24}$$

As expected, this interval gets larger as the lead time l becomes larger, although the exact pattern depends on the weights ψ_j.

Forecasts of y_t, together with a typical 66 percent confidence interval ($n = 1$) and 95 percent confidence interval ($n = 2$), are shown for a hypothetical ARMA model ($d = 0$) in Fig. 19.1. Note that the forecasts (denoted by crosses)

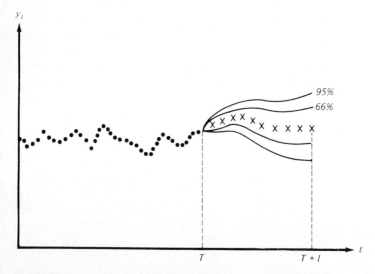

Figure 19.1 Forecasts and confidence intervals for a stationary ARMA process.

first are increasing but then decline to the constant mean level of the series. We know that the forecast will approach the mean of the series as the lead time l becomes large because the process is stationary. The confidence intervals, of course, increase as the forecast lead time becomes longer.

19.5 PROPERTIES OF ARIMA FORECASTS

We now examine the properties of the forecasts derived from some simple ARIMA models. In all the cases that follow we assume that the parameters of the particular ARIMA model are known with certainty.

19.5.1 The AR(1) Process

Let us begin with the stationary first-order autoregressive process, AR(1):

$$y_t = \phi_1 y_{t-1} + \delta + \varepsilon_t \tag{19.25}$$

For this process the one-period forecast is

$$\hat{y}_T(1) = E(y_{T+1}|y_T, \ldots, y_1) = \phi_1 y_T + \delta \tag{19.26}$$

Similarly, $\qquad \hat{y}_T(2) = \phi_1 \hat{y}_T(1) + \delta = \phi_1^2 y_T + (\phi_1 + 1)\delta \tag{19.27}$

And the l-period forecast is

$$\hat{y}_T(l) = \phi_1^l y_T + \left(\phi_1^{l-1} + \phi_1^{l-2} + \cdots + \phi_1 + 1\right)\delta \tag{19.28}$$

Note that in the limit as l becomes large, the forecast converges to the value

$$\lim_{l \to \infty} \hat{y}_T(l) = \delta \sum_{j=0}^{\infty} \phi_1^j = \frac{\delta}{1 - \phi_1} = \mu_y \tag{19.29}$$

We see, then, that the forecast tends to the mean of the series as l becomes large [recall Eq. (17.23) for the mean of the AR(1) process]. Of course this is not surprising, since the series is stationary. As the lead time l becomes very large, there is essentially no useful information in recent values of the time series, y_T, y_{T-1}, etc., that can be used to adjust the forecast away from the mean value. Thus for a very large lead time the best forecast is the stationary mean of the series.

Let us now calculate the forecast error for this process. The forecast error l periods ahead is given by

$$\begin{aligned} e_T(l) = y_{T+l} - \hat{y}_T(l) &= \phi_1 y_{T+l-1} + \delta + \varepsilon_{T+l} - \hat{y}_T(l) \\ &= \phi_1^2 y_{T+l-2} + (\phi_1 + 1)\delta + \varepsilon_{T+l} + \phi_1 \varepsilon_{T+l-1} - \hat{y}_T(l) \\ &\cdots\cdots\cdots\cdots\cdots\cdots\cdots\cdots\cdots\cdots\cdots \\ &= \phi_1^l y_T + \left(\phi_1^{l-1} + \phi_1^{l-2} + \cdots + \phi_1 + 1\right)\delta \\ &\quad + \varepsilon_{T+l} + \phi_1 \varepsilon_{T+l-1} + \cdots + \phi_1^{l-1}\varepsilon_{T+1} - \hat{y}_T(l) \end{aligned}$$

Now substituting Eq. (19.28) for $\hat{y}_T(l)$, we get

$$e_T(l) = \varepsilon_{T+l} + \phi_1 \varepsilon_{T+l-1} + \cdots + \phi_1^{l-1}\varepsilon_{T+1} \tag{19.30}$$

which has a variance

$$E[e_T^2(l)] = (1 + \phi_1^2 + \phi_1^4 + \cdots + \phi_1^{2l-2})\sigma_\varepsilon^2 \qquad (19.31)$$

Note that this forecast error variance increases (nonlinearly) as l becomes larger.

19.5.2 The MA(1) Process

Now let us examine the simple first-order moving average process, MA(1):

$$y_t = \delta + \varepsilon_t - \theta_1\varepsilon_{t-1} \qquad (19.32)$$

The one-period forecast for this process is

$$\hat{y}_T(1) = E(y_{T+1}|y_T, \ldots, y_1) = \delta - \theta_1\hat{\varepsilon}_T \qquad (19.33)$$

where $\hat{\varepsilon}_T$ is the actual residual from the current (and most recent) observation. On the other hand, the l-period forecast, for $l > 1$, is just

$$\hat{y}_T(l) = E(y_{T+l}|y_T, \ldots, y_1) = E(\delta + \varepsilon_{T+l} - \theta_1\varepsilon_{T+l-1}) = \delta \qquad (19.34)$$

This is also as expected, since the process MA(1) has a memory of only one period. Thus recent data are of no help in making a forecast two or more periods ahead, and the best forecast is the mean of the series, δ.

The variance of the forecast error for MA(1) is σ_ε^2 for the one-period forecast, and for the l-period forecast, $l > 1$, it is given by

$$E[e_T^2(l)] = E\{[y_{T+l} - \hat{y}_T(l)]^2\} = E[(\varepsilon_{T+l} - \theta_1\varepsilon_{T+l-1})^2] = (1 + \theta_1^2)\sigma_\varepsilon^2 \qquad (19.35)$$

Thus the forecast error variance is the same for a forecast two periods ahead, three periods ahead, etc. The forecast confidence intervals would appear as shown in Fig. 19.2.

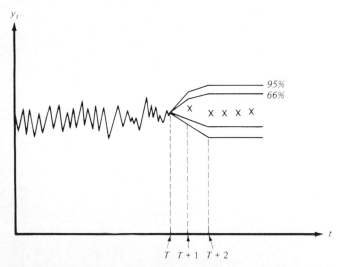

Figure 19.2 Forecasts and confidence intervals for an MA(1) process.

19.5.3 The ARMA(1, 1) Process

Let us now calculate and examine the forecasts generated by the simplest mixed autoregressive-moving average process, ARMA(1, 1):

$$y_t = \phi_1 y_{t-1} + \delta + \varepsilon_t - \theta_1 \varepsilon_{t-1} \tag{19.36}$$

The one-period forecast for the ARMA(1, 1) model is given by

$$\hat{y}_T(1) = E(\phi_1 y_T + \delta + \varepsilon_{T+1} - \theta_1 \varepsilon_T) = \phi_1 y_T + \delta - \theta_1 \hat{\varepsilon}_T \tag{19.37}$$

The two-period forecast is

$$\hat{y}_T(2) = E(\phi_1 y_{T+1} + \delta + \varepsilon_{T+2} - \theta_1 \varepsilon_{T+1}) = \phi_1 \hat{y}_T(1) + \delta$$
$$= \phi_1^2 y_T + (\phi_1 + 1)\delta - \phi_1 \theta_1 \hat{\varepsilon}_T \tag{19.38}$$

Finally, the *l*-period forecast is

$$\hat{y}_T(l) = \phi_1 \hat{y}_T(l - 1) + \delta = \phi_1^l y_T + (\phi_1^{l-1} + \cdots + \phi_1 + 1)\delta - \phi_1^{l-1} \theta_1 \hat{\varepsilon}_T \tag{19.39}$$

Note that the limiting value of the forecast as *l* becomes large is again the mean of the series:

$$\lim_{l \to \infty} \hat{y}_T(l) = \frac{\delta}{1 - \phi_1} = \mu_y \tag{19.40}$$

Examining these forecasts for different lead times, we see that the current disturbance (i.e., the current measured residual $\hat{\varepsilon}_T$) helps to determine the one-period forecast, and in turn serves as a starting point from which the remainder of the forecast profile, which is autoregressive in character, decays toward the mean $\delta/(1 - \phi_1)$.

The fact that forecasts from ARMA models approach the (constant) mean value of the series as the lead time becomes large indicates an important limitation of these models. As we will see in the examples in this chapter and the next, time-series models are useful largely for short-term forecasting. If one is interested in a long forecasting horizon, a structural econometric model is likely to be a more useful tool.

19.5.4 The ARI(1, 1, 0) Process

Now we examine a simple nonstationary process, the integrated autoregressive process ARI(1, 1, 0)

$$w_t = \phi_1 w_{t-1} + \delta + \varepsilon_t \tag{19.41}$$

with
$$w_t = \Delta y_t = y_t - y_{t-1} \tag{19.42}$$

Forecasts for y_t are related to forecasts of the differenced series w_t as follows:

$$\hat{y}_T(1) = y_T + \hat{w}_T(1) \tag{19.43}$$

and
$$\hat{y}_T(l) = y_T + \hat{w}_T(1) + \cdots + \hat{w}_T(l) \tag{19.44}$$

Since the differenced process w_t is AR(1), its forecasts are given by

$$\hat{w}_T(l) = \phi_1^l w_T + \left(\phi_1^{l-1} + \phi_1^{l-2} + \cdots + \phi_1 + 1\right)\delta$$
$$= \phi_1^l y_T - \phi_1^l y_{T-1} + \left(\phi_1^{l-1} + \cdots + \phi_1 + 1\right)\delta \qquad (19.45)$$

Then the one-period forecast for y_t is

$$\hat{y}_T(1) = y_T + \phi_1(y_T - y_{T-1}) + \delta = (1 + \phi_1)y_T - \phi_1 y_{T-1} + \delta \qquad (19.46)$$

The two-period forecast for y_t is

$$\hat{y}_T(2) = y_T + \hat{w}_T(1) + \hat{w}_T(2) = \hat{y}_T(1) + \hat{w}_T(2)$$
$$= \hat{y}_T(1) + \phi_1^2 w_T + (\phi_1 + 1)\delta$$
$$= \left(1 + \phi_1 + \phi_1^2\right)y_T - \left(\phi_1 + \phi_1^2\right)y_{T-1} + (\phi_1 + 1)\delta + \delta \qquad (19.47)$$

A more instructive way to look at this forecast, however, is in terms of its *changes*. Since

$$\hat{w}_T(2) = \phi_1 \hat{w}_T(1) + \delta \qquad (19.48)$$

we can write the forecast $\hat{y}_T(2)$ as

$$\hat{y}_T(2) = \hat{y}_T(1) + \phi_1 \hat{w}_T(1) + \delta \qquad (19.49)$$

Similarly, $\qquad \hat{y}_T(l) = \hat{y}_T(l - 1) + \phi_1 \hat{w}_T(l - 1) + \delta \qquad (19.50)$

Now let us examine the properties of this forecast. Since w_t is an AR(1) process, we know from Eq. (19.29) that

$$\lim_{l \to \infty} \hat{w}_T(l) = \frac{\delta}{1 - \phi_1} \qquad (19.51)$$

Thus as the forecast horizon l becomes large, the forecast profile approaches a straight line with slope $\delta/(1 - \phi_1)$. In other words, as the horizon becomes large, the forecast becomes dominated by the *deterministic drift* of the process. For a short forecast horizon this would not be so. It might have been the case, for example, that the last few differences w_T, w_{T-1}, w_{T-2} were negative (i.e., the series had been decreasing in the recent past), although δ was positive so that the series had an overall upward drift. In this case the short-term forecasts $\hat{w}_T(1)$ and $\hat{w}_T(2)$ might be negative, even though $\hat{w}_T(l)$ would tend toward $\delta/(1 - \phi_1)$ as l became larger. The forecasts for y_t, then, would first be decreasing, but then would *change direction*, ultimately approaching a straight line with slope $\delta/(1 - \phi_1)$. This hypothetical ARI(1, 1, 0) forecast is shown graphically in Fig. 19.3.

One thing that becomes immediately clear about ARIMA forecasts is that they are *adaptive*. As can be seen from Fig. 19.3, the forecast makes use of the most recent data, and adapts accordingly. Another example of the adaptive nature of ARIMA forecasts is shown in Fig. 19.4. This process is also ARI(1, 1, 0), and is identical to the process in Fig. 19.3, for $t \le T$. The crosses in Fig. 19.4 represent the forecasts made at time T. Now suppose that the series *increases* in periods $T + 1$, $T + 2$, and $T + 3$ and a *new* set of forecasts is made in period $T + 3$. These forecasts are denoted by circles, and, as can be seen in

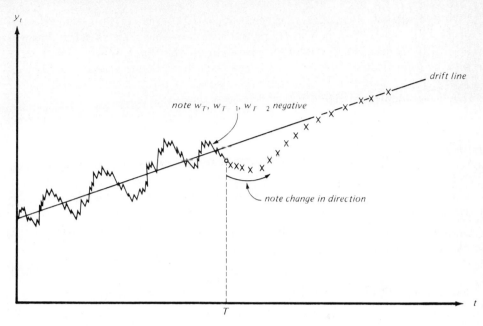

Figure 19.3 Hypothetical forecasts for an ARI(1, 1, 0) process.

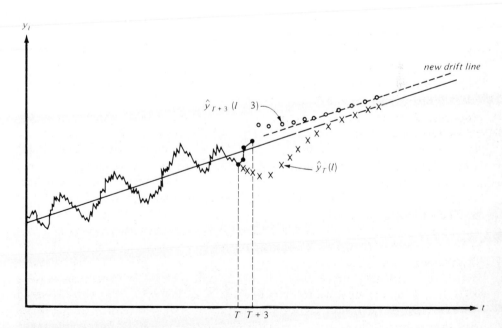

Figure 19.4 Adaptive nature of ARI(1, 1, 0) forecast.

Fig. 19.4, they first *increase* and then *decrease*. Ultimately they will also approach a drift line. This new drift line will have the same slope as before but will be slightly higher as a result of the new data points. What we observe, then, is that the forecast has "adapted" to the new data that became available in periods $T + 1$, $T + 2$, and $T + 3$. Notice that the values of this forecast for a long lead time have adapted as well.

19.5.5 Confidence Intervals for the ARI(1, 1, 0) Forecast

We now calculate the forecast error and its variance for the ARI(1, 1, 0) process, so that we can obtain a forecast confidence interval. As we will see, the forecast confidence interval for y_t is related to the forecast confidence interval for the differenced series w_t.

We begin with the forecast error for the one-period forecast, $\hat{y}_T(1)$:

$$e_T(1) = y_{T+1} - \hat{y}_T(1) = y_T + w_{T+1} - y_T - \hat{w}_T(1)$$

$$= w_{T+1} - \hat{w}_T(1) = \varepsilon_{T+1} \tag{19.52}$$

which has a variance σ_ε^2. The two-period forecast error is given by

$$e_T(2) = y_{T+2} - \hat{y}_T(2) = y_T + w_{T+1} + w_{T+2} - y_T - \hat{w}_T(1) - \hat{w}_T(2)$$

$$= \left[w_{T+1} - \hat{w}_T(1) \right] + \left[w_{T+2} - \hat{w}_T(2) \right]$$

$$= (1 + \phi_1)\varepsilon_{T+1} + \varepsilon_{T+2} \tag{19.53}$$

and this has a variance

$$E\left[e_T^2(2) \right] = \sigma_\varepsilon^2 \left[(1 + \phi_1)^2 + 1 \right] \tag{19.54}$$

Note that this forecast error (and its variance) is cumulative; i.e., it is equal to the two-period error for $\hat{w}_T(2)$ in *addition* to the one-period error for $\hat{w}_T(1)$. Thus the error in $\hat{y}_T(2)$ is an *accumulation* of the errors in $\hat{w}_T(1)$ and in $\hat{w}_T(2)$. Now observe this cumulative phenomenon in the l-period forecast:

$$e_T(l) = \left[w_{T+1} - \hat{w}_T(1) \right] + \left[w_{T+2} - \hat{w}_T(2) \right] + \cdots + \left[w_{T+l} - \hat{w}_T(l) \right]$$

$$= \varepsilon_{T+1} + (\varepsilon_{T+2} + \phi_1\varepsilon_{T+1}) + \cdots + \left(\varepsilon_{T+l} + \phi_1\varepsilon_{T+l-1} + \cdots + \phi_1^{l-1}\varepsilon_{T+1} \right)$$

$$= \left(1 + \phi_1 + \phi_1^2 + \cdots + \phi_1^{l-1} \right)\varepsilon_{T+1} + \left(1 + \phi_1 + \cdots + \phi_1^{l-2} \right)\varepsilon_{T+2}$$

$$+ \cdots + (1 + \phi_1)\varepsilon_{T+l-1} + \varepsilon_{T+l}$$

$$= \sum_{i=1}^{l} \varepsilon_{T+i} \sum_{j=0}^{l-i} \phi_1^j \tag{19.55}$$

and this has a variance

$$E\left[e_T^2(l) \right] = \sigma_\varepsilon^2 \sum_{i=1}^{l} \left(\sum_{j=0}^{l-i} \phi_1^j \right)^2 \tag{19.56}$$

Thus the error in $\hat{y}_T(l)$ is an accumulation of errors in $\hat{w}_T(1)$, $\hat{w}_T(2)$, ..., $\hat{w}_T(l)$. This can be seen graphically in Figs. 19.5 and 19.6, which compare confidence

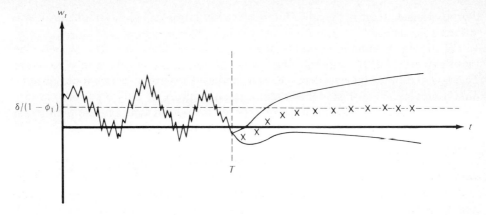

Figure 19.5 Confidence interval for $\hat{w}_T(l)$ for ARI(1, 1, 0) process.

intervals for forecasts of the differenced series w_t with confidence intervals for forecasts of y_t. Note the relationship between the forecasts of the differenced series w_t and the forecasts of y_t. w_{T-2} and w_{T-1} are decreasing, and w_T is negative, so that $\hat{w}_T(1)$ and $\hat{w}_T(2)$ are also negative [$\hat{y}_T(1)$ and $\hat{y}_T(2)$ are decreasing], $\hat{w}_T(3)$, $\hat{w}_T(4)$, etc., are positive [$\hat{y}_T(3)$ is larger than $\hat{y}_T(2)$], and finally $\hat{w}_T(l)$ approaches the mean $\delta/(1 - \phi_1)$ as l becomes large [so that $\hat{y}_T(l)$ approaches the drift line]. Observe that the confidence interval for $\hat{y}_T(l)$ grows

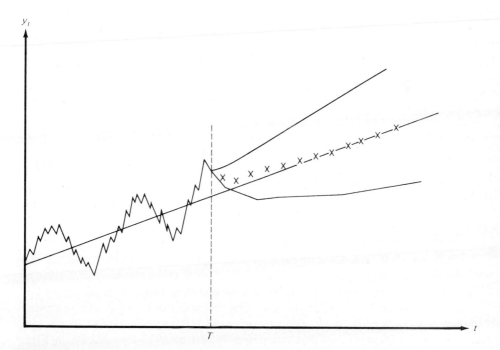

Figure 19.6 Confidence interval for $\hat{y}_T(l)$ for ARI(1, 1, 0) process.

rapidly, since it must account for the accumulation of forecast errors in the differenced series.

We have examined some of the properties of the forecasts of only the simplest of ARIMA models, but some of our conclusions apply to more complicated (i.e., higher-order) ARIMA models. In particular we should observe that a moving average model of order q has a memory of only q periods, so that the observed data will affect the forecast only if the lead time l is less than q. An autoregressive model has a memory of infinite length, so that all past observations will have some effect on the forecast, even if the lead time l is long. But although all past observations have *some* effect on the forecast, only more recent observations will have a large effect. Thus even with autoregressive (or mixed autoregressive–moving average) models, past observations have little effect on the forecast if the lead time is long. The conclusion, then, is that ARIMA models are best suited to *short-term forecasting*, i.e., forecasting with a lead time l not much longer than $p + q$.

19.6 TWO EXAMPLES

In the last chapter we estimated ARIMA models for two time series; we found that the first series, which consisted of quarterly data for the interest rate on 4- to 6-month commercial paper, could be represented using an ARIMA(4, 2, 2) model. The estimated version of that model is

$$(1 - .1675B + .1867B^2 + .0915B^3 - .2100B^4) \, \Delta^2 y_t$$

$$= -.0008 + (1 - .3627B - .6372B^2)\varepsilon_t \qquad (18.34)$$

The second time series consisted of data on monthly hog production in the United States, which we represented by applying an ARIMA(3, 1, 0) model to a twelfth-differencing of the original series. The estimated version of that model is

$$(1 + .6681B + .2015B^2 - .1298B^3)(1 - B)(1 - B^{12})y_t = .0014 + \varepsilon_t$$

$$(18.35)$$

Recall that the twelfth-differencing $(1 - B^{12})$ accounts for seasonal (annual) cycles in the data. We now generate forecasts of the interest rate and hog production using these two ARIMA models.

Example 19.1 Interest-rate forecast Recall that the ARIMA model for the interest rate was estimated using data that ran through the second quarter of 1972. In this example we generate two *ex post* forecasts that cover the end of the estimation period. The forecasts are presented in terms of the twice-differenced stationary series, and compared with the actual data.

A 10-period *ex post* forecast (from 1970-1 to 1972-2) is shown in Figs. 19.7 and 19.8, a 6-period forecast (1971-1 to 1972-2) is shown in Figs. 19.9

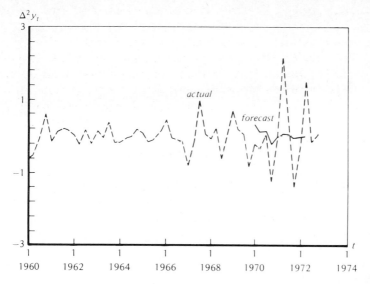

Figure 19.7 ARIMA(4, 2, 2): ten-period forecast of interest rate.

and 19.10, and a 7-period forecast that begins in 1972-2 and ends in 1973-4 is shown in Figs. 19.11 and 19.12. Note that in all these figures we are examining a series that has been differenced twice; i.e., we are examining a forecast of the second difference of the interest rate variable, rather than the level of the variable itself.

An evaluation of the model's forecast is somewhat difficult because the period over which we have forecasted was one of considerable fluctuation in

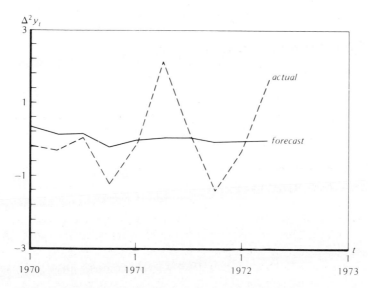

Figure 19.8 ARIMA(4, 2, 2): ten-period forecast (enlarged).

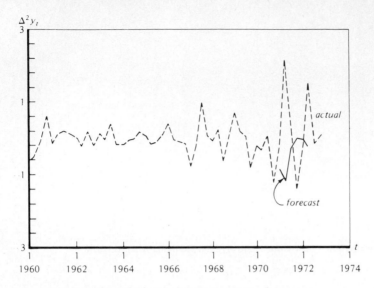

Figure 19.9 ARIMA(4, 2, 2): six-period forecast of interest rate.

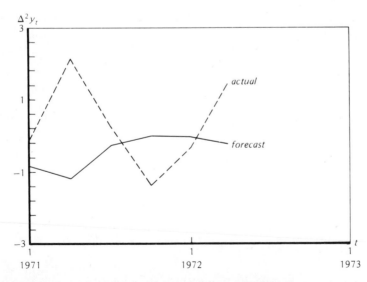

Figure 19.10 ARIMA(4, 2, 2): six-period forecast (enlarged).

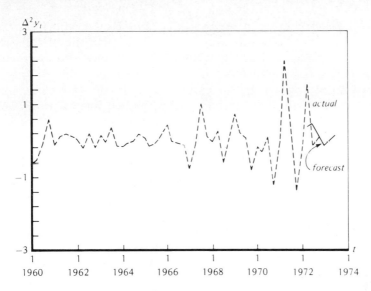

Figure 19.11 ARIMA(4, 2, 2): forecast to end of 1973 of interest rate.

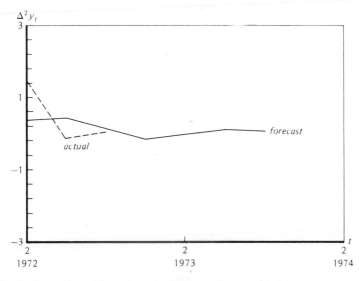

Figure 19.12 ARIMA(4, 2, 2): forecast to end of 1973 (enlarged).

interest rates. What we do see, however, is that the ARIMA model captures trends, but fails to predict sharp turns. This is characteristic of forecasts generated by time-series models. Nonetheless, the usefulness of this particular ARIMA model as a forecasting tool can be seriously evaluated only in comparison with other available forecasting tools. In the case of a short-term interest rate, particularly during a period when interest rates were fluctuating considerably, one might expect a structural regression model to show a better forecasting performance than a time-series model. (In the next chapter we will demonstrate how a time-series model can be combined with a regression model to improve the forecast of interest rates.)

Example 19.2   Hog production forecast Recall that the ARIMA model for hog production in Eq. (18.35) was estimated using data from the beginning of 1960 to the end of 1967. We generate our forecast out over a 2-year horizon, beginning in January 1968 and ending in January 1970. Since data on hog production are available for this period, we can compare the 25 months of forecasted production with the actual data.

The forecasted and actual series for hog production are shown in Fig. 19.13. The reader can observe that our model has generated forecasts which are quite accurate. The model not only correctly forecasts changing trends in the series but also picks up the broad seasonal cycle (as it should, since the model includes a twelfth-difference of the series to explain seasonality). Usually the forecast is within 10 or 15 percent of the actual series, and reproduces most of the turning points in the actual series. This model would be quite acceptable as a forecasting tool. Unlike our interest rate example, hog production can probably be forecasted better using a time-series model

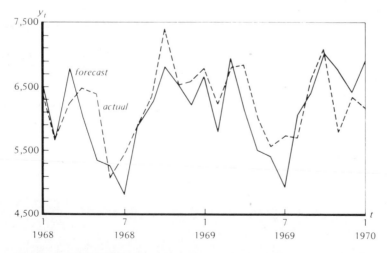

Figure 19.13 Two-year (25-month) forecast of hog production. Time bounds: January 1968 to January 1970.

than by using a single-equation regression model. The reason for this is that the economics of hog production are rather complicated and cannot be represented easily by a single structural equation. Although hog production could probably be modeled rather well by a multi-equation simulation model, constructing such a model would probably be rather difficult and time-consuming. The time-series model, on the other hand, can be constructed easily and quickly and does a reasonable job of forecasting.

In the next chapter we will look at some other examples of time-series models as applied to problems in economic and business forecasting. In each case we will go through the complete process of specifying, estimating, and checking an ARIMA model, and will then use the model to produce forecasts. This should provide the reader with more of a feeling for the properties and characteristics of time-series models and forecasts.

EXERCISES

19.1 Write the equation that determines the forecast $\hat{y}_T(l)$ in terms of $\hat{w}_T(1)$, $\hat{w}_T(2)$, . . . , for a third-order homogeneous nonstationary process; i.e., derive the equivalent of Eq. (19.18) for an ARIMA model with $d = 3$.

19.2 Does it seem reasonable that for any ARIMA specification the forecast error variance one period ahead is always the variance of the error term? Offer an intuitive explanation for why Eq. (19.22) must always hold.

19.3 Derive expressions for the one-, two-, and three-period forecasts, $\hat{y}_T(1)$, $\hat{y}_T(2)$, and $\hat{y}_T(3)$, for the second-order moving average process MA(2). What are the variances of the errors for these forecasts? What is the variance of the error for the l-period forecast, with $l > 3$?

19.4 Derive expressions for the one-, two-, and three-period forecasts for the second-order autoregressive process AR(2). What are the error variances of these forecasts?

19.5 Repeat Exercise 19.4 for the ARMA(2, 1) process.

19.6 Suppose that a particular nonstationary time series y_t can be modeled as a stochastic process that is ARIMA(1, 1, 1).

(a) After you have estimated the model's parameters, how would you forecast y_t one period ahead? Express this one-period forecast, $\hat{y}_t(1)$, as a function of observable data. In what sense is this forecast adaptive?

(b) How would you calculate the standard error of the one-period forecast $\hat{y}_t(1)$ *assuming that the parameters of the model are known perfectly*? Note that this is analogous to calculating the standard error of a regression forecast under the assumption that the coefficients β are known perfectly.

(c) What will be the *difference* between the l-period forecast $\hat{y}_t(l)$ and the $(l + 1)$-period forecast $\hat{y}_t(l + 1)$ *when l is very large*?

APPLICATIONS OF TIME-SERIES MODELS

In this chapter we present several detailed examples of the construction and use of time-series models. We hope that these examples will help convey a better understanding of how an analyst can decide what specification to use for a time-series model, how to estimate the model, and finally how to check the model and use it for forecasting. In addition, we would like to acquaint the reader with the usefulness of time-series models in applied forecasting problems. We will see that time-series models can be used in forecasting applications not only by themselves but also in combination with regression models.

We have seen that econometric model building is as much an art as it is a science. Even when constructing a simple single-equation econometric model, one must make judgments as to which explanatory variables should and should not be included, what functional form to specify for the equation, how the statistical fit of the model should be interpreted, and how useful the resulting model is for forecasting or explanation purposes. In building a regression model for predicting interest rates, for example, there might be many explanatory variables (with and without lags) that could be justified on theoretical grounds and thus included in the model. The analyst must decide which of those variables to include, and there are usually no well-defined rules for doing so. Also, the evaluation of the model's predictive performance is not straightforward. One can calculate confidence intervals for predictions of the dependent variable based on the assumption that the independent variables will be known with certainty, but these confidence intervals assume that the structural relationship will be stable over the forecasting period. Since this may not be the case, the analyst must make a judgment as to the applicability of the model to forecasting.

The situation is very much the same with time-series models. It is usually not obvious what the proper specification for an ARIMA model should be. For example, if one looks at the autocorrelation functions for a short-term interest rate and its differences, it may not be clear whether the model should be ARIMA(4, 0, 2), ARIMA(2, 2, 2), or some other specification. In general, many different specifications might be reasonable for a single time series and its autocorrelation function, so that sound judgment must be used together with a certain amount of experimentation. As in the regression case, one will often specify and estimate more than one ARIMA model, and check each of them individually. In general, the usefulness of an ARIMA model for forecasting purposes is difficult to ascertain. While confidence intervals can be determined for the model's forecasts, one must still decide whether any significant structural change in the determination of the variable under study might occur and thus alter the future movement of the time series.

In this chapter we consider the application of time-series analysis to several forecasting problems. We begin with a model for an aggregate economic variable, nonfarm inventory investment, and then turn to a model for forecasting seasonal telephone data. One might argue that inventory investment can be better explained by a structural econometric model, but such a model can be difficult and time-consuming to build. The seasonal telephone data that we examine are cyclical, highly fluctuating, and difficult to explain using a structural econometric model, so that a time-series model provides a natural vehicle for forecasting.

As a final application, we show in two examples how it is possible to combine a time-series model with a structural econometric model. To do so, we first construct a regression model and then develop a time-series model for the regression residuals (i.e., for the unexplained noise terms). This combined regression–time-series model is sometimes called a *transfer function* model, and if it is used with proper care, it can provide an extremely effective forecasting tool.

20.1 REVIEW OF THE MODELING PROCESS

Let us begin by briefly reviewing the steps involved in the construction, evaluation, and use of time-series models. One begins with the *specification* of the model. This first requires a decision as to the degree of homogeneity in the time series, i.e., how many times the time series must be differenced before a stationary series results. The decision is made by looking at the autocorrelation functions for the time series and its differences. (We have seen, however, that the correct degree of homogeneity is not always obvious.) After the degree of homogeneity has been specified, the orders of the moving average and the autoregressive parts of the model must be determined. In other words, values for p and q must be chosen for the ARMA model that will be used to represent the differenced series. One can get some guidance on the choice of p and q from examination of the total and partial autocorrelation functions, but often the correct choice will not be clear and several alternative specifications must be estimated.

Once a model (or a group of models) has been specified it must then be *estimated*. If the number of observations in the time series is large relative to the order of the model, this estimation process involves a straightforward nonlinear regression. In such cases, problems associated with the initialization of the time series can be ignored when performing the estimation.

After the model has been estimated, one must then perform a *diagnostic check* on it. This usually involves looking at the autocorrelation function of the residuals from the estimated model (i.e., the series determined by subtracting the actual series from the estimated series). A simple chi-square test can be performed to determine whether or not the residuals are themselves uncorrelated. In addition, one should check that the parameter estimates are consistent with *stationarity*, e.g., that the autoregressive parameters sum to a number smaller than 1 in magnitude.

If the model passes the diagnostic check, it must then be *evaluated* and *analyzed*. Evaluation and analysis are done to determine the ability of the model to forecast accurately and to provide a better understanding of its forecasting properties. For example, the model may pass a diagnostic check but have a very poor statistical fit, and this would seriously limit its usefulness for forecasting. If the model's estimated parameters have large standard errors, the standard error of forecast will be increased.

Unfortunately, the evaluation of the model is complicated by the fact that a nonlinear estimation has been performed. As a result the standard statistics of fit (that is, R^2, t statistics, etc.) have meaning only in the context of the last linearization in the iterative estimation process. Nonetheless, even if a model passes a diagnostic check on its residuals, an R^2 near 0 would indicate that the model is of very limited use for forecasting purposes. A useful rule of thumb is to drop from the equation terms whose coefficients have t statistics that are small (e.g., below 1). Often, one might want to respecify and reestimate a model, with the hope that the new version will also pass the diagnostic check, while yielding a better statistical fit.

Another method of evaluation and analysis is to perform an *historical simulation* of the model beginning at different points in time, i.e., to simulate the model over the historic time period but beginning at different instants in time. One can then examine such statistics as the rms simulation error and the Theil inequality coefficient and its decomposition. (See Chapter 12 for a review of these and other model evaluation statistics.) In addition, one can perform an *ex post forecast*, comparing the forecast to actual data to evaluate its performance. This kind of analysis can help the researcher decide how far into the future the model can be used for forecasting. This is extremely important if a time-series model is to be used in conjunction with a structural econometric model. Typically, the time-series model will provide a better forecast over the very short term, but the structural econometric model will provide a better forecast over the longer term.

20.2 MODELS OF ECONOMIC VARIABLES: INVENTORY INVESTMENT

In this section we construct and examine some time-series models for the level of nonfarm inventory investment. This variable is difficult to explain and forecast using structural econometric models, so that the construction of an ARIMA model seems appropriate.

We construct our models using quarterly data beginning in 1946 and ending in the second quarter of 1972. The time series is shown in Fig. 20.1, and its sample autocorrelation function is shown in Fig. 20.2. Note that the time series seems stationary, since there are no long-run trends either upward or downward. The autocorrelation function also exhibits (at least roughly) the properties of a stationary series. Its highest value (for a nonzero displacement lag) is .7 (at $k = 1$), and after a displacement lag of 3 or 4 it quickly goes down to values that are between $\pm.2$.

Before deciding on a stationary specification for the model, we choose to difference the time series and examine the sample autocorrelation functions of the series that result. A first difference of the series is shown in Fig. 20.3, and the corresponding autocorrelation function is shown in Fig. 20.4. Note that the autocorrelation function drops immediately to a value of $-.5$, and then oscillates, without any apparent damping, between values of $\pm.3$. The autocorrelation function has few clear-cut patterns, making it difficult to specify an ARIMA model.

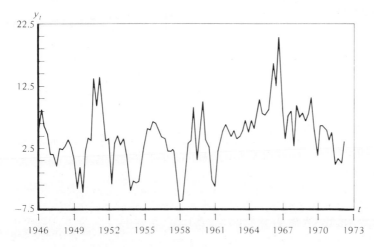

Figure 20.1 Nonfarm inventory investment.

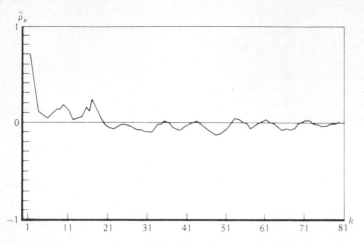

Figure 20.2 Nonfarm inventory investment: sample autocorrelation function.

The time series is differenced a second time, and the resulting series and its autocorrelation function are shown in Figs. 20.5 and 20.6. This autocorrelation function also lacks definitive qualities that would make an ARIMA specification possible and exhibits no more stationarity than the autocorrelation function for the undifferenced series in Fig. 20.2. It would probably be most logical to assume that our time series is stationary, i.e., to use a value of $d = 0$ in our ARIMA model. We do this, but for the purposes of comparison we also specify and estimate one or two models using a value of $d = 2$ (i.e., differencing the series twice).

Let us begin with a stationary specification. Looking at the autocorrelation function in Fig. 20.2 closely, we see that it begins to decay exponentially after about two or three displacement lags. It would thus be reasonable to specify the

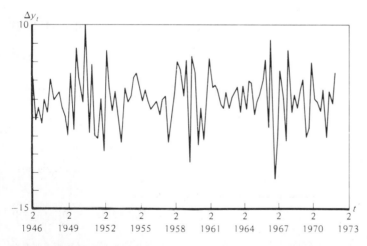

Figure 20.3 Nonfarm inventory investment: Δy_t.

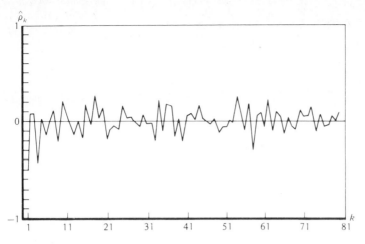

Figure 20.4 Nonfarm inventory investment: autocorrelation function of Δy_t.

moving average portion of the model as second order. The autoregressive portion of the model is somewhat more difficult to specify, since the autocorrelation function seems to exhibit oscillations with a period of about eight lags. Since these oscillations are somewhat damped, we might ignore them and specify the autoregressive portion of the model as first or second order. On the other hand, we could take them into account using a fourth-order autoregressive specification (which could have generated the observed oscillations). A fourth-order autoregressive specification would also be reasonable, since it would help account for any annual cycles in the original time series. Thus, there are at least three specifications that could be candidates for our ARIMA model: (1, 0, 2), (2, 0, 2), and (4, 0, 2). We estimate all three models and then compare them.

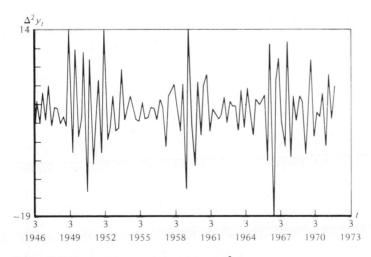

Figure 20.5 Nonfarm inventory investment: $\Delta^2 y_t$.

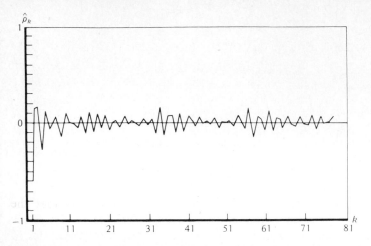

Figure 20.6 Nonfarm inventory investment: autocorrelation function of $\Delta^2 y_t$.

Upon reexamining the autocorrelation function in Fig. 20.6 for the twice-differenced series, we note that the autocorrelation function is a damped sinusoid after the second displacement lag. Thus, it appears that a moving average specification of second order would be appropriate. The autoregressive portion of the model could be specified as either second or fourth order; to be complete, we will estimate ARIMA models that are (2, 2, 2) and (4, 2, 2).

All five ARIMA models were estimated, with the results as shown in Eqs. (20.1) to (20.5) below. In each equation, the R^2 is shown, but its usefulness is limited because of the nature of the estimation process. After each model was estimated, a residual series was formed by subtracting the series predicted by the model from the actual time series. A sample autocorrelation function was then calculated for the residual series, after which a chi-square statistic was determined [see Eq. (18.31)] from the first 20 values of the autocorrelation function. The results are as follows:

ARIMA(1, 0, 2):

$$(1 - .6330B)y_t = 1.6055 + (1 - .0677B + .2880B^2)\varepsilon_t \qquad (20.1)$$

$$R^2 = .399 \qquad \chi^2(3, 20) = 14.77$$

ARIMA(2, 0, 2):

$$(1 - .8824B + .2686B^2)y_t = 1.685 + (1 - .3015B + .4280B^2)\varepsilon_t \quad (20.2)$$

$$R^2 = .519 \qquad \chi^2(4, 20) = 14.01$$

ARIMA(4, 0, 2):

$$(1 - .2622B - .2554B^2 - .1991B^3 + .2473B^4)y_t$$

$$= 2.333 + (1 + .3632B + .1822B^2)\varepsilon_t$$

$$(20.3)$$

$$R^2 = .236 \qquad \chi^2(6, 20) = 13.97$$

ARIMA(2, 2, 2):

$$(1 + .8938B + .2603B^2) \Delta^2 y_t = -.0175 + (1 - .380B - .620B^2)\varepsilon_t \quad (20.4)$$

$$R^2 = .523 \qquad \chi^2(4, 20) = 24.55$$

ARIMA(4, 2, 2):

$$(1 + .7478B + .1695B^2 + .0317B^3 + .1848B^4) \Delta^2 y_t$$

$$= -.0166 + (1 - .480B - .520B^2)\varepsilon_t \quad (20.5)$$

$$R^2 = .459 \qquad \chi^2(6, 20) = 22.38$$

Remember that the chi-square test is a test of the hypothesis that the residuals are not white noise, i.e., that they are correlated with each other. Since the statistic is a measure of correlation among the residuals, we would expect (if the model is correctly specified) it to be as small as possible. On the basis of this chi-square test alone, we can eliminate the two models (2, 2, 2) and (4, 2, 2). Consider, for example, the ARIMA(4, 2, 2) model. The chi-square statistic has 14 degrees of freedom (20 lags minus 6 estimated parameters) and a value of 22.38, falling above the 90 percent point (21.1) on the distribution (so that the probability that the residuals are not white noise is 90 percent). On the other hand, all three stationary ARIMA models have chi-square statistics that are low enough to fall at about the 50 percent point on the distribution. Thus, we were correct in our initial hypothesis that a stationary specification would have been most appropriate for the model.

For purposes of comparison, we retain the ARIMA(2, 0, 2) and the ARIMA(4, 0, 2) models, and examine their forecasting properties. The residual series for the ARIMA(4, 0, 2) model and the autocorrelation function of the residuals are shown in Figs. 20.7 and 20.8. The reader can observe that the

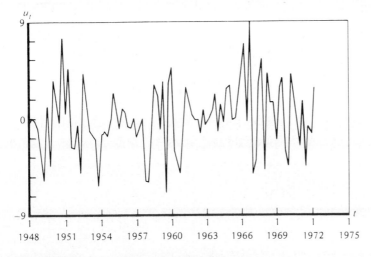

Figure 20.7 ARIMA(4, 0, 2) model: residual series.

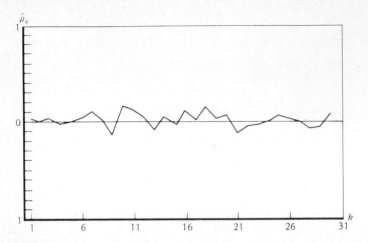

Figure 20.8 Autocorrelation function of ARIMA(4, 0, 2) residuals.

autocorrelation function has small values for most displacement lags, and no prominent peaks that would suggest the addition of more autoregressive or moving average terms. We have used this ARIMA(4, 0, 2) model to produce a 10-period forecast, beginning in the first quarter of 1970 and ending in the second quarter of 1972. The forecasted series is shown (in comparison with the actual series) in Figs. 20.9 and 20.10. Note that the ARIMA model predicted that the level of inventory investment in the first quarter of 1970 would be close to its mean value, thus failing to predict the sharp downturn in inventory investment that occurred in that period. The model does, however, predict a gradual decline over the entire 10 periods. The forecast is rather close to the

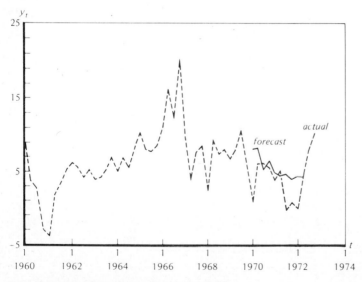

Figure 20.9 ARIMA(4, 0, 2): ten-period forecast.

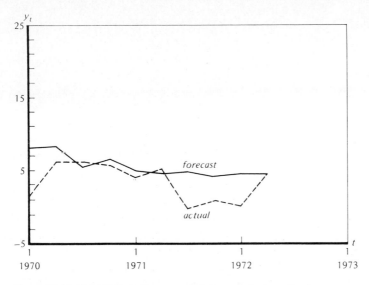

Figure 20.10 ARIMA(4, 0, 2): ten-period forecast (enlarged).

actual performance of inventory investment during the last three quarters of 1970 and the first two quarters of 1971, but it fails to predict the sharp drop in inventory investment during the last two quarters of 1971 and the first quarter of 1972.

Would the model have predicted the downturn in inventory investment during the second half of 1971 if we had begun the forecast at a later date? To answer this question, let us examine the six-period forecast that begins in the first quarter of 1971 and ends in the second quarter of 1972. This forecast is

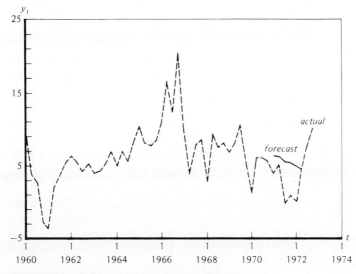

Figure 20.11 ARIMA(4, 0, 2): six-period forecast.

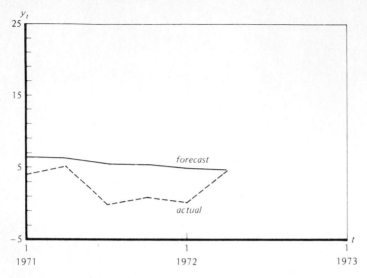

Figure 20.12 ARIMA(4, 0, 2): six-period forecast (enlarged).

shown in Figs. 20.11 and 20.12. What we find is that the six-period forecast is not very different from the ten-period forecast; i.e., it also predicts a gradual decline in inventory investment, but fails to predict the sharp downturn that actually occurred. This is not very surprising, since the original model was specified in an attempt to capture the overall trends and cycles in the original time series. Thus we should expect its predictive power to be limited largely to overall trends and cycles. (Had the inventory downturn at the end of 1971 been cyclical—which it was not—the time-series model probably would have captured it.)

A seven-period forecast, beginning in the second quarter of 1972 and ending in the fourth quarter of 1973, is shown in Figs. 20.13 and 20.14. Data on the actual time series were available only through the fourth quarter of 1972, but this is sufficient to allow us to observe that the ARIMA forecast only replicates overall trends in the series, and thus fails to predict the upturn in inventory investment that took place at the end of 1972.

For comparison, forecasts were also produced using the ARIMA(2, 0, 2) model: 10-period forecasts (1970-1 to 1972-2) are shown in Figs. 20.15 and 20.16; six-period forecasts (1971-1 to 1972-2) are shown in Figs. 20.17 and 20.18; and seven-period forecasts running through the end of 1973 are shown in Figs. 20.19 and 20.20. We observe that the ARIMA(2, 0, 2) model is a better predictor in the short term (two or three periods) but less able to predict longer-run trends. The 10-period ARIMA(2, 0, 2) forecast does, for example, predict the sharp downturn in the beginning of 1970, but its predictive power after the second quarter of 1970 is no better than that of the ARIMA(4, 0, 2) model [although its overall performance over 10 periods is slightly better; the rms forecast error is 2.25 versus 2.43 for the (4, 0, 2) model].†

---

† The rms error is defined and explained in Chapter 12.

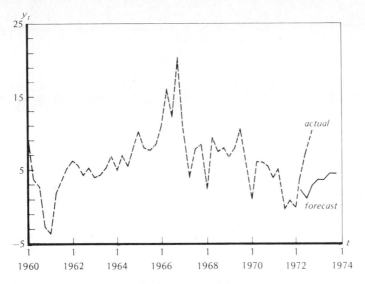

Figure 20.13 ARIMA(4, 0, 2): forecast to 1974.

Would the ARIMA(2, 0, 2) model be a better choice for actual use in forecasting? The answer to this question would probably be yes, particularly if the model were going to be used for short-term forecasts (i.e., two or three periods). The decision as to which model should be used would be made by comparing the forecasting performance of both models over recent years. If you in fact make this comparison, you would probably choose the (2, 0, 2) model, at least for short term forecasting purposes.

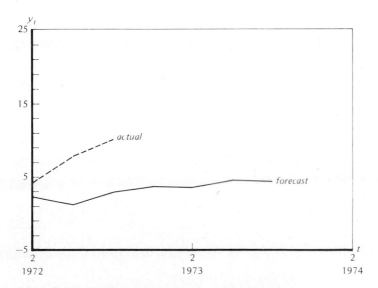

Figure 20.14 ARIMA(4, 0, 2): forecast to 1974 (enlarged).

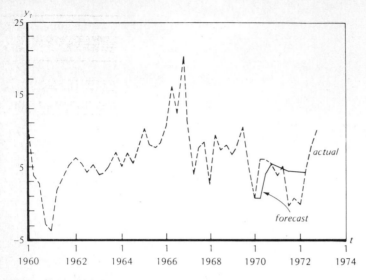

Figure 20.15 ARIMA(2, 0, 2): ten-period forecast.

The inability of both our ARIMA models to predict sharp downturns and upturns in inventory investment limits their value for forecasting. But before they are discarded as forecasting tools, they must be compared with alternative forecasting tools that are available. Many single- and multi-equation regression models have been constructed to forecast inventory investment, some with a performance not much better than that of our simple ARIMA model. Because inventory investment is dependent on several other macroeconomic variables,

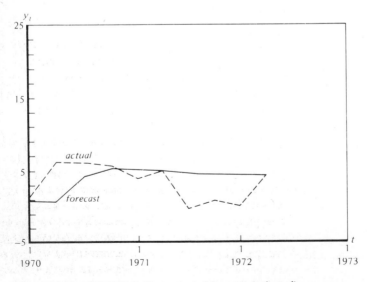

Figure 20.16 ARIMA(2, 0, 2): ten-period forecast (enlarged).

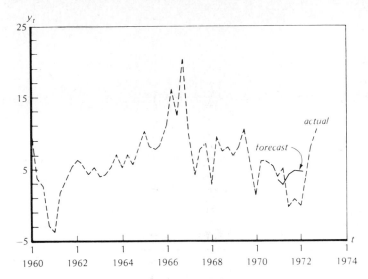

Figure 20.17 ARIMA(2, 0, 2): six-period forecast.

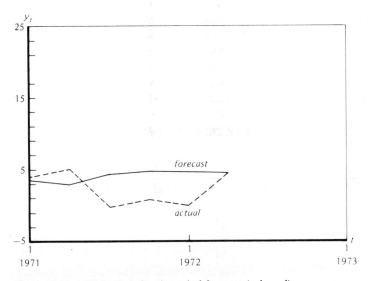

Figure 20.18 ARIMA(2, 0, 2): six-period forecast (enlarged).

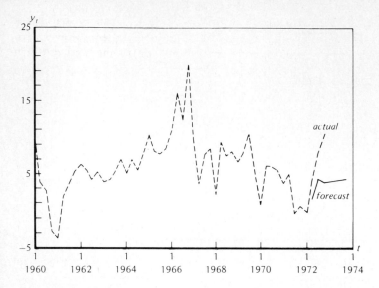

Figure 20.19 ARIMA(2, 0, 2): forecast to 1974.

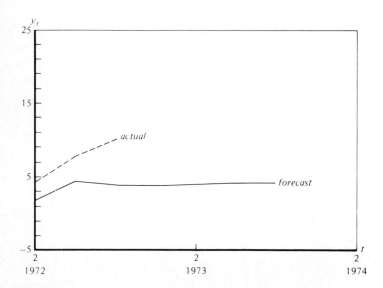

Figure 20.20 ARIMA(2, 0, 2): forecast to 1974 (enlarged).

which are themselves dependent on inventory investment, it can probably best be explained and forecasted using a complete simultaneous equation macro-econometric model. Such a model, however, is time-consuming and costly to build, so that a time-series model might provide an economical forecasting alternative.†

20.3 FORECASTING SEASONAL TELEPHONE DATA

An article by Thompson and Tiao provides another interesting case study for the application of time-series analysis.‡ In the study forecasting models were constructed for the inward and outward station movements of the Wisconsin Telephone Company using monthly data from January 1951 to October 1966. The inward station movement in a given month is the sum of residence and business telephone installations, while the outward station movement consists of removals and disconnects of telephones. It is important to the telephone company to obtain reasonably accurate forecasts of station movements, since these forecasts are used as fundamental inputs to both short- and long-term company planning. The difference between inward and outward station movements represents the net increase or (decrease) of telephones in service, so that an expected positive difference would lead to a sequence of capital expenditures. Under-estimating the difference might create a shortage in the supply of telephones and associated facilities, while overestimating it would result in a premature expansion of facilities and thus added cost to the company.

The data used by Thompson and Tiao for inward and outward station movements are shown in Figs. 20.21 and 20.22. The data show a very distinct seasonal pattern, with a peak and a trough reached each year. Note that the *level* of each series tends to increase over time *and that the variance of the data tends to increase as the level increases*. In order to reduce this dependence of the variance on the level, the authors applied a logarithmic transformation to both

---

† There have been several studies made of time-series models as a forecasting alternative to large-scale econometric models of the macroeconomy. The more interesting and illuminating studies include C. R. Nelson, "The Prediction Performance of the FRB-MIT-PENN Model of the U.S. Economy," *American Economic Review*, vol. 62, December 1972; and T. H. Naylor, T. G. Seaks, and D. W. Wichern, "Box-Jenkins Methods: An Alternative to Econometric Models," *International Statistical Review*, vol. 40, no. 2, 1972. In both these studies the authors found that time-series models can often provide better forecasts of macroeconomic variables than some of the better-known large econometric models. It is hard to say whether this should be taken as a compliment to time-series analysis or a comment on the state of the art of macroeconometric modeling! A more detailed discussion (including examples) of the use of time-series models for macroeconomic forecasting is given in C. R. Nelson, *Applied Time Series Analysis* (San Francisco: Holden-Day, 1973).

‡ H. E. Thompson and G. C. Tiao, "Analysis of Telephone Data: A Case Study of Forecasting Seasonal Time Series," *Bell Journal of Economics and Management Science*, vol. 2, no. 2, Autumn 1971.

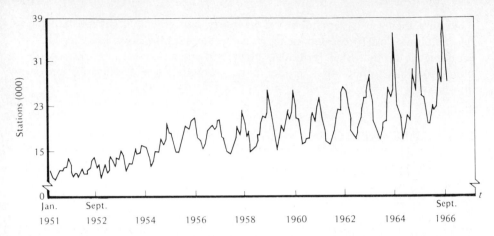

Figure 20.21 Monthly inward station movements, January 1951 to October 1966. (*Bell Journal of Economics and Management Sciences, vol. 2, no. 2, Autumn* 1971.)

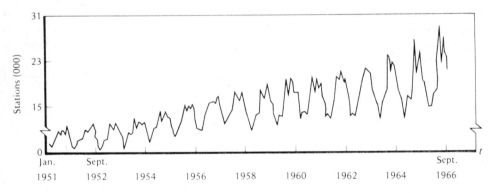

Figure 20.22 Monthly outward station movement, January 1951 to October 1966 (y_t). (*Bell Journal of Economics and Management Sciences, vol. 2, no. 2, Autumn* 1971.)

series. Thus, the analysis that follows is given in terms of transformed logarithmic data. (Logarithmic transformations are often used in time-series analysis as a means of removing growth over time of the variance of the data.)

Time-series models can easily be constructed to account for seasonality; in fact, we treated seasonality earlier when we constructed a time-series model for hog production.† It is reasonable to expect a seasonal pattern in station

---

† For a detailed treatment of seasonal time-series models, see G. E. P. Box, G. M. Jenkins, and D. W. Bacon, "Models for Forecasting Seasonal and Non-Seasonal Time Series," in *Spectral Analysis of Time Series* (New York: Wiley, 1967), and C. R. Nelson, *Applied Time Series Analysis* (San Francisco: Holden-Day, 1973), chap. 7.

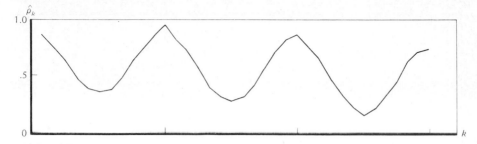

Figure 20.23 Sample autocorrelation function of y_t. (*Bell Journal of Economics and Management Sciences, vol. 2, no. 2, Autumn 1971.*)

movements, i.e., similarities in observations of the same month in different years. Thus, we would expect observations 12 periods apart to be highly correlated (as in our hog production example). We can express this seasonal relationship with the simple autoregressive model

$$(1 - \phi^* B^{12})y_t = e_t \tag{20.6}$$

where e_t is a random shock. While this equation explains observations between years, observations in successive months may also be dependent. This dependence might be represented by a second autoregressive model:

$$(1 - \phi B)e_t = \varepsilon_t \tag{20.7}$$

where ε_t is a random shock. Equation (20.6) can be substituted into (20.7) to eliminate e_t:

$$(1 - \phi^* B^{12})(1 - \phi B)y_t = \varepsilon_t \tag{20.8}$$

or $$y_t - \phi y_{t-1} - \phi^* y_{t-12} + \phi\phi^* y_{t-13} = \varepsilon_t \tag{20.9}$$

Equation (20.9) is a simple autoregressive model. It serves to describe, however, both seasonal and nonseasonal dependence between observations.†

In this case we present Thompson and Tiao's model of the *logarithmic outward series*. The reader interested in the rest of their results may refer to the original paper. Our purpose is simply to demonstrate how a seasonal time-series model might be constructed.

We represent the logarithm of monthly outward station movements by the variable y_t. The sample autocorrelation function of y_t is shown in Fig. 20.23.

---

† This equation can be generalized to yield a class of models for seasonal series:

$$\phi_{p1}^*(B^{12})\phi_p(B)(1 - B^{12})^{d_1}(1 - B)^d(y_t - \mu) = \theta_q(B)\varepsilon_t$$

where $\phi_{p1}^*(B^{12})$ is a polynomial in B^{12} of order p_1, and $\phi_p(B)$ is a polynomial of order p. The parameters $\phi_1^*, \ldots, \phi_{p1}^*$ can be called seasonal autoregressive parameters. In the preliminary model-building stage, particular attention is given to peaks in the sample autocorrelation functions which occur at multiples of 12 lags. Generally, differencing 12 periods apart (one or more times) is needed when ρ_k is persistently large for $k = 12, 24, 36, \ldots$.

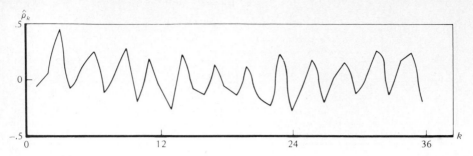

Figure 20.24 Sample autocorrelation function for w_t. (*Bell Journal of Economics and Management Sciences, vol. 2, no. 2, Autumn 1971.*)

Note that this autocorrelation function peaks at $k = 12$, 24, and 36, which is not surprising in view of the seasonal pattern in the data. We thus calculate 12-period differences in the series, and call this new series w_t:

$$w_t = (1 - B^{12})y_t \tag{20.10}$$

The sample autocorrelation function for w_t is shown in Fig. 20.24. Note that the seasonal dependence between years has been removed and the magnitude of the autocorrelations has been dampened considerably. Also, note that this autocorrelation function has peaks at every third lag, thus suggesting the autoregressive model†

$$(1 - \phi_3 B^3)w_t = \varepsilon_t \tag{20.11}$$

Thompson and Tiao fitted a third-order autoregressive model to the series w_t and then calculated the autocorrelation function for the residuals of this model. They found peaks at $k = 9$, 12, and 13, suggesting the addition of three moving average parameters. Thus, their final ARIMA model for y_t was of the form

$$(1 - \phi_3 B^3)(1 - \phi_{12} B^{12})y_t = (1 - \theta_9 B^9 - \theta_{12} B^{12} - \theta_{13} B^{13})\varepsilon_t \tag{20.12}$$

The five parameters ϕ_3, ϕ_{12}, θ_9, θ_{12}, and θ_{13} were estimated, and the resulting model was used to forecast the logarithmic outward series for the 36 months from November 1966 to October 1969. The forecast, together with the 95 percent confidence interval, is shown in Fig. 20.25.

Note that the model does a rather good job of forecasting outward station movements, even over a period of 36 months. In fact, the model seems to perform considerably better than our models of the level of inventory investment did. The reason for this is that the telephone data used in Thompson and Tiao's study were particularly amenable to time-series analysis. Time-series

---

† Cycles every third period could also be generated by a second-order autoregressive model (with the proper parameter values). The authors may have tested a second-order model and found Eq. (20.11) to be preferable. In general, however, if a distinct peak occurs in the autocorrelation function at every nth lag, we suggest including an nth-order autoregressive term in the specification of the ARIMA model.

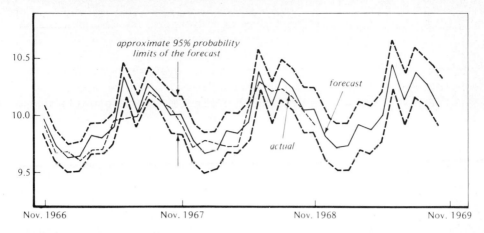

Figure 20.25 Forecasts of log outward series for the 36 months, November 1966 to October 1969, made in October 1966. (*Bell Journal of Economics and Management Sciences, vol. 2, no. 2, Autumn 1971.*)

analysis works best when a persistent pattern (seasonal or otherwise) exists in the data, and such a pattern is present in the telephone data.

20.4 COMBINING REGRESSION ANALYSIS WITH A TIME-SERIES MODEL: TRANSFER FUNCTION MODELS

At the end of Chapter 18 we estimated a time-series model for a short-term interest rate. Although we used the model to produce a forecast in Chapter 19, we suggested that a better forecast could have been obtained by using a single-equation structural regression model (as in Chapter 8). We will soon see how time-series analysis and regression analysis can be combined to produce a better forecast than would be possible through the use of either of these techniques alone.

Suppose that one would like to forecast the variable y_t using a regression model. Presumably such a model would include all those independent variables which could provide an explanation for movements in y_t but which are not themselves collinear. Let us suppose, for example, that the best regression model contains two independent variables, x_1 and x_2, as follows:

$$y_t = a_0 + a_1 x_{1t} + a_2 x_{2t} + \varepsilon_t \tag{20.13}$$

This equation has an implicit additive error term that accounts for *unexplained* variance in y_t; that is, it accounts for that part of the variance of y_t that is not explained by x_1 and x_2. The equation can be estimated, and an R^2 will result which (unless by some chance y_t is perfectly correlated with the independent variables) will be less than 1. The equation can then be used to forecast y_t. As we saw in Chapter 8, one source of forecast error would come from the additive noise term whose future values cannot be predicted.

By subtracting the estimated values of y_t from the actual values, we can calculate a residual series u_t which represents unexplained movements in y_t, i.e., pure noise. One effective application of time-series analysis is to construct an ARIMA model for the residual series u_t of the regression. We would then substitute the ARIMA model for the implicit error term in the original regression equation. When using the equation to forecast y_t, we would also be able to make a forecast of the error term ε_t using the ARIMA model. The ARIMA model provides some information as to what future values of ε_t are likely to be; i.e., it helps "explain" the unexplained variance in the regression equation. The combined regression–time-series model is

$$y_t = a_0 + a_1 x_{1t} + a_2 x_{2t} + \phi^{-1}(B)\theta(B)\eta_t \qquad (20.14)$$

where η_t is a normally distributed error term which may have a different variance from ε_t. This model is likely to provide much better forecasts than the regression equation (20.13) alone or a time-series model alone since it includes a structural (economic) explanation of that part of the variance of y_t that can be explained structurally, and a time-series "explanation" of that part of the variance of y_t that cannot be explained structurally.

Equation (20.14) is actually an example of what is sometimes referred to as a *transfer function model* or, alternatively, a *multivariate autoregressive–moving average model* (MARMA model). A transfer function model simply relates a dependent variable to lagged values of itself, current and lagged values of one or more independent variables, and an error term which is partially "explained" by a time-series model. Thus the general form for a univariate (only one independent variable) transfer function model could be written as

$$y_t = v^{-1}(B)\omega(B)x_t + \phi^{-1}(B)\theta(B)\eta_t \qquad (20.15)$$

The technique of transfer function modeling involves examination of partial and total autocorrelation functions for the independent variable x_t as well as the dependent variable y_t in an effort to specify the lag polynomials $v(B)$, $\omega(B)$, $\phi(B)$, and $\theta(B)$.† One problem with the technique, however, is that the specification of the structural part of the model, i.e., the polynomials $v(B)$ and $\omega(B)$ is done mechanically, rather than by appeal to economic theory and logic. Structural models that are consistent with intuition and economic theory are usually more reliable (and defensible) than models in which the structure is arrived at mechanically. For this reason we suggest that models of the form of Eq. (20.15) be used, but that the structural part of the model be arrived at through the mixture of economic theory and econometric method discussed in Part One, while the time-series part of the model, that is, $\phi(B)$ and $\theta(B)$, be arrived at through an analysis of the residuals of the structural model.

---

† The techniques are discussed in detail in G. E. P. Box and G. M. Jenkins, *Time Series Analysis* (San Francisco: Holden-Day, 1970), chaps. 10 and 11; and S. Makridakis and S. C. Wheelwright, *Forecasting Methods and Applications* (New York: Wiley, 1978), chap. 11.

Let us now turn back to the simple model of Eq. (20.14). First, note that specifying a time-series model for the error term is just a generalization of the technique described in Chapter 8 for forecasting with regression models that have serially correlated errors. [If the time-series model is AR(1), it is exactly equivalent to forecasting with first-order serially correlated errors.] Second, note that the parameters a_0, a_1, and a_2 of the structural regression equation and the parameters ϕ and θ of the time-series model should be estimated *simultaneously*. (Failure to estimate all the parameters simultaneously can lead to a loss of efficiency.) Unfortunately, the simultaneous estimation of all of the parameters can sometimes entail considerable computational expense, and therefore is often not done in practice.

This combined use of regression analysis with a time-series model of the error term is a particularly powerful approach to forecasting that in some cases can provide the best of both worlds. To demonstrate the technique and its usefulness, we now turn to two examples.

20.5 A COMBINED REGRESSION–TIME-SERIES MODEL TO FORECAST INTEREST RATES

As a first example of the combined use of regression analysis with time-series models, let us construct a model to forecast, on a monthly basis, the interest rate on 3-month Treasury bills. We begin by examining the regression model that was developed for that interest rate in Chapter 8. The regression equation related the interest rate R to disposable income YD, a moving sum of changes in the money supply M, and a moving sum of monthly inflation rates $\Delta P/P$ (note that the time unit is 1 month):

$$R = - \underset{(-9.45)}{3.662} + \underset{(14.76)}{.053} \, \text{YD} - \underset{(-6.13)}{.280} \, (\Delta M + \Delta M_{-1} + \Delta M_{-2})$$

$$+ \underset{(5.23)}{104.38} \left(\frac{\Delta P}{P} + \frac{\Delta P_{-1}}{P_{-1}} + \frac{\Delta P_{-2}}{P_{-2}} \right) \tag{20.16}$$

$$R^2 = .853 \qquad \text{SER} = .552 \qquad F = 271.9 \qquad \text{DW} = .24$$

A historical simulation of the regression model was performed over the 24-month period January 1968 to January 1970 and is shown in Fig. 20.26. That simulation had an rms error of .542 (the mean value of the interest rate over the period was 6.138). Next, the regression model was used to produce an *ex post* forecast of the interest rate over the 6-month period January 1970 to June 1970, and the results are shown in Fig. 20.27. The rms error for this forecast was .750 (the actual series had a mean value in this period of 6.943).

We now attempt to improve upon the forecasting performance of this model by constructing and applying a time-series model to the residual series. Sample autocorrelation functions are shown in Figs. 20.28 and 20.29 for the series of regression residuals undifferenced and differenced once. The reader can observe

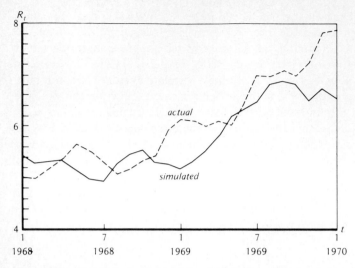

Figure 20.26 Historical simulation of Eq. (20.16). Time bounds: January 1968 to January 1970.

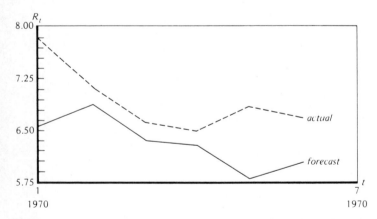

Figure 20.27 *Ex post* interest rate forecast using Eq. (20.16). Time bounds: January 1970 to June 1970.

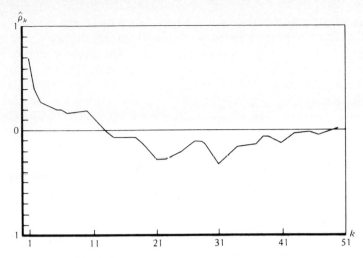

Figure 20.28 Autocorrelation function of residual series u_t.

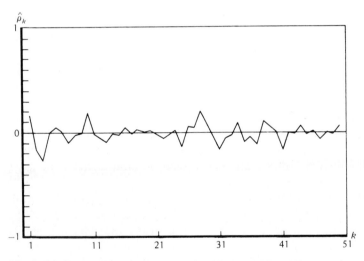

Figure 20.29 Autocorrelation function of residual series first-differenced (Δu_t).

that the autocorrelation function for the undifferenced series has the properties one would expect for a stationary time series, so that differencing the series one or more times is unnecessary to create a stationary series. The autocorrelation function appears to be autoregressive, since it decays exponentially, and also has some cyclical characteristics. This suggests the use of three models: ARIMA(2, 0, 0), ARIMA(4, 0, 0), and ARIMA(8, 0, 0). The estimation results for these three models, together with R^2, chi-square statistics, and t statistics, are:

ARIMA(2, 0, 0):

$$u_t = \underset{(.24)}{.0066} + \underset{(9.50)}{1.036}\, u_{t-1} - \underset{(-2.09)}{.238}\, u_{t-2} + \eta_t \tag{20.17}$$

$$R^2 = .670 \qquad \chi^2(2, 22) = 16.25$$

ARIMA(4, 0, 0):

$$u_t = \underset{(.53)}{.0143} + \underset{(9.52)}{1.028}\, u_{t-1} - \underset{(-1.16)}{.180}\, u_{t-2} - \underset{(-1.87)}{.290}\, u_{t-3} + \underset{(2.87)}{.324}\, u_{t-4} + \eta_t$$

$$\tag{20.18}$$

$$R^2 = .701 \qquad \chi^2(4, 24) = 11.99$$

ARIMA(8, 0, 0):

$$u_t = \underset{(.70)}{.019} + \underset{(8.81)}{1.014}\, u_{t-1} - \underset{(-.85)}{.140}\, u_{t-2} - \underset{(-2.10)}{.344}\, u_{t-3} + \underset{(1.69)}{.283}\, u_{t-4}$$

$$+ \underset{(.77)}{.131}\, u_{t-5} - \underset{(-.69)}{.117}\, u_{t-6} - \underset{(-.43)}{.075}\, u_{t-7} + \underset{(1.39)}{.171}\, u_{t-8} + \eta_t \tag{20.19}$$

$$R^2 = .712 \qquad \chi^2(8, 28) = 11.25$$

Because the models do not contain moving average terms, a linear regression can be used to estimate them, and the t statistics and R^2 retain their usual meaning. The resulting statistics seem to indicate that the ARIMA(4, 0, 0) model is most favorable. High-order terms in the eighth-order model are largely insignificant, and the second-order model has a lower R^2 and higher chi-square statistic. We therefore use the (4, 0, 0) model for forecasting.

Before we combine this ARIMA model with the regression model from Eq. (20.16), let us see how well it forecasts the residual series. In Fig. 20.30 we present a historical simulation of the residual series using the ARIMA model over the period 1968 to 1970, as well as the actual series. The reader can observe that the model tracks the actual series fairly closely. In Fig. 20.31, we use the ARIMA model to produce an *ex ante* forecast of the residuals over the time period January 1970 to January 1972. Since the regression equation was esti- mated only through the end of 1969, we do not have an actual residual series with which to compare this forecasted series, but we can observe the characteris- tics of the ARIMA forecast. Notice that the forecasted series drops off, increases slightly, and then goes toward 0 as the time horizon expands outward. An autoregressive model has an infinite memory, but the farther out in time one

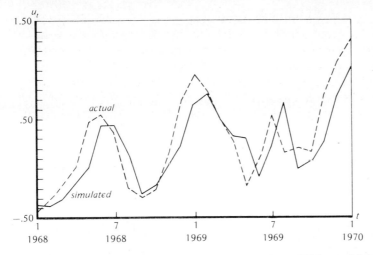

Figure 20.30 Historical simulation of residual series using ARIMA model. Time bounds: January 1968 to January 1970.

goes, the less influence past events have on our forecast, and the closer to 0 (the mean value of the residuals u_t) our forecast becomes.

We can now combine the ARIMA(4, 0, 0) model with our regression model and use the combined model to produce forecasts of the interest rate. First, we performed a historical simulation of the interest rate using the combined regression–time-series model over the period January 1968 to January 1970. These results are shown in Fig. 20.32, where one can observe that the simulated series is much closer to the actual series than was the case when the regression

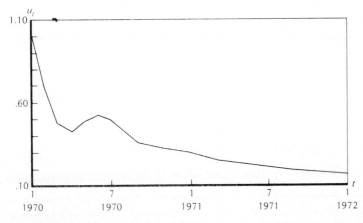

Figure 20.31 *Ex ante* forecast of residual series using ARIMA model. Time bounds: January 1970 to January 1972.

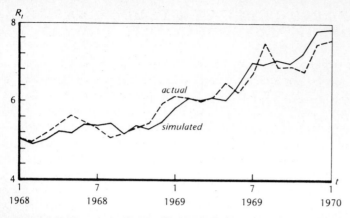

Figure 20.32 Historical simulation of interest rate using combined regression–time-series model. Time bounds: January 1968 to January 1970.

model was used alone. In fact, the rms simulation error has now been reduced by almost half—to a value of .269. A 6-month *ex post* forecast, from January 1970 to June 1970, using the combined regression–time-series model is shown in Fig. 20.33. Once again the reader can observe that the forecast is closer to the actual series than was the case with the regression model alone. Again, the rms forecast error has been reduced by a factor of almost 2, to a value of .340. This increase in forecasting accuracy gives an illustration of the usefulness of this application of time-series analysis.

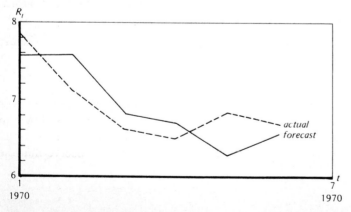

Figure 20.33 *Ex post* forecast of interest rate using combined regression–time-series model. Time bounds: January 1970 to June 1970.

20.6 A COMBINED REGRESSION–TIME-SERIES MODEL TO FORECAST SHORT-TERM SAVINGS DEPOSIT FLOWS

We now examine a second example of an application of time-series analysis in combination with regression analysis. This example, based on a study by Ludwig,† involves a forecast of the monthly flow of deposits into Massachusetts mutual savings banks. As in the last example, a regression model is first constructed (to explain deposit flows), and then a time-series model is developed to "explain" the residual series (i.e., the error term) in the regression equation.

We begin with a regression equation that provides a structural explanation for mutual savings deposit flows. Ludwig used the ratio of deposit flows S to personal wealth W as the dependent variable, and chose monthly Massachusetts personal income as a proxy variable for wealth. He found that his best regression equation included three explanatory variables: the effective percentage return (including dividends) on mutual savings deposits r_{ms}, the interest rate on 3-month Treasury bills r_m, and the ratio of the previous month's stock of mutual savings deposits A_{-1} to the wealth variable. His equation, estimated using monthly data for the state of Massachusetts over the period February 1968 to June 1973, is

$$\frac{S}{W} = \underset{(1.89)}{.16} + \underset{(2.98)}{.019} \, r_{ms} - \underset{(-5.27)}{.011} \, r_m - \underset{(-2.23)}{.032} \, \frac{A_{-1}}{W} \tag{20.20}$$

$$R^2 = .41 \qquad \text{SER} = .016 \qquad F = 14.42 \qquad \text{DW} = 1.55$$

As one would expect, there is a positive relationship between savings deposit flows and the effective percentage return on deposits. The interest rate on 3-month Treasury bills, used as a market rate of interest, represents the return on competing risk-free investment alternatives for savings, and thus should have a negative impact on savings deposit flows. Finally, the negative relationship between deposit flows and the stock of deposits represents a stock adjustment effect; savings deposits should be proportional to that part of personal wealth that has not already been placed in a savings bank; i.e.,

$$S_t = A_t - A_{t-1} = a(W_t - A_{t-1}) \tag{20.21}$$

so that
$$\frac{S_t}{W_t} = a - a\frac{A_{t-1}}{W_t} \tag{20.22}$$

An historical simulation of Eq. (20.20) is shown in Fig. 20.34, and an *ex post* forecast of the equation over the period July 1973 to October 1973 is shown in Fig. 20.35. The historical simulation has an rms *percent* error of 75.1, and the *ex post* forecast has an rms percent error of 157.‡ The reader can observe that the

---

† R. S. Ludwig, "Forecasting Short-Term Savings Deposit Flows: An Application of Time Series Models and a Regional Analysis," unpublished Master's thesis. Sloan School of Management, M.I.T., June 1974.

‡ The rms percent error is defined and explained in Chapter 12.

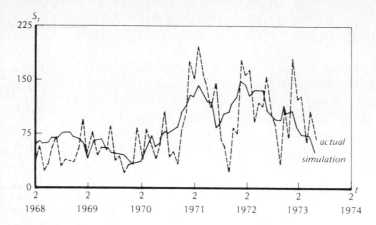

Figure 20.34 Historical simulation of Eq. (20.20) for deposit flows.

simulation tracks the general movement of the series but leaves much of the variance unexplained. The regression model does well in forecasting deposit flows in July 1973 but fails to capture the strong downward trend in deposits in August of that year.

Let us now see how to improve the forecast by constructing a time-series model for the residual series of the regression equation. The sample autocorrelation function for the residual series is shown in Fig. 20.36. The reader can observe that high-order correlations damp toward 0, so that the residual series can be considered stationary. The autocorrelation function does, however, contain peaks at monthly lags which are multiples of 12, indicating annual seasonality. In Fig. 20.37 we show the sample autocorrelation function for a series which is a 12-month difference of the original residual series, i.e., for the series $(1 - B^{12})u_t$. This autocorrelation function has a damped sinusoidal shape which is indicative of a purely autoregressive process of order 2 or greater.

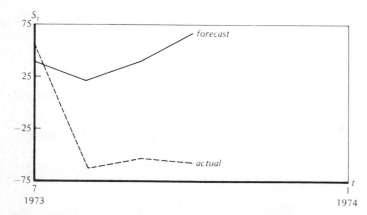

Figure 20.35 *Ex post* forecast of Eq. (20.20) for deposit flows.

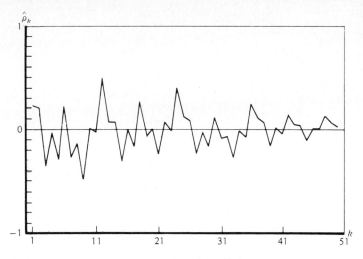

Figure 20.36 Autocorrelation function of residuals u_t from Eq. (20.20).

Ludwig estimated a variety of autoregressive models for this residual series, and found the best model to be of the form

$$\left(1 - \phi_{12}B^{12}\right)\left(1 - \phi_1 B - \phi_2 B^2 - \phi_3 B^3 - \phi_4 B^4 - \phi_5 B^5 - \phi_6 B^6\right)u_t = \eta_t$$
(20.23)

which in its expanded and estimated form is

$$(1 - .736B - .025B^2 - .055B^3 - .009B^4 + .310B^5 - .128B^6 - .782B^{12}$$
$$+ .532B^{13} + .081B^{14} + .125B^{15} - .213B^{16} - .103B^{17} - .060B^{18})u_t = \eta_t$$
(20.24)

$$R^2 = .78 \qquad \chi^2 = 14.5$$

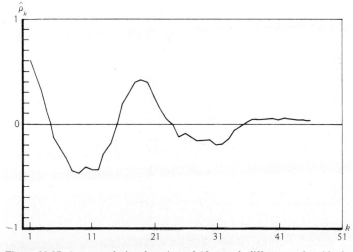

Figure 20.37 Autocorrelation function of 12-month difference of residuals $(1 - B^{12})u_t$.

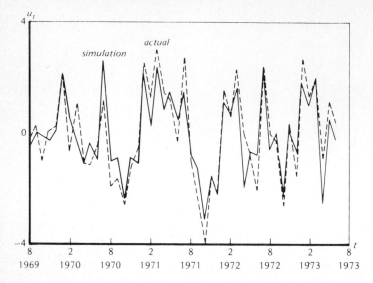

Figure 20.38 Historical simulation of time-series model for residuals.

An historical simulation of the time-series model alone is shown in Fig. 20.38. The reader can observe that the residual series is reproduced closely.

Now the time-series model for the residual series can be combined with the regression model of Eq. (20.20). An historical simulation of the combined regression–time-series model is shown in Fig. 20.39. The reader can observe that savings deposits are tracked much more closely than before. Indeed, the rms percent error has been reduced by a factor of more than 3, to 29.3.

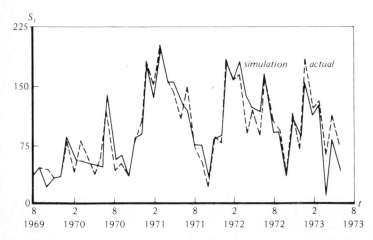

Figure 20.39 Historical simulation of combined regression–time-series model for savings deposit flows.

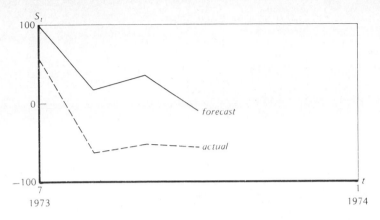

Figure 20.40 *Ex post* forecast of savings deposit flows using combined regression–time-series model.

Finally, an *ex post* forecast of savings flows is made using the combined regression–time-series model, again for the 4-month period July 1973 to October 1973. This forecast, shown in Fig. 20.40, is closer to the actual data than when the regression model alone was used. (The rms percent error has been reduced from 157 to 118.) Although the forecast does not capture the extent of the downturn in savings deposit flows in August 1973, it does predict general movements in the variable.

STATISTICAL TABLES

Table 1 Standardized normal distribution

z	.00	.01	.02	.03	.04	.05	.06	.07	.08	.09
0.0	.5000	.4960	.4920	.4880	.4840	.4801	.4761	.4721	.4681	.4641
0.1	.4602	.4562	.4522	.4483	.4443	.4404	.4364	.4325	.4686	.4247
0.2	.4207	.4168	.4129	.4090	.4052	.4013	.3974	.3936	.3897	.3859
0.3	.3821	.3873	.3745	.3707	.3669	.3632	.3594	.3557	.3520	.3483
0.4	.3446	.3409	.3372	.3336	.3300	.3264	.3228	.3192	.3156	.3121
0.5	.3085	.3050	.3015	.2981	.2946	.2912	.2877	.2843	.2810	.2776
0.6	.2743	.2709	.2676	.2643	.2611	.2578	.2546	.2514	.2483	.2451
0.7	.2420	.2389	.2358	.2327	.2296	.2266	.2236	.2206	.2217	.2148
0.8	.2119	.2090	.2061	.2033	.2005	.1977	.1949	.1922	.1894	.1867
0.9	.1841	.1814	.1788	.1762	.1736	.1711	.1685	.1660	.1635	.1611
1.0	.1587	.1562	.1539	.1515	.1492	.1469	.1446	.1423	.1401	.1379
1.1	.1357	.1335	.1314	.1292	.1271	.1251	.1230	.1210	.1190	.1170
1.2	.1151	.1131	.1112	.1093	.1075	.1056	.1038	.1020	.1003	.0985
1.3	.0968	.0951	.0934	.0918	.0901	.0885	.0869	.0853	.0838	.0823
1.4	.0808	.0793	.0778	.0764	.0749	.0735	.0721	.0708	.0694	.0681
1.5	.0668	.0655	.0643	.0630	.0618	.0606	.0594	.0582	.0571	.0559
1.6	.0548	.0537	.0526	.0516	.0505	.0495	.0485	.0475	.0465	.0455
1.7	.0446	.0436	.0427	.0418	.0409	.0401	.0392	.0384	.0375	.0367
1.8	.0359	.0351	.0344	.0366	.0329	.0322	.0314	.0307	.0301	.0294
1.9	.0287	.0281	.0274	.0268	.0262	.0256	.0250	.0244	.0239	.0233
2.0	.0228	.0222	.0217	.0212	.0207	.0202	.0197	.0192	.0188	.0183
2.1	.0179	.0174	.0170	.0166	.0162	.0158	.0154	.0150	.0146	.0143
2.2	.0139	.0136	.0132	.0129	.0125	.0122	.0119	.0116	.0113	.0110
2.3	.0107	.0104	.0102	.0099	.0096	.0094	.0091	.0089	.0087	.0084
2.4	.0082	.0080	.0078	.0075	.0073	.0071	.0069	.0068	.0066	.0064
2.5	.0062	.0060	.0059	.0057	.0055	.0054	.0052	.0051	.0049	.0048
2.6	.0047	.0045	.0044	.0043	.0041	.0040	.0039	.0038	.0037	.0036
2.7	.0035	.0034	.0033	.0032	.0031	.0030	.0029	.0028	.0027	.0026
2.8	.0026	.0025	.0024	.0023	.0023	.0022	.0021	.0020	.0020	.0019
2.9	.0019	.0018	.0018	.0017	.0016	.0016	.0015	.0015	.0014	.0014
3.0	.0013	.0013	.0013	.0012	.0012	.0011	.0011	.0010	.0011	.0010

The table plots the cumulative probability $Z \geq z$.

SOURCE: Produced from Edward J. Kane, *Economic Statistics and Econometrics: An Introduction to Quantitative Economics* (New York: Harper & Row, Publishers, 1968).

Table 2 Percentiles of the χ^2 distribution

df	\multicolumn{10}{c}{Percent}
	0.5	1	2.5	5	10	90	95	97.5	99	99.5
1	0.000039	0.00016	0.00098	0.0039	0.0158	2.71	3.84	5.02	6.63	7.88
2	0.0100	0.0201	0.0506	0.1026	0.2107	4.61	5.99	7.38	9.21	10.60
3	0.0717	0.115	0.216	0.352	0.584	6.25	7.81	9.35	11.34	12.84
4	0.207	0.297	0.484	0.711	1.064	7.78	9.49	11.14	13.28	14.86
5	0.412	0.554	0.831	1.15	1.61	9.24	11.07	12.83	15.09	16.75
6	0.676	0.872	1.24	1.64	2.20	10.64	12.59	14.45	16.81	18.55
7	0.989	1.24	1.69	2.17	2.83	12.02	14.07	16.01	18.48	20.28
8	1.34	1.65	2.18	2.73	3.49	13.36	15.51	17.53	20.09	21.96
9	1.73	2.09	2.70	3.33	4.17	14.68	16.92	19.02	21.67	23.59
10	2.16	2.56	3.25	3.94	4.87	15.99	18.31	20.48	23.21	25.19
11	2.60	3.05	3.82	4.57	5.58	17.28	19.68	21.92	24.73	26.76
12	3.07	3.57	4.40	5.23	6.30	18.55	21.03	23.34	26.22	28.30
13	3.57	4.11	5.01	5.89	7.04	19.81	22.36	24.74	27.69	29.82
14	4.07	4.66	5.63	6.57	7.79	21.06	23.68	26.12	29.14	31.32
15	4.60	5.23	6.26	7.26	8.55	22.31	25.00	27.49	30.58	32.80
16	5.14	5.81	6.91	7.96	9.31	23.54	26.30	28.85	32.00	34.27
18	6.26	7.01	8.23	9.39	10.86	25.99	28.87	31.53	34.81	37.16
20	7.43	8.26	9.59	10.85	12.44	28.41	31.41	34.17	37.57	40.00
24	9.89	10.86	12.40	13.85	15.66	33.20	36.42	39.36	42.98	45.56
30	13.79	14.95	16.79	18.49	20.60	40.26	43.77	47.98	50.89	53.67
40	20.71	22.16	24.43	26.51	29.05	51.81	55.76	59.34	63.69	66.77
60	35.53	37.48	40.48	43.19	46.46	74.40	79.08	83.30	88.38	91.95
120	83.85	86.92	91.58	95.70	100.62	140.23	146.57	152.21	158.95	163.64

SOURCE: Reprinted with permission from W. J. Dixon and F. J. Massey Jr., *Introduction to Statistical Analysis*, 3d ed. (New York: McGraw-Hill, 1969).

Table 3 Percentiles of the *t* distribution

df	.80	.60	.40	.20	.10	.05	.02	.01
					Pr			
1	0.325	0.727	1.376	3.078	6.314	12.706	31.821	63.657
2	0.289	0.617	1.061	1.886	2.920	4.303	6.965	9.925
3	0.277	0.584	0.978	1.638	2.353	3.182	4.541	5.841
4	0.271	0.569	0.941	1.533	2.132	2.776	3.747	4.604
5	0.267	0.559	0.920	1.476	2.015	2.571	3.365	4.032
6	0.265	0.553	0.906	1.440	1.943	2.447	3.143	3.707
7	0.263	0.549	0.896	1.415	1.895	2.365	2.998	3.499
8	0.262	0.546	0.889	1.397	1.860	2.306	2.896	3.355
9	0.261	0.543	0.883	1.383	1.833	2.262	2.821	3.250
10	0.260	0.542	0.879	1.372	1.812	2.228	2.764	3.169
11	0.260	0.540	0.876	1.363	1.796	2.201	2.718	3.106
12	0.259	0.539	0.873	1.356	1.782	2.179	2.681	3.055
13	0.259	0.538	0.870	1.350	1.771	2.160	2.650	3.012
14	0.258	0.537	0.868	1.345	1.761	2.145	2.624	2.977
15	0.258	0.536	0.866	1.341	1.753	2.131	2.602	2.947
16	0.258	0.535	0.865	1.337	1.746	2.120	2.583	2.921
17	0.257	0.534	0.863	1.333	1.740	2.110	2.567	2.898
18	0.257	0.534	0.862	1.330	1.734	2.101	2.552	2.878
19	0.257	0.533	0.861	1.328	1.729	2.093	2.539	2.861
20	0.257	0.533	0.860	1.325	1.725	2.086	2.528	2.845
21	0.257	0.532	0.859	1.323	1.721	2.080	2.518	2.831
22	0.256	0.532	0.858	1.321	1.717	2.074	2.508	2.819
23	0.256	0.532	0.858	1.319	1.714	2.069	2.500	2.807
24	0.256	0.531	0.857	1.318	1.711	2.064	2.492	2.797
25	0.256	0.531	0.856	1.316	1.708	2.060	2.485	2.787
26	0.256	0.531	0.856	1.315	1.706	2.056	2.479	2.779
27	0.256	0.531	0.855	1.314	1.703	2.052	2.473	2.771
28	0.256	0.530	0.855	1.313	1.701	2.048	2.467	2.763
29	0.256	0.530	0.854	1.311	1.699	2.045	2.462	2.756
30	0.256	0.530	0.854	1.310	1.697	2.042	2.457	2.750
40	0.255	0.529	0.851	1.303	1.684	2.021	2.423	2.704
60	0.254	0.527	0.848	1.296	1.671	2.000	2.390	2.660
120	0.254	0.526	0.845	1.289	1.658	1.980	2.358	2.617
∞	0.253	0.524	0.842	1.282	1.645	1.960	2.326	2.576

†Pr represents the probability that the *t* value will exceed each number in the table in absolute value. This is appropriate for two-tailed tests. For one-tailed tests simply divide each probability in half. For example, .325 in row 1, column 1 tells us that the probability of *t* being less than −.325 *or* greater than .325 is .8.

SOURCE: Obtained from Table III of Fisher and Yates, *Statistical Tables for Biological, Agricultural and Medical Research*, with the permission of the authors and publishers (Edinburgh: Oliver & Boyd, Ltd.)

Table 4a *F* distribution, 5 percent significance

Degrees of freedom for denominator	\ Degrees of freedom for numerator																		
	1	2	3	4	5	6	7	8	9	10	12	15	20	24	30	40	60	120	∞
1	161	200	216	225	230	234	237	239	241	242	244	246	248	249	250	251	252	253	254
2	18.5	19.0	19.2	19.2	19.3	19.3	19.4	19.4	19.4	19.4	19.4	19.4	19.5	19.5	19.5	19.5	19.5	19.5	19.5
3	10.1	9.55	9.28	9.12	9.01	8.94	8.89	8.85	8.81	8.79	8.74	8.70	8.66	8.64	8.62	8.59	8.57	8.55	8.53
4	7.71	6.94	6.59	6.39	6.26	6.16	6.09	6.04	6.00	5.96	5.91	5.86	5.80	5.77	5.75	5.72	5.69	5.66	5.63
5	6.61	5.79	5.41	5.19	5.05	4.95	4.88	4.82	4.77	4.74	4.68	4.62	4.56	4.53	4.50	4.46	4.43	4.40	4.37
6	5.99	5.14	4.76	4.53	4.39	4.28	4.21	4.15	4.10	4.06	4.00	3.94	3.87	3.84	3.81	3.77	3.74	3.70	3.67
7	5.59	4.74	4.35	4.12	3.97	3.87	3.79	3.73	3.68	3.64	3.57	3.51	3.44	3.41	3.38	3.34	3.30	3.27	3.23
8	5.32	4.46	4.07	3.84	3.69	3.58	3.50	3.44	3.39	3.35	3.28	3.22	3.15	3.12	3.08	3.04	3.01	2.97	2.93
9	5.12	4.26	3.86	3.63	3.48	3.37	3.29	3.23	3.18	3.14	3.07	3.01	2.94	2.90	2.86	2.83	2.79	2.75	2.71
10	4.96	4.10	3.71	3.48	3.33	3.22	3.14	3.07	3.02	2.98	2.91	2.85	2.77	2.74	2.70	2.66	2.62	2.58	2.54
11	4.84	3.98	3.59	3.36	3.20	3.09	3.01	2.95	2.90	2.85	2.79	2.72	2.65	2.61	2.57	2.53	2.49	2.45	2.40
12	4.75	3.89	3.49	3.26	3.11	3.00	2.91	2.85	2.80	2.75	2.69	2.62	2.54	2.51	2.47	2.43	2.38	2.34	2.30
13	4.67	3.81	3.41	3.18	3.03	2.92	2.83	2.77	2.71	2.67	2.60	2.53	2.46	2.42	2.38	2.34	2.30	2.25	2.21
14	4.60	3.74	3.34	3.11	2.96	2.85	2.76	2.70	2.65	2.60	2.53	2.46	2.39	2.35	2.31	2.27	2.22	2.18	2.13
15	4.54	3.68	3.29	3.06	2.90	2.79	2.71	2.64	2.59	2.54	2.48	2.40	2.33	2.29	2.25	2.20	2.16	2.11	2.07
16	4.49	3.63	3.24	3.01	2.85	2.74	2.66	2.59	2.54	2.49	2.42	2.35	2.28	2.24	2.19	2.15	2.11	2.06	2.01
17	4.45	3.59	3.20	2.96	2.81	2.70	2.61	2.55	2.48	2.45	2.38	2.31	2.23	2.19	2.15	2.10	2.06	2.01	1.96
18	4.41	3.55	3.16	2.93	2.77	2.66	2.58	2.51	2.46	2.41	2.34	2.27	2.19	2.15	2.11	2.06	2.02	1.97	1.92
19	4.38	3.52	3.13	2.90	2.74	2.63	2.54	2.48	2.42	2.39	2.31	2.23	2.16	2.11	2.07	2.03	1.98	1.93	1.88
20	4.35	3.49	3.10	2.87	2.71	2.60	2.51	2.45	2.39	2.35	2.28	2.20	2.12	2.08	2.04	1.99	1.95	1.90	1.84
21	4.32	3.47	3.07	2.84	2.68	2.57	2.49	2.42	2.37	2.32	2.25	2.18	2.10	2.05	2.01	1.96	1.92	1.87	1.81
22	4.30	3.44	3.05	2.82	2.66	2.55	2.46	2.40	2.34	2.30	2.23	2.15	2.07	2.03	1.98	1.94	1.89	1.84	1.78
23	4.28	3.42	3.03	2.80	2.64	2.53	2.44	2.37	2.32	2.27	2.20	2.13	2.05	2.01	1.96	1.91	1.86	1.81	1.76
24	4.26	3.40	3.01	2.78	2.62	2.51	2.42	2.36	2.30	2.25	2.18	2.11	2.03	1.98	1.94	1.89	1.84	1.79	1.73
25	4.24	3.39	2.99	2.76	2.60	2.49	2.40	2.34	2.28	2.24	2.16	2.09	2.01	1.96	1.92	1.87	1.82	1.77	1.71
30	4.17	3.32	2.92	2.69	2.53	2.42	2.33	2.27	2.21	2.16	2.09	2.01	1.93	1.89	1.84	1.79	1.74	1.68	1.62
40	4.08	3.23	2.84	2.61	2.45	2.34	2.25	2.18	2.12	2.08	2.00	1.92	1.84	1.79	1.74	1.69	1.64	1.58	1.51
60	4.00	3.15	2.76	2.53	2.37	2.25	2.17	2.10	2.04	1.99	1.92	1.84	1.75	1.70	1.65	1.59	1.53	1.47	1.39
120	3.92	3.07	2.68	2.45	2.29	2.18	2.09	2.02	1.96	1.91	1.83	1.75	1.66	1.61	1.55	1.50	1.43	1.35	1.25
∞	3.84	3.00	2.60	2.37	2.21	2.10	2.01	1.94	1.88	1.83	1.75	1.67	1.57	1.52	1.46	1.39	1.32	1.22	1.00

SOURCE: Reproduced with the permission of the Biometrika Trustees from M. Merrington, C. M. Thompson, "Tables of Percentage Points of the Inverted Beta (F) Distribution," *Biometrika*, vol. 33, p. 73, 1943.

Table 4b F distribution, 1 percent significance

Degrees of freedom for numerator

	1	2	3	4	5	6	7	8	9	10	12	15	20	24	30	40	60	120	∞
1	4,052	5,000	5,403	5,625	5,746	5,859	5,928	5,982	6,023	6,056	6,106	6,157	6,209	6,235	6,261	6,287	6,313	6,339	6,366
2	98.5	99.0	99.2	99.2	99.3	99.3	99.4	99.4	99.4	99.4	99.4	99.4	99.4	99.5	99.5	99.5	99.5	99.5	99.5
3	34.1	30.8	29.5	28.7	28.2	27.9	27.7	27.5	27.3	27.2	27.1	26.9	26.7	26.6	26.5	26.4	26.3	26.2	26.1
4	21.2	18.0	16.7	16.0	15.5	15.2	15.0	14.8	14.7	14.5	14.4	14.2	14.0	13.9	13.8	13.7	13.7	13.6	13.5
5	16.3	13.3	12.1	11.4	11.0	10.7	10.5	10.3	10.2	10.1	9.89	9.72	9.55	9.47	9.38	9.29	9.20	9.11	9.02
6	13.7	10.9	9.78	9.15	8.75	8.47	8.26	8.10	7.98	7.87	7.72	7.56	7.40	7.31	7.23	7.14	7.06	6.97	6.88
7	12.2	9.55	8.45	7.85	7.46	7.19	6.99	6.84	6.72	6.62	6.47	6.31	6.16	6.07	5.99	5.91	5.82	5.74	5.65
8	11.3	8.65	7.59	7.01	6.63	6.37	6.18	6.03	5.91	5.81	5.67	5.52	5.36	5.28	5.20	5.12	5.03	4.95	4.86
9	10.6	8.02	6.99	6.42	6.06	5.80	5.61	5.47	5.35	5.26	5.11	4.96	4.81	4.73	4.65	4.57	4.48	4.40	4.31
10	10.0	7.56	6.55	5.99	5.64	5.39	5.20	5.06	4.94	4.85	4.71	4.56	4.41	4.33	4.25	4.17	4.08	4.00	3.91
11	9.65	7.21	6.22	5.67	5.32	5.07	4.89	4.74	4.63	4.54	4.40	4.25	4.10	4.02	3.94	3.86	3.78	3.69	3.60
12	9.33	6.93	5.95	5.41	5.06	4.82	4.64	4.50	4.39	4.30	4.16	4.01	3.86	3.78	3.70	3.62	3.54	3.45	3.36
13	9.07	6.70	5.74	5.21	4.97	4.62	4.44	4.30	4.19	4.10	3.96	3.82	3.66	3.59	3.51	3.43	3.34	3.25	3.17
14	8.86	6.51	5.56	5.04	4.70	4.46	4.28	4.14	4.03	3.94	3.80	3.66	3.51	3.43	3.35	3.27	3.18	3.09	3.00
15	8.68	6.36	5.42	4.89	4.56	4.32	4.14	4.00	3.89	3.80	3.67	3.52	3.37	3.29	3.21	3.13	3.05	2.96	2.87
16	8.53	6.23	5.29	4.77	4.44	4.20	4.03	3.89	3.78	3.69	3.55	3.41	3.26	3.18	3.10	3.02	2.93	2.84	2.75
17	8.40	6.11	5.19	4.67	4.34	4.10	3.93	3.79	3.68	3.59	3.46	3.31	3.16	3.08	3.00	2.92	2.83	2.75	2.65
18	8.29	6.01	5.09	4.58	4.25	4.01	3.84	3.71	3.60	3.51	3.37	3.23	3.08	3.00	2.92	2.84	2.75	2.66	2.57
19	8.19	5.93	5.01	4.50	4.17	3.94	3.77	3.63	3.52	3.43	3.30	3.15	3.00	2.92	2.84	2.76	2.67	2.58	2.49
20	8.10	5.85	4.94	4.43	4.10	3.87	3.70	3.56	3.46	3.37	3.23	3.09	2.94	2.86	2.78	2.68	2.61	2.52	2.42
21	8.02	5.78	4.87	4.37	4.04	3.81	3.64	3.51	3.40	3.31	3.17	3.03	2.88	2.80	2.72	2.64	2.55	2.46	2.36
22	7.95	5.72	4.82	4.31	3.99	3.76	3.59	3.45	3.35	3.26	3.12	2.98	2.83	2.75	2.67	2.58	2.50	2.40	2.31
23	7.88	5.66	4.76	4.26	3.94	3.71	3.54	3.41	3.30	3.21	3.07	2.93	2.78	2.70	2.62	2.54	2.45	2.35	2.26
24	7.82	5.61	4.72	4.22	3.90	3.67	3.50	3.36	3.26	3.17	3.03	2.89	2.74	2.66	2.58	2.49	2.40	2.31	2.21
25	7.77	5.57	4.68	4.18	3.86	3.63	3.46	3.32	3.22	3.13	2.99	2.85	2.70	2.62	2.53	2.45	2.36	2.27	2.17
30	7.56	5.39	4.51	4.02	3.70	3.47	3.30	3.17	3.07	2.98	2.84	2.70	2.55	2.47	2.39	2.30	2.21	2.11	2.01
40	7.31	5.18	4.31	3.83	3.51	3.29	3.12	2.99	2.89	2.80	2.66	2.52	2.37	2.29	2.20	2.11	2.02	1.92	1.80
60	7.08	4.98	4.13	3.65	3.34	3.12	2.95	2.82	2.72	2.63	2.50	2.35	2.20	2.12	2.03	1.94	1.84	1.73	1.60
120	6.85	4.79	3.95	3.48	3.17	2.96	2.79	2.66	2.56	2.47	2.34	2.19	2.03	1.94	1.86	1.76	1.66	1.53	1.38
∞	6.63	4.61	3.78	3.32	3.02	2.80	2.64	2.51	2.41	2.32	2.18	2.04	1.88	1.79	1.70	1.59	1.47	1.32	1.00

Degrees of freedom for denominator

Table 5 Five percent significance points of d_l and d_u for Durbin-Watson test†

N	$k = 1$ d_l	d_u	$k = 2$ d_l	d_u	$k = 3$ d_l	d_u	$k = 4$ d_l	d_u	$k = 5$ d_l	d_u
15	1.08	1.36	0.95	1.54	0.82	1.75	0.69	1.97	0.56	2.21
16	1.10	1.37	0.98	1.54	0.86	1.73	0.74	1.93	0.62	2.15
17	1.13	1.38	1.02	1.54	0.90	1.71	0.78	1.90	0.67	2.10
18	1.16	1.39	1.05	1.53	0.93	1.69	0.82	1.87	0.71	2.06
19	1.18	1.40	1.08	1.53	0.97	1.68	0.86	1.85	0.75	2.02
20	1.20	1.41	1.10	1.54	1.00	1.68	0.90	1.83	0.79	1.99
21	1.22	1.42	1.13	1.54	1.03	1.67	0.93	1.81	0.83	1.96
22	1.24	1.43	1.15	1.54	1.05	1.66	0.96	1.80	0.86	1.94
23	1.26	1.44	1.17	1.54	1.08	1.66	0.99	1.79	0.90	1.92
24	1.27	1.45	1.19	1.55	1.10	1.66	1.01	1.78	0.93	1.90
25	1.29	1.45	1.21	1.55	1.12	1.66	1.04	1.77	0.95	1.89
26	1.30	1.46	1.22	1.55	1.14	1.65	1.06	1.76	0.98	1.88
27	1.32	1.47	1.24	1.56	1.16	1.65	1.08	1.76	1.01	1.86
28	1.33	1.48	1.26	1.56	1.18	1.65	1.10	1.75	1.03	1.85
29	1.34	1.48	1.27	1.56	1.20	1.65	1.12	1.74	1.05	1.84
30	1.35	1.49	1.28	1.57	1.21	1.65	1.14	1.74	1.07	1.83
31	1.36	1.50	1.30	1.57	1.23	1.65	1.16	1.74	1.09	1.83
32	1.37	1.50	1.31	1.57	1.24	1.65	1.18	1.73	1.11	1.82
33	1.38	1.51	1.32	1.58	1.26	1.65	1.19	1.73	1.13	1.81
34	1.39	1.51	1.33	1.58	1.27	1.65	1.21	1.73	1.15	1.81
35	1.40	1.52	1.34	1.53	1.28	1.65	1.22	1.73	1.16	1.80
36	1.41	1.52	1.35	1.59	1.29	1.65	1.24	1.73	1.18	1.80
37	1.42	1.53	1.36	1.59	1.31	1.66	1.25	1.72	1.19	1.80
38	1.43	1.54	1.37	1.59	1.32	1.66	1.26	1.72	1.21	1.79
39	1.43	1.54	1.38	1.60	1.33	1.66	1.27	1.72	1.22	1.79
40	1.44	1.54	1.39	1.60	1.34	1.66	1.29	1.72	1.23	1.79
45	1.48	1.57	1.43	1.62	1.38	1.67	1.34	1.72	1.29	1.78
50	1.50	1.59	1.46	1.63	1.42	1.67	1.38	1.72	1.34	1.77
55	1.53	1.60	1.49	1.64	1.45	1.68	1.41	1.72	1.38	1.77
60	1.55	1.62	1.51	1.65	1.48	1.69	1.44	1.73	1.41	1.77
65	1.57	1.63	1.54	1.66	1.50	1.70	1.47	1.73	1.44	1.77
70	1.58	1.64	1.55	1.67	1.52	1.70	1.49	1.74	1.46	1.77
75	1.60	1.65	1.57	1.68	1.54	1.71	1.51	1.74	1.49	1.77
80	1.61	1.66	1.59	1.69	1.56	1.72	1.53	1.74	1.51	1.77
85	1.62	1.67	1.60	1.70	1.57	1.72	1.55	1.75	1.52	1.77
90	1.63	1.68	1.61	1.70	1.59	1.73	1.57	1.75	1.54	1.78
95	1.64	1.69	1.62	1.71	1.60	1.73	1.58	1.75	1.56	1.78
100	1.65	1.69	1.63	1.72	1.61	1.74	1.59	1.76	1.57	1.78

†N = number of observations; k = number of explanatory variables (excluding the constant term).

SOURCE: Reprinted with permission from J. Durbin and G. S. Watson, "Testing for Serial Correlation in Least Squares Regression," *Biometrika*, vol. 38, pp. 159–177, 1951.

SOLUTIONS TO SELECTED PROBLEMS

1.1 (*a*) The regression line is $Y = 1.17 + 1.72X$.

(*b*) The slope tells us that on average a \$1 million increase in the quantity of money will lead to a \$1.72 million increase in national income. Interpreted literally, the intercept tells us that if the money supply fell to zero, national income would be \$1.17 million. However, since no observations were available for values of X near zero, we cannot place any reliance on such an interpretation.

(*c*) We would set the money supply at \$6.3 million.

1.3 (*a*) The slope will be reduced by a factor of 10, and the intercept will remain unchanged.

(*b*) To evaluate the effects of the transformation on the slope and intercept, substitute the equations describing the transformed variables into the least-squares estimators:

$$\hat{b}^* = \frac{\Sigma(X_i^* - \bar{X}^*)(Y_i^* - \bar{Y}^*)}{\Sigma(X_i^* - \bar{X}^*)^2} \qquad \hat{a}^* = \bar{Y}^* - \hat{b}^* \bar{X}^*$$

(You should check that $\bar{Y}^* = c_1 + c_2\bar{Y}$ and $\bar{X}^* = d_1 + d_2\bar{X}$.) After some elementary algebra, it follows that

$$\hat{b}^* = \frac{c_2}{d_2}\hat{b} \qquad \hat{a}^* = \left(c_1 - \frac{c_2 d_1}{d_2}\hat{b}\right) + c_2\hat{a}$$

1.4 The least-squares intercept and slope are both undefined. When all independent-variable observations are identical, Σx_i^2 equals zero. Since there is no change in the independent variable (in the sample), it is impossible to tell how the dependent variable would respond to a change in the independent variable.

1.7 (*a*)

$$\hat{\alpha} = 2.88 \qquad \hat{\beta} = -.0185$$

(*b*)

$$\hat{\alpha} = 1.47 \qquad \hat{\beta} = .11$$

2.1

$$\overline{\text{RENT}} = 318.16 \qquad \overline{\text{NO}} = 2.44 \qquad \overline{\text{RPP}} = 138.17$$

$$\frac{\overline{\text{RENT}}}{\overline{\text{NO}}} = 130.39 \neq \overline{\text{RPP}}$$

2.3 (a)

$$Z = \frac{\overline{\text{RPP}} - 135.00}{\left(\sigma^2_{\text{RPP}}/N\right)^{1/2}} = .387$$

Since Prob ($|Z| > 1.96) = .05$ from the normal table, we fail to reject the null hypothesis.
(b)

$$t = (\overline{\text{RPP}} - 135.00)\frac{\sqrt{N}}{s} = .381$$

Since Prob ($|t| > 2.042) = .05$ from the t table, we again fail to reject the null hypothesis.
2.4 The correct statistic is

$$Z = \frac{\overline{X}^m - \overline{X}^f}{\left(\sigma^{2m}_{\text{RPP}}/N^m + \sigma^{2f}_{\text{RPP}}/N^f\right)^{1/2}} = -2.44$$

Using a normal table, we reject at the 5 percent level of significance.
2.6 The correct statistic is

$$V = \frac{(N-1)s^2}{2,150} = 32.01$$

Using a chi-square table, we fail to reject the null hypothesis.
2.9 Prob ($x \geq 30) = .2119$.
2.12 $[(X - \mu)/\sigma]^2$ follows a chi-square distribution.
3.1 $s^2 = .14$ and $t_c = 2.3$. Therefore, the 95 percent confidence interval for the intercept is

$$1.17 \pm (2.3)(.484) = 1.17 \pm 1.11 = (.06, 2.28)$$

The 95 percent confidence interval for the slope is

$$1.72 \pm (2.3)(.126) = 1.72 \pm .29 = (1.43, 2.01)$$

Yes, you can reject the null hypothesis in both cases.
3.4 $R^2 = \hat{b}^2 \Sigma x_i^2 / \Sigma y_i^2$. If $R^2 = 1$, $\hat{b}^2 = \Sigma y_i^2 / \Sigma x_i^2$. But, by construction, $\hat{b} = \Sigma x_i y_i / \Sigma x_i^2$. Therefore

$$\Sigma x_i^2 = \frac{(\Sigma x_i y_i)^2}{\Sigma y_i^2} \qquad \text{and} \qquad \hat{b} = \frac{\Sigma y_i^2}{\Sigma x_i y_i} = \frac{1}{\hat{B}}$$

3.8 $\Sigma x_i \hat{\varepsilon}_i = \Sigma x_i(y_i - \hat{\beta}x_i) = \Sigma x_i y_i - \hat{\beta}\Sigma x_i^2$. But, $\hat{\beta} = \Sigma x_i y_i / \Sigma x_i^2$. Therefore, $\Sigma x_i \hat{\varepsilon}_i = \hat{\beta}\Sigma x_i^2 - \hat{\beta}\Sigma x_i^2 = 0$.
3.9 From data in deviations form, $y_i^* = a_2 y_i$ and $x_i^* = b_2 x_i$ (since $\overline{Y}^* = a_1 + a_2\overline{Y}$, $\overline{X}^* = b_1 + b_2\overline{X}$). Then from transformed data

$$(R^*)^2 = \frac{\hat{\beta}^{*2}\Sigma x_i^{*2}}{\Sigma y_i^{*2}}$$

But from Exercise 1.3, $\hat{\beta}^{*2} = (a_2/b_2)^2\hat{\beta}^2$. Substituting, we find that $(R^*)^2 = R^2$.
3.10 (a) B is the slope of the straight line passing through the points $(\overline{X}_1, \overline{Y}_1)$ and $(\overline{X}_2, \overline{Y}_2)$. Dividing the data into two groups is sufficient to allow for fitting a straight line, which yields an estimate of the slope.

(b) B does not equal $\hat{\beta}$, but it is an unbiased estimator of β. To prove this, use the original model to calculate that

$$\bar{Y}_1 = \alpha + \beta\bar{X}_1 + \bar{\epsilon}_1 \quad \text{and} \quad \bar{Y}_2 = \alpha + \beta\bar{X}_2 + \bar{\epsilon}_2$$

Then

$$E(\bar{Y}_2 - \bar{Y}_1) = \beta(\bar{X}_2 - \bar{X}_1)$$

and

$$E(B) = \frac{E(\bar{Y}_2 - \bar{Y}_1)}{\bar{X}_2 - \bar{X}_1} = \beta$$

(c) We know that Var $(B) \geq$ Var $(\hat{\beta})$ from the Gauss-Markov theorem, which states that $\hat{\beta}$ is the *best* linear unbiased estimator of β. (It is easy to show that B is a linear estimator.) In this particular case, it is possible to show that Var $(B) = .157\sigma^2$, while Var $(\hat{\beta}) = .115\sigma^2$.

4.1 (a) Let $Z_i = Y_i - X_{2i}$; then by substitution into Eqs. (4.3) to (4.5) we find that

$$\hat{\beta}_2' = \hat{\beta}_2 - \frac{(\Sigma x_{2i}^2 \Sigma x_{3i}^2) - (\Sigma x_{2i} x_{3i})^2}{(\Sigma x_{2i}^2)(\Sigma x_{3i}^2) - (\Sigma x_{2i} x_{3i})^2} = \hat{\beta}_2 - 1$$

Likewise $\hat{\beta}_3' = \beta_3$ and $\hat{\beta}_1' = \bar{Y} - \bar{X}_2 - \hat{\beta}_2\bar{X}_2 + \bar{X}_2 - \hat{\beta}_3\bar{X}_3 = \hat{\beta}_1$.

(b) In model I

$$\hat{\epsilon}_i = Y_i - \hat{\beta}_1 - \hat{\beta}_2 X_{2i} - \hat{\beta}_3 X_{3i}$$

In model II

$$\hat{\epsilon}_i' = Y_i - X_{2i} - \hat{\beta}_1' - \hat{\beta}_2' X_{2i} - \hat{\beta}_3' X_{3i} = Y_i - X_{2i} - \hat{\beta}_1 - \hat{\beta}_2 + X_{2i} - \hat{\beta}_3' X_{3i} = \hat{\epsilon}_i$$

(c) $R^2 = 1 - \Sigma\hat{\epsilon}_i^2/\Sigma(Y_i - \bar{Y})^2$ in model I; and $R'^2 = 1 - \Sigma\hat{\epsilon}_i'^2/\Sigma(Z_i - \bar{Z})^2$ in model II. Since the regression residuals are identical, the relationship between R^2 and R'^2 will depend directly on the relationship between the variance of Y and the variance of Z.

4.2 From the regression $X_{2i} = \alpha_1 + \alpha_2 X_{3i} + \epsilon_i'$, the residuals $\hat{\epsilon}_i' = X_{2i} - \hat{\alpha}_1 - \hat{\alpha}_2 X_{3i}$. Substituting into the regression $Y_i = \beta_1' + \beta_2'\hat{\epsilon}_i + \beta_3' X_{3i} + \epsilon_i^*$, we find that $Y_i = (\beta_1' - \beta_2'\hat{\alpha}_1) + \beta_2' X_{2i} + (\beta_3' - \beta_2'\hat{\alpha}_2)X_{3i} + \epsilon_i^*$. Comparing this with the original regression makes it clear that $\beta_2' = \beta_2$. The intuition behind this result lies in the fact that $\hat{\epsilon}_i$ measures the portion of X_{2i} which is uncorrelated with X_{3i}.

4.4 Each beta coefficient will equal the corresponding regression parameter, except for the intercept, which does not exist.

4.7 In the two-variable model,

$$\hat{\beta}^* = \hat{\beta}\frac{s_x}{s_y} = \frac{\Sigma x_i y_i}{\Sigma x_i^2}\left(\frac{\Sigma x_i^2}{\Sigma y_i^2}\right)^{1/2} = \frac{\Sigma x_i y_i}{(\Sigma x_i^2)^{1/2}(\Sigma y_i^2)^{1/2}} = r_{XY}$$

5.2

$$\hat{\beta}_2^* = \frac{\Sigma x_{2i} y_i}{\Sigma x_{2i}^2} = \beta_2 + \beta_3\frac{\Sigma x_{2i}^3}{\Sigma x_{2i}^2}$$

Therefore, the specification bias is equal to $\beta_3\Sigma x_{2i}^3/\Sigma x_{2i}^2$. Thus, the slope coefficient will be biased upward when $\beta_3\Sigma x_{2i}^3$ is positive and biased downward when $\beta_3\Sigma x_{2i}^3$ is negative.

5.3

$$\hat{\beta}_3^* = \frac{(\Sigma x_{3i} y_i)(\Sigma x_{2i}^2) - \beta_2(\Sigma x_{2i} y_i)(\Sigma x_{2i} x_{3i})}{(\Sigma x_{2i}^2)(\Sigma x_{3i}^2) - (\Sigma x_{2i} x_{3i})^2}$$

Substituting for $y_i = \beta_2 x_{2i} + \epsilon_i$ and taking expected values, we get

$$E(\hat{\beta}_3^*) = \frac{\beta_2(\Sigma x_{2i} x_{3i})(\Sigma x_{2i}^2) - (\Sigma x_{2i}^2)(\Sigma x_{2i} x_{3i})}{(\Sigma x_{2i}^2)(\Sigma x_{3i}^2) - (\Sigma x_{2i} x_{3i})^2} + \frac{E(\Sigma x_{3i}\epsilon_i)(\Sigma x_{2i}^2) - E(\Sigma x_{2i}\epsilon_i)(\Sigma x_{2i} x_{3i})}{(\Sigma x_{2i}^2)(\Sigma x_{3i}^2) - (\Sigma x_{2i} x_{3i})^2} = 0$$

5.6

$$\beta_2 = \frac{\partial \log Y}{\partial \log X_2} = \frac{1/Y \, dY}{1/X_2 \, dX_2} = \frac{dY}{dX_2} \frac{X_2}{Y_2}$$

Thus, $\hat\beta_2$ provides an estimate of the elasticity of Y with respect to X_2. The analogous result holds for $\hat\beta_3$. These elasticities are constant because the least-squares slope estimates are constant.

5.7 (a) $t = 3.02$ (on the coefficient ROOM PER), so we reject the null hypothesis using a one-tailed test.

(b) $t = -1.35$ (on the coefficient DIST), so we fail to reject using a one-tailed test.

(c) $t = 1.21$, so we fail to reject. The corresponding F test leads to an identical result.

5.8 (a) $t = -.96$ (on the coefficient [(ROOM PER)(SEX)], so we fail to reject.

(b) We calculate $F = A/B$, where $A = (ESS_I - ESS_{III})/2$ and $B = ESS_{III}/26$, so that $F = 2.61$. Using an F distribution with $(2, 26)$ degrees of freedom, we fail to reject.

(c)

$$\bar R^2 = \begin{cases} .29 & \text{model I} \\ .28 & \text{model II} \\ .37 & \text{model III} \end{cases}$$

5.12 $\hat\beta_2^* = .20$, $\hat\beta_3^* = .48$, $\hat\beta_4^* = -.22$.

6.2 Yes, we might expect that the error terms associated with communities with high educational expenditures would have larger variances than the error terms associated with communities with low educational expenditures. The Goldfeld-Quandt test might be more useful than Bartlett's test because there is no natural way to group the data to estimate sample error variances. To use the Goldfeld-Quandt test we might order the observations by level of median income in the community.

6.4 In cross-section studies there is usually no natural sequence to the data. In such a case, there is no reason to expect that errors associated with different observations will be correlated. However, serial correlation may be present if, for example, observations are geographically related. In a regional model of economic growth or a metropolitan model of local government behavior, errors corresponding to geographically related units of observation may be correlated.

6.6 The test statistic is $\hat\sigma^2_{male}/\hat\sigma^2_{female} = 1.47$ which follows an F distribution with $(19, 7)$ degrees of freedom. At the 5 percent level we fail to reject the null hypothesis.

6.9 (a)

$$\widehat{IRC} = 13.05 + .05 \, YD + .49 \, DEL - .041 \, PIRC$$
$$\quad\quad\quad\; 5.76 \quad\;\; 7.22 \quad\;\;\; 1.01 \quad\quad\; -1.06$$

(b) DW $= .1387$, so we reject the null hypothesis.

(c) $\hat\rho = .931$

(d) $t = (1 - \hat\rho)/(SE \, \hat\rho) = 1.89$ so we reject using a one-tailed test.

(e)

$$\widehat{IRC'} = -.664 + .066 YD' - .027 DEL' - .10 PIRC'$$

so

$$\hat\beta_1 = 9.52 \quad\quad \hat\beta_2 = .066 \quad\quad \hat\beta_3 = -.027 \quad\quad \hat\beta_4 = -.10$$

(f)

$$\hat\beta_1 = 8.14 \quad\quad \hat\beta_2 = .068 \quad\quad \hat\beta_3 = -.026 \quad\quad \hat\beta_4 = -.111 \quad\quad \hat\rho = .932$$

7.1 Measurement error in the dependent variable results in increased error variance, but as long as the measurement error is uncorrelated with the independent variable, parameter estimates will be unbiased and consistent. When an independent variable is measured with error, however, the measurement error will be correlated with the independent variable, causing parameter estimates to be biased and inconsistent.

7.2

$$\hat\beta = \frac{\Sigma y_i z_i}{\Sigma z_i^2} = \beta \frac{\Sigma x_i z_i}{\Sigma z_i^2} + \frac{\Sigma z_i \epsilon_i}{\Sigma z_i^2}$$

If z is an instrument, the second term will approach zero as the sample size gets large, but the first term will approach β only when $\Sigma x_i z_i / \Sigma z_i^2$ approaches 1.

7.6 Ordinary least squares will yield biased and inconsistent estimates of the parameters in the first equation. Indirect least squares, instrumental variables, and two-stage least squares all yield biased but consistent parameter estimates (there are two possible estimates for each parameter in the indirect least-squares case). However, two-stage least-squares estimation is more efficient than either indirect least squares or instrumental variables. This regression of Y on Z_1 and Z_2 will not yield estimates of either parameter in the first equation.

8.2 At least two explanations could be offered. First, one could argue that the narrowly defined money stock (currency plus demand deposits) used in the model is not the appropriate variable to explain interest rates and that the broadly defined money stock (including time deposits as well) should be used instead. Time deposits in fact did increase much more rapidly than demand deposits in the second half of 1970, so that use of the broadly defined money stock in the model would probably have resulted in a better forecast during that period. A second argument that could be made is that the time relationship between the interest rate and income, the money stock, and the inflation rate is not a linear one as specified in the model, and a nonlinear specification would forecast the downturn more closely.

9.3 Using time as an instrument, $\hat{X}_T = \hat{\alpha}_1 + \hat{\alpha}_2 T$ and $\hat{X}_t = X_t$ $t = 1, 2, \ldots, T - 1$, where $\hat{\alpha}_2 = \Sigma x_t t / \Sigma t^2$. The least-squares slope estimate is $\hat{\beta} = \Sigma \hat{x}_t y_t / \Sigma \hat{x}_t^2$. Now, substituting $y_t = \beta \hat{x}_t + \beta (x_t - \hat{x}_t) + \varepsilon_t$, we get

$$\hat{\beta} = \beta + \frac{\beta \Sigma \hat{x}_t (x_t - \hat{x}_t)}{\Sigma \hat{x}_t^2} + \frac{\Sigma \hat{x}_t \varepsilon_t}{\Sigma \hat{x}_t^2}$$

$$\text{plim } \hat{\beta} = \beta + \beta \text{ plim } \frac{\hat{x}_T (x_T - \hat{x}_T)}{\Sigma \hat{x}_t^2} + \text{plim } \frac{\Sigma \hat{x}_t \varepsilon_t}{\Sigma \hat{x}_t^2} = \beta$$

if time is a proper instrument. However, if the error term is serially correlated, time t and the error will be correlated and the consistency of $\hat{\beta}$ will disappear.

9.4 The appropriate test statistic is

$$F_{N-1, \, NT-N-1} = \frac{(\text{ESS}_1 - \text{ESS}_2) / (N - 1)}{(\text{ESS}_2) / (NT - N - 1)}$$

where ESS_1 is the residual sum of squares using ordinary least squares and ESS_2 is the residual sum of squares using cross-section dummies.

9.7 Using a second-degree polynomial specification, we assume that

$$w_i = C_0 + C_1 i + C_2 i^2 \qquad i = 0, 1, 2, 3$$

Substituting into the original specification, we get

$$Y_t = \alpha + \beta C_0 X_t + \beta (C_0 + C_1 + C_2) X_{t-1} + \beta (C_0 + 2C_1 + 4C_2) X_{t-2}$$
$$+ \beta (C_0 + 3C_1 + 9C_2) X_{t-3} + \varepsilon_t$$

Combining terms gives

$$Y_t = \alpha + \beta C_0 (X_t + X_{t-1} + X_{t-2} + X_{t-3}) + \beta C_1 (X_{t-1} + 2X_{t-2} + 3X_{t-3})$$
$$+ \beta C_2 (X_{t-1} + 4X_{t-2} + 9X_{t-3}) + \varepsilon_t$$

which can be estimated using ordinary least squares if there are no endpoint restrictions. If the tail and the head are set equal to zero, then $W_{-1} = C_0 - C_1 + C_2 = 0$ and $W_4 = C_0 + 4C_1 + 16C_2 = 0$. Solving, we find that $C_1 = -3C_2$ and $C_0 = -4C_2$. Then we can rewrite the original equation to be estimated by eliminating C_0 and C_1

$$Y_t = \alpha - \beta C_2 (4X_t + 6X_{t-1} + 6X_{t-2} + 4X_{t-3}) + \varepsilon_t$$

Using least squares we can estimate one of the lag weights, and by substitution we can determine the remaining two.

9.9

$$S = \sum_{t=1}^{T} (C_t - a_0 - a_1 YD_t^{a_2})^2$$

The normal equations are

$$\sum_{t=1}^{T} (C_t - a_0 - a_1 YD_t^{a_2}) = 0 \qquad \sum_{t=1}^{T} YD_t^{a_2}(C_t - a_0 - a_1 YD_t^{a_2}) = 0$$

$$\sum_{t=1}^{T} YD_t^{a_2} \log YD_t (C_t - a_0 - a_1 YD_t^{a_2}) = 0$$

Solution of these equations for a_0, a_1, and a_2 would typically require a computer algorithm that iteratively linearizes the normal equations around values for the parameters. Thus this direct optimization method of estimation can be computationally more expensive than the iterative linearization method suggested in Section 9.4.

10.1 There is a *unique* error variance associated with each observation on X_i and Y_i. It is impossible to obtain an estimate of each error variance from a single residual observation.

10.2 All coefficients will be doubled. This suggests that the estimated least-squares parameters are meaningful only relative to the magnitude of the other parameters and to the units of the dependent variable.

10.4 Assume that there exists an index Z_i, a linear function of the attributes of the ith community, which measures the probability that a community will default. Associated with each community is a normally distributed random variable Z_i^* which determines the cutoff point between default and nondefault. Then, the probit estimation procedure is appropriate for estimating the probability that a community will default. The probit model will yield predicted probabilities that lie within the (0, 1) interval, but it does necessitate a nonlinear estimation procedure.

10.6 The regression line is $\hat{Y} = \frac{1}{2} + \frac{3}{8}X$, $R^2 = .75$, and the number of correct classifications is five.

11.2 Let G = number of predetermined variables in system
$\quad G_1$ = number of predetermined variables in equation being considered
$\quad H$ = number of endogenous variables in system
$\quad H_1$ = number of endogenous variables in equation being considered
The first form of the order condition is equivalent to

$$G - G_1 \geq H_1 - 1$$

The second form of the order condition is equivalent to

$$(G - G_1) + (H - H_1) \geq H - 1$$

Subtracting $H - H_1$ from both sides of the second condition yields the first.

11.4 There are four endogenous variables and three predetermined variables in the system. Thus, according to the order condition, a necessary condition for identifiability is that the number of excluded predetermined variables be three or more. According to this criterion the first equation is just identified, while the second and third equations are unidentified. The first equation can be estimated by using two-stage least squares.

11.6 Write the model equations as $y_1 = \alpha x + u_1$ and $y_2 = \beta x + u_2$ with $\sigma_{12} = $ Cov $(u_1, u_2) = 0$. Then the derivation follows as in the text, except that $z^* = x^*$. Thus, Eqs. (11.36) and (11.37) simplify as

$$\hat{\alpha} = \frac{1}{C} A \sigma_1^2 \Sigma x^2 \qquad \hat{\beta} = \frac{1}{C} B \sigma_2^2 \Sigma x^2$$

$$A = \sigma_2^2 \Sigma xy_1 \qquad B = \sigma_1^2 \Sigma xy_2 \qquad C = \sigma_1^2 \sigma_2^2 (\Sigma x^2)^2$$

Substituting, we find that $\hat{\alpha} = \Sigma xy_1 / \Sigma x^2$ and $\hat{\beta} = \Sigma xy_2 / \Sigma x^2$, both of which are the ordinary least-squares parameter estimates.

12.1 The rms error is usually a better performance criterion when the variable of interest exhibits fluctuations and turning points; if the simulated series misses a turning point in the actual series, one would like to penalize heavily for the larger error that results. The mean absolute error might be preferred if the variable of interest exhibits a steady trend, in which case the concern is only how far above or below the actual trend line the simulated series is. Since we usually construct models to explain fluctuations in economic variables, the rms error is the standard statistic calculated in most computer simulation programs.

12.4 The underprediction of GNP is largely the result of the inability of the model to predict turning points in the interest rate, combined with a negative error in the estimated propensity to consume resulting in a general underprediction of consumption. In the historical simulation consumption is usually below the actual series. (Consumption and GNP are close to the actual series in 1970–1971 because of a positive error in simulated investment, resulting in turn from large negative errors in the simulated interest rate in 1969–1970.) Observe in the *ex post* forecast that the interest rate is overpredicted in 1972 so that investment is underpredicted in 1973. Consumption is underpredicted throughout the *ex post* forecast. The result is an underprediction of GNP.

13.2 (*a*) The fundamental dynamic equation for the model is given by

$$Y_t - (a_2 + b_2 a_2) Y_{t-1} + b_2 a_2 Y_{t-2} = a_1 + b_1 + G_t$$

so that the characteristic equation is

$$\lambda^2 - (a_2 + b_2 a_2)\lambda + b_2 a_2 = 0$$

The characteristic roots are therefore

$$\lambda_1, \lambda_2 = \frac{a_2 + b_2 a_2}{2} \pm \frac{1}{2}\sqrt{(a_2 + b_2 a_2)^2 - 4b_2 a_2}$$

(*b*) The solution will oscillate if the characteristic roots are complex, i.e., if $4b_2 a_2 > (a_2 + b_2 a_2)^2$. The solution will explode if the roots are greater than 1 in magnitude. The type of solution will depend on a_2 and b_2 as follows:

$$a_2 > \frac{4b_2}{(1 + b_2)^2} \qquad b_2 < 1 \qquad \text{stable, nonoscillatory solution}$$

$$a_2 > \frac{4b_2}{(1 + b_2)^2} \qquad b_2 > 1 \qquad \text{explosive, nonoscillatory solution}$$

$$\frac{1}{b_2} < a_2 < \frac{4b_2}{(1 + b_2)^2} \qquad \text{explosive, oscillatory solution}$$

$$a_2 < \frac{1}{b_2} \qquad \text{stable, oscillatory solution (damped cycles)}$$

14.1 The increase in government spending increases GNP and most of its components through the multiplier effect. The higher rate of growth of GNP directly increases the rate of price inflation [see Eq. (14.28)] and decreases the rate of unemployment [see Eq. (14.30)]. The higher rate of price inflation and the lower rate of unemployment together act to increase the rate of wage inflation [see Eq. (14.29)]. However, the higher rate of inflation and the increased GNP have the effect of pushing up interest rates, and this in turn dampens both residential and nonresidential investment. In the case of residential investment, the dampening effect of higher interest rates just about offsets the stimulating effect of higher GNP.

14.4 An increase in the support price will result in an increase in the amount of leaf pledged under the support program, from Eqs. (14.42) and (14.43). This in turn results in a drop in SQNET, the ratio of inventory stock to sales, which produces an increase in the actual leaf price as producers try to raise the inventory-sales ratio back to its desired level; see Eqs. (14.37) and (14.39). Finally, this increase in price results in an increase in the dollar value of producing acreage, an increase in the amount of acreage planted, and an increase in production; see Eqs. (14.31) to (14.36).

An increase in the government acreage allotment AL results in an increase in underage [from Eqs. (14.34) and (14.35)]. In Eq. (14.36) observe that the increase in underage has a negative effect on acreage planted but the increase in the allotment has a direct positive effect. The net effect is positive: a 1-acre increase in AL results in an increase of $1 - .016 = .984$ acres planted. Thus production increases. This will raise the inventory-sales ratio, however, so that the actual leaf price will fall.

14.6 To use the financial simulation model to determine the breakeven point for sales, make earnings before tax (EBT) an exogenous input parameter and rewrite the equations for operating income (OI) and EBT in block I of the model as follows:

1. Replace the third equation (for OI) with

$$\text{SALES} = \text{OI} + \text{CGS} + \text{OC}$$

2. Replace the seventh equation (for EBT) with

$$\text{OI} = \text{EBT} + \text{INT} + \text{DEP}$$

To determine the breakeven point for sales, simulate the new model setting EBT equal to zero.

15.3 Observe from the derivation of Eq. (15.25) that if an *actual* value of y_{T+1} is available, the forecast $\hat{y}_{T+2}$ will take this data point into account. The forecast will then be

$$\hat{y}_{T+2} = \alpha \sum_{\tau=0}^{\infty} (1 - \alpha)^{\tau} y_{T-\tau+1}$$

rather than as given by Eq. (15.25).

16.1 We know that the process given by Eq. (16.8) is nonstationary since its mean and variance increase indefinitely. It is first-order homogeneous since

$$w_t = \Delta y_t = d + \varepsilon_t$$

This process has a constant mean d and a constant variance σ_ε^2 and is stationary.

17.1 The variance and covariances for the MA(3) process are

$$\gamma_0 = \sigma_\varepsilon^2(1 + \theta_1^2 + \theta_2^3 + \theta_3^2) \qquad \gamma_1 = \sigma_\varepsilon^2(-\theta_1 + \theta_2\theta_1 + \theta_3\theta_2)$$

$$\gamma_2 = \sigma_\varepsilon^2(-\theta_2 + \theta_3\theta_1) \qquad \gamma_3 = -\theta_3\sigma_\varepsilon^2 \qquad \gamma_k = 0, \quad k > 3$$

17.2 Observe in Fig. 17.2 that y_t tends to be positively correlated with adjacent values; e.g., a positive value is more likely to be preceded and followed by a positive value than by a negative value. The correlation, however, does not extend more than one period out, so that the realization appears very "noisy." A realization of the process $y_t = 1 + \varepsilon_t - .8\varepsilon_{t-1}$ would show negative correlations between adjacent values, so that a positive value of y_t would be more likely to be followed by a negative value.

17.4

$$\rho_1 = \frac{\phi_1}{1 - \phi_2} - \frac{\theta_1(1 - \phi_1^2\phi_2 - \phi_1^2 - \phi_2)}{(1 - \phi_2)^2(1 - 2\phi_1\theta_1 + \theta_2^2) - 2\phi_1\phi_2\theta_1(1 - \phi_2)}$$

$$\rho_2 = \phi_2 + \phi_1\rho_1 \qquad \rho_3 = \phi_1\rho_2 + \phi_2\rho_1$$

17.6

$$y_t = \Sigma w_t \qquad \text{and so} \qquad E(y_t) = \Sigma E(w_t)$$

$$E(w_t) = \frac{1}{1 - .9} = 10$$

Then

$$E(y_t) = 10t$$

18.2 (*a*) This misspecification will result in residuals that are autocorrelated. The diagnostic check described in Section 18.2 can be used, and the statistic Q is likely to be above the 90 percent point on the chi-square distribution.

(*b*) Let us assume that the parameters of the process are known with certainty. Write the true ARMA(1, 2) process as

$$\varepsilon_t = y_t - \phi_1 y_{t-1} + \theta_1 \varepsilon_{t-1} + \theta_2 \varepsilon_{t-2}$$

and write the ARMA(0, 2) model as

$$\tilde{\varepsilon}_t = y_t + \theta_1 \varepsilon_{t-1} + \theta_2 \varepsilon_{t-2}$$

The error term for the model is thus related to the error term for the true process by

$$\tilde{\varepsilon}_t = \varepsilon_t + \phi_1 y_{t-1}$$

The error term $\tilde{\varepsilon}_t$ will therefore be autocorrelated:

$$E(\tilde{\varepsilon}_t \tilde{\varepsilon}_{t-1}) = E[(\varepsilon_t + \phi_1 y_{t-1})(\varepsilon_{t-1} + \phi_1 y_{t-2})] = \phi_1 \sigma_\varepsilon^2 + \phi_1^2 \gamma_1$$

where γ_1 is the covariance (for displacement 1) of the true process ARMA(1, 2). Generally $\phi_1^2 \gamma_1$ will be much smaller than $\phi_1 \sigma_\varepsilon^2$, so that we can write

$$E(\tilde{\varepsilon}_t \tilde{\varepsilon}_{t-1}) \approx \phi_1 \sigma_\varepsilon^2$$

Similarly $E(\tilde{\varepsilon}_t \tilde{\varepsilon}_{t-2}) \approx \phi_1^2 \sigma_\varepsilon^2$, and so on. Thus the residual autocorrelations for the ARMA(0, 2) model will look like those for a *first-order autoregressive process*, and this would indicate that ARMA(1, 2) is a more correct specification.

19.2 Reexamine Eqs. (19.10) and (19.11) for the ARIMA(p, d, q) model. Note that in making a forecast one period ahead, the only missing information is the value of the error term ε_t in the next period, i.e., the value of ε_{T+1} (the values of $w_T, w_{T-1}, \ldots, \varepsilon_T, \varepsilon_{T-1}, \ldots$ are all known, assuming that the parameters of the model are known). Therefore the forecast error variance for the one-period forecast should simply be the variance of ε_t.

19.4 The one-, two-, and three-period forecasts for the AR(2) process are

$$\hat{y}_T(1) = \phi_1 y_T + \phi_2 y_{T-1} + \delta$$

$$\hat{y}_T(2) = \phi_1 \hat{y}_T(1) + \phi_2 y_T + \delta = (\phi_1^2 + \phi_2) y_T + \phi_1 \phi_2 y_{T-1} + (1 + \phi_1)\delta$$

$$\hat{y}_T(3) = (\phi_1^3 + 2\phi_1 \phi_2) y_T + (\phi_1^2 \phi_2 + \phi_2^2) y_{T-1} + (1 + \phi_1 + \phi_1^2 + \phi_2)\delta$$

These forecasts have error variances:

$$E[e_T^2(1)] = \sigma_\varepsilon^2 \qquad E[e_T^2(2)] = (1 + \phi_1^2)\sigma_\varepsilon^2$$

$$E[e_T^2(3)] = [1 + \phi_1^4 + \phi_1^2(1 + 2\phi_2) + \phi_2^2]\sigma_\varepsilon^2$$

Adaptive expectations model, 234–235
Adaptive forecasts, 483, 564–566
Analysis of covariance, 253
Analysis of variance, 64
ARIMA (integrated autoregressive–moving average) models, 529–532
ARMA (autoregressive–moving average) models, 526–529
Autocorrelation (*see* Serial correlation)
Autocorrelation function, 499–504, 545, 549
  of autoregressive–moving average process, 527–528
  of autoregressive process, 523
  of moving average process, 518–519
  of nonstationary process, 503–504
  partial, 524–526
Automobile demand, 396–398
Autoregressive error process, 154
Autoregressive models, 519–526
Autoregressive–moving average (ARMA) models, 526–529
Autoregressive operator, 530
Autoregressive trend model, 476

Backcasting, 360
Backward shift operator, 528–530
Bartlett's test, 147–148, 500, 524
Best linear unbiased estimation, 51–55, 77
Beta coefficients, 90–91
Bias proportion, 365
Binary-choice models, 274–301
Block diagram, 402–403

Block recursive equation systems, 323
Bureau of the Census, U.S., 486n, 488

Census II method, 488
Characteristic equation, 385, 536
  computer solution of, 389–390
Characteristic roots, 385, 399–400
Chi-square distribution, 33
Chi-square test, 549 550, 580 581
Choice models:
  binary-, 274–301
  estimation of, 310–312
  forecasting with, 300–301
  multiple-, 301–310
Classical linear regression model, 48, 76
Cochrane-Orcutt procedure, 157, 456–457
Collinearity, perfect, 87–88
Combined regression–time-series models, 593–605
Conditional expectation, 556–557
Conditional forecasting, 204–205, 221, 224
Conditional log likelihood function, 541
Conditional operators, 450
Confidence intervals, 36–37
  for long-run elasticities, 269–270
  for random walk, 495–496
Consistency, estimator, 30–31
Convergence number, 544
Corporate financial planning, simulation models for, 447–456
Corrected R^2 ($\bar{R}^2$), 80–81, 105

Correlation:
  and causality, 64–65
  partial, 91–94
  simple, 26
  (*See also* Serial correlation)
Correlation coefficient, 22
Covariance, 22
Covariance analysis, 253
Covariance model, 254–255
Covariance proportion, 365
Cross-product matrix, 101
Cross-section data (*see* Pooling of cross-section
    and time-series data)
Cumulative probability function, 280

Data-less approach to modeling, 379
Data series for macroeconometric model, 458–
    466
Degrees of freedom, 25, 64n.
Dependent variables, 8
Deterministic drift, 564
Deterministic models of time series, 473–479
Deviations, 4
Deviations form, 10–11
Diagnostic checking, 532, 540, 548–550, 576
Difference equations, 356, 384–388
Distributed lag, 231–245
  geometric, 232–238, 368
  polynomial, 238–244
  rational, 245n.
  tests for causality, 244–245
Double exponential smoothing, 485
Dummy variables, 111–116
  in macroeconomic model, 424–425
Durbin h test, 194–195
Durbin procedure, 158–161
Durbin-Watson statistic, 159
Durbin-Watson test, 158–161
Dynamic elasticities, 395–398
Dynamic multipliers, 392–395, 400–401
  for macroeconometric model, 433–434
Dynamic response of simulation model, 366

Efficiency, 28–29
Elasticity, 91
  definition of, 395n.
Endogenous variables, 181
Error components model, 253, 256–261
Error sum of squares, 55
Errors:
  serially correlated, forecasting with, 215–221

Errors:
  simulation error statistics, 362–363, 380
  sum of squared, 540–543
  Type I and Type II, 39–40
  in variables, 176–178
  (*See also* Forecast error; Specification error)
Estimation:
  of choice models, 310–312
  of simulation models, 374–378
  of time-series models, 539–548
Estimators:
  best linear unbiased, 51–55, 77
  consistent, 30–31
  efficient, 28–29
  full-information maximum-likelihood (FIML),
      352
  generalized least-squares (GLS), 164–168
  indirect least-squares, 185
  instrumental-variables (IV), 178–180, 199–201
  least generalized residual variance (LGRV),
      352
  least-variance ratio, 351
  limited-information maximum-likelihood
      (LIML), 349–352
  maximum-likelihood, 69–71, 77, 310–312
  minimum mean square error, 29
  nonlinear (*see* Nonlinear estimation)
  robust, 8n.
  three-stage least-squares (3SLS), 334–335
  two-stage least squares (2SLS), 191–193, 330–
      331, 344–347
  unbiased, 24–28
  Zellner, 331–333, 347–349
Ex ante forecast, 360
Ex ante forecasting, 204–205, 360
Exogenous variables, 181
Expectations operator, 20–21, 40–43
Exponential growth curve, 475
Exponential model, 109
Exponential smoothing, 484–487
Ex post forecast error, 364
Ex post forecast of macroeconomic model, 425–
    440
Ex post forecasting, 204, 364
Ex post simulation, 358
Extrapolation methods, 473–487

F distribution, 35–36
F test, 65–66, 81, 105, 117–120, 123–126
Feedback loops, 403
Financial planning model, 447–456
Financial simulation models, 378

First-differencing, 156
Forecast(s):
　adaptive, 483, 564–566
　best, 205
　ex ante, 360
　ex post, 425–440
　interval, 203
　point, 203
　of telephone data, 589–593
Forecast confidence intervals for time-series
　　model, 559–561
Forecast error, 205–206
　ex post, 364
　minimum mean square, 556–557
　for random walk, 495–496
　for time-series model, 558–559
　variance of, 206–207
Forecasting, 203
　with choice model, 300–301
　conditional, 204–205, 221, 224
　ex ante, 204–205, 360
　ex post, 204, 364
　with linear model, 206–228
　with multivariate regression model, 224–228
　with nonlinear model, 266–269
　with serially correlated errors, 215–221
　unconditional, 204, 206–215
Forward lag operator, 553
Full-information maximum-likelihood (FIML) es-
　timation, 352
Fundamental dynamic equation, 384

Gauss-Markov theorem, 52, 102–103
Generalized differencing, 155–156
Generalized least-squares (GLS) estimation, 164–
　168
GNP, potential, 421
Goldfeld-Quandt test, 148–150
Goodness of fit, 61–64
　nonlinear model, 265–266

Heteroscedasticity, 49, 140–142
　consequence of, 141–142
　corrections for, 142–146
　tests for, 146–152
Hildreth-Lu procedure, 157–158, 375
Historical simulation, 358
Holt's exponential smoothing method, 485
Homogeneous nonstationary processes, 502–504,
　529–531
Homoscedasticity, 49

Housing starts, 486–487, 489–491
Hypothesis testing, 36–39

Identification, 186–190, 324–328, 339–344
　order condition for, 326–327, 344
　rank condition for, 327*n.,* 344
Independent variables, 8
Indirect least-squares estimation, 185
Inequality coefficient, Theil's, 364–365
Inflation in macroeconomic model, 420, 424–425
Inherently linear models, 107
Inherently nonlinear models, 107
Initialization of time series, 541–542, 552–554
Instrumental-variables (IV) estimation, 178–180,
　199–201
Instruments, 174–179
Integrated autoregressive–moving average
　(ARIMA) models, 529–532
Interaction model, 110
Interaction term (interaction variable), 110
Interest rate:
　long-term, 420, 424–425
　short-term, 420, 424, 595
Interval forecasts, 203
Invertibility, 521*n.,* 535–537
Investment:
　inventory, 419–420, 423–424, 577–589
　nonresidential, 418–419, 422–423
　residential, 419, 423–424

Koyck lag (geometric distributed lag), 232–238,
　368

Lag distribution (*see* Distributed lag)
Lagged endogenous variables, 181
Lagged variables:
　adaptive expectations model, 234–235
　stock adjustment model, 235–236
　(*See also* Distributed lag)
Least generalized residual variance (LGRV) esti-
　mation, 352
Least-variance ratio, 351
Limited-information maximum-likelihood (LIML)
　estimation, 349–352
Linear probability model, 275–280
Linear trend model, 475
Logarithmic autoregressive trend model, 476
Logarithmic transformations, 590
Logistic growth curve, 476–477
Logit model, 287–300
Lyapunov's direct method, 391*n.*

Macroeconometric model, 414–440
 data series for, 458–466
 dynamic multipliers for, 433–434
 policy analysis using, 434–440
 simulation of, 425–440
Markov process, 494
MARMA (multivariate autoregressive–moving
 average) models, 594
Maximum-likelihood estimation, 69–71, 77, 310–
 312
Mean, 20
Mean absolute error, 363n., 380
Mean lag, 232
Mean percent error, 362
Mean simulation error, 362
Mean square error, 29
Measurement errors, 176–178
Median lag, 233
Memory:
 of autoregressive process, 521
 of moving average process, 517–518
Minimum mean square error forecast, 556–557
Missing observations, 245–252
MIT–Federal Reserve–Penn econometric model,
 418
Mixed autoregressive–moving average models,
 526–529
Model(s):
 autoregressive, 519–526
 exponential, 109
 inherently linear, 107
 inherently nonlinear, 107
 interaction, 110
 linear probability, 275–280
 logit, 287–300
 moving average, 481–487, 515–519
 multiplicative, 109
 piecewise linear, 126–127
 polynomial, 108
 probit, 280–287
 reciprocal, 109
 semilog, 110
 simultaneous-equation, 180–184, 320–337
 structural, 182
 time-series, 469–472
 (See also specific models)
MODSIM simulation package, 358n., 394n.
Monte Carlo simulation, 406
Moving average models, 481–487, 515–519
 exponentially weighted, 481–487
Moving average operator, 530
Multicollinearity, 87–90
Multiple-choice models, 301–310
Multiplicative model, 109

Multiplier-accelerator model, 356, 384, 387
Multivariate autoregressive–moving average
 (MARMA) models, 594
Multivariate regression model, forecasting with,
 224–228

Nonlinear estimation, 261–269
 direct optimization, 263
 direct search, 262
 iterative linearization, 263–265
 steepest descent, 263
 of time-series models, 542–545, 547–548
Nonlinear models:
 dynamic analysis of, 390–391
 forecasting with, 266–269
 goodness of fit, 265–266
Normal distribution, 31–33

Operator(s):
 autoregressive, 530
 backward shift, 528–530
 conditional, 450
 expectations, 20–21, 40–43
 forward lag, 553
 moving average, 530
 summation, 13–16, 529–531, 558
Order condition for identification, 326–327, 344
Outliers, 6–8

Park-Glejser test, 150–152
Partial autocorrelation function, 524–526
Partial correlation, 91–94
Partial regression coefficients, 77, 97–98
Perfect collinearity, 87–88
Piecewise linear model, 126–127
Point forecasts, 203
Policy analysis using macroeconometric model,
 434–440
Political behavior, models of, 354
Polynomial model, 108
Pooling of cross-section and time-series data,
 252–261
 covariance model, 254–255
 error components model, 253, 256–261
 time-series autocorrelation model, 258–259
Potential GNP, 421
Predetermined variables, 181

Prediction (*see* Forecasting)
Principal components, 330
Probability limit (plim), 30n.
Probit model, 280–287
Pro forma balance sheet, 447, 449, 455
Pro forma income statement, 447, 449, 455
Proportions of inequality, 365

Q statistic, 500, 549–550
Quadratic trend model, 476

R square (R^2), 62, 78–79, 104
  corrected (R^{-2}), 80–81, 105
Random variable, 19–20
Random walk, 494–497
Rank condition for identification, 327n.,
  344
Reciprocal model, 109
Recursive equation systems, 322–323
Reduced form model, 182
Regression coefficients:
  partial, 77, 97–98
Regression–time-series models, combined, 593–
  605
Residual sum of squares, 55
Residuals, 47, 55
  time-series, model of, 593–595, 598, 603
  of time-series model, 540, 549–550
RMS percent error, 362
RMS simulation error, 362
Robust estimation, 8n.

St. Louis model, 394–395
Sample, defined, 4
Sample autocorrelation function, 499–500,
  549
Saturation models, 478
Seasonal adjustment methods, 487–491
Seasonal indices, 489–490
Seasonality, 509–511
Seemingly unrelated equation systems, 323–324,
  347–349
Semilog model, 110
Sensitivity of simulation model, 366
Serial correlation, 49, 152–153
  consequences of, 153–154
  corrections for, 154–158, 421, 456–458
  in the presence of lagged dependent variables,
    193–199
  tests for, 158–164

Serially correlated errors, forecasting with, 215–
  221
Simulation, 356
  ex post (historical), 358
  of macroeconometric model, 425–440
  Monte Carlo, 406
  stochastic, 405–413
  of tobacco industry model, 445–447
Simulation models:
  dynamic behavior, 382–405
  estimation of, 374–378
  evaluation of, 360–367
  solution of, 356–358
  tuning and adjusting, 401–405
Simulation process, 356–360
Simultaneity in financial planning models, 454
Simultaneous-equation models, 180–184, 320–
  337
Smoothing techniques, 484–487
Specification of ARIMA models, 531–532
Specification error, 128–133
  irrelevant variable, 130–131
  nonlinearities, 131
  omitted variables, 128–130
Stability, 357
Standard deviation, 21
Standard error, 55n.
Standard error of coefficient, 55, 78
Standard error of the forecast, 207n.
Standard error of the regression (SER), 55n.
Stationarity, 497–498, 535–537
Stepwise regression, 93–94
Stochastic explanatory variables, 134
Stochastic process, 494–497
Stochastic simulation, 405–413
Stock adjustment effect, 398
Stock adjustment model, 235–236
Strict-sense stationarity, 498n.
Structural model, 182
Student's t distribution, 33–34
Sum of squared errors, 540–543
Summation operator, 13–16, 529–531, 558
Surtax, 417

t distribution, 33–34
t test, 38–39, 57–58, 103–104, 121–123
Tax surcharge, 417n.
Taylor series expansion, 264, 543
Telephone data, forecasts of, 589–593
Theil's inequality coefficient, 364–365
Three-stage least-squares (3SLS) estimation, 334–
  335
Time horizon of model simulation, 358–360

Time series:
  deterministic models of, 473–479
  homogeneous nonstationary, 502–504
  initialization of, 541–542, 552–554
  nonstationary, 497, 502–504
  stationary, 497–498, 503–504
  (*See also* Pooling of cross-section and time-series data)
Time-series autocorrelation model, 258–259
Time-series models, 469–472
  estimation of, 539–548
  forecast confidence intervals for, 559–561
  forecast error for, 558–559
  (*See also under* Residuals)
Tobacco industry, model of, 440–447
Tobit analysis, 294n.
Transfer function models, 593–595
Transient solution, 384
TROLL system, 358n.
Turning points, 363
Two-stage least-squares, 421, 456–458
Two-stage least-squares (2SLS) estimation, 191–193, 330–331, 344–347
Type I error, 39–40
Type II error, 39–40

Unbiased estimators, 24–28
Unconditional forecasting, 204, 206–215
Unemployment rate in macroeconomic model, 421, 425
Unrelated equations, seemingly, 323–324, 347–349

Variables:
  dependent, 8
  dummy, 111–116, 424–425
  endogenous, 181
  errors in, 176–178
  exogenous, 181
  independent, 8
  interaction, 110
  lagged (*see* Lagged variables)
  predetermined, 181
  random, 19–20
  stochastic explanatory, 134
Variance, 20
  of autoregressive process, 521–523
  of forecast error, 206–207
  of mixed autoregressive–moving average process, 526–527
  of moving average process, 516–518
Variance analysis, 64
Variance-covariance matrix, 100
Variance proportion, 365

Weak hypothesis test, 550n.
Weighted least squares, 142–144
White noise process, 500, 515
Wide-sense stationarity, 498n.

Yule-Walker equations, 523, 525, 546–547
Yule-Walker estimates, 546

Zellner estimation, 331–333, 342–349

Afifi, A. A., 249n.
Aigner, D., 79n.
Aitchinson, A., 303n.
Aldrich, J., 283n.
Allen, R. G. D., 384n.
Almon, S., 239
Amemiya, T., 294n., 295n..
Andersen, L. C., 394
Ando, A., 414n.
Andrews, F., 163n.
Anscombe, F. J., 140n.
Anstrom, K., 406n.
Anthonyson, R. B., 450n.

Bacon, D. W., 590n.
Baily, M. N., 440n.
Balestra, P., 256n.
Barro, R., 245n.
Barth, J., 126n.
Bartlett, M. S., 500
Baumol, W. J., 356n., 384n.
Beals, R. E., 33n.
Belsley, D. A., 89n.
Berkson, J., 290n.
Blalock, H. M., 44n.
Boschan, C., 367n.
Bowen, W. G., 114n.
Box, G. E. P., 471n., 500n., 521n., 549n., 590n., 594n.
Brehm, C. T., 335
Brewer, G. D., 354n., 380n.
Brunk, H. D., 140n.

Brunner, K., 394n.
Brunner, R. D., 354n.

Cacappolo, G. J., 354n.
Carlson, K. M., 394
Chan, L., 126n.
Chaudry, M. A., 354n.
Chiang, A. C., 356n., 384n.
Choucri, N., 354n.
Chow, G. C., 123n., 132, 338n., 387n., 391n.
Cnudde, C. F., 283n.
Cochrane, D., 157n.
Collier, P., 132n.
Cooper, J. P., 450n.
Cootner, P. H. 440n., 494n.
Cox, D. R., 290n.
Cragg, J. G., 295n.
Crecine, J. P., 380n.
Crenson, M. A., 354n.
Crissey, B. L., 354n.

Dagenais, M. G., 249n.
Davis, B. E., 354n.
Dean, J., 110n.
Dhrymes, P. J., 80n., 232n., 237n., 367n.
Domencich, T., 247n.
Dornbusch, R., 394n.
Draper, N., 94n., 263n.
Duesenberry, J., 198n., 330n.
Duggal, V. G., 414n.
Durbin, J., 158n., 194n.
Dutton, J. M., 380n.

Eisner, M., 230*n*., 263*n*.
Elashoff, R. M., 249*n*.
Elliott, J. W., 354*n*.
Evans, M. K., 367*n*., 415*n*.

Fair, R. C., 194*n*., 295*n*., 330*n*., 366*n*., 375*n*., 377, 377*n*., 414*n*.
Fama, E. F., 494*n*.
Farrar, D. E., 89*n*.
Feldstein, M., 221*n*.
Finegan, T. A., 114*n*.
Finney, D. J., 281*n*.
Fischer, S., 394*n*.
Fisher, F. M., 123*n*., 198*n*., 326*n*., 330*n*., 440*n*.
Fisher, R. A., 270*n*.
Forrester, J. W., 379*n*.
Fox, K., 391*n*.
Freund, J. E., 33*n*.
Fromm, G., 198*n*., 330*n*., 359*n*.

Giesel, M. S., 237*n*.
Gilbert, R. F., 334*n*.
Glasser, M., 250*n*.
Glauber, R. R., 89*n*.
Glejser, H., 150*n*.
Goldberger, A., 99*n*., 123*n*., 201*n*., 217*n*., 352*n*., 392*n*.
Goldfeld, S., 148*n*., 150*n*., 265*n*.
Goodman, L., 290*n*.
Granger, C., 244*n*., 485*n*., 521*n*.
Graybill, F. A., 33*n*., 70*n*.
Greenberger, M., 354*n*.
Grenander, U., 537*n*.
Griffin, J. M., 440*n*.
Griliches, Z., 232*n*., 237*n*.
Gupta, P., 132*n*.

Haitovsky, Y., 249*n*., 367*n*., 404*n*.
Halvorsen, R., 195*n*.
Hanushek, E. A., 287*n*., 307*n*.
Harvey, A., 132*n*.
Heckman, J., 294*n*., 295*n*.
Heller, P., 259*n*.
Hickman, B., 367*n*.
Hildreth, G., 157*n*.
Hoel, P. G., 148*n*.
Holt, C. C., 485*n*.
Hood, W. C., 350*n*.
Houthakker, H., 141*n*.
Husby, R. D., 268*n*.

Hussain, A., 256*n*.
Hwa, E. C., 414*n*.
Hymans, S. H., 396, 414*n*.

Jackson, J. E., 287*n*., 307*n*.
Jacobi, L., 244*n*.
Jaffee, D. M., 205*n*.
Jenkins, G. M., 471*n*., 499*n*., 500*n*., 521*n*., 590*n*., 594*n*.
Johnston, J., 90*n*., 99*n*., 178*n*., 208*n*., 236*n*., 338*n*., 350*n*.
Jorgenson, D. W., 245*n*.

Kane, E. J., 147*n*.
Klein, L., 198*n*., 330*n*., 337, 366*n*., 414*n*.
Kloek, T., 128*n*., 141*n*., 178*n*., 237*n*., 330*n*., 334*n*., 352*n*.
Kmenta, J., 237*n*., 398
Kohn, M. G., 298*n*.
Koopmans, T. C., 350*n*.
Koutsoyiannis, A., 92*n*.
Koyck, L. M., 232*n*.
Kraft, A., 126*n*.
Kraft, J., 126*n*.
Kuh, E., 89*n*., 198*n*., 245*n*., 252*n*., 330*n*., 414*n*., 415*n*.

Laird, M., 354*n*.
Lancaster, K., 225*n*.
Leamer, E., 132*n*., 244*n*.
Lee, T. H., 303*n*.
Leuthold, R., 507*n*.
Liu, T. C., 414*n*.
Liviatan, N., 237*n*.
Lu, J. Y., 157*n*.
Ludwig, R. S., 601*n*.

Maasoumi, E., 132*n*.
MacAvoy, P. W., 359*n*., 440*n*.
McCallum, B. T., 90*n*.
McCarthy, M. D., 414*n*.
MacCormick, A., 507*n*.
McFadden, D., 274*n*.
McKelvey, R. D., 307*n*.
Madansky, A., 335*n*.
Maddala, G. S., 140*n*., 194*n*., 245*n*., 256*n*.
Makridakis, S., 485*n*., 594*n*.
Malinvaud, E., 329*n*.
Manski, C. F., 298*n*.

Marquardt, D. W., 265n.
Mason, A., 126n.
Maynes, E. S., 301n.
Meadows, D. L., 354n., 379n.
Mennes, L. B., 330n.
Miller, R. L., 128n.
Modigliani, F., 414n.
Mood, A. M., 33n., 70n., 147n.
Moore, G. H., 367n.
Morgan, J., 136n.
Morrison, D. G., 301n.
Mundel, D., 298n.
Murphy, J. L., 239n.

Naylor, T. H., 354n., 358n., 359n., 378n., 440, 589n.
Nelson, C. R., 521n., 589n., 590n.
Nerlove, M., 194n., 232n., 256n., 278n.
Neter, J., 301n.
Newbold, P., 485n., 521n.
Newhouse, J. P., 133
Nordhaus, W. D., 379n.

Okun, A. M., 421n.
Orcutt, G. H., 157n.

Pagan, A., 245n.
Park, R. E., 150n.
Pierce, D. A., 549n.
Pindyck, R. S., 110n., 263n., 359n., 421n., 440n.
Poirier, D., 126n.
Prais, S. J., 141n.
Press, S. J., 278n.

Quandt, R. E., 114n., 148n., 150n., 265n.

Ramsey, J., 147n.
Rao, P., 128n.
Rives, N. W., 440
Roberts, S., 110n.
Rosenblatt, M., 537n.
Rosenstone, S. J., 285n.
Ross, A. M., 114n.
Rubinfeld, D., 278n., 295n.

Salzman, L., 488n.
Samuelson, P. A., 387n.

Sargent, T., 244n., 245n.
Sasser, W. E., 440
Saving, T. R., 335
Schiller, R., 245n.
Schmalensee, R., 245n., 414n., 415n.
Schmidt, P., 305n.
Schmitz, A., 507n.
Seaks, T. G., 589n.
Sengupta, J., 391n.
Shapiro, H. T., 366n., 414n.
Shelton, J. P., 378n.
Siegel, S., 159n.
Silvey, S., 303n.
Sims, C., 244n.
Smith, H., 94n., 263
Smith, P. E., 398
Sonquist, S., 136n.
Spang, H. A., 263n.
Starbuck, W. H., 380n.
Strauss, R. P., 305n.
Suits, D., 126n.
Summers, R., 338n.
Swamy, P. A. V. B., 254n.

Taubman, P., 359n.
Taylor, L. D., 133
Theil, H., 128n., 140n., 159n., 182n., 225n., 254n., 290n., 301n., 303n., 334n., 365n.
Thompson, H. E., 589n.
Thorbecke, E., 391n.
Tiao, G. C., 589n.
Tobin, J., 281n., 294n.
Toro-Vizcarrondo, C., 89n.
Treyz, G., 367n., 404n.
Trotter, H. F., 265n.
Tukey, J. W., 140n.

Van Duyne, C., 358n.
Vernon, J. M., 440
Vinod, H. D., 90n.

Walker, G., 546n.
Wallace, T. D., 89n., 208n., 256n.
Wallace, W. H., 440n.
Wallis, K. F., 194n., 237n.
Ward, M. P., 244n.
Warner, S., 277n.
Warren, J. M., 378n.
Watson, G. S., 157n.

Watts, D. G., 499*n*., 507*n*.
Welsch, R. E., 89*n*.
Wheelwright, S. C., 485*n*., 594*n*.
Wichern, D. W., 589*n*.
Wolfinger, R. E., 285*n*.

Yule, G. U., 546*n*.

Zarembka, P., 274*n*.
Zarnowitz, V., 367*n*.
Zavoina, W., 307*n*.
Zellner, A., 132*n*., 237*n*., 303*n*., 332, 347